Lecture Notes in Co 3274

Commenced Publication in 1973
Founding and Former Series Editor
Gerhard Goos, Juris Hartmanis, and ... van Leeuwen

Rachid Guerraoui (Ed.)

Distributed Computing

18th International Conference, DISC 2004
Amsterdam, The Netherlands, October 4-7, 2004
Proceedings

 Springer

Volume Editor

Rachid Guerraoui
EPFL, I&C – LPD, Bât. IN
1015 Lausanne, Switzerland
E-mail: rachid.guerraoui@epfl.ch

Library of Congress Control Number: 2004112514

CR Subject Classification (1998): C.2.4, C.2.2, F.2.2, D.1.3, F.1.1, D.4.4-5

ISSN 0302-9743
ISBN 3-540-23306-7 Springer Berlin Heidelberg New York

Springer is a part of Springer Science+Business Media

springeronline.com

© Springer-Verlag Berlin Heidelberg 2004
Printed in Germany

Typesetting: Camera-ready by author, data conversion by Olgun Computergrafik
Printed on acid-free paper   SPIN: 11328841   06/3142   5 4 3 2 1 0

Preface

DISC, the International Symposium on Distributed Computing, is an annual conference for the presentation of research on the theory, design, analysis, implementation, and application of distributed systems and network. DISC 2004 was held on October 4–7, 2004, in Amsterdam, The Netherlands.

There were 142 papers submitted to DISC this year. These were read and evaluated by the program committee members, assisted by external reviewers. The quality of submissions was high and we were unable to accept many deserving papers. Thirty one papers were selected at the program committee meeting in Lausanne to be included in these proceedings. The proceedings include an extended abstract of the invited talk by Ueli Maurer. In addition, they include a eulogy for Peter Ruzicka by Shmuel Zaks.

The Best Student Paper Award was split and given to two papers: the paper "Efficient Adaptive Collect Using Randomization", co-authored by Hagit Attiya, Fabian Kuhn, Mirjam Wattenhofer and Roger Wattenhofer, and the paper "Coupling and Self-stabilization", co-authored by Laurent Fribourg, Stephane Messika and Claudine Picaronny.

The support of the CWI and EPFL is gratefully acknowledged. The review process and the preparation of this volume were done using CyberChairPRO. I also thank Sebastien Baehni and Sidath Handurukande for their crucial help with these matters.

August 2004 Rachid Guerraoui

Peter Ruzicka 1947–2003

Peter died on Sunday, October 5, 2003, at the age of 56, after a short disease. He was a Professor of Informatics at the Faculty of Mathematics, Physics and Informatics in Comenius University, Bratislava, Slovakia. Those of us who knew him through DISC and other occasions mourn his death and cherish his memory. These words are written in Peter's honor, as a farewell to a true colleague of our community. Peter's death came as a shock to everyone who knew him. His tragic death is an immense loss to his wife Marta and his daughter Kristina. I hope these words bring some comfort to them.

Peter worked in several research areas of theoretical computer science throughout his long career. His earlier works cover topics that include formal languages, unification, graph pebbling and others. Most of his research works since the early 1990s were in the areas of communication networks and distributed computing, and these works connected Peter to our community. These works include studies of complexity issues for various problems and models of interval routing, and for various problems and topics in distributed computing (like oriented and unoriented networks) and in interconnection networks. Peter was a true hard worker, always choosing difficult and challenging problems. His works always use deep and interesting mathematical tools, and are always presented very clearly and precisely. Peter was very persistent in setting up his research goals and following them. His papers contain many original ideas, and cover all relevant aspects comprehensively. Peter did some of these works together with Stefan Dobrev and Rastislav Kralovic, whom he devotedly supervised as his Ph.D. students in this research area, and he did joint works with many other colleagues.

Peter was a regular participant in many conferences in this area, including DISC and SIROCCO; he was on the program committees of DISC 1998 and 2000 and SIROCCO 1999. He participated and was very actively involved in other conferences, including ICALP, SOFSEM and MFCS. These activities included co-chairing MFCS 1994, chairing MFCS 1997 and chairing SOFSEM 2001, and being on the program committees of MFCS 2000 and SOFSEM 1997. In 1998, when I was the chair of DISC, I approached Peter, suggesting that he organize DISC in Bratislava, thus bringing DISC, for its first time, to an East-European country. Peter accepted this challenge enthusiastically, and with no hesitation whatsoever. Together with his local team, he then devoted the following year to the organization of DISC 1999 in Bratislava. I was in touch with Peter throughout that year and noticed his conscientious efforts to ensure that the conference would be successful. Indeed, this conference proved to be a great success, and Peter and his team were consequently highly appreciated by the Steering Committee and the whole audience.

I knew that Peter was sick, and I contacted him by email before I left home to attend DISC 2003 in Sorrento, at the end of September. When I returned home, a message waited for me, in which his wife Marta informed me about his death. It turned out that on the same days that we all met in Sorrento, Peter was fighting for his life. He died on Sunday, October 5, 2003, when we all made our way back home from the conference. I learnt from his wife that to the very end Peter proved very strong and was full of hope.

Personally, I found Peter an excellent colleague. I spent a few weeks with Peter, during our common visits to each other's place. The time I spent with him was of the highest value to me. He was always open to discussions of new ideas, very skillful as a researcher, very friendly, and very patient and gentle. I will always cherish Peter and Marta's warm hospitality during my visits to Bratislava.

We will all miss a very precious member of our community. I will miss a dear colleague and friend.

Prof. Shmuel Zaks
Department of Computer Science
Technion, Israel

Organization

DISC, the International Symposium on Distributed Computing, is an annual forum for research presentations on all facets of distributed computing. The symposium was called the International Workshop on Distributed Algorithms (WDAG) from 1985 to 1997. DISC 2004 was organized in cooperation with the European Association for Theoretical Computer Science (EATCS).

Conference Chairs	Jaap-Henk Hoepman, University of Nijmegen
	Paul Vitányi, CWI and University of Amsterdam
Program Chair	Rachid Guerraoui, EPFL
Organizing Committee	Wilmy van Ojik, CWI

Program Committee

Mustaque Ahamad	Georgia Tech
Lorenzo Alvisi	UT Austin
James Anderson	University of North Carolina at Chapel Hill
Paul Attie	Northeastern University
Ozalp Babaoglu	University of Bologna
Carole Delporte	University of Paris VII
Shlomi Dolev	Ben-Gurion University
Pierre Fraigniaud	CNRS
Felix Gaertner	University of Aachen
Maurice Herlihy	Brown University
Nancy Lynch	MIT
Michael Merritt	AT&T
Achour Mostefaoui	IRISA
Mike Reiter	CMU
Robert van Renessee	Cornell University
Luis Rodrigues	University of Lisbon
Paul Spirakis	University of Patras
Philippas Tsigas	Chalmers University
Paul Vitányi	CWI and University of Amsterdam
Roman Vitenberg	UCSB

Referees

Maha Abdallah
Ittai Abraham
Uri Abraham
Adnan Agbaria
Divyakant Agrawal
Marcos Aguilera
Amitanand S. Aiyer
Emmanuelle Anceaume
Krzysztof Apt
Luciana Arantes
Filipe Araujo
James Aspnes
Hagit Attiya
Yossi Azar
R. Badrinath
Sebastien Baehni
Mahesh Balakrishnan
Roberto Baldoni
Amos Beimel
Zinaida Benenson
Mark Bickford
Costas Busch
Gregory Chockler
Allen Clement
Sylvie Delaët
Yefim Dinitz
Frederick Ducatelle
Partha Dutta
Rui Fan
Panagiota Fatourou
Hugues Fauconnier
Dimitris Fotakis
Roy Friedman
Charles Fry
Juan A. Garay
Anders Gidenstam
Garth Goodson
Eric Goubault
Maria Gradinariu
Abishek Gutta
Phuong Ha
Martin Haenggi
David Hales
Sidath Handurukande

Mor Harchol-Balter
Yinnon Haviv
Jean-Michel Hélary
Ted Herman
Phuong Hoai Ha
Michel Hurfin
Amos Israeli
Michael A. Jaeger
Mark Jelasity
Colette Johnen
Alon Kama
Ronen I. Kat
Idit Keidar
Anne-Marie Kermarrec
Alex Kesselman
Roger Khazan
Boris Koldehofe
Lei Kong
Spyros Kontogiannis
Petr Kouznetsov
Danny Krizanc
Limor Lahiani
Kofi Laing
Subramanian
    Lakshmanan
Gerard Le Lann
Ron Levy
Feng Li
Xiaozhou (Steve) Li
Zvi Lotker
Dahlia Malkhi
Deepak Manohar
Jean-Philippe Martin
Marios Mavronicolas
Maged Michael
Martin Mink
Hugo Miranda
Mark Moir
Alberto Montresor
Gero Mühl
Jeff Napper
Priya Narasimhan
Tina Nolte
Michael Okun

Rui Oliveira
Florin Oprea
Vicky Papadopoulou
Marina Papatriantafilou
Simon Patarin
Lucia Draque Penso
Sara Tucci Piergiovanni
Lexi Pimenidis
Stefan Pleisch
Bastian Pochon
Michel Raynal
Robert van Renessee
Matthieu Roy
Eric Ruppert
Asad Samar
Christian Scheideler
Elad Schiller
Pierre Sens
Noam Singer
Jesper Spring
Maarten van Steen
Frank Stomp
Gideon Stupp
Håkan Sundell
Mikkel Thorup
Sebastien Tixeuil
Peter Triantafillou
Nir Tzachar
Sankarapandian
    Vijayaraghavan
Jean-Marc Vincent
Antonino Virgillito
Ramesh Viswanath
Hagen Völzer
Jaksa Vuckovic
Marko Vukolic
Jay J. Wylie
Reuven Yagel
Praveen Yalagandula
Christos Zaroliagis
Zhiyuan Zhan
Yi Zhang
Lantian Zheng

Table of Contents

The Synchronous
Condition-Based Consensus Hierarchy*

Achour Mostefaoui[1], Sergio Rajsbaum[2], and Michel Raynal[1]

[1] IRISA, Campus de Beaulieu, 35042 Rennes Cedex, France
{achour,raynal}@irisa.fr
[2] Instituto de Matemáticas, UNAM, D.F. 04510, Mexico
rajsbaum@math.unam.mx

Abstract. In the context of a system made up of n processes where at most t can crash, the *condition-based approach* studies restrictions on the inputs of a distributed problem, called *conditions,* that make it solvable, or easier to solve (in case it is solvable without restricting its inputs). Previous work studied conditions for consensus and other agreement problems, mostly for asynchronous systems. This paper considers the condition-based approach for consensus in synchronous systems, and establishes a bridge between the asynchronous and synchronous models, with a hierarchy $\mathcal{S}_t^{[-t]} \subset \cdots \subset \mathcal{S}_t^{[0]} \subset \cdots \subset \mathcal{S}_t^{[t]}$ where $\mathcal{S}_t^{[t]}$ includes all conditions (and in particular the trivial one made up of all possible input vectors). For a condition $C \in \mathcal{S}_t^{[d]}$, $-t \leq d \leq t$, we have:

- For values of $d \leq 0$ we have the hierarchy of conditions (we introduced in PODC'01) where consensus is solvable by more and more efficient protocols in an asynchronous system with t failures, as we go from $d = 0$ to $d = -t$.
- For values of $d > 0$ consensus is not solvable in an asynchronous system with t failures, but it is solvable in a synchronous system with more and more rounds, as we go from $d = 1$ (two rounds) to $d = t$ ($t + 1$ rounds).
- $d = 0$ is the borderline case where consensus is solvable in an asynchronous system with t failures, and optimally in a synchronous system (we proved this in DISC'03).

The two main results of this paper are proving the second item above. For the upper bound, the paper presents a generic synchronous early-deciding uniform consensus protocol. When instantiated with a condition $C \in \mathcal{S}_t^{[d]}$, $1 \leq d \leq t < n$, the processes decide in at most $\min(\alpha+1, f+2, t+1)$ rounds, where f is the number of actual crashes, and $\alpha = d$ if the input vector belongs to C, or $\alpha = +\infty$ otherwise. The paper establishes a corresponding lower bound stating that $d+1$ rounds are necessary to get a decision when the input vector belong to C.

Keywords: Condition, Consensus, Early deciding, Input Vector, Message passing, Process crash failure, Synchronous distributed system.

* This work has been supported by a grant from LAFMI (Franco-Mexican Lab in Computer Science). Proofs ommitted here for lack of space appear in [26].

R. Guerraoui (Ed.): DISC 2004, LNCS 3274, pp. 1–15, 2004.

1 Introduction

Context of the paper. The *consensus* problem is a central paradigm of fault-tolerant distributed computing informally stated as follows. Each process proposes a value, and each non-faulty process has to decide a value in such a way that a decided value is a proposed value and the non-faulty processes decide the same value. *Uniform consensus* is a stronger version of the problem where it is required that no two processes (correct or faulty) decide distinct values.

This paper considers a synchronous distributed model with n processes. A process can be faulty only by crashing, and at most t ($1 \leq t < n$) processes can crash in a run. There are many papers with algorithms and lower bounds for consensus in this model (e.g., see [29] for a survey). It has been shown that both consensus and uniform consensus require $t + 1$ rounds in the worst case [11, 12, 20]. Let f be the number of processes that actually crash during a given run ($0 \leq f \leq t$). For *early deciding* consensus, it has been shown that consensus requires at least $f + 1$ rounds [2, 21, 22], while early deciding uniform consensus requires at least $\min(f + 2, t + 1)$ rounds ($f < t - 1$) [7, 19]. Protocols that meet those lower bounds have been designed, thereby showing that they are tight.

In contrast to synchronous systems, consensus (hence, also uniform consensus) cannot be solved in asynchronous systems even if only a single crash failure is possible [13]. Several approaches have been proposed to circumvent this impossibility result, such as probabilistic protocols (e.g., [4]), failure detectors and partially synchronous models (e.g., [6, 10, 17, 27]), stronger communication primitives (e.g., [16]) and weaker versions of consensus (e.g., [5, 8]). More recently, the *condition-based* approach to circumvent the consensus impossibility result has been studied (e.g., [1, 14, 23, 25]). This approach restricts the possible inputs to a distributed problem to make it solvable, or to solve it more efficiently. For example, if we assume that "more than a majority of processes propose the same value" then consensus is solvable for $t = 1$ in an asynchronous system. A subset of inputs is called a *condition* and consists of a set of vectors; each entry of a vector contains the private input value of one process.

Motivation. In a previous work [23] we identified the conditions for which consensus is solvable in an asynchronous distributed system with t failures, and called them *t-legal*. Roughly, C is x-legal if its associated graph $G(C, x)$ satisfies the following condition. The graph contains as vertices the input vectors of C, and two vertices are connected with an edge iff their Hamming distance is at most x. Then, C is x-legal if for every connected component of $G(C, x)$ there is a value v that appears more than x times in every one of its vertices. Thus, there are connections with coding theory [14].

Very recently, two papers [24, 30] started investigating the condition-based approach in synchronous systems. In [24] we discovered that uniform consensus is solvable in two rounds with any t-legal condition. More precisely, we presented (1) a condition-based uniform consensus protocol that terminates in two rounds when the input vector belongs to the condition whatever the actual number of failures f (and in one round when additionally $f = 0$), and in $t + 1$ rounds otherwise, and (2) a theorem showing that if uniform consensus is solvable for a condition C in two rounds when the input vector belongs to C, whatever the number f of crashes ($f \leq t < n$), then C is $(t-1)$-legal. Thus, these results relate synchronous and asynchronous systems where t processes can crash: uniform consensus in an asynchronous system is solvable for a condition C if and only if it is solvable optimally in a synchronous system (optimally because any uniform consensus algorithm needs at least two rounds to decide [19]).

Another bridge between synchrony and asynchrony was discovered in [30]. Considering a slightly weaker synchronous model (see Section 3.1) and assuming $t < n/2$, that paper presents a protocol that solves consensus in $d + 2$ rounds for any $(t - d)$-legal condition, for $0 \leq d \leq t$, when the input belongs to the condition, and in $t + 1$ rounds when the input does not belong to the condition. These two papers thus leave open the general situation of $0 < d \leq t$, both for designing condition-based *early deciding* protocols, and proving lower bounds on the number of rounds needed to solve condition-based synchronous consensus. The goal of this paper is to answer these questions as well as to explore further the relation between synchronous and asynchronous systems.

Results. This paper introduces a full classification of conditions for consensus, establishing a continuum between the asynchronous and synchronous models, with the hierarchy

$$\mathcal{S}_t^{[-t]} \subset \cdots \subset \mathcal{S}_t^{[y]} \subset \mathcal{S}_t^{[y+1]} \subset \cdots \subset \mathcal{S}_t^{[0]} \subset \cdots \subset \mathcal{S}_t^{[x]} \subset \mathcal{S}_t^{[x+1]} \subset \cdots \subset \mathcal{S}_t^{[t]}.$$

A condition C is in $\mathcal{S}_t^{[d]}$, $-t \leq d \leq t$ iff it is $(t - d)$-legal. This hierarchy exposes further relations with the asynchronous model:

- For values of $d \leq 0$ consensus is solvable in an asynchronous system with t failures, and we get a hierarchy of conditions described in [25], where it is possible to solve asynchronous consensus with more and more efficient protocols as we go from $d = 0$ to $d = -t$ (where it is solved optimally).
- For values of $d > 0$ consensus is not solvable in an asynchronous system with t failures, but we get a hierarchy of conditions where consensus is solvable in a synchronous system with more and more rounds as we go from $d = 1$ (which requires only two rounds) to $d = t$ (which requires $t + 1$ rounds, but where any condition is possible).
- $d = 0$ is the borderline case where consensus is solvable in an asynchronous system with t failures, and optimally in a synchronous system. We proved this in [24].

The two main results presented in this paper are proving the second item above. For the upper bound, the paper presents a generic synchronous early-deciding uniform consensus protocol. When instantiated with a condition C in $\mathcal{S}_t^{[d]}$, $1 \leq d \leq t$, the protocol[1] solves the problem in at most $\min(\alpha+1, f+2, t+1)$ rounds, where $\alpha = d$ if the input vector belongs to C, or $\alpha = +\infty$ otherwise. The

---

[1] For clarity, we leave out from this extended abstract the simple extension to $d = 0$.

second result is a lower bound for synchronous consensus conditions, namely, when $d \geq 1$, any consensus protocol based on a condition $C \in \mathcal{S}_t^{[d]}$ has a run in which at least $d + 1$ rounds are necessary to get a decision.

The design of a synchronous condition-based consensus protocol that keeps the early deciding property is not an easy challenge. An early-deciding protocol must somehow reconcile two potentially conflicting values: the value possibly decided from the condition and the value possibly decided from the early deciding mechanism. Handling this conflict without requiring additional rounds reveals to be far from being trivial.

The investigation of relations between synchronous and asynchronous models is an important question (e.g., [15, 18, 22]). For our lower bound we use techniques from [19, 22]. Gafni's relation (that an asynchronous system with at most k failures can implement the first $\lfloor t/k \rfloor$ rounds of a synchronous system with t failures) [15] does not seem to imply our results. In [18] it is identified a mathematical structure that can be used to model both synchronous and asynchronous systems, useful to prove k-set agreement lower bounds.

This paper is organized as follows. General background about the condition-based approach and consensus in asynchronous systems appear in Section 2. The synchronous model and corresponding condition-based definitions appear in Section 3. The condition-based synchronous protocols are described in Section 4. The lower bound is proved in Section 5. (Proofs appear in [26].)

2   The Condition-Based Approach to Solve Consensus

2.1   The Consensus Problem

In the *uniform consensus* problem every process p_i *proposes* a value v_i and the processes have to *decide* on a value v, such that the following three properties are satisfied:

- Termination: Every correct process eventually decides.
- Validity: If a process decides v, then v was proposed by some process.
- Uniform Agreement: No two (correct or not) processes decide

different values. In the following $\mathcal{V}$ denotes the set of values that can be proposed by the processes, $|\mathcal{V}| \geq 2$.

2.2   The Condition-Based Approach in Asynchronous Systems

An *input vector* is a size n vector, whose i-th entry contains the value proposed by p_i, or $\perp$ if p_i did not take any step in the execution, $\perp \notin \mathcal{V}$. It will be convenient to assume that $\forall a \in \mathcal{V}$, $\perp < a$. We usually denote with I an input vector with all entries in $\mathcal{V}$, and with J an input vector that may have some entries equal to $\perp$; such a vector J is called a *view*. The set $\mathcal{V}^n$ consists of all the possible input vectors with all entries in $\mathcal{V}$, and $\mathcal{V}_x^n$ denotes the set of all possible input vectors with all entries in $\mathcal{V} \cup \{\perp\}$ and at most x entries equal to $\perp$.

For $I \in \mathcal{V}^n$, $\mathcal{I}_x$ denotes the set of possible views J such that J is equal to I except for at most x entries that are equal to $\perp$. A *condition* C is a subset of $\mathcal{V}^n$, i.e., $C \subseteq \mathcal{V}^n$. Given C, C_x denotes the union of the $\mathcal{I}_x$'s over all $I \in C$, i.e., $C_x = \bigcup_{I \in C} \mathcal{I}_x$.

For any pair of vectors $J1, J2 \in \mathcal{V}_x^n$, $J1$ is *contained* in $J2$ (denoted $J1 \leq J2$) if $\forall k : J1[k] \neq \perp \Rightarrow J1[k] = J2[k]$. Finally, $\#_a(J)$ denotes the number of occurrences of a value a in the vector J, with $a \in \mathcal{V} \cup \{\perp\}$. Finally, $dist(J, J')$ is the Hamming distance separating J and J', where J and J' are two vectors of $\mathcal{V}_x^n$. We can now present the main definition of [14, 23] as formulated in [30]:

Definition 1. *A condition C is x-legal if there exists a mapping $h : C \mapsto \mathcal{V}$ with the following properties:*

- $\forall I \in C$: $\#_{h(I)}(I) > x$, *and*
- $\forall I1, I2 \in C$: $h(I1) \neq h(I2) \Rightarrow dist(I1, I2) > x$.

A main result of [23] is the following.

Theorem 1. [23] *A condition C allows to solve consensus in an asynchronous system prone to up to t process crashes if and only if it is t-legal.*

A general method to define t-legal conditions is described in [25] where two natural t-legal conditions are defined. By way of example, we present here one of them, $C1_t$. Let $\max(I)$ denote the greatest value of I. Then

$$(I \in C1_t) \overset{def}{=} \#_{\max(I)}(I) > t.$$

It is easy to check that $C1_t$ is t-legal with $h(I) = \max(I)$, and, when at least $t + 1$ entries of the input vector I are equal to its greatest entry, consensus can be solved despite up to t process crashes using h. Moreover, it is shown in [23] that $C1_t$ is maximal.

Definition 2. *An x-legal condition C is* maximal *if any vector added to C makes it non x-legal.*

While legality has been useful to prove lower bound results, an equivalent formulation called acceptability in [23] is more convenient to design protocols. This formulation is in terms of a predicate P and a function S that are required to satisfy the following:

- Property $T_{C \to P}$: $I \in C \Rightarrow \forall J \in \mathcal{I}_x : P(J)$.
- Property $V_{P \to S}$: $\forall J \in \mathcal{V}_x^n$:
  $P(J) \Rightarrow S(J) =$ a non-$\perp$ value of J (determ. chosen).
- Property $A_{P \to S}$: $\forall J1, J2 \in \mathcal{V}_x^n$:
  $P(J1) \wedge P(J2) \wedge (J1 \leq J2) \Rightarrow S(J1) = S(J2)$.

Assume up to x processes can crash in the system. Then every $I \in \mathcal{V}^n$ is a possible input vector, and any J such that $J \leq I$ and $J \in \mathcal{V}_x^n$ can be a view of it obtained by a process p_i. Intuitively, the first property allows p_i to test from its view if the input vector may belong to C. The second property is used to guarantee validity. The third property is used to guarantee agreement.

Definition 3. *A condition C is x-acceptable if there exist a predicate P and a function S satisfying the properties* $T_{C \to P}$, $A_{P \to S}$ *and* $V_{P \to S}$.

We have the following equivalence:

Theorem 2. [23] *A condition C is x-acceptable if and only if it is x-legal.*

It is shown in [23] that $C1_t$ is t-acceptable with the following predicate P and function S:

- $P1(J) \equiv \#_{\max(J)}(J) > t - \#_\perp(J)$, and
- $S1(J) = \max(J)$.

2.3   Hierarchy in Asynchronous Systems

Let us define $\mathcal{S}_t^{[d]}$ to be the set of all $(t - d)$-legal conditions, for $-t \leq d \leq 0$. As stated in Theorem 1, consensus is solvable in an asynchronous system prone to up to t process crashes for C if and only if $C \in \mathcal{S}_t^{[0]}$. It is easy to check that $\mathcal{S}_t^{[d-1]} \subset \mathcal{S}_t^{[d]}$. Thus, if C is $(t-d)$-legal, for $d < 0$, then consensus is also solvable for C. It turns out [25] that in fact it is possible to solve asynchronous consensus with more and more efficient protocols as we go from $d = 0$ to $d = -t$, where it is solved optimally. In this sense we have the hierarchy

$$\mathcal{S}_t^{[-t]} \subset \cdots \subset \mathcal{S}_t^{[y]} \subset \mathcal{S}_t^{[y+1]} \subset \cdots \subset \mathcal{S}_t^{[0]}.$$

3   Hierarchy of Conditions for Synchronous Systems

3.1   Computation Model

The system model consists of a finite set of processes, $\Pi = \{p_1, \ldots, p_n\}$, that communicate by sending and receiving messages through channels. Every pair of processes p_i and p_j is connected by a channel denoted (p_i, p_j). The underlying communication system is assumed to be failure-free: there is no creation, alteration, loss or duplication of message. An execution consists of a sequence of *rounds*. For the processes, the current round number appears as a global variable r that they can read, and whose progress is managed by the underlying system. A round is made up of three consecutive phases: (1) A send phase in which each process sends messages; (2) A receive phase in which each process receives all the messages that were sent to it in the round, (3) A computation phase in which each process processes the messages it received during that round.

A process is *faulty* during an execution if it prematurely stops its execution (crash). After it has crashed, a process does nothing. We assume that at most t processes can crash, while f denotes the actual number of faulty processes during a run, with $0 \leq f \leq t$ and $1 \leq t < n$.

In a send phase a process sends the same message to each process in a predetermined order. We use this to obtain views of input vectors ordered by containment. In contrast, some other synchronous models, like the one considered in [30], the adversary can choose any subset of the messages sent by a crashed process to be lost. To obtain an effect similar to the containment property, [30] assumes $t < n/2$.

3.2 $(t, d)_{synch}$-Acceptability

This section shows that the acceptability notion that has been used in the past to study asynchronous systems is also suited to synchronous systems where up to t processes can crash ($t < n$). As we are interested in a hierarchy of classes of conditions, we introduce a parameter d ($0 \leq d \leq t$) related to the position of the class in the hierarchy.

Definition 4. *A condition C is $(t, d)_{synch}$-acceptable if it is $(t - d)$-acceptable.*

Thus, when we consider a synchronous system where up to t processes can crash, it is possible to associate a pair of parameters P and S with a $(t, d)_{synch}$-acceptable condition C such that

- Property $T_{C \rightarrow P}$: $J \in \mathcal{C}_{t-d} \Rightarrow P(J)$.
- Property $V_{P \rightarrow S}$: $\forall J \in \mathcal{V}^n_{t-d}$: $P(J) \Rightarrow S(J)=$ a non-$\perp$ value of J.
- Property $A^{[d]}_{P \rightarrow S}$: $\forall J1, J2 \in \mathcal{V}^n_{t-d}$:
  $P(J1) \wedge P(J2) \wedge (J1 \leq J2) \Rightarrow S(J1) = S(J2)$.

3.3 A Hierarchy of Classes of Conditions

Let $\mathcal{S}^{[d]}_t$ be the set of all the $(t, d)_{synch}$-acceptable conditions. The class of $(t, t)_{synch}$-acceptable conditions is the largest one and includes every condition, while the class of $(t, 0)_{synch}$-acceptable conditions is the smallest one is equal to the class of t-acceptable conditions.

Theorem 3. *If C is $(t, d)_{synch}$-acceptable then it is also $(t, d+1)_{synch}$-acceptable. Moreover, there exists at least one condition that is $(t, d+1)_{synch}$-acceptable but not $(t, d)_{synch}$-acceptable.*

That is, we have $\mathcal{S}^{[0]}_t \subset \cdots \subset \mathcal{S}^{[d]}_t \subset \mathcal{S}^{[d+1]}_t \subset \cdots \subset \mathcal{S}^{[t]}_t$. The proof of this result follows from the equivalent result for asynchronous systems in [23], since by definition a $(t, d)_{synch}$-acceptable condition is $(t - d)$-acceptable. It is proved there that $C1_{t-d-1}$ is $(t, d + 1)_{synch}$-acceptable but not $(t, d)_{synch}$-acceptable.

4   A Condition-Based Synchronous Protocol

The aim of this section is to present a synchronous uniform consensus protocol that, when instantiated with a $(t, d)_{synch}$-acceptable condition $C_t^{[d]}$, allows the processes to decide in at most $\min(\alpha + 1, f + 2, t + 1)$, where $\alpha = d$ if the input vector I belong to $C_t^{[d]}$, and $\alpha = +\infty$ otherwise. As already noticed, when $I \in C_t^{[d]}$, decision occurs by round $d + 1$ whatever the number $f \leq t$ of actual process crashes, and their occurrence pattern (i.e., even if there is a crash per round).

The protocol is presented in an incremental way. The first step enriches a flood set protocol to take into account $(t, d)_{synch}$-acceptable conditions. It is not early-deciding: the processes decide in at most $d+1$ rounds when the input vector belongs to the condition, and in at most $t + 1$ rounds otherwise. Then, this basic protocol is in turn enriched to take into account the early deciding possibilities, providing a protocol where the processes decide by round $\min(\alpha+1, f+2, t+1)$.

Notations. UP^r denotes the set of processes that have not crashed by the end of round r. V_i^r denotes the value of V_i after it has been updated by p_i during round r (e.g., after line 111 in the protocol described in Figure 1). Similarly, w_i^r denotes the value of w_i at the end of round r.

4.1   Basic Protocol: Principles and Description

A synchronous uniform consensus condition-based protocol that tolerates t crashes is described in Figure 1. It is assumed to be instantiated with the pair (P, S) of parameters associated with a $(t, d)_{synch}$-acceptable condition C $(1 \leq d \leq t)$. It terminates in at most $d+1$ rounds when the input vector belongs to C, and in at most $t + 1$ rounds otherwise.

As previously indicated, this first protocol can be seen as the composition of two sub-protocols, the round number r $(1 \leq r \leq t+1)$ acting as the composition glue. More precisely, we have the following. The first sub-protocol is the classical flood set uniform consensus protocol [3, 21, 29] which ensures the $t + 1$ lower bound when the input vector does not belong to $C_t^{[d]}$ (the condition the protocol is instantiated with). The second sub-protocol addresses the condition part. It is based on the following principles. Let p_i and p_j be two processes in UP^r.

- At the beginning of a round (line 104), a process p_i sends to the other processes (in a predetermined order, namely, first to p_1, then p_2, etc.) the set new_i of the new values it has learnt during the previous round. It also sends two other values: w_i that is its current knowledge on the value that should be decided from the condition, and a boolean flag $too\_much\_f_i$ (see below).
- Then (line 105), p_i decides the value w_i determined from the condition (if there is such a value). Let us observe that this can happen only from the second round.

- A process p_i then enriches its current view V_i of the input vector (lines 109-112). This view is used to compute the value w_i determined from the condition (if any) or to deterministically extract from this view and decide a value (see the lines 120 and 124 when $w_i = \perp$).
- The lines 113-122 constitute the core of the protocol as far as the condition approach is concerned. As we can see it is made up of two parts according to the current round number.
  - $r = 1$. If p_i has got a view V_i of the input vector with at most $(t - d)$ crashes (line 114), it looks if V_i could be from an input vector I belonging to the condition C. If it is the case, p_i computes the corresponding value w_i determined from the $(t - d)$-acceptable condition C.

    If p_i has got a view V_i of the input vector with more than $(t-d)$ crashes (line 115), it sets the flag $too\_much\_f_i$ thereby indicating there are too many failures for it to test whether the view could be from an input vector of the condition.
  - $r > 1$. In that case, p_i adopts the value that has to be decided from the condition (line 118), if it is possible ($v \in W_i$) and has not already been done ($w_i = \perp$).

    Then, if the predicate $r = d + 1 \ \wedge \ TOO\_MUCH\_F_i$ is satisfied, p_i decides (line 119). If there is a value determined from the condition, p_i decides it. Otherwise, p_i decides a value deterministically chosen from its current view V_i.

    The predicate $r = d + 1 \ \wedge \ TOO\_MUCH\_F_i$ states that at least one process has seen more than $(t - d)$ crashes during the first round. As we will see (Lemma 1), in that case two processes $p_i, p_j \in UP^{d+1}$ have necessarily the same view at $r = d + 1$. Thus, the processes decide the same value that is either the value v determined from the condition (they have it in their w_i local variables), or the same value deterministically extracted from the same view $V_i = V_j$.

Theorem 4. *Let us assume that the input vector belongs to the condition. The protocol described in Figure 1 terminates in: (i) 2 rounds when no more than $(t-d)$ processes crash by the end of the first round, (ii) and at most $d+1$ rounds otherwise.*

The following lemma is a key lemma for establishing consensus agreement.

Lemma 1. *Let x_1 be the number of processes that have crashed by the end of the first round. Either (i) $V_i^r \in V_{t-(r-1)}^n$ for every $p_i \in UP^r$, or else (ii) $x_1 > t - (r - 1)$. Moreover, if $x_1 > t - (r - 1)$ then $V_i^r = V_j^r$, for every $p_i, p_j \in UP^r$.*

Theorem 5. *When instantiated with a condition $C \in \mathcal{S}_t^{[d]}$, the protocol described in Figure 1 solves the uniform consensus problem.*

Function $CB^{[d]}\_Consensus(v_i)$

(101) $V_i \leftarrow [\bot, \ldots, \bot]; V_i[i] \leftarrow v_i; new_i \leftarrow \{(v_i, i)\};$
$\quad\quad\quad w_i \leftarrow \bot; too\_much\_f_i \leftarrow false;$
(102)   **when** $r = 1, 2, \ldots, t + 1$ **do**
(103)   **begin_round**
(104) $\quad$ **send** $(new_i, w_i, too\_much\_f_i)$ to $p_1, \ldots, p_n$ **in that order;**
(105) $\quad$ **if** $(w_i \neq \bot)$ **then** *return* (w_i) **end_if;**
(106) $\quad$ **let** $rec\_from_i[j] = new_j$ set received from p_j (if any), otherwise $\emptyset$;
(107) $\quad$ **let** $W_i =$ the set of w_j values received; % $W_i = \{v\}$ or $\{\bot\}$ or$\{v, \bot\}$ %
(108) $\quad$ **let** $TOO\_MUCH\_F_i = \vee_j \, too\_much\_f_j$ ("oring" of the rec. values);
(109) $\quad$ $new_i \leftarrow \emptyset;$
(110) $\quad$ **for_each** j **do for_each** $(x, k) \in rec\_from_i[j]$ **do**
(111) $\quad\quad\quad$ **if** $(V_i[k] = \bot)$ **then** $V_i[k] \leftarrow x; new_i \leftarrow new_i \cup \{(x, k)\}$ **end_if**
(112) $\quad$ **end_do end_do;**
(113) $\quad$ **case** $(r = 1)$ **then**
(114) $\quad\quad\quad$ **case** $(\#_\bot(V_i) \leq t - d)$ **then if** $P(V_i)$ **then** $w_i \leftarrow S(V_i)$ **end_if**
(115) $\quad\quad\quad\quad\quad$ $(\#_\bot(V_i) > t - d)$ **then** $too\_much\_f_i \leftarrow true$
(116) $\quad\quad\quad$ **end_case**
(117) $\quad\quad$ $(r > 1)$ **then**
(118) $\quad\quad\quad$ **if** $(w_i = \bot \wedge (v \in W_i \text{ with } v \neq \bot))$ **then** $w_i \leftarrow v$ **end_if;**
(119) $\quad\quad\quad$ **if** $(r = d + 1 \, \wedge \, TOO\_MUCH\_F_i)$ **then**
(120) $\quad\quad\quad\quad$ **if** $(w_i \neq \bot)$ **then** *return* (w_i) **else** *return* $(\min(V_i))$ **end_if**
(121) $\quad\quad\quad$ **end_if**
(122) $\quad$ **end_case**
(123)   **end_round;**
(124)   **if** $(w_i \neq \bot)$ **then** *return* (w_i) **else** *return* $(\min(V_i))$ **end_if**

Fig. 1. A Synchronous Condition-Based Uniform Consensus Protocol $(1 \leq d \leq t < n)$

4.2   Adding Early Decision to Condition: A Generic Protocol

This section enriches the previous protocol to get a protocol that decides in $\min(\alpha + 1, f + 2, t + 1)$, where $\alpha = d$ if the input vector I belong to $C_t^{[d]}$, and $\alpha = +\infty$ otherwise. As already noticed, when $I \in C_t^{[d]}$, decision occurs by round $d + 1$ even if there is a crash per round. In that sense, this protocol benefits from the best of both possible worlds (early decision and condition).

As indicated in the Introduction, the main difficulty in combining early decision (that comes from the fact that f is smaller than t), and the use of a condition, lies in a correct handling of the possible conflict between the value possibly decided from the early decision mechanism and the value possibly decided from the condition.

To keep the structure clear and makes the understanding and the proof relatively easy, we enrich the basic protocol (Figure 1) only with additional statements that do not interfere with previous statements (i.e., this means that there is no modification of existing statements and the new statement reads and writes its "own" variables). The resulting general protocol is described in Figure 2.

The additional lines are the lines 205-a, 205-b, and 205-c. These lines define a new local variable, namely, $nb_i[r]$, that counts the number of processes from which p_i has received a message during the round r ($nb_i[-1]$ and $nb_i[0]$ are appropriately initialized for consistency purpose). A new predicate ($early\_dec_i$) on the values of these local variables is defined. The aim of the $early\_dec_i$ predicate, namely,

$$((nb_i[r] \geq n - r + 2) \vee (r > 2) \wedge (nb_i[r - 2] = nb_i[r - 1]))$$

is to provide early decision whenever it is possible. This predicate is made up of two parts.

- Assuming that there are at most f crashes, the worst case is when there is one crash per round from the first round until round f (so, there is no more crash after round f). The aim of the first predicate, namely $(nb_i[r] \geq n - r + 2)$, is to ensure that no more than $f + 2$ rounds can be executed. As $(n - f)$ processes do not crash, we have $(nb_i[r] \geq n - f)$ at any round r; therefore, using $(nb_i[r] \geq n - r + 2)$ as a decision predicate guarantees that a process decides at the latest at the round $r = f + 2$.
- The second part of the predicate aims at ensuring termination as early as possible, and not only at the end of the round $f + 2$. This can occur when several processes crash during the same round. For example if f processes crash before the protocol execution and no process crashes later, we do not want to delay the decision until round $f + 2$. This kind of very early decision is ensured by the predicate $nb_i[r-2] = nb_i[r-1]$ which states that p_i received messages from the same set of processes during two consecutive rounds [9, 20, 29]. When this occurs, p_i can safely conclude that it knows all the values that can be known (as it got messages from all the processes that were not crashed at the beginning of $r - 1$). In order to prevent a possible conflict between the value decided by the early decision mechanism and the value decided from the condition (if any), the predicate $nb_i[r-2] = nb_i[r-1]$ must not be evaluated during the first two rounds. (This particular case motivated the first part of the predicate, namely $(nb_i[r] \geq n - r + 2)$, which works for any round r, but cannot ensures early decision before the round $f + 2$.)

Early decision makes possible that several processes do not decide during the same round. So, it is crucial to prevent a process p_i to erroneously consider as crashed a process p_j that decided in a previous round. To prevent such a possibility, a process p_j that decides during a round r is required to execute an additional round after deciding, thereby informing any other process p_i not to consider it as crashed in the rounds $r' \geq r + 1$. In order not to overload the presentation of the protocol, this additional round and the associated management of the variable nb_i are not described in Figure 2.

Theorem 6. *The protocol described in Figure 2 allows the processes to decide in at most $min(\alpha + 1, f + 2, t + 1)$ rounds, where $\alpha = d$ if the input vector I belongs to $C_t^{[d]}$, and $\alpha = +\infty$ otherwise.*

Function $ED\_CB^{[d]}\_Consensus(v_i)$

$(201)\ V_i \leftarrow [\bot, \ldots, \bot];\ V_i[i] \leftarrow v_i;\ new_i \leftarrow \{(v_i, i)\};\ w_i \leftarrow \bot;\ too\_much\_f_i \leftarrow false;$
$(202)\ \textbf{when } r = 1, 2, \ldots, t+1 \textbf{ do}$
$(203)\ \textbf{begin\_round}$
$(204)\ \quad \textbf{send } (new_i, w_i, too\_much\_f_i) \textbf{ to } p_1, \ldots, p_n \textbf{ in that order;}$
$(205)\ \quad \textbf{if } (w_i \neq \bot) \textbf{ then } return\ (w_i) \textbf{ end\_if;}$

$(205)\text{-a}\ \textbf{let } nb_i[r] = \text{number of proc. from which } p_i \text{ received msgs during } r;$
$\qquad\qquad \text{Initial values: } nb_i[-1] \leftarrow (n+1);\ nb_i[0] \leftarrow n;$
$(205)\text{-b}\ \textbf{let } early\_dec_i =$
$\qquad\qquad\qquad \big(nb_i[r] \geq n - r + 2\big) \vee \big((r > 2) \wedge (nb_i[r-2] = nb_i[r-1])\big);$
$(205)\text{-c}\ \textbf{if } (early\_dec_i) \textbf{ then } return\ (min(V_i)) \textbf{ end\_if;}$

$(206)\ \quad \textbf{let } rec\_from_i[j] = new_j \text{ set received from } p_j \text{ (if any), otherwise } \emptyset;$
$(207)\ \quad \textbf{let } W_i = \text{the set of } w_j \text{ values received; } \%\ W_i = \{v\} \text{ or } \{\bot\} \text{ or} \{v, \bot\}\ \%$
$(208)\ \quad \textbf{let } TOO\_MUCH\_F_i = \vee_j\ too\_much\_f_j \text{ ('oring'' of the values received);}$
$(209)\ \quad new_i \leftarrow \emptyset;$
$(210)\ \quad \textbf{for\_each } j \textbf{ do for\_each } (x, k) \in rec\_from_i[j] \textbf{ do}$
$(211)\ \qquad\qquad \textbf{if } (V_i[k] = \bot) \textbf{ then } V_i[k] \leftarrow x;\ new_i \leftarrow new_i \cup \{(x, k)\} \textbf{ end\_if}$
$(212)\ \quad \textbf{end\_do end\_do;}$
$(213)\ \quad \textbf{case } (r = 1) \textbf{ then}$
$(214)\ \qquad\qquad \textbf{case } (\#_\bot(V_i) > t - d) \textbf{ then } too\_much\_f_i \leftarrow true$
$(215)\ \qquad\qquad\quad (\#_\bot(V_i) \leq t - d) \textbf{ then if } P(V_i) \textbf{ then } w_i \leftarrow S(V_i) \textbf{ end\_if}$
$(216)\ \qquad\qquad \textbf{end\_case}$
$(217)\ \qquad (r > 1) \textbf{ then}$
$(218)\ \qquad\qquad \textbf{if } \big(w_i = \bot \wedge (v \in W_i \text{ with } v \neq \bot)\big) \textbf{ then } w_i \leftarrow v \textbf{ end\_if;}$
$(219)\ \qquad\qquad \textbf{if } (r = d+1 \wedge TOO\_MUCH\_F_i) \textbf{ then}$
$(220)\ \qquad\qquad\qquad \textbf{if } (w_i \neq \bot) \textbf{ then } return\ (w_i) \textbf{ else } return\ (min(V_i)) \textbf{ end\_if}$
$(221)\ \qquad\qquad \textbf{end\_if}$
$(222)\ \quad \textbf{end\_case}$
$(223)\ \textbf{end\_round;}$
$(224)\ \textbf{if } (w_i \neq \bot) \textbf{ then } return\ (w_i) \textbf{ else } return\ (min(V_i)) \textbf{ end\_if}$

Fig. 2. Early Deciding Condition-Based Uniform Consensus Protocol $(1 \leq d \leq t < n)$

Theorem 7. *When instantiated with a condition* $C \in \mathcal{S}_t^{[d]}$, *the protocol described in Figure 2 solves the uniform consensus problem.*

5   Lower Bound

Consider the protocol of Figure 1, instantiated with the pair of parameters (P, S) associated with a $(t, d)_{synch}$-acceptable condition C. Theorem 4 states that this protocol has a worst case round complexity of $t + 1$ rounds. This is known to be optimal [12, 20]. Theorem 4 also states that the protocol terminates in $d + 1$

rounds when the input vector belongs to the condition. Assuming the input vector always belongs to the condition, this section proves a corresponding lower bound.

We would like to prove that, given any $(t, d)_{synch}$-acceptable condition C, there is no protocol that terminates in less than $d + 1$ rounds on all input vectors that belong to the condition. However, this is clearly not true. Consider the condition $C = \{0^n\}$, which is trivially x-legal for every $x < n$. Taking $d = 1$, C is $(t, 1)_{synch}$-acceptable, and hence, the protocol of Figure 1 always terminates in two rounds with input 0^n (Theorem 4). But, when we assume that the input vector always belongs to C, there is a simple protocol that allows the processes to decide without executing rounds (namely, a process decides 0 without communicating with the other processes!). We avoid this anomaly by working with (t, d)-acceptable conditions that are maximal (Definition 2): any vector added to such a condition makes it non (t, d)-acceptable. We have the following straightforward lemma:

Lemma 2. *Let C be a $(t, d)_{synch}$-acceptable with the associated pair of parameters (P, S). Then, if $a = S(I)$ for $I \in C$, the value a must appear at least $t - d + 1$ times in I.*

As in [23, 25], it is convenient to work with a graph representation of legality. Given a condition C and a value of t, we associate with it a graph $G^{[d]}(C, t)$ defined as follows. Its vertices are the input vectors I of C plus all their views with at most $t - d$ entries equal to $\perp$ (i.e., all the views J such that $\exists I \in C : J \leq I \wedge \#_\perp(J) \leq (t - d)$). Two vertices $J1, J2$ are connected by an edge if and only if $J1 \leq J2$ and they differ in exactly one position. Notice that two vertices $I1, I2$ of C are connected (by a path) if their Hamming distance $dist(I1, I2) \leq (t - d)$. We have the following lemma [23, 25]:

Lemma 3. *A condition C is $(t, d)_{synch}$-acceptable if and only if for every connected component of $G^{[d]}(C, t)$ there is a value v that appears in every one of its input vectors.*

Thus, the function S of the acceptability definition identifies a value that appears in every one of the input vectors of a connected component. If C is a $(t, d)_{synch}$-acceptable condition with associated P, S, for any two vectors $I_0, I_1 \in C$, we have that if $S(I_0) \neq S(I_1)$, then $dist(I_0, I_1) \geq t - d + 1$. This bound is tight if C is maximal:

Lemma 4. *If C is a maximal $(t, d)_{synch}$-acceptable condition then for any associated pairs (P, S) of parameters, there exist two vectors I_0, I_1 in C such that $S(I_0) \neq S(I_1)$ and $dist(I_0, I_1) = t - d + 1$.*

The proof of our lower bound theorem uses the previous lemmas and the similarity notion defined below. It is fully described in [26]. From a technical point of view, it is based on the proof in [19] (and that proof is based on [22]). Lower bound and impossibility proofs for distributed algorithms are typically based on a notion of *similarity*. We use the following definition.

Definition 5. *States x and y are* similar, *denoted $x \sim y$, if they are identical, or if there exists a process p_j such that (a) x and y are identical except in the local state of p_j; and (b) there exists a process $p_i \neq p_j$ that is non-failed in both x and y (so, x and y are identical at least at p_i).*

A set X of states is similarity connected *if for every $x, y \in X$ there are states $x = x_0, \cdots, x_m = y$ such that $x_i \sim x_{i+1}$ for all $0 \leq i < m$.*

Given a state x, consider the execution extending x in which no failures occur after state x. Since the algorithm solves uniform consensus, then all correct processes must decide upon the same value in this execution. We denote this decision value by $val(x)$.

Lemma 5. *Let $t \leq n-2$, and X be a similarity connected set of states in which at most ℓ processes have failed, and assume that after $k+1$ rounds every process has decided, for $k + \ell \leq t - 1$. Then for every $x, x' \in X$, $val(x) = val(x')$.*

The following theorem states our lower bound result:

Theorem 8. *Consider an algorithm for uniform consensus with up to t failures, where $1 \leq t \leq n - 2$, and let C be a $(t, d)_{synch}$-acceptable condition. For every $1 \leq d \leq t$ there exists a run of the algorithm starting in C, in which it takes at least $d + 1$ rounds for a correct processes to decide.*

References

1. Attiya H., and Avidor Z., Wait-Free n-Set Consensus When Inputs Are Restricted. *16th Int. Symp. on DIStributed Computing*, Springer Verlag LNCS #2508, pp. 326-338, 2002.
2. Aguilera M.K. and Toueg S., A Simple Bivalency Proof that t-Resilient Consensus Requires $t + 1$ Rounds. *Information Processing Letters*, 71:155-178, 1999.
3. Attiya H. and Welch J., *Distributed Computing: Fundamentals, Simulations and Advanced Topics,* McGraw–Hill, 451 pages, 1998.
4. Ben Or M., Another Advantage of Free Choice: Completely Asynchronous Agreement Protocols. *2nd ACM Symposium on Principles of Distributed Computing (PODC'83)*, pp. 27-30, Montréal (CA), 1983.
5. Chaudhuri S., More *Choices* Allow More *Faults:* set Consensus Problems in Totally Asynchronous Systems. *Information and Computation,* 105:132-158, 1993.
6. Chandra T.K. and Toueg S., Unreliable Failure Detectors for Reliable Distributed Systems. *Journal of the ACM,* 43(2):225-267, March 1996.
7. Charron-Bost B. and Schiper A., Uniform Consensus is Harder than Consensus. *Technical Report DSC/2000/028,* EPFL, Lausanne (Switzerland), May 2000.
8. Dolev, D., Lynch, N. A., Pinter, S. S., Stark, E. W., and Weihl, W. E., Reaching Approximate Agreement in the Presence of Faults. *JACM,* 33(3):499-516, 1986.
9. Dolev D., Reischuk R. and Strong R., Early Stopping in Byzantine Agreement. *JACM,* 37(4):720-741, April 1990.
10. Dwork C., Lynch N. and Stockmeyer L., Consensus in the Presence of Partial Synchrony. *JACM,* 35(2):288-323, April 1988.
11. Dwork C. and Moses Y., Knowledge and Common Knowledge in a Byzantine Environment: Crash Failures. *Information Computation,* 88(2):156-186, 1990.

12. Fischer M.J. and Lynch N., A Lower Bound for the Time to Assure Interactive Consistency. *Information Processing Letters*, 71:183-186, 1982.
13. Fischer M.J., Lynch N.A. and Paterson M.S., Impossibility of Distributed Consensus with One Faulty Process. *JACM*, 32(2):374-382, 1985.
14. Friedman R., Mostefaoui A., Rajsbaum S. and Raynal M., Asynchronous Distributed Agreement and its Relation with Error Correcting Codes. *16th Int. Symp. on DIStributed Computing*, Springer Verlag LNCS #2508, pp. 63-87, 2002.
15. Gafni E., Round-by-round fault detectors: Unifying synchrony and asynchrony. *17th ACM Symp. on Principles of Distributed Computing*, pp. 143-152, 1998.
16. Herlihy M.P., Wait-Free Synchronization. *ACM TOPLAS*, 11(1):124-149, 1991.
17. Hurfin M., Mostefaoui A. and Raynal M., A Versatile Family of Consensus Protocols Based on Chandra-Toueg's Unreliable Failure Detectors. *IEEE Transactions on Computers*, 51(4):395-408, 2002.
18. Herlihy M.P., Rajsbaum S., and Tuttle M.R., Unifying synchronous and asynchronous message-passing models. *17th ACM Symp. on Principles of Distributed Computing*, pp. 133-142, 1998.
19. Keidar I. and Rajsbaum S., A Simple Proof of the Uniform Consensus Synchronous Lower Bound. *Information Processing Letters*, 85:47-52, 2003.
20. Lamport L. and Fischer M., Byzantine Generals and Transaction Commit Protocols. *Unpublished manuscript*, 16 pages, April 1982.
21. Lynch N.A., Distributed Algorithms. *Morgan Kaufmann Pub.*, San Francisco (CA), 872 pages, 1996.
22. Moses, Y. and Rajsbaum, S. A Layered Analysis of Consensus, *SIAM Journal of Computing* 31(4):989-1021, 2002.
23. Mostefaoui A., Rajsbaum S. and Raynal M., Conditions on Input Vectors for Consensus Solvability in Asynchronous Distributed Systems. *JACM*, 50(6):922-954, 2003.
24. Mostefaoui A., Rajsbaum S. and Raynal M., Using Conditions to Expedite Consensus in Synchronous Systems. *17th Int. Symposium on Distributed Computing*, Springer-Verlag LNCS #2848, pp. 249-263, 2003.
25. Mostefaoui A., Rajsbaum S., Raynal M. and Roy M., Condition-based Consensus Sovability: a Hierarchy of Conditions and Efficient Protocols. *Distributed Computing*, 17:1-20, 2004.
26. Mostefaoui A., Rajsbaum S. and Raynal M., The Synchronous Condition-Based Consensus Hierarchy. *Tech Report 1584*, 26 pages, IRISA, Univ. de Rennes 1, December 2003. (http://www.irisa.fr/bibli/publi/pi/2003/1584/1584.html).
27. Mostefaoui A. and Raynal M., Leader-Based Consensus. *Parallel Processing Letters*, 11(1):95-107, 2001.
28. Neiger G. and Toueg S., Automatically Increasing the Fault-Tolerance of Distributed Algorithms. *Journal of Algorithms*, 11:374-419, 1990.
29. Raynal M., Consensus in Synchronous Systems: a Concise Guided Tour. *9th IEEE Pacific Rim Int. Symp. on Dependable Computing*, pp. 221-228, 2002.
30. Zibin Y., Condition-Based Consensus in Synchronous Systems. *17th Int. Symp. on Distributed Computing*, Springer-Verlag LNCS #2848, pp. 239-248, 2003.

Synchronous Condition-Based Consensus Adapting to Input-Vector Legality

Taisuke Izumi and Toshimitsu Masuzawa

Graduate School of Information Science and Technology, Osaka University
1-3 Machikaneyama, Toyonaka, 560-8531, Japan
{t-izumi,masuzawa}@ist.osaka-u.ac.jp

Abstract. This paper proposes a novel condition-based algorithm for the uniform consensus in synchronous systems. The proposed algorithm is *adaptive* in the sense that its execution time depends on actual difficulty of input vectors, *legality level*, which is newly formalized in this paper. On the assumption that majority of processes are correct, the algorithm terminates within $\min\{f + 2 - l, t + 1\}$ rounds if $l < f$, where f and t is the actual and the maximum numbers of faults respectively, and l is the legality level of input vectors. Moreover, the algorithm terminates in 1 round if $l \geq t$ and $f = 0$, and terminates within 2 rounds if $l \geq f$ holds. Compared with previous algorithms, for the case of $t < n/2$, the algorithm achieves the best time complexity in almost all situations.

1 Introduction

The *consensus* problem is a fundamental and important problem for designing fault-tolerant distributed systems. Informally, the consensus problem is defined as follows: each process proposes a value, and all non-faulty processes have to agree on a common value that is proposed by a process. The *uniform consensus*, a stronger variant of the consensus, further requires that faulty processes are disallowed to disagree (Uniform Agreement). The (uniform) consensus problem has many applications, e.g., atomic broadcast [2][6], shared object [1][7], weak atomic commitment [5] and so on. However, despite of the variety of its applications, it has no deterministic solution in asynchronous systems subject to only a single crash fault [4]. Thus, several approaches to circumvent this impossibility have been proposed.

As one of such new approaches, the *condition-based approach* is recently introduced [9]. This approach is to restrict inputs so that the generally-unsolvable problem can be solved. A *condition* represents some restriction to inputs. In the case of the consensus problem, it is defined as a subset of all possible *input vectors* whose entries correspond to the proposal of each process. The first result of the condition-based approach clarifies the condition for which the uniform consensus can be solved in asynchronous systems subject to crash faults [9]. More precisely, this result proposed a class of conditions, called *d-legal conditions*, and proved that *d*-legal conditions is the class of necessary and sufficient conditions

R. Guerraoui (Ed.): DISC 2004, LNCS 3274, pp. 16–29, 2004.

to solve the (uniform) consensus in asynchronous systems where at most d process can crash. More recent researches focus on application of the concept of conditions to synchronous systems. However, it is well-known that the uniform consensus problem can be solved in synchronous systems. Thus, these researches try to improve time complexity by introducing conditions. While it is known that any synchronous uniform consensus algorithm takes at least $\min\{f + 2, t + 1\}$ rounds, where f and t is the actual and the maximum numbers of faults respectively [3], more efficient algorithms can be realized if the condition-based approach is introduced. For example, the algorithm proposed in [11] terminates within $\min\{f + 2, t + 1 - d\}$ rounds if the input vector is in some d-legal condition, and terminates within $\min\{f + 2, t + 1\}$ rounds otherwise. To the best of our knowledge, three synchronous condition-based uniform consensus algorithms have been proposed [10][11][14].

We also investigate condition-based uniform consensus algorithms in synchronous systems. Especially, we focus on *adaptiveness* to conditions, which is a novel notion this paper introduces. Intuitively, the adaptiveness is the property that the execution time of algorithms depends on actual difficulty of input vectors. As we mentioned, inputs in some d-legal condition can make algorithms terminate early by at most d rounds. Then, roughly speaking, the value d can be regarded as the difficulty of the inputs. On the other hand, in [12], it is shown that a d-legal condition can contain a $(d + 1)$-legal condition as a subset. This implies that a d-legal condition can include the input vector whose difficulty is lower than d. Our adaptiveness concept guarantees that such easier input make algorithms terminate earlier. To explain adaptiveness more precisely, we present an example for the d-legal condition $C_d^{\max}$: The condition $C_d^{\max}$ consists of the vectors in which the largest value in the vector appears at more than d entries. From the result in [11], we can construct, for any fixed d, an efficient condition-based uniform consensus algorithm that terminates within $t + 1 - d$ rounds for any input vector in $C_d^{\max}$. Now let $\mathcal{A}$ be such an algorithm for $d = 2$, and consider the three vectors $I_1 =< 0, 1, 1, 1, 1 >$, $I_2 =< 0, 1, 2, 2, 2 >$, and $I_3 =< 0, 1, 2, 3, 3 >$. Clearly, the vectors I_1, and I_2 are in $C_2^{\max}$, and thus for the input vectors I_1 and I_2, the algorithm $\mathcal{A}$ terminates within $t - 1$ rounds. On the other hand, since I_3 is not in $C_2^{\max}$, the algorithm $\mathcal{A}$ terminates within $\min\{f + 2, t + 1\}$ rounds. However, from the definition, I_1 is also contained in $C_3^{\max}$, and I_3 is contained in $C_1^{\max}$. Therefore, the execution for I_1 and I_3 is expected to terminate within $t - 2$ rounds and t rounds respectively: This is what we call adaptiveness. However, in this sense, none of existing algorithms is adaptive.

This paper formalizes the adaptiveness to conditions, and proposes a condition-based uniform consensus algorithm that achieves the adaptiveness. To define actual difficulty of input vectors, we introduce the notion of *legal condition sequence* and *legality level*. Intuitively, the legal condition sequence is a hierarchical sequence of the d-legal conditions. The legality level is defined for a legal condition sequence, and represents the location of input vectors in the hierarchy[1]. In

---

[1] The notion of the legal condition sequence and the legality level is similar to that of the *hierarchy* and the *degree* proposed in [12].

Table 1. Comparison about worst-case round complexity between this paper's algorithm and existing algorithms. The variable f, t, respectively represents the actual and maximum number of faulty processes, l represents legality level of the input vector, and d is the design parameter of each algorithm.

	$l \geq t$	$t > l \geq f$	$f > l$	Assumption
[14]	$t+2-d$ (if $l \geq d$) $t+1$ (otherwise)	$t+2-d$ (if $l \geq d$) $t+1$ (otherwise)	$t+2-d$ (if $l \geq d$) $t+1$ (otherwise)	$t < n/2$
[10]	1 if $f = 0$ 2 otherwise	$\min\{f+2, t+1\}$	$\min\{f+2, t+1\}$	nothing
[11]	2	$\min\{t+1-d, f+2\}$ (if $l \geq d$) $\min\{f+2, t+1\}$ (otherwise)	$\min\{t+1-d, f+2\}$ (if $l \geq d$) $\min\{f+2, t+1\}$ (otherwise)	nothing
this paper	1 if $f = 0$ 2 otherwise	2	$\min\{f+2-l, t+1\}$	$t < n/2$

the previous example, the legal condition sequence is $< C_0^{\max}, C_1^{\max}, \cdots, C_5^{\max} >$, and the legality levels of I_1, I_2 and I_3 are respectively 3, 2, and 1. The proposed algorithm is instantiated by a legal condition sequence. For any input vector with legality level l, it terminates within $\min\{f + 2 - l, t + 1\}$ rounds if $l < f$ holds, within 2 rounds if $l \geq f$ holds, and within 1 round if $f = 0$ and $l \geq t$ holds. The comparison of our algorithm with existing algorithms is summarized in Table 1, where l is the legality level of input vectors, and d is the design parameter of each algorithm. From the table, we can see that only our algorithm is adaptive to the conditions. Notice that our algorithm works on the assumption that $t < n/2$ holds. For the case $t < n/2$, our algorithm achieves the best time complexity in almost all cases. Only in the case that both $l = d$ and $f = t$ hold, the algorithm in [11] terminates faster.

The paper is organized as follows: In section 2, we introduce the system model, the definition of problem, and other necessary formalizations. Section 3 provides the adaptive condition-based consensus algorithm. We conclude this paper in Section 4.

2   Preliminaries

2.1   Distributed System

We consider a round-based synchronous distributed system consisting of n processes $P = \{p_0, p_1, p_2, \cdots, p_{n-1}\}$ in which any pair of processes can communicate with each other by exchanging messages. All channels are reliable: each channel correctly transfers messages. The system is round-based, that is, its execution is a sequence of synchronized *rounds* identified by $1, 2, 3 \cdots$. Each round r consists of three phases:

Send phase. Each process p_i sends messages.
Receive phase. Each process p_i receives all the messages sent to p_i at the beginning of round r.
Local processing phase. Each process p_i executes local computation.

Processes can crash. If a process p_i crashes during round r, it makes no operation subsequently. Then, messages sent by p_i at round r may or may not be received. We say a process is *correct* if it never crashes, and say "a round r is correct" when no process crashes during round r. There are an upper bound t on the number of processes that can crash. We also denote the actual number of crash processes by f ($\leq t$). In the rest of the paper, we assume that $t < n/2$ holds.

2.2 Uniform Consensus

In a consensus algorithm, each correct process initially proposes a value, and eventually chooses a decision value from the values proposed by processes so that all processes decide the same value. The *uniform consensus* is a stronger variant of the consensus. It disallows faulty processes to disagree on the decided value. More precisely, the uniform consensus is specified as follows:

Termination: Every correct process eventually decides.
Uniform Agreement: No two processes decide different values.
Validity: If a process decides a value v, then, v is a value proposed by a process.

The set of values that can be proposed is denoted by $\mathcal{V}$. Moreover, we assume that $\mathcal{V}$ is a finite ordered set.

2.3 Legality Level

Notations. An *input vector* is a vector in $\mathcal{V}^n$, where the i-th entry represents p_i's proposal value. We usually denote an input vector for an execution by I. We also define *view* J to be a vector in $(\mathcal{V} \cup \{\bot\})^n$ obtained by replacing the several entries in I by $\bot$ ($\bot$ is a default value such that $\bot \notin \mathcal{V}$). Let $\bot^n$ be the view such that all entries are $\bot$. We denote $J_1 \leq J_2$ if $\forall k : J_1[k] \neq \bot \Rightarrow J_1[k] = J_2[k]$ holds. For two views J_1 and J_2 such that $J_1 \leq J_2$ or $J_2 \leq J_1$ holds, we define their union $J = J_1 \cup J_2$ as follows: $\forall k : J[k] = a \neq \bot \Leftrightarrow J_1[k] = a$ or $J_2[k] = a$. For a vector J ($\in (\mathcal{V} \cup \{\bot\})^n$) and a value a, $\#_a(J)$ denotes the number of entries of value a in the vector J. For a vector J and a value a, we often describe $a \in J$ if there exists a value k such that $J[k] = a$. Finally, for two vectors J_1 and J_2, we denote the Hamming distance between J_1 and J_2 by $\text{dist}(J_1, J_2)$.

Conditions and Legality. A *condition* is formally defined as a subset of $\mathcal{V}^n$. First, as an important class of conditions, we introduce (d, h)-legal conditions[2].

Definition 1 ((d, h)-legal conditions) A condition C is (d, h)-legal (where h is a mapping $h : C \mapsto \mathcal{V}$) if h, d, and C satisfy the following properties:

1. $\forall I \in C : \#_{h(I)}(I) > d$,
2. $\forall I_1, I_2 \in C : h(I_1) \neq h(I_2) \Rightarrow \text{dist}(I_1, I_2) > d$.

---

[2] The (d, h)-legal conditions is a subclass of d-legal conditions (the condition C is d-legal if there exists a mapping h such that C is (d, h)-legal). This difference does not restrict the class of condition applicable to our algorithm because our algorithm can be instantiated with any h.

Intuitively, (d, h)-legal condition is the set of input vectors I such that $h(I)$ can be calculated even when at most d entries of I are lost. From the definition, $\mathcal{V}^n$ can be $(0, h)$-legal, and (n, h)-legal condition is only the empty set. Notice that (d, h)-legal condition is not uniquely determined by d and h (For instance, for a (d, h)-legal condition, its subset is also a (d, h)-legal condition). In recent researches, it is shown that (d, h)-legal conditions reduce the worst-case execution time of synchronous consensus algorithms. To be more precise, for any (d, h)-legal condition, there exists a consensus algorithm that terminates (1) within $\min\{t + 1 - d, f + 2\}$ rounds for input vector satisfying the condition, and (2) within $\min\{f + 2, t + 1\}$ rounds otherwise [11]. In this sense, we can regard d as a characteristic value representing difficulties of input vectors in (d, h)-legal condition. However, from the definition, a (d, h)-legal condition can include a $(d + 1, h)$-legal condition. This implies that a (d, h)-legal condition can include easier input vectors. Therefore, to define actual difficulty of input vectors, we introduce *legality levels* of input vectors as follows:

Definition 2 (Legal condition sequence) A sequence of conditions $\mathcal{C} =< C_0, C_1, \cdots C_n >$ is an h-legal condition sequence if the following properties are satisfied:

- $C_0 = \mathcal{V}^n$, $C_n = \emptyset$,
- $\forall k$ $(0 \leq k \leq n - 1)$: C_k is (k, h)-legal and $C_{k+1} \subseteq C_k$,
- $\forall k$ $(0 \leq k \leq n - 1)$: $(\nexists C' : C'$ is $(k + 1, h)$-legal and $C_{k+1} \subset C' \subseteq C_k)$.

Definition 3 (Legality level) For a h-legal condition sequence $\mathcal{C}$, the legality level of a input vector I is l if $I \in C_l$ and $I \notin C_{l+1}$ holds.

Since C_n is empty and C_0 is the set of all possible input vectors, for any input vector, its legality level can be defined necessarily. The legality level represents the actual difficulties of input vectors in the sense that we previously mentioned.

Example. An example of a (d, h)-legal condition is $C_d^{\max}$:

$$C_d^{\max} = \{I \in \mathcal{V}^n | \#_a(I) > d, \text{ where } a \text{ is the maximum value in } I\}$$

The condition $C_d^{\max}$ is a (d, h)-legal condition defined by d and $h = \max$. Moreover, it is *maximal*, that is, there is no (d, h)-legal condition C such that $C_d^{\max} \subset C$ [9][3]. Therefore, for $C_d^{\max}$, we can define legal condition sequence $\mathcal{C}^{\max} =< C_0^{\max}, C_1^{\max}, \cdots C_n^{\max} >$. As an example, we consider two input vectors, $I_1 =< 0, 0, 1, 3, 3 >$ and $I_2 =< 0, 0, 2, 2, 2 >$. Both vectors are contained in $C_1^{\max}$. However, whereas I_2 is contained in $C_2^{\max}$, I_1 is not. Therefore, for $\mathcal{C}^{\max}$, legality levels of vectors I_1 and I_2 are respectively 1 and 2.

The algorithm proposed in this paper is instantiated with a legal condition sequence, that is the legal condition sequence (which includes the mapping h)

---

[3] Actually, the definition of maximality in [9] is stronger: The (d, h)-legal condition C is maximal if $C \cup \{I'\}$ is not (d, h')-legal for any mapping h' and input vector $I' \notin C$.

is given and can be used in the algorithm. In all following discussions, let the algorithm be instantiated with $\mathcal{C} = < C_0, C_1, \cdots, C_n >$, where each C_k is (k, h)-legal. In addition, we denote the legality level of an input vector I for $\mathcal{C}$ by $l(I)$.

3   Condition-Based Consensus Algorithm Adapting to Legality Level

In this section, we propose a condition-based consensus algorithm that adapts to the legality level of input vectors. More precisely, the algorithm terminates in 1 round if $f = 0$ and $l(I) \geq t$ holds, (2)within 2 rounds if $l(I) \geq f$ holds, and (3) within $\min\{f + 2 - l(I), t + 1\}$ rounds otherwise.

We present the algorithm in an incremental way: Before the presentation of the algorithm, we first introduce the fundamental function decode, which is used as the subroutine of our algorithm. Then, we propose a basic adaptive algorithm. This algorithm is relatively simple and easy to understand, but is not optimized in some points. Thus, after that, we modify the basic algorithm to obtain the optimized algorithm.

3.1   Function decode

The function decode has two arguments J and d, which are respectively a view and legality level. Informally, the role of the function decode(J, d) is to obtain the value $h(I)$ from J. The behavior of decode is as follows: When a process invokes decode(J, d), it first supposes that legality level of the input vector is d, and tries to construct the vector $I' \geq J$ such that $h(I) = h(I')$ holds. Notice that this trial may fail. If the trial succeeds, decode returns the value $h(I')$, where I' is a constructed vector. On the other hand, if the trial fails, decode re-supposes that legality level of the input vector is $d - 1$, and tries to construct again.

The algorithm decode(J, d) is presented in Figure 1. To handle the case that the trial fails, the algorithm is described as the recursive function. First, the algorithm constructs the candidates of vector $I' \in C_d$ such that $h(I') \in J$ and $J \leq I'$ (line 4). These candidate vectors are stored in the variable $\mathcal{E}$. If more than one candidate are stored, the algorithm deterministically chooses one vector (in Figure 1, the algorithm chooses the vector I' with the largest $h(I')$). For the chosen vector I', the algorithm returns $h(I')$.

Properties of Function decode. We prove several properties of the function decode. Let $\mathcal{E}(J, d)$ be the value stored in $\mathcal{E}$ immediately after the line 4 is processed in the execution of decode(J, d).

Lemma 1 If $\mathcal{E}(J, d)$ is nonempty, the condition $\text{dist}(I_1, I_2) \leq \#_\perp(J)$ holds for any $I_1, I_2 \in \mathcal{E}(J, d)$.

Proof Since $J \leq I_1$ and $J \leq I_2$, this lemma clearly holds.   □

```
1: Function decode(J, d) :
2:   variable
3:     E : init ∅

4:   E ← {I ∈ C_d|h(I) ∈ J and J ≤ I}
5:   if E = ∅ then return(decode(J, d − 1))
6:   else return(max{h(I)|I ∈ E}) endif
```

Fig. 1. Function decode(J, d).

Lemma 2 (Decode Validity) For any $J \neq \perp^n$ and $d \ (\geq 0)$, the execution of decode(J, d) necessarily terminates, and its return value is contained in J.

Proof Clearly, return values are included in J. We prove the termination by showing that decode($J, 0$) is necessarily terminates. Since we assume that $J \neq \perp^n$, $\mathcal{E}(J, 0)$ is necessarily nonempty (any vector obtained by replacing $\perp$ by a non-$\perp$ value in J is necessarily contained in $\mathcal{E}(J, 0)$), and thus the execution terminates. □

Lemma 3 (Decodability) Let I be an input vector, and J be a vector such that $J \leq I$ and $\#_\perp(J) \leq l(I)$ holds. Then, for any value $d \geq \#_\perp(J)$, decode(J, d) $= h(I)$ holds.

Proof We consider the following two cases:

- **(Case1)** When $d \leq l(I)$ holds: Then, $I \in C_{l(I)} \subseteq C_d$ holds. In addition, $h(I) \in J$ holds from $\#_\perp(J) \leq l(I) < \#_{h(I)}(I)$. These implies that $I \in \mathcal{E}(J, d)$ holds. On the other hand, for any vector $I' \in \mathcal{E}(J, d)$, dist(I', I) $\leq \#_\perp(J) \leq d$ holds from Lemma 1. Then, we obtain $h(I') = h(I)$ because both I' and I are in C_d. This implies that decode(J, d) $= h(I)$ holds.
- **(Case2)** When $d > l(I)$ holds: We prove this case by induction for d. **(Basis)** We consider the case of $d = l(I)$ as the basis. It clearly holds from the proof of Case1. **(Inductive Step)** Assume as induction hypothesis that decode($J, d − 1$) $= h(I)$ holds. If $\mathcal{E}(J, d) = \emptyset$ holds, decode(J, d) returns the value from decode($J, d − 1$). Then, decode(J, d) $= h(I)$ holds from the induction hypothesis. Thus, we consider the case of $\mathcal{E}(J, d) \neq \emptyset$. Letting I' be a vector in $\mathcal{E}(J, d)$, dist(I, I') $\leq \#_\perp(J) \leq l(I)$ holds from Lemma 1. Then, we obtain $h(I) = h(I')$ because both I' and I are in $C_{l(I)}$. This implies that decode(J, d) $= h(I)$ holds. □

Lemma 4 (Transitivity) For any $d \geq \#_\perp(J)$, decode(J, d) $=$ decode($J, d + 1$) holds.

Proof We consider the following three cases:

- **(Case1)** When $\mathcal{E}(J, d+1) = \emptyset$ holds: Clearly, decode($J, d+1$) $=$ decode(J, d) holds.

- (**Case2**) When $\mathcal{E}(J, d) = \emptyset$ holds: There exists no vector I such that $J \leq I$, $h(I) \in J$, and $I \in C_d$ holds. Therefore, there also exists no vector I such that $J \leq I$, $h(I) \in J$, and $I \in C_{d+1}$ holds, because $C_{d+1} \subseteq C_d$ holds. This implies that $\mathcal{E}(J, d+1) = \emptyset$ holds. Afterward, the proof is same as Case1.
- (**Case3**) When neither $\mathcal{E}(J, d)$ nor $\mathcal{E}(J, d+1)$ is $\emptyset$: Let I_1 be the vector such that $I_1 \in \mathcal{E}(J, d)$ and $h(I_1) = \mathsf{decode}(J, d)$ holds, and I_2 be the vector such that $I_2 \in \mathcal{E}(J, d+1)$ and $h(I_2) = \mathsf{decode}(J, d+1)$ holds. Since both $J \leq I_2$ and $J \leq I_1$ holds, $\mathsf{dist}(I_1, I_2) \leq \#_\perp(J) \leq d$ holds from Lemma 1. In addition, the vector I_2 is also in C_d because $C_{d+1} \subseteq C_d$ holds. From the definition of C_d, we can conclude $h(I_1) = h(I_2)$, and thus, $\mathsf{decode}(J, d) = \mathsf{decode}(J, d+1)$ holds. □

3.2   Algorithm ACC

In this subsection, we propose a simple adaptive algorithm ACC. The algorithm is based on the well-known floodset algorithm [8] [13]. The typical floodset algorithm is as follows: Each process maintains its own view, which stores only its proposal at round 1. In each round, each process sends its own view to all processes, receives views from other processes, and updates its own view by the union of the current view and all received views. The primary objective of the floodset algorithm is to guarantee that each process has a same view after the execution by an appropriate round. In non-condition-based algorithm, $f+1$ rounds is sufficient for each process to have a same view. This relies on the fact that $f+1$ rounds' execution includes at least one correct round and the fact that each process have a same view at round r if a round r is correct. On the other hand, considering the input vector condition, $f + 1 - l(I)$ rounds is sufficient [11][14]. In this case, at the end of round $f + 1 - l(I)$, each process may have different views. However, then, it is guaranteed that a common value (that is $h(I)$) can be calculated from each view. Notice that the value f and $l(I)$ is unknown. Thus, the primary issues the algorithm ACC must consider is to execute the floodset algorithm till an appropriate round according to the value of f and $l(I)$.

The behavior of ACC is as follows: The algorithm executes floodset algorithm as an underlying task. In each round r, each process p_i supposes that legality level of the input vector is $t + 1 - r$, and estimates a decision value by executing $\mathsf{decode}(J_i, t + 1 - r)$, where J_i is the view maintained by p_i. This estimation can be wrong, and thus, at the next round, each process checks whether its estimation is correct or not. More precisely, at round $r + 1$, each process p_i sends its estimation to all processes (including itself). If all messages received by p_i has a same estimation w, p_i decide a value w. Then, each process terminates at round $f + 2 - l(I)$ or earlier. However, if a process p_j accidentally decides a round earlier than round $f + 2 - l(I)$ while another process p_i decides at round $f + 2 - l(I)$, those decision may differ. Hence, to avoid this inconsistency, we introduce the scheme of overwriting views into the algorithm: If p_i receives more than $n/2$ messages containing a common value w, before the estimation for next round, it overwrites its own view by the view J from other processes such that $\mathsf{decode}(J, t + 1 - r) = w$ holds. This implies if a process decides a value w at

```
Algorithm ACC(v_i) for h-legal condition sequence and t crashes (t < n/2)
Code for p_i:

1:   variable:
2:       J_i, S_i : init ⊥^n and J_i[i] ← v_i
3:       s_i : init ⊥
4:       Views_i : init <⊥^n, ⊥^n, · · · , ⊥^n>

5:   for each round r = 1, 2, · · · , t + 2 do :
6:       send (J_i, s_i) to all processes (including p_i)
7:       Let (Views_i[j], S_i[j]) be the message received from p_j
             (if no message is received from p_j, Views_i[j] =⊥^n)
8:       J_i ← ⋃_{k=0}^{n-1} Views_i[k]                              /* Updating the view */
9:       if r > 1 then
10:          if ∃w ≠⊥: #_w(S_i) + #_⊥(S_i) = n then decide(w) and exit endif
11:          if ∃w ≠⊥: #_w(S_i) > n/2 then
12:              Let y be a value in S_i[y] ≠⊥ (deterministically chosen)
13:              J_i ← Views_i[y]                                    /* Overwriting the view */
14:          endif
15:      endif
16:      s_i ← decode(J_i, t + 1 − r) /* Estimation of decision value */
17:  endfor
```

Fig. 2. Algorithm ACC: Adaptive Condition-based Consensus.

round $r + 1$, all other processes necessarily have such a view as J at the end of round $r+1$ because at least $n − f(> n/2)$ correct processes necessarily sends the same estimation w at round $r + 1$. Then, all other processes are guaranteed to decide a value w at round $r+2$ (the detail is explained in the correctness proof). It may be wondered that the view-overwriting scheme may prevent the floodset algorithm from working correctly, because the view maintained by the floodset algorithm can be changed. However, in this scheme, such problem never occurs: As we mentioned, the principle that the floodset algorithm uses is that each view becomes equal at the end of correct rounds. Even though the view-overwriting schemes is introduced, this principle is not violated at all.

Figure 2 presents the code of the algorithm ACC for process p_i. The view of each process p_i is maintained in the variable J_i. The variable $Views_i$ and S_i respectively denotes views and estimations received from other processes at current round. The line 9-15 corresponds to the view-overwriting scheme. The line 16 corresponds to the estimation of a decision value. Notice that the estimation is done after view-overwriting.

Correctness of ACC. In this subsection, we prove the correctness of the algorithm ACC. For the proof, we define the following notations and terms: J_i^r, $Views_i^r$ and S_i^r respectively denote the value of J_i, $Views_i$ and S_i at the end of round r. Let P^r be the set of processes that neither crash nor terminate at the end of round r, and P_c be the set of correct processes. For short, let F be $\max\{2, f + 2 − l(I)\}$.

Lemma 5 (Validity) If a process decides a value w, then w is a value proposed by a process.

Proof This lemma clearly holds from Lemma 2.   □

Lemma 6 If a round r ($1 \leq r \leq t+2$) is correct, then $J_i^k = J_j^k$ holds for any $p_i, p_j \in P^k$ and $k \geq r$.

Proof We prove this lemma by induction for k. (**Basis**) We consider the case of $r = k$. Since round $k(=r)$ is correct, each process in P^k receives a same set of messages at round k. Thus, for any $p_i, p_j \in P^k$, $Views_i^k = Views_j^k$ and $S_i^k = S_j^k$ holds. Since the value of J_i^k is deterministically calculated from the values of $Views_i^k$ and S_i^k, $J_i^k = J_j^k$ holds for any $p_i, p_j \in P^k$. (**Inductive step**) Suppose as induction hypothesis that $J_i^k = J_j^k$ holds for some $k(\geq r)$ and any $p_i, p_j \in P^k$ (let J be the value of J_*^k). Since each process in P^k sends a message $(J, *)$ at round $k+1$ unless it crashes, for each p_i, $Views_i^{k+1}$ contains only values J and $\perp^n$. Then, the value of J_i^{k+1} is either $\bigcup_{x=0}^{n-1} Views_i^{k+1}[x] = J$ (assignment at line 8) or $J^{k+1} = Views_i^k[x] = J$ (assignment at line 13). In any cases, J_i^{k+1} has a value J. This implies that $J_i^{k+1} = J_j^{k+1}$ holds for any $p_i, p_j \in P^{k+1}$.   □

Lemma 7 If a round r ($1 \leq r \leq t+2$) is correct, then every process $p_i \in P^r$ decides at round $r+1$ or earlier unless it crashes by the end of round $r+1$

Proof From Lemma 6, the variable J_i^r has a common value (say J) for any $p_i \in P^r$. This implies that each process sends the same message (J, w) at round $r+1$ (letting $w = \mathsf{decode}(J, t+1-r))$). Then, since S_i^{r+1} contains only w and $\perp$, each process $p_i(\in P^{r+1})$ decides a value w at round $r+1$.   □.

Lemma 8 (Termination) Each process p_i decides a value at round $\max\{2, f+2-l(I)\}$ or earlier.

Proof If there exists a correct round r up to $F-1$, the lemma clearly holds from Lemma 7. Thus, we have only to consider the case that every round up to $F-1$ is not correct. Since at least one process crashes in each round up to $F-1(\geq f+1-l(I))$, at most $l(I)$ processes can crash at round 1. Then, $\#\perp(J_i^{F-1}) \leq l(I)$ holds for any $p_i \in P^{F-1}$ (notice that if a process p_k does not crash at round 1, all processes receive p_k's proposal at round 1, and thus, $J[k] \neq \perp$ holds for every view in the execution). In addition, $t+1-(F-1) = t-f+l(I) \geq l(I) \geq \#\perp(J_i^{F-1})$ also holds. Therefore, from Lemma 3, we obtain $\mathsf{decode}(J_i^{F-1}, t+1-(F-1)) = h(I)$. Then, since every process in P^{F-1} sends message $(*, h(I))$, S_i^F contains only $h(I)$ and $\perp$. This implies that each process p_i in P^F decides $h(I)$ at round F.   □

Lemma 9 (Uniform Agreement) No two processes decide different values.

Proof Let p_i and p_j be the processes that decide. We prove that both p_i and p_j decide a common value. Without loss of generality, we assume that p_i is the first process that decides. Let r and w respectively denote the round when p_i decides and the value p_i decides. (**Case1**) When p_j decides at round r: Since the process p_i decides a value w at round r, S_i^r contains only w and $\bot$. This implies that every process $p_k \in P_c$ sends a message (J_k^{r-1}, w) at round r because no process in P_c terminates at the beginning of round r. Then, clearly $S_j^r[k] = w$ holds, and thus p_j decides w. (**Case2**) When p_j does not decides at round r: In the same way as the case1, we can show that every process $p_k \in P_c$ sends a message (J_k^{r-1}, w) at round r. Then, since $t < n/2$ holds, we obtain $\#_w(S_k^r) > n/2$ for any $p_k \in P^r$. Therefore, each process p_k overwrites its own variable J_k by a vector V_k such that $\mathsf{decode}(V_k, t + 1 - (r - 1)) = w$ holds. On the other hand, from Lemma 7, every round up to $r - 1$ is not correct because if not, p_j decides at round r or earlier. This implies that at most $f + 2 - r$ processes can crash at round 1. Hence, $\#_\bot(V_k) \leq f + 2 - r \leq t + 2 - r$ holds. Then, from Lemma 4, we obtain $\mathsf{decode}(V_k', t + 1 - r) = \mathsf{decode}(V_k', t + 1 - (r - 1)) = w$. Since every process $p_k \in P^r$ sends a message (V_k', w) at round $r + 1$ (or is crashed at the beginning of round $r + 1$), S_j^{r+1} contains only w and $\bot$ for any $p_j \in P^{r+1}$. This implies that p_j decides a value w at round $r + 1$.   □.

From lemma 5, 8, and 9, the following theorem holds.

Theorem 1 For any input vector I, the algorithm ACC solves the uniform consensus (1) within $f + 2 - l(I)$ rounds if $f > l(I)$ holds, or (2)within 2 rounds if $f \leq l(I)$ holds.

3.3   Optimized Algorithm

In this subsection, we introduce the algorithm ACCF, which is an optimized version of ACC. The algorithm ACCF terminates within the same number of rounds ($\max\{2, f + 2 - l(I)\}$) as ACC. In addition, it terminates within only 1 round if $l(I) \geq t$ holds, and within terminates within $t + 1$ rounds if $f = t$ and $l(I) = 0$ holds.

The idea of modification from ACC to ACCF is to add two exceptional decision schemes, which is called *fast decision* and *slow decision* afterward. Each scheme is as follows:

Fast decision. This scheme is same as that in [10]. At round 1 if a process p_i gathers all proposals and recognizes that legality level of the input vector is greater than or equal to t, it immediately decides a value $\mathsf{decode}(J_i, t)$ ($= h(I)$). In this case, even though up to t processes crash, all other processes can calculate $h(I)$. This implies that each process eventually decides a value $h(I)$, and thus then uniform agreement is guaranteed.

Slow decision. This scheme is that each process p_i simply decides a value $\mathsf{decode}(J_i, 0)$ at the end of round $t+1$. Then, since there $t+1$ rounds contains at least one correct round, each process no longer has to check its estimation.

The algorithm ACCF is presented in Figure 3. It is described as the additional code to Figure 2. The fast decision part (the lines 8.1 - 8.3) is inserted into the position after the line 8 of ACC. The slow decision part (the lines 16.1 - 16.3) is inserted into the position after the line 16 of ACC.

Algorithm ACC(v_i) for h-legal condition sequence and t faults ($t < n/2$)
(**Additional Code to ACC**)
Code for p_i

8.1	**if** $r = 1$ **and** $\#_\perp(J_i) = 0$ **and** $l(J_i) \geq t$ **then**	
8.2	decide(decode(J_i, t)) and exit	/* Fast decision */
8.3	**endif**	
16.1	**if** $r = t + 1$ **then**	
16.2	decide(decode($J_i, 0$)) and exit	/* Slow decision */
16.3	**endif**	

Fig. 3. Algorithm ACCF: Adaptive Condition-based Consensus with Fast/Slow decision.

Correctness of ACCF. In this subsection, we prove the correctness of ACCF. Lemmas 5, 6 ,and 7 also hold for ACCF (the proofs are same as that for ACC). Lemmas 8 and 9 are slightly modified as follows:

Lemma 10 (Regular and Slow Termination) Each process p_i decides a value at round $\min\{F, t + 1\}$ or earlier.

Proof This lemma clearly holds from Lemma 8. □

Lemma 11 (Regular Agreement) Let p_i be the first process that decides, w be the decision of p_i, and r be the round when p_i decides ($2 \leq r \leq t$). Then, for each process $p_j \in P^r$, p_j decides w at round r or $r + 1$ unless it crashes by the end of round $r + 1$.

Proof The proof is same as that of Lemma 9. □

Lemma 12 (Fast Termination) If $l(I) > t$ and $f = 0$ holds, each process p_i decides a common value at round 1.

Proof Since $f = 0$ holds, p_i receives the message from every process. This implies that $J_i^1 = I$ holds, and thus, p_i decides decode(I, t) at round 1 (line 8.5). □

Lemma 13 (Slow Agreement) If processes p_i and p_j decide at round $t + 1$, then, p_i and p_j decides a common value.

Proof From Lemma 7, every round up to $t - 1$ is not correct because p_i and p_j decide at round $t + 1$. Then, either round t or round $t + 1$ is correct. (**Case1**) Round t is correct: From Lemma 6, J_k^t has same value for each p_k (letting J be the value of J_*^t). Then, each process in P^t sends a same message (J, w) (unless it crashes), where w is decode($J, 1$). This implies that both p_i and p_j decide w. (**Case2**) Round $t + 1$ is correct: Then, $Views_i^{t+1} = Views_j^{t+1}$ and $S_i^{t+1} = S_j^{t+1}$ hold. This implies that p_i and p_j decide a same value. □

Lemma 14 (Fast Agreement) (1)If a process p_i decides w at round 1, each p_j decides w, or crashes.

Proof Since p_i decides at round 1, $l(I) \geq t$ clearly holds. Then, for any $k \leq t$ and J such that $\#_{\perp}(J) \leq t$, $\mathsf{decode}(J,k) = h(I) = \mathsf{decode}(I,t) = w$ holds. This implies that p_j decides w unless it crashes.   □

From Lemmas, 11, 13 and 14, we obtains the uniform agreement property:

Corollary 1 (Uniform Agreement) No two processes decide different values.

From Corollary 1, and, Lemmas 5, 10, and 12, the following theorem holds.

Theorem 2 The algorithm ACCF solves the uniform consensus (1) within one round if $l(I) \geq t$ and no process crashes, (2) within two rounds if $l(I) \geq f$, and (3) within $\min\{f + 2 - l(I), t + 1\}$ rounds otherwise.

4   Concluding Remarks

This paper considered condition-based consensus algorithms adapting to difficulty of input vectors. We formalized difficulty of input vectors as legality level, and proposed an adaptive condition-based uniform consensus algorithm. The proposed algorithm terminates within $\min\{f + 2 - l(I), t + 1\}$ rounds if $l(I) \leq f$, and within 2 rounds if $l(I) \geq f$, where $l(I)$ is legality level of the input vector. Moreover, this algorithm terminates with one round if $l(I) \geq t$ and $f = 0$ holds (fast decision), Compared with existing algorithm, the proposed algorithm is the fastest in almost all cases.

Acknowledgment

This work is supported in part by a JSPS, Grant-in-Aid for Scientific Research ((B)(2)15300017), and "The 21st Century Center of Excellence Program" of the Ministry of Education, Culture, Sports, Science and Technology, Japan.

References

1. H. Attiya and J. L. Welch. Sequential consistency versus linearizability. *ACM Transactions on Computer Systems*, 12(2):91–122, 1994.
2. T. D. Chandra and S. Toueg. Unreliable failure detectors for reliable distributed systems. *Journal of the ACM*, 43(2):225–267, 1996.
3. B. Charron-Bost and A. Schiper. Uniform consensus is harder than consensus (extended abstract). Technical Report DSC/2000/028, EPFL, Lausanne(Switzerland), May 2000.
4. M. J. Fischer, N. A. Lynch, and M. S. Paterson. Impossibility of distributed consensus with one faulty process. *Journal of the ACM*, 32(2):374–382, 1985.

5. R. Guerraoui. Revisiting the relationship between non-blocking atomic commitment and consensus. In *Proc. of 9th International Workshop on Distributed Algorithms(WDAG)*, volume 972 of *LNCS*, Sep 1995.
6. V. Hadzilacos and S. Toueg. Fault-tolerant broadcasts and related problems. In S. Mullender, editor, *Distributed Systems*, chapter 5, pages 97–145. Addison-Wesley, 1993.
7. M. Herlihy. Wait-free synchronization. *ACM Transactions on Programming Languages and Systems*, 13:124–149, 1991.
8. N. Lynch. *Distributed Algorithms*. Morgan Kaufmann, 1996.
9. A. Mostefaoui, S. Rajsbaum, and M. Raynal. Conditions on input vectors for consensus solvability in asynchronous distributed systems. *Journal of the ACM*, 50(6):922–954, 2003.
10. A. Mostefaoui, S. Rajsbaum, and M. Raynal. Using conditions to exppedite consensus in synchronous distributed systems. In *Proc. of 17th International Conference on Ditributed Computing(DISC)*, volume 2848 of *LNCS*, pages 249–263, Oct 2003.
11. A. Mostefaoui, S. Rajsbaum, and M. Raynal. The synchronous condition-based consensus hierarchy. In *Proc. of 18th International Conference on Distributed Computing(DISC)*, Oct 2004. (to appear).
12. A. Mostefaoui, S. Rajsbaum, M. Raynal, and M. Roy. Condition-based consensus solvability: a hierarchy of conditions and efficient protocols. *Distributed Computing*, 17(1):1–20, 2004.
13. M. Raynal. Consensus in synchronous systems: A concise guided tour. In *Proc. of Pacific Rim International Symposium on Dependable Computing(PRDC)*, pages 221–228, 2002.
14. Y. Zibin. Condition-based consensus in synchronous systems. In *Proc. of 17th International Conference on Ditributed Computing(DISC)*, volume 2848 of *LNCS*, pages 239–248, Oct 2003.

Group-Solvability
(Extended Abstract)

Eli Gafni

University of California Los Angeles, Dept. of Computer Science
Los Angeles, CA 90095-1596
eli@cs.ucla.edu

Abstract. Recent advances in Network Attached Storage (NAS) devices has given rise to research on tasks in which the number of potentially participating processors is not known or even bounded in advance. In many of such situations the output of processors depends upon the *group* the processor belongs to, rather than upon the individual.

Case in point: the renaming task in which processors dynamically acquire unique individual slots. In the group version of the renaming task, processors from the same group are allowed to share a slot. Sharing slots by processors for the same group may be applicable when processors are to post information and processors of the same group possess the same information. The difficulty in reducing the group version to the individual version arises from the fact that in an asynchronous READ-WRITE wait-free model of computation, a group cannot elect a leader to acquire slot on the group's behalf and post the information.

This paper generalizes the notion of a standard task solvability to solvability by groups. It is mainly concerned with solvability by groups of infinite size. It shows that the notion of group solvability by infinite size groups is proper restriction of standard solvability by proving that the Immediate Snapshots task on three processors is not group solvable. The paper's main technical contribution is in reducing a question about infinite size groups to finite size. It characterizes group solvability of a task T_n over $n + 1$ processors via solvability by groups of size n. Finally, it poses a challenging lower-bound conjecture on a proposed group-solvable version of the renaming task.

1 Introduction

Consider the renaming task [1]. In this task, if the participating set is of size k, the task requires each of the k processors to output a unique number in the range 1 to $f(k) = 2k - 1$. The renaming task allows for dynamically assigning dedicated slots to processors. Suppose we allocate slots in order for processors to post some information in their possession: consider a situation in which processors that belong to the same group are in possession of the same information. In this case, we need only one posting per group, but we cannot elect a leader in a group to post its information. A possible solution is to have each slot acquired in the renaming be a Multi-writer Multi-Reader (MWMR) register. Have processors

R. Guerraoui (Ed.): DISC 2004, LNCS 3274, pp. 30–40, 2004.
© Springer-Verlag Berlin Heidelberg 2004

acquire slots so that a slot is shared only by processors of the same group. Thus, processors overwriting each other do not alter the information. Is the renaming task as stated above solvable for groups? If it is not, and the range $f(k)$ of numbers has to grow faster than $2k - 1$ in order to render the task solvable, how does the growth in the size of the groups affect solvability? Does $f(k)$ have to grow without bound as the sizes of the groups grow? Or is it true that beyond some threshold any increase in the group size does not affect solvability? Does the fact that the number of groups is finite but the group sizes may be infinite allow us to solve the problem using only finite number of MWMR registers?

This paper answers some of these questions by introducing the notion of group solvability for tasks and investigating the necessary and sufficient conditions for it. A task dictates the allowed output tuples for each participating set. A protocol solves a task, if after executing it, each processor in the participating set halts with an output, and the collection of outputs constitutes an output tuple in the task for that participating set. We extend this notion to group solvability by equating a group with a processor and by requiring that any collection of outputs one from each processor in a distinct group out of the participating groups constitutes an output tuple for that participating groups.

Of special interest is when a task is solvable independent of the group size. When a task is solvable for any group size, we call the task group-solvable. In this paper we are concerned with asynchronous wait-free group solvability. Our model of computation is the Single-Writer Multi-Reader (SWMR) Atomic-Snapshots model. We investigate the solvability of tasks as the group sizes grow. Our main result is that if a task T_n on $n + 1$ processors is solvable for groups of size n then it is group-solvable.

Yet, group-solvability in SWMR model may mean that we need larger and larger memory as the size of the groups grow. Another corollary of our characterization is that if a task is group-solvable, it is solvable using a finite $(F(n, (T_n)))$ number of Multi-Writer Multi-Reader registers.

Related to our work is the work on group mutual-exclusion [2,3] and recent works on models and protocols when the number or universe of processors is not bounded a priori [4–6]. While the group mutual-exclusion is in the more difficult long-lived computation domain rather than one-shot task domain, solvability there is investigated in the fault-free model. While much work has been done with respect to wait-free solvability with unbounded number of processors, the group notion was not investigated in that model. Thus, this paper fills the gap. It investigates groups in the context of wait-free computation.

Our first step is to show that the group-solvability notion requires special study. It is a proper restriction of solvability. The task of 3 processors Immediate-Snapshots [7] is solvable, but not group-solvable.

We then invoke the characterization of wait-free solvability, which categorizes a task is solvable if and only if it is solvable in the Iterated Immediate Snapshots model [8,9]. Using it, we show that if a task T_n on $n + 1$ processors is solvable for group sizes of n then it is solvable for any group size. However, we conjecture that below the threshold n, for every k there is a task T_k, which is rendered unsolvable if we increase the size of any group.

This paper raises more questions than provides answers: We give a version of the renaming algorithm that is group-solvable. We conjecture that any restriction of this version (i.e., reducing $f(k)$) renders the task unsolvable for groups. This renaming algorithm is very simple and was first proposed in [10] as an interesting curiosity. In addition to the challenging lower bound, having distinct algorithms for groups and individuals leaves open the quest for an explicit algorithm that will seamlessly solve renaming in a conjectured optimal slot space, as a function of the actual number of processors in a group that are participating, i.e. a uniform algorithm [5].

The paper is organized as follows: We first present a Model section where we formally define terms and introduce machinery needed here. Then we show that the 3 processors Immediate Snapshots task is not group-solvable. In the following main section we present our simulation of groups of n processor by infinite groups, establishing the necessary and sufficient conditions for group-solvability. Then in a short section we discuss group solvability of the renaming task, and finally we conclude with a section of open questions and conjectures.

2   Model

The model of distributed computation in which group-solvability studied in this paper, is the standard asynchronous wait-free SWMR Atomic Snapshots model [11]. W.l.o.g we consider only computations in which processor's input is its distinct id (as we can consider distinct processor for any distinct input/processor pair), and the protocols are full-information [12]. Thus, an execution is an infinite sequence of processor IDs. The odd appearance of a processor id in the sequence is a WRITE while the even is a snapshot SCAN. The state of a processor in a position in the sequence are all the prefix compatible executions, where a READ commutes with READs and a WRITE commutes with WRITES. The distinct processors that appear in an execution comprise the *participating set* of processors in that execution.

A *task* T_n over processors $p_0, ..., p_n$ is a relation Δ from vectors of processor IDs, to matching-size vectors of outputs. The interpretation being that in an execution of participating set vector Q, if processor p_i appears in Q and outputs value v_i, then $(Q, V) \in \Delta$, where V is a vector $V = (v_{i_0}, ... v_{i_{|Q|-1}})$ such that a processor's position in Q and its output's position in V match.

The wait-free model requires that if a processor p_i appears infinitely often in an execution, than eventually it outputs a value. Correspondingly, a *protocol* for T_n is a partial map from a full-information state of a processor to an output that satisfies the requirement above. A protocol for T_n is said to *solve* T_n.

A task is solvable in a model, if there exists a protocol in the model that solves it.

Of particular interest are *simplex convergence* tasks [8]. A simplex convergence task SC_n on processors $p_0, ..., p_n$ is defined as follows: We are given an n-dimensional subdivided simplex S^n. We assume that S^n is colored properly by processor IDs such that each simplex $s^n \in S^n$ contains all IDs. The $n + 1$

0-dimensional faces of S^n are colored by distinct IDs, and each simplex on a face defined by a subset of the 0-dimensional faces is colored only by the corresponding IDs. A subdivided simplex thus colored is called *chromatic*.

The convergence task assigns to a vector of participating processors corresponding to a face $F \subseteq S^n$ all the simplexes in S^n that appear on that face. For example, the 3-processor Immediate Snapshots $SCD^0{}_2$ or IS_2 is depicted in Figure 1. If processor i, $i = 1, 2, 3$ goes solo, it returns the vertex $i : i$. In an execution of i and j $i < j$ with the corresponding participating set vector (i, j) they return either $(i : i, \ j : i, j)$ or $(i : i, j, \ j : i, j)$ or $(i : i, j, \ j : j)$, and if the participating set is all of them, they return any triangle, with processor i returning a vertex of the type $i : *$.

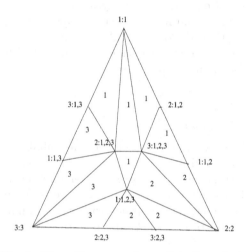

Fig. 1. Three Processors Immediate Snapshots.

Let T_n be a task on $n + 1$ task-processors $p_0, ..., p_n$. Let $G_0, ..., G_n$ be groups of processors with $|G_i| = k_i$, $i = 0, ..., n$ and $G_i = p_{(0,i)}, .., p_{(k_i-1,i)}$. Let P be the participating set of processors. The *participating groups* is the projection of the participating set over the groups. A protocol for the processors in the groups k_i-*group-solve* T_n w.r.t. $G_0, ..., G_n$ if arbitrarily choosing an output of processors one for each participating group constitutes an output tuple in T_n for the participating set of the task-processors that correspond to the $n + 1$ groups. The task T_n is *group-solvable* if it is solvable w.r.t. any group size k.

2.1   Immediate Snapshot Model

The immediate snapshot model introduced in [13,14] is a restriction of the atomic snapshot model (and thus potentially more powerful) in the sense that its set of executions is a subset of the atomic snapshot model. It comprises executions in the atomic snapshot model in which each maximal run of writes is followed by a maximal run of snapshots by the same processors. Consequently, we can condense the odd-followed-by-even appearance of a processor as a single operation called WriteRead(*value*). Thus, an execution is a sequence of *sets* of processors. In [7], it was proven that immediate snapshots model can be simulated by the atomic snapshot model and therefore cannot solve anything not solvable in the atomic snapshot model.

2.2   Iterated Immediate Snapshot Model

A one-shot immediate snapshot is an immediate snapshot model that allows each processor to WriteRead only once. In the iterated immediate snapshot model, we have a sequence of one-shot immediate snapshot memories, $M_0, M_1, \ldots$. The full-information protocol execution starts by p_i WriteReading its input to M_0. It then applies the output from M_i, $i > 0$, as an input value (i.e., it "pretends" to be a processor with that id) to M_{i+1}, ad infinitum.

Formally, one-shot immediate snapshot is specified as follows. Processor p_i outputs a subset S_i of the participating set P, such that

1. $p_i \in S_i$,
2. $S_i \subseteq S_j$ or $S_j \subseteq S_i$, $\forall p_i, p_j \in P$
3. $p_i \in S_j \Rightarrow S_i \subseteq S_j$, $\forall p_i, p_j \in P$

A full-information execution in the model is an infinite sequence, each element of which is an ordered partition of the set of processors p_i, $i = 0, \ldots, n$. Inductively, if the local state of processor p_i after its appearance in element j is v_{ij}, then its local state after its $j + 1$ appearance is the result of inputting (p_i, v_{ij}) to a one-shot immediate snapshot with S_i including all the tuples of processors in the $j + 1$ partition, which appear in the order in sets that precede or include p_i.

A task is solvable wait-free in the iterated immediate snapshot model if for b large enough, the output of p_i for all i from M_b can be mapped to an output-value satisfying the task.

In this paper we use the following characterization of wait-free solvability [9]:

Proposition 1. *A task T_n is read-write wait-free solvable if and only if there exits a bound $b(T_n, n)$ such that the task is solvable in b iteration of the Iterated Immediate Snapshots model.*

3   Three-Processor Immediate Snapshot Task Is Not Group-Solvable

3.1   The Task

A three-processor Immediate Snapshots task is a convergence task $SCD^0{}_2$ depicted in Figure 1.

Theorem 1. *The three-processor Immediate Snapshots task is not group-solvable.*

Proof. The idea of the proof is simple. The set of nodes returned cumulatively by the groups can reside, at most, in two triangles that share a face. Otherwise, we will have a combination of outputs that is not a triangle. We associate triangles with processors as in figure 1. Then we take three simulators each simulating three distinct processors, one from each group, by that each simulator delineates a triangle. Each simulator outputs the id of the processor associated with that triangle. Since there are, at most two distinct output triangles, the simulators have solved 2-set consensus wait-free, which is impossible [8,14,13].

Let the simulators be Sim_i, $i = 1, 2, 3$. Processor Sim_i executes first a member from group G_i and then, in an arbitrary order, two distinct members: one from each of the other groups. By that it delineated a triangle. It then outputs the value to which this triangle has been mapped.

Obviously, if Sim_i runs alone, it will output i. If it runs just with Sim_j, it will output i or j. Now, if the three simulators output three distinct numbers, then we can choose vertices of distinct color from these three triangles to obtain a collection which is not a triangle – thereby contradicting solvability. Thus, we conclude that the three simulators will output at most two distinct numbers. But then their outputs constitute a solution to the three-processors 2-set consensus, which is impossible.

Corollary 1. *Any non-trivial convergence task is not group-solvable.*

Obviously, the existence of a span [8] is necessary but strictly not sufficient for group-solvability. The next section gives a finite characterization of those necessary and sufficient conditions.

3.2   Solvability with "Small" Group Sizes

It can be seen that the Immediate Snapshot task for three processors, IS_2, is not group solvable, and holds for groups of size three. That is all that we used in the proof above. What about group-size of two? Our characterization in the next section implies that IS_2, since it is not group-solvable, is not solvable for groups of size 2, either. We relegate an explicit proof to the full paper.

In general, we conjecture that for every n and $k < n$, there exists a task T_n that is solvable for groups of size k but not solvable for groups of size $k+1$. Indeed, if we take a convergence task on IS_7 and equate p_i and $p_{(i+1)}$, $i = 0, 2, 4, 6$, to make it a task on 4 processors, our conjecture is that this task is solvable for group-size of 2 but not for group-size of 3.

4   Necessary and Sufficient Conditions for Group-Solvability

Theorem 2. *Let T_n be a task on $n + 1$ processors, then T_n is group-solvable if and only if it is solvable for groups $G_0, ... G_n$ of size $|G_i| \geq n$, $i = 0, ..., n$.*

4.1   The Idea – Informally

Obviously, if T_n is group-solvable then it is solvable for any finite-size groups. This establishes the necessity direction.

For sufficiency, we know that the Immediate Snapshots task is not group solvable since it is a convergence task. Yet a variation of the Immediate Snapshot task, which we will call *Relaxed Immediate Snapshots* (RIS) is group solvable. This variation requires a processor p_i to output a pair (p_j, S_j), where p_j is a participating processor id, and S_j is a subset of the participating processors, so that the collection of pairs returned constitutes an immediate snapshots (i.e., a processor may output on behalf of another processor and not necessarily return its own immediate snap.)

Thus, assume that T_n is group-solvable. Then it is solvable for any group size and in particular for groups $G_0, ..., G_n$, each of size n. Let processors in group G_j be $p_{(0,j)}, ..., p_{(n-1,j)}$. We now consider how groups of size n solve T_n, and show how infinite groups may simulate groups of size n in solving T_n. The infinite groups simulate the Iterated Immediate Snapshot computation by processors $p_{(0,0)}, ..., p_{(n-1,n)}$. To that end, we group-solve the Relaxed Immediate Snapshots for the $n + 1$ simulated processors $p_{(0,0)}, p_{(0,1)}, ..., p_{(0,n)}$, with simulating group $\bar{G}_j$ starting with $p_{(0,j)}$. This simulates the behavior of processors $p_{(0,0)}, p_{(0,1)}, ..., p_{(0,n)}$ at memory M_0 of the Iterated Immediate Snapshots by solving RIS. Then a simulator processor takes output from M_0, where now cumulatively there may be only few distinct outputs, as inputs for the next memory M_1 and group-solve the Relaxed Immediate Snapshots in that memory M_1. Continuing this way, we reach memory M_b, where we have an output, therefore, for at least one processor out of simulated processors $p_{(0,0)}, p_{(0,1)}, ..., p_{(0,n)}$, say $p_{(0,j)}$. Processors in group $\bar{G}_j$ can now adopt an output from M_b and drop out of the computation!

How do we continue? Since in the Relaxed Immediate Snapshot a processor obtains an output on behalf of possibly another processor, it may be that all the simulating groups "simulated" a single processor, $p_{(0,j)}$. To get an output for itself, after a processor of group $\bar{G}_k$ simulate a processor to M_b, it observes whether it can obtain an output for itself, and if not, it now inserts processor $p_{(1,k)}$ into the computation, so that there is a guarantee that it can simulate a processor that does not belong to a group for which an output has been obtained.

To this end, after a simulator p_i simulated some processor from G_j at M_b, it posts the output and view for the processor. It then take a snapshot of the posted outputs, and posts that snapshot. A simulator group terminates if its output is the intersections of all these output vectors. A simulator continues to the next stage "suspecting" that groups that correspond to the largest posted snapshot, have terminated.

Thus, when simulating $p_{(1,k)}$ we go to a new stage. We take a "fresh" copy of $M_0, M_1, ..., M_b$ where all the processors $p_{(1,*)}$ will be simulated. Yet, to be consistent to what was simulated in the first copy of $M_0, M_1, ..., M_b$, after inserting $p_{(1,k)}$, to level $2(n+1)$ of M_0, simulator p_k first drops all the processors in $p_{(0,0)}, p_{(0,1)}, ..., p_{(0,n)}$ to their appropriate levels according to the views of outputs observed in the previous M_b. Only after finishing pushing these processors down to full levels, does it start pushing down simulated processor $p_{(1,k)}$. The idea being that if $p_{(1,k)}$ gets to a full level and cannot be continued to be simulated, as explained below, there is some $p_{(1,*)}$ at a level above it that can be simulated.

Thus, at each stage at least one group drops out of the computation. so a the worst we need n stages (since in the last $n+1$ stage a group is simulating alone, and therefore just need to pick out an output compatible with all the outputs it has observed in the n'th stage.).

We now elaborate on the building blocks used in the sketch above.

We introduce the relaxed Immediate Snapshot Task RIS_n on processors $p_0, ..., p_n$.

Let P be the participating set. processor p_i returns a pair (p_j, S_j) such that:

1. $p_j \in P$, and $S_j \subseteq P$,
2. if p_i returns (p_j, S_j), and p_l returns (p_k, S_k), then $S_j \subseteq S_k$ or $S_k \subseteq S_j$.
3. if $k \in S_j$ then $S_k \subseteq S_j$.

Lemma 1. RIS_n *is group-solvable.*

Proof. A generalization of the lemma is to say that any "colorless" convergence task, i.e., one in which processors converge to a simplex, but in which a processor may return vertex of different color then its color, is group-solvable. A way of proving this is to show that colorless convergence on the barycentric-subdivision [15] is solvable, and then invoke the Simplicial Approximation Theorem [15]. But this will amount to rather an existence proof. Here we strive for an explicit distributed algorithm:

We prepare $n+1$ *levels*, level $n+1$ down to level 1. Each level i contains $n+1$ pairs of MWMR registers $(CG_{(i,j)}, CR_{(i,j)})$, $i, j = 0, ..., n$, (CellGreen,CellRed) all initialized to $\bot$.

At level i a processor from group $\bar{G}_j$ sets $CG_{(i,j)}$ to 1. It then takes a snapshot of the level and counts for how many registers $CG_{(i,k)}$ are set to 1. If it is less then i, defined as observation that the *level is not full*, it signals it intends to continue down to level $i-1$ by setting $CR_{(i,j)}$ to 1. It then takes another snapshot to observe whether the level has now become full due to other processors' arrival to the level. If the level is not full, the processor continues, inductively, to level $i-1$.

If, at any of the two snapshots, it observes level i as full, the processor stops. We argue that there exists at least one index l such that $CG_{(i,l)} = 1$, and $CR_{(i,l)} = \bot$. Indeed, consider the last $CG_{(i,k)}$ that was set to 1. All the processors writing this register will observe the level as full and will not continue on to set $CR_{(i,k)}$ to 1. The processor then returns (p_l, S_l), where S_l is the set of processors p_k such that $CG_{(i,k)} = 1$.

The algorithm starts with processors beginning at level $n+1$.

Standard inductive argument shows that $|S_l| = i$, i.e., the number of simulated processors arriving at level i is at most i. Furthermore, if a processor in group $\bar{G}_j$ returns (p_l, S_l) at level i, then no processors from group $\bar{G}_l$ will continue to level $i-1$. That follows since the processor from group $\bar{G}_j$ observes the level full and $CR_{(i,l)} = \perp$. If processor from group G_l will later set $CR_{(i,l)}$ to 1, then since no 1 is ever changes to $\perp$, it will also observe the level full, and stop.

Finally, to see that the sets are related by containment, notice that for simulated processor k to go to levels below i, $CG_{(i,k)}$ must be set to 1. Since $CG_{(i,k)}$ cannot be set from $\perp$ to 1 after the level was observed as full, it must be 1 in any observation of the level as full, and therefore it will be returned in S_l. Thus, the Immediate Snapshots relation between returned pairs is satisfied.

The other building block we need to consider is the Relaxed Immediate Snapshots with Immediate Snapshot Inputs. Let A and B be two distinct set of processors each of size n, and assume processors in A are to solve the RIS over processors in A, but yet, each processor in A has a snapshot of processors from B as inputs. Among the participating processors, let IS_B be the smallest input snapshot from B. Participating processors in A have to output a relaxed immediate snapshot of processors from A that are compatible with IS_B. The way to solve this problem is for processors to first go down the level of the IS implementation, pushing down first "token" for processors from B in their input IS_B until they get to a full level or until they get to the level of the input IS_B.

5   Renaming

The Renaming Task [1] has different versions. The version RN_n we consider here is specified by a function $RN(i)$, $i = 1, ..., n + 1$ which requires processors in a participating set of size i to a acquire a unique slot in the range 1 to $RN(i)$. It was shown [8] that the function $RN(i) = 2i - 1$ is solvable, while any function that minorizes it at any point is not. We conjecture that $RN(i) = 2i - 1$ is not group solvable, while we show that the function $RN(i) = i(i + 1)/2$ is.

The algorithm that solves $RN(i) = i(i+1)/2$ appears in [10]. Here, we adapt it to groups. Processors take group-snapshots. We set MWMR registers each dedicated to a group, initialized to $\perp$. A processor at group G_j sets its register to 1, and double scans until success. Let it return a set S_j. Lets the rank of G_j within the group IDs in S_j be k. It then acquires slot $|S_i|(|S_i| - 1)/2 + k$. Since two processors which have the same-size snapshot have the same snapshot, the correctness of this algorithm is obvious: Processors that obtain snapshot of size $|S_i|$ acquire slots in $|S_i|(|S_i| - 1)/2 + 1$ to $|S_i|(|S_i| - 1)/2 + |S_i|$. It is clear that processors of the same-size snapshot do not collide; the same is true for processors from different snapshots since each snapshot size is allocated it own slots.

Let n be $n \gg c$; then, for groups of size c we can employ the original renaming algorithm from []. In that algorithm, a processor tries to capture a slot by raising a flag for that slot and observing whether collision with other flags at the slot has occurred. If no collision(s) has occurred, the processor takes the slot. Otherwise, it removes its flag and raises it anew for the k's free slot, where k is its rank among the participating processors. It can be easily seen that that algorithm will work if the ranking is performed by group rank rather than by processor rank. Thus, the number of slots we need at the most for n classes is $cn + (n - 1) << n(n + 1)/2$. This algorithm is also adjusting to the number of the processors in a group that actually participate.

Thus, it opens the quest for a seamlessly adjusting renaming protocol, that on the one extreme will require, at most, $2i - 1$ slots (when there are exactly i participating processors from distinct groups), and on the other hand will require, at the most, $i(i+1)/2$ slots when the number of participating processors from the participating groups grows without bound.

6 Conclusion

This paper opens a new line of research, that of group-solvability. This paper established the first two results: (1) group-solvability is distinct from solvability, and (2) beyond a threshold, solvability of group-size k implies solvability for group-size $k + 1$. What happens in between these two extremes is not clear.

Our notion of group-solvability can be construed as the "for-all" version: a version the requires correctness of all combinations of outputs. With one from each group, the outputs constitute an output tuple. We may also consider the "there exists" version of the problem: there exists a representative from each group so the the combination of outputs is an output tuple. We conjecture that the two notions are equivalent; i.e., every task solvable for the latter notion is solvable for the former.

Thus, it leaves more question than answers:

1. Is n tight? Perhaps a better characterization of group-solvability is that if a task is solvable for group sizes $n - 1$ then it is group solvable.
2. Is the "there exists" notion of solvability equivalent to the "for all"?
3. As the number of group grows how should the range $RN(i)$ grow to make renaming group-solvable?
4. Is there a uniform algorithm [5] for group-solvable space-optimal renaming?

Finally, earlier drafts of this paper argued the main result using algebraic topology. It only later occurred to us that since the duality between algebraic topology and distributed algorithm goes both ways there may be a way to argue the result strictly algorithmically. Nevertheless, the first glimpse of why the result may hold was motivated completely by topological reasoning. And perhaps that is the way it should be.

Acknowledgement

Part of this work was conducted while visiting EPFL Lausanne. I am in debt to Rachid Guerraoui, Bastian Pochon, and Petr Kouznetsov, for many hours of discussion and even more hours of jogging.

References

1. H. Attiya, A. Bar-Noy, D. Dolev, D. Koller, D. Peleg, and R. Reischuk, "Achievable Cases in an Asynchronous Environment," in *Proceedings of the 28th Symposium on Foundations of Computer Science*, pp. 337–346, 1987.
2. Y. Joung, "Asynchronous group mutual-exclusion," *Distributed Computing*, vol. 13, pp. 189–206, 2000.
3. V. Hadzilacos, "A note on group mutual-exclusion," in *Proceedings of the 20th ACM Symposium on Principles of Distributed Computing*, pp. 100–106, 2001.
4. M. Merritt and G. Taubenfeld, "Computing with infinitly many processes," *Proceeding of the 14th International Symposium on Distributed Computing: LNCS 1914*, pp. 164–178, Oct. 2000.
5. E. Gafni, "A simple algorithmic characterization of uniform solvability," *Proceedings of the 43rd Annual IEEE Symposium On Foundation of Computer Science (FOCS2002)*, pp. 228–237, 2002.
6. G. Chockler and D. Malkhi, "Active disk paxos with infinitely many processes," in *In Proceedings of the 21th ACM Symposium on Principles of Distributed Computing (PODC 2002)*, pp. 78–87, 2002.
7. E. Borowsky and E. Gafni, "Immediate Atomic Snapshots and Fast Renaming," in *Proceedings of the 12th ACM Symposium on Principles of Distributed Computing*, pp. 41–51, 1993.
8. M. Herlihy and N. Shavit, "The topological structure of asynchronous computability," *Journal of the ACM*, vol. 46(6), pp. 858–923, 1999.
9. E. Borowsky and E. Gafni, "A simple algorithmically reasoned characterization of wait-free computations," *PODC97*, pp. 189–198, 1997.
10. A. Bar-Noy and D. Dolev, "Shared-memory vs. message-passing in an asynchronous distributed environment," *PODC 1989*, pp. 307–318, 1989.
11. Y. Afek, H. Attiya, D. Dolev, E. Gafni, M. Merrit, and N. Shavit, "Atomic Snapshots of Shared Memory," in *Proceedings of the 9th ACM Symposium on Principles of Distributed Computing*, pp. 1–13, 1990.
12. G. Frederickson and N. Lynch, "Electing a Leader in a Synchronous Ring," *Journal of the ACM*, vol. 34, no. 1, pp. 98–115, 1987.
13. E. Borowsky and E. Gafni, "Generalized FLP Impossibility Result for t-Resilient Asynchronous Computations," in *Proceedings of the 25th ACM Symposium on the Theory of Computing*, pp. 91–100, 1993.
14. M. Saks and F. Zaharoglou, " Wait-Free k-Set Agreement is Impossible: The Topology of Public Knowledge," in *Proceedings of the 26th ACM Symposium on the Theory of Computing*, pp. 101–110, 1993.
15. E. H. Spanier, *Algebraic Topology*. Springer-Verlag, New York, 1966.

The Notion of Veto Number
and the Respective Power of $\Diamond\mathcal{P}$ and $\Diamond\mathcal{S}$
to Solve One-Shot Agreement Problems

Roy Friedman[1], Achour Mostefaoui[2], and Michel Raynal[2]

[1] Computer Science Department, Technion, Haifa 32000, Israel
[2] IRISA, Campus de Beaulieu, 35042 Rennes Cedex, France
roy@cs.technion.ac.il, {achour,raynal}@irisa.fr

Abstract. Unreliable failure detectors are abstract devices that, when added to asynchronous distributed systems, allow to solve distributed computing problems (e.g., Consensus) that otherwise would be impossible to solve in these systems. This paper focuses on two classes of failure detectors defined by Chandra and Toueg, namely, the classes denoted $\Diamond\mathcal{P}$ (*eventually perfect*) and $\Diamond\mathcal{S}$ (*eventually strong*). Both classes include failure detectors that eventually detect permanently all process crashes, but while the failure detectors of $\Diamond\mathcal{P}$ eventually make no erroneous suspicions, the failure detectors of $\Diamond\mathcal{S}$ are only required to eventually not suspect a single correct process.

In such a context, this paper addresses the following question related to the comparative power of these classes, namely: "Are there one-shot agreement problems that can be solved in asynchronous distributed systems with reliable links but prone to process crash failures augmented with $\Diamond\mathcal{P}$, but cannot be solved when those systems are augmented with $\Diamond\mathcal{S}$?" Surprisingly, the paper shows that the answer to this question is "no". An important consequence of this result is that $\Diamond\mathcal{P}$ cannot be the weakest class of failure detectors that enables solving one-shot agreement problems in unreliable asynchronous distributed systems. These results are then extended to the case of more severe failure modes.

Keywords: Agreement Problem, Asynchronous Distributed System, Consensus, Computational Power, Input Vector, One-Shot Problem, Process Crash, Unreliable Failure Detector, $\Diamond\mathcal{P}$, $\Diamond\mathcal{S}$, Veto Number.

1 Introduction

Context of the study. The design and implementation of reliable applications on top of asynchronous distributed systems (sometimes called *time-free* asynchronous systems) prone to process or link failures is a difficult and complex task. One of the main issues one has to cope with lies in the impossibility of correctly detecting process crash failures in those systems. In such a context, some problems become very difficult or even impossible to solve. The most famous of these problems is the *Consensus* problem. It is known that there is no deterministic solution to Consensus in asynchronous distributed system if a single process (or more) may crash [16].

Overcoming the impossibility result associated with the Consensus problem requires augmenting the underlying asynchronous system with additional assumptions.

R. Guerraoui (Ed.): DISC 2004, LNCS 3274, pp. 41–55, 2004.
© Springer-Verlag Berlin Heidelberg 2004

Those are often related to synchrony. That is, they often state, in some way or another, "timing" assumptions that make the system no longer purely time-free, thereby allowing us to solve Consensus in those augmented systems (e.g, systems with partial synchrony [11], or minimal synchronism [14]).

A more abstract approach to circumvent impossibility results was introduced by Chandra and Toueg who have introduced the concept of an *Unreliable Failure Detector* [5]. All the synchrony or timing assumptions are hidden in the implementation of a failure detector that appears to the upper layer as a set of abstract properties. From an operational point of view, a failure detector can be seen as an oracle made up of a set of modules, each associated with a process. The failure detector module attached to a process provides it with a list of processes it suspects of having crashed (so, the output of a failure detector module is bounded). A failure detector can make mistakes by not suspecting a crashed process or erroneously suspecting a non crashed process. To be useful, a failure detector cannot be allowed to behave in a completely arbitrary way. So, its possible behaviors are defined by properties that restrict the mistakes it can make. In their seminal paper [5], Chandra and Toueg introduced several classes of failure detectors, each class being defined by two abstract properties, namely a *Completeness* property and an *Accuracy* property. Completeness specifies the ability to detect crashes, while accuracy restricts erroneous suspicions.

As defined and advocated by Chandra and Toueg [5], the failure detector approach is particularly attractive. This is because failure detectors are not defined in terms of a particular implementation involving network topology, message delays, local clocks, etc., but in terms of abstract properties related to the detection of failures. The failure detector approach favors a modular decomposition that not only simplifies protocol design but also provides general solutions. More specifically, during a first step, a protocol is designed and proved correct assuming only the properties provided by a failure detector class. So, this protocol is not expressed in terms of low-level parameters, but depends only on a well defined set of abstract properties. The implementation of a failure detector FD of the assumed class can then be addressed independently: additional assumptions can be investigated and the ones that are sufficient to implement FD can be added to the underlying distributed system in order to get an augmented system on top of which FD can be implemented. With this, FD can be implemented in one way in some context and in another way in another context, according to the particular features of the underlying system. It follows that this layered approach favors the design, the proof and the portability of protocols.

$\mathcal{P}$, $\Diamond\mathcal{P}$, and $\Diamond\mathcal{S}$ are three classes of Chandra-Toueg's failure detectors that define a hierarchy. $\mathcal{P}$ is the class of *perfect* failure detectors, i.e., those that never make a mistake: a process that crashes is suspected (completeness) and a process is not suspected before it crashes (accuracy). It has been shown that $\mathcal{P}$ is the weakest class of failure detectors that enables solving the *Interactive Consistency* problem in asynchronous distributed systems prone to process crash failures [21]. Interactive consistency [27] is a one-shot agreement problem (so, each process proposes a value) such that each correct process[1] decides a vector (termination), and no two processes decide different vectors (agreement). The decided vector has one entry per process and each entry contains ei-

---

[1] A *correct* process is a process that does not crash; otherwise, it is *faulty*. See Section 2.

ther the value proposed by the corresponding process or a default value $\perp$. Moreover, if a process is correct, its entry in the vector cannot be $\perp$ (validity).

The class $\Diamond P$ contains all the failure detectors that, after some unknown but finite time, no longer make mistakes. This means that those failure detectors can behave arbitrarily during a finite period, but that period terminates and then the failure detector behaves as a failure detector of the class P. This class of failure detectors is called the class of *eventually perfect* failure detectors. It has been shown that, among the classes of failure detectors that outputs lists of suspects, $\Diamond P$ is the weakest class that allows to solve the *Quiescent Reliable Communication* problem [1]. This problem is a one-shot *communication* problem that consists of achieving reliable communication with quiescent algorithms despite lossy links and process crashes. Quiescence means here that, at the protocol level, the sending (or broadcast) of each application message must generate only a finite number of protocol messages in spite of link or process failures.

The class $\Diamond S$ contains all the failure detectors that, after some unknown but finite time, suspect all processes that crash and do not suspect one correct process. It is important to notice that failure detectors of this class can make an infinite number of mistakes by repeatedly suspecting correct processes. There is only a single correct process that from some point on should never be suspected and this can start only after an arbitrary finite time. This class of failure detectors is called the class of *eventually strong* failure detectors. It has been shown that $\Diamond S$ is the weakest class of failure detectors that allows to solve the *Consensus* problem, assuming a majority of correct processes [4]. In the Consensus problem, each process proposes a value, and all correct processes have to decide a value (termination), such that a decided value is a proposed value (validity) and no two processes decide differently (uniform agreement). As a counter example, the *Atomic Broadcast* problem is both a communication problem and an agreement problem, but it is not one-shot. It is a communication problem because it allows processes to reliably broadcast messages, and it is an agreement problem because it requires that the processes agree on the same message delivery order. Yet, it is not one-shot, as it is a *continuous* problem that can be solved by repeated Consensus invocations [5].

Motivation and content of the paper. In this paper we are interested in asynchronous distributed systems made up of n processes communicating through reliable links, but where up to f ($\leq n - 1$) processes may crash. Moreover, we are interested in *one-shot* agreement problems. The Consensus problem, and the interactive consistency problem are examples of one-shot agreement problems (each process is assumed to propose a value).

Although $\Diamond S$ appears to be weaker than $\Diamond P$ (yet, most implementations of $\Diamond S$ in fact attempt to provide $\Diamond P$), an interesting problem concerns the computational power of those classes of failure detectors. On one hand, up to date, no one has exhibited a one-shot agreement problem that can be solved with $\Diamond P$ and cannot with $\Diamond S$. On the other hand, the properties defining $\Diamond S$ are weaker than the ones defining $\Diamond P$. Hence the following fundamental question:

"*In asynchronous distributed systems with reliable links but prone to process crash failures, are there one-shot agreement problems that can be solved when those systems are augmented with $\Diamond P$, but cannot be solved when they are augmented only with $\Diamond S$?*"

Surprisingly, this paper shows that the answer to this question is "*no*". It is important to notice that this does *not* mean that the classes $\Diamond P$ and $\Diamond S$ are equivalent in the sense that it could be possible to simulate a failure detector of the class $\Diamond P$ in an asynchronous system equipped with a failure detector of the class $\Diamond S$ [2]. The intuition underlying this apparent contradiction can be explained by the fact that the problem domain is not continuous. Interestingly, this result has an important consequence that answers an open problem, namely, it shows that $\Diamond P$ cannot be the weakest class of failure detectors that enables solving one-shot agreement problems in asynchronous distributed systems prone to process crash failures.

To prove this, we introduce new notions related to distributed one-shot agreement problems. The first is the notion of *veto* number associated with those problems. Intuitively, the veto number of a one-shot agreement problem P is the smallest number ℓ of processes that control the decision value. For example, $\ell = 1$ for the interactive consistency problem; if a process changes its input value, the decided vector becomes different. Differently, $\ell = n$ for the Consensus problem; in the worst case, all processes have to change the value they propose to force a different decided value [3].

The main result of the paper can be stated as follows. Let P be a one-shot agreement problem, with veto number ℓ, that cannot be solved without the help of a failure detector:

- If $\ell > f$ and $f < n/2$, then P can be solved in asynchronous distributed systems equipped with a failure detector of the class $\Diamond S$ (i.e., $\Diamond S$ is sufficient to solve P),
- If $\ell \leq f$ or $f \geq n/2$, then P cannot be solved in asynchronous distributed systems equipped with a failure detector of the class $\Diamond P$ (i.e., $\Diamond P$ is not "strong" enough to solve P).

To formally define the veto number of a problem, and to prove the main theorem, a (new) notion of *irreconcilable input vectors* is introduced. This notion generalizes in some way the notion of valence that has been introduced to show the impossibility to deterministically solve Consensus despite process crashes.

The full version of the paper [17] also addresses more severe failures than process crashes. It first shows that the previous results hold in presence of message omission failures, and then focuses on Byzantine failures. In such a context, it considers failure detectors that are capable of detecting only *silence* failures (a process is silent if there is a time after which it no longer sends protocol messages; notice that a Byzantine process can be silent or not, and a crashed process is silent [13]).

1.1 Related Work

Implementation of Chandra-Toueg's failure detectors. Several works have considered the implementation of some or all of Chandra-Toueg's classes of failure detectors (e.g., [5, 15, 22, 23]). Basically, these works consider that, eventually, the underlying system behaves in a synchronous way. More precisely, they consider the *partially synchronous*

---

[2] In particular, an example of an environment in which $\Diamond S$ can be implemented but $\Diamond P$ cannot was given in [2].

[3] Additional ℓ-veto problems with $1 < \ell < n$ are discussed in a followup paper [18].

system model [5] which is a generalization of the models proposed in [14]. A partially synchronous system assumes that there are bounds on process speeds and message transfer delays, but these bounds are not known and hold only after some finite but unknown time (called *Global Stabilization Time*).

A new look at the implementation of Chandra and Toueg's failure detectors classes is proposed in [25]. Differently from the previous approaches that are based on timing assumptions that are (eventually) satisfied, this approach allows communication delays to always increase. It is based on a query-response mechanism and assumes that, for each query, the associated response messages obey a pattern where the responses from some processes always arrive among the $(n - f)$ first ones. Also, as shown in [2], there are systems in which $\Diamond S$ can be implemented while $\Diamond P$ cannot.

Other types of failure detectors. *Restricted* failure detectors are studied in [28]. Unreliable failure detectors with a *limited scope accuracy* are investigated in [3]. The notion of *realistic* failure detectors has been introduced and investigated in [9]. The evaluation of the quality of service of failure detectors is addressed in [7] (namely, how *fast* a failure detector detects failures, and how *well* it avoids false detection). *Heartbeat* failure detectors have unbounded outputs; they have been introduced to implement quiescent reliable communication despite process and link failures [1].

Weakest failure detectors. We consider here timeless failure detectors (i.e., those that do not provide information on the time at which failures occur). As indicated previously, it has been shown in that $\Diamond S$ is the weakest failure detector class to solve the Consensus problem [4] when $f < n/2$, while P is the weakest failure detector class to solve the Interactive Consistency problem [21] (for $f < n$). Differently, neither P, $\Diamond P$ or $\Diamond S$ is the weakest failure detector class to solve the Non-Blocking Atomic Commit problem. The weakest class to solve this problem [20] when $f < n/2$ is the the class $?P + \Diamond S$ introduced in [19]. This class satisfies the properties defining $\Diamond S$ plus the properties denoted $?P$ (anonymous perfect failure detection), namely, each correct process is eventually safely informed about process crashes but without knowing which processes have actually crashed.

Consensus stability. A notion of *stability* for long-lived Consensus has been introduced in [12]. This notion reflects how sensitive to changes the decisions of the system are, from one invocation of Consensus to the next, with respect to input changes. So, this type of stability is related to successive Consensus invocations.

Characterizations of agreement problems. Moran and Wolfstahl investigated the relation between the solvability of a problem and the number of output values an external observer should know in order to guess the remaining output values [24]. This is different from ℓ-veto which looks at how changing several bits in the input vectors affect the set of allowed output values. Also, several binary agreement problems were characterized using the notion of k-*Tag* [6]. Yet, the notion of k-Tag is limited to binary problems and depends on the impact of failures on the allowed decision values. Differently, ℓ-veto is defined for problems over any alphabet, and does not care about the behavior in faulty runs. Finally, neither the work of [24] nor [6] discussed the impact of such a characterization on the solvability with respect to a given failure detector class.

Roadmap. The paper is made up of five sections. Section 2 presents the computation model, and the failure detector classes we are interested in. Section 3 defines one-shot agreement problems, and introduces the notions of veto number and irreconcilable configurations. Then Section 4 states and proves the main result. Section 5 provides concluding remarks.

2   Computation Model

2.1   Asynchronous Distributed Systems with Process Crash Failures

We consider a system consisting of a finite set Π of n processes, namely, $\Pi = \{p, q, \ldots\}$. A process can fail by *crashing*, i.e., by prematurely halting. It behaves correctly (i.e., according to its specification) until it (possibly) crashes. By definition, a *correct* process is a process that does not crash. A *faulty* process is a process that is not correct. As previously indicated, f denotes the maximum number of processes that can crash $(1 \leq f < n)$.

Processes communicate and synchronize by sending and receiving messages through channels. Every pair of processes is connected by a channel. Channels are assumed to be reliable: they do not create, alter or lose messages. There is no assumption about the relative speed of processes or message transfer delays.

2.2   Chandra-Toueg's Unreliable Failure Detectors

Failure detectors have been formally defined by Chandra and Toueg who have introduced eight classes of failure detectors [5]. As already indicated in the Introduction, a failure detector class is formally defined by two abstract properties, namely a *Completeness* property and an *Accuracy* property. In this paper, we are interested in the following properties:

- Strong Completeness: Eventually, every process that crashes is permanently suspected by every correct process.
- Perpetual Strong Accuracy: No process is suspected before it crashes.
- Eventual Strong Accuracy: There is a time after which no correct process is suspected.
- Eventual Weak Accuracy: There is a time after which some correct process is never suspected.

Combining the completeness property with every accuracy property provides us with the following three classes of failure detectors [5]:

- $\mathcal{P}$: The class of *Perfect* failure detectors. This class contains all the failure detectors that satisfy strong completeness and perpetual strong accuracy.
- $\Diamond\mathcal{P}$: The class of *Eventually Perfect* failure detectors. This class contains all the failure detectors that satisfy strong completeness and eventual strong accuracy.
- $\Diamond\mathcal{S}$: The class of *Eventually Strong* failure detectors. This class contains all the failure detectors that satisfy strong completeness and eventual weak accuracy.

2.3   Notation

In the following, by a slight abuse of language, we sometimes use $\mathcal{X}$ to denote a failure detector of the class $\mathcal{X}$ ($\mathcal{X}$ standing for $\mathcal{P}$, $\Diamond\mathcal{P}$ or $\Diamond\mathcal{S}$). Moreover, we will also use the following notation: $AS_{n,f}(\mathcal{X})$ denotes an asynchronous distributed system made up of n processes communicating through reliable links, where up to f processes may crash, and equipped with a failure detector of the class $\mathcal{X}$. $AS_{n,f}(\emptyset)$ is used to denote a purely asynchronous system (without additional failure detector). So, in terms of failure detection, $AS_{n,f}(\emptyset)$ is weaker than $AS_{n,f}(\Diamond\mathcal{S})$, which in turn is weaker than $AS_{n,f}(\Diamond\mathcal{P})$, which in turn is weaker than $AS_{n,f}(\mathcal{P})$.

3   Definitions

3.1   One-Shot Agreement Problems

In a one-shot agreement problem, each process p starts with an individual input value v_p. The input values are from a particular value set $\mathcal{V}_{in}$. Moreover, let $\perp$ denote a default value (such that $\perp \notin \mathcal{V}_{in}$), and $\mathcal{V}_{in,\perp}$ denote the set $\mathcal{V}_{in} \cup \{\perp\}$. All the correct processes are required to produce outputs from a value set $\mathcal{V}_{out}$. We say that a process "decides" when it produces an output value.

Let $I = [v_1, \ldots, v_p, \ldots, v_n] \in \mathcal{V}_{in}^n$ be a vector whose pth entry contains the value proposed by process p. Such a vector is called an *input vector* [26]. Let $\mathcal{B}_{fail}$ be a subset of processes, and let $\mathcal{F}(I, \mathcal{B}_{fail})$ be a mapping from $\mathcal{V}_{in}^n$ into a non-empty subset of $\mathcal{V}_{out}$. The mapping $\mathcal{F}(I, \mathcal{B}_{fail})$ associates a set of possible output values with each input vector in runs in which the processes of $\mathcal{B}_{fail}$ fail. For simplicity, we denote $\mathcal{F}(I) = \mathcal{F}(I, \emptyset)$, or in other words, $\mathcal{F}(I)$ is the set of possible decision values from I when there are no failures. The results of this paper, in fact, rely only on properties of $\mathcal{F}(I)$, yet the definition of agreement problems below requires $\mathcal{F}(I, \mathcal{B}_{fail})$ for completeness. Also, we assume that for any $\mathcal{B}_{fail}^1$ and $\mathcal{B}_{fail}^2$, if $\mathcal{B}_{fail}^1 \subset \mathcal{B}_{fail}^2$, then for any vector I, we have $\mathcal{F}(I, \mathcal{B}_{fail}^1) \subseteq \mathcal{F}(I, \mathcal{B}_{fail}^2)$. Essentially, this means that having a certain number of failures cannot prevent a decision value that is allowed with fewer (or no) failures. $\mathcal{F}(I)$ is called the *decision value set* associated with I. If it contains x values, the corresponding input vector I is said to be *x-valent*. For $x = 1$, I is said to be *univalent*.

Definition.   A one-shot agreement problem is characterized by a set $\mathcal{V}_{in}$, a set $\mathcal{V}_{out}$, and a particular mapping $\mathcal{F}(I, \mathcal{B}_{fail})$ with the following properties:

- *Termination.* Each correct process decides.
- *Agreement.* No two processes decide different values[4].
- *Validity.* In runs in which processes in $\mathcal{B}_{fail}$ fail, the value decided on from the input vector I is a value from the set $\mathcal{F}(I, \mathcal{B}_{fail})$. In particular, in failure free runs, the value decided on from the input vector I is a value from the set $\mathcal{F}(I)$.

Examples.   We consider here three examples of well-known one-shot agreement problems. Each is defined by specific values of $\mathcal{V}_{in}$, $\mathcal{V}_{out}$, and a particular function $\mathcal{F}()$.

- Consensus:
  - $\mathcal{V}_{in} = \mathcal{V}_{out} =$ the set of values that can be proposed.
  - $\forall I$ (an input vector): $\forall \mathcal{B}_{fail} : \mathcal{F}(I, \mathcal{B}_{fail}) = \{x \mid x \text{ appears in } I\}$.

---

[4] This footnote property is sometimes called *Uniform Agreement*.

– Interactive Consistency:
- $\mathcal{V}_{in}$ is the set of values that can be proposed, $\mathcal{V}_{out} = \mathcal{V}_{in,\perp}^n$.
- $\forall I, \forall \mathcal{B}_{fail}$: $\mathcal{F}(I, \mathcal{B}_{fail})$ is the set of all vectors J that satisfy the following:
  $\forall k$: if $k \notin \mathcal{B}_{fail}$ then $\forall J$: $J[k] = I[k]$,
  $\forall k$: if $k \in \mathcal{B}_{fail}$ then $J[k] \in \{I[k], \perp\}$.
  In particular, this means that $\forall I$: $\mathcal{F}(I) = I$.
– Non-Blocking Atomic Commit:
- $\mathcal{V}_{in} = \{yes, no\}$, $\mathcal{V}_{out} = \{commit, abort\}$.
- $\mathcal{F}([yes, \dots, yes]) = commit$.
- $\forall \mathcal{B}_{fail} \neq \emptyset$: $\mathcal{F}([yes, \dots, yes], \mathcal{B}_{fail}) = \{commit, abort\}$.
- $\forall \mathcal{B}_{fail}, \forall I$ such that I includes at least one abort : $\mathcal{F}(I, \mathcal{B}_{fail}) = abort$.

Thus, in the Consensus problem, there is no distinction between the allowed set of decision values in runs with and without failures. On the other hand, Non-Blocking Atomic Commit and Interactive Consistency allow a different output when there are failures. Surprisingly, our results rely only on a characterization of $\mathcal{F}(I)$. In other words, as shown in Section 4 below, the set of allowed decision values when there are failures does not affect the solvability of a one-shot agreement problem, regardless of whether the underlying distributed system is augmented with $\Diamond \mathcal{S}$ or $\Diamond \mathcal{P}$.

Remark. Note that not all agreement problems are one-shot. As an example, the membership problem [8] is an agreement problem that is not one-shot: its specification is not limited to a single invocation of a membership primitive, but rather involves the entire execution of the application in which it is used. Such problems are *continuous* agreement problems. Our results address one-shot agreement problems.

3.2   Irreconcilable Input Vectors

Let $\{I_i\}_{1 \le i \le k}$ $(k > 1)$ be a set of k input vectors, $\{V_i\}_{1 \le i \le k}$ the corresponding set of decision value sets, i.e., $V_i = \mathcal{F}(I_i)$ for $1 \le i \le k$.

Definition 1. *Set* $\{I_i\}_{1 \le i \le k}$ *of input vectors is said to be irreconcilable if* $\bigcap_{1 \le i \le k} V_i = \emptyset$.

Intuitively, when a set of input vectors is irreconcilable, then there does not exist an allowed decision value that can be reached from all of them. The other way of looking at this is that if the set of input vectors is not irreconcilable, then there is always one safe value that can be decided on regardless of the exact input vector from which the system started. For example, if no set of allowed input vectors is irreconcilable, then the problem has a trivial solution, which is to always pick the smallest value that can be decided by starting from all allowed input vectors. Moreover, note that when the set of decision values $\mathcal{V}_{out}$ is binary, only sets of univalent input vectors can be irreconcilable. The following claim directly follows from the above definition:

Claim. Let $\{I_i\}$ be a minimal irreconcilable set of input vectors, and let $I_1 \in \{I_i\}$. For any decision value $v_1 \in V_1 = \mathcal{F}(I_1)$, there is a vector I_2 in $\{I_i\}$ such that $v_1 \notin V_2 = \mathcal{F}(I_2)$.

We then say that I_2 *counters* I_1 on v_1.

3.3   Veto Number

The intuition that underlies the veto number notion is simple. It is defined for failure-free runs, and concerns the minimal number of processes such that the decided value can no longer be the same when each of these processes changes its mind on the value it proposes. So, the veto number ℓ of a one-shot agreement problem is the size of the smallest set of processes that, in worst case scenarios, control the decision value.

For example, in the non-blocking atomic commit problem, as soon as a single process votes *no*, the decision is *abort* whatever the votes of the other processes. Hence, $\ell = 1$ for this problem. Similarly, the veto number of the interactive consistency problem is 1: if a single process changes its initial value, the decided vector changes accordingly. Differently, the veto number of the binary Consensus problem is n, since in failure-free runs, the only input vectors that enforce specific decision values are when all processes propose the same input value.

More formally, to have a veto number, a one-shot agreement problem P needs to have at least one irreconcilable set of input vectors. Given S_x a minimal irreconcilable set of input vectors of a problem P, let $\ell(S_x)$ be the number of distinct entries for which at least two vectors of S_x differ[5], i.e., the number of entries k such that there are two vectors I_a and I_b of S_x with $I_a[k] \neq I_b[k]$. As an example let $S_x = \{[a, a, a, a, e, b, b], [a, a, a, a, e, c, c], [a, a, a, f, e, b, c]\}$. We have $\ell_x = 3$.

Definition 2. *Let P be a one-shot agreement problem whose minimal irreconcilable sets of input vectors are $\{S_x\}$, $1 \leq x \leq m$. The veto number of P is the integer $\ell = \min(\ell(S_1), \ldots, \ell(S_m))$.*

When we consider the previous example, this means that there is a set of 3 processes that control the decision value. Therefore, intuitively, we show that no decision can be made without first consulting these processes, or knowing definitely that a failure has occurred.

If a one-shot agreement problem has no irreconcilable set of input vectors, we say that its veto number is $+\infty$ (by definition). We also say that a one-shot agreement problem is an ℓ-veto problem if its veto number is ℓ.

Claim. Let P be a one-shot agreement problem for which there is no irreconcilable set of input vectors (hence, its veto number is $+\infty$). Then P can be solved in $AS_{n,f}(\emptyset)$ with $f < n$.

Proof Since there is no irreconcilable set of input vectors, there is at least one value that appears in the decision sets of all possible input vectors. Therefore, it is always possible to deterministically decide on the smallest such value. $\square_{Claim\ 3.3}$

4   Main Theorem

The main result presented in the paper is the following: there is no one-shot agreement problem that can be solved in $AS_{n,f}(\Diamond\mathcal{P})$ and cannot be solved in $AS_{n,f}(\Diamond\mathcal{S})$. This

---

[5] Let us notice that the Hamming distance is defined on pair of vectors: it measures the number of their entries that differ. Here we consider the whole set of vectors defining S_x.

means that, for any such problem, either $\Diamond\mathcal{S}$ is strong enough to solve the problem or $\Diamond\mathcal{P}$ is too weak to solve it.

The proof of the theorem is composed of three lemmas, that respectively show the following. Let P be a one-shot agreement problem whose veto number is ℓ.

- If $\ell \leq f$ then P cannot be solved in $AS_{n,f}(\Diamond\mathcal{P})$ (Lemma 1).
- If $\ell > f$ and $f < n/2$, then P can be solved in $AS_{n,f}(\Diamond\mathcal{S})$ (Lemma 2).
- If $\ell > f$ and $f \geq n/2$, then P cannot be solved in $AS_{n,f}(\Diamond\mathcal{P})$ (Lemma 3).

Lemma 1. *Let P be an ℓ-veto problem. If $\ell \leq f$, P cannot be solved in $AS_{n,f}(\Diamond\mathcal{P})$.*

Proof Let us assume, by way of contradiction, that there is a protocol $\mathcal{A}$ that solves P in $AS_{n,f}(\Diamond\mathcal{P})$ while $\ell \leq f$. So, $\mathcal{A}$ satisfies the termination, agreement and validity properties stated in Section 3.1.

Since P is an ℓ-veto problem and $\ell \leq f < +\infty$, there is a minimal irreconcilable set of input vectors $\{I_i\}$ and a subset D of $n - \ell$ processes such that the entries of all processes of D in all vectors of $\{I_i\}$ are the same.

Observe that, as $\mathcal{A}$ solves P in $AS_{n,f}(\Diamond\mathcal{P})$, it solves it with any failure detector in $\Diamond\mathcal{P}$. In particular, we can introduce a family of failure detectors $FD(t, D)$ such that in every run, $FD(t, D)$ always suspects all processes outside D (and only those processes) for the first t time units and afterwards behaves as a perfect failure detector (that detects crashes immediately as they occur).

Consider now a run σ of $\mathcal{A}$, equipped with a failure detector $FD(0, D)$, that starts with some vector $I_1 \in \{I_i\}$ and in which the ℓ processes outside D fail immediately and before sending any message (recall that $\ell \leq f$). Due to the termination and agreement properties of $\mathcal{A}$, the correct processes decide in σ, and they decide the same value v. Let p be the first such process and let t_1 be the time at which p decides.

By replacing the failure detector in σ with $FD(t_1, D)$, we can obtain a possible run σ_1 of $\mathcal{A}$ that, as far as p can tell, is indistinguishable from σ until time t_1. In fact, due to the asynchronous nature of the system, it is possible that during σ_1, no process fails, yet all the messages sent by any process outside D take more than t_1 time units to arrive, and all other events are timed as in σ. Thus, p must decide on v as well at time t_1 in σ_1. It then follows from the validity property of $\mathcal{A}$ that $v \in V_1$.

Recall that the set $\{I_i\}$ is assumed to be irreconcilable. Due to Claim 3.2, the assumption $f \leq \ell$ and the definition of D, there has to be at least one vector in $I_2 \in \{I_i\}$ with a corresponding value set V_2 such that all processes in D have the same entry in both I_1 and I_2, yet $v \notin V_2$. Also, let us notice that p does not receive any message from any process outside D until it decides in σ_1, and all processes in σ_1 continuously suspect all processes outside D until time t_1. Thus, by replacing the input vector of σ_1 with I_2, we obtain a possible run σ_2 of $\mathcal{A}$ that, as far as p can tell, is indistinguishable from σ_1 until time t_1. Thus, p also decides on the value v_1 at time t_1 in σ_2. It then follows from the validity property of $\mathcal{A}$ that $v \in V_2$. A contradiction to the assumption stating that $v \notin V_2$. $\square_{Lemma\ 1}$

Lemma 2. *Let P be an ℓ-veto problem. If $\ell > f$ and $f < n/2$, then P can be solved in $AS_{n,f}(\Diamond\mathcal{S})$.*

Proof The proof of this lemma is by reduction to the Consensus problem. More specifically, let us consider the following three step reduction protocol executed by each process p:

1. p sends its initial value to all processes, and waits until it receives values from $(n - f)$ processes (including itself).
2. Let I_p^f be the vector such that $I_p^f[q]$ includes the value p received from q if one was received, or $\perp$ otherwise. Let $\{I_p\}$ be the set of input vectors obtained by replacing each $\perp$ value in I_p^f with a value from $\mathcal{V}_{in}$. Let $\{V_p\}$ be the set of value sets $\mathcal{F}(I)$ for each $I \in \{I_p\}$.

   Each process p selects one value v_p that appears in the intersection of all value sets in $\{V_p\}$ (we show below that such a value always exists, when we discuss validity).
3. Then, the processes run a Consensus protocol in $AS_{n,f}(\Diamond \mathcal{S})$. Let us notice that, as $f < n/2$, such protocols do exist (e.g., [5]). Each process p uses v_p as its Consensus input value, and decides on the value decided by the Consensus protocol.

We claim that this three step reduction protocol solves $\mathcal{P}$ in $AS_{n,f}(\Diamond \mathcal{S})$ with $f < n/2$. Specifically, we need to show that the protocol ensures the termination, validity, and agreement properties stated in Section 3.1.

- Termination. As at most f processes fail, no correct process can block forever in step 1 or 2. Moreover, due to the termination of the underlying Consensus protocol, no correct process can block forever in step 3 of the reduction.
- Agreement. This property follows directly from the Consensus agreement, namely, no two processes that terminate the Consensus protocol decide differently.
- Validity. For all p, let us notice that, by definition, one of the input vectors in $\{I_p\}$ is the actual input vector. Since p waits for $(n - f)$ values in step 1, the Hamming distance between each pair of input vectors in $\{I_p\}$ is at most f. It follows from the definition of ℓ and the assumption $f < \ell$, that there is at least one value in the intersection of the sets in $\{V_p\}$ (otherwise, it will contradict the fact that ℓ is the veto number of the problem). Thus, the value that is proposed to Consensus, and therefore the value that is decided on, is a value that is allowed by the actual input vector I, i.e., a value of $\mathcal{F}(I)$.

$\square_{Lemma\ 2}$

Lemma 3. *Let P be an ℓ-veto problem. If $\ell > f$ and $f \geq n/2$, then either P can be solved in $AS_{n,f}(\emptyset)$, or P cannot be solved in $AS_{n,f}(\Diamond \mathcal{P})$.*

Proof Let P be a one-shot agreement problem that cannot be solved in $AS_{n,f}(\emptyset)$. The proof is a generalization of the proof showing that the Consensus problem cannot be solved in $AS_{n,f}(\Diamond \mathcal{P})$ when $f > n/2$ (Theorem 6.3.1, pages 247-248 in [5]).

Assume, by contradiction, that P can be solved in $AS_{n,f}(\Diamond \mathcal{P})$ when $f > n/2$, using some protocol $\mathcal{A}$. Hence, it can be solved in $AS_{n,f}(\Diamond \mathcal{P})$ with any failure detector from $\Diamond \mathcal{P}$. Next, we define a family of failure detectors $FD(t, C_1, C_2)$ accepting as parameters a time t and two subsets of processes C_1 and C_2, which has the following behavior (Π denotes the set of all processes):

- Until time t:
  - for each process in C_1, $FD(t, C_1, C_2)$ continuously suspects all processes in $\Pi \setminus C_1$;
  - for each process in C_2, $FD(t, C_1, C_2)$ continuously suspects all processes in $\Pi \setminus C_2$.
- After time t: $FD(t, C_1, C_2)$ behaves like a perfect failure detector (that detects failures immediately as they occur).

Let $\{I_i\}$ be an irreconcilable set of input vectors of P. Since P cannot be solved in $AS_{n,f}(\emptyset)$ and by the contrapositive of Claim 3.3, such a set does exist. Moreover, let I_1 be one of its vectors.

Consider now a run σ_1 of $\mathcal{A}$ with $FD(0, \emptyset, \emptyset)$ that starts in I_1 and in which f processes fail immediately and before sending any message. Due to the termination property satisfied by $\mathcal{A}$ (assumption), all correct processes must eventually decide. Let p_1 be the first correct process that decides, v_1 the value it decides, and t_1 the time of this decision. Moreover, denote the set of correct processes in σ_1 by D_1, and all other processes by D_2 (so, $D_1 \cap D_2 = \emptyset$, $D_1 \cup D_2 = \Pi$ -the set of all processes-, $|D_1| = n - f \leq f$ and $|D_2| = f$).

Due to the asynchrony of the system, we can construct a fail-free run σ_1' of $\mathcal{A}$ with $FD(t_1, D_1, D_2)$, in which all messages of processes of D_2 are delayed until after time t_1. Thus, as far as p_1 is concerned, the runs σ_1 and σ_1' are indistinguishable, so p_1 decides the same value v_1 at time t_1 in both σ_1 and σ_1'. Moreover, as σ_1' is fail-free and $\mathcal{A}$ is correct, its validity property implies that $v_1 \in V_1$.

Since $\{I_i\}$ is an irreconcilable set of input vectors, due to claim 3.2, there is also an input vector $I_2 \in \{I_i\}$ such that I_2 counters I_1 on v_1 (i.e., $v_1 \notin V_2 = \mathcal{F}(I_2)$). Using symmetric arguments, we can construct a fail-free run σ_2' that starts with I_2, in which some process p_2 in D_2 decides a value $v_2 \in V_2$ at time t_2. (The failure detector used in σ_2' is $FD(t_2, D_1, D_2)$ and all messages from processes of D_1 are delayed until after time t_2.)

Let I_3 be a vector that has (1) the same entries as I_1 for processes in D_1, and (2) the same entries as I_2 for processes in D_2. Moreover, let $t' = \max(t1, t2)$. By using a failure detector $FD(t', D_1, D_2)$, we construct a fail-free run σ' of $\mathcal{A}$ that starts in I_3 and in which messages from D_1 to D_2 and messages from D_2 to D_1 are delayed until after time t'. Moreover, the messages among the processes in D_1 are timed as in σ_1', and the messages among the processes in D_2 are timed as in σ_2'. Clearly, p_1 cannot distinguish between σ_1' and σ' until time t_1 and p_2 cannot distinguish between σ_2' and σ' until time t_2. Thus, p_1 decides v_1 in σ' and p_2 decides v_2 in σ'. However, as I_2 counters I_1 on v_1, we have $v_1 \notin V_2$, from which we conclude $v_1 \neq v2$. A contradiction of the agreement property of $\mathcal{A}$.

It follows that, when $l > f \geq n/2$, any one-shot agreement problem not solvable in $AS_{n,f}(\emptyset)$ is not solvable in $AS_{n,f}(\Diamond \mathcal{P})$ either. $\square_{Lemma\ 3}$

Theorem 1. $\forall f$, *there is no one-shot agreement problem that can be solved in* $AS_{n,f}(\Diamond \mathcal{P})$ *and cannot be solved in* $AS_{n,f}(\Diamond \mathcal{S})$.

The proof of the theorem follows from Lemma 1, Lemma 2 and Lemma 3. Observe also that Lemma 2 provides us with another insight on the fact that Consensus is a central problem when we consider one-shot agreement problems in asynchronous distributed systems equipped with failure detectors. Finally, the following corollary is an immediate consequence of Theorem 1.

Corollary 1. $\Diamond\mathcal{P}$ *cannot be the weakest class of failure detectors that enables solving any one-shot agreement problems in asynchronous distributed systems prone to process crash failures.*

5   Additional Remarks

As already indicated, $\Diamond\mathcal{S}$ is the weakest failure detector to solve Consensus when $f < n/2$ [4]. An interesting related question is then the following: *"Are there problems that are more "restricted" than Consensus and can still be solved in $AS_{n,f}(\Diamond\mathcal{S})$ when $f < n/2$?"* Given two one-shot agreement problems (that cannot be solved without failure detectors), $P1$ and $P2$ with veto numbers $\ell 1$ and $\ell 2$, respectively, we say *"P1 is more restricted than P2"* if $\ell 1 < \ell 2$. As an example, Interactive Consistency ($\ell = 1$) is more restricted than Consensus ($\ell = n$). Intuitively, a problem $P1$ is more restricted than a problem $P2$ if its decision is controlled by fewer processes than the decision of $P2$, i.e., $P1$ is more sensitive to failures than $P2$. From this definition and Theorem 1 we get that it is possible to have problems more restricted than Consensus and can still be solved in $AS_{n,f}(\Diamond\mathcal{S})$.

When we consider asynchronous distributed systems with a majority of correct processes, and timeless failure detectors (the ones that do not provide information on the occurrence time of failures [20]), as already noticed, $\Diamond\mathcal{S}$ is the weakest class of failure detectors to solve Consensus ($\ell = n$) [4], while $?\mathcal{P} + \Diamond\mathcal{S}$ is the weakest to solve non-blocking atomic commit ($\ell = 1$) [20]. We trivially have $?\mathcal{P} + \Diamond\mathcal{S} \subset \Diamond\mathcal{S}$. Moreover, $\mathcal{P} \subset \Diamond\mathcal{P} \subset \Diamond\mathcal{S}$.

Additionally, Corollary 1 states that $\Diamond\mathcal{P}$ is not strong enough to enable solving non-blocking atomic commit. So, when considering one-shot agreement problems that cannot be solved in purely asynchronous systems, we get from this corollary and [20] that $?\mathcal{P} + \Diamond\mathcal{S}$ is "stronger" than $\Diamond\mathcal{P}$ for solving such problems in asynchronous distributed systems with a majority of correct processes. It is important to notice that this does not mean that we can construct a failure detector of the class $\Diamond\mathcal{P}$ from a failure detector of the class $?\mathcal{P} + \Diamond\mathcal{S}$ (notice that such a transformation is not a one-shot problem). Similarly, recall that $\Diamond\mathcal{S}$ cannot simulate $\Diamond\mathcal{P}$, even though we showed in this paper that for one-shot agreement problems, their power is the same. (A similar observation can be done when we consider the class of failure detectors, denoted $P^f \times \Diamond\mathcal{S}$, introduced in [10]. Such a class -that is stronger than $\Diamond\mathcal{S}$-[6]enables solving the Consensus problem for any value of f, i.e., $f < n$.)

As already mentioned, the veto number notion (ℓ) relies only on the set of input vectors in failure-free runs. This means that the inability to solve problems such as Non-Blocking Atomic Commit and Interactive Consistency in $AS_{n,f}(\Diamond\mathcal{P})$ has nothing to do with the decision values in runs with failures. However, in our characterization,

---

[6] P^f is the weakest class of realistic failure detectors that enables solving the *Register* problem in presence of up to f process crashes [10].

both problems have a veto number $\ell = 1$. As indicated above, Non-Blocking Atomic Commit can be solved with the class $?\mathcal{P} + \diamond\mathcal{S}$ while Interactive Consistency requires the stronger class $\mathcal{P}$. This suggests an interesting open problem, namely, defining a characterization of the allowed decision values in failure-prone runs that will explain this difference. In particular, one can notice that, in the Non-Blocking Atomic Commit problem, the allowed decision values in runs prone to failures do not depend on which process has failed. This can be thought of as "failure anonymity". Yet, in Interactive Consistency, the set of allowed decision values depends on the exact identity of the processes that failed.

References

1. Aguilera M.K., Chen W. and Toueg S., On Quiescent Reliable Communication. *SIAM Journal of Computing*, 29(6):2040-2073, 2000.
2. Aguilera M.K., Delporte-Gallet C., Fauconnier H. and Toueg S., On Implementing Ω with Weak Reliability and Synchrony Assumptions. *Proc. 22h ACM Symposium on Principles of Distributed Computing (PODC'03)*, ACM Press, Boston (MA), July 2003.
3. Anceaume E., Fernandez A., Mostefaoui A., Neiger G. and Raynal M., A Necessary and Sufficient Condition for Transforming Limited Accuracy Failure Detectors. *Journal of Computer and Systems Science*, 68:123-133, 2004.
4. Chandra T.D., Hadzilacos V. and Toueg S., The Weakest Failure Detector for Solving Consensus. *Journal of the ACM*, 43(4):685-722, 1996.
5. Chandra T.D. and Toueg S., Unreliable Failure Detectors for Reliable Distributed Systems. *Journal of the ACM*, 43(2):225-267, 1996.
6. Charron-Bost B. and Le Fessant F., Validity conditions in agreement problems, and time complexity. *SOFSEM 2004*, LNCS 2932, pp. 187-207, 2004.
7. Chen W., Toueg S. and Aguilera M.K., On the Quality of Service of Failure Detectors. *IEEE Transactions on Computers*, 51(5):561-580, 2002.
8. Chockler G., Keidar I. and Vitenberg R., Group Communication Specifications: a Comprehensive Study. *ACM Computing Surveys*, 33(4):427-469, 2001.
9. Delporte-Gallet C., Fauconnier H. and Guerraoui R., A Realistic Look at Failure Detectors. *Proc. IEEE Inter. Conference on Dependable Systems and Networks (DSN'02)*, IEEE Computer Society Press, pp. 345-352, Washington D.C., 2002.
10. Delporte-Gallet C., Fauconnier H. and Guerraoui R., Failure Detection Lower Bounds on Registers and Consensus. *Proc. Symposium on Distributed Computing (DISC'02)*, Springer-Verlag LNCS #2508, pp. 237-251, 2002.
11. Dolev D., Dwork C. and Stockmeyer L., On the Minimal Synchronism Needed for Distributed Consensus. *Journal of the ACM*, 34(1):77-97, 1987.
12. Dolev S. and Rajsbaum S., Stability of Long-Lived Consensus. *Proc. 19th ACM Symposium on Principles of Distributed Computing (PODC'03)*, ACM Press, pp. 309-318, Portland (OR), July 2000.
13. Doudou A. and Schiper A., Muteness Detectors for Consensus with Byzantine Processes. *Brief Annoucement, Proc. 17th ACM Symposium on Principles of Distributed Computing (PODC'98)*, ACM Press pp. 315, Puerto Vallarta (Mexico), 1998.
14. Dwork C., Lynch N. and Stockmeyer L., Consensus in the Presence of Partial Synchrony. *Journal of the ACM*, 35(2):288-323, 1988.
15. Fetzer Ch., Raynal M. and Tronel F., An Adaptive Failure Detection Protocol. *Proc. 8th IEEE Pacific Rim Int. Symposium on Dependable Computing (PRDC'01)*, pp. 146-153, 2001.

16. Fischer M.J., Lynch N. and Paterson M.S., Impossibility of Distributed Consensus with One Faulty Process. *Journal of the ACM*, 32(2):374-382, 1985.

17. Friedman R., Mostefaoui A. and Raynal M., On the Respective Power of $\Diamond P$ and $\Diamond S$ to Solve One-Shot Agreement Problems. *Tech Report #1547*, 20 pages, IRISA, Université de Rennes 1, (France), 2003. http://www.irisa.fr/bibli/publi/pi/2003/1547/1547.html.

18. Friedman R., Mostefaoui A. and Raynal M., The Notion of Veto Number for Distributed Agreement Problems. Invited Paper. *6th International Workshop on Distributed Computing (IWDC'04)*, Springer Verlag LNCS, Kolkata (India), December 2004.

19. Guerraoui R., Non-Blocking Atomic Commit in Asynchronous Distributed Systems with Failure Detectors. *Distributed Computing*, 15:17-25, 2002.

20. Guerraoui R. and Kouznetsov P., On the Weakest Failure Detector for Non-Blocking Atomic Commit. *Proc. 2nd Int. IFIP Conference on Theoretical Computer Science (TCS'02)*, pp. 461-473, Montréal (Canada), August 2002.

21. Hélary J.-M., Hurfin M., Mostefaoui A., Raynal M. and Tronel F., Computing Global Functions in Asynchronous Distributed Systems with Process Crashes. *IEEE Transactions on Parallel and Distributed Systems*, 11(9):897-909, 2000.

22. Larrea M., Arèvalo S. and Fernández A., Efficient Algorithms to Implement Unreliable Failure Detectors in Partially Synchronous Systems. *13th Symposium on Distributed Computing (DISC'99)*, Springer Verlag LNCS #1693, pp. 34-48, 1999.

23. Larrea M., Fernández A. and Arèvalo S., Optimal Implementation of the Weakest Failure Detector for Solving Consensus. *Proc. 19th Symposium on Reliable Distributed Systems (SRDS'00)*, pp. 52-60, 2000.

24. Moran S., and Wolfstahl Y., Extended Impossibility Results for Asynchronous Complete Networks. *Information Processing Letters*, 26:145-151, 1987.

25. Mostefaoui A., Mourgaya E. and Raynal M., Asynchronous Implementation of Failure Detectors. *Proc. Int. IEEE Conference on Dependable Systems and Networks (DSN'03)*, pp. 351-360, June 2003.

26. Mostefaoui A., Rajsbaum S. and Raynal M., Conditions on Input Vectors for Consensus Solvability in Asynchronous Distributed Systems. *Journal of the ACM*, 50(6):922-954, 2003.

27. Pease L., Shostak R. and Lamport L., Reaching Agreement in Presence of Faults. *Journal of the ACM*, 27(2):228-234, 1980.

28. Raynal M. and Tronel F., Restricted Failure Detectors: Definition and Reduction Protocols. *Information Processing Letters*, 72:91-97, 1999.

The Black-White Bakery Algorithm
and Related Bounded-Space, Adaptive,
Local-Spinning and FIFO Algorithms

Gadi Taubenfeld

The Interdisciplinary Center, P.O.Box 167
Herzliya 46150, Israel
tgadi@idc.ac.il

Abstract. A mutual exclusion algorithm is presented that has four
desired properties: (1) it satisfies FIFO fairness, (2) it satisfies local-
spinning, (3) it is adaptive, and (4) it uses finite number of bounded size
atomic registers. No previously published algorithm satisfies all these
properties. In fact, it is the first algorithm (using only atomic registers)
which satisfies both FIFO and local-spinning, and it is the first bounded
space algorithm which satisfies both FIFO and adaptivity.
All the algorithms presented are based on Lamport's famous Bakery
algorithm [27], which satisfies FIFO, but uses unbounded size registers
(and does not satisfy local-spinning and is not adaptive). Using only one
additional shared bit, we bound the amount of space required by the
Bakery algorithm by *coloring* the tickets taken in the Bakery algorithm.
The resulting Black-White Bakery algorithm preserves the simplicity and
elegance of the original algorithm, satisfies FIFO and uses finite number
of bounded size registers. Then, in a sequence of steps (which preserve
simplicity and elegance) we modify the new algorithm so that it is also
adaptive to point contention and satisfies local-spinning.

1 Introduction

Motivation and Results

Several interesting mutual exclusion algorithms have been published in recent
years that are either adaptive to contention or satisfy the local-spinning property
[3, 4, 6, 7, 9, 10, 14, 21, 24, 34, 37, 41, 44]. (These two important properties are defined in the sequel.) However, each one of these algorithms either does not satisfy
FIFO, uses unbounded size registers, or uses synchronization primitives which
are stronger than atomic registers. We presents an algorithm that satisfies all
these four desired properties: (1) it satisfies FIFO fairness, (2) it is adaptive, (3)
it satisfies local-spinning, and (4) it uses finite number of bounded size atomic
registers. The algorithm is based on Lamport's famous Bakery algorithm [27].

The Bakery algorithm is based on the policy that is sometimes used in a
bakery. Upon entering the bakery a customer gets a number which is greater
than the numbers of other customers that are waiting for service. The holder

R. Guerraoui (Ed.): DISC 2004, LNCS 3274, pp. 56–70, 2004.
© Springer-Verlag Berlin Heidelberg 2004

of the lowest number is the next to be served. The numbers can grow without bound and hence its implementation uses unbounded size registers.

Using only one additional shared bit, we bound the amount of space required in the Bakery algorithm, by *coloring* the tickets taken in the original Bakery algorithm with the colors black and white. The new algorithm, which preserves the simplicity and elegance of the original algorithm, has the following two desired properties, (1) it satisfies FIFO: processes are served in the order they arrive, and (2) it uses finite number of bounded size registers: the numbers taken by waiting processes can grow only up to n, where n is the number of processes.

Then, in a sequence of steps which preserve simplicity and elegance, we modify the new algorithm so that it satisfies two additional important properties. Namely, it satisfies *local-spinning* and is *adaptive* to point contention. The resulting algorithm, which satisfies all theses four properties, is the first algorithm (using only atomic registers) which satisfies both FIFO and local-spinning, and it is the first bounded space algorithm which satisfies both FIFO and adaptivity.

Mutual Exclusion

The mutual exclusion problem is to design an algorithm that guarantees mutually exclusive access to a critical section among a number of competing processes [Dij65]. It is assumed that each process is executing a sequence of instructions in an infinite loop. The instructions are divided into four continuous sections: the remainder, entry, critical and exit. The problem is to write the code for the entry and the exit sections in such a way that the following two basic requirements are satisfied (assumed a process always leaves its critical section),

Mutual exclusion: *No two processes are in their critical sections at the same time.*

Deadlock-freedom: *If a process is trying to enter its critical section, then some process, not necessarily the same one, eventually enters its critical section.*

A stronger liveness requirement than deadlock-freedom is,

Starvation-freedom: *If a process is trying to enter its critical section, then this process must eventually enter its critical section.*

Finally, the strongest fairness requirement is FIFO. In order to formally define it, we assume that the entry section consists of two parts. The first part, which is called the *doorway*, is *wait-free*: its execution requires only bounded number of atomic steps and hence always terminates; the second part is a *waiting* statement: a loop that includes one or more statements. A *waiting process* is a process that has finished the doorway code and reached the waiting part in its entry section.

First-in-first-out (FIFO): *No beginning process can pass an already waiting process. That is, a process that has already passed through its doorway will enter its critical section before any process that has just started.*

Notice that FIFO does not imply deadlock-freedom. (It also does not exactly guarantee bounded bypass, [32] pages 277 and 296.) Throughout the paper, it is assumed that there may be up to n processes potentially contending to enter their critical sections. Each of the n processes has a unique identifier which is a positive integer taken from the set $\{1, ..., n\}$, and the only atomic operations on the shared registers are reads and writes.

Local-Spinning

All the mutual exclusion algorithms which use atomic registers (and many algorithms which use stronger primitives) include busy-waiting loops. The idea is that in order to wait, a process *spins* on a flag register, until some other process terminates the spin with a single write operation. Unfortunately, under contention, such spinning may generate lots of traffic on the interconnection network between the process and the memory. Hence, by consuming communication bandwidth spin-waiting by some process can slow other processes.

To address this problem, it makes sense to distinguish between *remote* access and *local* access to shared memory. In particular, this is the case in *distributed shared memory* systems where the shared memory is physically distributed among the processes. I.e., instead of having the "shared memory" in one central location, each process "owns" part of the shared memory and keeps it in its own local memory. For algorithms designed for such systems, it is important to minimize the number of *remote access*. That is, the number of times a process has to reference a shared memory location that does not physically resides on its local memory. In particular, we would like to avoid remote accesses in busy-waiting loops.

Local-spinning: *Local Spinning is the situation where a process is spinning on locally-accessible registers. An algorithm satisfies local-spinning if it is possible to physically distribute the shared memory among the processes in such a way that the only type of spinning required is local-spinning.*

The advantage of local-spinning is that it does not require remote accesses. In the above definition, it does not make any difference if the processes have coherent caches. In cache-coherent machines, a reference to a remote register r causes communication if the current value of r is not in the cache. Since we are interested in proving upper bounds, such a definition would only make our results stronger. (Coherent caching is discussed in Section 4.)

Adaptive Algorithms

To speed the entry to the critical section, it is important to design algorithms in which the time complexity is a function of the actual number of contending processes rather than a function of the total number of processes. That is, the time complexity is independent of the total number of processes and is governed only by the current degree of contention.

Adaptive algorithm: *An algorithm is adaptive with respect to time complexity measure ψ, if its time complexity ψ is a function of the actual number of contending processes.*

Our time complexity measures involve counting remote memory accesses. In Section 4, we formally define time complexity w.r.t. two models: one that assumes cache-coherent machines, and another that does not. Our algorithms are also adaptive w.r.t. other common complexity measures, such as *system response time* in which the longest time interval where some process is in its entry section while no process is in its critical section is considered, assuming there is an upper bound of one time unit for step time in the entry or exit sections and no lower bound [38]. In the literature, adaptive, local-spinning algorithms are also called scalable algorithms.

Two notions of contention can be considered: *interval contention* and *point contention*. The interval contention over time interval T is the number of processes that are active in T. The point contention over time interval T is the maximum number of processes that are active at the *same time* in T. Our adaptive algorithms are adaptive w.r.t. both point and interval contention.

Related Work

Dijksta's seminal paper [15] contains the first statement and solution of the mutual exclusion problem. Since than it has been extensively studied and numerous algorithms have been published. Lamport's Bakery algorithm is one of the best known mutual exclusion algorithms [27]. Its main appeal lies in the fact that it solves a difficult problem in such a simple and elegant way. All the new algorithms presented in this paper are based on Lamport's Bakery algorithm. For comprehensive surveys of many algorithms for mutual exclusion see [8, 39].

The Bakery algorithm satisfies FIFO, but uses unbounded size registers. Few attempts have been made to bound the space required by the Bakery algorithm. In [43], the integer arithmetic in the original Bakery algorithm is replaced with modulo arithmetic and the *maximum* function and the *less than* relation have been redefined. The resulting published algorithm is incorrect, since it does not satisfy deadlock-freedom. Also in [25], modulo arithmetic is used and the *maximum* function and the *less than* relation have been redefined. In addition, an additional integer register is used. Redefining and explaining these two notions in [25] requires over a full page and involve the details of another unbounded space algorithm. The Black-White Bakery algorithms use integer arithmetic, and do not require to redefine any of the notions used in the original algorithm.

Another attempt to bound the space required by the Bakery algorithm is described in [40]. The algorithm presented is incorrect when the number of processes n is too big; the registers size is bigger than 2^{15} values; and the algorithm is complicated. In [1], a variant of the Bakery algorithm is presents, which uses $3^n + 1$ values per register (our algorithm requires only $2n + 2$ values per register). Unlike the Bakery algorithm (and ours), the algorithm in [1] is not symmetric: process p_i only reads the values of the lower processes. It is possible to replace the unbounded timestamps of the Bakery algorithm (i.e., taking a number) with bounded timestamps, as defined in [22] and constructed in [16, 17, 20], however the resulting algorithm will be rather complex, when the price of implementing bounded timestamps is taken into account.

Several FIFO algorithms which are not based on the Bakery algorithm and use bounded size atomic registers have been published. These algorithms are more complex than the Black-White Bakery algorithm, and non of them is adaptive or satisfies local-spinning. We mention five interesting algorithms below. In [26], an algorithm that requires n (3-valued) shared registers plus two shared bits per process is presented. A modification of the algorithm in [26], is presented in [29] which uses n bits per process. In [30, 31], an algorithm that requires five shared bits per process is presented, which is based on the One-bit algorithm that was devised independently in [12, 13] and [29]. In [42], an algorithm that requires four shared bits per process is presented, which is based on a scheme similar to that of [33]. Finally, in [2] a first-in-first-enabled solution to the ℓ-exclusion problem is presented using bounded timestamps. We are not aware of a way to modify these algorithms, so that they satisfy adaptivity and local-spinning.

In addition to [27], the design of the Black-White Bakery algorithm was inspired by two other papers [18, 19]. In [18], an ℓ-exclusion algorithm for the FIFO allocation of ℓ identical resources is presented, which uses a single read-modify-write object. The algorithm uses colored tickets where the number of different colors used is only $\ell+1$, and hence only *two* colors are needed for mutual exclusion. In [19], a starvation-free solution to the mutual exclusion problem that uses *two* weak semaphores (and two shared bits) is presented.

Three important papers which have investigated local-spinning are [9, 21, 34]. The various algorithms presented in these papers use strong synchronization primitives (i.e., stronger than atomic registers), and require only a constant number of remote accesses for each access to a critical section. Performance studies done in these papers have shown that local-spinning algorithms scale well as contention increases. More recent local-spinning algorithms using objects which are stronger than atomic registers are presented in [24, 41], these algorithms have unbounded space complexity. Local-spinning algorithms using only atomic registers are presented in [4–6, 44], and a local-spinning algorithm using only non-atomic registers is presented in [7], these algorithms do not satisfy FIFO.

The question whether there exists an adaptive mutual exclusion algorithm using atomic registers was first raised in [36]. In [35], it is shown that is no such algorithm when time is measured by counting all accesses to shared registers. In [10, 14, 37] adaptive algorithms using atomic registers, which do not satisfy local-spinning, are presented. In [4, 6], local-spinning and adaptive algorithms are presented. None of these adaptive algorithms satisfy FIFO. In [3], an interesting technique for collecting information is introduced, which enables to transform the Bakery algorithm [27] into its corresponding adaptive version. The resulting FIFO algorithm is adaptive, uses unbounded size registers and does not satisfy local-spinning. We use this technique to make our algorithms adaptive.

The time complexity of few known adaptive and/or local-spinning non-FIFO algorithms, and in particular the time complexity of [6], is better than the time complexity of our adaptive algorithms. This seems to be the prices to be paid for satisfying the FIFO property. We discuss this issue in details in Section 5.

2   Lamport's Bakery Algorithm

We first review Lamport's Bakery algorithm [27]. The algorithm uses a boolean array $choosing[1..n]$, and an integer array $number[1..n]$ of *unbounded* size registers. The entries $choosing_i$ and $number_i$ can be read by all the processes but can be written only by process i. The relation "$<$" used in the algorithm on ordered pairs of integers is the *lexicographic order* relation and is defined by $[a, b] < [c, d]$ if $a < c$, or if $a = c$ and $b < d$. The statement **await** *condition* is used as an abbreviation for **while** $\neg condition$ **do** *skip*. The algorithm is given below.

Algorithm 1. THE BAKERY ALGORITHM: process i's code

Shared variables:
    $choosing[1..n]$: boolean array
    $number[1..n]$: array of type $\{0, ..., \infty\}$
    Initially $\forall i : 1 \leq i \leq n : choosing_i = \texttt{false}$ and $number_i = 0$

```
1   choosing_i := true                          /* beginning of doorway */
2   number_i := 1 + maximum({number_j | 1 ≤ j ≤ n})
3   choosing_i := false                          /* end of doorway */
4   for j = 1 to n do
5       await choosing_j = false
6       await (number_j = 0) ∨ ([number_j, j] ≥ [number_i, i])
7   od
8   critical section
9   number_i := 0                                /* exit code */
```

As Lamport has pointed out, the correctness of the Bakery algorithm depends on how the maximum is computed [28]. We assume a simple correct implementation in which a process first reads into local memory all the n *number* registers, one at a time, and then computes the maximum over these n values.

3   The Black-White Bakery Algorithm

Using only one additional shared bit, called *color* of type $\{\texttt{black}, \texttt{white}\}$, we bound the amount of space required in the Bakery algorithm, by *coloring* the tickets taken with the colors black and white. In the new algorithm, the numbers of the tickets used can grow only up to n, where n is the number of processes.

The first thing that process i does in its entry section is to take a colored ticket $ticket_i = (mycolor_i, number_i)$, as follows: i first reads the shared bit *color*, and sets its ticket's color to the value read. Then, it takes a number which is greater than the numbers of the tickets which have the same color as the color of its own ticket. Once i has a ticket, it waits until its colored ticket is the *lowest* and then it enters its critical section. The order between colored tickets is defined as follows: If two tickets have different colors, the ticket whose color is *different* from the value of the shared bit *color* is smaller. If two tickets have the same color, the ticket with the smaller number is smaller. If tickets of two processes have the same color and the same number then the process with the smaller identifier enters its critical section first. Next, we explain when the shared *color* bit is written. The first thing that a process i does when it leaves its critical section (i.e., its first step in the exit section) is to set the *color* bit to a value which is different from the color of its ticket. This way, i gives priority to waiting processes that hold tickets with the same color as the color of i's ticket.

Until the value of the *color* bit is first changed, all the tickets have the same color, say white. The first process to enter its critical section flips the value of the *color* bit (i.e., changes it to black), and hence the color of all the new tickets taken thereafter (until the color bit is modified again) is black. Next, *all* the processes which hold white colored tickets enter and then exit their critical sections one at a time until there are no processes holding white tickets in the system. Only then the process with the lowest black ticket is allowed to enter its critical section, and when it exits it changes to white the value of the *color* bit, which gives priority to the processes with black tickets, and so on.

Three data structures are used: (1) a single shared bit named *color*, (2) a boolean array *choosing*[1..n], and (3) an array with n entries where each entry is a colored ticket which ranges over $\{\texttt{black}, \texttt{white}\} \times \{0, ..., n\}$. We use $mycolor_i$ and $number_i$ to designate the first and second components, respectively, of the ordered pair stored in the ith entry.

Algorithm 2. THE BLACK-WHITE BAKERY ALGORITHM: process i's code

Shared variables:
    color: a bit of type $\{\texttt{black}, \texttt{white}\}$
    choosing[1..n]: boolean array
    $(mycolor, number)$[1..n]: array of type $\{\texttt{black}, \texttt{white}\} \times \{0, ..., n\}$
    Initially $\forall i : 1 \leq i \leq n : choosing_i = \texttt{false}$ and $number_i = 0$,
    the initial values of all the other variables are immaterial.

```
1   choosing_i := true                      /* beginning of doorway */
2   mycolor_i := color
3   number_i := 1 + max({number_j | (1 ≤ j ≤ n) ∧ (mycolor_j = mycolor_i)})
4   choosing_i := false                      /* end of doorway */
5   for j = 1 to n do
6       await choosing_j = false
7       if mycolor_j = mycolor_i
8       then await (number_j = 0) ∨ ([number_j, j] ≥ [number_i, i]) ∨
                  (mycolor_j ≠ mycolor_i)
9       else await (number_j = 0) ∨ (mycolor_i ≠ color) ∨
                  (mycolor_j = mycolor_i) fi
10  od
11  critical section
12  if mycolor_i = black then color := white else color := black fi
13  number_i := 0
```

In line 1, process i indicates that it is contending for the critical section by setting its *choosing* bit to true. Then it takes a colored ticket by first "taking" a color (step 2) and then taking a number which is greater by one than the numbers of the tickets with the same color as its own (step 3). For computing the maximum, we assume a simple implementation in which a process first reads into local memory all the n tickets, one at a time atomically, and then computes the maximum over numbers of the tickets with the same color as its own.

After passing the doorway, process i waits in the *for loop* (lines 5–10), until it has the lowest colored ticket and then it enters its critical section. We notice that each one of the three terms in each of the two await statements is evaluated separately. In case processes i and j have tickets of the same color (line 8), i waits until it notices that either (1) j is not competing any more, (2) i has a smaller number, or (3) j has reentered its entry section. (If two processes have the same number then the process with the smaller identifier enters first.) In case processes i and j have tickets with different colors (line 9), i waits until it notices that either (1) j is not competing any more, (2) i has priority over j because i's color is *different* than the value of the color bit, or (3) j has reentered its entry section.

In the exit code (line 12), i sets the *color* bit to a value which is different than the color of its ticket, and sets its ticket number to 0 (line 13). The algorithm is also correct if we replace the order of lines 11 and 12, allowing process i to write the color bit immediately before it enters its critical section. We observe that the order of lines 12 and 13 is crucial for correctness; and that without the third clause in the await statement in line 9 the algorithm can deadlock. Although the color bit is not a purely single-writer registers, there is at most one write operation pending on it at any time.

The following lemma captures the effect of the tickets' colors on the order in which processes enter their critical sections. For lack of space all the proofs are omitted from this abstract.

Lemma 1. *Assume that at time t, the value of the color bit is $c \in \{black, white\}$. Then, any process which at time t is in its entry section and holds a ticket with a color different than c must enter its critical section before any process with a ticket of color c can enter its critical section.*

For example, if the value of the *color* bit is white, then no process with a white ticket can enter its critical section until all the processes which hold black tickets enter their critical sections. The following corollary follows immediately from Lemma 1.

Corollary 1. *Assume that at time t, the value of the color bit has changed from $c \in \{black, white\}$ to the other value. Then, at time t, every process that is in its entry section has a ticket of color c.*

The following theorem states the main properties of the algorithm.

Theorem 1. *The Black-White Bakery Algorithm satisfies mutual exclusion, deadlock-freedom, FIFO, and uses finite number of bounded size registers (each of size one bit or $\log(2n + 2)$ bits).*

4   Adaptive FIFO Algorithm with Bounded Space

In [3], a new object, called an *active set* was introduced, together with an implementation which is wait-free, adaptive and uses only bounded number of bounded size atomic registers. Notice that wait-freedom implies local spinning, as a wait-free implementation must also be spinning-free. The authors of [3], have shown how to transform the Bakery algorithm into its corresponding adaptive version using the active set object. We use the same efficient transformation.

Active set: *An active set S object supports the following operations:*

- join(S): *which adds the id of the executing process to the set S. That is, when process i executes this operation the effect is to execute, $S := S \cup \{i\}$.*
- leave(S): *which removes the id of the executing process from the set S. That is, when process i executes this operation the effect is to execute, $S := S - \{i\}$.*
- getset(S): *which returns the current set of active processes. More formally, the following two conditions must be satisfied,*
  - *the set returned includes all the processes that have finished their last* join(S) *before the current* getset(S) *has started, and did not start* leave(S) *in the time interval between their last* join(S) *and the end of the current* getset(S).
  - *the set returned does not includes all the processes that have finished their last* leave(S) *before the current* getset(S) *has started, and did not start* join(S) *in the time interval between their last* leave(S) *and the end of the current* getset(S).

The implementation in [3] of the active set object is both wait-free and adaptive w.r.t. the number of steps required. That is, the number of steps depends only on the number of active processes – the number of processes that finished join(S) and have not yet started leave(S). Next we transform the Black-white Bakery algorithm into its corresponding adaptive version. The basic idea is to use an active set object in order to identify the active processes and then to ignore the other processes. The code of the *adaptive* Black-White Bakery algorithm (Algorithm 3) is shown on the next page.

For computing the maximum, we assume that a process first reads into local memory *only* the tickets of processes in S, one at a time atomically, and then computes the maximum over numbers of the tickets with the same color as its own. Algorithm 3 is adaptive only if we assume that spinning on a variable while its value does not change, is counted only as one operation (i.e., only remote uncached accesses are counted.) In the next section we modify the algorithm so that it is adaptive even without the above assumption.

In order to be able to formally claim that Algorithm 3 is adaptive, we need to formally define time complexity. As discussed in the introduction, for certain shared memory systems, it makes sense to distinguish between *remote* and *local* access to shared memory. Shared registers may be locally-accessible as a result of coherent caching, or when using distributed shared memory where shared memory is physically distributed among the processors.

Algorithm 3. THE ADAPTIVE BLACK-WHITE BAKERY ALGORITHM: i's code

Shared variables:

S: adaptive active set, initially $S = \emptyset$

$color$: a bit of type $\{\texttt{black}, \texttt{white}\}$

$choosing[1..n]$: boolean array

$(mycolor, number)[1..n]$: array of type $\{\texttt{black}, \texttt{white}\} \times \{0, ..., n\}$

Initially $\forall i : 1 \leq i \leq n : choosing_i = \texttt{false}$ and $number_i = 0$,

the initial values of all the other variables are immaterial.

```
                                              /* beginning of doorway */
1    join(S)                                  /* S := S ∪ {i} */
2    choosing_i := true
3    localS := getset(S) − {i}                /* reads S into local variable */
4    mycolor_i := color
5    number_i := 1 + max({number_j | (j ∈ localS) ∧ (mycolor_j = mycolor_i)})
6    choosing_i := false
7    localS := getset(S) − {i}                /* reads S into local variable */
                                              /* end of doorway */
8    for every j ∈ localS do
9        await choosing_j = false
10       if mycolor_j = mycolor_i
11       then await (number_j = 0) ∨ ([number_j, j] ≥ [number_i, i]) ∨
                       (mycolor_j ≠ mycolor_i)
12       else await (number_j = 0) ∨ (mycolor_i ≠ color) ∨
                       (mycolor_j = mycolor_i) fi
13   od
14   critical section
15   if mycolor_i = black then color := white else color := black fi
16   number_i := 0
17   leave(S)                                 /* S := S − {i} */
```

Remote access: *We define a remote access by process p as an attempt to access a memory location that does not physically resides on p's local memory. The remote memory location can either reside in a central shared memory or in some other process' memory.*

Next, we define when remote access causes *communication*.

Communication: *Two models are possible,*

1. Distributed Shared Memory (DSM) Model: *Any remote access causes communication;*
2. Coherent Caching (CC) Model: *A remote access to register r causes communication if (the value of) r is not (the same as the value) in the cache. That*

is, communication is caused only by a remote write access that overwrites a different process' value or by the first remote read access by a process that detects a value written by a different process.

It is important to notice that spinning on a remote variable while its value does not change, is counted only as one remote operation that causes communication in the CC model, while it is counted as many operations that causes communication in the DSM model. Next we define time complexity. This complexity measure is defined with respect to either the DSM Model or the CC model, and whenever it is used, we will say explicitly which model is assumed.

Time complexity: *The maximum number of remote accesses which cause communication that a process, say p, may need to perform in its entry and exit sections in order to enter and exit its critical section since p started executing the code of its entry section.*

Theorem 2. *Algorithm 3 satisfies mutual exclusion, deadlock-freedom, FIFO, uses finite number of bounded size registers, and is adaptive w.r.t. time complexity in the CC model.*

Algorithm 3 is adaptive in the CC model, even if it is assumed that every write access causes communication. The Bakery algorithm uses single-writer safe registers. Our adaptive algorithm requires using multi-writer registers and atomic registers. The following results show that this is unavoidable.

Theorem 3 (Anderson and Kim [7]). *There is no adaptive mutual exclusion algorithms, in both the CC and the DSM models, if registers accesses are non-atomic.*

Theorem 4. *There is no adaptive mutual exclusion algorithm, in both the CC and the DSM models, using only single-writer registers.*

Algorithm 3 is not adaptive w.r.t. time complexity in the DSM model, and it does not satisfy local-spinning. This is due to the fact that in Algorithm 3 two processes may spin on the same shared variable. Our next algorithm satisfies these two additional properties: (1) it is adaptive also w.r.t. time complexity in the DSM model, and (2) it satisfies local-spinning.

5   Adaptive and Local-Spinning Black-White Bakery Algorithm

We modify Algorithm 3, so that the new algorithm is: (1) adaptive w.r.t. time complexity in the DSM model, (2) satisfies local-spinning, (3) satisfies FIFO, and (4) uses bounded space. In Algorithm 3, process i may need to busy-wait for another process, say j, in one of two cases:

1. Process i might need to wait until the value of $choosing_j$ changes (line 9).
2. Process i has lower priority than j and hence i has to wait until j exits its critical section.

Algorithm 3 does not satisfy local-spinning since in each one of these two cases process i waits by spinning on remote registers. To overcome this difficulty, in Algorithm 4, process i uses two new single-reader shared bits, $spin.ch[i,j]$ and $spin.nu[i,j]$, which are both assumed to be locally accessible for process i.

1. In the first case, instead of spinning on $choosing_j$, process i spins locally on $spin.ch[i,j]$, waiting for j to notify it that the value of $choosing_j$ has been changed. Process j notifies i of such a change by writing into $spin.ch[i,j]$.
2. In the second case, instead of waiting for j to exit its critical section by spinning on the variables $number_j$, $color$ and $mycolor_j$, process i spins locally on $spin.nu[i,j]$, waiting for j to notify it that j has exited its critical section. Process j notifies i when it exits by writing into $spin.nu[i,j]$.

To implement all the (single-reader) spin bits, we use the two dimensional arrays $spin.ch$ and $spin.nu$. To keep the algorithm adaptive we use one active set S which records at any moment the set of active processes. As in Algorithm 3, a process uses S in order to know which processes are concurrent with it when it either takes a number or when it compares its ticket with the tickets of the other active processes. In addition, in Algorithm 4, the adaptive active set S is used to know which are the waiting processes that need to be notified of a change in one of the shared variables. The code of the *adaptive and local-spinning* Black-White Bakery algorithm (Algorithm 4) is shown on the next page.

Theorem 5. *Algorithm 4 satisfies mutual exclusion, deadlock-freedom, FIFO, uses finite number of bounded size registers, is adaptive w.r.t. time complexity in the DSM model, and satisfies local-spinning.*

The time complexity in the CC model of both Algorithms 3 and Algorithm 4, is dominated by the complexity of the active set, and is $O(\max(k, comp.S))$, where k is the point contention and $comp.S$ is the step complexity of the active set. Since Algorithm 3 does not satisfy local-spinning its time complexity in the DSM model is unbounded, however, the time complexity of Algorithm 4 is $O(\max(k, comp.S))$ also in the DSM model. The step complexity of the active set implementation from [3] is $O(k^4)$. However, a more efficient implementation exists which has only $O(k^2)$ step complexity [11,23]. (This is an implementation of *collect* which is a stronger version of active set.) Thus, using this implementation, the time complexity of Algorithm 4 is $O(k^2)$ for both the CC and DSM model, where k is the point contention. As already mentioned, few other adaptive algorithms which do not satisfy FIFO have better time complexity.

The time complexity of the algorithm in [6] is $O(\min(k, \log n))$ for both the CC and DSM model, where k is point contention (this is also its system response time). The time complexity of the algorithm in [4] is $O(\min(k^2, k \log n))$ for both the CC and DSM model, however here k is interval contention. The time complexity of the algorithm in [3] is $O(k^4)$ for the CC mode, and since it does not satisfy local-spinning its time complexity in the DSM model is unbounded. The time complexity of the algorithm in [14] for the CC model is $O(N)$, however its system response time is $O(k)$. In [10], it is assumed that busy-waiting is counted as a single operation (even if the value of the lock changes several times while waiting). The step complexity of the algorithm in [10] is $O(k)$ and its system response time is $O(\log k)$. The system response time of the algorithm in [37] (which works for infinitely many processes) is $O(k)$.

Algorithm 4. THE ADAPTIVE AND LOCAL-SPINNING BLACK-WHITE BAKERY ALGORITHM: process i's code

Shared variables:
> S: adaptive active set, initially $S = \emptyset$
> $spin.ch[1..n, 1..n]$: two dimensional boolean array /*spin on choosing*/
> $spin.nu[1..n, 1..n]$: two dimensional boolean array /* spin on number */
> $color$: a bit of type {black, white}
> $choosing[1..n]$: boolean array
> $(mycolor, number)[1..n]$: array of type {black, white} $\times \{0, ..., n\}$
> Initially $\forall i : 1 \leq i \leq n : choosing_i = \text{false}$ and $number_i = 0$,
> the initial values of all the other variables are immaterial.

```
                                            /* beginning of doorway */
1    join(S)                                        /* S := S ∪ {i} */
2    choosing_i := true
3    localS := getset(S) − {i}            /* reads S into local variable */
4    mycolor_i := color
5    number_i := 1 + max({number_j | (j ∈ localS) ∧ (mycolor_j = mycolor_i)})
6    choosing_i := false
7    localS := getset(S) − {i} /* notifyAll that choosing_i has changed */
8    for every j ∈ localS do spin.ch[j, i] := false od
                                                 /* end of doorway */
9    for every j ∈ localS do
10       spin.ch[i, j] := true          /* waits until choosing_i = false */
11       if choosing_j = true then await spin.ch[i, j] = false fi
12       spin.nu[i, j] := true    /* writes first to avoid race cond. */
13       if mycolor_j = mycolor_i /* waits until i has priority over j */
14       then if (number_j = 0) ∨ ([number_j, j] ≥ [number_i, i]) ∨
                       (mycolor_j ≠ mycolor_i)
15            then skip else await spin.nu[i, j] = false fi
16       else if (number_j = 0) ∨ (mycolor_i ≠ color) ∨ (mycolor_j = mycolor_i)
17            then skip else await spin.nu[i, j] = false fi
18       fi
19   od
20   critical section
21   if mycolor_i = black then color := white else color := black fi
22   number_i := 0
23   leave(S)                                         /* S := S − {i} */
24   localS := getset(S)                       /* notifyAll of i's exit */
25   for every j ∈ localS do spin.nu[j, i] := false od
```

References

1. U. Abraham. Bakery algorithms. In *Proc. of the Concurrency, Specification and Programming Workshop*, pages 7–40, 1993.
2. Y. Afek, D. Dolev, E. Gafni, M. Merritt, and N. Shavit. A bounded first-in, first-enabled solution to the ℓ-exclusion problem. *ACM Transactions on Programming Languages and Systems*, 16(3):939–953, 1994.
3. Y. Afek, G. Stupp, and D. Touitou. Long-lived adaptive collect with applications. In *Proc. 40th IEEE Symp. on Foundations of Computer Science*, 262–272, 1999.
4. Y. Afek, G. Stupp, and D. Touitou. Long lived adaptive splitter and applications. *Distributed Computing*, 30:67–86, 2002.
5. J. H. Anderson. A fine-grained solution to the mutual exclusion problem. *Acta Informatica*, 30(3):249–265, 1993.
6. J.H. Anderson and Y.-J. Kim. Adaptive mutual exclusion with local spinning. *Proceedings of the 14th international symposium on distributed computing. Lecture Notes in Computer Science*, 1914:29–43, oct 2000.
7. J.H. Anderson and Y.-J. Kim. Nonatomic mutual exclusion with local spinning. In *Proc. 21st ACM Symp. on Principles of Distributed Computing*, pages 3–12, 2002.
8. J. Anderson, Y.-J. Kim, and T. Herman. Shared-memory mutual exclusion: Major research trends since 1986. *Distributed Computing*, 16:75–110, 2003.
9. T. E. Anderson. The performance of spin lock alternatives for shared-memory multiprocessor. *IEEE Trans. on Parallel and Distributed Systems*, 1(1):6–16, 1990.
10. H. Attiya and V. Bortnikov. Adaptive and efficient mutual exclusion. *Distributed Computing*, 15(3):177–189, 2002.
11. H. Attiya and A. Fouren. Algorithms adapting to point contention. *Journal of the ACM*, 50(4):144–468, 2003.
12. J. E. Burns and A. N. Lynch. Mutual exclusion using indivisible reads and writes. In *18th annual allerton conf. on comm., control and computing*, 833–842, 1980.
13. J. N. Burns and N. A. Lynch. Bounds on shared-memory for mutual exclusion. *Information and Computation*, 107(2):171–184, December 1993.
14. M. Choy and A.K. Singh. Adaptive solutions to the mutual exclusion problem. *Distributed Computing*, 8(1):1–17, 1994.
15. E. W. Dijkstra. Solution of a problem in concurrent programming control. *Communications of the ACM*, 8(9):569, 1965.
16. D. Dolev and N. Shavit. Bounded concurrent time-stamping. *SIAM Journal on Computing*, 26(2):418–455, 1997.
17. C. Dwork and O. Waarts. Simple and efficient bounded concurrent timestamping or bounded concurrent timestamp systems are comprehensible! In *Proc. 24rd ACM Symp. on Theory of Computing*, pages 655–666, May 1992.
18. M. J. Fischer, N. A. Lynch, J. E. Burns, and A. Borodin. Distributed FIFO allocation of identical resources using small shared space. *ACM Trans. on Programming Languages and Systems*, 11(1):90–114, January 1989.
19. S. A. Friedberg and G. L. Peterson. An efficient solution to the mutual exclusion problem using weak semaphores. *Info. Processing Letters*, 25(5):343–347, 1987.
20. R. Gawlick, N. A. Lynch, and N. Shavit. Concurrent timestamping made simple. In *Israel Symposium on Theory of Computing Systems*, pages 171–183, 1992.
21. G. Graunke and S. Thakkar. Synchronization algorithms for shared-memory multiprocessors. *IEEE Computers*, 28(6):69–69, June 1990.
22. A. Israeli and M. Li. Bounded time-stamps. *Distributed Computing*, 6(4):205–209, 1993.

23. M. Inoue, S. Umetani, T. Masuzawa, and H. Fujiwara. Adaptive long-lived $O(k^2)$-renaming with $O(k^2)$ steps. In *15th international symposium on distributed computing*, 2001. *LNCS 2180* Springer Verlag 2001, 123–135.

24. P. Jayanti. Adaptive and efficient abortable mutual exclusion. In *Proc. 22nd ACM Symp. on Principles of Distributed Computing*, pages 295–304, July 2003.

25. P. Jayanti, K. Tan, G. Friedland, and A. Katz. Bounding Lamport's Bakery algorithm. In *28 annual conference on current trends in theory and practice of informatics*, December 2001. *LNCS 2234* Springer Verlag 2001, 261–270.

26. H.P. Katseff. A new solution to the critical section problem. In *Proc. 10th ACM Symp. on Theory of Computing*, pages 86–88, May 1978.

27. L. Lamport. A new solution of Dijkstra's concurrent programming problem. *Communications of the ACM*, 17(8):453–455, August 1974.

28. L. Lamport. A bug in the Bakery algorithm. Technical Report CA–7704–0611, Massachusette computer associates, inc., April 1977.

29. L. Lamport. The mutual exclusion problem: Part II – statement and solutions. *Journal of the ACM*, 33:327–348, 1986.

30. E. A. Lycklama. A first-come-first-served solution to the critical section problem using five bits. M.Sc. thesis, University of Toronto, October 1987.

31. E. A. Lycklama and V. Hadzilacos. A first-come-first-served mutual exclusion algorithm with small communication variables. *ACM Trans. on Programming Languages and Systems*, 13(4):558–576, 1991.

32. N. A. Lynch. *Distributed Algorithms*. Morgan Kaufmann Publishers, Inc., 1996.

33. J. M. Morris. A starvation-free solution to the mutual exclusion problem. *Information Processing Letters*, 8(2):76–80, 1979.

34. J. M. Mellor-Crummey and M. L. Scott. Algorithms for scalable synchronization on shared-memory multiprocessors. *ACM Trans. on Computer Systems*, 9(1):21–65, 1991.

35. R. Alur and G. Taubenfeld. Results about fast mutual exclusion. In *Proceedings of the 13th IEEE Real-Time Systems Symposium*, pages 12–21, December 1992.

36. M. Merritt and G. Taubenfeld. Speeding Lamport's fast mutual exclusion algorithm. *Information Processing Letters*, 45:137–142, 1993. (Published as an AT&T technical memorandum, May 1991.)

37. M. Merritt and G. Taubenfeld. Computing with infinitely many processes. In *14th international symposium on distributed computing*, October 2000. *LNCS 1914* Springer Verlag 2000, 164–178.

38. G. L. Peterson and M. J. Fischer. Economical solutions for the critical section problem in a distributed system. In *Proc. 9th ACM Symp. on Theory of Computing*, pages 91–97, 1977.

39. M. Raynal. *Algorithms for mutual exclusion*. The MIT Press, 1986.

40. S. Vijayaraghavan. A variant of the bakery algorithm with bounded values as a solution to Abraham's concurrent programming problem. In *Proc. of Design, Analysis and Simulation of Distributed Systems*, 2003.

41. M.L. Scott. Non-blocking timeout in scalable queue-based spin locks. In *Proc. 21th ACM Symp. on Principles of Distributed Computing*, pages 31–40, July 2002.

42. B. K. Szymanski. Mutual exclusion revisited. In *Proc. of the 5th Jerusalem Conf. on Information Technology*, pages 110–117, October 1990.

43. T. Woo. A note on Lamport's mutual exclusion algorithm. *Operating Systems Review (ACM)*, 24(4):78–80, October 1990.

44. J-H. Yang and J.H. Anderson. Fast, scalable synchronization with minimal hardware support. In *Proc. 12th ACM Symp. on Principles of Distributed Computing*, pages 171–182, 1993.

Local-Spin Group Mutual Exclusion Algorithms*
(Extended Abstract)

Robert Danek[1] and Vassos Hadzilacos[2]

[1] IBM Toronto Lab
[2] Department of Computer Science
University of Toronto

Abstract. Group mutual exclusion (GME) is a natural generalisation of the classical mutual exclusion problem. In GME, when a process leaves the non-critical section it requests a "session"; processes are allowed to be in the critical section simultaneously if they have requested the same session. We present GME algorithms (where the number of sessions is not known a priori) that use $O(N)$ remote memory references in distributed shared memory (DSM) multiprocessors, where N is the number of processes, and prove that this is asymptotically optimal even if there are only two sessions that processes can request. We also present an algorithm for two-session GME that requires $O(\log N)$ remote memory references in cache-coherent (CC) multiprocessors. This establishes a complexity separation between the CC and DSM models: there is a problem (two-session GME) that is provably more efficiently solvable in the former than in the latter.

1 Introduction

Group mutual exclusion (GME) [1] is a generalisation of the classical mutual exclusion problem [2, 3]. In GME there are N processes $1, 2, \ldots, N$, each having the structure shown in Figure 1. Each process alternates between a (possibly nonterminating) **non-critical section** (NCS) and a (terminating) **critical section** (CS). Each time a process leaves the NCS to enter the CS, it "requests" a positive integer (not necessarily the same each time) called a **session**. Two processes are said to **conflict** if they are requesting different sessions. Processes coordinate their entry to the CS by executing the **trying** and **exit protocols** so that the following properties are satisfied:

Mutual exclusion: No two conflicting processes are in the CS simultaneously.
Lockout freedom: A process that leaves the NCS eventually enters the CS.
Bounded exit: A process completes its exit protocol in a bounded number of its own steps.
Concurrent entering: If process p is in the trying protocol while no process is requesting a conflicting session, then p completes the trying protocol in a bounded number of its own steps.

---
* Research supported in part by the Natural Sciences and Engineering Research Council of Canada.

R. Guerraoui (Ed.): DISC 2004, LNCS 3274, pp. 71–85, 2004.

---

repeat
  NCS
  Trying Protocol $\left\{\begin{array}{l}\text{Doorway (bounded)}\\\text{Waiting room}\end{array}\right.$
  CS
  Exit Protocol
forever

Fig. 1. GME process structure

The ordinary mutual exclusion problem is the special case where each process p always requests session p, and thus any two processes conflict.

In some applications it may be important that processes enter the CS in a "fair" manner – i.e., roughly in the order in which they leave the NCS. To formalise this we assume that the trying protocol starts with a *bounded* section of code (i.e., one that contains no unbounded loops), called the **doorway**; the rest of the trying protocol is called the **waiting room** (see Figure 1). The fairness requirements can now be stated as follows:

First-come-first served (FCFS): If process p completes the doorway before a conflicting process q starts the doorway, then q does not enter the CS before p [3, 4].

First-in-first-enabled (FIFE): If process p completes the doorway before a non-conflicting process q starts the doorway, and q enters the CS before p, then p enters the CS in a bounded number of its own steps [5, 6].

We can also strengthen the concurrent entering property to:

Strong concurrent entering: If process p completes the doorway before any conflicting process q starts the doorway, then p enters the CS in a bounded number of its own steps [6].

Model: We work in the context of the asynchronous, shared-memory model of computation. More precisely, we consider a system consisting of N processes, named $1, 2, \ldots, N$, and a set of shared variables. Each process also has its own private variables. Processes can communicate only by accessing the shared variables by means of read, write and COMPARE&SWAP operations. (COMPARE&SWAP(x, v, w) atomically reads the shared variable x, writes w into it iff its old value was v, and returns the old value.) One of our algorithms additionally uses FETCH&ADD(x, v), which atomically adds v to shared variable x and returns the old value of x. An execution is modeled as a sequence of process steps. In each step, a process either performs some local computation affecting only its private variables, or accesses a shared variable by applying one of the available operations. Processes take steps asynchronously: there is no bound on the number of other processes' steps that can be executed between two successive steps of a process. Every process, however, is *live*: if it has not terminated, it will eventually execute its next step.

Within this general framework, there are two models of shared memory: the *distributed shared-memory* (DSM) model and the *cache-coherent* (CC) model. These differ on where shared variables are physically stored and how processes can access them. These models are important for our results and we describe them next.

In the DSM model, each process has an associated memory module. Every shared variable is stored at the memory module associated with exactly one process. Accessing a variable stored at a different process's memory module causes the process to make a *remote memory reference.*

In the CC model, all shared variables are stored in a global store that is not associated with any particular process. Every time a process reads a shared variable, it does so using a local (cached) copy of the variable. Whenever the cached variable is no longer valid – either because the process has never read the variable before, or because some process overwrote it in the global store – the process makes a remote memory reference and copies the variable into its local store (i.e., it caches the variable). Also, every time a process writes a variable, the process writes the variable to the global store (thereby invalidating all cached copies), which involves a remote memory reference. In our complexity analysis of algorithms under the CC model we assume that unsuccessful COMPARE&SWAP operations, i.e., ones that do not update the shared variable they access, do not invalidate cached copies of the variable.

Remote memory references are orders of magnitude slower than accesses to the local memory module (or cache); they also generate traffic on the processor-to-memory interconnect, which can be a bottleneck. For these reasons, the performance of many algorithms for shared memory multiprocessor systems depends critically on the number of remote memory references they generate [7]. In such systems, it is therefore important to design algorithms that minimise the number of remote memory references. An ordinary or group mutual exclusion algorithm is called *local spin* (under the DSM or CC model) if the maximum number of remote memory references made in any passage is bounded. (A *passage* is the sequence of steps executed by a process between the time it leaves the NCS and the time it next returns to it.) Many such algorithms have been devised for ordinary mutual exclusion; see [8] for a survey. In this paper we present local-spin algorithms for *group* mutual exclusion under the DSM model. To our knowledge, these are the first such algorithms (but see "Related Work" below for a caveat).

In the pseudocode description of algorithms we use the construct

$$\textbf{cobegin } S_1 \parallel \ldots \parallel S_k \textbf{ coend}$$

where $S_1, \ldots, S_k$ are "threads", i.e., statements typically containing one or more unbounded loops. The meaning of this construct is that the threads are executed concurrently in an arbitrary fair interleaving. (A fair interleaving is one which, if infinite, contains an infinite number of instructions of *every* thread.) Furthermore, if one of the threads terminates, then the execution of the remaining threads is eventually suspended and the entire cobegin-coend statement terminates.

Outline of Results: In Section 2 we present three local-spin GME algorithms under the DSM model. Two of these algorithms satisfy strong fairness properties; the third sacrifices strong fairness to achieve greater concurrency. These three algorithms require $O(N)$ remote memory references per passage. We also prove that this is in some sense asymptotically optimal: In the DSM model, *any* GME algorithm (even for the special case of only two sessions and regardless of how powerful synchronisation primitives it may use), requires $\Omega(N)$ remote memory references for some passage. This is in sharp contrast to ordinary (as opposed to group) mutual exclusion, which can be solved in the DSM model using only $O(\log N)$ remote memory references, even if the shared variables can be accessed only by read and write operations [9].

In Section 3 we present an algorithm for two-session GME that requires only $O(\log N)$ remote memory references in the CC model. This algorithm uses COMPARE&SWAP and FETCH&ADD primitives to access shared memory. This result is interesting, as it provides a complexity separation between the DSM and CC models. We are not aware of other such separation results for these two models in asynchronous systems (but see "Related Work" below for similar results in synchronous systems)[1]. By using a tournament-tree technique, this algorithm can be used to solve the M-session GME problem, for any fixed M, with $O(\log M \log N)$ remote memory references in the CC model.

We omit proofs from this extended abstract. They can be found in [10].

Related Work: Group mutual exclusion was first formulated and solved by Joung [1]. Many algorithms for this problem (or variants of it) have been proposed [1, 11, 4, 12, 6]. The only one of these that is local-spin in the DSM model is that by Keane and Moir [11]; it requires $O(\log N)$ remote memory references per passage. This algorithm, however, does not satisfy concurrent entering: there are executions where, although all processes request the same session, some processes are delayed arbitrarily long in the trying protocol. It satisfies a weaker liveness property called **concurrent occupancy** [4]. The difference between concurrent entering and concurrent occupancy turns out to be substantial: as our lower bound shows, there is no GME algorithm that satisfies concurrent entering and requires only $o(N)$ remote memory references per passage.

Kim and Anderson studied local-spin algorithms for ordinary mutual exclusion in *synchronous* systems, where there is a known maximum delay on the time to access a shared variable, and processes have access to reasonably accurate timers [13]. Their results provide a complexity separation between the DSM and CC models in such systems. They show that to solve ordinary mutual exclusion in synchronous systems, $\Theta(1)$ remote memory references are sufficient in the DSM model, while $\Theta(\log \log N)$ remote memory references are necessary (and sufficient) in the CC model. Intriguingly, this separation in the synchronous

---

[1] Truth in advertising: This separation result is not as strong as one might hope. In particular, we are able to prove it only in the context where COMPARE&SWAP and FETCH&ADD are both available, and under the assumption that unsuccessful COMPARE&SWAP operations do not invalidate cached copies. We view this result as a modest first step in exploring the relationship between the CC and DSM models.

model is in the reverse direction than the separation we show in this paper for the asynchronous model.

All the GME algorithms we present in this paper use as a "black box" – i.e., without any assumptions about how it works – an **abortable** algorithm for ordinary mutual exclusion that satisfies the FCFS property. (This is the property stated above keeping in mind that, in ordinary mutual exclusion, any two processes conflict.) An abortable mutual exclusion algorithm has, in addition to the trying and exit protocols, an **abort protocol**. This can be invoked at any time while a process is waiting in its trying protocol and causes the process to re-enter the NCS in a bounded number of its own steps. Jayanti has devised an abortable FCFS mutual exclusion algorithm that requires $O(\log N)$ remote memory references per passage in the DSM and CC models [14]. We use this fact in our complexity analyses, and we refer to this algorithm as the **underlying mutual exclusion algorithm**.

2   Local-Spin GME Algorithms for the DSM Model

In this section we present GME algorithms that require $O(N)$ remote memory references per passage in the DSM model, and show a matching lower bound.

2.1   "Fair" GME Algorithms

In this section we present two algorithms that emphasise fairness. The first of these satisfies mutual exclusion, lockout freedom, bounded exit, strong concurrent entering and FCFS. This algorithm is conceptually simple, but it does not satisfy FIFE. The second algorithm is an elaboration of the first, and satisfies FIFE in addition to all the other properties. The two algorithms are shown together in pseudocode form in Figure 2. The first consists of the non-shaded portions of the pseudocode; the second also includes the shaded portions. We now give an informal but hopefully informative presentation of the algorithms, cross-referenced to the pseudocode, explaining the actions of each process at a high level.

We start with the simple version that satisfies FCFS but not FIFE. (Refer to Figure 2, ignoring the shaded portions.) Upon leaving the NCS, a process p makes public its session by writing it into a shared variable $statusCS[p]$ (line 4)[2]. It then executes the doorway portion of the underlying FCFS mutual exclusion algorithm denoted MUTEXDOORWAY (line 5), and notes the set of conflicting processes (lines 6–9). As p considers each process j to determine if they conflict, it sets to true a boolean variable $barricade[p, j]$ (line 8). This is a spin-lock used by p to wait for j, as we will see shortly. These actions comprise p's

---

[2] In all places where $statusCS[p]$ is written in the first version of the algorithm (initialisation, and lines 4 and 20), the second component *passage* is set to -1. So, in this version of the algorithm, we can think of this variable as containing only the first component *session*. The component *passage* plays a role in the second version of the algorithm.

shared variables:
statusCS: **array**$[1..N]$ **of record** *session*: **integer**; *passage*: **integer init** $(0, -1)$
barricade: **array**$[1..N][1..N]$ **of boolean** ▷ *barricade*$[p, j]$ is in p's memory, $\forall j$

capture: **array**$[1..N]$ **of integer init** 0 ▷ *capture*$[p]$ is in p's memory

private variables:
mysession: **integer** ▷ session p wants to attend, set when p leaves the NCS
conflict_set: **set of integer**

passage: **integer init** 0
L_status: **array**$[1..N]$ **of record** *session*: **integer**; *passage*: **integer**

repeat
1   **NCS**
2   *passage* := *passage* + 1
3   **for** $j \in \{1..N\} \setminus \{p\}$ **do** *L_status*$[j]$:= *statusCS*$[j]$

4   *statusCS*$[p]$:= (*mysession*, -1)
5   MutexDoorway
6   *conflict_set* := $\emptyset$
7   **for** $j = 1$ *to* N **do**
8   *barricade*$[p, j]$:= **true**
9   **if** *statusCS*$[j]$.*session* $\notin \{0, mysession\}$ **then** *conflict_set* := *conflict_set*$\cup\{j\}$

10   *statusCS*$[p]$:= (*mysession*, *passage*)

11   **cobegin**
12   MutexWaitingRoom
        ∥
13   **for each** $j \in$ *conflict_set* **do await** $\neg$*barricade*$[p, j]$

        ∥
14   **await** *capture*$[p]$ = *passage*

15   **coend**   ▷ when one co-routine terminates, go to the next line

16   **for** $j \in \{1..N\} \setminus \{p\}$ **do**
17   **if** $\exists v \neq -1 : statusCS[j] = L\_status[j] = (mysession, v)$ **then**
18   *capture*$[j]$:= *L_status*$[j]$.*passage*

19   **CS**
20   *statusCS*$[p]$:= $(0, -1)$
21   **for** $j = 1$ *to* N **do** *barricade*$[j, p]$:= **false**
22   **if** *mutex qualified* **then** MutexExit **else** MutexAbort
    forever

Fig. 2. "Fair" GME algorithms

doorway. The process then enters its waiting room, where it waits for one of two events: (a) the completion of the underlying mutual exclusion algorithm's waiting room, denoted MUTEXWAITINGROOM (line 12), or (b) the clearing of spinlocks $barricade[p, j]$ by every conflicting process j (line 13). At that time, p enters the CS. If it does so because of event (a) (respectively, (b)) we say that it enters the CS *mutex qualified* (respectively, *conflict-free qualified*).

When p leaves the CS it executes its exit protocol, which consists of the following actions: First p signals to other processes that it is no longer interested in a session by setting $statusCS[p]$ to 0 (line 20). For every process j, p then clears the spinlock $barricade[j, p]$ that j uses to wait for p (line 21). As a result, if j is waiting for p in line 13 of its waiting room (because j, in its doorway, found p to be conflicting) it stops doing so. Finally, p executes either the exit (MUTEXEXIT) or the abort (MUTEXABORT) protocol of the underlying mutual exclusion algorithm, depending on whether it entered the CS mutex qualified or conflict-free qualified (line 22).

This algorithm satisfies mutual exclusion, lockout freedom, bounded exit, FCFS, and strong concurrent entering. It does not, however, satisfy FIFE. We describe a scenario that shows how FIFE can be violated. The scenario involves processes p and q requesting the same session s and process r requesting a different session s'. Suppose that r enters the CS. Process p then leaves the NCS; while in the doorway, p notes the conflicting process r and completes the doorway. Process r leaves the CS and sets $session[r]$ to 0, but does not (yet) execute any more steps of its exit protocol. Process q leaves the NCS; in the doorway it notes no conflicting processes and so it enters the CS conflict free. However, because r has not yet cleared the spinlock $barricade[p, r]$, p is still waiting for r. Moreover, r has not yet executed MUTEXEXIT or MUTEXABORT and so p cannot become mutex qualified. Thus, we have a situation where p's doorway precedes q's and q enters the CS, but p cannot enter the CS in a bounded number of its own steps. This is a violation of FIFE.

To avoid this we embellish the algorithm with a "capturing mechanism". The overall idea is that a process such as q in the above scenario will, before entering the CS, "capture" a process such as p thereby enabling it to enter the CS without waiting. In more detail, the capturing mechanism, which is implemented by the shaded portions of pseudocode in Figure 2, works as follows. Each process p makes public in shared variable $statusCS[p]$ two pieces of information: the session number it is requesting and its current passage number. Process p starts its doorway by making a note of all other processes' $statusCS$ variables (line 3). It then makes public its session number but writes -1 as its current passage; this indicates that p is active but still in the doorway. Process p then executes the doorway of the underlying mutual exclusion algorithm and notes all conflicting processes j, setting the spinlocks $barricade[p, j]$; these play exactly the same role as before. Finally, p indicates that it has completed the doorway by writing its passage number in the second component of $statusCS[p]$ (line 10). These actions comprise p's doorway. The process then enters the waiting room, where it now waits for one of *three* events to happen:

(a) The waiting room of the underlying mutual exclusion algorithm finishes (line 12). As before, we say that p enters the CS mutex qualified.
(b) The spinlocks $barricade[p, j]$ have been cleared for every conflicting process j (line 13). This indicates that all conflicting processes noted in p's doorway are done. We say that p enters the CS conflict-free qualified.
(c) Variable $capture[p]$ equals p's passage number (line 14). As we will see shortly, this indicates that p has been captured and can enter the CS without (further) waiting. In this case, we say that p enters the CS **capture qualified**.

Just before entering the CS, p examines every other process j to determine whether to capture it (lines 16–18). Process p captures j iff: (i) p and j do not conflict; and (ii) $statusCS[j]$ has not changed since p made a note of it in its doorway (line 3) and, at that time, j had finished the doorway (and so the passage recorded in $statusCS[j]$ was not -1). If this is the case, p captures j by setting the spinlock $capture[j]$ to j's current passage number. (As we saw in case (c) above, a process completes the waiting room and becomes capture qualified when its $capture$ variable is set to its current passage.) The capturing mechanism completes p's entry protocol. The exit protocol is identical to the previous algorithm's.

The opening of a new pathway to the CS via the capturing mechanism is cause for concern regarding mutual exclusion: We have to verify that a captured process is not enabled to enter the CS while another process requesting a different session is in the CS. Fortunately, this is the case but some interesting machinery is needed to prove that mutual exclusion is never violated.

Theorem 1. *The algorithm in Figure 2 satisfies mutual exclusion, lockout freedom, bounded exit, strong concurrent entering, FCFS and FIFE. Furthermore, in the DSM model, it requires $O(N)$ remote memory references per passage in addition to those used by the underlying mutual exclusion algorithm. Thus, combining this algorithm with Jayanti's abortable FCFS mutual exclusion algorithm [14], yields a GME algorithm with the above properties that requires $O(N)$ remote memory references per passage in the DSM model.*

2.2 "High-Concurrency" GME Algorithms

A drawback of both algorithms in Section 2.1 is illustrated by the following scenario: Let S be a set of processes, and p be a process that is not in S. Suppose that all processes in S leave the NCS at about the same time requesting the same session s, while p requests a different session s'. Further suppose that p publicises its session (line 4) before any process in S goes through the loop in the doorway that checks for conflicting processes (lines 7–9). Thus every process in S detects conflict and cannot be conflict-free qualified until after p leaves the CS. Moreover, assume that all processes in S took a snapshot of the $statusCS$ variables (line 3) before any of them wrote its $statusCS$ variable (line 4), so that there is no opportunity for any process in S to be capture qualified. Finally, suppose that the processes in $S \cup \{p\}$ execute through the doorway and waiting room in such a way that all processes in S become mutex qualified before p. This means that all the processes in S execute through the CS sequentially, even though they could all enter the CS concurrently.

We will now describe a "high-concurrency" GME algorithm that alleviates this problem by using a capturing mechanism. A process that enters the CS mutex qualified "captures" other processes that have requested the same session and enables them to enter the CS wait free. In doing so, our algorithm sacrifices FCFS and FIFE, the strong fairness properties of the previous algorithms.

---

shared variables:
$statusCS$: **array**[1..N] **of** $\{(0, \text{OUT}), (\textbf{integer}, \text{IN}), (\textbf{integer}, \text{REQ})\}$ **init** $(0, \text{OUT})$
$barricade$: **array**[1..N][1..N] **of boolean init true**
$\qquad\qquad\qquad\qquad\qquad$ ▷ $barricade[p, j]$ is in p's memory, $\forall j$

private variables:
$mysession$: **integer**   ▷ session p wants to attend, set when p leaves the NCS
$conflict\_set$: **set of integer**

repeat
1   **NCS**
2     $statusCS[p] := (mysession, \text{REQ})$
3   MUTEXDOORWAY
4     $conflict\_set := \emptyset$
5   **for** $j = 1$ **to** N **do**
6       $barricade[p, j] := \textbf{true}$
7   **if** $statusCS[j] \notin \{(0, \text{OUT}), (mysession, \text{REQ}), (mysession, \text{IN})\}$ **then**
8         $conflict\_set := conflict\_set \cup \{j\}$
9   **cobegin**
10   MUTEXWAITINGROOM
        $\|$
11   **for each** $j \in conflict\_set$ **do await** $\neg barricade[p, j]$
        $\|$
12   **await** $statusCS[p] = (mysession, \text{IN})$
13   **coend**   ▷ when one co-routine terminates, go to the next line
14   **for** $j = 1$ **to** N **do**
15      $barricade[p, j] := \textbf{true}$
16   **if** $\exists s \neq mysession : statusCS[j] = (s, \text{IN})$ **await** $\neg barricade[p, j]$
17   **if** mutex qualified **then**
18   **for** $j \in \{1..N\} \setminus \{p\}$ **do**
19   COMPARE&SWAP($statusCS[j], (mysession, \text{REQ}), (mysession, \text{IN})$)
20   **CS**
21    $statusCS[p] := (0, \text{OUT})$
22   **for** $j = 1$ **to** N **do** $barricade[j, p] := \textbf{false}$
23   **if** mutex qualified **then** MUTEXEXIT **else** MUTEXABORT **forever**

Fig. 3. "High concurrency" GME algorithm using COMPARE&SWAP

The algorithm is shown in Figure 3. Each process p has a shared variable $statusCS[p]$ in which it publicises some information about itself in the form of a pair (s, v). The value of s is the session that p is requesting or 0; the value of v is one of OUT, REQ or IN. If $v =$ IN then p has been captured; if $v =$ REQ then p in in the trying protocol or the CS but has not been captured. If $v =$ OUT then p is in the NCS or in the exit protocol (and $s = 0$).

Upon leaving the NCS, p writes (s, REQ) into $statusCS[p]$, where s is the session it is requesting (line 2), and executes the doorway of the underlying mutual exclusion algorithm (line 3). It then records the name of every conflicting process j and sets the spinlock $barricade[p, j]$ on which it will wait for conflicting processes to finish, as in the previous algorithms (lines 4–8). These actions comprise the doorway.

Process p then enters the waiting room which consists of two phases. The first phase is as in the previous algorithm; p waits for one of three events (lines 9–13): (a) to be the winner in the underlying mutual exclusion algorithm (mutex qualified); (b) to find that all conflicting processes are done (conflict-free qualified); or (c) to be captured (capture qualified). In the second phase, p waits for captured conflicting processes to finish the CS (lines 14–16) and then, *if it completed the first phase of the waiting room mutex qualified*, p captures any processes that have requested the same session (lines 17–19). Waiting for captured conflicting processes is accomplished by (re)using the *barricade* spinlocks: p resets the spinlock $barricade[p, j]$, and then waits for j to clear the spinlock in its exit protocol (line 22) if j is conflicting. Capturing processes that have requested the same session s as p is accomplished by writing (s, IN) into $statusCS[j]$ for every process j whose $statusCS[j]$ was previously (s, REQ) (line 19). Note that here we use the COMPARE&SWAP operation, so that the reading of $statusCS[j]$ (to see if it is (s, REQ)) and its updating (to make it (s, IN)) are done in one atomic action. At this point, p has completed the trying protocol and enters the CS.

The exit protocol is very similar to the algorithms we have seen before: p indicates that it is out of the CS by writing $(0, \text{OUT})$ in $statusCS[p]$ (line 21), clears the spinlocks of every process j that could be waiting for it (line 22), and then executes the exit or abort procedure of the underlying mutual exclusion algorithm, depending on whether it entered the CS mutex qualified or not (line 23).

Theorem 2. *The algorithm in Figure 3 satisfies mutual exclusion, lockout freedom, bounded exit and concurrent entering. Furthermore, in the DSM model, it requires $O(N)$ remote memory references per passage in addition to those used by the underlying mutual exclusion algorithm. Thus, combining this algorithm with Jayanti's abortable FCFS mutual exclusion algorithm [14], yields a GME algorithm with the above properties that requires $O(N)$ remote memory references per passage in the DSM model.*

2.3   Lower Bound on Remote Memory References

We now show that, in some sense, the preceding algorithms are asymptotically optimal in terms of the number of remote memory references they generate in the DSM model.

Theorem 3. *Any algorithm that satisfies mutual exclusion, lockout freedom, bounded exit and concurrent entering, and is local-spin under the DSM model, must perform $\Omega(N)$ remote memory references in some passage. This holds even for the two-session GME problem, i.e., when each process can request one of only two sessions.*

We now sketch a proof of this lower bound. Let **A** be an algorithm for two-session GME that is local-spin under the DSM model. Consider the following execution of **A**: Some process p requests session s, while no other process is active. Process p enters the CS (because **A** is lockout-free). At this point the remaining $N - 1$ processes, each requesting the other session s', enter the trying protocol. Since p is in the CS and **A** satisfies mutual exclusion, none of the $N - 1$ processes requesting s' can enter the CS. There is no bound on the amount of time that p can spend in the CS, so we assume that p stays in the CS until each of the $N - 1$ processes in the trying protocol enters a busy-wait loop. Since **A** is local-spin under the DSM model, this implies that there are at least $N - 1$ distinct variables on which the processes in the trying protocol are busy-waiting. For any such process to enter the CS, the local-spin variable(s) it is busy-waiting on must be updated. Thus, when p leaves the CS and executes the exit protocol, it must update at least $N - 1$ remotely stored variables: If it updated any fewer then we could continue the execution in such a way that at least one process in the trying protocol would not enter the CS in a bounded number of its own steps after p is no longer active. This would violate the concurrent entering property that **A** is supposed to satisfy. Therefore, there is an execution of **A** in which a process executes $\Omega(N)$ remote memory references during a passage.

The difficulty in formalising this proof is that the idea of a process "entering a busy-wait loop", although intuitively clear, is not easy to express formally. A rigorous proof is given in [10] (see Chapter 3). Although the technical details of that proof are intricate, the basic intuition is contained in the simplified proof sketch we presented here.

3   Local-Spin Algorithms for GME in the CC Model

We now turn our attention to the CC model. We will describe a two-session GME algorithm that uses (as a black box) an abortable FCFS ordinary mutual exclusion algorithm and requires $O(1)$ remote memory references in addition to those used by the underlying mutual exclusion algorithm.

The algorithm is shown in pseudocode in Figure 4. We assume that the two sessions that processes can request are 1 and 2. If $s \in \{1, 2\}$, $\bar{s}$ denotes the "other" session than s – i.e., $\bar{s} = 3 - s$. We provide a high-level overview of the algorithm, cross-referenced to the pseudocode. We start by describing the shared variables used in the algorithm, and then explain how they are used.

Associated with each session $s \in \{1, 2\}$ are two shared variables: a counter, $active[s]$, and a spin-lock, $gate[s]$. Each process increments by one the counter of the session it is requesting when it enters the trying protocol (line 3) and atomically reads and decrements that counter by one when it leaves the CS (line 17). In addition, each process atomically reads and increments by $N + 1$ the counter of the *other* session when it enters the waiting room (line 9), and decrements that counter by the same amount when it leaves the waiting room (line 15). Thus, if $active[s] = a(N + 1) + b$, where $0 \leq b \leq N$, then there are exactly b processes requesting s in lines 4–17, and exactly a processes requesting $\overline{s}$ in lines 10–15. We will later see in more detail how this variable is used, but it is clear that by reading this variable a process can get some idea of how many active processes request each of the sessions.

---

shared variables:
gate: **array**[1..2] **of record** *tag* : {0..N}; *state* : {OPEN, CLOSED} **init** (0, CLOSED)
active: **array**[1..2] **of integer init** 0

private variables:
mysession : {1, 2}   ▷ *session p wants to attend, set when p leaves the NCS*
L_active: **array**[1..2] **of integer**   ▷ *private copy of active*
L_gate: **record** *tag* : {0..N}; *state* : {OPEN, CLOSED}   ▷ *and of gate[mysession]*

repeat
1   **NCS**
2   *othersession* := 3 − *mysession* ▷ *the opposite session than the one p requests*
3   FETCH&ADD(*active*[*mysession*], 1)
4   *L_gate* := *gate*[*othersession*]
5   **if** *L_gate* $\neq$ (0, CLOSED) **then**
6   COMPARE&SWAP(*gate*[*othersession*], *L_gate*, (0, CLOSED))
7   COMPARE&SWAP(*gate*[*othersession*], (0, OPEN), (0, CLOSED))
8   MUTEXDOORWAY
9   *L_active*[*othersession*] := FETCH&ADD(*active*[*othersession*], $N + 1$)
10   **cobegin**
11   MUTEXWAITINGROOM
        ||
12   **if** *L_active*[*othersession*] **mod** $(N + 1) > 0$ **then**
13   **await** *gate*[*mysession*] = (0, OPEN)
14   **coend**   ▷ *when one coroutine terminates, go to the next line*
15   FETCH&ADD(*active*[*othersession*], −(N + 1))
16   **CS**
17   *L_active*[*mysession*] := FETCH&ADD(*active*[*mysession*], −1)
18   **if** *L_active*[*mysession*] **mod** $(N + 1) = 1$ **and** *L_active*[*mysession*] $\geq (N + 1)$ **then**
19   *gate*[*othersession*] := (*p*, CLOSED)
20   **if** *active*[*mysession*] **mod** $(N + 1) = 0$ **then**
21   COMPARE&SWAP(*gate*[*othersession*], (*p*, CLOSED), (0, OPEN))
22   **if** *mutex qualified* **then** MUTEXEXIT **else** MUTEXABORT
forever

Fig. 4. Two-session GME algorithm for the CC model

To enter the CS, a process executes the doorway of the underlying mutual exclusion algorithm (line 8) and then waits for one of two events: (a) the waiting room of the underlying mutual exclusion algorithm completes (line 11), in which case we say that the process enters the CS mutex qualified; or (b) it detects that no conflicting process is active (lines 12–13), in which case we say that the process enters the CS conflict-free qualified. We now discuss how a process detects that no conflicting process is active.

As alluded to earlier, a process requesting s can detect that there are no active processes currently requesting $\bar{s}$ by checking that $active[\bar{s}] \bmod (N + 1) = 0$. Unfortunately, a mechanism for detecting absence of conflicting requests that spins on the value of $active[\bar{s}]$ does not give us the desired complexity of only $O(1)$ remote memory references in the CC model.

For this reason we need a different mechanism for processes to detect the absence of conflicting requests. The shared variable $gate[s]$ provides this mechanism. At a high level, the idea behind this mechanism is that as soon as a process requesting $\bar{s}$ leaves the NCS, it "closes" $gate[s]$ by setting it to $(0, \text{CLOSED})$ (lines 4–7), thereby preventing processes requesting s from entering the CS conflict-free qualified (line 13). We refer to this as the "gate-closing" phase of the trying protocol. The subsequent opening of $gate[s]$ is accomplished as follows: As each process requesting $\bar{s}$ leaves the CS, it checks whether (a) it is the last such process to do so, and (b) there are conflicting processes in the waiting room. Process p, requesting session $\bar{s}$, does this by looking at the old value v of $active[\bar{s}]$ when it decremented it (line 18): If $v \bmod (N+1) = 1$, then p is the last one requesting $\bar{s}$ to leave the CS; and if $v \geq (N + 1)$, then there are conflicting processes (requesting s) in the waiting room. If both of these conditions are satisfied, p attempts to "open" $gate[s]$ (lines 19–21). (The second condition, that a conflicting process be in the waiting room, is needed only to ensure that our algorithm makes $O(1)$ remote memory references in addition to those of the underlying mutual exclusion algorithm, not for any of the correctness properties.)

Process p should not "open" $gate[s]$ by using a simple assignment statement to set it to $(0, \text{OPEN})$. If p did this, there is the possibility that between the time when p reads $active[\bar{s}]$ (line 17) and the time when it writes $gate[s] = (0, \text{OPEN})$, some other process p' requesting session $\bar{s}$ executes its doorway (lines 2–9) and goes into its waiting room (lines 10–15) without closing the gate, since it already found it closed (lines 4–6). Process p could then set $gate[s] = (0, \text{OPEN})$ and return to the NCS, leaving us in a situation where $gate[s]$ is open, and a process requesting session $\bar{s}$ (i.e., p') has gotten past the gate-closing phase of the algorithm (lines 4–7) without ensuring that $gate[s]$ is closed. This is dangerous: after p' enters the CS, since $gate[s]$ is open, processes requesting session s can also enter the CS conflict-free (by completing line 13), thus violating mutual exclusion.

The preceding could be avoided if p, when it leaves the CS, could somehow do the following atomically: read and decrement the variable $active[\bar{s}]$, check if the value read meets the conditions for opening $gate[s]$ and, if it does, set $gate[s] = (0, \text{OPEN})$. This would ensure that other processes requesting session $\bar{s}$ (such as p' in the above scenario) could not race into the waiting room before p has the opportunity to set $gate[s] = (0, \text{OPEN})$. However, there is no realistic synchronization primitive that allows p to perform atomically all the required operations on $active[\bar{s}]$ and $gate[s]$. This leads us to devise a mechanism that achieves an equivalent effect.

Such a mechanism is located in lines 19–21. The first thing that p does in this fragment of the algorithm is to set $gate[s] = (p, \text{CLOSED})$. This essentially "tags" the $gate[s]$ variable with p's identifier. Using this tag, p can later determine if anyone else has written to $gate[s]$ since p last wrote to it. Process p then repeats the check of whether it is the last active process to leave the CS (line 20). If the recheck fails, then p knows that it should not open $gate[s]$ to processes requesting session s. If, however, the check succeeds, then p is still responsible for opening $gate[s]$. This is what p does in line 21. Again, however, p cannot use a simple assignment statement to set $gate[s] = (0, \text{OPEN})$ because of the danger of some other process requesting session $\bar{s}$ racing out of the NCS and into the waiting room. Instead, p makes use of the fact that it can safely assign $(0, \text{OPEN})$ to $gate[s]$ as long as no one wrote to $gate[s]$ since the time p performed the recheck. Specifically, by using COMPARE&SWAP, p atomically checks that its tag is still in $gate[s]$ (which it set before the recheck) and, if it is, it sets $gate[s] = (0, \text{OPEN})$ (line 21).

After a process carries out the "gate opening" procedure (lines 17–21), it completes the exit protocol by executing MUTEXEXIT or MUTEXABORT depending on whether it entered the CS mutex or conflict-free qualified (line 22).

Theorem 4. *The algorithm in Figure 4 solves the two-session FCFS GME problem. That is, it satisfies mutual exclusion, lockout freedom, bounded exit, concurrent entering and FCFS. Furthermore, in the CC model, it requires $O(1)$ remote memory references per passage in addition to those used by the underlying mutual exclusion algorithm. Thus, combining this algorithm with Jayanti's abortable FCFS mutual exclusion algorithm [14], yields a two-session GME algorithm that requires $O(\log N)$ remote memory references per passage in the CC model.*

Note that this "beats" the lower bound on the number of remote memory references per passage for the two-session GME problem in the DSM model (Theorem 3). Thus, two-session GME provides a complexity separation between the DSM and CC models. Consequently there is no general transformation that takes an algorithm that works in the CC model and turns it into one that solves the same problem and works as efficiently (within a constant factor) in the DSM model. This confirms the intuition that in general it is harder to design efficient local-spin algorithms for the DSM model than for the CC model.

Using the two-session GME algorithm as a building block, we can construct an algorithm for the M-session GME problem, for any fixed M, that requires $O(\log M \log N)$ remote memory references per passage in the CC model. The idea is to create a "tournament tree" with M leaves (one per session), and height $\lfloor \log_2 M \rfloor$. Each internal node of the tree corresponds to an instance of the two-session algorithm. A process p requesting session s starts at the leaf that corresponds to s and traces a path from that leaf to the root. At each internal node along that path, p executes the trying protocol of the corresponding two-session GME algorithm, using session 1 or 2 depending on whether p reached the node from its left or right child. When p completes the trying protocol of a node, it moves "up" to the node's parent; in the case of the root, p enters the CS. Upon leaving the CS, p retraces the same path in reverse order (from root to leaf) executing the exit protocols of the nodes it visits on the way "down" the tree. Yang and Anderson's algorithm for ordinary mutual exclusion [9] exhibits a similar recursive structure, though in that case the recursion is on the number of processes N, while here it is on the number of sessions M. A precise description of this algorithm, along with its correctness proof and remote memory reference complexity analysis in the CC model, can be found in [10].

Acknowledgments

We thank the anonymous referees for their comments.

References

1. Joung, Y.: Asynchornous group mutual exclusion. Distributed Computing **13** (2000) 189–206
2. Dijkstra, E.: Solution of a problem in concurrent programming control. Communications of the ACM **8** (1965) 569
3. Lamport, L.: The mutual exclusion problem: Parts I & II. Journal of the ACM **33** (1986) 313–348
4. Hadzilacos, V.: A note on group mutual exclusion. In: Proceedings of the 20th Annual Symposium on Principles of Distributed Computing. (2001) 100–106
5. Fischer, M., Lynch, N., Burns, J., Borodin, A.: Resource allocation with immunity to limited process failure. In: Proceedings of the 20th Annual Symposium on Foundations of Computer Science. (1979) 234–254
6. Jayanti, P., Petrovic, S., Tan, K.: Fair group mutual exclusion. In: Proceedings of the 22nd Annual Symposium on Principles of Distributed Computing. (2003)
7. Mellor-Crummey, J., Scott, M.L.: Algorithms for scalable synchronization on shared-memory multiprocessors. ACM Transactions on Computer Systems **9** (1991) 21–65
8. Anderson, J., Kim, Y.J., Herman, T.: Shared-memory mutual exclusion: major research trends since 1986. Distributed Computing **16** (2003) 75–110
9. Yang, J.H., Anderson, J.: A fast, scalable mutual exclusion algorithm. Distributed Computing **9** (1995) 51–60
10. Danek, R.: Local-spin group mutual exclusion algorithms. Master's thesis, University of Toronto (2004)
11. Keane, P., Moir, M.: A simple local-spin group mutual exclusion algorithm. IEEE Transactions on Parallel and Distributed Systems **12** (2001) 673–685
12. Vidyasankar, K.: A simple group mutual l-exclusion algorithm. Information Processing Letters **85** (2003) 79–85
13. Kim, Y., Anderson, J.: Timing-based mutual exclusion with local spinning. In: Proceedings of the 17th International Conference on Distributed Computing. (2003) 30–44
14. Jayanti, P.: Adaptive and efficient abortable mutual exclusion. In: Proceedings of the 22nd Annual Symposium on Principles of Distributed Computing. (2003)

On Quorum Systems for Group Resources with Bounded Capacity*

Yuh-Jzer Joung

Dept. of Information Management, National Taiwan University, Taipei, Taiwan

Abstract. We present a problem called $(m, 1, k)$-*resource allocation* to model group mutual exclusion with bounded capacity. Specifically, the problem concerns the scheduling of a resource among m groups of processes. The resource can be used by at most k processes of the same group at a time, but no two processes of different groups can use the resource simultaneously. The problem reduces to group mutual exclusion when k is equal to the group size. We then generalize quorum systems for mutual exclusion to the problem. We show that the study of quorum systems for $(m, 1, k)$-resource allocation is closely related to some classical problems in combinatorics and in finite projective geometries. By applying the results there, we are able to obtain some optimal/near-optimal quorum systems.

1   Introduction

l-exclusion [1] and group mutual exclusion [2–4] generalize mutual exclusion in two orthogonal directions. In mutual exclusion, every two processes conflict with each other when both are using a shared resource at the same time. So the resource must be accessed in an exclusive style. In l-exclusion, conflicts occur only when more than l processes are using the resource simultaneously. So up to l processes can concurrently use the resource. In group mutual exclusion, processes are divided into groups, and a conflict occurs only when two processes of different groups are attempting to use the shared resource. Any number of processes are allowed to use the resource concurrently so long as they belong to the same group.

Some applications, however, have properties captured by both l-exclusion and group mutual exclusion. For example, consider a multi-head CD jukebox in which up to l discs can be loaded for access simultaneously. When a disc is loaded, users interested in the disc can concurrently access the disc. By defining the set of users interested in the same disc as a group, we see that up to l groups of users can concurrently use the CD jukebox, and for each group, any number of users can concurrently access the disc they are interested in. Furthermore, to guarantee some quality of service, some system may impose a limit on the number of processes that can concurrently access a disc. A similar problem also occurs in wireless communication, where the communication channel consists of l sub-channels, each of which can allow up to k users to communicate.

---

* Part of this research was done when the author was visiting Lab for Computer Science, Massachusetts Institute of Technology (1999-2000). Research supported in part by the National Science Council, Taiwan, Grants NSC 92-2213-E-002-017.

R. Guerraoui (Ed.): DISC 2004, LNCS 3274, pp. 86–101, 2004.

To model the above resource allocation problems, we propose a family of problems called (m, l, k)-*resource allocation*. They concern the scheduling of l copies of a resource among m groups of processes. Each copy of the resource can be used by at most k processes of the same group at a time, but no two processes of different groups can use the same copy simultaneously. We replace k with ∞ when there is no limit on the number of processes that may concurrently access a copy of the resource. By assigning different values to the parameters, (m, l, k)-resource allocation can be used to model many existing resource allocation problems, as well as new problems illustrated above. For example, both $(1, 1, 1)$-resource allocation and $(n, 1, 1)$-resource allocation can be used to model n-process mutual exclusion, while both $(1, 1, l)$-resource allocation and $(n, l, 1)$-resource allocation are able to model l-exclusion among n processes. Moreover, $(m, 1, \infty)$-resource allocation reduces to group mutual exclusion.

To solve (m, l, k)-resource allocation, the concept of quorum systems comes to our mind, as they have been successfully applied to mutual exclusion (e.g., [5–7]) and l-exclusion (e.g., [8–10]) to reduce system load and to cope with site failures. Informally, a quorum system is a set of sets of processes with some intersection property. Each set in a quorum system is called a *quorum*. The quora provide some guard against conflicts in using a shared resource. To acquire the resource, a process must obtain permission from every member of a quorum. The quorum is usually chosen arbitrarily from the system, and a quorum member can give permission to only one process at a time. So for mutual exclusion, every two quora in a quorum system must intersect; while for l-exclusion, any collection of $l+1$ quora must contain a pair of intersecting quora. Note that a quorum usually involves only a subset of the processes in the underlying network of computation. So system load is reduced because when a process requests the resource, not all processes are involved in the scheduling. Failure resilience is increased as well because the resource can be accessed so long as not all quora are hit (a quorum is *hit* if one of its members has failed).

For a distinguishing purpose, we call quorum systems for mutual exclusion and l-exclusion 1-*coteries* and l-*coteries*, respectively. We can see that 1-coteries are not general enough to solve $(m, 1, k)$-resource allocation. A direct use of them would result in a degenerate solution in which only one copy of the resource can be used at a time and only one process can use the copy. For l-coteries, it is not clear how they can be applied to $(m, 1, k)$- or (m, l, k)-resource allocation.

The goal of this research is therefore to lay some groundwork for quorum systems for (m, l, k)-resource allocation. This paper presents the results for the $l = 1$ case. This case corresponds to group mutual exclusion with and without bounded capacity, i.e., the $(m, 1, k)$-resource allocation problem and the $(m, 1, \infty)$-resource allocation problem. We begin by establishing some basic and general results for quorum systems for $(m, 1, k)$-resource allocation, based on which quorum systems for the more general case, (m, l, k)-resource allocation, can be understood and constructed. We show that the study of quorum systems for $(m, 1, k)$-resource allocation is related to some classical problems in combinatorics and in finite projective geometries. By applying the results there, we are able to obtain some quorum systems that can provide optimal/near-optimal concurrency.

The paper is organized as follows. Section 2 defines quorum systems for $(m, 1, k)$-resource allocation, and presents composition methods for the quorum systems. Section 3 presents some optimal/near-optimal quorum systems for $(m, 1, k)$-resource allocation. Section 4 discusses failure resilience. Concluding remarks are offered in Section 5.

2   Fundamentals

2.1   Basic Definitions

Definition 1. *Let P be a finite set of elements. An $(m, 1)$-**coterie** over P, is a tuple $C = (C_1, \ldots, C_m)$, where each $C_i \subseteq 2^P$ is nonempty, such that the following conditions are satisfied:*

intersection: $\forall 1 \le i \ne j \le m, \forall Q_1 \in C_i, \forall Q_2 \in C_j : Q_1 \cap Q_2 \ne \emptyset.$
minimality: $\forall 1 \le i \le m, \forall Q_1, Q_2 \in C_i : Q_1 \not\subset Q_2$ [1].

*We call each C_i a **cartel**, and each $Q \in C_i$ a **quorum**.*

Note that by the intersection condition, no cartel can contain an empty set if $m > 1$; and by the minimality condition, no cartel can contain $\emptyset$ unless $C = (\{\emptyset\})$—the **empty** $(1, 1)$-coterie.

Definition 2. *The **degree** of a cartel C, denoted as $\deg(C)$, is the maximum number of pairwise disjoint quora in C. The **degree** of an $(m, 1)$-coterie C, denoted as $\deg(C)$, is defined to be the minimum degree of its cartels. C is of **uniform degree** k if all its cartels have the same degree k.*

We shall use $(m, 1, k)$-**coteries** to refer to $(m, 1)$-coteries of uniform degree k. For example, $(\{\{1, 2\}, \{3, 4\}\}, \{\{1, 3\}, \{2, 4\}\}, \{\{2, 3\}, \{1, 4\}\})$ is a $(3, 1, 2)$-coterie over $\{1, 2, 3, 4\}$.

For comparison, we present the definition of 1-coteries used for standard mutual exclusion. Formally, a 1-coterie over P is a nonempty set $C \subseteq 2^P$ of quora satisfying the following requirements:

intersection: $\forall Q_1, Q_2 \in C : Q_1 \cap Q_2 \ne \emptyset.$
minimality: $\forall Q_1, Q_2 \in C : Q_1 \not\subset Q_2.$

So each cartel in an $(m, 1, 1)$-coterie is a 1-coterie. Conversely, a 1-coterie C can be straightforwardly converted to an $(m, 1, 1)$-coterie as follows:

$$\boldsymbol{\tau}_m(C) = (C, \ldots, C)$$

To see how $(m, 1, k)$-coteries connect to the $(m, 1, k)$-resource allocation problem, let P be the set of processes in the problem, and let $C = (C_1, \ldots, C_m)$ be an $(m, 1, k)$-coterie over P. Each group of processes in P is assigned a cartel so

---

[1] For notational simplicity, throughout the paper, unless stated otherwise, by "$\forall a_1, \ldots, a_k \in S$" we assume that the k elements $a_1, \ldots, a_k$ are distinct. Similarly for "$\exists a_1, \ldots, a_k \in S$".

that when a process of group j wishes to use the shared resource, it must acquire an arbitrary quorum $Q \in C_j$ by locking every member of the quorum. Suppose a quorum member can be locked by one process at a time. Then the intersection property of C ensures that no processes of different groups can access the resource simultaneously. The degree of C ensures that k processes (and no more) can concurrently access the resource. The minimality property is used rather to enhance efficiency. As is easy to see, if $Q_1 \subset Q_2$, then a process that can lock Q_2 can also lock Q_1.

The above quorum-acquiring concept is essentially from Maekawa's well-known algorithm [5] for standard mutual exclusion. The number of messages needed for a process to access a shared resource is $O(|Q|)$, where Q is the quorum the process chooses. The minimum synchronization delay (i.e., the minimum time, in message transmission delay, for a process to access a shared resource) is 2. So by using Maekawa's algorithm, an $(m, 1, k)$-coterie corresponds directly to a distributed solution to $(m, 1, k)$-resource allocation. Also notice that the coterie is usually formed from the processes in the resource allocation problem.

By definition, an $(m, 1, k)$-coterie over an n-set guarantees that every cartel contains at least one unhit quorum even if $k - 1$ processes have failed. So high degree coteries provide better protection against faults. However, every quorum in an $(m, 1, k)$-coterie must have size at least k (unless $m = 1$). So the higher the degree, the larger the quorum size. Because every cartel in an $(m, 1, k)$-coterie contains k pairwise disjoint quora, and because every quorum has size at least k, the system must contain at least k^2 processes. So k is bounded by $\sqrt{n}$:

Theorem 1. *For every $(m, 1, k)$-coterie C over an n-set, $k \leq \sqrt{n}$ if $m > 1$.*

The above theoretical limit poses a problem to quorum-based solutions to $(m, 1, k)$-resource allocation with large value of k, in particular, the $(m, 1, \infty)$-resource allocation (group mutual exclusion). We shall return to this problem after we have constructed some $(m, 1, k)$-coteries with the maximum possible k in Section 3.2.

Some $(m, 1, k)$-coteries have a structure that is not only mathematically beautiful, but has also an important meaning in distributed computing. Below we define this structure. Section 3 will present construction of the coteries.

Definition 3. *Let $C = (C_1, \ldots, C_m)$ be an $(m, 1, k)$-coterie over P. C is **balanced** if all cartels have the same size. C is **regular** if all elements in P are involved in the same number of quora; i.e., $\forall p, q \in P : |n_p| = |n_q|$, where n_p is the multiset $\{Q \mid \exists 1 \leq i \leq m : Q \in C_i$ and $p \in Q\}$, and similarly for n_q. C is **uniform** if all quora have the same size.*

For example, the $(3, 1, 2)$-coterie $(\{\{1,2\}, \{3,4\}\}, \{\{1,3\}, \{2,4\}\}, \{\{2,3\}, \{1,4\}\})$ is balanced, uniform, and regular.

When used for $(m, 1, k)$-resource allocation, a balanced $(m, 1, k)$-coterie ensures that each group has an equal chance in competing for the resource. The regular property ensures that each process shares the same responsibility. The uniform property ensures that the number of messages needed per access to the resource is independent of the quorum a process chooses. Thus the three properties are desirable for a truly distributed algorithm for the problem [5].

2.2   Compositions of Coteries

In this section we provide some useful lemmas for constructing "large" $(m, 1, k)$-coteries from "small" ones. We begin with a composition that takes an $(m, 1, k_1)$-coterie over an n_1-element set, and an $(m, 1, k_2)$-coterie over an n_2-element set, and then constructs an $(m, 1, k_1 \cdot k_2)$-coterie over an $n_1 \cdot n_2$-element set. The composition is borrowed from MacNeish's technique for composing Latin Squares [11]. The same technique has also been used in the context of standard quorum systems [12, 13].

The composition needs the following notation. Let $\mathcal{C} = (C_1, \dots, C_m)$ be an $(m, 1, k)$-coterie over an n-element set $\{1, \dots, n\}$. Then, $\mathcal{C}(P)$ denotes the $(m, 1, k)$-coterie $\mathcal{C}$ obtained by replacing $\{1, \dots, n\}$ with another n-element set P (using some arbitrary bijection between $\{1, \dots, n\}$ and P). Note that $\mathcal{C}(P)$ is essentially the same as $\mathcal{C}$ subject to renaming of the elements. Similarly, quorum $Q(P)$ corresponds to the quorum obtained from Q by replacing the elements in Q with that in P.

Lemma 1. *Let* $P_1, \dots P_r$ *be* r *pairwise disjoint sets, each of size* s. *Let* $\mathcal{C} = (C_1, \dots, C_m)$ *be an* $(m, 1)$-coterie over an r-element set $\{1, \dots, r\}$, *and* $\mathcal{D} = (D_1, \dots, D_m)$ *be an* $(m, 1)$-coterie over an s-element set $\{1, \dots, s\}$. *Let* $\mathcal{C} \otimes \mathcal{D} = (E_1, \dots, E_m)$, *where each cartel* E_i, $1 \leq i \leq m$, *is defined as follows: Let* $C_i = \{Q_1^i, \dots, Q_{|C_i|}^i\}$, *and let* $D_i = \{R_1^i, \dots, R_{|D_i|}^i\}$. *Then* $E_i = \{S_{g,h}^i \mid 1 \leq g \leq |C_i|, 1 \leq h \leq |D_i|\}$, *where*

$$S_{g,h}^i = \bigcup_{j \in Q_g^i} R_h^i(P_j)$$

Then, $\mathcal{C} \otimes \mathcal{D}$ *is an* $(m, 1)$-coterie over $\bigcup_{1 \leq j \leq r} P_j$, *and* $\deg(E_i) = \deg(C_i) \cdot \deg(D_i)$.

Proof: We first show that $\mathcal{C} \otimes \mathcal{D}$ satisfies the intersection condition of Definition 1. Let $S_{a,b}^i$ be a quorum in E_i, and $S_{c,d}^j$ be a quorum in E_j, where $i \neq j$. By the intersection property of $\mathcal{C}$, there is a w such that $w \in Q_a^i$ and $w \in Q_b^j$. So $S_{a,b}^i$ contains a subset $R_b^i(P_w)$, and $S_{c,d}^j$ contains a subset $R_d^j(P_w)$. By the intersection property of $\mathcal{D}(P_w)$, $R_b^i(P_w)$ and $R_d^j(P_w)$ contain a common element. So $S_{a,b}^i \cap S_{c,d}^j \neq \emptyset$.

For the minimality condition, let $S_{a,b}^i$ and $S_{c,d}^i$ be two quora in E_i. If $a \neq c$, then by the minimality property of $\mathcal{C}$, there is some $w \in Q_a^i - Q_c^i$, and some $w' \in Q_c^i - Q_b^i$. So $S_{a,b}^i$ contains $R_b^i(P_w)$ and $S_{c,d}^i \cap R_b^i(P_w) = \emptyset$. Similarly, $S_{c,d}^i$ contains $R_d^i(P_{w'})$ and $S_{a,b}^i \cap R_d^i(P_{w'}) = \emptyset$. So $S_{a,b}^i \not\subset S_{c,d}^i$ and $S_{c,d}^i \not\subset S_{a,b}^i$. If $a = c$, then clearly $S_{a,b}^i \subset S_{c,d}^i$ implies $R_b^i \subset R_c^i$. By the minimality property of $\mathcal{D}$, we have $S_{a,b}^i \not\subset S_{c,d}^i$; and similarly $S_{c,d}^i \not\subset S_{a,b}^i$.

For the degree of $\mathcal{C} \otimes \mathcal{D}$, observe that if $Q_a^i \cap Q_c^i = \emptyset$, then $S_{a,b}^i \cap S_{c,d}^i = \emptyset$ for all $1 \leq b, d \leq |D_i|$. Moreover, if $R_b^i \cap R_d^i = \emptyset$, then $S_{a,b}^i \cap S_{c,d}^i = \emptyset$ for all $1 \leq a, c \leq |C_i|$. So $\deg(E_i) \geq \deg(C_i) \cdot \deg(D_i)$. On the other hand, if $R_b^i \cap R_d^i \neq \emptyset$, then $S_{a,b}^i \cap S_{c,d}^i \neq \emptyset$ if $Q_a^i \cap Q_c^i \neq \emptyset$. So $\deg(E_i) = \deg(C_i) \cdot \deg(D_i)$.   □

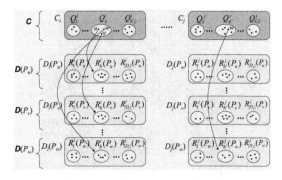

Fig. 1. Illustration of the composition in Lemma 1.

Figure 1 illustrates the composition. To see how a quorum $S^i_{g,h} \in E_i$ is constructed, consider the quorum $Q^i_g \in C_i$ which consists of three nodes u, v, w. Then $S^i_{g,h}$ is the union of $R^i_h(P_u), R^i_h(P_v)$, and $R^i_h(P_w)$. To see the intersection property of $C \otimes D$, let $S^j_{g',h'}$ be a quorum in $E_j, j \neq i$. By the intersection property of C, there is a common node between C_i and C_j, in this figure, w. Then $S^j_{g',h'}$ contains all nodes in $R^j_{h'}(P_w)$. By the intersection property of $D(P_w)$, there is a common node between $R^i_h(P_w)$ and $R^j_{h'}(P_w)$, say, x. So $x \in S^i_{g,h} \cap S^j_{g',h'}$.

The above composition allows one to build up a large degree $(m, 1, k)$-coterie from ones with smaller degree. The next two compositions we will present build up a coterie with larger number of cartels. The compositions need the following lemma.

Lemma 2. *Let $P_1, \ldots P_r$ be r pairwise disjoint sets, and let $P = \bigcup_{1 \leq j \leq r} P_j$. Let $C^j = (C^j_1, C^j_2, \ldots, C^j_m)$ be an $(m, 1)$-coterie over $P_j, 1 \leq j \leq r$. Let u and v be two vectors in $\{0, 1, \ldots, m\}^r$. Define $C_u \subset 2^P$ as follows:*

$$C_u = \left\{ \bigcup_{1 \leq j \leq r,\, u[j] \neq 0} Q_{u[j]} \,\middle|\, Q_{u[j]} \in C^j_{u[j]} \right\} \tag{1}$$

That is, each set in C_u is of the form: $Q_{u[1]} \cup Q_{u[2]} \cup \ldots \cup Q_{u[r]}$, where each $Q_{u[j]}$ is an arbitrary quorum taken from $C^j_{u[j]}$ if $u[j]$ (the jth element of vector u) is not zero, or is $\emptyset$ otherwise. Similarly for C_v. If there is an i such that $u[i] \neq 0, v[i] \neq 0$, and $u[i] \neq v[i]$ (i.e., u and v have a distinct nonzero ith element), then C_u and C_v satisfy the following two conditions:

intersection: $\forall S \in C_u, \forall T \in C_v : S \cap T \neq \emptyset$.
minimality: $\forall S, T \in C_u : S \not\subset T$. *Similarly for C_v.*

Moreover, $\deg(C_u) = \min\{\deg(C^j_{u[j]}) \mid u[j] \neq 0, 1 \leq j \leq r\}$. Similarly for C_v.

Proof. For the intersection condition, let i be such that $u[i] \neq 0, v[i] \neq 0$, and $u[i] \neq v[i]$. Let $S \in C_u$ and $T \in C_v$. Since $u[i] \neq 0$, by the definition of C_u, S

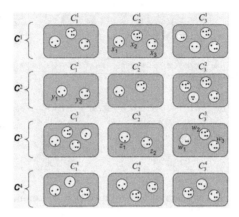

Fig. 2. Illustration of the composition in Lemma 2.

contains a subset $Q_{u[i]} \in C^i_{u[i]}$. Similarly T contains a subset $Q_{v[i]} \in C^i_{v[i]}$. Since $u[i] \neq v[i]$, by the intersection property of C^i, $Q_{u[i]} \cap Q_{v[i]} \neq \emptyset$. So $S \cap T \neq \emptyset$.

For the minimality condition, suppose otherwise $S, T \in C_u$ and $S \subset T$. Since $|C_u| \geq 2$, there is a j such that $u[j] \neq 0$ and $C^j_{u[j]}$ contains Q_1 and Q_2 such that $Q_1 \subset S$ and $Q_2 \subset T$. Since $\{P_1, \dots P_r\}$ is a partition of P, no C^i can involve an element in Q_1 and Q_2 if $i \neq j$. So $S \subset T$ implies that $Q_1 \subset Q_2$, contradicting the fact that quora in $C^j_{u[j]}$ also satisfy the minimality condition. The case for C_v is similar.

Finally, let $k = \min\{\deg(C^j_{u[j]}) \mid u[j] \neq 0, 1 \leq j \leq r\}$, and let h be such that $u[h] \neq 0$ and $\deg(C^h_{u[h]}) = k$. By the definition of C_u, every $S \in C_u$ contains some subset $Q \in C^h_{u[h]}$. So $\deg(C_u) \leq k$. On the other hand, it is easy to see that C_u contains k pairwise disjoint sets, as each $C^j_{u[j]}$, $u[j] \neq 0$, contains at least k pairwise disjoint sets. So $\deg(C_u) = k$. Similarly, $\deg(C_v) = \min\{\deg(C^j_{v[j]}) \mid v[j] \neq 0, 1 \leq j \leq r\}$. $\qquad\square$

To illustrate the lemma, consider Figure 2. Assume that $u = [2, 1, 2, 0]$. Then C_u consists of the following 12 sets: $x_i \cup y_j \cup z_k$, $i = 1, 2, 3$, $j = 1, 2$, and $k = 1, 2$. To see the intersection property, let $v = [2, 0, 3, 0]$. Then, the third elements of u and v are both nonzero and distinct. We see that every set in C_u must contain all the nodes in z_1, or all the nodes in z_2; and every set in C_v must contain all the nodes in w_1, w_2, or w_3. z_i's and w_j's are quora from different cartels of the same coterie C^3. By the intersection property of C^3, every z_i intersects every w_j. So every set in C_u intersects every set in C_v.

Let us say that two vectors u and v of size r 'hit' if they have a distinct nonzero ith element for some $i \leq r$. Lemma 2 then implies that given a collection of q pairwise hit vectors, we can construct a $(q, 1)$-coteries over P. In particular, if the vectors are from $\{1, \dots, m\}^r$, then any two different vectors must hit. So we immediately have the following lemma:

Lemma 3. *Let $\{P_1, \ldots P_r\}$ be a partition of P, i.e., $P = \bigcup_{1 \leq j \leq r} P_j$. Let $\mathcal{C}^j = (C_1^j, C_2^j, \ldots, C_m^j)$ be an $(m, 1, k)$-coterie over P_j, $1 \leq j \leq r$. Let u_i, $1 \leq i \leq q$, be q different vectors in $\{1, \ldots, m\}^r$, and C_{u_i} be defined as in Equation (1). Then $\mathcal{C} = (C_{u_1}, C_{u_2}, \ldots, C_{u_q})$ is a $(q, 1, k)$-coterie over P.*

Another way to construct a collection of q pairwise hit vectors is that if two vectors u and v from $\{0, 1, \ldots, m\}^r$ both have $\lfloor r/2 \rfloor + 1$ nonzero elements, then they must have a nonzero element in the same field. By requiring their elements in the field to be distinct, we can obtain such a collection. The following lemma follows from this observation:

Lemma 4. *Let $\{P_1, \ldots P_r\}$ be a partition of P. Let $\mathcal{C}^j = (C_1^j, C_2^j, \ldots, C_m^j)$ be an $(m, 1, k)$-coterie over P_j, $1 \leq j \leq r$. Let u_i, $1 \leq i \leq q$ be q different vectors in $\{0, 1, \ldots, m\}^r$ such that $\left| \{g \mid u_i(g) \neq 0\} \right| = \lfloor r/2 \rfloor + 1$, and for any two different vectors u_i and u_j, there is an h such that $u_i(h) \neq 0$, $u_j(h) \neq 0$, and $u_i(h) \neq u_j(h)$. Let C_{u_i} be defined as in Equation (1). Then $\mathcal{C} = (C_{u_1}, C_{u_2}, \ldots, C_{u_q})$ is a $(q, 1, k)$-coterie over P.*

The difference between the compositions in the above two lemmas is that in Lemma 3, every quorum S in C_{u_i} is formed by r sub-quora, one from $C_{u[1]}^1$, one from $C_{u[2]}^2$, ..., and one from $C_{u[r]}^r$. Thus, if each sub-quorum has size s, then S has size $r \cdot s$. In Lemma 4, the size of a quorum in C_{u_i} is reduced approximately by half by letting S be composed by only $\lfloor r/2 \rfloor + 1$ sub-quora. Note, however, that the maximum number of cartels one can obtain in the first composition is m^r, while in the second composition the number is reduced to $O(m^{r/2})$.

3 Constructions of $(m, 1, k)$-Coteries

Recall Theorem 1 that the degree of $(m, 1)$-coteries over an n-set is bounded by $\sqrt{n}$. In this section we show that the bound is tight by constructing an $(m, 1, \sqrt{n})$-coterie over an n-set. We also show that the coterie is balanced, uniform, and regular. Based on this coterie and the composition methods presented in the previous section, we show how other coteries with near-optimal degree can be constructed. Note that the existence of an $(m, 1, k)$-coterie implies the existence of $(m, 1, k')$-coteries for all $k' < k$ (and the existence of $(m', 1, k)$-coteries for all $m' < m$ as well). This is because for every cartel C in an $(m, 1, k)$-coterie, removing any subset of quora from C does not affect the intersection and minimality properties so long as the remaining cartel is not empty. So we start the construction of $(m, 1, k)$-coteries with some optimal degree.

3.1 $(m, 1)$-Coteries of Maximal Degree

The study of $(m, 1, \sqrt{n})$-coteries over an n-set is related to the study of finite projective geometries (see, e.g., [14]). The following definition and theorem can be found in the literature:

Definition 4. *An **affine plane** is an ordered pair* $(\mathcal{P}, \mathcal{L})$*, where* $\mathcal{P}$ *is a nonempty set of elements called **points**, and* $\mathcal{L}$ *is a nonempty collection of subsets of* $\mathcal{P}$ *called **lines** satisfying the following properties:*

- *Every two points lie on exactly one line. (A point* i ***lies*** *on a line* L *iff* $i \in L$*).*
- *Given a line* L *and a point* i *not on* L*, there is exactly one line* L' *such that* i *is on* L'*, and* L *and* L' *are **parallel** (i.e.,* $L \cap L' = \emptyset$*).*
- *Each line has at least two points, and there are at least two lines.*

If each line of an affine plane contains exactly x points, the plane is said to have **order** x.

Theorem 2. *An affine plane* $(\mathcal{P}, \mathcal{L})$ *of order* x *has the following properties:*

- $\mathcal{P}$ *has* x^2 *points.*
- $\mathcal{L}$ *has* $x^2 + x$ *lines.*
- *Each point is on* $x + 1$ *lines.*
- $\mathcal{L}$ *can be partitioned into* $x+1$ *classes such that each class contains* x *parallel lines, and every two lines of different classes intersect.*

For example, let the nine points $1, \ldots, 9$ be arranged as follows:

$$1\,2\,3$$
$$4\,5\,6$$
$$7\,8\,9$$

Then we can construct an affine plane of order 3 consisting of 4 classes $C_1, \ldots, C_4$, as follows:

$$C_1 = \big\{\{1,4,7\},\ \{2,5,8\},\ \{3,6,9\}\big\}$$
$$C_2 = \big\{\{1,2,3\},\ \{4,5,6\},\ \{7,8,9\}\big\}$$
$$C_3 = \big\{\{3,5,7\},\ \{1,6,8\},\ \{2,4,9\}\big\}$$
$$C_4 = \big\{\{1,5,9\},\ \{3,4,8\},\ \{2,6,7\}\big\}$$

To picture this, C_1 corresponds to the three vertical lines, C_2 corresponds to the three horizontal lines, and C_3 and C_4 correspond to the three "rounded" lines with slope 1 and -1, respectively.

It is known that an affine plane of order x exists if x is a power of a prime. So Theorem 2 immediately implies the following.

Theorem 3. *Let* $n = p^{2k}$*, where* p *is a prime, and* k *is a positive integer. Then there is an* $(m, 1, \sqrt{n})$*-coterie* $\mathcal{C}$ *over an* n*-set for every* $m \leq \sqrt{n} + 1$*. In particular,* $\mathcal{C}$ *is balanced, uniform, and regular, and each quorum has size* $\sqrt{n}$*.*

By Theorem 1, the above construction obtains $(m, 1)$-coteries with optimal degree. Moreover, by Lemma 1, given $n = p_1^{2c_1} \ldots p_l^{2c_l}$, and $m \leq \min\{p_1^{c_1}, \ldots, p_l^{c_l}\} + 1$, where $p_1, \ldots, p_l$ are primes and $c_1, \ldots, c_l$ are positive integers, a degree-optimal $(m, 1)$-coterie over an n-element set can also be constructed as well. The construction of finite affine planes (and thus the construction of $(m, 1)$-coteries with optimal degree) can be found in finite projective geometries.

Note that in the above construction m is at most $\sqrt{n} + 1$. By a combinatorial analysis, we can prove that the bound is also tight.

Theorem 4. *Let* $\mathcal{C} = (C_1, \ldots, C_m)$ *be an* $(m, 1, k)$-*coterie over an* n-*set. If* $k = \sqrt{n}$, *then* $m \leq k + 1$.

For $m > \sqrt{n} + 1$, we propose deterministic and randomized constructions. The deterministic constructions make use of the composition methods presented in Section 2.2. For example, by Lemma 3 and Theorem 3 we immediately have the following:

Theorem 5. *Given* $|P| = r \cdot k^2$, *where* k *is a power of a prime and* r *an integer, there is an* $(m, 1, k)$-*coterie* $\mathcal{C}$ *over* P *for every* $m \leq (k + 1)^r$.

So, taking r to be a constant, we can construct an $(m, 1)$-coterie that is near optimal in degree by only a constant factor of $\sqrt{r}$ for any m up to $\approx r^{-\frac{r}{2}} n^{\frac{r}{2}}$. In particular, in the $(m, 1, \infty)$-resource allocation problem, when groups are disjoint, m cannot be greater than the total number of processes n, and $m \leq n/2$ if each group consists of more than one process. In this case, we can let $r = 2$ and obtain an $(m, 1, \sqrt{n/2})$-coterie. Each quorum in the coterie has size only $\sqrt{2n}$.

When groups are not disjoint, m can be larger than n in the $(m, 1, \infty)$-resource allocation problem. In this case, the above construction gives an $(m, 1)$-coterie of degree $O(\sqrt{\frac{n \log n}{\log m}})$. Notice that the above construction requires s to be a power of a prime. However, by the distribution of primes in number theory (see, e.g., [15]), for any given $\epsilon > 0$, there is a prime p such that $x < p \leq (1 + \epsilon)x$ for all $x > x_0$, where x_0 is some constant depending on ϵ. So the construction can be generalized to arbitrary n when n is sufficiently large.

Similarly, Lemma 4 and Theorem 3 can be used to obtain some near-optimal constructions.

The above constructions require some knowledge about primes and projective geometries. In contrast, the following randomized construction is much simpler and requires less restriction on n and m.

Theorem 6. *Given any* n, m, *and* k *such that* n/k *is an integer, the following construction guarantees to generate, with probability one, an* $(m, 1, k)$-*coterie over* $P = \{1, \ldots, n\}$ *if* $k \leq \sqrt{\frac{n}{2 \log(nm)}}$:

1. **repeat**
2.   *randomly choose* m *sets* $C_1, \ldots, C_m$, *each of which is a random partition of* P *of* k *equal-size parts;*
3. **until** $\mathcal{C} = \{C_1, \ldots, C_m\}$ *is an* $(m, 1)$-*coterie over* P;
4. *output* $\mathcal{C}$;

Proof. It suffices to show that the probability that step 2 of the construction does not generate an $(m, 1)$-coterie over P is strictly less than one. For each $1 \leq i \leq m$, let $C_i = \{Q_i^j, 1 \leq j \leq k\}$ be the random partition of P chosen in step 2. Then the probability that step 2 does not generate an $(m, 1)$-coterie is equal to

Table 1. Comparison of 1-coteries vs. $(m,1)$-coteries for $(m,1,k)$-resource allocation. 'AP' denotes the affine plane coterie.

	FPP + Maekawa_M	AP + Maekawa	AP + Maekawa_M
$k \leq \sqrt{n}$	$O(\sqrt{n} \cdot k)$	$O(\sqrt{n})$	$-$
$k > \sqrt{n}$	$O(\sqrt{n} \cdot k)$	$-$	$O(k)$

$$Pr[\exists i,j,a,b, i \neq j, \text{ such that } Q_i^a \cap Q_j^b = \emptyset]$$

$$\leq \sum_{\substack{i,j,a,b \\ 1 \leq i \neq j \leq m \\ 1 \leq a,b \leq k}} Pr[Q_i^a \cap Q_j^b = \emptyset]$$

$$= k^2 \binom{m}{2} \frac{\binom{n-\frac{n}{k}}{\frac{n}{k}}}{\binom{n}{\frac{n}{k}}} = k^2 \binom{m}{2} (\frac{n-\frac{n}{k}}{n})(\frac{n-\frac{n}{k}-1}{n-1}) \cdots (\frac{n-\frac{n}{k}-(\frac{n}{k}-1)}{n-(\frac{n}{k}-1)})$$

$$\leq k^2 \binom{m}{2} (\frac{n-\frac{n}{k}}{n})^{\frac{n}{k}} = k^2 \binom{m}{2} \left((1-\frac{1}{k})^k\right)^{\frac{n}{k^2}}$$

$$\leq k^2 \binom{m}{2} e^{-\frac{n}{k^2}} < e^{2\log(km)-\frac{n}{k^2}} \leq e^{2\log(km)-2\log(nm)} < 1$$

$\square$

Theorem 5 constructs an $(m,1)$-coterie of a fixed degree determined by n. In contrast, the degree of the $(m,1)$-coterie constructed in Theorem 6 is part of the input parameters. Thus, although an $(m,1,k')$-coterie can be obtained from an $(m,1,k)$-coterie for any given $k' < k$ (by removing additional quora), the construction in Theorem 6 provides a more direct way in constructing an $(m,1)$-coterie of a given degree.

3.2 $(m,1,k)$-Coteries Versus 1-Coteries

As noted in Section 2, by using Maekawa's algorithm, an $(m,1,k)$-coterie corresponds directly to a distributed solution to the $(m,1,k)$-resource allocation problem, and the coterie is formed from the processes in the problem. Assume that there are n processes in the problem. Theorem 1, however, says that we cannot construct an $(m,1,k)$-coterie out of the n processes for any $k > \sqrt{n}$ (unless $m = 1$). This means that a different approach needs to be used to solve the problem when $k > \sqrt{n}$. We discuss two of them.

The first approach introduces auxiliary processes to act as quorum nodes. Since k cannot be greater than n, in the worst case (when $k = n$) we can add $n^2 - n$ auxiliary processes to construct an $(m,1,n)$-coterie over these n^2 actual and auxiliary processes, and then use Maekawa's algorithm to solve the problem. The message complexity is $O(n)$, and the total space overhead (for the auxiliary processes) is $O(n^2)$. Note that we can let the n actual processes act also as auxiliary processes, so that no extra physical process is added to the system.

The second approach is to adopt a different quorum-acquiring algorithm. Two algorithms, Maekawa_M and Maekawa_S, have been proposed in [16]. Both algorithms are modifications of Maekawa's algorithm, but they remove the restriction that a quorum node can be locked by only one process at a time. So, multiple processes (of the same group) may all acquire a quorum simultaneously, regardless of whether their quora intersect or not. Maekawa_M imposes no order on the locking sequence within a quorum, while a global ordering is used in Maekawa_S. As a result, the two algorithms trade off between message complexity and synchronization delay. Maekawa_M has message complexity $O(c \cdot k/d)$ and minimum synchronization delay 2, while Maekawa_S has message complexity and minimum synchronization delay both of $O(c)$, where c is the quorum size and d is the degree of the $(m, 1)$-coteries. When the affine plane $(m, 1, \sqrt{n})$-coterie constructed in Theorem 3 is used, Maekawa_M has message complexity $O(n)$, while Maekawa_S has message complexity and minimum synchronization delay both of $O(\sqrt{n})$.

At this point one may have observed that 1-coteries can also be used in Maekawa_M and Maekawa_S to solve $(m, 1, k)$-resource allocation. A natural question then is whether $(m, 1, k)$-coteries are beneficial over 1-coteries. The answer depends on applications. If applications need fast response time, then Maekawa_M should be chosen. If 1-coteries are used in the algorithm, then as commented above, the message complexity is $O(c \cdot k)$, because 1-coteries have degree one when converted to $(m, 1)$-coteries. For example, the FPP 1-coterie in [5] (which also supports a truly distributed solution) has $O(\sqrt{n} \cdot k)$ complexity. On the other hand, when $(m, 1, k)$-coteries are used, then Maekawa's original algorithm can be used for k up to $\sqrt{n}$. In this case, the affine plane coterie yields $O(\sqrt{n})$ message complexity. For $k > \sqrt{n}$, Maekawa_M together with the affine plane coterie yields $O(n)$ message complexity. Table 1 summarizes the comparison. Overall, the use of affine plane coterie has message complexity better than the FPP 1-coterie by an $O(\sqrt{n})$ factor.

If applications can tolerate long synchronization delay, then Maekawa_S can be used. In this case, there is not much difference in choosing between $(m, 1, k)$-coteries and 1-coteries. However, 1-coteries have been extensively studied in the literature, and they have been optimized in many possible ways; while $(m, 1, k)$-coteries are new concept and many of their properties remain to be exploited. We hope that our studies in the paper can initiate further research on a more general type of quorum systems.

4   Failure Resistance

Since there are many $(m, 1, k)$-coteries over a given set, some criteria are needed to evaluate them. In this section we compare $(m, 1, k)$-coteries based on their failure resilience. The notion we shall be using is *dominance*, which was first proposed by Garcia-Molina and Barbara [17] to compare the failure resilience of 1-coteries. Intuitively, a 1-coterie C *dominates* another 1-coterie D if whenever a quorum in D can survive some failures, then some quorum in C can certainly survive as well. Thus in this sense C is said to be superior to D because C provides more protection against failures. Formally, a 1-coterie D is nondominated if there is no other 1-coterie C such that $\forall Q \in D, \exists R \in C : R \subseteq Q$. Similarly, domination of $(m, 1, k)$-coteries can be defined as follows:

Definition 5. *An $(m, 1, k)$-coterie $C = (C_1, \ldots, C_m)$ over P **dominates** an $(m, 1, k')$-coterie D over P if*

1. $C \neq D$,
2. $\forall 1 \leq i \leq m, \forall Q \in D_i, \exists R \in C_i : R \subseteq Q$.

*D is **(strongly) nondominated** if there is no $(m, 1, k)$-coterie that dominates D. D is **weakly nondominated** if it is not dominated by any $(m, 1, k')$-coterie of the same degree.*

To illustrate dominance, the $(2, 1, 2)$-coterie $D = (\{\{1, 2\}, \{3, 4\}\}, \{\{1, 3\}, \{2, 4\}\})$ is dominated by the $(2, 1, 2)$-coterie $C = (\{\{1, 2\}, \{3, 4\}, \{1, 4\}, \{2, 3\}\}, \{\{1, 3\}, \{2, 4\}\})$. By a simple enumeration, it can be proved that C is nondominated.

If $C = (C_1, \ldots, C_m)$ dominates $D = (D_1, \ldots, D_m)$, then $\deg(C_i) \geq \deg(D_i)$ for all $1 \leq i \leq m$. For example, the $(2, 1, 1)$-coterie $D = (\{\{1, 2, 3\}, \{2, 3, 4\}\}, \{\{1, 2, 3\}, \{2, 3, 4\}\})$ is dominated by the $(2, 1, 2)$-coterie $C = (\{\{1, 2\}, \{3, 4\}, \{1, 4\}, \{2, 3\}\}, \{\{1, 3\}, \{2, 4\}\})$. So nondominated $(m, 1)$-coteries not only are more failure-resilient, but have degree no less than those they dominate. On the other hand, weak nondominance can be used to evaluate $(m, 1)$-coteries of a fixed degree.

It is often useful to discuss dominance with respect to a cartel, as defined below.

Definition 6. *Let $D = (D_1, \ldots, D_m)$ be an $(m, 1)$-coterie over P. D is **dominated** w.r.t. D_i if there exists some $C = (C_1, \ldots, C_m)$ such that C dominates D and $C_i \neq D_i$; otherwise D is **nondominated** w.r.t. D_i.*

It follows that if D is nondominated w.r.t. every D_i, then D must be nondominated as well. Similar to the theorem proposed by Garcia-Molina and Barbara for checking dominance of 1-coteries [17], the following can be used to check dominance of $(m, 1)$-coteries.

Lemma 5. *An $(m, 1)$-coterie $D = (D_1, \ldots, D_m)$ over P is dominated w.r.t. D_i if, and only if, there exists a set $H \subseteq P$ such that*

1. $\forall Q \in D_i, Q \nsubseteq H$.
2. $\forall Q \in D_j, j \neq i : Q \cap H \neq \emptyset$.

Proof: For the if-direction, there are two cases to consider. If there exists some $R \in D_i$ such that $H \subsetneq R$, then let D_i' be $D_i - \{S \in D_i \mid H \subseteq S\} \cup \{H\}$. It is easy to see that $D' = (D_1, \ldots, D_{i-1}, D_i', D_{i+1}, \ldots, D_m)$ is an $(m, 1)$-coterie and it dominates D. If there is no $R \in D_i$ such that $H \subsetneq R$, then let D_i' be $D_i \cup \{H\}$. Again, it is easy to see that $D' = (D_1, \ldots, D_{i-1}, D_i', D_{i+1}, \ldots, D_m)$ is an $(m, 1)$-coterie and it dominates D.

For the only-if direction, assume that $C = (C_1, \ldots, C_m)$ dominates D and $C_i \neq D_i$. There are two cases to consider. If $D_i \subsetneq C_i$, then let H be one of the elements in $C_i - D_i$. Then set H must satisfy conditions 1 and 2, or otherwise C would not be an $(m, 1)$-coterie. If $D_i - C_i \neq \emptyset$, then let $Q \in D_i - C_i$. Since C dominates D, there exists some $H \in C_i$ such that $H \subsetneq Q$. We claim that H satisfies both conditions 1 and 2. For condition 1, if the condition does not hold, then $Q' \subseteq H$ for some $Q' \in D_i$. But then we have $Q' \subseteq H \subsetneq Q$, contradicting the fact that $\mathcal{D}$ satisfies the minimality property. For condition 2, suppose otherwise that $Q' \cap H = \emptyset$ for some $Q' \in D_j$, $j \neq i$. Then since $\mathcal{C}$ dominates $\mathcal{D}$, there exists some $R \in C_j$ such that $R \subseteq Q'$. So $R \cap H = \emptyset$. Since $R \in C_j$ and $H \in C_i$, we have a contradiction that $\mathcal{C}$ does not satisfy the interaction property of $(m, 1)$-coteries.   □

Recall from Theorems 2, 3, and 4 that an affine plane $AP = (\mathcal{P}, \mathcal{L})$ of order x can be used to construct an $(m, 1, x)$-coterie over $\mathcal{P}$, for any $m \leq x+1$, by taking m classes of parallel lines from $\mathcal{L}$ as the m cartels of the coterie. All $(m, 1, x)$-coteries constructed in this way are identical subject to isomorphisms. As we do not need to distinguish isomorphic $(m, 1, x)$-coteries, we shall use $AP(x, m)$ to denote an $(m, 1, x)$-coterie of this form.

As also noted in Theorem 3, $AP(x, m)$ is balanced, uniform, and regular. The three properties are important to realize a truly distributed implementation of the $(m, 1, k)$-resource allocation problem. Unfortunately, $AP(x, m)$ is, in general, dominated.

Theorem 7. $AP(x, m)$ is dominated for all $x > 2$ and $m > 1$.

Proof. Let $AP(x, m) = (D_1, \ldots, D_m)$, and let P be the underlying x^2-element set. Without loss of generality, we show that $AP(x, m)$ is dominated w.r.t. D_1. By Lemma 5, it suffices to find a set $H \subseteq P$ such that

1. $\forall Q \in D_1, Q \nsubseteq H$.
2. $\forall Q \in D_j, j \neq 1 : Q \cap H \neq \emptyset$.

Let $D_i = \{Q_i^1, \ldots, Q_i^x\}$, $1 \leq i \leq m$. Note that D_i is a partition of P, and each block has size x. Let a_1 be an element in Q_1^1. By the incidence properties of affine planes, $Q_1^1 - \{a_1\}$ intersects all but one quorum in D_j for every $1 < j \leq m$. Without loss of generality, let Q_j^1, $1 < j \leq m$, be the quorum in D_j that does not intersect $Q_1^1 - \{a_1\}$. Again, by the incidence properties, $Q_j^1 \cap Q_1^h \neq \emptyset$ for all $h \leq x$. To construct H, there are two cases to consider. If $m \leq x$, then $H = Q_1^1 - \{a_1\} \cup \{a_2, \ldots, a_m\}$, where a_k is an arbitrary element in $Q_k^1 \cap Q_1^k$, $2 \leq k \leq m$. If $m = x + 1$, H additionally contains an element a_{x+1} such that $a_{x+1} \in Q_{x+1}^1 \cap Q_1^2$. Note that a_{x+1} may or may not be equal to a_2. So in either case ($m \leq x$ or $m = x + 1$), H contains $x - 1$ elements from Q_1^1, at most two elements from Q_1^2, and one element from each of $Q_1^3, \ldots, Q_1^{\min(m,x)}$. Since $x > 2$, $Q_1^2 \nsubseteq H$. Clearly, $Q_1^1, Q_1^3, Q_1^4, \ldots Q_1^x \nsubseteq H$. So H satisfies condition 1. It is also easy to see that H satisfies condition 2; the theorem is therefore proven.   □

Because $AP(x, m)$ has optimal degree for all $m > 1$, any $(m, 1)$-coterie that dominates $AP(x, m)$ must be of the same degree. So $AP(x, m)$ cannot be weakly nondominated, either. Theorem 7 excludes the case $x = 2$. For this case, $AP(2, 3)$ is nondominated. To see this, let $\mathcal{P} = \{1, 2, 3, 4\}$. Then $AP(2, 3) = (\{\{1, 2\}, \{3, 4\}\}, \{\{1, 3\}, \{2, 4\}\}, \{\{1, 4\}, \{2, 3\}\})$ (subject to isomorphisms). It is easy to verify that $AP(2, 3)$ is nondominated.

In [16] we presented another $(m, 1)$-coterie that is also balanced, uniform, and regular. The coterie minimizes processes' loads by letting each process be included in at most two quora. It has degree $\sqrt{\frac{2n}{m(m-1)}}$, and is also dominated. Except for some special cases, it remains open whether or not there exists a nondominated $(m, 1, k)$-coterie that is also balanced, uniform, and regular for any given k.

To cope with the apparently conflicting nature in between full distributedness and failure resilience, we observe that in real systems failures do not occur often. So distributedness and failure resilience need not be considered at the same time. Rather, we can focus on distributedness when failures do not occur, and turn into fault tolerance when failures do occur. In this case, we can design a quorum system such that some quora are used to facilitate a truly distributed implementation of the resource scheduling, while other quora are used to "back up" the system when failures occur. We will present the details in the full paper.

5 Concluding Remarks

We have studied quorum systems for $(m, 1, k)$-resource allocation, which corresponds to group mutual exclusion with and without bounded capacity (when $k = \infty$). The main benefit of our studies is that they reduced the design of distributed solutions for group resource allocation to combinatorial problems. Many interesting results in combinatorics can then be applied. For example, by using Maekawa's algorithm, the design of an $(m, 1, k)$-coterie provides an immediate solution to $(m, 1, k)$-resource allocation. To our knowledge, no solution for the problem has been proposed before. As we have also proved, no $(m, 1, k)$-coterie can be constructed out of an n-set if $k > \sqrt{n}$. For the corresponding $(m, 1, k)$-resource allocation problem involving n processes, the $(m, 1, \sqrt{n})$-coterie $AP(\sqrt{n}, m)$ constructed from an affine plane of order $\sqrt{n}$ in combination with a modification of Maekawa's algorithm, the Maekawa_M algorithm presented in [16], can be used. In this case, the algorithm has message complexity $O(n)$ and synchronization delay 2 message transmission time. For comparison, the message-passing solutions in [18–20] for group mutual exclusion all have message complexity $O(n)$, and synchronization delay 2 or $O(n)$ (if they use a ring architecture). Moreover, unlike quorum-based algorithms, none of them can tolerate a single process failure.

In light of the rich literature for quorum systems for mutual exclusion, l-exclusion, and replicated databases, there are many possible directions for future work, including constructions of other possible $(m, 1)$-coteries, availability analysis (cf., [21, 22]), and case studies/performance measurement.

Acknowledgments

I would like to thank Nancy Lynch for giving me a valuable opportunity to visit her TDS group in LCS at MIT, and to discuss this research with her, as well as with the other members of the TDS group, including Idit Keidar, Alex Shvartsman, and Victor Luchangco. I would also like to thank Yevgeniy Dodis, Adam D. Smith, Eric Lehman, Salil Vadhan, and Lenore J. Cowen of the TOC group for helpful discussion on the construction of $(m, 1)$-coteries, Dan J. Kleitman of the math department for pointing out related work in combinatorics, and Dahlia Malkhi of the Hebrew University of Jerusalem for providing several comments on the manuscript.

References

1. Fischer, M.J., Lynch, N.A., Burns, J.E., Borodin, A.: Resource allocation with immunity to limited process failure (preliminary report). In: 20th Annual Symposium on Foundations of Computer Science (1979) 234–254
2. Joung, Y.J.: Asynchronous group mutual exclusion. Distributed Computing **13** (2000) 189–206
3. Keane, P., Moir, M.: A simple local-spin group mutual exclusion algorithm. In: Proceedings of the 18th Annual ACM Symposium on Principles of Distributed Computing (PODC) (1999) 23–32
4. Hadzilacos, V.: A note on group mutual exclusion. In: Proceedings of the 20th Annual ACM Symposium on Principles of Distributed Computing (PODC) (2001)
5. Maekawa, M.: A $\sqrt{N}$ algorithm for mutual exclusion in decentralized systems. ACM Transactions on Computer Systems **3** (1985) 145–159
6. Barbara, D., Garcia-Molina, H.: Mutual exclusion in partitioned distributed systems. Distributed Computing **1** (1986) 119–132
7. Peleg, D., Wool, A.: Crumbling walls: A class of practical and efficient quorum systems. Distributed Computing **10** (1997) 87–97
8. Kakugawa, H., Fujita, S., Yamashita, M., Ae, T.: Availability of k-coterie. IEEE Transactions on Computers **42** (1993) 553–558
9. Kuo, Y.C., Huang, S.T.: A simple scheme to construct k-coteries with $O(\sqrt{N})$ uniform quorum sizes. Information Processing Letters **59** (1996) 31–36
10. Neilsen, M.L.: Properties of nondominated K-coteries. Journal of Systems and Software **37** (1997) 91–96
11. MacNeish, H.F.: Euler squares. The Annals of Mathematics **2nd series, 23** (1922) 221–227
12. Neilsen, M.L., Mizuno, M.: Coterie join algorithm. IEEE Transactions on Parallel and Distributed Systems **3** (1992) 582–590
13. Malkhi, D., Reiter, M.K., Wool, A.: The load and availability of Byzantine quorum systems. SIAM Journal on Computing **29** (2000) 1889–1906
14. Pedoe, D.: An Introduction to Projective geometry (1963)
15. Hardy, G.H., Wright, E.M.: An introduction to the theory of numbers (1965)
16. Joung, Y.J.: Quorum-based algorithms for group mutual exclusion. IEEE Transactions on Parallel and Distributed Systems **14** (2003) 463–476
17. Garcia-Molina, H., Barbara, D.: How to assign votes in a distributed system. Journal of the ACM **32** (1985) 841–860
18. Joung, Y.J.: The congenial talking philosophers problem in computer networks (extended abstract). In: Proceedings of the 13th International Symposium on DIStributed Computing (DISC99). LNCS 1693, Springer (1999) 195–209
19. Wu, K.P., Joung, Y.J.: Asynchronous group mutual exclusion in ring networks. IEE Proceedings–Computers and Digital Techniques **147** (2000) 1–8
20. Cantarell, S., Datta, A.K., Petit, F., Villain, V.: Token based group mutual exclusion for asynchronous rings. In: Proceedings of the 21st International Conference on Distributed Computing Systems (ICDCS) (2001) 691–694
21. Peleg, D., Wool, A.: The availability of quorum systems. Information and Computation **123** (1995) 210–223
22. Naor, M., Wool, A.: The load, capacity, and availability of quorum systems. SIAM Journal on Computing **27** (1998) 423–447

Bounded Version Vectors

José Bacelar Almeida*, Paulo Sérgio Almeida, and Carlos Baquero**

Departamento de Informática, Universidade do Minho
{jba,psa,cbm}@di.uminho.pt

Abstract. Version vectors play a central role in update tracking under optimistic distributed systems, allowing the detection of obsolete or inconsistent versions of replicated data. Version vectors do not have a bounded representation; they are based on integer counters that grow indefinitely as updates occur. Existing approaches to this problem are scarce; the mechanisms proposed are either unbounded or operate only under specific settings. This paper examines version vectors as a mechanism for data causality tracking and clarifies their role with respect to vector clocks. Then, it introduces bounded stamps and proves them to be a correct alternative to integer counters in version vectors. The resulting mechanism, bounded version vectors, represents the first bounded solution to data causality tracking between replicas subject to local updates and pairwise symmetrical synchronization.

1 Introduction

Optimistic replication is a critical technology in distributed systems, in particular when improving availability of database systems and adding support to mobility and partitioned operation [18]. Under optimistic replication, data replicas can evolve autonomously by incorporation new updates into their state. Thus, when contact can be established between two or more replicas, mutual consistency must be evaluated and potential divergence detected.

The classic mechanism for assessing divergence between mutable replicas is provided by *version vectors* which, since their introduction by Parker et al. [14], have been one of the cornerstones of optimistic data management. Version vectors associate to each replica a vector of integer counters that keeps track of the last update that is known to have been originated in every other replica and in the replica itself. The mechanism is simple and intuitive but requires a state of unbounded size, since each counter in the vector can grow indefinitely.

The potential existence of a bounded substitute to version vectors has been overlooked by the community. A possible cause is a frequent confusion of the roles played by *version vectors* and *vector clocks* (e.g. [17, 18]), that have the same representation [14, 5, 13], together with the existence of a minimality result by Charron-Bost [4], stating that vector clocks are the most concise characterization of causality among process events.

---

* Partially supported by FCT project POSI/ICHS/44304/2002.
** Supported in part by FCT under grant BSAB/390/2003.

R. Guerraoui (Ed.): DISC 2004, LNCS 3274, pp. 102–116, 2004.

Operation Init():
$$(V_i^k)' = 0.$$
Operation Upd(a):
$$(V_i^k)' = \begin{cases} V_i^k + 1 & \text{if } i = k = a; \\ V_i^k & \text{otherwise.} \end{cases}$$
Operation Sync(a, b):
$$(V_a^k)' = (V_b^k)' = V_a^k \sqcup V_b^k.$$

Fig. 1. Semantics of version vector operations.

In this article we show that a bounded solution is possible for the problem addressed by version vectors: the detection of mutual inconsistency between replicas subject to local updates and pairwise symmetrical synchronization. We present a mechanism, *bounded stamps*, that can be used to replace integer counters in version vectors, stressing that the minimality result that precludes bounded vector clocks does not apply to version vectors. Due to space limitations, proofs of Lemmas 1 and 3 are omitted. See [1] for full details.

2   Data Causality

Data causality on a set of replicas can be assessed via set inclusion of the sets of update events known to each replica. Data causality is the pre-order defined by:

$$r_a \leq r_b \quad \text{iff} \quad U_a \subseteq U_b \ ,$$

being U_a and U_b the sets of update events (globally unique events) known to replicas r_a and r_b.

When tracking data causality with version vectors in an N replica system, one associates to each replica $r_i \in \{r_0, \ldots, r_{N-1}\}$ a vector V_i of N integer counters. The order on version vectors is the standard pointwise (coordinatewise) order:

$$V_a \leq_V V_b \quad \text{iff} \quad \forall k. V_a^k \leq V_b^k \ ,$$

where V_i^k denotes component k of vector V_i.

The operations on version vectors, formally presented in Fig. 1, are as follows:

Initialization (Init()) establishes the initial system state. All vectors are initialized with zeroes.

Update (Upd(a)) an update event in replica r_a increments V_a^a.

Synchronization (Sync(a, b)) synchronization of r_a and r_b is achieved by taking the pointwise join (greatest element) of V_a and V_b.

This classic mechanism encodes data causality because comparing version vectors gives the same result as comparing sets of known update events. For all runs and replicas r_a and r_b:

$$r_a \leq r_b \quad \text{iff} \quad U_a \subseteq U_b \quad \text{iff} \quad V_a \leq_V V_b \ .$$

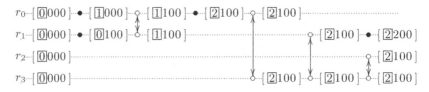

Fig. 2. Version Vectors: example run, depicting slice 0 counters by a boxed digit.

Figure 2 shows a run with version vectors in a four replica system. Updates are depicted by a "•" and synchronization by two "○" connected by a line.

2.1   Version Vector Slices

All operations over version vectors exhibit a pointwise nature: a given vector position is only compared or updated to the same position in other vectors, resulting from all information about updates originated in replica r_k being stored in component k of each version vector. This allows a decomposition of the replicated system into N *slices*, where each slice represents the updates that were originated in a given replica. Slice i for an N replica system is made up of the ith component of each version vector:

$$\langle V_0^i, \ldots, V_{N-1}^i \rangle \ .$$

This means that data causality in N replicas can be encoded by the concatenation of the representation for each of the N slices. It also means that it is enough to concentrate on a subproblem: encoding the distributed knowledge about a single source of updates, and the corresponding version vector slice (VVS). The source of updates increments its counter and all other replicas keep potentially outdated copies of that counter; this subproblem amounts to storing a distributed representation of a total order.

For the remainder of the paper we will concentrate, for notational convenience and without loss of generality, on finding a bounded representation for slice 0. In the run presented in Fig. 2 this slice is shown using boxed counters.

2.2   On Version Vectors and Vector Clocks

Asynchronous distributed systems track causality and logical time among communicating processes by means of several mechanisms [12, 19], in particular vector clocks [5, 13]. While structurally equivalent to version vectors, vector clocks serve a distinct purpose. Vector clocks track causality by establishing a strict partial order on the events of processes that communicate by message passing, and are known to be the most concise solution to this problem [4]. Vector clocks, being a vector of integer counters, are unbounded in size, but so is the number of events that must be ordered and timestamped by them. In short, *vector clocks order an unlimited number of events occurring in a given number of processes.*

If we consider the role of version vectors, data causality, there is always a limit to the number of possible relations that can be established on the set of replicas. This limit is independent on the number of update events that are considered on any given run. For example, in a two replica system $\{r_a, r_b\}$ only four cases can occur: $r_a = r_b$, $r_a < r_b$, $r_b > r_a$ and $r_a \parallel r_b$. If the two replicas are already divergent the inclusion of *new* update events on any of the replicas does not change their mutual divergence and the corresponding relation between them. In short, *version vectors order a given number of replicas, according to an unlimited number of update events.*

The existence of a limited number of relations is a necessary but not sufficient condition for the existence of a bounded characterization mechanism. A relation, which is a global abstraction, must be encoded and computed through local operations on replica pairs without the need for a global view. This is one of the important properties of version vectors.

3 Informal Presentation

We now give an informal presentation of the mechanism and give some intuition of how it works and how it accomplishes its purpose. Having shown that it is enough to concentrate on a subproblem (a single source of updates) and the corresponding slice of version vectors, we now present the stamp that will replace, in each replica, the integer counter of the corresponding version vector.

For problem size N, i.e. assuming N replicas, with r_0 the "primary" where updates take place and $r_1, \ldots, r_{N-1}$ the "secondary" replicas, we represent a stamp by something like

It has a representation of bounded size, as it consists of N rows, each with at most N symbols (letters here), taken from a finite set $\mathcal{L}_N$. An example run consisting of four replicas is presented in Fig. 3.

A stamp is, in abstract, a vector of totally ordered sets. Each of the N components (rows in our notation) represents a total order, with the greatest element on the left (the first row above means $c > b > a$). In a stamp for replica r_i, row i ($i \in \{0, \ldots N-1\}$) is what we call the *principal order* (displayed with a gray background), while the other rows are the *cached orders*. (Thus, the stamp above would belong to replica r_3.) The cached order in row j represents the principal order of replica j at some point in time, propagated to replica i (either directly or indirectly through several synchronizations).

The greatest element of the principal order (on the left, depicted in bold over gray) is what we call the *principal element*. It represents the most recent update (in the primary) known by the replica. In a representation using an infinite total ordered set instead of $\mathcal{L}_N$ nothing more would be needed. This element can be thought of as "corresponding" to the value of the integer counter in version vectors. The left column in a stamp (depicted in bold) is what we

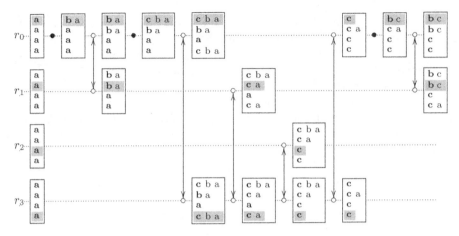

Fig. 3. Bounded stamps: example run.

call the *principal vector*; it is made up of the greatest element of each order (row). It represents the most recent local knowledge about the principal element of each replica (including itself). In a stamp, there is a relationship between the principal order and the principal vector: the elements in the principal vector are the same ones as in the principal order. In other words, the set of elements in the principal vector is ordered according to the principal order.

3.1   Comparison and Synchronization as Well Defined Local Operations

As we will show below, the mechanism is able to compare two stamps by a local operation on the respective principal orders. No global knowledge is used: not even a global order on the set of symbols $\mathcal{L}_N$ is assumed. For comparison purposes $\mathcal{L}_N$ is simply an unordered set, with elements that are ordered differently in different stamps. As an example, the comparison of

$$r_0 = \begin{array}{|c|} \hline \text{b c} \\ \text{c a} \\ \text{c} \\ \text{c} \\ \hline \end{array} \quad \text{with} \quad r_1 = \begin{array}{|c|} \hline \text{c b a} \\ \text{c a} \\ \text{a} \\ \text{c a} \\ \hline \end{array}$$

involves looking at `b c` and `c a`, and gives $r_0 > r_1$.

When synchronizing two stamps, in the positions of the two principal elements, the resulting value will be the maximum of the two principal elements; the rest of the resulting principal vector will be the pointwise maximum of the respective values. The comparisons are performed according to the principal orders of the two stamps involved.

It is important to notice that, in general, it is not possible to take two arbitrary total orders and merge them into a new total order. As such, it could be thought that computing the maximum as mentioned above is ill defined. As we will show, several properties of the model can be exploited that make these operations possible and well defined. We will also show that it is possible to totally order the elements in the resulting principal vector, i.e. to obtain a new principal order.

The update of cached-orders is trivial: if the element in the principal vector is updated to a new value, the whole cached order is updated to the corresponding one in the other replica; otherwise is remains as before.

3.2   Garbage Collection for Symbol Reuse

The boundedness of the mechanism is only possible through symbol reuse. When an update operation is performed, instead of incrementing an integer counter, some symbol is chosen to become the new principal element. By using a finite set of symbols $\mathcal{L}_N$, an update will eventually reuse a symbol that was already used in the past to represent some previous update that has been synchronized with other replicas.

However, by reusing symbols, an obvious problem arises that needs to be addressed: the symbol reuse cannot compromise the well-definedness of the comparison operations described above. As an example, it would not be acceptable that, due to reuse, the principal orders of two stamps end up being $\boxed{a\,b\,c}$ and $\boxed{c\,a}$, as it would not be possible to overcome the ambiguity between $a > b > c$ and $c > a$ and to infer which one is the greatest stamp.

To address the problem, the mechanism implements a distributed "garbage collection" of symbols. This is accomplished through the extra information in the cached orders. As we will show, any element in the principal order/vector of any replica is also present in the primary replica (in some principal or cached order). This is the key property towards symbol reuse: when an update is performed, any symbol which is not present in the primary replica is considered "garbage" and can be (re)used for the new principal element.

As an example, in Fig. 3, when the final update occurs, symbol b can be used for the new principal element because it is not present in the primary replica. Notice that the scheme only assures that b does not occur in the principal orders/vectors. In this example b occurs in some cached orders of replicas r_1 and r_2, but this is not a problem because those elements will not be used in comparisons; the "old" b will not be confused with the "new" b.

3.3   Synopsis of Formal Presentation

The formal presentation and proof of correctness will make use of an unbounded mechanism which we call the *counter mode principal vectors* (CMPV). This auxiliary mechanism represents what the evolution of the principal vector would be if we could afford to use integer counters. The mechanism makes use of the total order on natural numbers and does not encode orders locally. In Fig. 4 we present part of the run in Fig. 3 using the counter mode mechanism.

The bulk of the proof consists in establishing several properties of the CMPV model that allow the relevant comparison operations to be computed in a well-defined way using only local information. The key idea is that, exploiting these

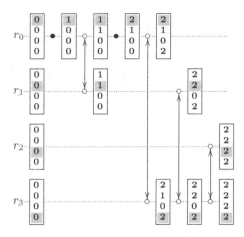

Fig. 4. Counter mode principal vectors.

properties, bounded stamps can be seen as an encoding of CMPV using a finite set $\mathcal{L}_N$, where the principal orders are used to encode the relevant order information.

4   Counter Mode Principal Vectors

Version Vector Slices (VVS) rely on an unbounded totally ordered set – the natural numbers. Their unbounded nature is actually a consequence of adopting a predetermined order relation (and hence globally known) to capture data causality among replicas. To overcome this, we enrich VVS in a way that order judgments become, in a sense, local to each replica. In this way, it will be possible to dynamically encode the causality order and open the perspective of bounding the "counters" domain.

For a replica index a, its stamp in the CMPV model is denoted by C_a and defined as the tuple $\langle a, a \rangle$ where a is a vector of integers with size N – the *principal vector* for C_a (see Fig. 4). The value in position k of vector a is denoted by a^k and represents the knowledge of stamp C_a concerning the most recent update known by stamp C_k. The element a^a plays a central role since it holds C_a's view about the more recent update – this is essentially the information contained in VVS counters and we call it the *principal element* for stamp C_a.

Figure 5 defines the semantics of the operations in the CMPV model.[1] Symbol $\sqcup$ denotes the join operation under integer ordering (i.e. taking the maximum element). Notice that the order information is only required to perform the synchronization operation. Moreover, comparisons are always between principal elements or pointwise (between the same position in two principal vectors).

---

[1] Recall that the problem under consideration is restricted to slice 0. In particular, this implies that one considers only update events for replica 0.

Operation Init():

$$(a^k)' = 0.$$

Operation Upd(0):

$$(a^k)' = \begin{cases} a^k + 1 & \text{if } a = k = 0; \\ a^k & \text{otherwise.} \end{cases}$$

Operation Sync(a, b):

$$(a^k)' = (b^k)' = \begin{cases} a^a \sqcup b^b & \text{if } k \in \{a, b\}; \\ a^k \sqcup b^k & \text{otherwise.} \end{cases}$$

Fig. 5. Semantics of operations in CMPV.

Occasionally, it will be convenient to write $a \sqcup b$ for the result of the synchronization on stamps C_a and C_b (i.e. the principal vector of one of these stamps after synchronization).

A *trace* consists of a sequence of operations starting with Init() and followed by an arbitrary number of updates and synchronizations. In the remainder, when stating properties in the CMPV, we will leave implicit that they only refer to reachable states, i.e. states that result from some trace of operations. Induction over the traces is the fundamental tool to prove invariance properties, as the following simple facts about CMPV.

Proposition 1. *For every stamp C_a, C_b and index k,*

1. $a^b \leq b^b$,
2. $a^a \leq 0^0$,
3. $a^k \leq a^a$.

Proof. Simple induction on the length of traces.   □

Given stamps C_a and C_b we define their *data causality order under CMPV* ($\leq_C$) as the comparison of their principal elements:

$$C_a \leq_C C_b \quad \text{iff} \quad a^a \leq b^b .$$

By Fig. 5 it can be seen that the computation of principal elements only depends upon principal elements. Moreover, if we restrict the impact of the operations to the principal element we recover the VVS semantics. This observation leads immediately to the correctness of CMPV as a data causality encoding for slice 0:

$$C_a \leq_C C_b \quad \text{iff} \quad V_a^0 \leq_V V_b^0 .$$

This result is not surprising since CMPV was defined as a semantics preserving extension of VVS.

Next we will show that the additional information contained in the CMPV model makes it possible to avoid relying on the integer order, and to replace it with a locally encoded order. For this, we will use a non-trivial invariant on the global state given by the following lemma.

Lemma 1. *For every stamp* C_a *and* C_b *and index* k,

$$a^a \leq b^b \quad and \quad b^k \leq a^k \quad implies \quad a^k \in b .$$

Recall that the order information is only required to perform the synchronization operation. Moreover, comparisons are always between principal elements or pointwise (between the same position in two principal vectors). In the following we will show that these comparisons can be performed without relying on integer order as long as we can order the elements in the principal vector of each stamp individually.

Comparison between principal elements reduces to a membership testing.

Proposition 2. *For every stamp* C_a, C_b,

$$a^a \leq b^b \quad iff \quad a^a \in b .$$

Proof. $\Longrightarrow$ If $a^a \leq b^b$ then, by Proposition 1(1) we have that $b^a \leq a^a$ and so, by Lemma 1, $a^a \in b$.

$\Longleftarrow$ If $a^a \in b$ then, by Proposition 1(3) we have that $a^a \leq b^b$.   □

For a stamp C_a, let us denote by $\leq^a$ the restriction of the intrinsic integer order to the values contained in the principal vector a:

$$x \leq^a y \quad iff \quad x \leq y \text{ and } x \in a \text{ and } y \in a .$$

Using these orderings, we define new ones that are appropriate to perform the required comparisons. For stamps C_a and C_b, let their combined order $\leq^{ab}$ be defined as:

$$x \leq^{ab} y \quad iff \quad (b^b \in a \text{ and } (x \in a \Rightarrow x \leq^a y)) \text{ or}$$
$$(a^a \in b \text{ and } (x \in b \Rightarrow x \leq^b y)) .$$

For convenience, we also define the corresponding join operation $\underset{ab}{\sqcup}$ as:

$$x \underset{ab}{\sqcup} y = \begin{cases} y & \text{if } x \leq^{ab} y, \\ x & \text{otherwise.} \end{cases}$$

The following proposition establishes the claimed properties for this ordering.

Proposition 3. *For every stamp* C_a *and* C_b *and index* k,

1. $a^a \leq b^b \quad iff \quad a^a \leq^{ab} b^b$,
2. $a^k \leq b^k \quad iff \quad a^k \leq^{ab} b^k$.

Proof. (1) Follows directly from Propositions 1 and 2.

(2) $\Longrightarrow$ Let $a^k \leq b^k$. When $b^b \leq a^a$ Proposition 2 guarantees that $b^b \in a$ and, by Lemma 1, we have $b^k \in a$ and then $a^k \leq^a b^k$, which establishes $a^k \leq^{ab} b^k$. The case $a^a < b^b$ is trivial since, either $a^k \in b$ (in which case $a^k \leq^b b^k$), or $a^k \notin b$ and so $a^k \leq^{ab} b^k$. $\Longleftarrow$ Let $a^k \not\leq b^k$ (that is, $b^k < a^k$). The proof proceeds as in the previous implication.   □

Restricted orders can be explicitly encoded (e.g. by a sequence) and can be easily manipulated. We now show that when a synchronization is performed, all the elements in the resulting principal vector were already present in the more up-to-date stamp. This means that the restricted order that results is a restriction of the one from the more up-to-date stamp.

Proposition 4. *Let* C_a *and* C_b *be stamps and* $C_x = C_a \sqcup C_b$. *If* $a^a \leq b^b$ *then, for all* k,

$$x^k \in b \ .$$

Proof. For the pointwise join $x^k = a^k \sqcup b^k$: if $a^k \leq b^k$ then $x^k = b^k \in b$; if $b^k \leq a^k$ then, by Lemma 1, $a^k \in b$. Otherwise, note that the resulting principal element (b^b) is already in b.   □

These observations together with the fact that the global state can only retain a bounded amount of integer values (an obvious limit is N^2) opens the way for a change in the domain from the integers in the CMPV model to a finite set.

5   Bounded Stamps

A migration from the domain of integer counters in CMPV to a finite set $\mathcal{L}_N$ is faced with the following difficulty: the update operation should be able to choose a value, that is not present in any principal vector, for the new principal element in the primary.

Adopting a set $\mathcal{L}_N$ sufficiently large (e.g. with N^2 elements) guarantees that such a choice exists under a global view. The problem lies in making that choice using only the information in the state of the primary. To overcome this problem we make a new extension of the model that allows the primary to keep track of all the values in use in the principal vectors of all stamps.

We will present this new model parameterized by a set $\mathcal{L}_N$ (the symbol domain), a distinguished element $\mathbf{0} \in \mathcal{L}_N$ (the initial element), and an oracle for new symbols $new(-)$ (satisfying an axiom described below). For each replica index a, its local state in the bounded stamps model is denoted by B_a and defined as $\langle a, \underline{a}, \overline{a} \rangle$ where:

- a is the replica index;
- $\underline{a}$ is a vector of values from $\mathcal{L}_N$ with size N – the principal vector;
- $\overline{a}$ is a vector of N total orders, encoded as sequences, representing the full bounded stamp.

This last component contains all the information in the principal vector, the principal order and the cached orders. Although the principle vector $\underline{a}$ is redundant (as each component $\underline{a}^k$ is also present in the first position of each $\overline{a}^k$), it is kept in the model for notational convenience in describing the operations and in establishing the correspondence between the models.

The intuitive idea is that the state for each stamp keeps an explicit representation of the restricted orders. More precisely, for stamp B_a, the sequence

Operation Init():
$$(\underline{a}^k)' = \mathbf{0},$$
$$(\boxed{a}^k)' = \langle \mathbf{0} \rangle.$$

Operation Upd(0):
$$(\underline{0}^0)' = \text{new}(\boxed{0}),$$
$$(\boxed{0}^0)' = \text{new}(\boxed{0}) \cdot \boxed{0}^0_{|(\underline{0})'}.$$

Operation Sync(a, b):
$$(\underline{a}^k)' = (\underline{b}^k)' = \begin{cases} \underline{a}^a \underset{ab}{\sqcup} \underline{b}^b & \text{if } k \in \{a, b\}, \\ \underline{a}^k \underset{ab}{\sqcup} \underline{b}^k & \text{otherwise,} \end{cases}$$

if $k \in \{a, b\}$:
$$(\boxed{a}^k)' = (\boxed{b}^k)' = \begin{cases} \boxed{b}^b_{|(\underline{b})'} & \text{if } \underline{a}^a \in \underline{b}, \\ \boxed{a}^a_{|(\underline{a})'} & \text{otherwise,} \end{cases}$$

if $k \neq a$ and $k \neq b$:
$$(\boxed{a}^k)' = \begin{cases} \boxed{b}^k & \text{if } (\underline{a}^k)' \neq \underline{a}^k, \\ \boxed{a}^k & \text{otherwise,} \end{cases}$$
$$(\boxed{b}^k)' = \begin{cases} \boxed{a}^k & \text{if } (\underline{b}^k)' \neq \underline{b}^k, \\ \boxed{b}^k & \text{otherwise.} \end{cases}$$

Fig. 6. Semantics of operations on BS model.

$\boxed{a}^a$ contains precisely the elements of $\underline{a}$ ordered downward (first element is $\underline{a}^a$). From that sequence one easily defines the restricted order for stamp B_a, what we call *principal order* to emphasize its explicit nature.

$$x \leq_{\mathsf{B}}^a y \quad \text{iff} \quad x = y \quad \text{or} \quad \langle y, x \rangle = \boxed{a}^a_{|\{x,y\}} \ ,$$

where $l_{|m}$ denotes the sequence l restricted to the elements in m, i.e. $\langle x \mid x \in l$ and $x \in m \rangle$. The combined order $\leq^{ab}$ and associated join are defined precisely as in counter mode, that is

$$x \leq^{ab} y \quad \text{iff} \quad \begin{aligned} &(\underline{b}^b \in \underline{a} \wedge (x \in \underline{a} \Rightarrow x \leq_{\mathsf{B}}^a y)) \quad \text{or} \\ &(\underline{a}^a \in \underline{b} \wedge (x \in \underline{b} \Rightarrow x \leq_{\mathsf{B}}^b y)) \ . \end{aligned}$$

The other sequences in $\boxed{a}$ keep information about (potentially outdated) principal orders of other stamps – these are called the *cached orders*.

Figure 6 gives the semantics for the operations in this model. The oracle for new symbols new($-$) is a function that gives an element of $\mathcal{L}_N$ satisfying the following axiom:

$$\text{For every stamp } \mathsf{B}_a, \qquad \text{new}(\boxed{0}) \notin \underline{a} \ .$$

The argument $\boxed{0}$ in the oracle new($-$) intends to emphasize that the choice of the new symbol should be made based on the primary local state.

Data causality ordering under the Bounded Stamps model is defined by

$$B_a \leq_B B_b \quad \text{iff} \quad \underline{a}^a \in \underline{b} \ .$$

The correctness of the proposed model follows from the observation that, apart from the cached orders used for the symbol reuse mechanism, it is actually an encoding of the CMPV model. To formalize the correspondence between both models, we introduce an encoding function $[\![-]\!]_-$ that maps each integer in the CMPV model into the corresponding symbol (in $\mathcal{L}_N$) in the state resulting from a given trace. This map is defined recursively on the traces.

$$
\begin{aligned}
[\![n]\!]_{\text{Init}()} &= \mathbf{0}, \\
[\![n]\!]_{\alpha \cdot \text{Upd}(0)} &= \begin{cases} \text{new}(\boxed{0}_\alpha) & \text{if } n = \left| \alpha_{|\text{Upd}(0)} \right| + 1, \\ [\![n]\!]_\alpha & \text{otherwise,} \end{cases} \\
[\![n]\!]_{\alpha \cdot \text{Sync}(x,y)} &= [\![n]\!]_\alpha.
\end{aligned}
$$

Where $\left| \alpha_{|\text{Upd}(0)} \right|$ is the number of update events in α, $\boxed{0}_\alpha$ is the bounded stamp for the primary after trace α, and $\text{new}(\boxed{0}_\alpha)$ gives a canonical choice for the new principal element on the primary after the update. When we discard the cached orders, the semantics of operations given in Fig. 6 are precisely the ones in CMPV (Figure 5) affected by the encoding map. Moreover, the principal orders are encodings for the restricted orders presented in the previous section.

Lemma 2. *For an arbitrary trace α, replicas index a and b:*

1. *$\underline{a}^k = [\![\mathsf{a}^k]\!]_\alpha$,*
2. *$[\![\mathsf{a}^i]\!]_\alpha = [\![\mathsf{a}^j]\!]_\alpha$ implies $\mathsf{a}^i = \mathsf{a}^j$,*
3. *$x \leq^a y$ iff $[\![x]\!]_\alpha \leq_B^a [\![y]\!]_\alpha$.*

Proof. This results from a simple induction on the length of traces. When the last operation was Init() it is trivial. When it was Upd(0), the result follows from the induction hypothesis and the axiom for the oracle new($-$). When it was Sync(x, y) the result follows from induction hypothesis, the fact that definitions on both models coincide since $\leq^{ab}$ computes the required joins (Proposition 3), and the correctness of the new restricted orders (Proposition 4).   □

As a simple consequence of the previous result, we can state the following correctness result.

Proposition 5. *For any arbitrary trace α and replica indexes a and b we have*

$$B_a \leq_B B_b \quad \text{iff} \quad C_a \leq_C C_b \ .$$

Proof. Immediate from Lemma 2 and the definitions of $\leq_B$ and $\leq_C$.   □

It remains to instantiate the parameters of the model. A trivial but unbounded instantiation would be: set $\mathcal{L}_N$ as the integers, $\mathbf{0}$ as value 0 and new($\boxed{0}$) $= \underline{0}^0 + 1$. In this setting, principal orders would be an explicit representation of counter mode restricted orders. Obviously, we are interested in bounded instantiations of $\mathcal{L}_N$. To show that such instantiations exists, we introduce the following lemma that puts in evidence the role of cached orders.

Lemma 3. *For every stamp* B_a *there exists an* i *such that*

$$\boxed{a}^a \subseteq \boxed{0}^i \ .$$

We are now able to present a bounded instantiation for the model. Let $\mathcal{L}_N$ be a totally ordered set with N^2 elements (we have observed by model-checking that not all N^2 elements are needed, but this is enough for our purpose of proving boundedness; the total order is here only to avoid making non-deterministic choices). We define:

$$\mathbf{0} = \sqcap \mathcal{L}_N,$$
$$\mathrm{new}(\boxed{a}) = \sqcap\{x \mid x \in \mathcal{L}_N \ \text{and} \ x \notin \boxed{a}\}.$$

Lemma 3 guarantees that new($\boxed{0}$) satisfies the axiom. It follows then that it acts as an encoding of counter mode model (Proposition 5). Thus we have constructed a bounded model for the data causality problem in a slice, which generalizes, by concatenating slices, to the full data causality problem addressed by version vectors.

6   Related Work

On what concerns bounded replacements for version vectors there is, up to our knowledge, no previous solution to the problem. The possible existence of a bounded substitute to version vectors was referred in [2] while introducing the version stamps concept. Version stamps allow the characterization of data causality in settings where version vectors cannot operate, namely when replicas can be created and terminated autonomously.

There have been several approaches to version vector compression. Update coalescing [15] takes advantage of the fact that several consecutive updates issued in isolation in a single replica can be made equivalent to a single large update. Update coalescing is intrinsic in bounded stamps since sequence restriction in the update operation discards non-propagated symbols. Dynamic compression [15] can effectively reduce the size of version vectors by removing a common minimum from all entries (along each slice). However, this technique requires distributed consensus on all replicas and therefore cannot progress if one or more replicas are unreachable. Unilateral version vector pruning [17] avoids distributed consensus by allowing unilateral deletion of inactive version vectors entries, but relies on some timing assumptions on the physical-clock's skew.

Lightweight version vectors [9] develop an integer encoding technique that allows a gradual increase of integer storage as counters increase. This technique is used in conjunction with update coalescing to provide a dynamic size representation. Hash histories [10] track data causality by collecting hash fingerprints of contents. This representation is independent of the number of replicas but grows in proportion to the number of updates.

The minimality of vectors clocks as a characterization of Lamport causality [12], presented by Charron-Bost [4] and recently re-addressed in [7], indicates particular runs where the full expressiveness of vectors clocks is required.

However there are cases in which smaller representations can operate: Plausible Clocks [20] offer a bounded substitute to vectors clocks that are accurate in a large percentage of situations and may be used in settings were deviations only impacts performance and not correctness; Resettable Vector Clocks [3] allow a bounded implementation of vector clocks under a specific communication pattern between processes.

The collection of cached copies of the knowledge in other replicas has been explored before in [6, 21] and used for optimization of message passing strategies. This concept is sometimes referred to as matrix clocks [16]. These clocks are based on integer counters and are similar to our intermediate "counter mode principal vector" representation.

7   Conclusions

Version vectors are the key mechanism in the detection of inconsistency and obsolescence among optimistically replicated data. This mechanism has been used extensively in the design of distributed file systems [11, 8], in particular for data causality tracking among file copies. It is well known that version vectors are unbounded due to their use of counters; some approaches in the literature have tried to address this problem.

We have brought the attention to the fact that causally ordering a limited number of replicas does not require the full expressive power of version vectors. Due to the limited number of configurations among replicas, data causality tracking does not necessarily imply the use of unbounded mechanisms. As a consequence, Charron-Bost's minimality of vector clocks cannot be transposed to version vectors. The key to bounded stamps was defining an intermediate unbounded mechanism and showing that it was possible to perform comparisons without requiring a global total order. Bounded stamps were then derived as an encoding into a finite set of symbols. This required the definition of a non-trivial symbol reuse mechanism that is able to progress even if an arbitrary number of replicas ceases to participate in the exchanges. This mechanism may have a broader applicability beyond its current use (e.g. log dissemination and pruning) and become a building block in other mechanisms for distributed systems.

Bounded version vectors are obtained by substituting integer counters on version vectors by bounded stamps. It represents the first bounded mechanism for detection of obsolescence and mutual inconsistency in distributed systems.

References

1. José Bacelar Almeida, Paulo Sérgio Almeida, and Carlos Baquero. Bounded version vectors. Technical Report UMDITR2004.01, Departamento de Informática, Universidade do Minho, July 2004.
2. Paulo Sérgio Almeida, Carlos Baquero, and Victor Fonte. Version stamps – decentralized version vectors. In *Proceedings of the 22nd International Conference on Distributed Computing Systems (ICDCS)*, pages 544–551. IEEE Computer Society, 2002.

3. A. Arora, S. S .Kulkarni, and M. Demirbas. Resettable vector clocks. In *19th Symposium on Principles of Distributed Computing (PODC'2000), Portland, 2000.* ACM, 2000.
4. Bernadette Charron-Bost. Concerning the size of logical clocks in distributed systems. *Information Processing Letters,* 39:11–16, 1991.
5. Colin Fidge. Timestamps in message-passing systems that preserve the partial ordering. In *11th Australian Computer Science Conference,* pages 55–66, 1989.
6. Michael J. Fischer and A. Michael. Sacrificing serializability to attain high availability of data. In *Proceedings of the ACM Symposium on Principles of Database Systems,* pages 70–75. ACM, 1982.
7. V. K. Garg and C. Skawratananond. String realizers of posets with applications to distributed computing. In *Proceedings of the ACM Symposium on Principles of Distributed Computing (PODC'01),* pages 72–80. ACM, 2001.
8. Richard G. Guy, John S. Heidemann, Wai Mak, Thomas W. Page, Gerald J. Popek, and Dieter Rothmeier. Implementation of the ficus replicated file system. In *USENIX Conference Proceedings,* pages 63–71. USENIX, June 1990.
9. Yun-Wu Huang and Philip Yu. Lightweight version vectors for pervasive computing devices. In *Proceedings of the 2000 International Workshops on Parallel Processing,* pages 43–48. IEEE Computer Society, 2000.
10. Brent ByungHoon Kang, Robert Wilensky, and John Kubiatowicz. The hash history approach for reconciling mutual inconsistency. In *Proceedings of the 23nd International Conference on Distributed Computing Systems (ICDCS),* pages 670–677. IEEE Computer Society, 2003.
11. James Kistler and M. Satyanarayanan. Disconnected operation in the coda file system. *ACM Transaction on Computer Systems,* 10(1):3–25, February 1992.
12. Leslie Lamport. Time, clocks and the ordering of events in a distributed system. *Communications of the ACM,* 21(7):558–565, July 1978.
13. Friedemann Mattern. Virtual time and global clocks in distributed systems. In *Workshop on Parallel and Distributed Algorithms,* pages 215–226, 1989.
14. D. Stott Parker, Gerald Popek, Gerard Rudisin, Allen Stoughton, Bruce Walker, Evelyn Walton, Johanna Chow, David Edwards, Stephen Kiser, and Charles Kline. Detection of mutual inconsistency in distributed systems. *Transactions on Software Engineering,* 9(3):240–246, 1983.
15. David Howard Ratner. *Roam: A Scalable Replication System for Mobile and Distributed Computing.* PhD thesis, 1998. UCLA-CSD-970044.
16. Frédéric Ruget. Cheaper matrix clocks. In *Proceedings of the 8th International Workshop on Distributed Algorithms,* pages 355–369. Springer Verlag, LNCS, 1994.
17. Yasushi Saito. Unilateral version vector pruning using loosely synchronized clocks. Technical Report HPL-2002-51, HP Labs, 2002.
18. Yasushi Saito and Marc Shapiro. Optimistic replication. Technical Report MSR-TR-2003-60, Microsoft Research, 2003.
19. R. Schwarz and F. Mattern. Detecting causal relationships in distributed computations: In search of the holy grail. *Distributed Computing,* 3(7):149–174, 1994.
20. F. J. Torres-Rojas and M. Ahamad. Plausible clocks: constant size logical clocks for distributed systems. *Distributed Computing,* 12(4):179–196, 1999.
21. G. T. J. Wuu and A. J. Bernstein. Efficient solutions to the replicated log and dictionary problems. In *Proceedings of the ACM Symposium on Principles of Distributed Computing (PODC'84),* pages 232–242. ACM, 1984.

An Optimistic Approach
to Lock-Free FIFO Queues

Edya Ladan-Mozes[1] and Nir Shavit[2]

[1] Department of Computer Science, Tel-Aviv University, Israel
[2] Sun Microsystems Laboratories and Tel-Aviv University

Abstract. First-in-first-out (FIFO) queues are among the most fundamental and highly studied concurrent data structures. The most effective
and practical dynamic-memory concurrent queue implementation in the
literature is the lock-free FIFO queue algorithm of Michael and Scott,
included in the standard $Java^{TM}$ *Concurrency Package*.
This paper presents a new dynamic-memory lock-free FIFO queue algorithm that performs consistently better than the Michael and Scott
queue. The key idea behind our new algorithm is a novel way of replacing the singly-linked list of Michael and Scott, whose pointers are inserted
using a costly compare-and-swap (CAS) operation, by an "optimistic"
doubly-linked list whose pointers are updated using a simple store, yet
can be "fixed" if a bad ordering of events causes them to be inconsistent.
We believe it is the first example of such an "optimistic" approach being
applied to a real world data structure.

1 Introduction

First-in-first-out (FIFO) queues are among the most fundamental and highly
studied concurrent data structures [1–12], and are an essential building block
of concurrent data structure libraries such as JSR-166, the $Java^{TM}$ Concurrency Package [13]. A concurrent queue is a linearizable structure that supports
enqueue and dequeue operations with the usual FIFO semantics. This paper
focuses on queues with dynamic memory allocation.

The most effective and practical dynamic-memory concurrent FIFO queue
implementation is the lock-free FIFO queue algorithm of Michael and Scott [14]
(Henceforth the *MS-queue*). On shared-memory multiprocessors, this compare-
and-swap (CAS) based algorithm is superior to all former dynamic-memory
queue implementations including lock-based queues [14], and has been included
as part of the $Java^{TM}$ Concurrency Package [13]. Its key feature is that it allows
uninterrupted parallel access to the head and tail of the queue.

This paper presents a new dynamic-memory lock-free FIFO queue algorithm
that performs consistently better than the MS-queue. It is a practical example of
an "optimistic" approach to reduction of synchronization overhead in concurrent
data structures. At the core of this approach is the ability to use simple stores
instead of CAS operations in common executions, and *fix* the data structure in
the uncommon cases when bad executions cause structural inconsistencies.

R. Guerraoui (Ed.): DISC 2004, LNCS 3274, pp. 117–131, 2004.
© Springer-Verlag Berlin Heidelberg 2004

1.1   The New Queue Algorithm

As with many finely tuned high performance algorithms (see for example CLH [15, 16] vs. MCS [17] locks), the key to our new algorithm's improved performance is in saving a few costly operations along the algorithm's main execution paths.

Figure 1 describes the MS-queue algorithm which is based on concurrent manipulation of a singly-linked list. Its main source of inefficiency is that while its dequeue operation requires a single successful CAS in order to complete, the enqueue operation requires *two* such successful CASs. This may not seem important, until one realizes that it increases the chances of failed CAS operations, and that on modern multiprocessors [18, 19], even the successful CAS operations cost an order-of-magnitude longer to complete than a load or a store, since they require exclusive ownership and flushing of the processor's write buffers.

The key idea in our new algorithm is to (literally) approach things from a different direction... by logically reversing the direction of enqueues and dequeues to/from the list. If enqueues were to add elements at the beginning of the list, they would require only a single CAS, since one could first direct the new node's next pointer to the node at the beginning of the list using only a store operation, and then CAS the tail pointer to the new node to complete the insertion. However, this re-direction would leave us with a problem at the end of the list: dequeues would not be able to traverse the list "backwards" to perform a linked-list removal.

Our solution, depicted in Figure 2, is to maintain a doubly-linked list, but to construct the "backwards" direction, the path of prev pointers needed by dequeues, in an optimistic fashion using only stores (and no memory barriers). This doubly-linked list may seem counter-intuitive given the extensive and complex work of maintaining the doubly-linked lists of lock-free deque algorithms using double-compare-and-swap operations [20]. However, we are able to store and follow the optimistic prev pointers in a highly efficient manner.

If a prev pointer is found to be inconsistent, we run a fixList method along the chain of next pointers which is guaranteed to be consistent. Since prev pointers become inconsistent as a result of long delays, not as a result of contention, the frequency of calls to fixList is low. The result is a FIFO queue based on a doubly-linked list where pointers in both directions are set using

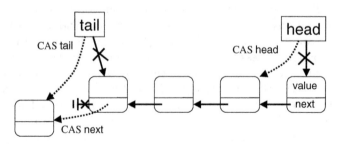

Fig. 1. The single CAS dequeue and costly two CAS enqueue of the MS-Queue algorithm.

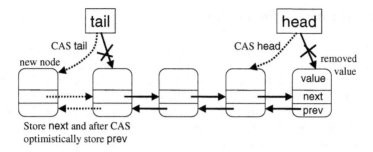

Fig. 2. The Single CAS **enqueue** and **dequeue** of the new algorithm.

simple stores, and both **enqueues** and **dequeues** require only a single successful CAS operation to complete.

1.2 Optimistic Synchronization

Optimistically replacing CAS with loads/stores was first suggested by Moir et al. [21] who show how one can replace the use of CAS with simple loads in good executions, using CAS only if a bad execution is incurred. However, while they show a general theoretical transformation, we show a practical example of a highly concurrent data structure whose actual performance is enhanced by using the optimistic approach.

Our optimistic approach joins several recent algorithms tailored to the good executions while dealing with the bad ones in a more costly fashion. Among these is the obstruction-freedom methodology of Herlihy et al. [22] and the lock-elision approach by Rajwar and Goodman [23] that use backoff and locking (respectively) to deal with bad cases resulting from contention. Our approach is different in that inconsistencies occur because of long delays, not as a result of contention. We use a special mechanism to fix these inconsistencies, and our resulting algorithm is lock-free.

1.3 Performance

We compared our new lock-free queue algorithm to the most efficient lock-based and lock-free dynamic memory queue implementations in the literature, the two-lock-queue and lock-free MS-queue of Michael and Scott [14]. Our empirical results, presented in Section 4, show that the new algorithm performs consistently better than the MS-queue. This improved performance is not surprising, as our enqueues require fewer costly CAS operations, and as our benchmarks show, generate significantly less failed CAS operations.

The new algorithm can use the same dynamic memory pool structure as the MS-queue. It fits with memory recycling methods such as ROP [24] or SMR [25], and it can be written in the Java^{TM} programming language without the need for a memory pool or ABA-tags. We thus believe it can serve as a viable practical alternative to the MS-queue.

2   The Algorithm in Detail

The efficiency of our new algorithm rests on implementing a queue using a doubly-linked list, which, as we show, allows enqueues and dequeues to be performed with a single CAS per operation. Our algorithm guarantees that this list is always connected and ordered by the enqueue order in one direction. The other direction is optimistic and may be inaccurate at various points of the execution, but can be reconstructed to an accurate state when needed.

Our shared queue data structure (see Figure 3) consists of a head pointer, a tail pointer, and nodes. Each node added to the queue contains a value, a next pointer and a prev pointer. Initially, a node with a predefined dummy value, hence forth called a dummy node, is created and both head and tail point to it. During the execution, the tail always points to the last (youngest) node inserted to the queue, and the head points to the first (oldest) node. When the queue becomes empty, both head and tail point to a dummy node. Since our algorithm uses CAS for synchronization, the ABA issue arises [14, 10]. In Section 2.1, we describe the enqueue and dequeue operations ignoring ABA issues. The tagging mechanism we added to overcome the ABA problem is explained in Section 3. The code in this section includes this tagging mechanism. Initially, the tags of the tail and head are zero. When a new node is created, the tags of the next and prev pointers are initiated to a predefined null value.

```
struct pointer_t {
  <ptr, tag>: <node_t *, unsigned integer>
};
```

```
struct node_t {                      struct queue_t {
  data_type value;                     pointer_t tail;
  pointer_t next;                      pointer_t head;
  pointer_t prev;                    };
};
```

Fig. 3. The queue data structures.

2.1   The Queue Operations

A FIFO queue supports two operations (or methods): enqueue and dequeue. The enqueue operation inserts a value to the queue and the dequeue operation deletes the oldest value in the queue.

The code of the enqueue method appears in Figure 4, and the code of the dequeue method appears in Figure 5. To insert a value, the enqueue method creates a new node that contains the value, and then tries to insert this node to the queue. As seen in Figure 2, the enqueue reads the current tail of the queue, and sets the new node's next pointer to point to that same node. Then it tries to atomically modify the tail to point to its new node using a CAS operation. If the CAS succeeded, the new node was inserted into the queue. Otherwise the enqueue retries.

```
void enqueue(queue_t* q, data_type val)
E01: pointer_t tail
E02: node_t* nd = new_node()                              # Allocate a new node
E03: nd->value = val                                      # Set enqueued value
E04: while(TRUE){                                         # Do till success
E05:    tail = q->tail                                    # Read the tail
E06:    nd->next = <tail.ptr, tail.tag+1>                 # Set node's next ptr
E07:    if CAS(&(q->tail), tail, <nd, tail.tag+1>){       # Try to CAS the tail
E08:       (tail.ptr)->prev = <nd, tail.tag>              # Success, write prev
E09:       break                                          # Enqueue done!
E10:    }
E11: }
```

Fig. 4. The enqueue operation.

To delete a node, a **dequeue** method reads the current **head** and **tail** of the queue, and the **prev** pointer of the node pointed by the **head**. It then tries to CAS the **head** to point to the node as that pointed by the **prev** pointer. If it succeeded, then the node previously pointed by the **head** was deleted. If it failed, it repeats the above steps. If the queue is empty then NULL is returned.

We now explain how we update the prev pointers of the nodes in a consistent and lock-free manner, assuming there is no ABA problem. The **prev** pointers are modified in two stages. The first stage is performed optimistically immediately after the successful insertion of a new node. An **enqueue** method that succeeded in atomically modifying the **tail** using a CAS, updates the **prev** pointer of the node previously pointed by the **tail** to point to the new node. This is done using a simple store operation. Once this write is completed, the **prev** pointer points to its preceding node in the list. Thus the order of operations to perform an enqueue is a write of the **next** in the new node, then a CAS of the **tail**, and finally a write of the **prev** pointer of the node pointed to by the **next** pointer. This ordering will prove crucial in guaranteeing the correctness of our algorithm.

Unfortunately, the storing of the **prev** pointer by an **enqueue** might be delayed for various reasons, and a dequeuing method might not see the necessary **prev** pointer. The second stage is intended to fix this situation. In order to fix the **prev** pointer, we use the fact that the **next** pointer of each node is set only by the **enqueue** method that inserted that node, and never changes until the node is dequeued. Thus, if ABA problems resulting from node recycling are ignored, this order is invariant. The fixing mechanism walks through the entire list from the **tail** to the **head** along the chain of **next** pointers, and corrects the **prev** pointers accordingly. Figure 7 provides the code of the **fixList** procedure. As can be seen, the fixing mechanism requires only simple load and store operations.

There are two special cases we need to take care of: when the last node is being deleted and when the the **dummy** node needs to be skipped.

- The situation in which there is only one node in the queue is encountered when the **tail** and **head** point to the same node, which is not a **dummy** node. Deleting this node requires three steps and two CAS operations, as seen in

```
data_type dequeue(queue_t* q)
D01: pointer_t tail, head, firstNodePrev
D02: node_t* nd_dummy
D03: data_type val
D04: while(TRUE){                              # Try till success or empty
D05:   head = q->head                          # Read the head
D06:   tail = q->tail                          # Read the tail
D07:   firstNodePrev = (head.ptr)->prev        # Read first node prev
D08:   val = (head.ptr)->value                 # Read first node val
D09:   if (head == q->head){                   # Check consistency
D10:     if (val != dummy_val){                # Head val is dummy?
D11:       if (tail != head){                  # More than 1 node?
D12:         if (firstNodePrev.tag != head.tag){  # Tags not equal?
D13:           fixList(q, tail, head)          # Call fixList
D14:           continue                        # Re-iterate (D04)
D15:         }
D16:       }
D17:       else{                               # Last node in queue
D18:         nd_dummy = new_node()             # Create a new node
D19:         nd_dummy->value = dummy_val       # Set it's val to dummy
D20:         nd_dummy->next = <tail.ptr, tail.tag+1>   # Set its next ptr
D21:         if CAS(&(q->tail), tail ,<nd_dummy, tail.tag+1>){# CAS tail
D22:           (head.ptr).prev = <nd_dummy, tail.tag>        # Write prev
D23:         }
D24:         else{                             # CAS failed
D25:           free(nd_dummy)                  # free nd_dummy
D26:         }
D27:         continue;                         # Re-iterate (D04)
D28:       }
D29:       if CAS(&(q->head), head, <firstNodePrev.ptr,head.tag+1>){# CAS
D30:         free (head.ptr)                   # Free the dequeued node
D31:         return val                        # Dequeue done!
D32:       }
D33:     }
D34:     else {                                # Head points to dummy
D35:       if (tail.ptr == head.ptr){          # Tail points to dummy?
D36:         return NULL;                       # Empty queue, done!
D37:       }
D38:       else{                               # Need to skip dummy
D39:         if (firstNodePrev.tag != head.tag){ # Tags not equal?
D40:           fixList(q, tail, head);         # Call fixList
D41:           continue;                       # Re-iterate (D04)
D42:         }
D43:         CAS(&(q->head),head,<firstNodePrev.ptr,head.tag+1>)#Skip dummy
D44:       }
D45:     }
D46:   }
D47: }
```

Fig. 5. The dequeue operation.

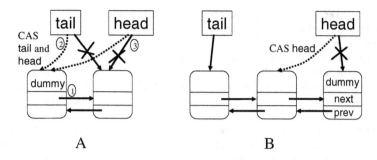

Fig. 6. A - A `dequeue` of the last node, B - Skipping the dummy node.

Figure 6 Part A. First, a new node with a dummy value is created, and its next pointer is set to point to the last node. Second, the `tail` is atomically modified using a CAS to point to this dummy node, and then, the `head` is atomically modified using a CAS to also point to this dummy node. The intermediate state in which the `tail` points to a dummy node and the `head` points to another node is special, and occurs only in the above situation.

This sequence of operations ensures that the algorithm is not blocked even if a `dequeue` method modified the `tail` to point to a dummy node and then stopped. We can detect the situation in which the `tail` points to a dummy node and the `head` does not, and continue the execution of the `dequeue` method. In addition, enqueuing methods can continue to insert new nodes to the queue, even in the intermediate state.

– In our algorithm, a dummy node is a special node with a dummy value. It is created and inserted to the queue when it becomes empty as explained above. Since a dummy node does not contain a real value, it must be skipped when nodes are deleted from the queue. The steps for skipping a dummy node are similar to those of a regular dequeue, except that no value is returned. When a `dequeue` method identifies that the `head` points to a dummy node and the `tail` does not, as in Figure 6 Part B, it modifies the `head` using a CAS to point to the node pointed by the `prev` pointer of this dummy node. Then it can continue to `dequeue` nodes.

3   Solving the ABA Problem

An ABA situation [10, 14] can occur when a process read some part of the shared memory in a given state and then was suspended for a while. When it wakes up the part it read could be in an identical state, however many insertions and deletions could have happened in the interim. The process may incorrectly succeed in performing a CAS operation, bringing the data structure to an inconsistent state. To identify such situation and eliminate ABA, we use the standard tagging-mechanism approach [26, 14].

In the tagging-mechanism, each pointer (`tail`, `head`, `next`, and `prev`) is added a `tag`. The `tags` of the `tail` and `head` are initiated to zero. When a new

```
F01:void fixList(queue_t* q, pointer_t tail, pointer_t head)
F02: pointer_t curNode , curNodeNext, nextNodePrev
F03: curNode = tail                              # Set curNode to tail
F04: while((head == q->head) && (curNode != head)){  # While not at head
F05:   curNodeNext = (curNode.ptr)->next         # Read curNode next
F06:   if (curNodeNext.tag !=  curNode.tag){      # Tags don't equal?
F07:     return;                                 # ABA, return!
F08:   }
F09:   nextNodePrev = (curNodeNext.ptr)->prev     # Read next node prev
F10:   if (nextNodePrev != <curNode.ptr, curNode.tag-1>){#Ptr don't equal?
F11:     (curNodeNext.ptr)->prev = <curNode.ptr, curNode.tag-1>; # Fix
F12:   }
F13:   curNode = <curNodeNext.ptr, curNode.tag-1>    # Advance curNode
F14: }
```

Fig. 7. The fixList procedure.

node is created, the next and prev tags are initiated to a predefined null value. The tag of each pointer is atomically modified with the pointer itself when a CAS operation is performed on the pointer.

Each time the tail or head is modified, its tag is incremented, also in the special cases of deleting the last node and skipping the dummy node. If the head and tail point to the same node, their tags must be equal. Assume that an enqueue method executed by a process P read that the tail points to node A and then was suspended. By the time it woke up, A was deleted, B was inserted and A was inserted again. The tag attached to the tail pointing to A will now be different (incremented twice) from the tag originally read by P. Hence P's enqueue will fail when attempting to CAS the tail.

The ABA problem can also occur while modifying the prev pointers. The tag of the next pointer is set by the enqueuing process to equal the tag of the new tail it tries to CAS. The tag of the prev pointer is set to equal the tag of the next pointer in the same node. Thus consecutive nodes in the queue have consecutive tags in the next and prev pointers. Assume that an enqueue method executed by process P inserted a node to the queue, and stopped before it modified the prev pointer of the consecutive node A (see Section 2.1). Then A was deleted and inserted again. When P woke up, it wrote its pointer and the tag to the prev pointer of A. Though the pointer is incorrect, the tag indicates this since it is smaller than the one expected. A dequeue method verifies that the tag of the prev pointer of the node it is deleting equals the tag of the head pointer it read. If the tags are different, it concludes that an ABA problem occurred, and calls a method to fix the prev pointer.

The fixing of the prev pointer after it was corrupted by an ABA situation is performed in the fixList procedure (Figure 7), in combination with the second stage of modifying the prev pointers, as explained in Section 2.1. In addition to using the fact that the next pointers are set locally by the enqueue method and never change, we use the fact that consecutive nodes must have consecutive tags attached to the next and prev pointers. The fixing mechanism walks through the entire list from the `tail` to the `head` along the `next` pointers of the nodes, correcting `prev` pointers if their `tags` are not consistent.

Finally we note that in garbage-collected languages such as the Java^{TM} programming language, ABA does not occur and the `tags` are not needed. When creating a new instance of a node, its `prev` pointer is set to NULL. Based on this, the fixing mechanism is invoked if the `prev` pointer points to NULL (instead of checking that the tags are equal). In this way we can detect the case in which an `enqueue` did not succeed in its optimistic update of the `prev` pointer of the consecutive node,and fix the list according to the `next` pointers.

4   Performance

We evaluated the performance of our FIFO queue algorithm relative to other known methods by running a collection of synthetic benchmarks on a 16 processor Sun Enterprise^{TM} 6500, an SMP machine formed from 8 boards of two 400MHz UltraSparc® processors, connected by a crossbar UPA switch, and running a Solaris^{TM} 9 operating system. Our C code was compiled by a Sun *cc* compiler 5.3, with flags `-x05 -xarch=v8plusa`.

4.1   The Benchmarks

We compare our algorithm to the two-lock queue and to MS-queue of Michael and Scott [14]. We believe these algorithms to be the most efficient known lock-based and lock-free dynamic-memory queue algorithms in the literature. We used Michael and Scott's code (referenced in [14]).

The original Michael and Scott paper [14] showed only an *enqueue-dequeue pairs* benchmark where a process repeatedly alternated between enqueuing and dequeuing. This tests a rather limited type of behavior. In order to simulate additional patterns, we implemented an internal memory management mechanism. As in Micheal and Scott's benchmark, we use an array of nodes that are allocated in advance. Each process has its own pool with an equal share of these nodes. Each process performs a series of `enqueues` on its pool of nodes and `dequeues` from the queue. A dequeued node is placed in dequeuing process pool for reuse. If there are no more nodes in its local pool, a process must first `dequeue` at least one node, and can then continue to `enqueue`. Similarly, a process cannot `dequeue` nodes if its pool is full. To guarantee fairness, we used the same mechanism for all the algorithms. We tested several benchmarks of which two are presented here:

- enqueue-dequeue pairs: each process alternately performed `enqueue` or `dequeue` operation.
- 50% enqueues: each process chooses uniformly at random whether to perform an enqueue or a dequeue, creating a random pattern of 50% `enqueue` and 50% dequeue operations.

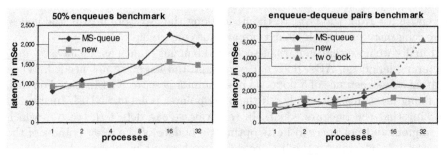

Fig. 8. Results of enqueue-dequeue pairs and 50% benchmarks.

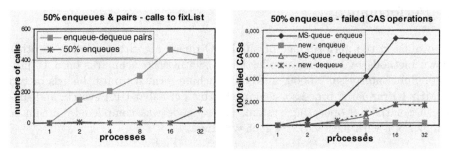

Fig. 9. The number of failed CASs and calls to fixList.

4.2   The Experiments

We repeated the above benchmarks delaying each process a random amount of time between operations to mimic local work usually performed by processes (in the range of 0 to 1000 increment operations in a loop).

We measured latency (in milliseconds) as a function of the number of processes: the amount of time that elapsed until the completion of a total of a million operations divided equally among processes. To counteract transient startup effects, we synchronized the start of the processes (i.e., no process can start before all others finished their initialization phase).

We pre-tested the algorithms on the given benchmarks by running hundreds of combinations of exponential backoff delays. The results we present were taken from the best combination of backoff values for each algorithm in each benchmark (although we found, similarly to Michael and Scott, that the exact choice of backoff did not cause a significant change in performance). Each of the presented data points in our graphs is the average of eight runs.

4.3   Empirical Results

As can be seen in Figure 8, the new algorithm consistently outperforms the MS-queue in both the 50% and the enqueue-dequeue pairs benchmarks when there are more than two processes. From the enqueue-dequeue pairs benchmark one can also see that the lock-based algorithm is consistently worst than the lock-free algorithms, and deteriorates when there is multiprogramming, that is, when there are 32 processes on 16 processors. Hence, in the rest of this section, we concentrate on the performance of the MS-queue and our new algorithm.

Figure 8 shows that the results in both enqueue-dequeue pairs and 50% enqueues benchmarks were very similar, except in the case of one or two processes. To explain this, let us consider the overhead of an empty queue, the number of calls to the fixList procedure as it appears in the left side of Figure 9, and the number failed CAS operations as it appears in the right side of Figure 9.

– As described in Section 2.1 (see also Figure 6), additional successful CASs are required by the new algorithm when the queue becomes empty. As the number of concurrent processes increases, their scheduling causes the queue to become empty less frequently, thus incurring less of the overhead of an empty queue. A benchmark which we do not present here shows that this phenomena can be eliminated if the enqueue-dequeue pairs benchmark is initiated with a non-empty queue. In the 50% enqueues benchmark, due to its random characteristics, the overhead of an empty queue is eliminated even in low concurrency levels.
– Overall, there were a negligible number of calls to fixlist in both benchmarks, no more than 450 calls for a million operations. This makes a strong argument in favor of the optimistic approach.
  Recall that the fixList procedure is called when a process tries to dequeue a node before the enqueuing process completed the optimistic update of the prev pointer of the consecutive node. This happens more frequently in the enqueue-dequeue pairs benchmark due to its alternating nature. In the 50% enqueues benchmark, due to its more random patterns, there are almost no calls to fixList when the concurrency level is low, and about 85 when there are 32 processes.
– The righthanded side of Figure 9 shows the number of failed CAS operations in the enqueue and dequeue methods. These numbers expose one of the key performance benefits of the new algorithm. Though the number of failed CASs in the dequeue operations in both algorithms is approximately the same, the number of failed CASes in the enqueue of MS-queue is about 20 to 40 times greater than in our new algorithm. This is a result of the additional CAS operation required by MS-queue's enqueue method, and is the main advantage allowed by our new optimistic doubly-linked list structure.

We conclude that in our tested benchmarks, our new algorithm outperforms the MS-queue. The MS-queue's latency is increased by the failed CASs in the enqueue operation, while the latency of our new algorithm is influenced by the additional CASs when the queue is empty. We note again that in our presented benchmarks we did not add initial nodes to soften the effect of encountering an empty queue.

5   Correctness Proof

This section contains a sketch of the formal proof that our algorithm has the desired properties of a concurrent FIFO queue. A sequential FIFO queue as defined in [27] is a data structure that supports two operations: enqueue and dequeue. The enqueue operation takes a value as an argument, inserts it to the queue, and does not return a value. The dequeue operation does not take an argument, deletes and returns the oldest value from the queue.

We prove that our concurrent queue is linearizable to the sequential FIFO queue, and that it is lock-free. We treat basic read/write (load/store) and CAS operations as atomic actions, and can thus take the standard approach of viewing them as if they occurred one after the other in sequence [28].

In the following we explain the FIFO queue semantics and define the linearization points for each enqueue and dequeue operation. We then define the insertion order of elements to the queue. The correctness proof and the lock freedom property proof are only briefly described out of space limitations.

5.1   Correct FIFO Queue Semantics

The queue in our implementation is represented by a head and a tail pointers, and uses a dummy node. Each node in the queue contains a value, a next pointer and a prev pointer. All pointers, head, tail, next and prev, are attached with a tag. Initially, all tags are zero and the head and tail point to the dummy node.

The Compare-And-Swap (CAS) operation used in our algorithm takes a register, an *old* value, and a *new* value. If the register's current content equals *old*, then it is replaced by *new*, otherwise the register remains unchanged [29]. A successful CAS operation is an operation that modified the register.

The successfulness of the enqueue and dequeue operations depends on the successfulness of CAS operations performed in the execution. For any process, the enqueue operation is always successful. The operation ends when a process successfully performed the CAS operation in line E07. A successful dequeue operation is one that successfully performed the CAS in D22. If the queue is empty, the dequeue operation is considered unsuccessful and it returns null.

Definition 1. *The linearization points of* enqueue *and* dequeue *operations are:*

- – Enqueue *operations are linearized at the successful CAS in line E07.*
- – *Successful* dequeue *operations are linearized at the successful CAS in line D29.*
- – *Unsuccessful* dequeue *operations are linearized in line D06.*

Definition 2. *In any state of the queue, the insertion order of nodes to the queue is the reverse order of the nodes starting from the tail, linked by the* next *pointers, to the head.*

If the dummy *node is linked before the* head *is reached, then the insertion order is the same from the* tail *to the* dummy *node, the* dummy *node is excluded, and the node pointed by the* head *is attached instead of the* dummy *node. If the* head *points to the* dummy *node then the* dummy *node is excluded.*

5.2   The Proof Structure

In the full paper we show that the insertion order is consistent with the linearization order on the enqueue operations. We do that by showing that the next pointer of a linearized enqueue operation always points to the node inserted by the previous linearized enqueue operation, and that the next pointers never change during the execution. We then show that the correctness of the prev pointers can be verified using the tags, and fixed if needed by the fixList procedure. We also prove that in any state of the queue there is at most one node with a dummy value in the queue, and that the queue is empty if both head and tail point to a dummy node.

To finish the proof we show that the deletion order of nodes from the queue is consistent with the insertion order. This is done by proving that we can detect the case in which the optimistic update of the prev pointer did not occur (and also the case of an ABA situation) and fix it using the tags and the fixList procedure. We then show that when a dequeue operation takes place, the prev pointer of the node pointed by the head, always point to the consecutive node as dictated by the next pointers.

From the above we can conclude that our concurrent implementation implements a FIFO queue.

5.3   Lock Freedom

In order to prove that our algorithm is lock-free we need to show that if one process fails in executing an enqueue or dequeue operation, then another process have modified the tail or the head, and thus the system as whole made progress. We also need to show that the fixList procedure eventually ends. These properties are fairly easy to conclude from the code.

5.4   Complexity

It can be seen from the code that each enqueue and dequeue operation takes a constant number of steps in the uncontended case. The fixList procedure, in a specific state of the queue, requires all the running dequeue processes to go over all the nodes in the queue in order to fix the list. However, once this part of the queue is fixed, when ABA does not occur, all the nodes in this part can be dequeued without the need to fix the list again.

6   Conclusion

In this paper we presented a new dynamic-memory lock-free FIFO queue. Our queue is based on an optimistic assumption of good ordering of operations in the common case, and on the ability to fix the data structure if needed. It requires only one CAS operation for each enqueue and dequeue operation and performs constantly better than the MS-queue. We believe that our new algorithm can serve as a viable alternative to the MS-queue for implementing linearizable FIFO queues.

References

1. Gottlieb, A., Lubachevsky, B.D., Rudolph, L.: Basic techniques for the efficient coordination of very large numbers of cooperating sequential processors. ACM Trans. Program. Lang. Syst. **5** (1983) 164–189
2. Herlihy, M., Wing, J.: Linearizability: A correctness condition for concurrent objects. ACM Transactions on Programming Languages and Systems **12** (1990) 463–492
3. Hwang, K., Briggs, F.A.: Computer Architecture and Parallel Processing. McGraw-Hill, Inc. (1990)
4. Lamport, L.: Specifying concurrent program modules. ACM Transactions on Programming Languages and Systems **5** (1983) 190–222
5. Mellor-Crummey, J.M.: Concurrent queues: Practical fetch-and-ϕ algorithms. Technical Report Technical Report 229, University of Rochester (1987)
6. Prakash, S., Lee, Y.H., Johnson, T.: Non-blocking algorithms for concurrent data structures. Technical Report 91–002, Department of Information Sciences, University of Florida (1991)
7. Prakash, S., Lee, Y.H., Johnson, T.: A non-blocking algorithm for shared queues using compare-and-swap. IEEE Transactions on Computers **43** (1994) 548–559
8. Stone, H.S.: High-performance computer architecture. Addison-Wesley Longman Publishing Co., Inc. (1987)
9. Stone, J.: A simple and correct shared-queue algorithm using compare-and-swap. In: Proceedings of the 1990 conference on Supercomputing, IEEE Computer Society Press (1990) 495–504
10. Treiber, R.K.: Systems programming: Coping with parallelism. Technical Report RJ 5118, IBM Almaden Research Center (1986)
11. Tsigas, P., Zhang, Y.: A simple, fast and scalable non-blocking concurrent fifo queue for shared memory multiprocessor systems. In: Proceedings of the thirteenth annual ACM symposium on Parallel algorithms and architectures, ACM Press (2001) 134–143
12. Valois, J.: Implementing lock-free queues. In: Proceedings of the Seventh International Conference on Parallel and Distributed Computing Systems. (1994) 64–69
13. Lea, D.: (The java concurrency package (JSR-166))
    `http://gee.cs.oswego.edu/dl/concurrency-interest/index.html`.
14. Michael, M.M., Scott, M.L.: Simple, fast, and practical non-blocking and blocking concurrent queue algorithms. In: Proceedings of the 15th Annual ACM Symposium on Principles of Distributed Computing (PODC '96), New York, USA, ACM (1996) 267–275
15. Craig, T.: Building FIFO and priority-queueing spin locks from atomic swap. Technical Report TR 93-02-02, University of Washington, Department of Computer Science (1993)
16. Magnussen, P., Landin, A., Hagersten, E.: Queue locks on cache coherent multiprocessors. In: Proceedings of the 8th International Symposium on Parallel Processing (IPPS), IEEE Computer Society (1994) 165–171
17. Mellor-Crummey, J., Scott, M.: Algorithms for scalable synchronization on shared-memory multiprocessors. ACM Transactions on Computer Systems **9** (1991) 21–65
18. Weaver, D., (Editors), T.G.: The SPARC Architecture Manual (Version 9). PTR Prentice Hall, Englewood Cliffs, NJ) (1994)
19. Intel: Pentium Processor Family User's Manual: Vol 3, Architecture and Programming Manual. (1994)

20. Agesen, O., Detlefs, D., Flood, C., Garthwaite, A., Martin, P., Moir, M., Shavit, N., Steele, G.: DCAS-based concurrent deques. Theory of Computing Systems **35** (2002) 349–386
21. Luchangco, V., Moir, M., Shavit, N.: On the uncontended complexity of consensus. In: Proceedings of Distributed Computing. (2003)
22. Herlihy, M., Luchangco, V., Moir, M.: Obstruction-free synchronization: Double-ended queues as an example. In: Proceedings of the 23rd International Conference on Distributed Computing Systems, IEEE (2003) 522–529
23. Rajwar, R., Goodman, J.: Speculative lock elision: Enabling highly concurrent multithreaded execution. In: Proceedings of the 34th Annual International Symposium on Microarchitecture. (2001) 294–305
24. Herlihy, M., Luchangco, V., Moir, M.: The repeat offender problem: A mechanism for supporting lock-free dynamic-sized data structures. In: Proceedings of the 16th International Symposium on DIStributed Computing. Volume 2508., Springer-Verlag Heidelberg (2002) 339–353 A improved version of this paper is in preparation for journal submission; please contact authors.
25. Michael, M.: Safe memory reclamation for dynamic lock-free objects using atomic reads and writes. In: The 21st Annual ACM Symposium on Principles of Distributed Computing, ACM Press (2002) 21–30
26. Moir, M.: Practical implementations of non-blocking synchronization primitives. In: Proceedings of the 16th Annual ACM Symposium on Principles of Distributed Computing. (1997) 219–228
27. Cormen, T., Leiserson, C., Rivest, R., Stein, C.: Introduction to Algorithms. Second edition edn. MIT Press, Cambridge, MA (2001)
28. Afek, Y., Attiya, H., Dolev, D., Gafni, E., Merritt, M., Shavit, N.: Atomic snapshots of shared memory. In Dwork, C., ed.: Proceedings of the 9th Annual ACM Symposium on Principles of Distributed Computing, Québec City, Québec, Canada, ACM Press (1990) 1–14
29. Herlihy, M.: Wait-free synchronization. ACM Transactions on Programming Languages and Systems (TOPLAS) **13** (1991) 124–149

A Single-Enqueuer Wait-Free
Queue Implementation

Matei David

Department of Computer Science, University of Toronto
matei@cs.toronto.edu

Abstract. We study wait-free linearizable Queue implementations in asynchronous shared-memory systems from other consensus number 2 objects, such as Fetch&Add and Swap. The best previously known implementation allows at most two processes to perform Dequeue operations. We provide a new implementation, when only one process performs Enqueue operations and any number of processes perform Dequeue operations. A nice feature of this implementation is the fact that both Enqueue and Dequeue operations take constant time.

1 Introduction

An asynchronous shared-memory distributed system provides the user with a collection of shared objects. Different systems might provide different types of shared objects, hence an algorithm written for one system might have to be completely rewritten to work in another system. A general way to make all algorithms written for a source system work in a target system is to use the objects of the target system in simulating every object of the source system. An *implementation* of an object consists of a set of procedures simulating the primitive operations of the implemented object, written using the objects in the target system.

The main tool determining whether objects of one type T' can be implemented from objects of another type T is the consesnsus hierarchy, introduced by Herlihy in [Her91] and refined by Jayanti in [Jay93]. If k is the consensus number of T, then it can be used to implement any other type in a system of at most k processes. Furthermore, if k' is the consensus number of type T' and $k < k'$, then there are objects of type T' which cannot be implemented from type T in a system of more than k processes.

There are some questions that the consensus hierarchy does not answer. If two types are on the same level k, it is not clear whether one type can implement the other in a system of more than k processes. Even for level 2, [Her91] leaves as an open problem whether Fetch&Add objects can be used to implement any other object whose type has consensus number 2 in a system of three or more processes.

The Queue is an important and well studied shared object type, used in many distributed algorithms. However, distributed systems usually provide lower-level

R. Guerraoui (Ed.): DISC 2004, LNCS 3274, pp. 132–143, 2004.

types, such as Register, Fetch&Add and Compare&Swap, so, in general, one has to implement a Queue object from the available base types. We know that the Queue type has consensus number 2, and from Herlihy's results in [Her91], we know that wait-free Queue implementations exist for any number of processes in systems providing consensus number ∞ types, such as Compare&Swap. But some (old) systems only provide types with consensus number 2, such as Test&Set, Fetch&Add and Swap. To this date, it is an open problem whether any of these types can be used to implement a wait-free Queue in a system with three or more processes.

In [AWW93], Afek, Weisberger and Weisman consider the class *Common2* of commutative and overwriting read-modify-write types of consensus number 2, which includes most familiar types such as Test&Set, Fetch&Add and Swap. They show that any type in Common2 can be implemented in a wait-free manner from any consensus number 2 type in a system with any number of processes. By transitivity of wait-free implementations, their result implies that a wait-free Queue implementation exists from Common2 types if and only if such an implementation exists from any consensus number 2 type.

Let *Basic2* denote the set of types of consensus number 2 that can be implemented from types in Common2 in a system with any number of processes. The results of [AWW93] imply that using only Basic2 types in an algorithm carries with it the guarantee that the algorithm can be ported to any system providing types of consensus number 2. It is not known whether Queue is in Basic2.

However, some restricted Queue implementations exist. Herlihy and Wing present in [HW90] a non-blocking implementation of a Limited-Queue object shared by n processes from Fetch&Add and Swap objects. The Limited-Queue object type is similar to the Queue object type with the exception that Dequeue operations are not defined when the queue is in the empty state. Li gives a regular, unlimited, non-blocking Queue implementation in [Li01] and observes that the implementation in [HW90] is in fact a single-dequeuer wait-free Queue implementation. That is, if only one process is allowed to perform Dequeue operations, the implementation becomes wait-free, and the Queue is no longer limited.

In [Her91], Herlihy showed that in a system of n processes, any object can be implemented from Consensus objects shared by all n processes. Using ideas from Herlihy's universal construction, Li modifies the implementation in [HW90] and obtains in [Li01] a two-dequeuer wait-free Queue implementation from Common2 types. Furthermore, Li conjectures that there is no Queue implementation from Common2 types which would allow three processes to perform both Enqueue and Dequeue operations. In an attempt to narrow down the difficulty involved in implementing one such object, Li proposes a stronger conjecture: there is no three-dequeuer Queue implementation from Common2 types.

In both wait-free implementations, the code for the Enqueue procedures is very simple. However, the number of accesses to shared objects during Dequeue procedures is not bounded by any constant, i.e. it is wait-free but not bounded wait-free.

In this paper, we present a new wait-free Queue implementation from Common2 types, for one enqueuer process and any number of dequeuer processes. This disproves the stronger of Li's conjectures. In our single-enqueuer Queue implementation, the conceptually difficult part of the computation is done by the Enqueue procedure, and the Dequeue procedures are very simple. Unlike Li's implementations, our implementation is very time efficient, using at most three accesses to shared objects for both Enqueue and Dequeue procedures. Although the algorithm is simple, proving its correctness is complicated.

This paper is organized as follows. In Sect. 2, we briefly talk about our model of computation. In Sect. 3, we present our new single-enqueuer Queue implementation from Common2 objects. The main ideas for the proof of correctness are presented in Sect. 4. Section 5 contains a discussion of possible extensions of our algorithm. In particular, we give a scheme which would reduce the space requirements of our algorithm, and we talk about why our single-enqueuer Queue implementation cannot be extended to allow for two enqueuer processes in a manner similar to that in which Li extends the single-dequeuer Queue implementation in [HW90] to a two-dequeuer Queue implementation.

2   System Model

The system we consider is an asynchronous shared-memory distributed system. It consists of a number of processes and a collection of shared objects. Processes start from their initial state, execute deterministic sequential programs and communicate by accessing shared objects. During an atomic *step*, a process performs an operation on a certain shared object and receives a response from that object. In this setting, the crash failure of a process can be simulated by considering executions in which that process is no longer taking any steps. Between steps, processes can perform an arbitrary amount of local computation. This assumption captures the fact that process P cannot get any information about the computation of process P' except for what is conveyed by the operations P' performs on shared objects.

Each shared object has a type, an initial state and a set of rules specifying what operations on this object are available to each process in the system. The *type* of an object contains its sequential specification, which defines how that object reacts as operations are sequentially applied on it. In this paper, the Queue type supports only Enqueue and Dequeue operations, and the Queue object we are implementing allows every process to apply either Enqueue or Dequeue operations, but not both. Afek et al. show that no generality is lost in assuming that for every Common2 object O used in our implementation, every processes can perform on O every operation specified by O's type [AWW93].

The Queue implementation consists of one Enqueue procedure $E : \text{Enqueue}(x)$ for the enqueuer process E, and one Dequeue procedure $D : \text{Dequeue}$ for every dequeuer process D. The Enqueue procedure always returns the special value OK. The Dequeue procedure returns either a value retrieved from the Queue, or the special value ε in case the Queue is empty.

In a *run* R of the implementation, each process P starts from its initial state and sequentially executes access procedures of the form $P : OP$, completing one before starting the next. Given a run R, one can partition the subsequence of steps taken by any process P into contiguous blocks, such that each block contains the steps that P is taking while executing some access procedure. We define a *procedure instance* to be the set of steps in one such block. We say that a procedure instance by process P is *complete* if, after P executes the last step of this instance appearing in R, the access procedure contains only local computation before returning a result.

The only correctness condition we consider is *linearizability* [HW90], which states that, no matter how the steps in the execution of the access procedure $P : OP$ are interleaved with the steps in the executions of other access procedures by other processes, $P : OP$ has to appear to be atomic, occurring at some moment between its first and last steps, in a way that respects the sequential specification of the implemented object. Our Queue implementation is linearizable.

An implementation is *wait-free* [Her91] if every process will complete the execution of every access procedure within finitely many steps, regardless of the steps performed by other processes in the system and, in particular, regardless of whether other processes have crashed. An implementation is *b-bounded wait-free* if no access procedure requires more than b steps. Notice that bounded wait-freedom is a stronger condition than wait-freedom. Our Queue implementation is 3-bounded wait-free.

3   Algorithm

The first attempt to implement a Queue object for one enqueuer E and n dequeuers $D_1, \ldots D_n$ would probably be to use an array of Register objects to store the values in the Queue, together with a pair of head and tail pointers. E would add items in the array at the location indicated by the tail pointer, while dequeue processes would retrieve values from the location indicated by the head pointer. This does not work because several dequeue processes may try to read the same location, and there is no easy way for them to agree which one should return that value. A slightly more elaborate approach would be to use a Fetch&Add object for the head pointer, and have each dequeue procedure reserve a unique cell to read by a simple Fetch&Add(1) operation. This does not work because dequeue procedures might end up reading a cell before the enqueuer process has a chance to write something there. Afterward, if the enqueuer puts an element in that location, it might happen that no dequeue procedure will ever read the cell again, causing the enqueued element to simply vanish. We have been able to fix this situation by using Swap objects instead of Registers as the array cells, a design which allows the enqueuer process to detect and adapt to the situation in which a dequeuer has overtaken it.

The algorithm in Fig. 1 is our Queue implementation from Common2 objects and Registers, for one enqueuer process E and n dequeuer processes $D_1, \ldots, D_n$. We are using a one-dimensional array HEAD of Fetch&Increment objects, each initialized to 0, a two-dimensional array ITEMS of Swap objects, each initialized to $\perp$, and one Register ROW initialized to 0. The set of values that may be held by a cell of ITEMS is $V \cup \{\perp, \top\}$, where V is the set of values that may be enqueued. The two variables *tail* and *enq_row* are two persistent local variables of E, initialized to 0. Elements enqueued by E are written in consecutive cells on the row ROW of ITEMS. When E detects that it has been overtaken by a dequeue process, it starts using a fresh row. Dequeue processes read the active row of ITEMS from ROW and order themselves on a given row using HEAD. Both arrays HEAD and ITEMS are infinite. Since in any run, any enqueue or dequeue instance has at most three steps, the implementation is clearly 3-bounded wait-free. The main ideas for the proof of correctness are given in Sect. 4.

Access procedure E : Enqueue(x), for all $x \in V$:

```
1. (step 1) val ⟵ Swap(ITEMS[enq_row, tail], x)
2.          if val = ⊤
            then
3.                  increment(enq_row)
4.                  tail ⟵ 0
5. (step 2)         Swap(ITEMS[enq_row, tail], x)
6. (step 3)         Write(ROW, enq_row)
            end if
7.          increment(tail)
8.          return OK
```

Access procedure D_i : Dequeue, for all $1 \leq i \leq n$:

```
1. (step 1) deq_row ⟵ Read(ROW)
2. (step 2) head ⟵ Fetch&Increment(HEAD[deq_row])
3. (step 3) val ⟵ Swap(ITEMS[deq_row, head], ⊤)
4.          if val = ⊥
            then
5.                  return ε
            else
6.                  return val
            end if
```

Fig. 1. Main Algorithm.

Informally, the algorithm works as follows. The cells in the two dimensional array ITEMS are initialized to a default value, $\perp \notin V$. Whenever they are accessed during an Enqueue procedure, their value is updated to contain the element to be enqueued. Whenever they are accessed by a Dequeue procedure, their value is updated to contain $\top \notin V$. By design, each cell in the array ITEMS will be used at most once by an Enqueue operation, and at most once by a Dequeue operation.

In order to perform a Dequeue operation, process D_i reads from ROW the value of the active row in the two-dimensional array ITEMS. This is the row which was last used to enqueue a value by an Enqueue procedure which has already finished. Having obtained the value of this row in its local variable deq_row, process D_i selects the column $head$ of a cell to query on this row using the Fetch&Increment object HEAD[deq_row]. It then proceeds to query the Swap object ITEMS[$deq\_row, head$] and update its value to $\top$. If the value retrieved is not $\perp$, then some value to be enqueued was written in this location and the process dequeues that value. Otherwise, this location was never used by an Enqueue operation, and in this case the dequeuer process finds an empty queue.

The process E performing Enqueue operations has two local *persistent* variables, enq_row and $tail$. They are persistent in the sense that their values are not lost from one invocation of the enqueue procedure to the next. The value of the variable enq_row mirrors the value of the shared register ROW, while $tail$ contains the smallest index of a Swap object not already used by an Enqueue procedure on row enq_row of ITEMS.

In order to perform an Enqueue operation, process E writes the value to be enqueued in the array location ITEMS[$enq\_row, tail$] and retrieves the latter's value. If this value was $\top$, then some Dequeue operation has already accessed this cell before E had a chance to write to it. In this case, the Enqueue procedure will abandon the current row and start using the next row for storing the values in the Queue. Notice that no dequeuer could have used the new row that the enqueuer writes to in its second step (line 5), because the index of that row appears in ROW only after the third step by the enqueuer. Hence, the result obtained by the enqueuer to its second step is always $\perp$.

The access procedures above consist of local computation and accesses to shared objects, that is, steps. A complete execution of the Enqueue procedure can consist of at most three steps, in lines 1, 5 and 6. A complete execution of the Dequeue procedure always consists of three steps, in its first three lines.

For example, Fig. 2 presents a possible state of the shared variables in this implementation. Exactly two Enqueue procedures with arguments 1 and 2 were started, both were completed, and neither of them executed the body of the if statement in lines 3 through 6. Exactly four Dequeue procedures were started and executed at least their first two steps. All four of them obtained the result 0 in their first step, and they obtained the results $0, 1, 2, 3$ in their second steps, respectively. The Dequeue procedures with ($deq\_row = 0, head = 0$) and ($deq\_row = 0, head = 2$) were completed and output the values 1 and ε, respectively. The Dequeue procedures with ($deq\_row = 0, head = 1$) and ($deq\_row = 0, head = 3$) only executed their first two steps, and if either was allowed to take another step, they would output 2 and ε, respectively.

In Fig. 3, a new Enqueue procedure with argument 3 is started and completed. This procedure applied a Swap operation with argument 3 to the cell ITEMS[0, 2], obtained the result $\top$ for that step, and it then executed the body of the if statement. This is the situation in which a dequeuer accesses a cell of ITEMS before the enqueuer.

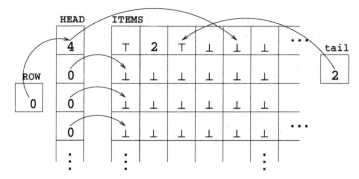

Fig. 2. A possible state of the shared variables in this implementation.

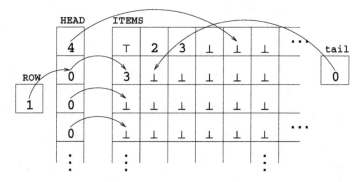

Fig. 3. The state after another Enqueue procedure is started and completed.

The state in Fig. 4 is the result of a possible execution extending the one which led to the state in Fig. 3. Three more Enqueue procedures with arguments $4, 5, 6$ were started, and all of them were completed. None of these Enqueue procedures executed the body of the `if` statement. One more Dequeue procedure was started and executed its first two steps, obtaining ($deq\_row = 1, head = 0$). This Dequeue procedure was completed, and it output 3. Furthermore, one of the two incomplete Dequeue procedures from the state in Fig. 2 was completed, the one with ($deq\_row = 0, head = 3$), and it output ε.

4   Proof of Linearizability

Due to space constraints, we only give the key ideas needed to prove that our algorithm is linearizable. More specifically, we explain how to assign linearization points for access procedures in an arbitrary run R of this implementation. A formal proof of linearizability is presented in [Dav04].

First, we introduce some notation. For π an enqueue instance in R, let enq_row_π and $tail_\pi$ denote the values of the local variables enq_row and $tail$, respectively, at the beginning of the execution of π. Let val_π denote the result of the first step of π (line 1). For ϕ a dequeue instance in R, let deq_row_ϕ denote

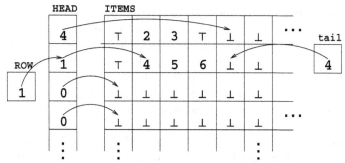

Fig. 4. Yet another possible state, extending the previous one.

the result of the first step of ϕ (line 1). If ϕ has at least two steps, let $head_\phi$ denote the result of its second step (line 2). If ϕ is complete, that is, if it contains three steps, let val_ϕ denote the result of its third step (line 3).

Enqueue Instances. We consider two kinds of enqueue instances. We say that an enqueue instance π is a *regular* enqueue instance if $val_\pi \neq \top$, so E does not execute the body of the **if** statement during π. A complete regular enqueue instance consists of only one step. We say that π is a *jump* enqueue instance if $val_\pi = \top$, referring to the fact that it "jumps" to the next row of the array ITEMS. A complete jump enqueue instance consists of three steps.

Since all enqueue instances in R are executed sequentially by the same process E, no two enqueue instances are concurrent. Furthermore, only the last enqueue instance in R can be incomplete, because in a run R, a process must finish the execution of an access procedure before starting the next one. If the value of ROW is r, then there was exactly one jump enqueue instance π with $enq\_row_\pi = i$, for every $i = 0, \ldots, r - 1$.

An Association Between Enqueue Instances and Dequeue Instances. We also need to classify dequeue instances. To do that, we need a method which associates a dequeue instance ϕ with the enqueue instance π which enqueued the value that ϕ is dequeuing.

For a dequeue instance ϕ with at least two steps, we say that ϕ *reserves* the cell at row deq_row_ϕ and column $head_\phi$ of ITEMS. This is the only cell of ITEMS that ϕ will access. Conversely, no dequeue instance other than ϕ will access that cell. We establish a relation between dequeue instances and enqueue instances as follows. Let ϕ be a dequeue instance with at least two steps. If there exists an enqueue instance π such that:

- π accesses the cell in ITEMS reserved by ϕ, and
- if ϕ has three steps, then π accesses that cell before ϕ (in its third step),

then we define $\rho(\phi) = \pi$. It can be shown that if π exists, then π is unique, so the definition is sound. If no such enqueue instance exists, we leave $\rho(\phi)$ undefined. The following correlation between a complete dequeue instance ϕ and $\rho(\phi)$ exists: if ϕ returns ε, then $\rho(\phi)$ is not defined; if ϕ returns a value other than ε, then that value was enqueued by $\rho(\phi)$.

Dequeue Instances. We consider three types of dequeue instances.

A dequeue instance ϕ consisting of at least two steps is a *type I* dequeue instance if $\rho(\phi) = \pi$ is defined and the step in which π accesses the cell reserved by ϕ occurs *after* step 2 of ϕ. By definition of ρ, the step in which π accesses that cell has to precede the third step of ϕ, should the latter exist in R. It can be shown that π is a regular enqueue instance. Informally, a complete type I dequeue instance ϕ will return a value other than ε, but when ϕ reserves a cell (in step 2), the value is not yet in the cell.

A dequeue instance ϕ consisting of at least two steps is a *type II* dequeue instance if there exists a complete jump enqueue instance π' such that $enq\_row_{\pi'} = deq\_row_\phi$ and the third step of π' precedes the second step of ϕ. It can be shown that π' is unique and that $\rho(\phi)$ is undefined, i.e. no enqueue instance is associated with ϕ. Hence, ϕ cannot also be a type I dequeue instance. Informally, between step 1 and step 2 of a type II dequeue instance, a jump enqueue instance has incremented ROW. If complete, ϕ will return ε.

A dequeue instance ϕ consisting of at least two steps is a *type III* dequeue instance if it is neither type I nor type II. A type III dequeue instance may or may not return ε.

Linearization Points. To show that our algorithm is linearizable, we assign linearization points for all complete enqueue instances and all dequeue instances which perform at least two steps in R. We argue that the linearization point of any procedure instance α occurs during the execution of α, i.e. at or after the first step of α and, if α is complete, at or before the last step of α.

- A complete regular enqueue instance is linearized at its first (and only) step, in line 1.
- A complete jump enqueue instance is linearized at its third (and last) step, in line 6.
- A type I dequeue instance ϕ is linearized at the first step (line 1) of $\pi = \rho(\phi)$, immediately *after* π. We know in this case that π is a regular enqueue instance, so by definition of a type I dequeue instance, the second step of ϕ precedes the first step of π. Furthermore, if ϕ is complete, then its third step occurs after the first step of π. Hence, the linearization point of ϕ occurs at some point during its execution.
- For a type II dequeue instance ϕ, let π' be the unique complete jump enqueue instance such that $enq\_row_{\pi'} = deq\_row_\phi$ and the third step of π' occurs before the second step of ϕ. We linearize ϕ at the third step (line 6) of π', immediately *before* π'. Clearly, the first step of ϕ precedes the third step of π', for otherwise $deq\_row_\phi \neq enq\_row_{\pi'}$.

  It turns out that many type II dequeue instances may be linearized at the same third step of some jump enqueue instance π'. In this case, we order these dequeue instances arbitrarily. Informally, this does not cause any problem because the queue is empty at that point and they all output ε.
- A type III dequeue instance is linearized at its second step, in line 2.

Responses of Incomplete Dequeue Instances. The linearization points we have defined provide us with a total order on the sequence of operations that are performed on the Queue object during a run of our implementation. To prove linearizability, we have to define responses for the incomplete instances we have chosen to linearize. In our case, the only incomplete instances we linearize are dequeue instances which perform at least two steps. Let ϕ be such a dequeue instance. If $\rho(\phi) = \pi$ is defined, let the response of ϕ to be the value enqueued by π. If $\rho(\phi)$ is undefined, let the response of ϕ be ε.

Completing the Proof of Linearizability. By defining linearization points and responses of incomplete linearized dequeue instances in a run R, we have generated a sequence $\sigma(R)$ of operations and responses on the implemented Queue object. To complete the proof of linearizability, we have to show that there exists a sequence of states of the Queue object, that starts with the empty state, and is consistent with $\sigma(R)$. This is formally done in [Dav04] by defining a Queue state based on the states of the shared objects in the system, followed by a somewhat tedious case analysis of how various steps of enqueue and dequeue procedures modify the states of the shared objects and, thus, the state of the Queue object.

5 Conclusions

The results in this paper, together with the ones in [Li01], establish that there exist wait-free linearizable Queue implementations from Common2 objects when there is either only one enqueuer or at most two dequeuers. The question whether there exists a wait-free linearizable fully-accessible Queue implementation from Common2 objects for three processes (or more) remains open, as is Herlihy's question about whether Fetch&Add objects can be used to implement every consensus number 2 type in a system of three (or more) processes.

Our implementation uses a one dimensional array HEAD and a two dimensional array ITEMS. Both arrays are assumed to be infinite. However, the array HEAD and one dimension (the number of rows) of ITEMS can both be made finite, with $O(n)$ rows, where n is the number of dequeuers. The idea is to reuse rows of ITEMS when it is safe to do so. We cannot reuse a row until we are sure that no dequeuer has reserved a cell on that row but not yet accessed it. To this end, every dequeuer will start by reading ROW, announcing the value retrieved in a single-writer Register, and then reading ROW again. If ROW changes between the two reads, the dequeuer outputs ε. Otherwise, it continues as before, with its Fetch&Increment and Swap operations. This way, whenever the enqueuer has to jump to the next row, it can read what row each dequeuer is operating on, and then select an unused row. This takes $O(n)$ steps, plus the time to reinitialize the cells of ITEMS on the selected row to $\bot$. Since any number of cells may have been previously used on that row, going through them all would be wait-free but not bounded wait-free. We can avoid this and maintain bounded wait-freedom by having the enqueuer increment a sequence number and storing it with a row index in the shared variable ROW. Every cell of ITEMS would then have a time-stamp of its own, and every time a process retrieves a value with an old time-stamp, it should treat that cell as being fresh (that is, containing $\perp$). The implementation will then be $O(n)$-bounded wait-free. We have not incorporated this scheme into the algorithm because the emphasis in this paper is on the existence of an algorithm rather than its efficiency.

Another interesting improvement, from a practical point of view, is to limit the size of each row by, say, the maximum number of items present in the Queue at any one time (should such a maximum exist). Even though we have been unable to design such a scheme, perhaps one could do it by somehow having the enqueuer jump to a new row when the current one becomes full. However, in this situation, it is unclear how to dequeue elements from the old row.

Li obtains in [Li01] a two-dequeuer Queue implementation by modifying the single-enqueuer implementation of [HW90], using ideas from Herlihy's universal construction in [Her91]. Specifically, he develops a mechanism by which two dequeuer processes agree on a total order on the Dequeue operations to be performed, and subsequently perform those operations much like they would in the original single-enqueuer case. We attempted to apply a similar mechanism in order to obtain a two-enqueuer implementation from our single-enqueuer implementation, but without success. Informally, the problem appears to lie with the interaction between the enqueuer and dequeuer processes: in the single-dequeuer implementation considered in [Li01], the communication between enqueuer processes and dequeuer processes is achieved exclusively through Register objects; while in our single-enqueuer implementation, this communication is achieved through both the Register object ROW, and the Swap objects in the array ITEMS. Li obtains a two-dequeuer implementation by (i) having the two dequeuer processes agree on a total order for the Dequeue operations; (ii) having each dequeuer execute the steps of each of the Dequeue operations, including those initiated by the other dequeuer process; and (iii) having the two dequeuer processes agree on the result of each Dequeue operation. When trying to extend our single-enqueuer implementation to allow two enqueuers, part (iii) is irrelevant (since all enqueue operations produce the same result, OK) and part (i) can be achieved by having the two enqueuer processes agree on a sequence of Enqueue operations. The problem lies with part (ii), specifically with the fact that we were unable to find any way in which two enqueuers can work together while performing a single Enqueue operation. In Li's extended implementation, each of the Register objects used for communication between enqueuer and dequeuer processes only influences the steps taken by the two dequeuer processes. If we were to apply the same method to our implementation, accesses to the shared Swap objects in the array ITEMS would influence not only the steps of the two enqueuer processes, but also the steps of one dequeuer process. For example, consider the situation in which enqueue processes E_1 and E_2 are working together to perform some enqueue operation. Suppose E_1 first applies its Swap operation to the cell ITEMS$[r, c]$, and then E_2 applies its own Swap operation to the same cell. At that moment, E_2 cannot tell if some dequeue process accessed that cell before E_1, so E_2 cannot tell if E_1 has to jump to the next row of ITEMS or not. This is merely an informal argument of why Li's method cannot be straightforwardly applied. The existence of an implementation for two enqueuers and three or more dequeuers remains open.

Acknowledgments

This work was supported by the Natural Sciences and Engineering Research Council of Canada. I thank my supervisor, Faith Ellen Fich, for her helpful advice, her constructive criticism and her relentless proofreading of my work.

References

[AWW93]   Yehuda Afek, Eytan Weisberger, and Hanan Weisman. A completeness theorem for a class of synchronization objects. In *Proceedings of the 12th ACM Symposium on Principles of Distributed Computing*, pages 159–170, 1993.

[Dav04]   Matei David. Wait-free linearizable queue implementations. Master's thesis, Univ. of Toronto, 2004.

[Her91]   Maurice Herlihy. Wait-free synchronization. *ACM Transactions on Programming Languages and Systems*, 13(1):124–149, January 1991.

[HW90]   Maurice Herlihy and Jeanette Wing. Linearizability: A correctness condition for concurrent objects. *ACM Transactions on Programming Languages and Systems*, 12(3):495–504, January 1990.

[Jay93]   Prasad Jayanti. On the robustness of Herlihy's hierarchy. In *Proceedings of the 12th ACM Symposium on Principles of Distributed Computing*, pages 145–158, 1993.

[Li01]   Zongpeng Li. Non-blocking implementation of queues in asynchronous distributed shared-memory systems. Master's thesis, Univ. of Toronto, 2001.

Practical Lock-Free and Wait-Free LL/SC/VL Implementations Using 64-Bit CAS

Maged M. Michael

IBM Thomas J. Watson Research Center, Yorktown Heights, New York, USA

Abstract. The ideal semantics of the instructions LL/SC/VL (Load-Linked, Store-Conditional, Validate) are inherently immune to the ABA problem which is a fundamental problem that affects most lock-free algorithms. This paper presents practical lock-free and wait-free implementations of arbitrary-sized LL/SC/VL variables using 64-bit CAS (Compare-and-Swap). The implementations improve on Jayanti and Petrovic's 64-bit wait-free implementations by reducing the space overhead per variable to a small constant, and not requiring advance knowledge of the maximum number of participating threads, while maintaining minimal amortized expected time and work complexities.

1 Introduction

A shared object is *lock-free* [3] if whenever a thread executes some finite number of steps toward an operation on the object, some thread must have completed an operation on the object during the execution of these steps. A lock-free shared object is also *wait-free* [2] if progress is also guaranteed per operation. Unlike conventional lock-based objects, lock-free objects are immune to deadlock and livelock, regardless of thread speeds, scheduling policies, and arbitrary termination, in addition to performance advantages such as tolerance to preemption.

A subtle problem that affects the design of most lock-free algorithms is the ABA problem. If not prevented, it can cause the corruption of lock-free objects as well as unrelated objects that happen to reuse dynamic memory removed from these objects, and it can cause the program to crash or return incorrect results. The ABA problem was first reported in the documentation of the Compare-and-Swap (CAS) instruction and its use for implementing lock-free freelists on the IBM System 370 [5]. CAS takes three arguments: the address of a memory location, an expected value, and a new value. If the memory location is found to hold the expected value, the new value is written to it, atomically. A Boolean return value indicates whether the write occurred. If CAS returns true, it is said to succeed, otherwise, it is said to fail.

The ABA problem occurs when a thread reads some value A from a shared variable, and then other threads write to the variable some value B, and then A again. Later, when the original thread checks if the variable holds the value A, using read or CAS, the comparison succeeds, while the intention of the algorithm designer is for such a comparison to fail in this case, and to succeed only if the

R. Guerraoui (Ed.): DISC 2004, LNCS 3274, pp. 144–158, 2004.

variable has not been written after the initial read. However, the semantics of read and CAS prevent them from distinguishing the two cases.

The theoretical semantics of the instructions LL/SC/VL (Load-Linked, Store-Conditional, Validate) make them inherently immune to the ABA problem. LL takes one argument: the address of a memory location, and returns its contents. SC takes two arguments: the address of a memory location and a new value. If the location was not written since the current thread last read it using LL, the new value is written to the memory location, atomically. A Boolean return value indicates whether the write occurred. VL takes one argument: the address of a memory location, and returns a Boolean value that indicates whether the memory location was not written since the current thread last read it using LL. If SC or VL returns true, it is said to succeed, otherwise, it is said to fail.

For practical architectural reasons, none of the architectures that support LL/SC (PowerPC, MIPS, Alpha) support the ideal semantics, and hence offer little or no help with preventing the ABA problem, and for most lock-free algorithms LL/SC with restricted semantics are used just to simulate CAS.

Until recently, implementations of LL/SC/VL variables [5, 1, 11] required atomic operations on both the implemented variable and an additional tag field. As most 32-bit architectures support 64-bit – as well as 32-bit – atomic instructions, these mechanisms are feasible to varying degrees in 32-bit applications running on 32-bit as well as 64-bit architectures. However, most current 64-bit architectures do not support atomic instructions on more than 64-bit blocks, thus it is no longer possible to pack a large tag with pointer-sized values in 64-bit applications.

Jayanti and Petrovic [7] address this problem by presenting wait-free implementations of 64-bit LL/SC/VL using 64-bit CAS. However, these implementations require space overhead per LL/SC/VL variable that is proportional to N, where N is the maximum number of threads that may operate on the LL/SC/VL variable. The implementations also require the use of N-sized arrays, which are problematic to implement without advance knowledge of the value of N or a conservative estimate of it. These requirements limit the practicality of these implementations to special cases where the maximum number of LL/SC/VL variables and the maximum number of threads in the program that may operate on these variables are known in advance to be small.

In this paper, we present lock-free and wait-free implementations of arbitrary-sized LL/SC/VL variables using 64-bit CAS (preliminary version in [8]). The implementations require only constant space overhead per LL/SC/VL variable (one word for the lock-free implementation and four words for the wait-free implementation), and in the worst case linear space in the number of participating threads per participating thread. The implementations do not require advance knowledge of the maximum number of participating threads.

In the wait-free implementation, LL and VL take constant time, and SC takes constant amortized expected time. In the lock-free implementation, VL takes constant time and SC takes constant amortized expected time, and in the absence of interfering successful SC operations, LL takes constant time. In both implementations – regardless of contention – concurrent LL, VL, and unsuccessful SC operations do not interfere with each other. Using the work performance measure, the amortized expected complexity of any set of LL/SC/VL operations using either of our implementations is the same (except for the amortized and expected qualifiers) as those assuming hypothetical hardware support for ideal LL/SC/VL.

The rest of this paper is organized as follows. In Section 2, we discuss the memory reclamation technique used to support the LL/SC/VL implementations and other related issues. In Section 3, we present the lock-free implementation, and in Section 4, we present the wait-free implementation. We discuss the complexity of the implementations in Section 5, and conclude with Section 6.

2   Preliminaries

Memory Reclamation. The memory reclamation problem is the problem of allowing dynamic blocks removed from lock-free objects to be freed, while guaranteeing that threads operating on these objects never access the memory of free blocks. The term *free* here is used in a broad sense, including reusing the block, dividing, coalescing, or unmapping its memory. Solutions for the memory reclamation problem have the side effect of partially – but not completely – preventing the ABA problem. In this paper, we make use of this feature of the hazard pointer memory reclamation method [9].

Briefly, the hazard pointer method uses single-writer shared pointers called hazard pointers. When a thread sets one of its hazard pointer to the address of a block, it in effect announces to other threads that if they happen to remove that block after the setting of the hazard pointer, then they must not free it as long as the hazard pointer continues to point to it. So, after a thread removes a block – and before it can free the block – it scans the list of hazard pointers and checks if any of them points to the block. Only if no match is found then the block is determined to be safe to free.

In a preferred implementation [9] using amortization, only constant amortized expected time is needed for processing each removed block until it is determined to be safe to free. A thread scans the hazard pointers after accumulating $H+\Theta(H)$ removed blocks, where H is the number of hazard pointers in the program. Then, the thread reads the H hazard pointers and organizes the non-NULL values read from them in an efficient private search structure such as a hash table with constant expected lookup time. Then, for each of the blocks that it has accumulated it searches the hash table for matching values. As described in [9], the procedure takes $O(H)$ expected time, and is guaranteed to identify $\Theta(H)$ blocks as safe to free. We use the hazard pointer method because it is portable across operating systems and architectures, it is wait-free, and it uses only pointer-sized instructions. Also, threads can join the method and retire dynamically, and acquire and release hazard pointers dynamically. Neither the number of participating threads N nor the number of hazard pointers H needs to be known in advance. See [9] for more details.

Definitions. A thread p is said to hold an *active reservation* for LL/SC/VL variable $\mathcal{O}$ at time t, if p has performed LL($\mathcal{O}$) at time $t_0 < t$ and it is possible for p to perform SC($\mathcal{O}$,v) or VL($\mathcal{O}$) at some time $t_1 \geq t$ without performing LL($\mathcal{O}$) during the interval $[t, t_1]$. We define K as the highest number of active reservations that p needs to hold concurrently. Typically, K is a small constant.

3   Lock-Free LL/SC/VL Implementation

In the lock-free implementation (Figure 1) the LL/SC/VL variable $\mathcal{O}$ is represented by a pointer X. The current value of $\mathcal{O}$ is always held in the dynamic block currently pointed to by X. Whenever $\mathcal{O}$ is written, a new block holding the new value replaces the old block pointed to by X.

The subscript i in some function and variable names is used to distinguish among the reservations that may be held concurrently by the same thread.

The basic idea of the implementation is for $LL_{p,i}(\mathcal{O})$ to read the value in the current block pointed to by X and use a hazard pointer to protect the block from being reused prematurely, i.e., while p is holding the reservation for $\mathcal{O}$. Subsequently, if $SC_{p,i}(\mathcal{O},v)$ or $VL_{p,i}(\mathcal{O})$ find X pointing to the same block, then it must be the case that $\mathcal{O}$ was not written since $LL_{p,i}(\mathcal{O})$ was performed.

$LL_{p,i}(\mathcal{O})$: The implementation of $LL_{p,i}(\mathcal{O})$ proceeds as follows. In line 2, thread p reads a pointer value from X into a persistent private variable $exp_{p,i}$, with the intention of reading $\mathcal{O}$'s value from $*exp_{p,i}$ (as in line 5). However, p cannot just proceed to read $*exp_{p,i}$, as it is possible that after line 2, another thread has replaced $exp_{p,i}$ (by performing a successful SC on $\mathcal{O}$) and then freed it before p manages to read its contents.

So, in line 3, p sets the hazard pointer $hp_{p,i}$ to $exp_{p,i}$ in order to prevent the block $exp_{p,i}$ from being freed before line 5 if it happens to be replaced by another thread. However, it is possible that $exp_{p,i}$ has already bean removed before p set the hazard pointer in line 3. Therefore, p checks X again in line 4. If $X \neq exp_{p,i}$, then it is possible that $exp_{p,i}$ was removed before p set $hp_{p,i}$ in line 3, and hence $exp_{p,i}$ might have been – or will be – freed before line 5. It is not safe to proceed to line 5 in this case, so p starts over from line 2.

If in line 4, p finds $X = exp_{p,i}$, then it is safe for p to read $*exp_{p,i}$ in line 5. This is true whether or not X has changed between line 2 and line 4. What matters is that at line 4, $X = exp_{p,i}$ (and hence $exp_{p,i}$ is not removed or free at that point) and $hp_{p,i} = exp_{p,i}$ already from line 3. Therefore, according to the hazard pointer method, from that point (line 4), if $exp_{p,i}$ is removed by another thread, it will not be freed as long as $hp_{p,i}$ continues to point to it, which is true as long as the current reservation is alive (i.e., beyond line 5).

$LL_{p,i}(\mathcal{O})$ is linearized [4] at line 4. At that point $X = exp_{p,i}$ and accordingly $\mathcal{O} = *exp_{p,i}$. By the hazard pointer method, the value of $*exp_{p,i}$ remains unchanged between lines 4 and 5. Therefore, $LL_{p,i}(\mathcal{O})$ returns the value of $\mathcal{O}$ at the time of the execution of line 4. Also, as described later, subsequent SC and VL operations – for the same reservation initiated by $LL_{p,i}(\mathcal{O})$ – will succeed if and only if $\mathcal{O}$ has not been written since line 4 of $LL_{p,i}(\mathcal{O})$.

Types
      blocktype = valuetype = arbitrary-sized value
Shared variables representing each LL/SC/VL variable $\mathcal{O}$
      X: pointer to blocktype   initially $(X = b \neq \text{NULL}) \wedge (*b = \mathcal{O}\text{'s initial value})$
Per-thread shared variables (for thread p)
      for $i \in \{0, \dots, K\text{-}1\}$ $hp_{p,i}$: hazard pointer
Per-thread persistent private variables (for thread p)
      for $i \in \{0, \dots, K\text{-}1\}$ $exp_{p,i}$: pointer to blocktype

$LL_{p,i}(\mathcal{O})$: valuetype		$SC_{p,i}(\mathcal{O},v)$: boolean
1: repeat	1:	$b := \text{GetSafeBlock}()$
2: $exp_{p,i} := X$	2:	$*b := v$
3: $hp_{p,i} := exp_{p,i}$	3:	$ret := \text{CAS}(X, exp_{p,i}, b)$
4: until $(X = exp_{p,i})$	4:	if (ret)
5: return $*exp_{p,i}$	5:	$\text{RetireNode}(exp_{p,i})$
	6:	else
$VL_{p,i}(\mathcal{O})$: boolean	7:	$\text{KeepSafeBlock}(b)$
1: return $(X = exp_{p,i})$	8:	return ret

Fig. 1. Lock-free implementation of LL/SC/VL using pointer-sized CAS.

As long as the reservation initiated by $LL_{p,i}(\mathcal{O})$ is alive, p must keep $hp_{p,i}$ and $exp_{p,i}$ unchanged. Once p reaches a point where it will not be possible to issue $SC_{p,i}(\mathcal{O})$ or $VL_{p,i}(\mathcal{O})$ corresponding to the current reservation, then p can simply reuse $hp_{p,i}$ and $exp_{p,i}$.

$SC_{p,i}(\mathcal{O},v)$: The implementation of $SC_{p,i}(\mathcal{O},v)$ proceeds as follows. In lines 1 and 2, p allocates a safe block and sets it to the new value v. A block b is safe if there is no thread q with any reservation j with $hp_{q,j} = b$. That is, if this SC succeeds, then the new pointer value of X – i.e., b – will be different from all the $exp_{q,j}$ pointer values associated with all live reservations at the time.

In line 3, the CAS succeeds if and only if $X = exp_{p,i}$. When SC is issued it is guaranteed that $hp_{p,i} = exp_{p,i}$ and that they were unchanged since the linearization of $LL_{p,i}(\mathcal{O})$ that initiated the reservation. By the hazard pointer method, if the block $exp_{p,i}$ was replaced after $LL_{p,i}(\mathcal{O})$, then no other thread could have subsequently allocated $exp_{p,i}$ as a safe block during the lifetime of the reservation. Therefore, the CAS succeeds if and only if, $\mathcal{O}$ was not written since $LL_{p,i}(\mathcal{O})$. So, $SC_{p,i}(\mathcal{O},v)$ is linearized at line 3.

If $SC_{p,i}(\mathcal{O},v)$ succeeds (i.e., the CAS in line 3 succeeds), the old block removed from X (i.e., $exp_{p,i}$) cannot be reused immediately and its value should not be changed until it is determined to be safe to free by going through the hazard pointer method by calling RetireNode (defined in [9]). If $SC_{p,i}(\mathcal{O},v)$ fails, then the block b can be reused immediately safely, as it was already safe in line 1 and it has not been observed by other threads since then.

The functions GetSafeBlock and KeepSafeBlock can be replaced with malloc and free, respectively, which can be implemented in user-level in an efficient completely lock-free manner [10]. Furthermore, our LL/SC/VL implementations have the feature that as long as N (the number of participating threads) is stable (which is an implicit requirement in Jayanti and Petrovic's implementations [7]), the number of blocks needed per thread remains stable, and so these functions can be completely private and without calling malloc and free. Each participating thread maintains two persistent private lists of *safe* and *not-safe-yet* blocks with combined maximum size equal to the batch size of the hazard pointer method. GetSafeBlock pops a block from the *safe* list. KeepSafeBlock pushes a block into that list. When the thread calls RetireNode and processes the blocks in the *not-safe-yet* list, it moves the blocks identified to be safe to the *safe* list.

$\underline{\text{VL}_{p,i}(\mathcal{O})}$: The implementation of $\text{VL}_{p,i}(\mathcal{O},v)$ simply checks if X is equal to $exp_{p,i}$. As argued regarding $\text{SC}_{p,i}(\mathcal{O},v)$, this is true if and only if $\mathcal{O}$ has not been written since the linearization of $\text{LL}_{p,i}(\mathcal{O})$. $\text{VL}_{p,i}(\mathcal{O})$ is linearized at line 1.

4   Wait-Free LL/SC/VL Implementation

In the LL/SC/VL implementation in Section 3, $\text{LL}_{p,i}(\mathcal{O})$ is not wait-free because thread p is always trying to capture the value of $\mathcal{O}$ from a specific block $exp_{p,i}$. However, by the time p reads the pointer value to $exp_{p,i}$ from X and is about to protect it using the hazard pointer $\text{hp}_{p,i}$, the block $exp_{p,i}$ might have already been removed and possibly freed, and p is forced to start over.

Unlike hazard pointers which prevent specific blocks from being freed, we introduce the notion of a *trap* which can capture *some block* (not a specific one) that satisfies certain criteria. In $\text{LL}_{p,i}(\mathcal{O})$, we use a trap to guarantee that in a constant number of steps, *some block* holding some value of $\mathcal{O}$ will be guaranteed not to be freed until p reads a value of $\mathcal{O}$ from it.

To be linearizable, LL needs to return a value that was held by $\mathcal{O}$ between LL's invocation and its response [4]. Therefore, a trap must avoid capturing a block that holds an old value of $\mathcal{O}$ that was overwritten before LL's invocation. For that purpose, we maintain a sequence number for each LL/SC/VL variable. The sequence number is incremented after every successful SC. When a thread sets a trap for a variable, it specifies the minimum acceptable sequence number.

4.1   Trap Functionality

Our wait-free LL/SC/VL implementation uses the following interface with the trap mechanism: $\text{SetTrap}_p(\mathcal{O},seq)$, $\text{ReleaseTrap}_p()$, $\text{GetCapturedBlock}_p()$, and $\text{ScanTraps}_p(b)$. Between every two calls to SetTrap_p there must be a call to ReleaseTrap_p. Thread p's trap is said to be active after a call to SetTrap_p and before the corresponding call to ReleaseTrap_p. $\text{GetCapturedBlock}_p$ is called only when p's trap is active. A block b is passed as argument of ScanTraps only after b has been removed from a LL/SC/VL variable. Blocks passed to ScanTraps are only freed (i.e., determined to be safe) by ScanTraps. The trap mechanism offers the following guarantees:

1. If thread p's call to GetCapturedBlock$_p$(), between calls to SetTrap$_p$($\mathcal{O}$,seq) and the corresponding ReleaseTrap$_p$(), returns b then either $b =$ NULL or b holds the nth value of $\mathcal{O}$, where $n \geq seq$.
2. If thread p calls SetTrap$_p$($\mathcal{O}$,seq) at time t, and block b is removed from $\mathcal{O}$ (before or after t), and b holds the nth value of $\mathcal{O}$, and $n \geq seq$, and b is passed to ScanTraps$_q$ by some thread q after t, then b will not be freed before p calls ReleaseTrap$_p$(), and/or p's trap captures a block b' different from b.

First we present the wait-free LL/SC/VL functions assuming this trap functionality, then we describe the trap implementation in detail.

4.2   LL/SC/VL Functions

Figure 2 shows the structures and functions of the wait-free LL/SC/VL implementation. We start with the sequence number. An additional variable Seq is used per LL/SC/VL variable $\mathcal{O}$. Between every two consecutive successful SC operations on $\mathcal{O}$, Seq must be incremented exactly once. Therefore, if Seq $= n$, then there must have been either n or $n+1$ successful SC operations performed on $\mathcal{O}$ so far.

Two additional fields are added to the block structure. The field Var points to the LL/SC/VL variable, and the field Seq holds a sequence number. If the nth successful SC on $\mathcal{O}$ sets X to b, then it must be the case that at that point $b{\rightarrow}$Seq $= n$ and $b{\rightarrow}$Var $= \mathcal{O}$. The purpose of these two fields is to enable a trap to capture only a block that holds a value for a specific LL/SC/VL variable with a sequence number higher than some value.

LL$_{p,i}$($\mathcal{O}$): Lines 1–4 of LL$_{p,i}$($\mathcal{O}$) are similar to the lock-free implementation in Figure 1. In the absence of intervening successful SC operations by other threads between p's execution of line 1 and line 3, LL$_{p,i}$($\mathcal{O}$) returns at line 4. In such a case LL$_{p,i}$($\mathcal{O}$) is linearized at line 3. If intervening successful SC operations are detected in line 3, p sets a trap before it tries to read X again, to ensure completion in constant time even if more successful SC operations occur.

In line 5, p reads Seq into a local variable seq. At that point, there must have been so far either seq or $seq+1$ successful SC operations performed on $\mathcal{O}$. In line 6, p sets a trap for $\mathcal{O}$ with a sequence number seq. The trap guarantees that from that point until the release of the trap, either the trap has captured a block that contains a value of $\mathcal{O}$ with a sequence number greater than or equal to seq, or no block that contains a value of $\mathcal{O}$ with a sequence number greater than or equal to seq has been freed. Then, p proceeds to read X again into $exp_{p,i}$ in line 7, and in line 8 it sets hp$_{p,i}$ to $exp_{p,i}$. At this point, it must be the case that $exp_{p,i}{\rightarrow}$Seq $\geq seq$.

If the trap set in line 6 does not capture a block before the setting of the hazard pointer in line 8, then $exp_{p,i}$ could not have been freed after line 7 and

Types

    valuetype = arbitrary-sized value

    seqnumtype = 64-bit unsigned integer

    blocktype = record Value: valuetype; Seq: seqnumtype;

                      Var: pointer to LL/SC/VL variable end

Shared variables representing each LL/SC/VL variable $\mathcal{O}$

    X: pointer to blocktype

    Seq: seqnumtype

        initially $(X = b \neq$ NULL$) \wedge (b{\rightarrow}$Value $= \mathcal{O}$'s initial value$) \wedge$

                $(b{\rightarrow}$Seq $=$ Seq $= 0) \wedge (b{\rightarrow}$Var $= \mathcal{O})$

Per-thread shared variables (for thread p)

    for $i \in \{0, \ldots, K\text{-}1\}$ $\mathrm{hp}_{p,i}$: hazard pointer

Per-thread persistent private variables (for thread p)

    for $i \in \{0, \ldots, K\text{-}1\}$ $exp_{p,i}$: pointer to blocktype

$LL_{p,i}(\mathcal{O})$: valuetype		$SC_{p,i}(\mathcal{O},v)$: boolean	
1:	$exp_{p,i} := X$	1:	if $(exp_{p,i} =$ NULL$)$ return FALSE
2:	$\mathrm{hp}_{p,i} := exp_{p,i}$	2:	$b :=$ GetSafeBlock()
3:	if $(X = exp_{p,i})$	3:	$b{\rightarrow}$Value $:= v$
4:	return $exp_{p,i}{\rightarrow}$Value	4:	$b{\rightarrow}$Var $:= \mathcal{O}$
5:	$seq :=$ Seq	5:	$seq := exp_{p,i}{\rightarrow}$Seq
6:	SetTrap$_p(\mathcal{O},seq)$	6:	$b{\rightarrow}$Seq $:= seq+1$
7:	$exp_{p,i} := X$	7:	CAS(Seq,seq-1,seq)
8:	$\mathrm{hp}_{p,i} := exp_{p,i}$	8:	$ret :=$ CAS(X,$exp_{p,i}$,b)
9:	$b :=$ GetCapturedBlock$_p()$	9:	if (ret)
10:	if $(b =$ NULL$)$	10:	ScanTraps$_p(exp_{p,i})$
11:	$v := exp_{p,i}{\rightarrow}$Value	11:	else
12:	else	12:	KeepSafeBlock(b)
13:	$v := b{\rightarrow}$Value	13:	return ret
14:	$exp_{p,i} :=$ NULL		
15:	ReleaseTrap$_p()$		$VL_{p,i}(\mathcal{O})$: boolean
16:	return v	1:	return $(X = exp_{p,i})$

Fig. 2. Wait-free implementation of LL/SC/VL using 64-bit CAS.

will not be freed as long as $\mathrm{hp}_{p,i}$ continues to point to it. Therefore, if p finds in line 9 that no block has been captured yet by the trap, then it must be safe to read $exp_{p,i}{\rightarrow}$Value in line 11. In such a case, $LL_{p,i}(\mathcal{O})$ is linearized at line 7.

This is correct for the following reasons: First, at line 7, $X = exp_{p,i}$ and $exp_{p,i}{\rightarrow}$Value remains unchanged after line 7 (throughout the life of the reservation). Therefore, $LL_{p,i}(\mathcal{O})$ returns the value of $\mathcal{O}$ at the time of p's execution of line 7. Second, by the guarantee of the memory reclamation method, $exp_{p,i}$ will not be freed after line 7 until the end of the reservation. Therefore, subsequent calls to SC and VL for the same reservation are guaranteed to succeed (by finding $X = exp_{p,i}$) iff $\mathcal{O}$ has not been written since p's execution of line 7.

If p finds in line 9 that the trap set in line 6 has indeed captured some block b (may or may not be the same as $exp_{p,i}$), then it might be possible that $exp_{p,i}$ has already been removed before setting the hazard pointer in line 8. Therefore, it may not be safe to access $exp_{p,i}$. However, as long as the trap is not released, it is safe to access b. So, p proceeds to read $b{\rightarrow}$Value in line 13.

In this case (i.e., a block b was captured before line 9), $LL_{p,i}(\mathcal{O})$ is linearized just before the SC that removed b from X, which is guaranteed to have occurred between p's execution of line 1 and line 9. If $b{\rightarrow}$Seq $> seq$ then b must have been removed from X after p's execution of line 5. If $b{\rightarrow}$Seq $= seq$ then b must have been removed from X after p's execution of line 1.

In line 14 $exp_{p,i}$ is set to NULL in order to guarantee the failure of subsequent $SC_{p,i}(\mathcal{O},v)$ and $VL_{p,i}(\mathcal{O})$ operations for the same reservation, as they should. At this point we are already certain that $\mathcal{O}$ has been written after the linearization point of $LL_{p,i}(\mathcal{O})$, as only removed blocks get trapped.

After reading a valid value either in line 11 or line 13, it is safe to release the trap in line 15. Therefore, each participating thread needs only one trap, even if it may hold multiple reservations concurrently.

$SC_{p,i}(\mathcal{O},v)$: In line 1, p checks if $LL_{p,i}(\mathcal{O})$ has already determined that this SC will certainly fail (by setting $exp_{p,i}$ to NULL). If so, $SC_{p,i}(\mathcal{O},v)$ returns FALSE and is linearized immediately after its invocation.

Otherwise, $LL_{p,i}(\mathcal{O})$ must have read its return value from $exp_{p,i}{\rightarrow}$Value and $exp_{p,i}$ has been continuously protected by $hp_{p,i}$. Therefore, the same arguments for the lock-free implementation apply here too, and $SC_{p,i}(\mathcal{O},v)$ is linearized at the time of applying CAS to X (line 8). However, care must be taken to maintain the invariant that when the $n + 1^{th}$ successful SC on $\mathcal{O}$ is linearized, Seq $= n$.

In lines 2 and 3, as in the SC implementation in Section 3, p allocates a safe block b and sets its Value field to the new value v. Also, p sets $b{\rightarrow}$Var to $\mathcal{O}$ in line 4 to allow the trap implementation to associate b with $\mathcal{O}$.

In lines 5 and 6, p reads the value seq from $exp_{p,i}{\rightarrow}$Seq and then sets $b{\rightarrow}$Seq to $seq+1$ for the following reason. The current SC can succeed only if it replaces $exp_{p,i}$ in X with b in line 8. Since $exp_{p,i}$ holds the seq^{th} value of $\mathcal{O}$, then if the current SC succeeds, b will be holding the $(seq+1)^{th}$ value of $\mathcal{O}$. So, p sets $b{\rightarrow}$Seq to $seq+1$ to allow the trap implementation to associate b with the $(seq+1)^{th}$ value of $\mathcal{O}$.

We now discuss the update of Seq. Seq is monotonically increasing and always by increments of 1. Correctness requires that between every two successful SC operations, Seq must be incremented exactly once. That is, if this SC succeeds in line 8, then Seq must be equal to seq at that point. By an induction argument, if this SC is to succeed then at line 7 either Seq $= seq$-1 or Seq $= seq$. So, whether the CAS in line 7 succeeds or fails, immediately after line 7 Seq $= seq$, if this SC is to succeed. An optional optimization is to test for Seq $= seq$-1 before issuing CAS in line 7.

We then argue that if Seq is incremented by another thread between lines 7 and 8, then this SC must fail. If Seq $= n > seq$ at line 8, then some other thread q must have performed CAS on Seq with a new value n, then q must have observed $X = exp_{q,j}$ with $exp_{q,j} \rightarrow$ Seq $= n$, which implies that at least n SC operations on $\mathcal{O}$ have already succeeded before line 8, then this SC cannot be the $(seq+1)^{th}$ successful SC on $\mathcal{O}$, and so this SC must fail.

We now move to line 8. As in the lock-free LL/SC/VL implementation, SC succeeds if and only if the CAS on X succeeds. Line 8 is the linearization point of SC if $exp_{p,i} \neq$ NULL. If SC succeeds, p passes the removed block $exp_{p,i}$ to ScanTraps so that it will be freed but not prematurely. If SC fails, then block b remains safe and can be freed or kept for future use without going through traps or hazard pointers.

$VL_{p,i}(\mathcal{O})$: As in the lock-free implementation in Section 3, $X = exp_{p,i}$ if and only if $\mathcal{O}$ has not been written since the linearization of $LL_{p,i}(\mathcal{O})$.

Wrap-around: Implementing sequence numbers as 64-bit variables makes wrap-around impossible for all practical purposes. Even if 1,000,000 successful SC operations are performed on $\mathcal{O}$ every second, the 64-bit sequence number would still not wrap around after 584,000 years!

4.3   Trap Implementation

The trap implementation is shown in Figure 3. Each participating thread p owns a trap record $trap_p$ and an additional hazard pointer $traphp_p$.

SetTrap$_p(\mathcal{O},seq)$: This function starts by setting $trap_p \rightarrow$ Var to $\mathcal{O}$ and setting $trap_p \rightarrow$ Seq to seq in lines 1 and 2, in order to indicate that the trap is set for blocks that contain a value of $\mathcal{O}$ with a sequence number not less than seq.

The purpose of the field $trap_p \rightarrow$ Captured is to provide other threads with a location to offer a block that matches the criteria of this trap. When p sets a trap, it cannot just set $trap_p \rightarrow$ Captured to NULL, otherwise a slow thread trying to set $trap_p \rightarrow$ Captured in relation to an earlier trap might offer the wrong block for the current trap. We need to guarantee that only a thread that intends to offer a block that satisfies the criteria of the current trap succeeds in setting $trap_p \rightarrow$ Captured.

For that purpose, p uses a unique tag every time it sets a trap. Since arbitrary 64-bit numbers might match pointer values captured by the trap, we use only non-pointer values for the tag. By convention and as required by most current processor architectures, the addresses of dynamic blocks must be 8-byte aligned. So, tag numbers not divisible by 8 are guaranteed not to match any block addresses. By convention, NULL = 0. Thus, a 64-bit word can hold 7×2^{61} different tag values. The variable tag_p keeps track of the tag values already used by $trap_p$. Similar to the sequence number, even if $trap_p$ is used 1,000,000 times per second to perform LL operations where each LL is interfered with by a successful SC, and this continues for 511,000 years, tag_p would still not wrap around. So, wrap-around is not a practical concern in this case either.

In line 3, p sets $trap_p \rightarrow$ Captured to tag_p, and in line 4 it sets $traphp_p$ to the same tag value. We discuss $traphp_p$ in detail when discussing ScanTraps.

Setting the trap takes effect only when p sets $trap_p \rightarrow$ Active to TRUE in line 5. Finally, in line 6, p prepares a new tag value in tag_p for the next trap.

Types
        tagtype = 64-bit unsigned integer
        traptype = record Active: boolean; Var: pointer to LL/SC/VL variable;
            Seq: seqnumtype; Captured: tagtype or pointer to blocktype end
Per-thread shared variables (for thread p)
        trap_p: traptype   initially $\text{trap}_p \to$ Active = FALSE
        traphp_p: hazard pointer
Per-thread persistent private variables (for thread p)
        tag_p: tagtype   initially tag_p = non-pointer value (e.g. 1)
        $list_p$: list of block addresses

SetTrap$_p(\mathcal{O}, seq)$

1: $\text{trap}_p \to$ Var := $\mathcal{O}$
2: $\text{trap}_p \to$ Seq := seq
3: $\text{trap}_p \to$ Captured := tag_p
4: traphp_p := tag_p
5: $\text{trap}_p \to$ Active := TRUE
6: tag_p := next non-pointer value

ReleaseTrap$_p()$

1: $\text{trap}_p \to$ Active := FALSE
2: $\text{trap}_p \to$ Captured := NULL
3: traphp_p := NULL

ScanTraps$_p(list_p)$

1: for all q
2:      if $\neg\text{trap}_q \to$ Active skip
3:      tag := $\text{trap}_q \to$ Captured
4:      if (tag is a pointer value) skip
5:      var := $\text{trap}_q \to$ Var
6:      seq := $\text{trap}_q \to$ Seq
7:      b := $list_p$.lookup(var, seq)
8:      if (b = NULL) skip
9:      if CAS($\text{trap}_q \to$ Captured, tag, b)
10:         CAS(traphp_q, tag, b)
11: RetireNode($list_p$)

GetCapturedBlock$_p()$: pointer to blocktype

1: b := $\text{trap}_p \to$ Captured
2: if (b is a pointer value) return b else return NULL

Fig. 3. Trap structures and functions.

ReleaseTrap$_p()$: In this function, p simply sets $\text{trap}_p \to$ Active to FALSE and is ready to reuse the trap if needed. It is essential that $\text{trap}_p \to$ Active = FALSE whenever p updates the other fields of trap_p or traphp_p. Lines 2 and 3 are optional optimizations.

GetCapturedBlock$_p()$: In this function, p simply checks if any other thread has replaced the tag value it has put in $\text{trap}_p \to$ Captured in SetTrap$_p$ with a pointer value (block address). If so, GetCapturedBlock returns the address of the captured block, otherwise it returns NULL to indicate that no block has been captured yet by this trap.

ScanTraps$_p(list_p)$: Every successful SC$_{p,i}$ requires scanning the traps of the other thread for criteria matching the removed block $exp_{p,i}$ that held the value of $\mathcal{O}$ just before the success of SC. The ScanTraps function can be implemented in several ways. A simple implementation would be to scan the traps upon every successful SC, but this would take linear time per successful SC.

We show an amortized implementation that takes constant amortized expected time per successful SC. In this implementation, instead of calling ScanTraps for every successful SC, p accumulates replaced blocks in a persistent private list $list_p$. When $list_p$ contains enough removed blocks for amortization ($O(N)$ blocks or less if the trap structures are integrated with the hazard pointer method), p proceeds to scan the trap structures of others participating threads. First, p organizes the addresses of the blocks in $list_p$ in an efficient private search structure (hash table) that allows constant expected lookup time. If $list_p$ contains multiple blocks that hold values for the same LL/SC/VL variable, the lookup can just return the block with the highest sequence number.

Now we describe the scanning process. For each participating thread q, p starts by checking $trap_q \rightarrow$Active in line 2. If it is FALSE, then it is certain that q does not have an active trap that was set before any of the blocks in $list_p$ were removed. Therefore, p can skip this trap and move on to the next one if any.

If $trap_q \rightarrow$Active is TRUE, p proceeds to line 3 and reads $trap_q \rightarrow$Captured into the local variable tag. If tag is a pointer value, then it is either NULL or actually a block's address and not a tag. If it is NULL, then the trap must have already been released. If it is an actual block, then it must be the case that $trap_q$ has already captured a block. Therefore p need not be concerned about providing a block to $trap_q$ whether or not $list_p$ contains blocks that match the criteria of $trap_q$. So, whether $trap_q$ has been released or has captured a block, p can skip this trap and move on to the next one if any.

If tag is a non-pointer value, then $trap_q$ has not captured a block and so p needs to proceed to lines 5 and 6, to read $trap_q \rightarrow$Var and $trap_q \rightarrow$Seq. In line 7, p performs a lookup in $list_p$ (in constant expected time) for a block that matches the criteria of $trap_q$. If none are found, then p moves on to the next trap if any.

If p finds a block b in $list_p$ that matches the criteria of $trap_q$, then p tries to install b in $trap_q \rightarrow$Captured using CAS in line 9. If the CAS fails then it must be the case that either the trap has been released or some other thread has installed a block in $trap_q \rightarrow$Captured, and so p can move on to the next trap if any. If the CAS (in line 9) succeeds, then $trap_q$ has captured b. In this case p needs to ensure that b is not freed before the release of $trap_q$. Therefore it tries to set $traphp_q$ to b in line 10 using CAS.

If the CAS in line 10 fails, then q must have already released the trap. Therefore, neither b nor possibly the other blocks in $list_p$ that matched the criteria in $trap_q$ need to be prevented from being free (at least as far as $trap_q$ is concerned). So, p moves on to the next trap if any.

If the CAS in line 10 succeeds, then the hazard pointer method guarantees that b will not be freed as long as $traphp_q$ remains unchanged, i.e., not before $trap_q$ is released.

After scanning the trap records of all participating threads, p is guaranteed that all the blocks in $list_p$ can be passed safely to the hazard pointer method (through RetireNode) for ultimate determination of when they are safe to be freed. If a block b has been captured by one or more traps then it will not be freed as long as any of these traps has not been released. If a block b has not been captured by any traps, then either it did not match the criteria of any of the traps set before its removal, or it did match the criteria of one or more traps but in each case either the trap has been released or some other block has been captures by the trap. In any case, it is safe to pass b to RetireNode.

The trap structures can be maintained dynamically and in a wait-free manner similar to the hazard pointer structures in [9, Figure 4]. Threads can participate (i.e., acquire and release trap structures) dynamically and in a wait-free manner, and do not require advance knowledge of the maximum value of N. Furthermore, the trap structures can be integrated in the hazard pointer structures, and the blocks accumulated in $list_p$ can be counted together with the blocks accumulated for the sake of amortization in the hazard pointer method. For example, The blocks in $list_p$ can be counted with other removed blocks awaiting processing by the hazard pointer method (i.e., those in the *not-safe-yet* list mentioned in Section 3). When the combined count of these two lists reaches the (dynamically determined) batch size for the hazard pointer method, blocks in $list_p$ scan the trap structures, and then blocks in both lists scan the hazard pointers, all in a wait-free manner and with constant amortized expected time per freed block.

5   Complexity and Implementation Issues

Time and Work Complexities. In the wait-free LL/SC/VL implementation LL, VL, and unsuccessful SC operations take constant time, and successful SC operations take constant amortized expected time. In the lock-free LL/SC/VL implementation, SC and VL are wait-free. Successful SC operations take constant amortized expected time, and VL and unsuccessful SC operations take constant time. LL takes constant time in the absence of intervening successful SC operations.

The conventional performance measure for lock-free algorithms is work, the total number of steps executed by N threads to perform some number r of operations. In our implementations LL, VL, and unsuccessful SC operations do not interfere with each other and all operations take at most constant amortized expected time in the absence of contention. So, the amortized expected work complexity of our implementations is the same (except for the amortized and expected qualifiers) as that of a hypothetical hardware implementation of ideal LL/SC/VL. For example, consider r LL operations, r LL/SC pairs, and as many LL/SC operations as needed to result in r successful SC operations. Assuming hardware support for ideal LL/SC/VL, the work is $O(r)$, $O(r)$, and $O(r.N)$, respectively. Using either of our LL/SC/VL implementations, the amortized expected work is $O(r)$, $O(r)$, and $O(r.N)$, respectively.

Space Complexity. The worst-case space complexity of our LL/SC/VL implementations consists of two components: (1) space overhead per LL/SC/VL variable, and (2) space per participating thread.

Component (1): For both implementations the space overhead per variable is a small constant, one word (variable X) for the lock-free implementation and four words (variables X and Seq, and the Var and Seq fields of the current block) for the wait-free implementation. Component (2): For both implementations, the space per participating thread is $O(N.K)$.

Component (1) is obviously reasonable and constitutes a clear and significant improvement over the space complexity of Jayanti and Petrovic's implementations [7]. Whether the number of LL/SC/VL variables in a program is large or not is no longer a concern.

We now argue that in the vast majority of cases, component (2) is – or can be made – within acceptable practical limits. If the maximum number of threads (active at the same time) in the program is in the order of hundreds or less, then the space overhead is within acceptable limits for 64-bit applications. Otherwise, we argue that optimizations can be applied to the hazard pointer method and to the trap structures and functions in order to reduce the expected space overhead to acceptable levels.

If a program may have a large number of threads active concurrently, a two-track (or more) organization can be used for hazard pointer and trap structures, in order to keep the number of participating threads N acceptable. High priority threads that operate frequently on LL/SC/VL variables use the first track, while threads that operate infrequently on LL/SC/VL variable use the other tracks. Threads in the first track keep their hazard pointer and trap structures between operations on lock-free objects. The other threads participate in the LL/SC/VL mechanism and hazard pointer method dynamically (still in a wait-free manner as in [9, Figure 4]) and use the other track(s). These threads acquire hazard pointer and trap structures dynamically before operating on lock-free objects and then release them after they are done with the operation.

Let N_1 be the maximum number of threads using the first track concurrently. Let n_2 be the number of threads that are participating concurrently in the LL/SC/VL mechanism using the second track at some time t. Let N_2 be the maximum value of n_2. Then, N is at most $N_1 + N_2$. As threads that use the second track are expected to operate infrequently on LL/SC/VL variables, the value of N is expected to be much less than the actual total number of threads. The amortized expected time for the operations of the first track threads remains constant, while for threads using the second track it is $O(n_2)$ (to acquire hazard pointer and trap structures dynamically as in [9]). Again, as second track threads are not expected to operate frequently on LL/SC/VL variables, then n_2 is expected to be small.

Supporting Reads and Writes: By supporting arbitrary-sized LL/SC/VL variables, it is straightforward to extend our implementations to support LL/SC/VL variables that also support reads and writes, by using Jayanti's constructions of LL/SC/VL/Read/Write from LL/SC/VL [6].

Using Restricted LL/SC: On architectures which support restricted LL/SC rather than CAS, CAS(a,e,v) can be implemented as follows [12]:

do { if (LL(a) ≠ e) return FALSE } until SC(a,v); return TRUE

Supporting Persistent Reservations: Our implementations can be easily extended to support what we call *persistent reservations*, which may be needed for lock-free traversal. With persistent reservations, a successful SC does not end a reservation, but rather a thread can perform multiple successful SC operations during the lifetime of the same reservation. This can be achieved without increase in the time, work, or space complexity of the implementations, by using a total of $K + 1$ hazard pointers per thread and by swapping hazard pointer labels after successful SC operations, if reservation persistence is desired.

6   Conclusion

Ideal LL/SC/VL offer a complete solution for the ABA problem. In this paper, we presented practical lock-free and wait-free implementations of LL/SC/VL that improve on Jayanti and Petrovic's implementations [7] by limiting the space requirements to practically acceptable levels, and eliminating the need for advance knowledge of the number of threads that may operate on these variables, while still using only 64-bit CAS, and maintaining low time and work complexities and low latency.

References

1. J. H. Anderson and M. Moir. Universal constructions for multi-object operations. In *Proceedings of the Fourteenth Annual ACM Symposium on Principles of Distributed Computing*, pages 184–193, 1995.
2. M. P. Herlihy. Wait-free synchronization. *ACM Transactions on Programming Languages and Systems*, 13(1):124–149, Jan. 1991.
3. M. P. Herlihy. A methodology for implementing highly concurrent objects. *ACM Transactions on Programming Languages and Systems*, 15(5):745–770, Nov. 1993.
4. M. P. Herlihy and J. M. Wing. Linearizability: A correctness condition for concurrent objects. *ACM Transactions on Programming Languages and Systems*, 12(3):463–492, July 1990.
5. *IBM System/370 Extended Architecture, Principles of Operation*, 1983. Publication No. SA22-7085.
6. P. Jayanti. A complete and constant time wait-free implementation of CAS from LL/SC and vice versa. In *Proceedings of the Twelfth International Symposium on Distributed Computing*, pages 216–230, Sept. 1998.
7. P. Jayanti and S. Petrovic. Efficient and practical constructions of LL/SC variables. In *Proceedings of the Twenty-Second Annual ACM Symposium on Principles of Distributed Computing*, pages 285–294, July 2003.
8. M. M. Michael. ABA prevention using single-word instructions. Technical Report RC 23089, IBM T. J. Watson Research Center, Jan. 2004.
9. M. M. Michael. Hazard pointers: Safe memory reclamation for lock-free objects. *IEEE Transactions on Parallel and Distributed Systems*, 15(6):491–504, June 2004. Earlier version in *21st PODC*, pages 21–30, July 2002.
10. M. M. Michael. Scalable lock-free dynamic memory allocation. In *Proceedings of the 2004 ACM SIGPLAN Conference on Programming Language Design and Implementation*, pages 35–46, June 2004.
11. M. Moir. Practical implementations of non-blocking synchronization primitives. In *Proceedings of the 16th Annual ACM Symposium on Principles of Distributed Computing*, pages 219–228, Aug. 1997.
12. *PowerPC Microprocessor Family: The Programming Environment*, 1991.

Efficient Adaptive Collect Using Randomization

Hagit Attiya[1], Fabian Kuhn[2], Mirjam Wattenhofer[2], and Roger Wattenhofer[2]

[1] Department of Computer Science, Technion
[2] Department of Computer Science, ETH Zurich

Abstract. An *adaptive* algorithm, whose step complexity adjusts to the number of active processes, is attractive for distributed systems with a highly-variable number of processes. The cornerstone of many adaptive algorithms is an adaptive mechanism to collect up-to-date information from all participating processes. To date, all known collect algorithms either have non-linear step complexity or they are impractical because of unrealistic memory overhead.

This paper presents new randomized collect algorithms with asymptotically optimal $O(k)$ step complexity and polynomial memory overhead only. In addition we present a new deterministic collect algorithm which beats the best step complexity for previous polynomial-memory algorithms.

1 Introduction and Related Work

To solve certain problems, processes need to collect up-to-date information about the other participating processes. For example, in a typical *indulgent* consensus algorithm [9, 10], a process needs to announce its preferred decision value and obtain the preferences of all other processes. Other problems where processes need to collect values are in the area of atomic snapshots [1, 4, 8], mutual exclusion [2, 3, 5, 6], and renaming [2]. A simple way that information about other processes can be communicated is to use an array of registers indexed by process identifiers. An active process can update information about itself by writing into its register. A process can collect the information it wants about other participating processes by reading the entire array of registers. This takes $O(n)$ steps, where n is the total number of processes.

When there are only a few participating processes, it is preferable to be able to collect the required information more quickly. An *adaptive* algorithm is one whose step complexity is a function of the number of participating processes. Specifically, if it performs at most $f(k)$ steps when there are k participating processes, we say that it is f-adaptive. An algorithm is *wait-free* if all processes can complete their operations in a finite number of steps, regardless of the behavior of the other processes [11].

Several adaptive, wait-free collect algorithms are known [2, 7, 8]. In particular, there is an algorithm that features an asymptotically optimal $O(k)$-adaptive collect, but its memory consumption is exponential in the number of potential processes [8], which renders the algorithm impractical. Other algorithms have polynomial (in the number of potential processes) memory complexity, but the collect costs $\Theta(k^2)$ steps [8, 14][1]. The lower bound of Jayanti, Tan and Toueg [12] implies that the step complexity of a collect algorithm is $\Omega(k)$. This raises the question of the existence of a collect algorithm

---

[1] Moir and Anderson [14] employ a matrix structure to solve the renaming problem. The same structure can be used to solve the collect problem, following ideas of [8].

R. Guerraoui (Ed.): DISC 2004, LNCS 3274, pp. 159–173, 2004.

that features an asymptotically optimal $O(k)$ step complexity and needs polynomial memory size only.

This paper suggests that randomization can be used to make adaptive collect algorithms more practical, in contrast to known deterministic algorithms with either superlinear step complexity or unrealistic memory overhead. We present wait-free algorithms that take $O(k)$ steps to store and collect, while having polynomial memory overhead only. The algorithms are randomized, and their step complexity bounds hold "with high probability" as well as "in expectation." We believe that randomization may bring a fresh approach to the design of adaptive shared-memory algorithms.

Analogously to previous approaches, both randomized algorithms use *splitters* as introduced by Moir and Anderson to govern the algorithmic decisions of processes [14]. Our first algorithm (Section 4) uses a *randomized* splitter, and operates on a complete binary tree of depth $c \log n$, for carefully chosen constant c. A process traverses the tree of random splitters as in the linear collect algorithm [8]. We prove that with high probability the process stops at some vertex in this shallow tree; in (the low-probability) case that a process reaches the leaves of the tree, it falls back on a deterministic *backup* structure. A binary tree of radomized splitters was previously used by Kim and Anderson [13] for adaptive mutual exclusion.

Our second algorithm (Section 5) uses standard, deterministic splitters [14]. The splitters are connected in a random graph (with out-degree two), that is, the randomization is in the topology rather than in the actual algorithm executed by the processes. A process traverses the random graph by accessing the splitters. However, if the process suspects that it has stayed in the graph for too long, it immediately moves to a deterministic backup structure. We prove that with high probability, the graph traversed by the processes does not contain a cycle, and the backup structure is not accessed at all. This relies on the assumption that the adversarial scheduler is not allowed to inspect this graph.

The crux of the step complexity analysis of both algorithms is a balls-into-bins game, and it requires a probabilistic lemma estimating the number of balls in bins containing more than one ball.

In addition, Section 3 introduces a new wait-free, deterministic algorithm that improves the trade-off between collect time and memory complexity: Using polynomial memory only, we achieve $o(k^2)$ collect. The randomized algorithms fall back on this algorithm. For any integer $\gamma > 1$, the algorithm provides a STORE with $O(k)$ step complexity, a COLLECT with $O(k^2/((\gamma - 1) \log n))$ step complexity and $O(n^{\gamma+1}/((\gamma - 1) \log n))$ memory complexity. Interestingly, by choosing γ accordingly, our deterministic algorithm achieves the bounds of both previously known algorithms [8, 14].

All new algorithms build on the basic collect algorithm on a binary tree [8]. To employ this algorithm in a more versatile manner than its original design, we rely on a new and simplified proof for the linear step complexity of COLLECT (Section 3.1).

2   Model

We assume a standard asynchronous shared-memory model of computation. A system consists of n *processes*, $p_1, \ldots, p_n$, communicating by reading from and writing to shared *registers*.

Processes are state machines, each with a (possibly infinite) set of local states, which includes a unique *initial state*. In each *step*, the process determines which operation to perform according to its local state, and subsequently changes its local state according to the value returned by the operation.

A *register* provides two operations: *read*, returning the value of the register; and *write*, changing the register value to the value of its input. A *configuration* consists of the states of the processes and the values of the registers. In the *initial configuration*, every process is in the initial state and all registers are $\bot$. A *schedule* is a (possibly infinite) sequence $p_{i_1}, p_{i_2}, \ldots$ of process identifiers. An *execution* consists of the initial configuration and a schedule, representing the interleaving of steps by processes.

An *implementation* of an object of type X provides for every operation OP of X a set of n procedures $F_1, \ldots, F_n$, one for each process. (Typically, the procedures are the same for all processes.) To execute OP on X, process p_i calls procedure F_i. The worst-case number of steps performed by some process p_i executing procedure F_i is the *step complexity* of implementing OP.

An operation OP_i *precedes* operation OP_j (and OP_j *follows* operation OP_i) in an execution α, if the call to the procedure of OP_j appears in α after the return from the procedure of OP_i.

Let α be a finite execution. Process p_i is *active* during α if α includes a call of a procedure F_i. The *total contention* during α is the number of all processes that are active during α. Let f be a non-decreasing function. An implementation is f-*adaptive* to total contention if the step complexity of each of its procedures is bounded from above by $f(k)$, where k is the total contention.

A *collect algorithm* provides two operations: A STORE(val) by process p_i sets val to be the latest value for p_i. A COLLECT operation returns a *view*, a partial function V from the set of processes to a set of values, where $V(p_i)$ is the latest value stored by p_i, for each process p_i. A COLLECT operation cop should not read from the future or miss a preceding STORE operation sop. Formally, the following validity properties hold for every process p_i:

- If $V(p_i) = \bot$, then no STORE operation by p_i precedes cop.
- If $V(p_i) = v \neq \bot$, then v is the value of a STORE operation sop of p_i that does not follow cop, and there is no STORE operation by p_i that follows sop and precedes cop.

3 Deterministic Adaptive Collect

3.1 The Basic Binary Tree Algorithm

Associated to each vertex in the complete binary tree of depth $n - 1$ is a *splitter* [14]: A process entering a splitter exits with either **stop**, **left** or **right**. It is guaranteed that if a single process enters the splitter, then it obtains **stop**, and if two or more processes enter the splitter, then there are two processes that obtain different values. Thus the set of processes is "split" into smaller subsets, according to the values obtained.

To perform a STORE in the algorithm of [8], a process writes its value in its acquired vertex. In case it has no vertex acquired yet it starts at the root of the tree and moves down the data structure according to the values obtained in the splitters along the path: If it receives a **left**, it moves to the left child, if it receives a **right**, it moves to the right child. A process marks each vertex it accesses by raising a flag associated with the vertex. We call a vertex *marked*, if its flag is raised. A process i acquires a vertex v, or stops in v, if it receives a **stop** at v's splitter. It then writes its id into $v.id$ and its value in $v.value$. In later invocations of STORE, process i immediately writes its value in $v.value$, clearly leading to a constant step complexity $O(1)$. This leaves us to determine the step complexity of the first invocation of STORE.

In order to perform a COLLECT, a process traverses the part of the tree containing marked vertices in DFS order and collects the values written in the marked vertices.

A complete binary tree of depth $n - 1$ has $2^n - 1$ vertices, implying the following lemma.

Lemma 1. *The memory complexity is $\Theta(2^n)$.*

Lemma 2 ([8]). *Each process writes its id in a vertex with depth at most $k - 1$ and no other process writes its id in the same vertex.*

Lemma 3. *The step complexity of COLLECT at most $2k - 1$.*

Proof. In order to perform a collect, a process traverses the marked part of the tree. Hence, the step complexity of a collect is equivalent to the number of marked (visited) vertices.

Let x_k be the number of marked vertices in a tree, where k processes access the root. The splitter properties imply the following recursive equations:

$$x_k = x_i + x_{k-i-1} + 1, \qquad (i \geq 0) \qquad (1)$$
$$x_k = x_i + x_{k-i} + 1, \qquad (i > 0) \qquad (2)$$

depending on whether (1) or not (2) a process stops in the splitter.

We prove the lemma by induction; note that the lemma trivially holds for $k = 1$. For the induction step, assume the lemma is true for $j < k$, that is, $x_j \leq 2j - 1$. Then we can rewrite Equation (1):

$$x_k \leq (2i - 1) + (2(k - i - 1) - 1) + 1 \leq 2k - 1$$

and Equation (2) becomes:

$$x_k \leq (2i - 1) + (2(k - i) - 1) + 1 \leq 2k - 1.$$

$\square$

3.2   The Cascaded Trees Algorithm

We present a spectrum of algorithms, each providing a different trade-off between memory complexity and step complexity. For an arbitrary constant $\gamma > 1$, the *cascaded trees algorithm* provides a STORE with $O(k)$ step complexity, a COLLECT with $O(k^2/((\gamma - 1)\log n))$ step complexity and $O(n^{\gamma+1})$ memory complexity.

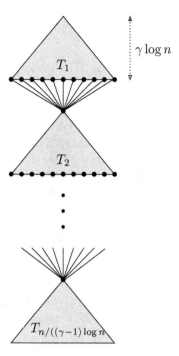

Fig. 1. Organization of splitters in the cascaded trees algorithm.

The Algorithm. The algorithm is performed on a sequence of $n/((\gamma-1)\lceil \log n \rceil)$ complete binary splitter trees of depth $\gamma \log n$, denoted $T_1, \ldots, T_{n/((\gamma-1)\lceil \log n \rceil)}$. Except for the last tree, each leaf of tree T_i has an edge to the root of tree T_{i+1} (Figure 1).

To perform a STORE, a process writes in its acquired vertex. If it has not acquired a vertex yet, it starts at the root of the first tree and moves down the data structure as in the binary tree STORE (described in the previous section). A process that does not stop at some vertex of tree T_i continues to the root of the next tree. Note that both the right and the left child of a leaf in tree T_i, $1 \le i \le n/((\gamma - 1)\lceil \log n \rceil) - 1$, are the root of the next tree.

The splitter properties guarantee that no two processes stop at the same vertex.

To perform a COLLECT, a process traverses the part of tree T_i containing marked vertices in DFS order and collects the values written in the marked vertices. If any of the leaves of tree i are marked, the process also collects in tree T_{i+1}.

Analysis. We have $n/((\gamma - 1) \log n)$ trees, each of depth $\gamma \log n$, implying the following lemma.

Lemma 4. *The memory complexity is*

$$O\left(\frac{n^{\gamma+1}}{(\gamma - 1) \log n} \right).$$

Let k be the number of processes that call STORE at least once and k_i be the number of processes that access the root of tree T_i.

Lemma 5. *At least* $\min\{k_i, (\gamma - 1)\lceil \log n \rceil\}$ *processes stop in some vertex of tree* T_i, *for every* i, $1 \leq i \leq n/(\gamma - 1) \log n$.

Proof. Let m_i be the number of marked leaves in tree T_i. Consider the tree T_i' that is induced by all the paths from the root to the marked leaves of T_i.

A non-leaf vertex $v \in T_i'$ with one marked child in T_i' corresponds to at least one process that does not continue to T_{i+1}. If only one child of v is visited in T_i, then some process obtained **stop** at v and does not continue. Otherwise, processes reaching v are split between left and right. Since only one path leads to a leaf, say, the one through the left child, at least one process (that obtained **right** at v) does not access the left child of v and does not reach a leaf of T_i.

The number of vertices in T_i' with two children is exactly $m_i - 1$, since at each such node, the number of paths to the leaves increases by one.

To count the number of vertices with one child, we estimate the total number of vertices in T_i' and then subtract $m_i - 1$.

Starting from the leaves, the number of vertices on each preceding level is at least half the number at the current level. For the number of non-leaf vertices n_i of tree T_i', we therefore get:

$$n_i \geq \underbrace{\frac{m_i}{2} + \frac{m_i}{4} + \cdots + \frac{m_i}{2^{\lceil \log m_i \rceil}}}_{m_i - 1} + \underbrace{1 + \cdots + 1}_{\gamma \lceil \log n \rceil - \lceil \log m_i \rceil},$$

where the number of ones in the equation follows from the fact that the tree T_i hast depth $\gamma \log n$ and after $\lceil \log m_i \rceil$ levels the number of vertices on the next level can be lower bounded by one. The claim follows since $m_i \leq n$. □

Lemma 6. *A process writes its id in a vertex at depth at most* $k \cdot \gamma/(\gamma - 1)$.

Proof. If $k \leq (\gamma - 1)\lceil \log n \rceil$, the claim follows from Lemma 2.

If $k = m \cdot (\gamma - 1)\lceil \log n \rceil$, for some $m > 1$, then we know by Lemma 5 that in each tree, at least $(\gamma - 1)\lceil \log n \rceil$ processes will stop in a vertex. Thus, at most $(\gamma - 1)\lceil \log n \rceil$ processes access tree T_m. By Lemma 2, a process stops in a vertex with total depth at most $\gamma \log n \cdot (m - 1) + \gamma \log n = k \cdot \gamma/(\gamma - 1)$. □

Since each splitter requires a constant number of operations, by Lemma 6, the step complexity of the first invocation of STORE is $O(\gamma/(\gamma - 1)k)$ and all invocations thereafter require $O(1)$ steps.

By Lemma 3, the time to collect in tree T_i is $2k_i - 1$. By Lemma 6, all processes stop after at most $k/((\gamma - 1) \log n)$ trees. This implies the next lemma:

Lemma 7. *The step complexity of a* COLLECT *is*

$$O\left(\frac{k^2}{(\gamma - 1)\log n}\right).$$

Remark: The cascaded-trees algorithm provides a spectrum of trade-offs between memory complexity and step complexity. Choosing $\gamma = 1+1/\log n$ gives an algorithm with $O(k^2)$ step complexity for COLLECT and $O(n^2)$ memory complexity; this matches the complexities of the matrix algorithm [14]. Setting $\gamma = n/\log n + 1$ yields a single binary tree of height n; namely, an algorithm where the step complexity of COLLECT is linear in k but the memory requirements are exponential, as in the algorithm of [8].

4   Adaptive Collect with Randomized Splitters

The next two sections present two algorithms that allow to STORE and COLLECT with $O(k)$ step complexity and polynomial memory complexity. For the first algorithm, we use a new kind of randomized splitters, arranged in a binary tree of small size. The second algorithm uses classical splitters (Section 3.1) which are interconnected at random.

For both algorithms, we need the following lemma.

Lemma 8. *Assume k balls are thrown into N bins, i.e. the bins for all balls are chosen independently and uniformly at random. Let C denote the number of balls ending up in bins containing more than one ball. We have*

$$\frac{k(k-1)}{N} - \frac{k^3}{2N^2} \le \mathrm{E}[C] \le \frac{k(k-1)}{N} \tag{3}$$

and

$$\Pr\left(C \ge t + \frac{k^2}{N}\right) \le \frac{6k^2}{t^2 N} \tag{4}$$

under the condition that $k \le N^{2/3}$.

Proof. Let us first prove the bounds (3) on the expected value $\mathrm{E}[C]$. The random variable B_m denotes the number of bins containing exactly m balls. Further, P is the number of pairs (i, j) of balls for which ball i and ball j end up in the same bin. The variable T is defined accordingly for triples. Clearly, we have

$$C = \sum_{m=2}^{\infty} m B_m,$$

as well as

$$P = \sum_{m=2}^{\infty} \binom{m}{2} B_m \quad \text{and} \quad T = \sum_{m=3}^{\infty} \binom{m}{3} B_m.$$

We get $2P - 3T \le C \le 2P$ because

$$2P - 3T = 2B_2 + \sum_{m=3}^{\infty} m(m-1)\left(1 - \frac{m-2}{2}\right) B_m$$

$$\le 2B_2 + 3B_3 \le C \le \sum_{m=2}^{\infty} m(m-1) B_m = 2P.$$

Let p_{ij} be the probability that a pair of balls i and j are in the same bin. Accordingly, p_{ijl} denotes the probability that balls i, j, and l are in the same bin. We have $p_{ij} = 1/N$ and $p_{ijl} = 1/N^2$. Using p_{ij} and p_{ijl}, we can compute the expected values of P and T as

$$E[P] = \binom{k}{2} p_{ij} = \frac{k(k-1)}{2N} \quad \text{and}$$

$$E[T] = \binom{k}{3} p_{ijl} \leq \frac{k^3}{6N^2}.$$

Using $2P - 3T \leq C \leq 2P$ and linearity of expectation, the bounds on $E[C]$, claimed in (3), follow.

We prove Inequality (4) using the Chebyshev inequality. In order to do so, we need to know an upper bound on the variance $\mathrm{Var}[C]$ of C. Let $\mathcal{E}_i$ be the event that ball i is in a bin with at least two balls. Further, $\mathcal{E}_{ij}$ is the event that i and j are together in the same bin whereas $\overline{\mathcal{E}_{ij}}$ denotes the complement, i.e. the event that i and j are in different bins. $\mathrm{Var}[C]$ can be written as $\mathrm{Var}[C] = E[C^2] - E[C]^2$. The expected value of C^2 can be computed as follows:

$$E[C^2] = E\left[\left(\sum_{i=1}^{k} X_i\right)^2\right] = E\left[\sum_{i=1}^{k} X_i^2 + 2\sum_{1 \leq i < j \leq k} X_i X_j\right]$$
$$= E[C] + 2 \cdot \sum_{1 \leq i < j \leq k} \Pr(\mathcal{E}_i \cap \mathcal{E}_j). \tag{5}$$

We have $\Pr(\mathcal{E}_i \cap \mathcal{E}_j) = \Pr(\mathcal{E}_i) \cdot \Pr(\mathcal{E}_j | \mathcal{E}_i)$ and

$$\Pr(\mathcal{E}_j | \mathcal{E}_i) = \Pr(\mathcal{E}_{ij} | \mathcal{E}_i) + \Pr(\mathcal{E}_j \cap \overline{\mathcal{E}_{ij}} | \mathcal{E}_i)$$
$$= \frac{\Pr(\mathcal{E}_{ij})}{\Pr(\mathcal{E}_i)} + \Pr(\mathcal{E}_2 \cap \overline{\mathcal{E}_{12}} | \mathcal{E}_{13}) \tag{6}$$
$$\leq \frac{\Pr(\mathcal{E}_{ij})}{\Pr(\mathcal{E}_i)} + \Pr\left(\bigcup_{\ell=4}^{k} \mathcal{E}_{2\ell} \,\middle|\, \mathcal{E}_{13}\right)$$
$$= \frac{\Pr(\mathcal{E}_{ij})}{\Pr(\mathcal{E}_i)} + \Pr\left(\bigcup_{\ell=4}^{k} \mathcal{E}_{2\ell}\right). \tag{7}$$

For Equation (6), we assume that w.l.o.g., ball 1 is in the same bin as ball 3 and that ball 2 shares the bin with some ball i for $i = 4, \ldots, k$. Equation (7) holds because $\mathcal{E}_{13}$ and $\mathcal{E}_{2\ell}$ are independent for $\ell \geq 4$. The probability that two balls i and j are in the same bin is $\Pr(\mathcal{E}_{ij}) = 1/N$. Using the bounds (3) on $E[C]$ and linearity of expectation, we get the following bounds for the probability of E_i:

$$\frac{k-1}{N} - \frac{k^2}{2N^2} \leq \Pr(\mathcal{E}_i) \leq \frac{k-1}{N}. \tag{8}$$

Therefore, we have

$$\frac{\Pr(\mathcal{E}_{ij})}{\Pr(\mathcal{E}_i)} \leq \frac{\frac{1}{N}}{\frac{k-1}{N} - \frac{k^2}{2N^2}} \leq \frac{2}{k-1} \tag{9}$$

where the second inequality of (9) holds for $k \leq N^{2/3}$ and $N \geq 5$. The second term of Equation (7) can be bounded as

$$\Pr\left(\bigcup_{\ell=4}^{k} \mathcal{E}_{2\ell}\right) \leq \sum_{\ell=4}^{k} \Pr(\mathcal{E}_{2\ell}) = \frac{k-3}{N}. \tag{10}$$

Combining (7), (8), (9), and (10), we get

$$\Pr(\mathcal{E}_i \cap \mathcal{E}_j) \leq \frac{k-1}{N} \cdot \left(\frac{2}{k-1} + \frac{k-3}{N}\right) \leq \frac{2}{N} + \frac{k^2}{N^2}.$$

Applying Equation (5), we have

$$\mathrm{E}[C^2] \leq \frac{k(k-1)}{N} + 2\binom{k}{2}\left(\frac{2}{N} + \frac{k^2}{N^2}\right) \leq \frac{3k^2}{N} + \frac{k^4}{N^2}$$

and therefore

$$\mathrm{Var}[C] \leq \frac{3k^2}{N} + \frac{k^4}{N^2} - \left(\frac{k(k-1)}{N} - \frac{k^3}{2N^2}\right)^2 \leq \frac{3k^2}{N} + \frac{2k^3}{N^2} + \frac{k^5}{N^3} \underset{(k \leq N^{3/2})}{\leq} \frac{6k^2}{N}.$$

Using the bounds for $\mathrm{E}[C]$ and $\mathrm{Var}[C]$, we can now apply Chebyshev in order to bound the probability of the upper tail of C:

$$\Pr\left(C \geq t + \frac{k^2}{N}\right) \leq \frac{6k^2}{t^2 N}.$$

This concludes the proof.   □

4.1   The Algorithm

The algorithm presented in this section provides STORE and COLLECT with $O(k)$ step complexity and polynomial memory complexity. It uses a new kind of splitter that makes a random choice in order to partition the processes to left and right. The algorithm operates on a complete binary tree of depth $c \log n$ ($c \geq 3/2$) with randomized splitters (see Algorithm 1) in the vertices. The algorithm uses the cascaded trees structure (of Section 3.2) as well as an array of length n as deterministic backup structures. The cascaded trees have height $2 \log(4\sqrt{n})$ and there are $4\sqrt{n}/\log(4\sqrt{n})$ such trees. That is, we build the structure with the parameter $\gamma = 2$ but only for $4\sqrt{n}$ processes.

As in the previous algorithms, a process tries to acquire a vertex by moving down the data structure according to the values obtained from the randomized splitters. If a process does not stop at a leaf of the tree, it enters the cascaded trees backup structure. If a process also fails to stop at a vertex of the first backup structure (the cascaded trees), it raises a flag, indicating that the array structure is used, and stores its value in the array at the index corresponding to the process ID. That is, process i stores its value at position i in the array for $1 \leq i \leq n$.

The COLLECT works analogously to the previous algorithms. The marked part (visited splitters) of the randomized splitter tree is first traversed in DFS order. Then, if necessary, the first backup structure is traversed as described in Section 3.2. Finally, if the flag of the array is set, the whole array is read.

Algorithm 1 Randomized Splitter.

1: $X = id_i$
2: if Y then return randomly **right** or **left**
3: Y = true
4: **if** $(X == id_i)$ **then**
5:     return **stop**
6: **else**
7:     return randomly **right** or **left**
8: **fi**

4.2   Analysis

Clearly, the tree of randomized splitters needs $O(n^c)$ randomized splitters and therefore $O(n^c)$ registers. By Lemma 4, the first backup structure requires $O((\sqrt{n})^3/\log\sqrt{n}) = O(n^{3/2}/\log n)$ registers; the array takes n additional registers, implying the following lemma.

Lemma 9. *The memory complexity is $O(n^c)$ for $c > 3/2$.*

Lemma 10. *The probability that more than $4\sqrt{k}$ processes enter the first backup structure is at most k/n^c.*

Proof. In order to get an upper bound on the probability that at least a certain number of processes reach a leaf of the randomized splitter tree, we can assume that whenever at least two processes visit a splitter, none of them stops and all of them are randomly forwarded to the left or the right child. Assume that we extend the random walk of stopping processes until they reach a leaf. If we do this, the set of processes which stops in the tree corresponds to the set of processes which arrive at a leaf that is not reached by any other processes. On the other hand, all processes which are not alone when arriving at their leaf have to enter the backup structure. Because the leaves of the processes are chosen independently and uniformly at random, we can view it as a 'balls-into-bins' game and the lemma follows by applying Lemma 8 with $N = n^c$ and $t = 3\sqrt{k}$. Note that $k \leq (n^c)^{2/3}$, since $c \geq 3/2$.   □

Lemma 11. *The number of marked nodes in the random splitter tree is at most $3k$ in expectation and no more than $7k$ with probability at least $1 - 1/2^k$.*

Proof. We partition the marked vertices into vertices where the processes are split (there are processes going left *and* processes going right *or* some process stops at the node) and into vertices where all processes proceed into the same direction. If we contract all the paths of vertices which do not split the processes to single edges, we obtain a binary tree where all vertices behave like regular splitters (not all processes go into the same direction). Hence, by Lemma 3, there are at most $2k - 1$ of those vertices. At most $k - 1$ of them are visited by more than one process. All paths of non-splitting vertices are preceding one of those $k - 1$ splitting vertices. That is, there are at most $k - 1$ paths of consecutive vertices where all processes proceed in the same direction. As there are at least two processes traversing such paths, in the worst case, the length Z_i of each path i is geometrically distributed with probability $\Pr(Z_i = \ell) \leq 1/2^{\ell+1}$. Thus, the distribution of the total number X of vertices where processes are not split can be by estimated by the distribution of the sum of $k-1$ independent geometrically distributed random variables. Let $Y := \sum_{i=1}^{k-1} Z_i$, we have

$$E[X] \leq E[Y] = (k-1)E[Z_i] = k-1.$$

and therefore, the total number of marked nodes is at most $3k$ in expectation. For the tail probability, we have

$$\Pr(X \geq x) \leq \Pr(Y \geq x). \tag{11}$$

The random variable Y can be seen as the number of Bernoulli trials with success probability $1/2$ until there are $k-1$ successes, i.e., the distribution of Y is a negative binomial distribution. We have

$$\Pr(Y = y) = \binom{y-1}{k-2}\left(\frac{1}{2}\right)^y.$$

For $y \geq 5k$, we have

$$\frac{\Pr(Y = y+1)}{\Pr(Y = y)} = \frac{y}{y-k+2} \cdot \frac{1}{2} \leq \frac{5}{8}.$$

Therefore, for $y \geq 5k$, $\Pr(Y \geq y)$ can be upper bounded by a geometric series and we get

$$\Pr(Y \geq 5k) \leq \frac{8}{3}\Pr(Y = 5k) \leq \frac{8}{3}\binom{5k}{k}\frac{1}{2^{5k}} \leq \frac{8}{3}\left(\frac{5ek}{2^5 k}\right)^k \underset{(k \geq 2)}{\leq} \frac{1}{2^k}.$$

Adding the $2k-1$ vertices where processes are split completes the proof. $\qquad \square$

Lemma 12. *The step complexity of the first invocation of* STORE *requires* $O(k)$ *steps in expectation and with high probability.*

Proof. A process visits at most $c \log n$ vertices in the randomized structure. With probability $1 - k/n^c$ at most $4\sqrt{k}$ processes enter the first backup structure and hence stop there. Applying Lemma 6, we conclude that with high probability the step complexity of the first store is linear in k. For the expectation we get

$$E[\text{STORE}] \leq \left(1 - \frac{k}{n^c}\right)(c \log n + 2k) + \frac{k}{n^c}(c \log n + 2 \log 4\sqrt{n} \cdot \frac{4\sqrt{n}}{\log 4\sqrt{n}} + 1)$$
$$= O(k).$$

$\qquad \square$

Lemma 13. *An invocation of* COLLECT *requires* $O(k)$ *steps with high probability and in expectation. In any case, the step complexity of* COLLECT *is* $O(k^2 + k \log n)$.

Proof. Let $\mathcal{A}$ be the event that more than $7k$ nodes are marked in the random splitters tree. By Lemma 11, $\Pr(\mathcal{A}) \leq 1/2^k$. Further, let $\mathcal{B}$ be the event that more than $4\sqrt{k}$ processes enter the cascaded trees backup structure. By Lemma 10 we have $\Pr(\mathcal{B}) \leq k/n^c$ and therefore $\Pr(\mathcal{A} \cup \mathcal{B}) \leq 1/2^k + k/n^c$. Hence, with probability at least $1 - 1/2^k - k/n^c$, the step complexity of a collect is at most $7k + (4\sqrt{k})^2/\log n = O(k)$.

We compute the expected step complexity of a COLLECT operation in each of the three data structures separately. By linearity of expectation, we can sum up those results and get the total expected step complexity. Let S_T, S_C, and S_A denote the number of steps of a COLLECT operation, performed on the randomized splitter tree, the cascaded trees, and the array, respectively. By Lemma 11, we immediately have $\mathrm{E}[S_T] \leq 3k$. For the cascaded trees structure we get

$$\mathrm{E}[S_C] \leq \left(1 - \frac{k}{n^c}\right) \cdot \frac{(4\sqrt{k})^{2^{\min(k, 4\sqrt{n})}}}{\log n} + \sum_{j=4\sqrt{k}}^{} O\left(\frac{j^2}{\log n} \cdot \frac{6k^2}{(j - \sqrt{k})^2 n^{3/2}}\right)$$

$$+ O\left(\frac{6k^2}{n(4\sqrt{n} - \sqrt{n})^2 \cdot n^{3/2}} \cdot (\sqrt{n})^3\right)$$

$$\leq O\left(\frac{k}{\log n} + \frac{\min(k, \sqrt{n})}{\sqrt{n}} \cdot \frac{k^2}{n} + k\right) = O(k),$$

where we applied Lemma 8, Lemma 10 and the fact that the number of nodes in the cascaded trees structure is $O((\sqrt{n})^3)$. For the second backup structure, the linear array, we get $\mathrm{E}[S_A] \leq k/n^c \cdot n = O(k/\sqrt{n})$. Summing up, we get $\mathrm{E}[\text{COLLECT}] = O(k)$.

The worst-case number of vertices marked in the binary tree of randomized splitters is $O(k \log n)$ because each process can mark at most $3/2 \log n$ vertices. The step complexity in the cascaded-tree structure is at most $k^2/\log n$ by Lemma 7. If the linear array is accessed, the step complexity is $O(n)$. However, this can only happen if $k > 4\sqrt{n}$, and therefore the lemma follows. $\square$

5   Randomized Construction for Deterministic Collect

In this section, we show that instead of having processes, which have access to a random source, it is also possible to have a pre-computed ramdom splitter structure and keep the processes themselves deterministic. The random structure upon which the STORE and COLLECT is performed is constructed in a pre-processing phase. It is a random directed graph with n^3 vertices and out-degree 2 at all vertices. To each of the vertices, there is an deterministic splitter (cf. Section 3) associated. That is, we are given n^3 vertices, each of which chooses two random successors among the other vertices. The two successors of a vertex v are associated with **left** and **right** of v's splitter. One of the vertices is singled out and called the *root*.

The processes traverse the data structure as described in Section 3.1. Additionally, each process counts the number of visited splitters. If this number exceeds n, the process immediately leaves the random data structure and enters the backup structure. In the backup structure the process will then raise a flag at the root, indicating that the backup structure has been used, and then traverse the cascaded tree structure, as described in the Section 3.2.

To perform a COLLECT a process traverses the part of the random data structure containing marked vertices by simply visiting the children of a marked vertex in DFS order. The process furthermore memorizes which vertices it has already accessed and will not access a vertex twice. Additionally, it checks whether the flag in the backup structure is raised and, if that is the case, collects the values in the backup structure as described in the previous section.

To prove the correctness and complexity of the algorithm, we will proceed as in the previous section. Let k be the number of processes that call STORE at least once.

We have n^3 vertices in the randomized structure and $n^{\gamma+1}/\log n$, $\gamma > 1$ vertices in the backup structure. With $\gamma \leq 2$, we get the following lemma.

Lemma 14. *The memory complexity is* $O(n^3)$.

Lemma 15. *The probability that a process enters the backup structure is at most* $O(1/n)$.

Proof. A process traverses the data structure according to the values it is given in the splitters and leaves the random structure if it accessed more than n vertices. We want to show that, with high probability, the marked part of the data structure is a tree (that is, we do not have a cycle) and consequently a process stops with high probability after at most $k \leq n$ steps (see Lemma 2). Taking into account that by Lemma 3 in a tree at most $2k - 1$ vertices are being marked, this leaves us to prove that the first $2k - 1$ visited vertices are distinct and hence do not form a cycle with high probability.

We may model the way how the data structure is traversed by the processes as a 'balls-into-bins' game, since the children of a vertex were chosen uniformly at random. The number of balls is $2k - 1$ and the number of bins is $N = n^3$. If we let C be the number of balls ending up in a bin containing more than one ball, by Lemma 8 the probability that C is at least one can be estimated as

$$\Pr(C \geq 1) \leq \frac{6(2k - 1)^2}{(1 - k^2/n^3)^2 n^3} \leq O(1/n).$$

$\square$

Lemma 16. *The step complexity of the first invocation of* STORE *requires expected and with high probability* $O(k)$ *steps.*

Proof. By the previous lemma we know that with high probability the marked subgraph of our randomized data structure is a tree and hence, by Lemma 2, a store takes at most $k - 1$ steps. Since a process makes at most n steps in the randomized structure and, by Lemma 6, k steps in the cascaded tree structure, we have:

$$E[\text{STORE}] \leq \left(1 - \frac{1}{n}\right) \cdot k + \frac{1}{n} \cdot (n + k) = O(k).$$

$\square$

Lemma 17. *With high probability and in expectation the step complexity of* COLLECT *is* $O(k)$. *In any case, the step complexity is at most* $O(n^2)$.

Proof. The collect time in the backup structure is at most $n^2/\log n$ and the processes leave the randomized structure after at most n steps. Hence, the step complexity of the COLLECT will never exceed $O(n^2)$.

With probability $\left(1 - \frac{1}{n}\right)$ the marked data structure is a tree and no process enters the backup structure. Hence, we can apply Lemma 3 and the step complexity of a collect is with high probability at most $(2k-1)$. If it enters the backup structure, a collect costs by Lemma 7 at most $k^2/\log n$ and furthermore at most kn vertices are marked in the randomized structure. Hence, for the expected step complexity we get

$$E[\text{COLLECT}] \leq \left(1 - \frac{1}{n}\right) \cdot (2k-1) + \left(\frac{1}{n}\right) \cdot \left(kn + \frac{k^2}{\log n}\right) = O(k).$$

$\square$

6 Conclusions

We presented new deterministic and randomized adaptive collect algorithms. Table 1 compares the three algorithms presented in this paper with previous work. The algorithms are adaptive to so-called *total contention*, that is, to the maximum number of processes that were ever active during the execution. There are other contention definitions which are more fine-grained, such as point contention. The *point contention* during an execution interval is the maximum number of processes that were simultaneously active at some point in time during that interval. We believe that some of our new techniques carry over to algorithms that adapt to point contention [2, 4, 7].

Table 1. Summary of the complexities achieved by different collect algorithms. Note that the kind of randomization used in the two randomized algorithms is inherently different. For the algorithm of Section 4, the processes need access to a random source while the algorithm of Section 5 works on a random graph which can be precomputed.

Algorithm	Step Complexity		Memory Complexity	
	COLLECT	STORE		
triangular matrix [14]	$O(k^2)$	$O(k)$	$O(n^2)$	deterministic
tree [8]	$O(k)$	$O(k)$	$O(2^n)$	deterministic
cascaded trees (Sec. 3.2)	$O(k^2/(\varepsilon \log n))$	$O(k/\varepsilon)$	$O(n^{2+\varepsilon})$	deterministic
randomized splitters (Sec. 4)	$O(k)$	$O(k)$	$O(n^{3/2})$	randomized
randomized graph (Sec. 5)	$O(k)$	$O(k)$	$O(n^3)$	randomized

Our paper shows that it is possible to perform a COLLECT operation in $O(k)$ time with polynomial memory using randomization. We believe that there is no deterministic algorithm, using splitters, that achieves linear COLLECT and polynomial memory. To determine the best possible step complexity for COLLECT achievable by a deterministic algorithm with polynomial memory is an interesting open problem.

References

1. Y. Afek and M. Merritt. Fast, wait-free $(2k - 1)$-renaming. In *Proceedings of the 18th Annual ACM Symposium on Principles of Distributed Computing (PODC)*, pages 105–112, 1999.

2. Y. Afek, G. Strupp, and D. Touitou. Long-lived Adaptive Collect with Applications. In *Proceedings of the 40th IEEE Symposium on Foundations of Computer Science (FOCS)*, pages 262–272. IEEE Computer Society Press, 1999.

3. Y. Afek, G. Strupp, and D. Touitou. Long-lived and adaptive splitters and applications. volume 15, pages 444–468, 2002.

4. Y. Afek, G. Stupp, and D. Touitou. Long-lived and adaptive atomic snap-shot and immediate snapshot. In *Proceedings of the 19th Annual ACM Symposium on Principles of Distributed Computing (PODC)*, pages 71–80, 2000.

5. J. Anderson, Y.-J. Kim, and T. Herman. Shared-memory mutual exclusion: Major research trends since 1986. *Distributed Computing*, 16:75–110, 2003.

6. H. Attiya and V. Bortnikov. Adaptive and efficient mutual exclusion. *Distributed Computing*, 15(3):177–189, 2002.

7. H. Attiya and A. Fouren. Algorithms Adaptive to Point Contention. *Journal of the ACM (JACM)*, 50(4):444–468, July 2003.

8. H. Attiya, A. Fouren, and E. Gafni. An adaptive collect algorithm with applications. *Distributed Computing*, 15(2):87–96, 2002.

9. R. Guerraoui. Indulgent algorithms. In *Proceedings of the 19th Annual ACM Symposium on Principles of Distributed Computing (PODC)*, number 289–297, 2000.

10. R. Guerraoui and M. Raynal. A generic framework for indulgent consensus. In *Proceedings of the 23rd International Conference on Distributed Computing Systems (ICDCS)*, pages 88–95, 2003.

11. M. Herlihy. Wait-free synchronization. *ACM Transactions on Programming Languages and Systems*, 13(1):124–149, January 1991.

12. P. Jayanti, K. Tan, and S. Toueg. Time and space lower bounds for nonblocking implementations. *SIAM Journal on Computing*, 30(2):438–456, 2000.

13. Y.-J. Kim and J. Anderson. A time complexity bound for adaptive mutual exclusion. In *Proceedings of the 14th International Symposium on Distributed Computing (DISC)*, Lecture Notes in Computer Science, pages 1–15, 2001.

14. M. Moir and J. H. Anderson. Wait-free algorithms for fast, long-lived renaming. *Science of Computer Programming*, 25(1):1–39, October 1995.

Nonblocking Concurrent Data Structures
with Condition Synchronization*

William N. Scherer III and Michael L. Scott

Department of Computer Science
University of Rochester
Rochester, NY 14627-0226
{scherer,scott}@cs.rochester.edu

Abstract. We apply the classic theory of linearizability to operations that must wait for some other thread to establish a precondition. We model such an operation as a *request* and a *follow-up*, each with its own linearization point. Linearization of the request marks the point at which a thread's wishes become visible to its peers; linearization of the follow-up marks the point at which the request is fulfilled and the operation takes effect. By placing both linearization points within the purview of object semantics, we can specify not only the effects of operations, but also the order in which pending requests should be fulfilled.

We use the term *dual data structure* to describe a concurrent object implementation that may hold both data and *reservations* (registered requests). By reasoning separately about a request, its successful follow-up, and the period in-between, we obtain meaningful definitions of nonblocking dual data structures. As concrete examples, we present lock-free *dualstacks* and *dualqueues*, and experimentally compare their performance with that of lock-based and nonblocking alternatives.

1 Introduction

Since its introduction nearly fifteen years ago, linearizability has become the standard means of reasoning about the correctness of concurrent objects. Informally, linearizability "provides the illusion that each operation... takes effect instantaneously at some point between its invocation and its response" [3, abstract]. Linearizability is "nonblocking" in the sense that it never requires a call to a total method (one whose precondition is simply **true**) to wait for the execution of any other method. (Certain other correctness criteria, such as serializability [10], may require blocking, e.g. to enforce coherence across a multi-object system.) The fact that it is nonblocking makes linearizability particularly attractive for reasoning about nonblocking *implementations* of concurrent objects, which provide guarantees of various strength regarding the progress of method calls in practice. In a *wait-free* implementation, every contending thread is guaranteed to complete its method call within a bounded number of its own time steps [4]. In a *lock-free* implementation, *some* some contending thread is guaranteed to complete its method call within a bounded number of steps (from any thread's point of view) [4]. In

---

* This work was supported in part by NSF grants numbers EIA-0080124, CCR-9988361, and CCR-0204344, by DARPA/AFRL contract number F29601-00-K-0182, and by Sun Microsystems Laboratories.

R. Guerraoui (Ed.): DISC 2004, LNCS 3274, pp. 174–187, 2004.

an *obstruction-free* implementation, a thread is guaranteed to complete its method call within a bounded number of steps in the absence of contention, i.e. if no other threads execute competing methods concurrently [2].

These various *progress conditions* all assume that every method is total. As Herlihy puts it [4, p. 128]:

> We restrict our attention to objects whose operations are total because it is unclear how to interpret the wait-free condition for partial operations. For example, the most natural way to define the effects of a partial *deq* in a concurrent system is to have it wait until the queue becomes nonempty, a specification that clearly does not admit a wait-free implementation.

To avoid this problem the designers of nonblocking data structures typically "totalize" their methods by returning an error flag whenever the current state of the object does not admit the method's intended behavior.

But partial methods are important! Many applications need a `dequeue`, `pop`, or `deletemin` operation that waits when its structure is empty; these and countless other examples of *condition synchronization* are fundamental to concurrent programming.

Given a nonblocking data structure with "totalized" methods, the obvious spin-based strategy is to embed each call in a loop, and retry until it succeeds. This strategy has two important drawbacks. First, it introduces unnecessary contention for memory and communication bandwidth, which may significantly degrade performance, even with careful backoff. Second, it provides no fairness guarantees.

Consider a total queue whose `dequeue` method waits until it can return successfully, and a sequence of calls by threads A, B, C, and D:

    C enqueues a 1
    D enqueues a 2
    A calls dequeue
    A's call returns the 2
    B calls dequeue
    B's call returns the 1

This is clearly a "bad" execution history, because it returns results in the wrong (non-FIFO) order; it implies an incorrect implementation. The following is clearly a "good" history:

    A calls dequeue
    B calls dequeue
    C enqueues a 1
    D enqueues a 2
    A's call returns the 1
    B's call returns the 2

But what about the following:

    A calls dequeue
    B calls dequeue
    C enqueues a 1
    D enqueues a 2
    B's call returns the 1
    A's call returns the 2

If the first line is known to have occurred before the second (this may be the case, for example, if waiting threads can be identified by querying the scheduler, examining a thread control block, or reading an object-specific flag), then intuition suggests that while this history returns results in the right order, it returns them to the wrong threads. If we implement our queue by wrapping the nonblocking "totalized" `dequeue` in a loop, then this third, questionable history may certainly occur.

In the following section we show how to apply the theory of linearizability in such a way that object semantics can specify the order in which pending requests will be fulfilled. We then propose that data structures implement those semantics by explicitly representing the set of pending requests. Borrowing terminology from the BBN Butterfly Parallel Processor of the early 1980s [1], we define a *dual* data structure to be one that may hold *reservations* (registered requests) instead of, or in addition to, data. A *nonblocking* dual data structure is one in which (a) every operation either completes or registers a request in a nonblocking fashion, (b) fulfilled requests complete in a nonblocking fashion, and (c) threads that are waiting for their requests to be fulfilled do not interfere with the progress of other threads.

As concrete examples, we introduce two lock-free dual data structures in Section 3: a *dualstack* and a *dualqueue*. The dualstack both returns results and fulfills requests in LIFO order; the dualqueue does both in FIFO order. Both structures are attractive candidates for "bag of tasks" programming on multiprocessor systems. The dualqueue also subsumes scalable queue-based spin locks and semaphores, and can be used in conjunction with a small-scale test-and-set lock to obtain a *limited contention* spin lock that embodies an explicit tradeoff between fairness and locality on distributed shared memory machines. Preliminary performance results for dualstacks and dualqueues appear in section 4. We summarize our findings and suggest directions for future work in Section 5.

2   Definitions

2.1   Linearizable Objects

Following Herlihy and Wing [3], a *history* of an object is a (potentially infinite) sequence of method invocation events $\langle m(args)\, t \rangle$ and response (return) events $\langle r(val)t \rangle$, where m is the name of a method, r is a return condition (usually "ok"), and t identifies a thread. An invocation *matches* the next response in the sequence that has the same thread id. Together, an invocation and its matching response are called an *operation*. The invocation and response of operation o may also be denoted $inv(o)$ and $res(o)$, respectively. If event e_1 precedes event e_2 in history H, we write $e_1 <_H e_2$.

A history is *sequential* if every response immediately follows its matching invocation. A non-sequential history is *concurrent*. A *thread subhistory* is the subsequence of a history consisting of all events for a given thread. Two histories are *equivalent* if all their thread subhistories are identical. We consider only *well-formed* concurrent histories, in which every thread subhistory is sequential, and begins with an invocation.

We assume that the semantics of an object (which we do not consider formally here) uniquely determine a set of *legal* sequential histories. In a queue, for example, items must be inserted and removed in FIFO order. That is, the nth successful `dequeue` in a legal history must return the value inserted by the nth enqueue. Moreover at any given point the number of prior enqueues must equal or exceed the number of successful dequeues. To permit dequeue calls to occur at any time (i.e., to make dequeue a *total* method—one whose precondition is simply **true**), one can allow unsuccessful dequeues [$\langle deq(\ ) \ t\rangle \ \langle no(\bot) \ t\rangle$] to appear in the history whenever the number of prior enqueues equals the number of prior successful dequeues.

A (possibly concurrent) history H induces a partial order $\prec_H$ on operations: $o_i \prec_H o_j$ if $res(o_i) <_H inv(o_j)$. H is *linearizable* if (a) it is equivalent to some legal sequential history S, and (b) $\prec_H \subseteq \prec_S$.

Departing slightly from Herlihy and Wing, we introduce the notion of an *augmented history* of an object. A (well-formed) augmented history H' is obtained from a history H by inserting a *linearization point* $\langle m^l(args, val) \ t\rangle$ (also denoted $lin(o)$) somewhere between each response and its previous matching invocation: $inv(o) <_{H'} lin(o) <_{H'} res(o)$.

If H is equivalent to some legal sequential history S and the linearization points of H' appear in the same order as the corresponding operations in S, then H' embodies a linearization of H: the order of the linearization points defines a total order on operations that is consistent with the partial order induced by H. Put another way: $res(o_i) <_H inv(o_j) \Rightarrow lin(o_i) <_{H'} lin(o_j)$. Given this notion of augmented histories, we can define legality without resort to equivalent sequential histories: we say that an augmented history is *legal* if its sequence of linearization points is permitted by the object semantics. Similarly, H is *linearizable* if it can be augmented to produce a legal augmented history H'.

2.2 Implementations

We define an *implementation* of a concurrent object as a pair $(\mathcal{E}, \mathcal{I})$, where

1. $\mathcal{E}$ is a set of valid *executions* of some operational system, e.g. the possible interleavings of machine instructions among threads executing a specified body of C code on some commercial multiprocessor. Each execution takes the form of a series of *steps* (e.g., instructions), each of which is identified with a particular thread and occurs atomically. Implementations of nonblocking concurrent objects on real machines typically rely not only on atomic loads and stores, but on such *universal* atomic primitives [4] as compare_and_swap or load_linked and store_conditional, each of which completes in a single step.

2. $\mathcal{I}$ is an *interpretation* that maps each execution $E \in \mathcal{E}$ to some augmented object history $H' = \mathcal{I}(E)$ whose events (including the linearization points) are identified with steps of E in such a way that if $e_1 <_{H'} e_2$, then $s(e_1) \leq_E s(e_2)$, where $s(e)$ for any event e is the step identified with e.

We say an implementation is *correct* if $\forall E \in \mathcal{E}, \mathcal{I}(E)$ is a legal augmented history of the concurrent object.

In practice, of course, steps in an execution have an observable order only if they are executed by the same thread, or if there is a data dependence between them [7]. In particular, while we cannot in general observe that $s(inv(o_i)) <_E s(inv(o_j))$, where o_i and o_j are performed by different threads, we can observe that $s(res(o_i)) <_E s(inv(o_j))$, because o_i's thread may write a value after its response that is read by o_j's thread before its invocation. The power of linearizability lies in its insistence that the semantic order of operations on a concurrent object be consistent with such externally observable orderings.

In addition to correctness, an implementation may have a variety of other properties of interest, including bounds on time (steps), space, or remote memory accesses; the suite of required atomic instructions; and various *progress conditions*. An implementation is *wait-free* if we can bound, for all executions E and invocations $inv(o)$ in $\mathcal{I}(E)$, the number of steps between (the steps identified with) $inv(o)$ and $res(o)$. An implementation is *lock-free* if for all invocations $inv(o_i)$ we can bound the number of steps between (the steps identified with) $inv(o_i)$ and the (not necessarily matching) first subsequent response $res(o_j)$. An implementation is *obstruction-free* if for all threads t and invocations $inv(o)$ performed by t we can bound the number of consecutive steps performed by t (with no intervening steps by any other thread) between (the steps identified with) $inv(o)$ and $res(o)$. Note that the definitions of lock freedom and obstruction freedom permit executions in which an invocation has no matching response (i.e., in which threads may starve).

2.3 Adaptation to Objects with Partial Methods

When an object has partial methods, we divide each such method into a *request* method and a *follow-up* method, each of which has its own invocations and responses. A total queue, for example, would provide `dequeue_request` and `dequeue_followup` methods. By analogy with Lamport's bakery algorithm [6], the request method returns a *ticket*, which is then passed as an argument to the follow-up method. The follow-up, for its part, returns either the desired result or, if the method's precondition has not yet been satisfied, an error indication.

The history of a concurrent object now consists not only of invocation and response events $\langle m(args)\ t \rangle$ and $\langle ok(val)\ t \rangle$ for total methods m, but also request invocation and response events $\langle p_{req}(args)\ t \rangle$ and $\langle ok(tik)\ t \rangle$, and follow-up invocation and response events $\langle p_{fol}(tik)\ t \rangle$ and $\langle r(val)\ t \rangle$ for partial methods p. A request invocation and its matching response are called a *request operation*; a follow-up invocation and its matching response are called a *follow-up operation*. The request invocation and response of operation o may be denoted $inv(o^r)$ and $res(o^r)$; the follow-up invocation and response may be denoted $inv(o^f)$ and $res(o^f)$.

A follow-up with ticket argument k *matches* the previous request that returned k. A follow-up operation is said to be *successful* if its response event is $\langle ok(val)\ t \rangle$; it is said to be *unsuccessful* its its response event is $\langle no(\bot)\ t \rangle$. We consider only well-formed histories, in which every thread subhistory is sequential, and is a prefix of some string in the regular set $(ru^\star s)^\star$, where r is a request, u is an unsuccessful follow-up that matches the preceding r, and s is a successful follow-up that matches the preceding r.

Because it consists of a sequence of operations (beginning with a request and ending with a successful response), a call to a partial method p has a sequence of linearization points, including an *initial* linearization point $\langle p^i(args)\ t \rangle$ somewhere between the invocation and the response of the request, and a *final* linearization point $\langle p^f(val)\ t \rangle$

somewhere between the invocation and the response of the successful matching follow-up. The initial and final linearization points for p may also be denoted $in(p)$ and $fin(p)$.

We say an augmented history is *legal* if its sequence of linearization points is among those determined by the semantics of the object. This definition allows us to capture partial methods in object semantics. In the previous section we suggested that the semantics of a queue might require that (1) the nth successful dequeue returns the value inserted by the nth enqueue, and (2) the number of prior enqueues at any given point equals or exceeds the number of prior successful dequeues. We can now instead require that (1') the nth final linearization point for dequeue contains the value from the linearization point of the nth enqueue, (2') the number of prior linearization points for enqueue equals or exceeds the number of prior final linearization points for dequeue, and (3') at the linearization point of an unsuccessful dequeue_followup, the number of prior linearization points for enqueue exactly equals the number of prior final linearization points for dequeue (i.e., linearization points for successful dequeue_followups). These rules ensure not only that the queue returns results in FIFO order, but also that pending requests for partial methods (which are now permitted) are fulfilled in FIFO order.

As before, a history H is linearizable if it can be augmented to produce a legal augmented history H', and an implementation $(\mathcal{E}, \mathcal{I})$ is correct if $\forall E \in \mathcal{E}, \mathcal{I}(E)$ is a legal augmented history of the concurrent object.

Given the definition of well-formedness above, a thread t that wishes to execute a partial method p must first call $p\_$request and then call $p\_$followup in a loop until it succeeds. This is very different from calling a traditional "totalized" method until it succeeds: linearization of a distinguished request operation is the hook that allows object semantics to address the order in which pending requests will be fulfilled.

As a practical matter, implementations may wish to provide a $p\_$demand method that waits until it can return successfully, and/or a plain p method equivalent to $p\_$demand($p\_$request). The obvious implementation of $p\_$demand contains a busy-wait loop, but other implementations are possible. In particular, an implementation may choose to use scheduler-based synchronization to put t to sleep on a semaphore that will be signaled when p's precondition has been met, allowing the processor to be used for other purposes in the interim. We require that it be possible to provide request and follow-up methods, as defined herein, with no more than trivial modifications to any given implementation. The algorithms we present in Section 3 provide only a plain p interface, with internal busy-wait loops.

Progress Conditions. When reasoning about progress, we must deal with the fact that a partial method may wait for an arbitrary amount of time (perform an arbitrary number of unsuccessful follow-ups) before its precondition is satisfied. Clearly we wish to require that requests and follow-ups are nonblocking. But this is not enough: we must also prevent unsuccessful follow-ups from interfering with progress in other threads. We do so by prohibiting such operations from accessing remote memory. On a cache-coherent machine, an access by thread t within operation o is said to be *remote* if it writes to memory that may (in some execution) be read or written by threads other than t more than a constant number of times between $inv(o^r)$ and $res(o^f)$, or if it reads memory that may (in some execution) be written by threads other than t more than a constant number of times between $inv(o^r)$ and $res(o^f)$. On a non-cache-coherent machine, an access by thread t is also remote if it refers to memory that t itself did not allocate.

2.4 Dual Data Structures

We define a *dual data structure* D to be a concurrent object implementation that may hold *reservations* (registered requests) instead of, or in addition to, data. Reservations correspond to requests that cannot be fulfilled until the object satisfies some necessary precondition. A reservation may be removed from D, and a call to its follow-up method may return, when some call by another thread makes the precondition true. D is a *nonblocking* dual data structure if

1. It is a correct implementation of a linearizable concurrent object, as defined above.
2. All operations, including requests and follow-ups, are nonblocking.
3. Unsuccessful follow-ups perform no remote memory accesses.

Nonblocking dual data structures may be further classified as wait-free, lock-free, or obstruction-free, depending on their guarantees with respect to condition (2) above. In the following section we consider concrete lock-free implementations of a dualstack and a dualqueue.

3   Example Data Structures

Space limitations preclude inclusion of pseudocode in the conference proceedings. Both example data structures can be found on-line at www.cs.rochester.edu/u/scott/synchron-ization/pseudocode/duals.html. Both use a double-width compare_and_swap (CAS) instruction (as provided, for example, on the Sparc) to create "counted pointers" that avoid the ABA problem: each vulnerable pointer is paired with a serial number, which is incremented every time the pointer is updated to a non-NULL value. We assume that no thread can stall long enough to see a serial number repeat. On a machine with (single-word) load_linked/store_conditional (LL/SC) instructions, the serial numbers would not be needed.[1]

3.1   The Dualstack

The dualstack is based on the standard lock-free stack of Treiber [13]. So long as the number of calls to pop does not exceed the number of calls to push, the dualstack behaves the same as its non-dual cousin.

---

[1] CAS takes an address, an expected value, and a new value as argument. If the expected value is found at the given address, it is replaced with the new value, atomically; a Boolean return value indicates whether the replacement occurred. The ABA problem [5] can arise in a system in which memory is dynamically allocated, freed, and then reallocated: a thread that performs a load followed by a CAS may succeed when it should not, if the value at the location in question has changed *and then changed back* in-between. LL reads a memory location and makes a note of having done so. SC stores a new value to the location accessed by the most recent LL, provided that no other thread has modified the location in-between. Again, a Boolean return value indicates whether the store occurred.

When the stack is empty, or contains only reservations, the pop method pushes a reservation, and then spins on the data_node field within it. A push method always pushes a data node. If the previous top node was a reservation, however, the two adjacent nodes "annihilate each other": any thread that finds a data node and an underlying reservation at the top of the stack attempts to (a) write the address of the former into the data_node field of the latter, and then (b) pop both nodes from the stack. At any given time, the stack contains either all reservations, all data, or one datum (at the top) followed by reservations.

Both the head pointer and the next pointers in stack nodes are *tagged* to indicate whether the next node in the list is a reservation or a datum and, if the latter, whether there is a reservation beneath it in the stack. We assume that nodes are word-aligned, so that these tags can fit in the low-order bits of a pointer. For presentation purposes the on-line pseudocode assumes that data values are integers, though this could obviously be changed to any type (including a pointer) that will fit, together with a serial number, in the target of a double-width CAS (or in a single word on a machine with LL/SC). To differentiate between the cases where the topmost data node is present to fulfill a request and where the stack contains all data, pushes for the former case set both the data and reservation tags; pushes for the latter set only the data tag.

As mentioned in Section 2.3 our code provides a single pop method that subsumes the sequence of operations from a pop request through its successful follow-up. The initial linearization point in pop, like the linearization point in push, is the CAS that modifies the top-of-stack pointer. For pops when the stack is non-empty, this CAS is also the final linearization point. For pops that have to spin, the final linearization point is the CAS (in some other thread) that writes to the data_node field of the requester's reservation, terminating its spin.

The code for push is lock-free, as is the code from the beginning of pop to the initial linearization point, and from the final linearization point (the read that terminates the spin) to the end of pop. Moreover the spin in pop (which would comprise the body of an unsuccessful follow-up operation, if we provided it as a separate method), is entirely local: it reads only the requester's own reservation node, which the requester allocated itself, and which no other thread will write except to terminate the spin. The dualstack therefore satisfies conditions 2 and 3 of Section 2.4.

Though we do not offer a proof, inspection of the code confirms that the dualstack satisfies the usual LIFO semantics for total methods: if the number of previous linearization points for push exceeds the number of previous initial linearization points for pop, then a new pop operation p will succeed immediately, and will return the value provided by the most recent previous push operation h such that the numbers of pushes and pops that linearized between h and p are equal. In a similar fashion, the dualstack satisfies pending requests in LIFO order: if the number of previous initial linearization points for pop exceeds the number of previous linearization points for push, then a push operation h will provide the value to be returned by the most recent previous pop operation p such that the numbers of pushes and pops that linearized between p and h are equal. This is condition 1 from Section 2.4.

The spin in pop is terminated by a CAS in some other thread (possibly the fulfilling thread, possibly a helper) that updates the data_node field in the reservation. This

CAS is the final linearization point of the spinning thread. It is not, however, the final linearization point of the fulfilling thread; that occurs earlier, when the fulfilling thread successfully updates the top-of-stack pointer to point to the fulfilling datum. Once the fulfilling push has linearized, no thread will be able to make progress until the spinning pop reaches its final linearization point. It is possible, however, for the spinning thread to perform an unbounded number of (local, spinning) steps in a legal execution before this happens: hence the need to separate the linearization points of the fulfilling and fulfilled operations.

It is tempting to consider a simpler implementation in which the fulfilling thread pops a reservation from the stack and then writes the fulfilling datum directly into the reservation. This implementation, however, is incorrect: it leaves the requester vulnerable to a failure or stall in the fulfilling thread subsequent to the pop of the reservation but prior to the write of the datum. Because the reservation would no longer be in the stack, an arbitrary number of additional pop operations (performed by other threads, and returning subsequently pushed data) could linearize before the requester's successful follow-up.

One possible application of a dualstack is to implement a "bag of tasks" in a locality-conscious parallel execution system. If newly created tasks share data with recently completed tasks, it may make sense for a thread to execute a newly created task, rather than one created long ago, when it next needs work to do. Similarly, if there is insufficient work for all threads, it may make sense for newly created tasks to be executed by threads that became idle recently, rather than threads that have been idle for a long time. In addition to enhancing locality, this could allow power-aware processors to enter a low-power mode when running spinning threads, potentially saving significant energy. The LIFO ordering of a dualstack will implement these policies.

3.2 The Dualqueue

The dualqueue is based on the M&S lock-free queue [9]. So long as the number of calls to dequeue does not exceed the number of calls to push, it behaves the same as its non-dual cousin. It is initialized with a single "dummy" node; the first real datum (or reservation) is always in the second node, if any. At any given time the second and subsequent nodes will either all be reservations or all be data.

When the queue is empty, or contains only reservations, the dequeue method enqueues a reservation, and then spins on the request pointer field of the former tail node. The enqueue method, for its part, fulfills the request at the head of the queue, if any, rather than enqueue a datum. To do so, the fulfilling thread uses a CAS to update the reservation's request field with a pointer to a node (outside the queue) containing the provided data. This simultaneously fulfills the request and breaks the requester's spin. Any thread that finds a fulfilled request at the head of the queue removes and frees it. (NB: acting on the head of the queue requires that we obtain a *consistent snapshot* of the head, tail, and next pointers. Extending the technique of the original M&S queue, we use a two-stage check to ensure sufficient consistency to prevent untoward race conditions.)

As in the dualstack, queue nodes are tagged as requests by setting a low-order bit in pointers that point to them. We again assume, without loss of generality, that data values are integers, and we provide a single dequeue method that subsumes the sequence of operations from a dequeue request through its successful follow-up.

The code for enqueue is lock-free, as is the code from the beginning of dequeue to the initial linearization point, and from the final linearization point (the read that terminates the spin) to the end of dequeue. The spin in dequeue (which would comprise the body of an unsuccessful follow-up) accesses a node that no other thread will write except to terminate the spin. The dualqueue therefore satisfies conditions 2 and 3 of Section 2.4 on a cache-coherent machine. (On a non-cache-coherent machine we would need to modify the code to provide an extra level of indirection; the spin in dequeue reads a node that the requester did not allocate.)

Though we do not offer a proof, inspection of the code confirms that the dualqueue satisfies the usual FIFO semantics for total methods: if the number of previous linearization points for enqueue exceeds the number of previous initial linearization points for dequeue, then a new, nth dequeue operation will return the value provided by the nth enqueue. In a similar fashion, the dualqueue satisfies pending requests in FIFO order: if the number of previous initial linearization points for dequeue exceeds the number of previous linearization points for enqueue, then a new, nth enqueue operation will provide a value to the nth dequeue. This is condition 1 from Section 2.4.

The spin in dequeue is terminated by a CAS in another thread's enqueue method; this CAS is the linearization point of the enqueue and the final linearization point of the dequeue. Note again that a simpler algorithm, in which the enqueue method could remove a request from the queue and then fulfill it, would not be correct: the CAS operation used for removal would constitute the final linearization point of the enqueue, but the corresponding dequeue could continue to spin for an arbitrary amount of time if the thread performing the enqueue were to stall.

Dualqueue Applications. Dualqueues are versatile. They can obviously be used as a traditional "bag of tasks" or a producer–consumer buffer. They have several other uses as well:

Mutual exclusion. A dualqueue that is initialized to hold a single datum is a previously unknown variety of queue-based mutual exclusion lock. Unlike the widely used MCS lock [8], a dualqueue lock has no spin in the release code: where the MCS lock updates the tail pointer of the queue and then the next pointer of the predecessor's node, a dualqueue lock updates the next pointer first, and then swings the tail to cover it.

Semaphores. A dualqueue that is initialized with k data nodes constitutes a contention-free spin-based semaphore. It can be used, for example, to allocate k interchangeable resources among a set of competing threads.

Limited contention lock. As noted by Radovic and Hagersten [11], among others, the strict fairness of queue-based locks may not be desirable on a non-uniform memory access (distributed shared memory) multiprocessor. At the same time, a test-and-set lock, which tends to grant requests to physically nearby threads, can be unacceptably unfair (not to mention slow) when contention among threads is high: threads that are physically distant may starve. An attractive compromise is to allow waiting threads to bypass each other in line to a limited extent. A dualqueue paired with a test-and-set lock provides a straightforward implementation of such a "limited contention" lock. We initialize the dualqueue with k tokens, each of which grants permission to contend for the test-and-set lock. The value of k determines the balance between fairness and locality. The acquire operation first dequeues a token from the dualqueue and then contends for the test-and-set lock. The release operation enqueues a token in the dualqueue and releases the test-and-set lock. Starvation is still possible, though less likely than with an ordinary test-and-set lock. We can eliminate it entirely, if desired, by reducing k to one on a periodic basis.

4   Experimental Results

In this section we compare the performance of the dualstack and dualqueue to that of Treiber's lock-free stack [13], the M&S lock-free queue [9], and four lock-based alternatives. With Treiber's stack and the M&S queue we embed the calls to pop and dequeue, respectively, in a loop that repeats until the operations succeed. Two lock-based alternatives, the "locked stack" and the "locked queue" employ similar loops. The remaining two alternatives are lock-based dual data structures. Like the nonblocking dualstack and dualqueue, the "dual locked stack" and "dual locked queue" can contain either data or requests. All updates, however, are protected by a test-and-set lock.

Our experimental platform is a 16-processor SunFire 6800, a cache-coherent multiprocessor with 1.2Ghz UltraSPARC III processors. Our benchmark creates $n+1$ threads for an n thread test. Thread 0 executes as follows:

```
while time has not expired
   for i = 1 to 3
      insert -1 into data structure
   repeat
      pause for about 50μs
   until data structure is empty
   pause for about 50μs
```

Other threads all run the following:

```
while time has not expired
   remove val from data structure
   if val == -1
      for i = 1 to 32
         insert i into data structure
   pause for about 0.5μs
```

These conventions arrange for a series of "rounds" in which the data structure alternates between being full of requests and being full of data. Three threads, chosen more or less at random, prime the structure for the next round, and then join their peers in emptying it. We ran each test for two seconds, and report the minimum per-operation run time across five trials. Spot checks of longer runs revealed no anomalies. Choosing the minimum effectively discards the effects of periodic execution by kernel daemons.

Code for the various algorithms was written in C (with embedded assembly for CAS), and was compiled with gcc version 3.3.2 and the -O3 level of optimization. We use the fast local memory allocator from our 2002 *PODC* paper [12].

Stack results appear in Figure 1. For both lock-based and lock-free algorithms, dualism yields a significant performance improvement: at 14 worker threads the dual locked stack is about 9% faster than (takes 93% as much time as) the locked stack that retries failed pop calls repeatedly; the nonblocking dualstack is about 20% faster than its nondual counterpart. In each case the lock-based stack is faster than the corresponding lock-free stack due, we believe, to reduced contention for the top-of-stack pointer.

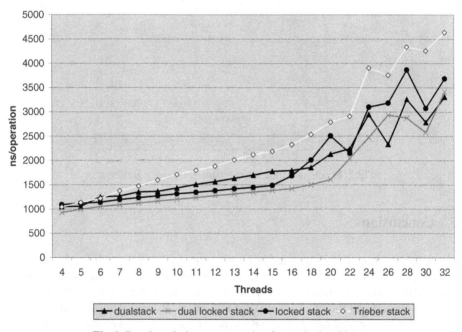

Fig. 1. Benchmark time per operation for stack algorithms.

Queue results appear in Figure 2. Here dualism again yields significant improvements: at 14 worker threads the dual locked queue is about 14% faster than the locked queue that retries failed dequeue calls repeatedly; the nonblocking dualqueue is more than 40% faster than its non-dual counterpart. Unlike the stacks, the nonblocking dualqueue outperforms the dual locked queue by a significant margin; we attribute this difference to the potential concurrency between enqueues and dequeues. The M&S queue is slightly faster than the locked queue at low thread counts, slightly slower for 12–15 threads, and significantly faster once the number of threads exceeds the number of processors, and the lock-based algorithm begins to suffer from preemption in critical sections. Performance of the nonblocking dualqueue is almost flat out to 16 threads (the size of the machine), and reasonable well beyond that, despite an extremely high level of contention in our benchmark; we can recommend this algorithm without reservation on any cache-coherent machine.

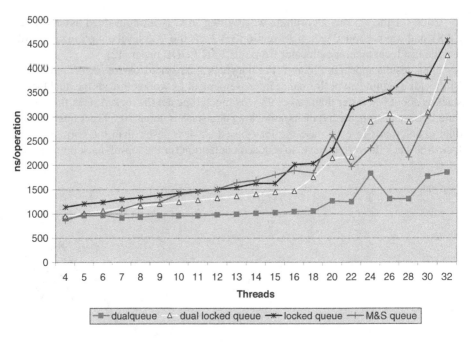

Fig. 2. Benchmark time per operation for queue algorithms.

5   Conclusions

Linearizability is central to the study of concurrent data structures. It has historically been limited by its restriction to methods that are total. We have shown how to encompass partial methods by introducing a *pair* of linearization points, one for the registration of a request and the other for its later fulfillment. By reasoning separately about a request, its successful follow-up, and the period in-between, we obtain meaningful definitions of wait-free, lock-free, and obstruction-free implementations of concurrent objects with condition synchronization.

We have presented concrete lock-free implementations of a *dualstack* and a *dualqueue*. Performance results on a commercial multiprocessor suggest that dualism can yield significant performance gains over naive retry on failure. The dualqueue, in particular, appears to be an eminently useful algorithm, outperforming the M&S queue in our experiments by almost a factor of two for large thread counts.

Nonblocking dual data structures could undoubtedly be developed for double-ended queues, priority queues, sets, dictionaries, and other abstractions. Each of these may in turn have variants that embody different policies as to which of several pending requests to fulfill when a matching operation makes a precondition true. One could imagine, for example, a stack that grants pending requests in FIFO order, or (conceivably) a queue that grants them in LIFO order. More plausibly, one could imagine an arbitrary system of thread priorities, in which a matching operation fulfills the highest priority pending request.

Further useful structures may be obtained by altering behavior between a request and its subsequent successful follow-up. As noted in Section 2.3, one could deschedule waiting threads, thereby effectively incorporating scheduler-based condition synchronization into nonblocking data structures. For real-time or database systems, one might combine dualism with timeout, allowing a spinning thread to remove its request from the structure if it waits "too long".

Acknowledgments

We are grateful to the anonymous referees for several helpful suggestions, and in particular to referee 4, who suggested that requests and follow-ups be full-fledged operations, thereby significantly simplifying the description of progress conditions between initial and final linearization points.

References

1. BBN Laboratories. Butterfly Parallel Processor Overview. BBN Report #6148, Version 1, Cambridge, MA, March 1986.
2. M. Herlihy, V. Luchangco, and M. Moir. Obstruction-Free Synchronization: Double-Ended Queues as an Example. In *Proceedings of the Twenty-Third International Conference on Distributed Computing Systems*, Providence, RI, May, 2003.
3. M. P. Herlihy and J. M. Wing. Linearizability: A Correctness Condition for Concurrent Objects. *ACM Transactions on Programming Languages and Systems*, 12(3):463–492, July 1990.
4. M. Herlihy. Wait-Free Synchronization. *ACM Transactions on Programming Languages and Systems*, 13(1):124–149, January 1991.
5. *System/370 Principles of Operation*. IBM Corporation, 1983.
6. L. Lamport. A New Solution of Dijkstra's Concurrent Programming Problem. *Communications of the ACM*, 17(8):453–455, August 1974.
7. L. Lamport. Time, Clocks, and the Ordering of Events in a Distributed System. *Communications of the ACM*, 21(7):558–565, July 1978.
8. J. M. Mellor-Crummey and M. L. Scott. Algorithms for Scalable Synchronization on Shared-Memory Multiprocessors. *ACM Transactions on Computer Systems*, 9(1):21–65, February 1991.
9. M. M. Michael and M. L. Scott. Simple, Fast, and Practical Non-Blocking and Blocking Concurrent Queue Algorithms. In *Proceedings of the Fifteenth ACM Symposium on Principles of Distributed Computing*, pages 267–275, Philadelphia, PA, May 1996.
10. C. H. Papadimitriou. The Serializability of Concurrent Database Updates. *Journal of the ACM*, 26(4):631–653, October 1979.
11. Z. Radovic and E. Hagersten. Hierarchical Backoff Locks for Nonuniform Communication Architectures. In *Proc of the Ninth International Symposium on High Performance Computer Architecture*, pages 241–252, Anaheim, CA, February 2003.
12. M. L. Scott. Non-blocking Timeout in Scalable Queue-based Spin Locks. In *Proceedings of the Twenty-Second ACM Symposium on Principles of Distributed Computing*, pages 31–40, Monterey, CA, July 2002.
13. R. K. Treiber. Systems Programming: Coping with Parallelism. RJ 5118, IBM Almaden Research Center, April 1986.

Dynamic Memory ABP Work-Stealing

Danny Hendler[1], Yossi Lev[2], and Nir Shavit[2]

[1] Tel-Aviv University
[2] Sun Microsystems Laboratories & Tel-Aviv University

Abstract. The non-blocking work-stealing algorithm of Arora, Blumofe, and Plaxton (hencheforth *ABP work-stealing*) is on its way to becoming the multiprocessor load balancing technology of choice in both Industry and Academia. This highly efficient scheme is based on a collection of array-based deques with low cost synchronization among local and stealing processes. Unfortunately, the algorithm's synchronization protocol is strongly based on the use of fixed size arrays, which are prone to overflows, especially in the multiprogrammed environments which they are designed for. This is a significant drawback since, apart from memory inefficiency, it means users must tailor the deque size to accommodate the effects of the hard-to-predict level of multiprogramming, and add expensive blocking overflow-management mechanisms.

This paper presents the first *dynamic memory* work-stealing algorithm. It is based on a novel way of building non-blocking dynamic memory ABP deques by detecting synchronization conflicts based on "pointer-crossing" rather than "gaps between indexes" as in the original ABP algorithm. As we show, the new algorithm dramatically increases robustness and memory efficiency, while causing applications no observable performance penalty. We therefore believe it can replace array-based ABP work-queues, eliminating the need to add application specific overflow mechanisms.

1 Introduction

The ABP work-stealing algorithm of Arora, Blumofe, and Plaxton [1] has been gaining popularity as the multiprocessor load-balancing technology of choice in both Industry and Academia [2, 1, 3, 4]. The scheme implements a provably efficient work-stealing paradigm due to Blumofe and Leiserson [5] that allows each process to maintain a local work deque, and steal an item from others if its deque becomes empty. It has been extended in various ways such as stealing multiple items [6] and stealing in a locality-guided way [2]. At the core of the ABP algorithm is an efficient scheme for stealing an item in a non-blocking manner from an array-based deque, minimizing the need for costly Compare-and-Swap (CAS) synchronization operations when fetching items locally.

Unfortunately, the use of fixed size arrays[1] introduces an inefficient memory-size/robustness tradeoff: for n processes and total allocated memory size m, one

---

[1] One may use cyclic array indexing but this does not help in preventing overflows.

R. Guerraoui (Ed.): DISC 2004, LNCS 3274, pp. 188–200, 2004.
© Springer-Verlag Berlin Heidelberg 2004

can tolerate at most $\frac{m}{n}$ items in a deque. Moreover, if overflow does occur, there is no simple way to malloc additional memory and continue. This has, for example, forced parallel garbage collectors using work-stealing to implement an application specific blocking overflow-management mechanism [3, 7]. In multi-programmed systems, the main target of ABP work-stealing [1], even inefficient over-allocation based on an application's maximal execution-DAG depth [1,5] may not always work. If a small subset of non-preempted processes end up queuing most of the work items, since the ABP algorithm sometimes starts pushing items from the middle of the array even when the deque is empty, this will lead to overflow.[2]

This state of affairs leaves open the question of designing a dynamic memory algorithm to overcome the above drawbacks, but to do so while maintaining the low-cost synchronization overhead of the ABP algorithm. This is not a straightforward task, since the the array-based ABP algorithm is quite unique: it is possibly the only real-world algorithm that allows one to transition in a lock-free manner from the common case of using loads and stores to using a costly CAS *only* when a potential conflict requires processes to reach consensus. This somewhat-magical transition rests on the ability to detect these boundary synchronization cases based on the relative gap among array indexes. There is no straightforward way of translating this algorithmic trick to the pointer based world of dynamic data structures.

1.1 The New Algorithm

This paper introduces the first lock-free[3] *dynamic-memory* version of the ABP work-stealing algorithm. It provides a near-optimal memory-size/robustness tradeoff: for n processes and total pre-allocated memory size m, it can potentially tolerate up to $O(m)$ items in a single deque. It also allows one to malloc additional memory beyond m when needed, and as our empirical data shows, it is far more robust than the array-based ABP algorithm in multiprogrammed environments.

An ABP style work-stealing algorithm consists of a collection of **deque** data structures with local processes performing pushes and pops on the "bottom" end of the deque and multiple thieves performing pops on the "top" end. The new algorithm implements the deque as a doubly-linked list of $\Theta(m)$ nodes, each of which is a short array that is allocated and freed dynamically from a shared pool. It can also use malloc to add nodes to the shared pool in case its node supply is exhausted.

The main technical difficulties in the design of the new algorithm arise from the need to provide performance comparable to that of ABP. This means the doubly linked list must be manipulated using only loads and stores in the common case, and transition in a lock-free manner to using a costly CAS *only* when a potential conflict requires consensus.

---

[2] The ABP algorithm's built-in "reset on empty" heuristic may help in some, but not all, of these cases.

[3] Our abstract Deque definition is such that the original ABP algorithm is also lock-free.

The potential conflict which requires CAS-based synchronization occurs when a pop by a local process and a pop by a thief might both be trying to remove the same item from the deque. The original ABP algorithm detects this scenario by examining the gap between the Top and Bottom array indexes, and uses a CAS operation only when they are "too close." Moreover, in the original algorithm, the empty deque scenario is checked simply by checking whether Bottom ≤ Top.

A key algorithmic feature of our new algorithm is the creation of an equivalent mechanism to allow detection of these boundary situations in our linked-list structures using the relations between the Top and Bottom pointers, even though these point to entries that may reside in different nodes. On a high level, our idea is to prove that one can restrict the number of possible ways the pointers interact, and therefore, given one pointer, it is possible to calculate the different possible positions for the other pointer which implies such a boundary scenario. The different empty deque scenarios are depicted in Figure 2.

The other key feature of our algorithm is that the dynamic insertion and deletion operations of nodes into the doubly linked-list (when needed in a push or pop) is performed so the local thread uses only loads and stores. This contrasts, at least intuitively, with the more general linked-list deque implementations [8, 9] which require a double-compare-and-swap synchronization operation [10] to insert and delete nodes.

1.2   Performance Analysis

We compared our new dynamic-memory work-stealing algorithm to the original ABP algorithm on a 16-node shared memory multiprocessor using the benchmarks of the style used by Blumofe and Papadopoulos [11]. We ran several standard *Splash2* [12] applications using the Hood scheduler [13] with the ABP and new work-stealing algorithms. Our results, presented in Section 3, show that the new algorithm performs as well as ABP, that is, the added dynamic-memory feature does not slow the applications down. Moreover, the new algorithm provides a better memory/robustness ratio: the same amount of memory provides far greater robustness in the new algorithm than the original array-based ABP work-stealing. For example, running Barnes-Hut using ABP work-stealing with an 8 fold level of multiprogramming causes a failure in 40% of the executions if one uses the deque size that works for stand-alone (non-multiprogrammed) runs. It causes *no failures* on using the new dynamic memory work-stealing algorithm.

2   The Algorithm

2.1   Basic Description

An ABP style work-stealing algorithm consists of a collection of deque data structures. Each deque is local to some process, which can perform LIFO Push and Pop operations on it (PushBottom and PopBottom on the "bottom" end of the deque), and is remote to multiple potential thieves, which can perform FIFO Pop operations on it (PopTop on the "top" end of the deque).

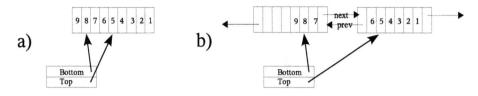

Fig. 1. The original ABP deque structure (a) vs. that of the new dynamic deque. (b) The structure after 9 `PushBottom` operations, 4 successful `PopTop` operations, and one `PopBottom` operation (In practice the original ABP deque uses cell indexes and not pointers as in our illustration).

The new algorithm implements the deque as a doubly-linked list of short arrays, as depicted in Figure 1 (the size of the arrays is a tuneable parameter). The nodes are allocated and freed from a shared pool, and the only case in which one may need to malloc additional storage is if the shared pool is exhausted.

The main technical difficulty in our design arises from the wish to maintain the same synchronization efficiency that characterizes the ABP algorithm; We use only loads and stores for `PushBottom` and `PopBottom` in the common case, and transition in a lock-free manner to using a costly CAS *only* when a potential conflict requires processes to reach consensus. This potential conflict occurs when the local `PopBottom` and a thieve's `PopTop` might concurrently try to remove the same item from the deque. The original ABP algorithm detects this scenario by examining the gap between the `Top` and `Bottom` array indexes, and uses a CAS operation only when they are "too close." Moreover, in the original algorithm, the empty deque scenario is checked simply by checking whether `Bottom` ≤ `Top`.

In the new linked-list structure, we need an equivalent mechanism to allow us to detect these situations even if the `Top` and `Bottom` pointers point to array entries that reside in different nodes. Our solution is to prove that one can restrict the number of possible scenarios among the pointers. Given some pointer, we show that the "virtual" distance of the other, ignoring which array it resides in, can be no more than 1. We can thus easily test for each of these scenarios. (Several such scenarios are depicted in parts (a) and (b) of Figure 2).

The next problem one faces is the maintenance of the deque's doubly-linked list structure. We wouldn't like to use CAS operations when updating the `next` and `previous` pointers, since this will cause a significant performance penalty. Our solution is to allow only the local process to update these fields, thus preventing `PopTop` operations from doing so when moving from one node to another. We would like to keep the deque dynamic, which means freeing old nodes when they're not needed anymore. This restriction immediately implies that an active list node may point to an already freed node, or even to a node which was freed and reallocated again, essentially ruining the list structure. As we prove, the algorithm can overcome this problem by having a `PopTop` operation that moves to a new node, free only the node preceding the old node and not the old node itself. This allows us to maintain the invariant that the doubly-linked list structure between the `Top` and `Bottom` pointers is preserved. This is true even in scenarios such as that in Figure 2 where the pointers cross over.

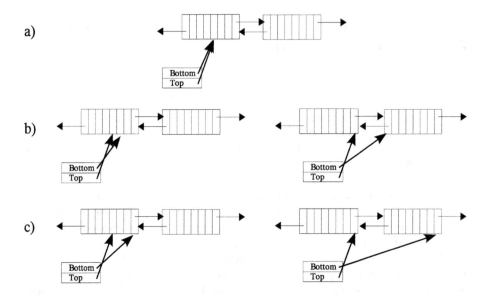

Fig. 2. The different types of empty deque scenarios. (a) Simple: `Bottom` and `Top` point to the same cell. (b) Simple Crossing: both the left and right scenarios are examples where `Bottom` passed over `Top` by one cell, but they still point to neighboring cells. (c) Non-Simple Crossing (with the reset-on-empty heuristic): both the left and right scenarios are examples of how pointers can cross given the reset-on-empty heuristic, between the reset of `Bottom` to the reset of `Top`.

Finally, given that the `PopTop` operation may be executed concurrently by many processes, the node that is pointed to by `Top` at the beginning of the method may be freed during the method execution. We must thus limit the `PopTop` method to read (in order to pop) array entries only within the `Top` node and not across nodes.

2.2   The Implementation

The `C++` like Pseudo Code for the different deque methods is given in Figures 3 and 4. The deque object saves the `Bottom` and `Top` pointers information in the `Bottom` and `Top` data members, and uses the *EncodeBottom, DecodeBottom, EncodeTop* and *DecodeTop* macros to encode/decode this information into a CAS-able size word. Underlined commands in the Pseudo Code stand for code blocks which will be described later. We now describe each of the methods.

PushBottom. The method begins by reading `Bottom` and storing the pushed value in the cell it is pointing to (Lines 1-2). Then it calculates the next value of `Bottom` linking a new node to the list if necessary (Lines 3-14). Finally the method updates `Bottom` to its new value (Line 15). As in the original ABP algorithm, this method is executed only by the owner process, and therefore regular writes suffice (both for the value and `Bottom` updates). Note that the new node is linked to the list before `Bottom` is updated, so the list structure is preserved for the nodes between `Bottom` and `Top`.

```
void DynamicDedeque::PushBottom(ThreadInfo theData)
{
1   <currNode, currIndex> = DecodeBottom(Bottom); // Read Bottom data
2   currNode->itsDataArr[currArrIndex] = theData; // Write data in current bottom cell
3   if (currIndex!=0)
4   {
5           newNode = currNode;
6           newIndex = currIndex-1;
7   }
8   else
9   {  // Allocate and link a new node:
10          newNode = AllocateNode();
11          newNode->next = currNode;
12          currNode->prev = newNode;
13          newIndex = DequeNode::ArraySize-1;
14  }
15  Bottom = EncodeBottom(newNode,newArrIndex);    // Update Bottom
}
```

```
ThreadInfo DynamicDedeque::PopTop()
{
16  currTop = Top;      // Read Top
17  <currTopTag, currTopNode, currTopIndex> = DecodeTop(currTop);
18  currBottom = Bottom; // Read Bottom
19  EmptinessTest(currBottom,currTop);

20  if (currTopIndex!=0)      // if deque isn't empty, calculate next top pointer:
21  {  // stay at current node:
22          newTopTag = currTopTag;
23          newTopNode = currTopNode;
24          newIndex = currIndex-1;
25  }
26  else
27  {  // move to next node and update tag:
28          newTopTag = currTopTag+1;
29          newTopNode = currTopNode->prev;
30          newTopIndex = DequeNode::ArraySize-1;
31  }
32  retVal = currTopNode->itsDataArr[currTopIndex]; // Read value
33  newTopVal = Encode(newTopTag,newTopNode,newTopIndex);
34  if (CAS(&Top, currTop, newTopVal))    //Try to update Top using CAS
35  {
36          FreeOldNodeIfNeeded();
37          return retVal;
38  }
39  else
40  {
41          return ABORT;
42  }
}
```

Fig. 3. Pseudo Code for the PushBottom and PopTop operations.

PopTop. The method begins by reading the Top and Bottom values, in that order (Lines 16-18). Then it checks whether these values indicate an EMPTY deque, and returns if they do (Line 19). Otherwise, it calculates the next position for Top (Lines 20-31). Before updating Top to its new value, the method must read the value which should be returned if the steal succeeds (Line 32) (this read

```
ThreadInfo DynamicDedeque::PopBottom()
{
43  <oldBotNode,oldBotIndex > = DecodeBottom(Bottom); // Read Bottom Data
44  if (oldBotIndex != DequeNode::ArraySize-1)
45  {
46              newBotNode = oldBotNode;
47              newBotIndex = oldBotIndex+1;
48  }
49  else
50  {
51              newBotNode = oldBotNode->next;
52              newBotIndex = 0;
53  }
54  retVal = newBotNode->itsDataArr[newBotIndex];       // Read data to be popped
55  Bottom = EncodeBottom(newBotNode,newBotIndex);      // Update Bottom
56  currTop = Top;                                      // Read Top
57  <currTopTag,currTopNode,currTopIndex> = DecodeTop(currTop);

58  if (oldBotNode == currTopNode &&          // Case 1: if Top has crossed Bottom
59      oldBotIndex == curTopIndex  )
60  {
        //Return bottom to its old possition:
61              Bottom = EncodeBottom(oldBotNode,oldBotIndex);
62              return EMPTY;
63  }
64  else if ( newBotNode == currTopNode &&   // Case 2: When popping the last entry
65            newBotIndex == currTopIndex )   //         in the deque (i.e. deque is
66  {                                         //         empty after the update of bottom).

        //Try to update Top's tag so no concurrent PopTop operation will also pop the same entry:
67              newTopVal = Encode(currTopTag+1, currTopNode, currTopIndex);
68              if (CAS(&Top, currTop, newTopVal))
69              {
70                  FreeOldNodeIfNeeded();
71                  return retVal;
72              }
73              else    // if CAS failed (i.e. a concurrent PopTop operation already popped the last entry):
74              {
                //Return bottom to its old possition:
75                  Bottom = EncodeBottom(oldBotNode,oldBotIndex);
76                  return EMPTY;
77              }
78  }
79  else // Case 3: Regular case (i.e. there was at least one entry in the deque after bottom's update):
80  {
81              FreeOldNodeIfNeeded();
82              return retVal;
83  }
}
```

Fig. 4. Pseudo Code for the PopBottom operation.

cannot be done after the update of Top since then the node may already be
freed by some other concurrent PopTop execution). Finally the method tries to
update Top to its new value using a CAS operation (Line 34), returning the
popped value if it succeeds, or ABORT if it failed. In case of success, the method
also checks if there is an old node that needs to be freed (Line 36). As explained
earlier, a node is released only if Top moved to a new node, and the node released
is not the old Top's node, but its preceding one.

PopBottom. The method begins by reading `Bottom` and updating it to its new value (Lines 43-55) after reading the value to be popped (Line 54). Then it reads the value of `Top` (Line 56), to check for the special cases of popping the last entry of the deque, and popping from an empty deque. If the `Top` value read points to the old `Bottom` position (Lines 58-63), then the method rewrites `Bottom` to its old position, and returns `EMPTY` (since the deque was empty even without this `PopBottom` operation). Otherwise, if `Top` is pointing to the new `Bottom` position (Lines 64-78), then the popped entry was the last in the deque, and like in the original algorithm, the method updates the `Top` tag value using a CAS, to prevent a concurrent `PopTop` operation from popping out the same entry. If neither of the above is true, then there was at least one entry in the deque after the `Bottom` update (lines 79-83), in which case the popped entry is returned. Note that, as in the original algorithm, most executions of the method will be short, and will not involve any CAS-based synchronization operations.

Memory Management. We implement the shared node pool using a variation of Scott's shared pool [14]. It maintains a local group of g nodes per process, from which the thread may allocate nodes without the need to synchronize. When the nodes in this local group are exhausted, it allocates a new group of g nodes from a shared LIFO pool using a CAS operation. When a thread frees a node, it returns it to its local pool, and if the size of the local group exceeds $2g$, it returns g nodes to the shared pool. In our benchmarks we used a group size of 1, which means that in case of a fluctuation between pushing and popping, the first node is always local and CAS is not necessary.

Omitted Code Blocks. We describe here the code segments that were not included in the pseudo code given in Figures 3 and 4:

- *The Emptiness Test in the* `PopTop` *method (Line 19):* This code segment is a possible return point from the `PopTop` method, if the `Bottom` and `Top` pointers, that were read in lines 16 and 18, respectively, indicate an empty deque. The code segment does the following:
  1. Checks if the `Top` and `Bottom` values read indicate an empty deque. The different possible empty deque scenarios will be discussed in the correctness proof.
  2. If an empty deque is detected, the `Top` pointer is read again to see if it was changed from the first read value. If it was indeed changed, ABORT is returned, otherwise EMPTY is returned.
  3. If the deque was not empty, the `PopTop` method continues at Line 20.

- *The reclamation of old list nodes by the* `Pop` *methods:* Nodes may be reclaimed both by `PopTop` and `PopBottom` operations, as follows:
  - *Reclamation of a node by the* `PopTop` *method (Line 36):* The `PopTop` method reclaims a list node if and only if it changed the `Top` pointer and the new `Top` pointer points to a different node than the old one. In this case, the method reclaims the node pointed to by the next pointer of the old `Top` node.

- *Reclamation of a node by the* PopBottom *method (Line 70 or 81):* The PopBottom method reclaims a list node if and only if it changed the Bottom pointer and the new Bottom pointer points to a different node than the old one. In this case, the method reclaims the old Bottom node.

2.3   Enhancements

We briefly describe two enhancements to the above dynamic-memory deque algorithm.

Reset-on-Empty. In the original ABP algorithm the PopBottom operation uses a heuristic that resets Top and Bottom to point back to the beginning of the array every time it detects an empty deque (including the case of popping the last entry by PopBottom). This reset operation is necessary in ABP since it is the only "anti-overflow" mechanism at its disposal.

Our algorithm does not need this method to prevent overflows, since it works with the dynamic nodes. However, adding a version of this resetting feature gives the potential of improving our space complexity, especially when working with large nodes.

There are two issues to be noted when implementing the reset-on-empty heuristic in our dynamic deque. The first issue is that while performing the reset operation, we create another type of empty deque scenario, in which Top and Bottom do not point to the same cells nor to neighboring ones (see part *c* of Figure 2). This scenario requires a more complicated check for the empty deque scenario by the PopTop method (Line 19). The second issue is that we must be careful when choosing the array node to which Top and Bottom point after the reset. In case the pointers point to the same node before the reset, we simply reset to the beginning of that node. Otherwise, we reset to the beginning of the node pointed to by Top. Note, however, that Top may point to the same node as Bottom and then be updated by a concurrent PopTop operation, which may result in changing on-the-fly the node to which we direct Top and Bottom.

Using a Base Array. In the implementation described, all the deque's nodes are identical and allocated from the shared pool. This introduces a trade-off between the performance of the algorithm and its space complexity: small arrays save space but cost in allocation overhead, while large arrays cost space but reduce the allocation overhead.

Our heuristic improvement is to use a large array for the initial base node, allocated for each of the deques, and use the pool only when overflow space is needed. This base node is used only by the process/deque it was originally allocated to, and is never freed to the shared pool. Whenever a Pop operation frees this node, it raises a local boolean flag, indicating that the base node is now free. When a PushBottom operation needs to allocate and link a new node, it first checks this flag, and if true, links the base node to the deque (instead of a regular node allocated from the shared pool).

3   Performance

We evaluated the performance of the new dynamic memory work-stealing algorithm in comparison to the original fixed-array based ABP work-stealing algorithm in an environment similar to that used by Blumofe and Papadopoulos [11] in their evaluation of the ABP algorithm. Our preliminary results include tests running several standard Splash2 [12] applications using the *Hood Library* [13] on a 16 node Sun Enterprise™ 6500, an SMP machine formed from 8 boards of two 400MHz UltraSparc® processors, connected by a crossbar UPA switch, and running a Solaris™ 9 operating system.

Our benchmarks used the work-stealing algorithms as the load balancing mechanism in Hood. The Hood package uses the original ABP deques for the scheduling of threads over processes. We compiled two versions of the Hood library, one using an ABP implementation, and the other using the new implementation. In order for the comparison to be fair, we implemented both algorithms in C++, using the same tagging method.

We present our results running the *Barnes Hut* and *MergeSort* Splash2 [12] applications. Each application was compiled with the minimal ABP deque size needed for a stand-alone run with the biggest input tested. For the Dynamic deque version we've chosen a base-array size of about 75% of the ABP deque size, a node array size of 6 items, and a shared pool size such that the total memory used (by the deques and the shared pool together) is no more than the total memory used by all ABP deques. In all our benchmarks the number of processes equaled the number of processors on the machine.

Figure 5 shows the total execution time of both algorithms, running stand-alone, as we vary the input size. As can be seen, there is no real difference in performance between the two approaches. This is in spite of the fact that our tests show that the deque operations of the new algorithm take as much as 30% more time on average than those of ABP. The explanation is simple: work stealing accounts for only a small fraction of the execution time in these (and in fact in most) applications. In all cases both algorithms had a 100% completion rate in stand-alone mode, i.e. none of the deques overflowed.

Figure 6 shows the results of running the *Barnes Hut* [12] application (on the largest input) in a multiprogrammed fashion by running multiple instances of Hood in parallel. The graph shows the completion rate of both algorithms as a function of the multiprogramming level (i.e. the number of instances run in parallel). One can clearly see that while both versions perform perfectly at a multiprogramming level of 2, ABP work-stealing degrades rapidly as the level of multiprogramming raises, while the new algorithm maintains its 100% completion rate. By checking Hood's statistics regarding the amount of work performed by each process, we noticed that some processes complete 0 work, which means much higher work loads for the others. This, we believe, caused the deque size which worked for a stand-alone run (in which the work was more evenly distributed between the processes) to overflow in the multiprogrammed run. We also note that as the work load on individual processes increases, the chances of a "reset-on-empty" decrease, and the likelihood of overflow increases. In the

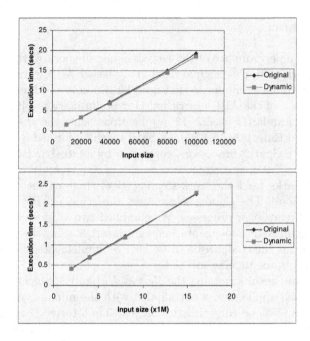

Fig. 5. *Barnes Hut* Benchmark on top and *Msort* on the bottom.

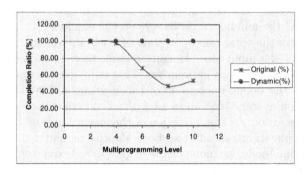

Fig. 6. *Barnes Hut* completion ratio vs. level of multiprogramming.

new dynamic version, because 25% of the memory is allocated in the common shared pool, there is much more flexibility in dealing with the work imbalance between the deques, and no overflow occurs.

Our preliminary benchmarks clearly show that for the same amount of memory, we get significantly more robustness with the new dynamic algorithm than with the original ABP algorithm, with a virtually unnoticeable effect on the application's overall performance. It also shows that the deque size depends on the maximal level of multiprogramming in the system, an unpredictable parameter which one may want to avoid reasoning about by simply using our new dynamic memory version of the ABP work stealing algorithm.

4   Proof

Our full paper will provide a proof that the algorithm is a linearizable implementation of an ABP style deque. Our specification differs slightly from that of ABP to allow one to use linearizability [15] as the consistency condition and not a weaker specialized form of serializability as used in the proof of the original ABP algorithm [1, 16]. Our revised specification is designed to allow an ABORT as a return value from PopTop, which does not affect the actual implementation algorithms, but serves to simplify their proofs.

There are two main claims that need to be proved about our algorithm: that it is lock-free, and that it is linearizable to the sequential specification of the ABP deque. The first claim is trivial, since the algorithm contains no loops, and the only case in which a PopTop operation returns ABORT is if some other concurrent operation changed Top and therefore made progress.

The linearizability proof, however, is much more complex. Here we provide only the linearization points of each of the deque's methods:

PushBottom. The linearization point of this method is always the Bottom update operation in the end of the method (Figure 3, Line 15).
PopBottom. The linearization point of this method depends on its returned value. In case the return value is:
  - EMPTY: The linearization point here is the read of the Top pointer (Figure 4, Line 56).
  - A deque entry: The linearization point here is the Bottom update (Figure 4, Line 55).
PopTop. The linearization point of this method depends on its returned value. In case the return value is:
  - EMPTY: The linearization point here is the read of the Bottom pointer (Figure 3, Line 18).
  - ABORT: The linearization point here is the operation that first observed the change of Top. This is either the CAS operation (Line 34), or a reread of Top done inside the emptiness test code block.
  - A deque entry: If the deque was not empty right before the CAS operation at Line 34, the linearization point is that CAS operation. Otherwise, it is the first operation that changed the deque to be empty, in the interval after the execution of Line 18, and right before the execution of the CAS operation at Line 34.

5   Conclusions

We have shown how to create a dynamic memory version of the ABP work stealing algorithm. It may be interesting to see how our dynamic-memory technique is applied to other schemes that improve on ABP-work stealing such as the locality-guided work-stealing of Blelloch [2] or the steal-half algorithm of Hendler and Shavit [6].

References

1. Arora, N.S., Blumofe, R.D., Plaxton, C.G.: Thread scheduling for multiprogrammed multiprocessors. Theory of Computing Systems **34** (2001) 115–144
2. Acar, U.A., Blelloch, G.E., Blumofe, R.D.: The data locality of work stealing. In: ACM Symposium on Parallel Algorithms and Architectures. (2000) 1–12
3. Flood, C., Detlefs, D., Shavit, N., Zhang, C.: Parallel garbage collection for shared memory multiprocessors. In: Usenix Java Virtual Machine Research and Technology Symposium (JVM '01), Monterey, CA (2001)
4. Leiserson, Plaat: Programming parallel applications in cilk. SINEWS: SIAM News **31** (1998)
5. Blumofe, R.D., Leiserson, C.E.: Scheduling multithreaded computations by work stealing. Journal of the ACM **46** (1999) 720–748
6. Hendler, D., Shavit, N.: Non-blocking steal-half work queues. In: Proceedings of the 21st Annual ACM Symposium on Principles of Distributed Computing. (2002)
7. Detlefs, D., Flood, C., Heller, S., Printezis, T.: Garbage-first garbage collection. Technical report, Sun Microsystems – Sun Laboratories (2004) To appear.
8. Agesen, O., Detlefs, D., Flood, C., Garthwaite, A., Martin, P., Moir, M., Shavit, N., Steele, G.: DCAS-based concurrent deques. Theory of Computing Systems **35** (2002) 349–386
9. Martin, P., Moir, M., Steele, G.: Dcas-based concurrent deques supporting bulk allocation. Technical Report TR-2002-111, Sun Microsystems Laboratories (2002)
10. Greenwald, M.B., Cheriton, D.R.: The synergy between non-blocking synchronization and operating system structure. In: 2nd Symposium on Operating Systems Design and Implementation. (1996) 123–136 Seattle, WA.
11. Blumofe, R.D., Papadopoulos, D.: The performance of work stealing in multiprogrammed environments (extended abstract). In: Measurement and Modeling of Computer Systems. (1998) 266–267
12. Arnold, J.M., Buell, D.A., Davis, E.G.: Splash 2. In: Proceedings of the fourth annual ACM symposium on Parallel algorithms and architectures, ACM Press (1992) 316–322
13. Papadopoulos, D.: Hood: A user-level thread library for multiprogrammed multiprocessors. In: Master's thesis, Department of Computer Sciences, University of Texas at Austin. (1998)
14. Scott, M.L.: Personal communication: Code for a lock-free memory management pool (2003)
15. Herlihy, M., Wing, J.: Linearizability: A correctness condition for concurrent objects. ACM Transactions on Programming Languages and Systems **12** (1990) 463–492
16. Blumofe, R.D., Plaxton, C.G., Ray, S.: Verification of a concurrent deque implementation. Technical Report CS-TR-99-11, University of Texas at Austin (1999)

Coupling and Self-stabilization

Laurent Fribourg, Stéphane Messika, and Claudine Picaronny

LSV, CNRS & ENS de Cachan,
61 av. du Prés. Wilson
94235 Cachan cedex, France

Abstract. A randomized self-stabilizing algorithm $\mathcal{A}$ is an algorithm
that, whatever the initial configuration is, reaches a set $\mathcal{L}$ of *legal configurations* in finite time with probability 1. The proof of convergence
towards $\mathcal{L}$ is generally done by exhibiting a potential function φ, which
measures the "vertical" distance of any configuration to $\mathcal{L}$, such that φ
decreases with non-null probability at each step of $\mathcal{A}$. We propose here a
method, based on the notion of coupling, which makes use of a "horizontal" distance δ between any pair of configurations, such that δ decreases
in expectation at each step of $\mathcal{A}$. In contrast with classical methods, our
coupling method does not require the knowledge of $\mathcal{L}$. In addition to the
proof of convergence, the method allows us to assess the convergence rate
according to two different measures. Proofs produced by the method are
often simpler or give better upper bounds than their classical counterparts, as examplified here on Herman's mutual exclusion and Iterated
Prisoner's Dilemma algorithms in the case of cyclic graphs.

1   Introduction

The notion of self-stabilization was introduced in computer science by Dijkstra
[4]. A distributed algorithm is self-stabilizing if, whatever the initial configuration it starts from, it reaches within a finite time a set $\mathcal{L}$ of "legal" configurations, i.e, configurations satisfying a desired property. Self-stabilizing systems
have notably received much attention because they propose an elegant way of
solving the problem of fault-tolerance [14]. Randomization is often employed in
self-stabilization to break the symmetry in anonymous systems (see [5]). With
randomized self-stabilizing algorithms, the convergence towards $\mathcal{L}$ is guaranteed
with probability 1.

We show here that we can use the notion of *coupling*, as used in the field
of Applied Probability, to prove the self-stabilization property and at the same
time, the rate of convergence to the set of legal configurations. Coupling is a
method used for analysing the rate of convergence to equilibrium in Markov
chain Monte Carlo experiments (see, e.g., [22]). The coupling time is the time
that two faithful copies of a stochastic process coalesce together. Coupling time is
generally used as an upper bound of the "mixing time" of a Markov chain $\mathcal{A}$, i.e.,
the time for the chain to be ε-close to its stationary distribution. Here we used
the coupling mechanism in an original manner in order to simultaneously prove

R. Guerraoui (Ed.): DISC 2004, LNCS 3274, pp. 201–215, 2004.
© Springer-Verlag Berlin Heidelberg 2004

the self-stabilization of an algorithm $\mathcal{A}$ w.r.t. the set of legal configurations $\mathcal{L}$, and analyze the rate of convergence to $\mathcal{L}$, assuming this set is strongly connected. The coupling time will be used as an upper bound of two measures of the rates of convergence of $\mathcal{A}$: the expected time of reaching $\mathcal{L}$ ("hitting time") and the time after which $\mathcal{L}$ has been reached with high probability ("ε-absorption time").

Comparison with related work. Classically, self-stabilization is shown by finding an integer-valued potential function φ on the set Ω of configurations that decreases with non-null probability until $\mathcal{L}$ is reached. The expected time of hitting is calculated independently (see, e.g., [20, 5, 16]). There is an other classical method for both showing self-stabilization w.r.t. $\mathcal{L}$ and analysing the rate of convergence, as examplified in [7], which consists in finding an integer-valued potential function φ on Ω such that, basically:

$\varphi(X) = 0$ iff $X \in \mathcal{L}$ and $E[\varphi(X_{t+1})] \leq \beta\varphi(X_t)$ for some β $(0 \leq \beta < 1)$.

This function φ can be seen as a "vertical" distance that separates X from $\mathcal{L}$.

Our new method consists in finding a coupling (X_t, Y_t) and a "horizontal" distance δ on $\Omega \times \Omega$ such that, basically:

$E[\delta(X_{t+1}, Y_{t+1})] \leq \beta\delta(X_t, Y_t)$, for some β $(0 \leq \beta < 1)$.

The advantages of our coupling method are the following:

- it provides us not only with a proof of self-stabilization, but also with an upper bound for the hitting time and the ε-absorption time,
- it does not rely on the knowledge of $\mathcal{L}$,
- the evaluation of β can be greatly simplified by using various optimizations of coupling, such as path coupling (see [3]),
- on Herman's mutual exclusion and Iterated Prisoner's Dilemma algorithms, proofs produced by our method are simpler or give better upper bounds than their classical counterparts.

Our method is limited in its applicability in the context of self-stabilization, because we have to assume the set of "legal" states to be strongly connected and the scheduling to be fixed (e.g., synchronous or randomized central).

Plan of the paper. After some preliminaries on randomized distributed algorithms (Sec. 2), we define self-stabilization in terms of ergodicity (Sec. 3). We then relate the notion of coupling to that of self-stabilization (Sec. 4), which yields a new method for proving self-stabilization (Sec. 5). The method is refined via the technique of Path Coupling (Sec. 6). We conclude in Sec. 7.

2   Randomized Distributed Algorithms as Markov Chains

In a distributed system, the topology of the network of machines is generally given under the form of a graph $G = (V, E)$, where the set $V = \{1, \cdots, N\}$ of vertices corresponds to the locations of the machines. There is an edge between two vertices when the corresponding machines can communicate together. All the machines are here identical finite state machines. The space of states is Q.

A *configuration* x of the network is the N-tuple of all the states of the machines. The set of configurations Q^N is denoted Ω. Given a configuration x of Ω, the state of the i-th machine is written $x(i)$. The communication between machines is done here through the reading of neighbors' states. Randomized distributed algorithms are characterized by a *scheduler* (or *adversary*), i.e., a mechanism which selects, at each step, a nonempty subset of machines, and a set of *actions* which applies simultaneously at each selected machine. In this paper, we suppose that the scheduler is fixed and memoryless (called "oblivious" in [21]): at each step, it selects a subset of machines depending on the current configuration only. For example, we will consider the case of a *synchronous scheduler* (resp. *randomized central scheduler*) which selects, at each step, all the machines (resp. a single machine randomly chosen). Once a machine is selected, its state (as well as possibly, the state of some of its neighbors) is changed by the action that applies. For a given memoryless scheduler, the randomized distributed algorithm can be seen as a Markov chain $\mathcal{A}$ on Ω (see [6]): the probability at each step to go from a configuration x to another one y is a constant, denoted $\mathbf{P}(x, y)$, that depends on x and y only. Suppose that all the configurations of Ω are of the form x_e with $e \in \{1, 2, \cdots, |\Omega|\}$. Then $\mathcal{A}$ is characterized by the matrix $\mathbf{P}$ on $\Omega \times \Omega$ which has $\mathbf{P}(x_e, x_f)$ as (e, f)-coordinate. The probability of going from x to y in t steps is $\mathbf{P}^t(x, y)$ (see, e.g., [12]).

Example 1. We consider Herman's mutual exclusion algorithm [10]. The topology is a cyclic graph (ring) of N vertices, and the scheduler synchronous. The set of states is $Q = \{0, 1\}$, and the number of machines N is odd. At each step, the state of every machine $x(i)$ ($1 \leq i \leq N$) is changed into $x'(i)$ as follows:

- if $x(i) \neq x(i-1)$ then $x'(i) = \neg x(i)$,
- if $x(i) = x(i-1)$ then $x'(i) = \begin{cases} 0 \text{ with probability } 1/2, \\ 1 \text{ with probability } 1/2. \end{cases}$

(When $i = 1$, $(i-1)$ stands for N. As usual, $\neg 0$ stands for 1, and $\neg 1$ for 0.)

Example 2. We consider the problem of the Iterated Prisoner's Dilemma, as modeled in [7]. The topology is a cyclic graph (ring) of N vertices, and the scheduler randomized central. The set of states is $Q = \{-, +\}$. At each each step, a vertex i ($1 \leq i \leq N$) is chosen uniformly at random, and the values $x(i)$ and $x(i+1)$ are changed into $x'(i)$ and $x'(i+1)$ respectively as follows:

- if $x(i) = x(i+1)$, then $x'(i) = x'(i+1) = +$,
- if $x(i) = \neg x(i+1)$, then $x'(i) = x'(i+1) = -$.

(When $i = N$, $(i+1)$ stands here for 1. Here, $\neg +$ stands for $-$, and $\neg -$ for $+$.)

3 Self-stabilization

3.1 Convergence

Let us consider a Markov chain $\mathcal{A}$. Two configurations x and y are in the same equivalence class if they are "strongly connected", i.e., if there exist t, u such that $\mathbf{P}^t(x, y) > 0$ and $\mathbf{P}^u(y, x) > 0$. Given two classes C and C', $C' \ll C$ means that $\mathbf{P}^t(x, y) > 0$ for some $x \in C, y \in C'$ and $t > 0$. The minimal classes for $\ll$ are called *ergodic sets*. More precisely:

Definition 1. *Let $\mathcal{M} \subset 2^\Omega$ be a set of configurations. $\mathcal{M}$ is an* ergodic set *if*
  1. *$\mathcal{M}$ is strongly connected, i.e.: $\forall x, y \in \mathcal{M}: \mathbf{P}^t(x, y) > 0$ for some t, and*
  2. *$\mathcal{M}$ is closed, i.e.: $(x \in \mathcal{M} \land \mathbf{P}(x, y) > 0) \Rightarrow y \in \mathcal{M}$.*

Every finite Markov chain has always at least one ergodic set (since finite partial ordering $\ll$ must have at least one minimal element). Furthermore, two distinct ergodic sets are disjoint (since they are both strongly connected). We focus here on Markov chains with a single ergodic set. As explained below, they correspond to the notion of "self-stabilizing" algorithms, as originally defined by Dijkstra in the deterministic framework [4].

In [4], Dijkstra defined the set $\mathcal{L}$ of *legal configurations* of a distributed algorithm as a set of configurations meeting a global correctness criterion (e.g., the uniqueness of "token") with the constraints of (1) strong connectivity and (2) closure. Therefore, in our context of Markov chains, a set of legal configurations is necessarily an ergodic set. An algorithm $\mathcal{A}$ is *convergent w.r.t* a set $\mathcal{L}$ of legal configurations if, starting from any initial configuration, the system is guaranteed to reach a configuration of $\mathcal{L}$ within a finite number of transitions. For example, in mutual exclusion problems, a legal configuration is a configuration with a single token, which expresses the fact that only one machine can enjoy the resource. Following Dijkstra's definition, we have:

Definition 2. *Given a set $\mathcal{L}$ of configurations, $\mathcal{A}$ is self-stabilizing w.r.t. $\mathcal{L}$, in Dijkstra's sense[1], if*
  1. *$\mathcal{L}$ is strongly connected,*
  2. *$\mathcal{L}$ is closed, and*
  3. *$\mathcal{A}$ is convergent w.r.t. $\mathcal{L}$.*

In the probabilistic context of Markov chains, the convergence property (3) has to be guaranteed with probability 1. Formally, $\mathcal{A}$ is *convergent w.r.t $\mathcal{L}$ (with probability 1)* if: $\forall x \sum_{y \in \mathcal{L}} \mathbf{P}^t(x, y) \to 1$ when $t \to \infty$. We have (see, e.g., [12]):

Proposition 1. *A finite Markov chain $\mathcal{A}$ converges with probability 1 to the union of the ergodic sets, whatever the initial configuration is.*

It follows:

Proposition 2. *A randomized distributed algorithm $\mathcal{A}$ is self-stabilizing (in Dijkstra's sense) w.r.t. a set $\mathcal{L}$ of configurations iff $\mathcal{L}$ is the unique ergodic set of $\mathcal{A}$.*

---

[1] The notion of self-stabilization has been relaxed since pioneering Dijkstra's work, and requirement (1) of strong connectivity for $\mathcal{L}$ is often dropped (see [20]). However, in this paper, we keep requirement (1) because it matches better with the notion of rapidly mixing Markov chains.

Proof: ($\Leftarrow$) Suppose that $\mathcal{L}$ is the unique ergodic set of $\mathcal{A}$. Then $\mathcal{L}$ satisfies the properties of closure and strong connectivity, and by Proposition 1, there is convergence with probability 1 to the union of the ergodic sets, viz. $\mathcal{L}$, whatever the initial configuration is. Hence $\mathcal{A}$ is self-stabilizing w.r.t. $\mathcal{L}$.

($\Rightarrow$) Suppose that $\mathcal{A}$ is self-stabilizing w.r.t. $\mathcal{L}$. Then $\mathcal{L}$ is closed and strongly connected, hence is an ergodic set. Let us show that $\mathcal{L}$ is the unique ergodic set by *reductio ad absurdum*: suppose that there is another (disjoint) ergodic set $\mathcal{L}'$, and let us show that $\mathcal{A}$ is not self-stabilizing w.r.t. $\mathcal{L}$. Consider an element $y \in \mathcal{L}'$. Every sequence of transitions starting from y stays in $\mathcal{L}'$ (since $\mathcal{L}'$ is closed). Hence no sequence of transitions starting from y can reach $\mathcal{L}$ (since $\mathcal{L}$ and $\mathcal{L}'$ are disjoint). So, for any starting configuration $y \in \mathcal{L}'$, the probability of reaching $\mathcal{L}$ is null. It follows that $\mathcal{A}$ is not convergent to $\mathcal{L}$, hence not self-stabilizing.   □

It is generally easy to check that a given set $\mathcal{L}$ of configurations is ergodic for $\mathcal{A}$, as illustrated in Examples 1 and 2. What is difficult is to show the *uniqueness* of the ergodic set, i.e., the absence of any other ergodic set, besides $\mathcal{L}$: for example, for a mutual exclusion algorithm, the absence of any subset of "looping" configurations with two tokens.

Example 3. Consider Herman's algorithm in the case where N is odd. In a configuration, a "token" at position i ($1 \leq i \leq N$) corresponds to the presence of two contiguous states of the same value (00 or 11) at position $i - 1$ and i. Since N is odd, any configuration contains always at least one token. It is easy to see that such a set is ergodic .

Example 4. In the Iterated Prisoner's Dilemma, the set $\mathcal{L}$ of legal configurations is the singleton made of the configuration $x^* = (+)^N$. Obviously, any action transforms x^* to itself. Hence, $\{x^*\}$ is trivially an ergodic set.

In the following, we assume that we are given a Markov chain $\mathcal{A}$ and an ergodic set $\mathcal{L}$, and we focus on the problem of proving the self-stabilization property of $\mathcal{A}$ w.r.t. $\mathcal{L}$. We are also interested in evaluating the rate of convergence of $\mathcal{A}$ to $\mathcal{L}$. We will use two different measures of convergence: the "expected hitting time" and the "ε-absorption time".

The expected hitting time is the standard rate of convergence used in the self-stabilization community (see, e.g., [5], p. 118). It is the expected time for $\mathcal{A}$ to reach $\mathcal{L}$, starting from the "worst" configuration, i.e.:

Definition 3. *Given a Markov chain $\mathcal{A}$ and a set $\mathcal{L}$, the expected hitting time of $\mathcal{L}$ (or more simply the hitting time) is:*
$$\mathbf{H}_\mathcal{L} = max_{x \in \Omega} \ E(H_{x\mathcal{L}}),$$
where $E(.)$ denotes expectation and $H_{x\mathcal{L}} = min\{t : \ X_t \in \mathcal{L} \mid X_0 = x\}$.

We will also use a different rate of convergence, called here "ε-absorption time", that gives the time after which $\mathcal{L}$ has been reached with high probability.

Definition 4. *Given a Markov chain $\mathcal{A}$ and an ergodic set $\mathcal{L}$, the time of ε-absorption by $\mathcal{L}$ (or simply the ε-absorption time) is:*
$$\Theta_{\mathcal{L}}(\varepsilon) = max_{x \in \Omega}\ \Theta_{x\mathcal{L}}(\varepsilon),$$
where $\Theta_{x\mathcal{L}}(\varepsilon) = min\{t :\ Pr(X_t \in \mathcal{L}) \geq 1 - \varepsilon \mid X_0 = x\}$.

So $\Theta_{\mathcal{L}}(\varepsilon)$ is the minimal number of steps in which $\mathcal{A}$ reaches $\mathcal{L}$ with probability at least $1 - \varepsilon$. This notion is, for example, used in [7], for measuring the rate of convergence of the Iterated Prisoner's Dilemma. The notion is closed to the notion of "mixing time", that measures the number of steps after which the chain is ε-close of the "stationary distribution" of $\mathcal{A}$. [2] An upper bound on the mixing time is often computed by finding the "coupling time" (see, e.g., [19, 22]), that is defined henceforth.

Remark. Various notions of convergence rates are compared together in [1] and [15], but these studies concern only the case of "irreducible" chains where $\mathcal{L}$ and Ω coincide (all the configurations are legal and inter-connected) while, here, we are concerned with "reducible" chains where $\mathcal{L}$ is a strict subset of Ω.

4   Coupling

Let us come back to $\mathcal{A}$ viewed as a Markov chain. It will be characterized by a sequence of random variables (X_t) taking their values on the space Ω of configurations. The method of "coupling" is an elementary probabilistic method for measuring the "agreement" time between the components of a stochastic process (see, e.g., [22, 19]).

Definition 5. *A coupling is a Markov chain on $\Omega \times \Omega$ defining a stochastic process $(X_t, Y_t)_{t=1}^{\infty}$ with the properties*
1. Each of the processes (X_t) and (Y_t) is a faithful copy of $\mathcal{A}$ (given initial configurations $X_0 = x$ and $Y_0 = y$).
2. If $X_t = Y_t$, then $X_{t+1} = Y_{t+1}$.

Condition 1 ensures that each process, viewed in isolation, is just simulating the original chain – yet the coupling updates them simultaneously so that they tend to move closer together, according to some notion of distance. Once the pair of configurations agree, condition 2 guarantees they agree from that time forward.

Definition 6. *Given a coupling (X_t, Y_t), the (expected) coupling time is:*
$$\mathbf{T} = max_{x \in \Omega, y \in \Omega}\ E(T_{x,y}),$$
where $T_{x,y} = min\{t : X_t = Y_t \mid X_0 = x, Y_0 = y\}$.

The coupling time is often computed as un upper bound on the mixing time, in order to show the property of "rapid mixing" for $\mathcal{A}$ (i.e, the fact that the mixing time is bounded above by a polynomial in N and $\ln(\frac{1}{\varepsilon})$). We show hereafter that the coupling time gives also an upper bound on the hitting time.

---

[2] Actually, the two notions coincide when the set $\mathcal{L}$ is reduced to a single configuration, as in the example of Iterated Prisoner's Dilemma.

Theorem 1. *Given a Markov chain $\mathcal{A}$ and an ergodic set $\mathcal{L}$, if there exists a coupling of finite expected time $\mathbf{T}$, then:*
  1. $\mathcal{A}$ is self-stabilizing w.r.t. $\mathcal{L}$.
  2. The hitting time $\mathbf{H}_{\mathcal{L}}$ is less than or equal to $\mathbf{T}$: $\mathbf{H}_{\mathcal{L}} \leq \mathbf{T}$.

Proof: 1. By *reductio ad absurdum*: Suppose that there are two non-empty ergodic sets $\mathcal{L}_1$ and $\mathcal{L}_2$ with two elements $X_0 = x \in \mathcal{L}_1$ and $Y_0 = y \in \mathcal{L}_2$. Then, for all $t > 0$, $X_t \in \mathcal{L}_1$ and $Y_t \in \mathcal{L}_2$ since $\mathcal{L}_1$ and $\mathcal{L}_2$ are closed. Therefore for all $t > 0$, $X_t \neq Y_t$ since $\mathcal{L}_1$ and $\mathcal{L}_2$ are disjoint. Hence $T_{x,y}$ is infinite. So is $\mathbf{T}$, which contradicts the assumption.

2. Let us show: $\mathbf{H}_{\mathcal{L}} \leq \mathbf{T}$. Recall that: $H_{x\mathcal{L}} = min\{t :\ X_t \in \mathcal{L} \mid X^0 = x\}$, and $T_{xy} = min\{t :\ X_t = Y_t \mid X^0 = x, Y^0 = y\}$. Suppose now that $y \in \mathcal{L}$. Then $Y_t \in \mathcal{L}$ since $\mathcal{L}$ is closed. Hence: $H_{x\mathcal{L}} \leq T_{xy}$ for all $x \in \Omega, y \in \mathcal{L}$. And by taking the expectations, then the maxima of the two sides: $\mathbf{H}_{\mathcal{L}} \leq \mathbf{T}$. □

5 Two Sufficient Criteria of Self-stabilization

By Theorem 1, finding an upper bound on the time of coupling T allows us to prove simultaneously the self-stabilization and to obtain an upper bound on the hitting time. Following classical results on mixing time (see e.g. [8]), we give hereafter two sufficient conditions for bounding the coupling time. In each case, this provides us additionally with an upper bound not only for the hitting time, but also for the ε-absorption time.

Theorem 2. *Given a Markov chain $\mathcal{A}$ and an ergodic set $\mathcal{L}$, suppose there exists a coupling (X_t, Y_t) and an integer-valued function δ on $\Omega \times \Omega$ which takes values in $\{0, 1, \cdots, B\}$ such that $\delta(X_t, Y_t) = 0$ iff $X_t = Y_t$, and:*
$$\exists \beta < 1 \ \ \forall (X_t, Y_t) \ \ E(\delta(X_{t+1}, Y_{t+1})) \leq \beta \delta(X_t, Y_t). \tag{$*$}$$
Then:
  1. $\mathcal{A}$ is self-stabilizing w.r.t. $\mathcal{L}$.
  2. The expected hitting time satisfies: $\mathbf{H}_{\mathcal{L}} \leq \frac{B}{1-\beta}$.
  3. The ε-absorption time satisfies: $\Theta_{\mathcal{L}}(\varepsilon) \leq \frac{\ln(B/\varepsilon)}{1-\beta}$.

Proof: See Appendix 1.

A similar theorem exists even when $\beta = 1$, i.e.: $E(\delta(X_{t+1}, Y_{t+1})) \leq \delta(X_t, Y_t)$, provided that the probability of $(X_{t+1}, Y_{t+1}) \neq (X_t, Y_t)$ can be bounded below.

Theorem 3. *Given a Markov chain $\mathcal{A}$ and an ergodic set $\mathcal{L}$, suppose there exists a coupling (X_t, Y_t) and an integer-valued function δ on $\Omega \times \Omega$ which takes values in $\{0, 1 \cdots, B\}$ such that $\delta(X_t = Y_t) = 0$ iff $X_t = Y_t$, and such that, there exists $\alpha > 0$ such that, for all (X_t, Y_t) with $X_t \neq Y_t$:*

$$E(\delta(X_{t+1}, Y_{t+1})) \leq \delta(X_t, Y_t) \ \wedge \ \ Pr(\delta(X_{t+1}, Y_{t+1}) \neq \delta(X_t, Y_t)) \geq \alpha. \tag{$**$}$$

Then:
1. *$\mathcal{A}$ is self-stabilizing w.r.t. $\mathcal{L}$.*
2. *The expected hitting time satisfies: $\mathbf{H}_{\mathcal{L}} \leq B^2/\alpha$.*
3. *The ε-absorption time satisfies: $\Theta_{\mathcal{L}}(\varepsilon) \leq \lceil e \frac{B^2}{\alpha} \rceil \lceil \ln(\frac{1}{\varepsilon}) \rceil$.*

Proof: See Appendix 2.

Therefore finding a coupling (X_t, Y_t) and a function δ such that $(*)$ (resp. $(**)$) holds allows us to prove that $\mathcal{A}$ is self-stabilizing and gives an upper bound on two different rates of convergence towards the (unique) ergodic set.

6   Refinement of Coupling

6.1   Path Coupling

As pointed out in [19], it is often cumbersome to measure the expected change in distance between two arbitrary configurations. The method of *path coupling*, introduced by Bubley and Dyer [3], simplifies the approach by showing that only pairs of configurations that are "close" need to be considered. Path coupling involves defining a coupling (X_t, Y_t) by considering a *path*, or sequence $X_t = Z_0, Z_1, \cdots, Z_r = Y_t$ between X_t and Y_t where the Z_i satisfy certain conditions. The following version of the path coupling method is convenient:

Lemma 1. (Dyer and Greenhill [8]) *Let δ be an integer valued metric defined on $\Omega \times \Omega$ which takes value in $\{0, \cdots, B\}$. Let U be a subset of $\Omega \times \Omega$ s.t., for all $(X_t, Y_t) \in \Omega \times \Omega$, there exists a path $X_t = Z_0, Z_1, \cdots, Z_r = Y_t$ between X_t and Y_t such that $(Z_i, Z_{i+1}) \in U$ for $0 \leq i < r$ and $\sum_{i=0}^{r-1} \delta(Z_i, Z_{i+1}) = \delta(X_t, Y_t)$.*
Suppose there exists a coupling $(X, Y) \mapsto (X', Y')$ of the Markov chain $\mathcal{A}$ on all pairs $(X, Y) \in U$, and a constant $\beta \leq 1$ such that, for all $(X, Y) \in U$:
$$E[\delta(X', Y')] \leq \beta\delta(X, Y). \qquad (***)$$
Then this coupling can be extended to a coupling of $\mathcal{A}$ on all pairs $(X, Y) \in \Omega \times \Omega$ which also satisfies $(***)$.

Two configurations X and Y are said to be *adjacent* if $(X, Y) \in U$. The advantage of this lemma is that it allows to check the crucial property $(***)$ only on the set U of adjacent pairs instead of the entire space $\Omega \times \Omega$. Lemma 1 combined with Theorem 2 (resp. Theorem 3) allows us to enhance our coupling method for proving self-stabilization.

6.2   Application to Herman

Let us come back to Herman's algorithm (see Example 1).

Theorem 4. *For Herman's algorithm and N odd, there exists a subset U of $\Omega \times \Omega$, an integer valued metric δ on $\Omega \times \Omega$ taking value in $\{0, \cdots, N\}$, and a coupling defined on U s.t.: $\forall (X_t, Y_t) \in U$ $E[\delta(X_{t+1}, Y_{t+1})] \leq \delta(X_t, Y_t)$, and $\forall (X_t, Y_t) \in \Omega \times \Omega$ (with $X_t \neq Y_t$) : $Pr[\delta(X_{t+1}, Y_{t+1}) \neq \delta(X_t, Y_t)] \geq 1/2$.*

Proof:

- *Metric δ*. We define δ as the Hamming distance, i.e.: $\delta(X_t, Y_t)$ is the number of positions at which X_t and Y_t differ. The couple (X_t, Y_t) belongs to U iff $\delta(X_t, Y_t) = 1$.
- *Coupling.* Coupling is such that if, for all i ($1 \leq i \leq N$), $X_t(i)$ and $Y_t(i)$ both perform *randomized* actions (i.e., when $X_t(i) = X_t(i-1)$ and $Y_t(i) = Y_t(i-1)$), the i-th machines of X_t and Y_t are forced to do the same probabilistic choice so that $X_{t+1}(i)$ and $Y_{t+1}(i)$ always coincide:

$$X_{t+1}(i) = Y_{t+1}(i) = \begin{cases} 0 \text{ with probability } 1/2, \\ 1 \text{ with probability } 1/2. \end{cases}$$

- *Proof of $E[\delta(X_{t+1}, Y_{t+1})] = \delta(X_t, Y_t)$ on U, and $Pr(\delta(X_{t+1}, Y_{t+1}) \neq \delta(X_t, Y_t)) \geq 1/2$ for all $(X_t, Y_t) \in \Omega \times \Omega$ with $X_t \neq Y_t$.*
  At each step, the state of all the machines at position $1, \cdots, N$ are updated. Let ℓ be the position of disagreement. In order to fix the ideas consider the following vector

$$\begin{pmatrix} X_t \\ Y_t \end{pmatrix} = \begin{pmatrix} \nu_1 \ \nu_2 \ \cdots \ \nu_{\ell-2} \ \mathbf{0} \ \mathbf{0} \ 0 \ \nu_{\ell+2} \ \cdots \ \nu_N \\ \nu_1 \ \nu_2 \ \cdots \ \nu_{\ell-2} \ 0 \ \mathbf{1} \ 0 \ \nu_{\ell+2} \ \cdots \ \nu_N \end{pmatrix}$$

where all the ν_i are in $\{0, 1\}$, the figures in bold font correspond to positions ℓ. (The other cases are similar.) After one step, we have:

$$\begin{pmatrix} X_{t+1} \\ Y_{t+1} \end{pmatrix} = \begin{pmatrix} \nu'_1 \ \nu'_2 \ \cdots \ \nu'_{\ell-2} \ \nu'_{\ell-1} \ \mathbf{0/1} \ 0/1 \ \nu'_{\ell+2} \ \cdots \ \nu'_N \\ \nu'_1 \ \nu'_2 \ \cdots \ \nu'_{\ell-2} \ \nu'_{\ell-1} \ \mathbf{0} \ 1 \ \nu'_{\ell+2} \ \cdots \ \nu'_N \end{pmatrix}$$

where '0/1' means "0 with prob. $1/2$ and 1 with prob. $1/2$". Note that, for $1 \leq i \leq \ell - 1$ and $\ell + 2 \leq i \leq N$, $X_{t+1}(i) = Y_{t+1}(i) = \nu'_i$ thanks to our coupling. So X_{t+1} and Y_{t+1} coincide everywhere except, perhaps, at positions ℓ or $\ell + 1$. We have:

$$\delta(X_{t+1}, Y_{t+1}) = \begin{cases} \delta(X_t, Y_t) = 1 & \text{with probability } 1/2, \\ \delta(X_t, Y_t) - 1 = 0 & \text{with probability } 1/4, \\ \delta(X_t, Y_t) + 1 = 2 & \text{with probability } 1/4. \end{cases}$$

Hence $E(\delta(X_{t+1}, Y_{t+1})) = \delta(X_t, Y_t)$, for all $(X_t, Y_t) \in U$. Furthermore, it is easy to show that $Pr(\delta(X_{t+1}, Y_{t+1}) \neq \delta(X_t, Y_t)) \geq 1/2$, for all $(X_t, Y_t) \in \Omega \times \Omega$ such that $X_t \neq Y_t$. $\qquad \square$

Since $\delta(X_t, Y_t)$ takes its values in $\{0, 1, \cdots, N\}$, it then follows from Theorem 3, Lemma 1 and Theorem 4:

Corollary 1. *For N odd, Herman's algorithm $\mathcal{A}$ is such that:*
1. *$\mathcal{A}$ is self-stabilizing w.r.t. the set $\mathcal{L}$ of configurations with a single token.*
2. *The hitting time satisfies:* $\mathbf{H}_\mathcal{L} \leq 2N^2$.
3. *The ε-absorption time satisfies:* $\Theta_\mathcal{L}(\varepsilon) \leq 2eN^2 \lceil \ln(\frac{1}{\varepsilon}) \rceil$.

Note that the metric δ on $\Omega \times \Omega$ found here (Hamming distance) is much simpler than the function φ on Ω used by Herman, which involves the number of tokens of a configuration x together with the minimal distance between two tokens of x. Our method gives also directly an upper bound for the hitting time with no need for a separate analysis as done in Herman's work [10]. Besides, it gives a quadratic bound for the ε-absorption time (not considered by Herman).

The method can be applied in the same manner to several other self-stabilizing algorithms on cyclic graphs (e.g., mutual exclusion Flatebo-Datta's algorithm [9] with central randomized scheduler, Mayer-Ostrovsky-Yung's binary clock algorithm with synchronous scheduler [17]).

6.3   Application to Iterated Prisoner's Dilemma

Let us come back to Iterated Prisoner's Dilemma algorithm (Example 2). Recall that, in this case, the set $\mathcal{L}$ made of the unique configuration x^*, with $x^*(i) = +$ for all $1 \leq i \leq N$, is ergodic. Let us show that the algorithm is self-stabilizing.

Theorem 5. *For the Prisoner's Dilemma algorithm, there exist a subset U of $\Omega \times \Omega$, an integer valued metric δ on $\Omega \times \Omega$ taking value in $\{0, \cdots, 11N\}$, and a coupling defined on U such that, for all $(X_t, Y_t) \in U$:*
$$E[\delta(X_{t+1}, Y_{t+1})] \leq (1 - \tfrac{1}{18N})\delta(X_t, Y_t).$$

Proof:

- *Adjacent pairs.* A pair (X, Y) belongs to U iff X and Y coincide everywhere except on k contiguous positions, with $k = 1, 2, 3, 4$ or 5, where they disagree.
- *Metric δ.* Consider a pair $(X, Y) \in U$ which disagrees exactly at k contiguous positions ($1 \leq k \leq 5$). Let $\delta(X, Y) = a_k$ where a_k is a positive constant that will be determined later. By convention, we let $a_0 = 0$. The function δ on U extends to the entire space $\Omega \times \Omega$ as explained hereafter. Consider $(X, Y) \in \Omega \times \Omega$ such that X and Y differ only on ℓ contiguous positions. We have: $\ell = 5m + r$ for some $m \geq 0$ and $0 \leq r \leq 4$. The function δ is then defined by: $\delta(X, Y) = ma_5 + a_r$. Suppose that X and Y disagree on n separated zones of contiguous positions W_p ($1 \leq p \leq n$). Let m_p and r_p be the quotient and the remainder of the length of W_p divided by 5 ($|W_p| = 5m_p + r_p$ with $0 \leq r_p \leq 4$). Then, for all $(X, Y) \in \Omega \times \Omega$, δ is defined by: $\delta(X, Y) = \sum_{p=1}^{n} m_p a_5 + a_{r_p}$. We will show later that, for appropriate values of a_k ($1 \leq k \leq 5$), function δ is a metric which satisfies the conditions required by Lemma 1 (i.e., for all path $X = Z_0, Z_1, \cdots, Z_r = Y$ where $(Z_j, Z_{j+1}) \in U$, $\sum_{j=0}^{r-1} \delta(Z_j, Z_{j+1}) = \delta(X, Y)$).
- *Coupling.* The coupling $(X, Y) \mapsto (X', Y')$ is defined such that, at each step, the position chosen uniformly at random coincides for X and Y. (So, at each step, the state of the machine of the selected position, say j, and the state of the $j + 1$-th machine are updated simultaneously in X and Y.)
- *Proof of $E[\delta(X', Y')] \leq \beta\delta(X, Y)$:* Consider a vector $(X_t, Y_t) \in U$ with k contiguous disagreeing positions. Let i be the first disagreeing position. The vector is of the form

$$\begin{pmatrix} X_t \\ Y_t \end{pmatrix} = \begin{pmatrix} \gamma_1 \cdots \gamma_{i-2}\ \gamma_{i-1}\ \gamma_i\ \cdots\ \gamma_{i+k-1}\ \gamma_{i+k} \cdots \gamma_N \\ \gamma_1 \cdots \gamma_{i-2}\ \gamma_{i-1}\ \neg\gamma_i\ \cdots\ \neg\gamma_{i+k-1}\ \gamma_{i+k} \cdots \gamma_N \end{pmatrix}$$

where the γ_ℓ are in $\{-,+\}$. Suppose that the selected position j is such that $1 \leq j \leq i-2$ or $i+k \leq j \leq N$. Then $X_t(j) = Y_t(j)$ and $X_t(j+1) = Y_t(j+1)$, so $X_{t+1}(j) = Y_{t+1}(j)$ and $X_{t+1}(j+1) = Y_{t+1}(j+1)$, and the disagreement zone is not modified. Suppose now that the selected position j is equal to $i-1$. Then, after one step, we have:

$$\begin{pmatrix} X_{t+1} \\ Y_{t+1} \end{pmatrix} = \begin{pmatrix} \gamma_1 \cdots \gamma_{i-2}\ \gamma'_{i-1}\ \gamma'_i\ \cdots\ \gamma_{i+k-1}\ \gamma_{i+k} \cdots \gamma_N \\ \gamma_1 \cdots \gamma_{i-2}\ \neg\gamma'_{i-1}\ \neg\gamma'_i\ \cdots\ \neg\gamma_{i+k-1}\ \gamma_{i+k} \cdots \gamma_N \end{pmatrix}$$

where $\gamma'_{i-1} = \gamma'_i = +$ if $\gamma_{i-1} = \gamma_i$, and $\gamma'_{i-1} = \gamma'_i = -$ otherwise. This means that the disagreement zone has progressed on position at the left. A symmetrical case exists for $j = i + k - 1$. We say that j is an "outer rim position". All the other possible cases for j are studied in Appendix 3. A simple case analysis shows that, for appropriate values of a_k ($1 \leq k \leq 5$), there exists β with $\beta \leq 1 - \frac{1}{18N}$ such that $E[\delta(X',Y')] \leq \beta\delta(X,Y)$. Furthermore, for these values of a_k, the maximal value B of δ on $\Omega \times \Omega$ is such that $B \leq 11N$. See Appendix 3. $\square$

Therefore, from Theorem 2, Lemma 1 and Theorem 5, it follows:

Corollary 2. *For Iterated Prisoner's Dilemma algorithm $\mathcal{A}$, we have:*
1. *$\mathcal{A}$ is self-stabilizing w.r.t. the set $\mathcal{L} = \{(+)^N\}$.*
2. *The hitting time satisfies: $\mathbf{H}_{\mathcal{L}} \leq 198N^2$.*
3. *The ε-absorption time satisfies: $\Theta_{\mathcal{L}}(\varepsilon) \leq 18N \ln(\frac{11N}{\varepsilon})$.*

Thus the quasi-linear bound on the ε-time of absorption is obtained, as found in [7]. Note that the linearity factor is better here (18 vs. 49/2). We retrieve also the quadratic bound on the hitting time found empirically in [13].

The proof presented here bears some resemblance with the proof by Dyer et al. in [7]: A function δ has been found here on $\Omega \times \Omega$ which satisfies $E\delta(X',Y') \leq \beta\delta(X,Y)$ (with $\beta < 1$), while they found a function φ on Ω satisfying $E\varphi(X') \leq \beta'\varphi(X)$ (with $\beta' < 1$) and $\varphi(\mathcal{L}) = 0$. Note that their function φ is somewhat simpler than δ (φ mainly involves isolated singletons $(-)$ and doublets $(--)$ while δ involves isolated sequences of disagreement of length up to 5). However, thanks to the path coupling method, it is easier to show the decrease in expectation for δ than for φ. Furthermore, we obtain here a better ε-absorption time ($\beta = 18 < \beta' = 49/2$).

7   Final Remarks

We have shown that the method of coupling, which is classically used to evaluate the rate of convergence to equilibrium of Monte Carlo Markov chains, can be used to prove self-stabilization of distributed algorithms in an original manner. It allows us also to analyse the rate of convergence of these algorithms according to two different measures. The method has been enhanced by using the refinement of coupling, called "path coupling". This suggests to explore applications of the method using other refinements of coupling, such as Huber's bounding chain method [11]. We believe that our method still applies when the set $\mathcal{L}$ of legal states is not strongly connected, in the case where the various ergodic sets of $\mathcal{L}$ can be abstracted together using symmetries (e.g., in the case of randomized consensus protocols [2]). Finally, we plan to adapt our method on algorithms working with arbitrary schedulers (modelled by Markov decision proceses [18]) using, for example, the technique of scheduler-luck games (see [5]).

Acknowledgment

We are grateful to Alistair Sinclair for helpful discussions on an earlier draft of this paper.

References

1. A. Aldous and J. Fill. *Reversible Markov Chains and Random Walks on Graph.* draft at http:/www.stat.Berkeley.EDU/users/aldous/book.html, To appear.
2. J. Aspnes and M. Herlihy. Fast randomized consensus using shared memory. *Journal of Algorithms*, 11(3):441–461, 1990.
3. R. Bubley and M. Dyer. Path coupling: A technique for proving rapid mixing in Markov chains. In *Proc. of the 38th Annual IEEE Symposium on Foundations of Computer Science (FOCS'97)*, pages 223–231, 1997.
4. E.W. Dijkstra. Self-stabilizing systems in spite of distributed control. *Communications of the ACM*, 17(11):643–644, Nov. 1974.
5. S. Dolev, A. Israeli, and S. Moran. Analyzing expected time by scheduler luck games. *IEEE transactions on Software Engineering*, 21(5):429–439, May 1995.
6. M. Duflot, L. Fribourg, and C. Picaronny. Randomized distributed algorithms as Markov chains. In *Proc. 15th Int. Conf. on Distributed Computing (DISC 2001), LNCS 2180*, pages 240–254. Springer, 2001.
7. M. Dyer, L.A. Goldberg, C. Greenhill, G. Istrate, and M. Jerrum. Convergence of the Iterated Prisoner's Dilemma Game. *Combinatorics, Probability and Computing*, 11(2), 2002.
8. M.E. Dyer and C. Greenhill. A more rapidly mixing Markov chain for graph colorings. *Random Structures and Algorithms*, 13:285–317, 1998.
9. M. Flatebo and A.K. Datta. Two-state self-stabilizing algorithms for token rings. *IEEE Transactions on Software Engineering*, 20(6):500–504, June 1994.
10. T. Herman. Probabilistic self-stabilization. *IPL*, 35(2):63–67, June 1990.
11. M. Huber. Exact sampling and approximate counting techniques. In *Proc. of the 30th Annual ACM Symp. on Theory of Computing (STOC'98)*, pages 31–40, 1998.
12. J.G. Kemeny and J.L. Snell. *Finite Markov Chains.* D. van Nostrand Co., 1969.
13. J.E. Kittock. Emergent conventions and the structure of multi-agent systems. In L. Nadel and D. Stein, editors, *Proc. of the 1993 Complex systems summer school.* Santa Fe Institute Studies in the Sciences of Complexity, Addison-Wesley, 1995.
14. L. Lamport. Solved problems, unsolved problems and non-problems in concurrency. In *Proc. of the 3rd ACM Symp. on Principles of Distributed Computing (PODC'84)*, pages 1–11, 1984.

15. L. Lovász and P. Winkler. Mixing Times. *Microsurveys in Discrete Probability*, pages 85–134, 1998.
16. N.A. Lynch. *Distributed Algorithms*. Morgan Kaufmann Publishers, Inc., 1997.
17. A. Mayer, R. Ostrovsky, and M. Yung. Self-Stabilizing Algorithms for Synchronous Unidirectional Rings. In *Proc. of the 7th ACM-SIAM Symp. on Discrete Algorithms (SODA-96)*, 1996.
18. Martin L. Puterman. *Markov Decision Processes : Discrete Stochastic Dynamic Programming*. Wiley-Interscience, 1994.
19. D. Randall. Mixing. In *Proc. of the 44th Annual IEEE Symp. on Foundations of Computer Science (FOCS'03)*, 2003.
20. M. Schneider. Self-stabilization. *ACM Computing Surveys*, 25:45–67, 1993.
21. R. Segala. *Modeling and Verification of Randomized Distributed Real-Time Systems*. PhD thesis, Massachusetts Institue of Technology, Jun. 1995.
22. A. Sinclair. Convergence rates for Monte Carlo experiments. In *Numerical Methods for Polymeric Systems*, pages 1–18. IMA Volumes in Mathematics & Its application, 1997.
23. D. Williams. *Probability with Martingales*. Cambridge University Press, 1991.

Appendix 1: Proof of Theorem 2

We will use the following Proposition that is easily proven by supermartingale theory, applying Doob's optional stopping Theorem (see for example [23]):

Proposition 3. *Suppose that* $D = (D_0, D_1, \cdots)$ *is a nonnegative stochastic process on* $\{0, 1, \cdots, B\}$ *such that* $E[D_{t+1}] \leq \beta D_t$ *(with* $0 < \beta < 1$*) when* $D_t > 0$. *Then if* τ *is the first time that* $D_t = 0$, *we have:* $E[\tau] \leq B/(1 - \beta)$.

Proof of Theorem 2

1. By *reductio ad absurdum*: Suppose that $\mathcal{A}$ is not self-stabilizing. Then there are two non-empty ergodic sets $\mathcal{L}_1$ and $\mathcal{L}_2$ with two elements $x \in \mathcal{L}_1$ and $y \in \mathcal{L}_2$. Then, for all $t > 0$, $X_t \in \mathcal{L}_1$ and $Y_t \in \mathcal{L}_2$ since $\mathcal{L}_1$ and $\mathcal{L}_2$ are closed. Therefore for all $t > 0$, $X_t \neq Y_t$ since $\mathcal{L}_1$ and $\mathcal{L}_2$ are disjoint. Hence, for all $t > 0$, $\delta(X_t, Y_t) \geq 1$. Therefore $\forall t\ E(\delta(X_t, Y_t)) \geq 1$. On the other hand, we have: $\forall t > 0\ E(\delta(X_t, Y_t)) \leq \beta^t \delta(x, y)) \leq \beta^t B$. This leads to: $\forall t > 0\ \beta^t B \geq 1$, which is false (e.g., for $t > \frac{\ln(B)}{\ln(1/\beta)}$).

2. Consider two elements $x, y \in \Omega$, and the coupling (X_t, Y_t) starting from $(X_0, Y_0) = (x, y)$. Let D_t be the process defined by $D_t = \delta(X_t, Y_t)$ for $t \geq 0$. Since $\delta(X_t, Y_t) = 0$ iff $X_t = Y_t$, the quantity $T_{x,y}$ is the time required for D_t to reach 0. Consider the coupling (X_t, Y_t) which starts from $(X_0, Y_0) = (x, y)$. Therefore by Proposition 3, we have, for all $x, y \in \Omega$, $E(T_{x,y}) \leq B/(1 - \beta)$. Now, by Theorem 1 (statement 2), $\mathbf{H}_\mathcal{L} \leq max_{x,y}\ E(T_{x,y})$. Hence $\mathbf{H}_\mathcal{L} \leq B/(1 - \beta)$.

3. Since $E(\delta(X_{t+1}, Y_{t+1})) \leq \beta\delta(X_t, Y_t)$, we have $E(\delta(X_t, Y_t)) \leq \beta^t \delta(X_0, Y_0) \leq \beta^t B$. But, by Markov's inequality ($P(X \geq a) \leq E[X]/a$): $Pr(\delta(X_t, Y_t) \geq 1) \leq E(\delta(X_t, Y_t))$. Hence, for all $X_0, Y_0 \in \Omega$ and all $t > 0$: $Pr(X_t \neq Y_t) = Pr(\delta(X_t, Y_t) > 0) = Pr(\delta(X_t, Y_t) \geq 1) \leq E(\delta(X_t, Y_t)) \leq \beta^t B$. Therefore, for all $X_0, Y_0 \in \Omega$ and all $t > 0$: $Pr(X_t = Y_t) \geq 1 - \beta^t B$.

Suppose that $Y_0 \in \mathcal{L}$. Then $Y_t \in \mathcal{L}$ (because $\mathcal{L}$ closed), and $X_t = Y_t$ implies $X_t \in \mathcal{L}$. So, for all $X_0 \in \Omega$ and all $t > 0$: $Pr(X_t \in \mathcal{L}) \geq 1 - \beta^t B$. It follows that $Pr(X_t \in \mathcal{L}) \geq 1 - \varepsilon$, as soon as $\beta^t B \geq \varepsilon$, i.e., $t \geq \frac{\ln(B/\varepsilon)}{\ln(1/\beta)}$. Hence $Pr(X_t \in \mathcal{L}) \geq 1 - \varepsilon$, as soon as $t \geq \frac{\ln(B/\varepsilon)}{1-\beta}$ (because $1 - \beta \leq \ln(\frac{1}{\beta})$). $\qquad\square$

Appendix 2: Proof of Theorem 3

The proof of Theorem 3 is analogous to that of Theorem 2, but relies on the following proposition (see for example [23]):

Proposition 4. *Suppose that $D = (D_0, D_1, \cdots)$ is a nonnegative stochastic process on $\{0, 1, \cdots, B\}$ such that $E[D_{t+1}] \leq D_t$ when $D_t > 0$. Furthermore suppose that $Pr(D_{t+1} \neq D_t) \geq \alpha$ (with $\alpha > 0$). Then if τ is the first time that $D_t = 0$, we have: $E[\tau] \leq B^2/\alpha$.*

Appendix 3: Proof of Theorem 5 ($E\delta(X', Y') \leq \beta\delta(X, Y)$)

Consider $(X, Y) \in U$. Let $[i, i + k - 1]$ be the interval of contiguous disagreeing positions between X and Y (with $1 \leq k \leq 5$). The random choice of the selected machine j modifies the zone of disagreement iff j corresponds to:

- *Outer rim position:* This means that $j = i - 1$ or $j = i + k - 1$. There are two outer rim positions for every $1 \leq k \leq 5$. Choosing an outer rim position extends the disagreement zone by one. This happens with probability $2/N$, and contributes to modify $E(\delta)$ by: $(a_{k+1} - a_k)(2/N)$. (For $k = 5$, $a_{k+1} = a_6$ stands for $a_5 + a_1$.)
- *Inner rim position:* This means that $j = i$ or $j = i + k - 2$. There are no inner rim position if $k = 1$, one inner rim position if $k = 2$, and two inner rim positions if $k = 3, 4, 5$. Choosing an inner rim position decreases the disagreement zone by two. This happens with probability $1/N$ (resp. $2/N$) when $k = 2$ (resp. $k = 3, 4, 5$). It contributes to modify $E(\delta)$ by $(a_0 - a_2)(1/N) = (-a_2)(1/N)$ when $k = 2$, and by $(a_{k-2} - a_k)(2/N)$ when $k = 3, 4, 5$.
- *Internal position:* This means that $j = i + 1$ or $j = i + k - 3$. There are no internal position if $k = 1, 2$ or 3, one internal position if $k = 4$, and two internal positions if $k = 5$. For $k = 4$, choosing an internal position ($j = i+1$) transforms the disagreement zone into two separated disagreement zones of length 1. This happens with probability $1/N$, and contributes to modify $E(\delta)$ by: $(2a_1 - a_4)(1/N)$. For $k = 5$, choosing an internal position ($j = i + 1$ or $j = i+2$) transforms the disagreement zone into two separated disagreement zones of length 1 and 2. This happens with probability $2/N$, and contributes to modify $E(\delta)$ by: $(a_1 + a_2 - a_5)(2/N)$.

Accordingly, we have the following cases:

1. *Case k=1.* Then:
   $E(\delta(X',Y')) - \delta(X,Y) = (a_2 - a_1)(2/N)$.
   Hence $E(\delta(X',Y')) = \beta_1\delta(X,Y)$ with $\beta_1 = (1 - \frac{2}{N}\frac{a_1-a_2}{a_1})$
   (using the fact that $\delta(X,Y)$ is equal here to a_1).

2. *Case k=2.* Then:
   $E(\delta(X',Y')) - \delta(X,Y) = (2(a_3 - a_2) + (a_0 - a_2))(1/N) = (2a_3 - 3a_2)(1/N)$.
   Hence $E(\delta(X',Y')) = \beta_2\delta(X,Y)$ with $\beta_2 = (1 - \frac{1}{N}\frac{3a_2-2a_3}{a_2})$
   (using the fact that $\delta(X,Y)$ is equal here to a_2).

3. *Case k=3.* Then:
   $E(\delta(X',Y'))-\delta(X,Y) = ((a_4-a_3)+(a_1-a_3))(2/N) = (a_4-2a_3+a_1)(2/N)$.
   Hence $E(\delta(X',Y')) = \beta_3\delta(X,Y)$ with $\beta_3 = (1 - \frac{2}{N}\frac{2a_3-a_4-a_1}{a_3})$
   (using the fact that $\delta(X,Y)$ is equal here to a_3).

4. *Case k=4.* Then:
   $$E(\delta(X',Y')) - \delta(X,Y) = (2(a_5 - a_4) + 2(a_2 - a_4) + (2a_1 - a_4))(1/N)$$
   $$= (2a_5 - 5a_4 + 2a_2 + 2a_1)(1/N).$$
   Hence $E(\delta(X',Y')) = \beta_4\delta(X,Y)$ with $\beta_4 = (1 - \frac{1}{N}\frac{5a_4-2a_5-2a_2-2a_1}{a_4})$
   (using the fact that $\delta(X,Y)$ is equal here to a_4).

5. *Case k=5.* Then:
   $$E(\delta(X',Y')) - \delta(X,Y) = ((a_5 + a_1 - a_5) + (a_3 - a_5) + (a_1 + a_2 - a_5))(2/N)$$
   $$= (-2a_5 + a_3 + a_2 + 2a_1)(2/N).$$
   Hence $E(\delta(X',Y')) = \beta_5\delta(X,Y)$ with $\beta_5 = (1 - \frac{2}{N}\frac{2a_5-a_3-a_2-2a_1}{a_5})$
   (using the fact that $\delta(X,Y)$ is equal here to a_5).

Therefore, for all $(X,Y) \in U$, $E(\delta(X',Y')) \leq \beta\delta(X,Y)$, with $\beta = max\{\beta_k\}_{1\leq k\leq 5}$. We have now to find $a_1,\cdots,a_5$ such that β satisfies $0 < \beta < 1$. A possible solution is: $a_1 = 21, a_2 = 20, a_3 = 29, a_4 = 36, a_5 = 48$.
It follows $\beta \leq 1 - (1/18N)$, hence $\frac{1}{1-\beta} \leq 18N$.
It remains to check that δ is a metric on $\Omega \times \Omega$, i.e.:
   1. $\delta(X,Y) = 0$ iff $X = Y$.
   2. $\forall x, y, z$ $\delta(x,z) \leq \delta(x,y) + \delta(y,z)$.
The first item holds because all the coefficients a_i are positive.
The proof of the second item relies on the following fact: For all $k = 1,2,3,4,5$ and all partition $i_1,..,i_\ell$ of k (i.e: $i_1+..+i_\ell = k$), we have: $a_k < a_{i_1}+a_{i_2}+...+a_{i_\ell}$. Finally, it remains to check that, for all $x,y \in \Omega \times \Omega$, there exists a path $x = z_0, z_1, \cdots, z_r = y$ where $(z_j, z_{j+1}) \in U$, $\sum_{j=0}^{r-1}\delta(z_j, z_{j+1}) = \delta(x,y)$. For all x, y in Ω, we consider the path from x to y as follows: We first eliminate all the disagreement zones of length 5 (beginning at the leftmost site of disagreement of each zone), then all the disagreement zones of length 4, 3, 2 and finally 1. It comes from the definition of our metric that for this path $x = z_0, z_1, \cdots, z_k = y$, we have: $\sum_{j=0}^{k-1}\delta(z_j, z_{j+1}) = \delta(x,y)$.
Finally, let us note that the maximal value B of δ on $\Omega \times \Omega$ is at most $a_1\lceil\frac{N}{2}\rceil \leq 11N$. $\square$

Optimal Randomized Self-stabilizing Mutual Exclusion on Synchronous Rings

Philippe Duchon[1,*], Nicolas Hanusse[1,**], and Sébastien Tixeuil[2,***]

[1] LaBRI, Université Bordeaux I, 351 Cours de la Libération, 33400 Talence
{duchon,hanusse}@labri.fr
[2] LRI – CNRS UMR 8623 & INRIA Grand Large, Université Paris-Sud XI, France
tixeuil@lri.fr

Abstract. We propose several self-stabilizing protocols for unidirectional, anonymous, and uniform synchronous rings of arbitrary size, where processors communicate by exchanging messages. When the size of the ring n is unknown, we better the service time by a factor of n (performing the best possible complexity for the stabilization time and the memory consumption). When the memory size is known, we present a protocol that is optimal in memory (constant and independant of n), stabilization time, and service time (both are in $\Theta(n)$).

1 Introduction

The mutual exclusion one is a fundamental problem in the area of distributed computing. Consider a distributed system of n processors. Every processor, from time to time, may need to execute a critical section in which exactly one processor is allowed to use some shared resource. A distributed system solving the mutual exclusion problem must guarantee the following two properties: *(i) Mutual Exclusion*: one and only one processor is allowed to execute its critical section at any time; *(ii) Fairness*: each processor must be able to execute its critical section infinitely often. A classical technique consists in having every processor passing a special message called *token*. Holding a token means that the processor may enter its critical section. This token must satisfy mutual exclusion constraints: be unique and pass infinitely often at each processor.

The concept of self-stabilization was first introduced by Edsger W. Dijkstra in 1974 [Dij74]. It is now considered to be the most general technique to design a system to tolerate arbitrary transient faults. A self-stabilizing system guarantees that starting from an arbitrary state, the system converges to a legal configuration in a finite number of steps and remains in a legal state until another fault occurs (see also [Dol00]). Intuitively, a self-stabilizing token passing protocol for

---

* Partially supported by EC's IHRP Program, grant HPRN-CT-2001-00272, "Algebraic Combinatorics in Europe".
** Partially supported by CNRS-JemSTIC "Mobicoop".
*** Partially supported by CNRS-JemSTIC "Mobicoop" and CNRS-JemSTIC "STAR".

R. Guerraoui (Ed.): DISC 2004, LNCS 3274, pp. 216–229, 2004.
© Springer-Verlag Berlin Heidelberg 2004

mutual exclusion guarantees that, even if the system is started from a global state where mutual exclusion specification is violated (zero or several tokens are present in the system), then within a finite number of steps, a unique token circulates fairly in the network.

In practise, we only prove that starting from a global state with several tokens, the system reaches in finite time a global state with a unique token. Indeed, it is proved in [KP93] that when processors communicate by exchanging messages, a *timeout* mechanism is required to spontaneously inject new tokens: if such a mechanism is not available, the system may not be self-stabilizing since it would be deadlocked when started from a message-free initial global state.

1.1   Previous Works

A network is *uniform* if every processor executes the same code, and it is *anonymous* if processors do not have identifiers that would enable executing different sections of code. If a protocol works in a uniform and anonymous network, then it works *a fortiori* in a non-uniform or non-anonymous network. Since the first three self-stabilizing protocols about tokens passing presented in the pioneering paper [Dij74], numerous works dealt with the same problem in various contexts: For the case of unidirectional anonymous and uniform rings., see [Her90,BCD95,BGJ99,DGT00,Ros00,KY02,Joh02].

A self-stabilizing token passing protocol is *transparent* to the application if it does not modify the format or the content of tokens that are exchanged by the application. Such a property is desirable *e.g.* whenever the token's content is used by the application (it is the case in *Token Ring* or *FFDI* networks, where the token also contains a piece of information to be transmitted to the destination). Indeed, a transparent protocol is easier to implement (it does not modify the frame format of the application that can thus be encrypted or compressed) and to integrate in heterogeneous networks (where some parts of the network use a different token passing protocol). Moreover, checking for message integrity can be delegated entirely to the calling application. Among the pre-cited protocols, only [Her90,BCD95] and the synchronous protocol of [DGT00] are transparent to the upper layer application. In order to ensure stabilization, the protocols presented in [BGJ99,DGT00,Ros00,KY02,Joh02] either make use of several types of tokens (thus adding a *type* field to application messages), or add information to each token in order to ensure stabilization.

A major criterion to evaluate the efficiency of self-stabilizing protocols is its *stabilization time* (or *convergence time*), noted T, that is the time needed to go from a global state with an arbitrary number of tokens to a global state with a unique token. As proved in [BP89], it is impossible to solve the problem of self-stabilizing token passing in a n-sized unidirectional anonymous and uniform ring using a deterministic protocol (except when n is prime, which is not a realistic assumption). Thus, the aforementioned solutions are probabilistic. Among those, [Her90,BCD95] do not provide any stabilization time calculus, and the expected stabilization times of [BGJ99,DGT00,KY02,Joh02] are of order n^3, where n denotes the size of the ring, and that of [Ros00] is of order n^2. It is obvious that the stabilization time for any algorithm is $\Omega(n)$: if the system is started from a configuration with two opposite tokens, at least $n/2$ time units are needed for a token to catch up with the other.

Another evaluation criterion is the *service time*, *i.e.* the time, in stabilized phase, between two tokens passing at the same processor. This criterion is important to evaluate the performance of the protocol when there are no faults and thus the overhead compared to a non stabilizing protocol. In a system with n processors, the service time is $\Omega(n)$, since if every processor waits the least amount of time, it waits as long as every other. The service time is not calculated in [Her90,BCD95,BGJ99], and it is respectively of order n^3, n^2, n, and n in [DGT00,Ros00,KY02,Joh02].

1.2   Our Contribution

We propose several self-stabilizing protocols for synchronous, anonymous, uniform and unidirectional ring networks, in which processors communicate by exchanging messages. The first two protocols are the transpositions in a message passing model of the protocols of [Her90,BCD95] (for the **0Memory** protocol) and [DGT00] (for the **1bitMemory** protocol) that were using a shared memory model. By a tight complexity analysis, we prove that the equivalent of [Her90,BCD95] stabilizes in expected time $\Theta(n^2)$, and that its service time is $\Theta(n)$ (those complexities were not calculated in the quoted papers). Then, we show that the equivalent of the synchronous protocol of [DGT00] converges in expected time $\Theta(n^2)$ (it was only proved $O(n^3)$ in the original paper) and has a service time of $\Theta(n)$. paper). The technique used for proving the **1bitMemory** protocol may be of independant interest for proving other complex probabilistic distributed algorithms using Markov chains (see also [FMP04]).

Then, we propose several new protocols based on the notion of *speed reducer*. Each processor may declare itself to be a speed reducer and slow down token it receives with some probability. According to the power that is given to the speed reducer (*i.e.* the quantity of memory it has), the complexity results are different, but both new protocols we present have an expected convergence time, noted $\mathbb{E}(T)$, and an expected service time in $\Theta(n)$.

All the protocols we present (see Figure 1) are transparent to the upper layer application. For some protocols (*i.e.* [Joh02,KY02],**1bitMemory**), not only the expected service time is upper bounded, but the bound is also certain (processors are ensured that the upper bound cannot be broken in any execution).

The protocols of [BGJ99,Joh02,KY02] work in shared memory systems, while the protocol of [Ros00] and ours perform in message passing systems. In shared memory systems, a combinatorial trick (see [BCD95]) permits to avoid any time-out mechanism (that is mandatory in message passing systems), at the cost of an extra variable that takes values between 0 and $\log n$ (thus requiring $O(\log \log n)$ bits). For fair comparison, the memory space used by [BGJ99,Joh02,KY02] has been decreased by $O(\log \log n)$ in Figure 1.

The protocol of [Ros00] works in asynchronous systems, but for fair comparison, the complexity measures presented here are for the synchronous setting (Those results are not presented in the original paper, but are easy to obtain).

Protocol	Knowledge of n	Stabilization time	Service time * certain	Memory	Synchronous	Transparent
[BGJ99]	yes	$\Theta(n^3)$	$O(n^3)$	$O(\log(n))$	no	no
[Joh02]	yes	$O(n^3)$	$^*O(n)$	$O(\log(n))$	no	no
[KY02]	yes	$O(n^3)$	$^*O(n)$	$O(\log(n))$	no	no
[Ros00]	no	$\Theta(n^2)$	$O(n^2)$	$O(1)$	yes	no
0Memory	no	$\Theta(n^2)$	$\Theta(n)$	0	yes	yes
1bitMemory	no	$\Theta(n^2)$	$^*\Theta(n)$	$O(1)$	yes	yes
SpeedReducer1	yes	$\Theta(n)$	$\Theta(n)$	$O(\log(n))$	yes	yes
SpeedReducer2	yes	$\Theta(n)$	$\Theta(n)$	$O(1)$	yes	yes

Fig. 1. Results summary.

When the size of the ring is unknown, the **1bitMemory** protocol is the most interesting (since the service time is certain). When the size of the ring is known, the **SpeedReducer2** protocol is the most interesting, being optimal according to the three evaluation criteria (memory consumption, stabilization time, and service time). Due to space limitations, some of the proofs are given in the appendix.

2   Preliminaries

2.1   Execution Model

We assume that processors are organized as a unidirectional ring of size n and communicate by exchanging messages. A processor may only receive messages from its predecessor and may only send messages to its successor. We consider a synchronous system where every processor takes an action at each *pulse* of a global clock. While processors are synchronized, there exists no global absolute time, only time pulses. Such a phase where all processors take action is called *round*. We also assume that any processor is able to query its underlying communication layer to know if a message (for example, a token) was delivered.

In this paper, we consider the problem of token passing. An algorithm is self-stabilizing for the token passing task if, starting from any configuration, after finite time there remains a unique token that pass forever at every processor. In the context of message passing systems, it is well known [KP93] that at least one timeout mechanism must be assumed in order to cope with initial configurations where no tokens are present. It is also assumed that those timeouts are activated at most once, and only at the begining of an execution. Thus, designing a self-stabilizing token passing algorithm is reduced to designing an algorithm that reduces tokens so that eventually, a single token remains. To ensure that the system never ends up in a deadlocked (*i.e.* message free) situation, all previous algorithms (and ours) use the technique of *token merging*: when two or more tokens are present at the same time at a single processor, all tokens are merged into one.

2.2   Markov Chains

We follow the terminology of [Nor97] about Markov Chains. The classical hypothesis can be used since the network has a synchronous behaviour; for an asynchronous setting, see [DFP01]. Let $P_{n \times n}$ be a stochastic matrix, that is the sum of every line is equal to 1. A *discrete Markov Chain*, denoted by $(X_t)_{t \leq 0}$ on a set of states X is a sequence of random variables $X_0, X_1, \dots$ with $X_i \in X$ and so that X_{i+1} only depends on X_i and $\Pr(X_{i+1} = y | X_i = x) = p_{x,y}$. The matrix P is called the *transition probability matrix*.

A node x *leads* to a node y if $\exists j \geq i, \Pr(X_j = y | X_i = x) > 0$. A state y is an *absorbing* state if y does not lead to any other state. The *expected hitting time* or *hitting time* $\mathbb{E}_x^y$ is the average number of steps starting from node x to reach node y for the first time.

We will make use of the following theorem for Markov chains:

Theorem 1. *The vector of hitting times* $\mathbb{E}^t = (\mathbb{E}_x^t : x \in V)$ *is the minimal non-negative solution of the following system of linear equations:*

$$\begin{cases} \mathbb{E}_t^t = 0 \\ \mathbb{E}_x^t = 1 + \sum_{y \neq t} p_{x,y} \mathbb{E}_y^t \text{ for } x \in V \end{cases}$$

and the following lemma:

Lemma 1 (cf. [Nor97] page 5). *Let* (X_t) *be a Markov Chain of two states* $\{1,2\}$ *with transition matrix* P *defined by:* $P = \begin{pmatrix} 1-\alpha & \alpha \\ \beta & 1-\beta \end{pmatrix}$ *then*

$$\Pr(X_t = 1 | X_0 = 1) = \begin{cases} \frac{\beta}{\alpha+\beta} + \frac{\alpha}{\alpha+\beta}(1-\alpha-\beta)^t & \text{for } \alpha + \beta > 0 \\ 1 & \text{for } \alpha = \beta = 0 \end{cases}$$

3   Algorithms: Without a Knowledge of n

The first protocol we propose is equivalent to a random walk of tokens in the ring, and can be seen as a transposition in the message passing model of the protocols of [Her90,BCD95]:

3.1   0Memory Protocol

Each processor i executes the following code: at each pulse, if i is currently holding a token, it transmits it to its successor with probability p, and keeps it with probability $1 - p$. Remark that the protocol runs without memory and without a knowledge of n.

Applying Theorem 1 to a specific Markov chain, we obtain a useful Lemma for the analysis of **0Memory** protocol:

Lemma 2. *Let C_d be a chain of $d+1$ states $0, 1, \ldots, d$ and $q \in]0, 1/2]$. If state 0 is absorbing and the transition matrix is of the form:*

$$\begin{cases} p_{i,i-1} = p_{i,i+1} = q \text{ for } 1 \leq i \leq d-1 \\ p_{i,i} = 1 - 2q \text{ for } 1 \leq i \leq d-1 \\ p_{d,d} = 1 - q \end{cases}$$

then the hitting time to state 0 starting from state i is $\mathbb{E}_i^0 = \frac{i}{2q}(2d - i + 1)$.

Proof. We make a use of Theorem 1 for the computation of $\mathbb{E}_i^0$. We have

$$\begin{cases} \mathbb{E}_1^0 = 1 + (1 - 2q)\mathbb{E}_1^0 + q\mathbb{E}_2^0 \\ \mathbb{E}_i^0 = 1 + q\mathbb{E}_{i-1}^0 + (1 - 2q)\mathbb{E}_i^0 + q\mathbb{E}_{i+1}^0 \text{ for } 2 \leq i \leq d-1 \\ \mathbb{E}_d^0 = 1 + (1 - q)\mathbb{E}_d^0 + q\mathbb{E}_{d-1}^0 \end{cases}$$

Noting that $\mathbb{E}_i^0 = \sum_{j=1}^i \mathbb{E}_j^{j-1}$, we are interested by $\mathbb{E}_j^{j-1}$ for $1 \leq j \leq d$. Therefore, $\mathbb{E}_d^{d-1} = 1 + (1 - q)\mathbb{E}_d^{d-1} = 1/q$ and

$$\begin{aligned} \mathbb{E}_j^{j-1} &= 1 + (1 - 2q)\mathbb{E}_j^{j-1} + q\mathbb{E}_{j+1}^{j-1} \\ &= 1 + (1 - 2q)\mathbb{E}_j^{j-1} + q(\mathbb{E}_{j+1}^j + \mathbb{E}_j^{j-1}) \\ &= 1/q + \mathbb{E}_{j+1}^j \\ &= \frac{d - j}{q} \end{aligned}$$

This implies that $\mathbb{E}_i^0 = \sum_{j=1}^i (d - j)/q = \frac{1}{q}(di - \frac{i(i-1)}{2})$.

Theorem 2. *In a unidirectional n-sized ring containing an arbitrary number k of tokens ($k \geq 2$), the stabilization time of protocol **0Memory** is $\frac{n^2}{8p(1-p)} < \mathbb{E}(T) < \frac{n^2}{2p(1-p)}(\frac{\pi^2}{6} - 1) + \frac{n \log n}{p(1-p)}$. For constant p, $\mathbb{E}(T) = \Theta(n^2)$.*

Proof. For any $k \geq 2$, the evolution of the ring with exactly k tokens under the **0Memory** protocol can be described by a Markov chain $\mathcal{S}_k$ whose state space is the set of k-tuples of positive integers whose sum is equal to n (these integers represent the distances betweeen successive tokens on the ring), with an additional state $\delta = (0, \ldots, 0)$ to represent transitions to a configuration with fewer than k tokens. To prove the upper bound of the theorem, we will prove an upper bound on the hitting time of this state δ, independently of the initial state.

Consider two successive tokens on the ring. On any given round, each will move forward, independently of the other, with probability p, and stay in place with probability $1 - p$. Thus, with probability $p(1 - p)$, the distance between them will decrease by 1; with the same probability, it will increase by 1; and, with probability $1 - 2p(1 - p)$, the distance will remain the same. Thus, locally, the distance between consecutive tokens follows the same evolution rule as that of the chain C_n of Lemma 2.

What follows is a formal proof, using the technique of *couplings* of Markov chains, that the expected time it takes for two tokens among k to collide is no longer than the expected time for $C_{n/k}$ to reach state 0.

For any state $\mathbf{x} = (x^1, \ldots, x^k)$ of S_k, let $m(\mathbf{x}) = \min_i x^i$ denote the minimum distance between two successive tokens, and let $i(\mathbf{x}) = \min\{j : x^j = m(\mathbf{x})\}$ denote the smallest index where this minimum is realized. Let $(X_t)_{t \geq 0}$ denote a realization of the Markov chain S_k. We define a *coupling* $(X_t, Y_t)_{t \geq 0}$ of the Markov chains S_k and C_d, where $d = \lfloor n/k \rfloor$ and $q = p(1 - p)$, as follows:

- $Y_0 = m(X_0)$;
- $Y_{t+1} = \min\{d, Y_t + (X_{t+1}^{i(X_t)} - X_t^{i(X_t)})\}$

In other words, the evolution of Y_t is determined by selecting two tokens that are separated by the minimum distance in X_t, and making the change in Y_t reflect the change in distance between these two tokens (while capping Y_t at d).

A trivial induction on t shows that $Y_t \geq m(X_t)$ holds for all t, so that (X_t) will reach state δ no later than (Y_t) reaches 0. Thus, *the time for S_k to reach δ (that is, the time during which the ring has exactly k tokens) is stochastically dominated by the time for C_d to reach 0.* By Lemma 2, the expectation of this time is no longer than

$$\frac{d(d+1)}{2q} \leq \frac{1}{2q}\left(\frac{n^2}{k^2} + \frac{n}{k}\right)$$

Summing over all values of k from 2 to n, we get, for the expected stabilization time T,

$$\mathbb{E}(T) \leq \frac{1}{2p(1-p)} \sum_{k=2}^{n} \frac{n^2}{k^2} + \frac{n}{k}$$

$$\leq \frac{1}{2p(1-p)}\left(\left(\frac{\pi^2}{6} - 1\right)n^2 + n\ln(n)\right)$$

The lower bound comes from the fact that, when $k = 2$, the expected time for $C_{n/2}$ to reach state 0 from state $n/2$ is at least $\frac{n^2}{8p(1-p)}$.

Remark 1. Our upper bound on the expected convergence time is minimal for $p = 1/2$. The precise study of the **0Memory** protocols show that the convergence time does not hardly depend on the initial number of tokens: for n high enough and $p = 1/2$, $\mathbb{E}(T) > n^2/2$ for two initial tokens at distance $n/2$, and $\mathbb{E}(T) < 1.3n^2$ for n tokens.

The expected service time is exactly n/p. The following protocol, **1bitMemory**, guarantees that the the service time can be upper bounded by $2n$ with probability 1. This allows to ease the implementation of the timeout mechanism by inserting a new token if no token has been encountered for $2n$ rounds.

3.2   1bitMemory Protocol

Each processor i executes the following code: at each pulse, if a token was just delivered to i, then i executes the **0Memory** protocol for one pulse. If a token was delivered to i at the previous round, then i transmits the token to its successor on the ring. Processor i needs only one bit of memory to store whether it received a token at the previous round. Remark that the protocol runs with one bit of memory and without a knowledge of n.

The analysis of this protocol leads to the following result:

Theorem 3. *In a unidirectional n-sized ring containing an arbitrary number k of tokens $(k \geq 2)$, the service time of protocol **1bitMemory** is between n et $2n$ with probability 1 and the stabilization time is $\mathbb{E}(T) = O(n^2)$ for constant p.*

Proof. The state of the ring with k tokens is described by a Markov chain $\mathcal{S}'_k$, whose states are of the form $\mathbf{x} = (x^1, s^1, \ldots, x^k, s^k)$. In such a state, x^i denotes the distance between tokens i and $i+1$, and $s^i \in \{0, 1\}$ keeps track of the current state of the node holding token i (0 corresponds to a node who just received a token, and 1, to a node that got its token one round ago). If we only look at two consecutive tokens – that is, the part (s^i, x^{i+1}, s^{i+1}) for some i – we can see that this will evolve according to a Markov chain $\mathcal{C}'_d$, part of whose state space and transition probabilities are represented in Figure 2.

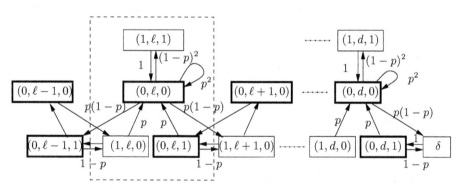

Fig. 2. Transition probabilities of chain $\mathcal{C}'_d$.

Our proof of the upper bound on the expected collision time (in the chain $\mathcal{S}'_k$) is in two steps. In the first part of the proof, we construct a kind of coupling between $\mathcal{S}'_k$ and $\mathcal{C}'_d$ (with the caveat that we have to use a trick where one of the chains in the coupling may have to be "stopped" from time to time while the other "catches up" with it; *i.e.*, until $Y_t = m(X_t)$); this allows us to prove that the expected collision time is lower than the expected hitting time of state $(0, 0, 1)$ in $\mathcal{C}'_d$. In the second step, we use yet another Markov chain to prove an upper bound on this expected hitting time.

First, we need to introduce some notation. If $\mathbf{x} = (x^1, s^1, \ldots, x^k, s^k)$ is some state of $\mathcal{S}'_k$ and $1 \leq i \leq k$, $d_i(\mathbf{x}) = x_i$, and $I_{\min}(\mathbf{x})$ is the smallest index j such that $d_j(\mathbf{x})$ is minimal. Also, $m_i(\mathbf{x}) = (x^i, s^i, x^{i+1})$ is a mapping of the states of $\mathcal{S}'_d$ to the states of $\mathcal{C}'_d$, with the special provision that, if $d_i(\mathbf{x}) > d$, then $m_i(\mathbf{x}) = \delta$. The set of "good" states A of $\mathcal{C}'_d$ is the set of states of the form $(0, \ell, 0)$ or $(0, \ell, 1)$, plus the special state δ; note that any transition from a state *not* in A is guaranteed to lead to a state in A – see Figure 2.

The idea of our coupling is as follows: we start with a copy (X_t) of the chain $\mathcal{S}'_k$, and initially select two consecutive tokens in the configuration; the distance between these two tokens will be used to define a copy (Y_t) of the chain $\mathcal{C}_d$. We have to be careful, however, if the two tokens ever get too far apart from each other (that is, their distance grows larger than d). In such a case, we select two "new" tokens with the minimal distance between them, and "stop" the chain (X_t), while still running the chain (Y_t) until it "catches up" with the distance between the two newly selected tokens in (X_t). This last part is only possible because of the special structure of the Markov chain $\mathcal{C}'_d$.

More precisely, our coupling will be a Markov chain $(X_t, Y_t, I_t, T_t)_{t \geq 0}$. Here, T_t indicates the number of transitions (X) has gone through when (Y) has gone through t transitions (it is a "change of time"); I_t simply keeps track of which two tokens of X_t we are currently "watching". The coupling is constructed as follows: X_0 is any state of $\mathcal{S}'_k$, $T_0 = 0$, $I_0 = I_{\min}(X_0)$, $Y_0 = m_{I_0}(X_0)$; then, the transition from time t to $t+1$ is done as follows:

– if $Y_t = m_{I_t}(X_t)$: this corresponds to the "normal" operation of the coupling. X_{t+1} is selected randomly, according to the evolution law of $\mathcal{S}'_k$, and we set $T_{t+1} = T_t + 1$, $Y_{t+1} = m_{I_t}(X_{t+1})$, then I_{t+1} is determined depending on $d_{I_t}(X_{t+1})$:
  - if $d_{I_t}(X_{t+1}) \leq d$, then $I_{t+1} = I_t$;
  - if $d_{I_t}(X_{t+1}) > d$ (in which case we have $Y_{t+1} = \delta$), then $I_{t+1} = I_{\min}(X_{t+1})$ (that is, I_{t+1} is now the index of a new pair of consecutive tokens in the configuration described by X_{t+1})
– if $Y_t \neq m_{I_t}(X_t)$, then we need to distinguish whether $X_t \in A$ (in which case we "stop" X_t) or not (in which case running X_t for one more round will ensure $X_{t+1} \in A$):
  - if $X_t \in A$, then we set $X_{t+1} = X_t$, $T_{t+1} = T_t$, $I_{t+1} = I_t$, and select Y_{t+1} randomly, according to the evolution law of $\mathcal{C}'_d$;
  - otherwise, we set $T_{t+1} = T_t$, $I_{t+1} = I_t$, and select X_{t+1} and Y_{t+1} independently, according to the evolution laws of $\mathcal{S}'_k$ and $\mathcal{C}'_d$, respectively.

It should be clear that $(Y_n)_{n \geq 0}$ is a faithful copy of the chain $\mathcal{C}'_d$. Next, if we set, for all $n \geq 0$, $\tau_n = \inf\{t : T_t \geq n\}$ (so that we have $T_{\tau_n} = n$ with probability 1, and thus $\tau_n \geq n$), then $(X_{\tau_n})_{n \geq 0}$ is a faithful copy of the chain $\mathcal{S}'_k$. Furthermore, $d_{I_t}(X_t) \leq d(Y_t)$ holds for all t (the only evolution rules where this might conceivably not be maintained are those that apply when $Y_t \neq m_{I_t}(X_t)$; the key observation is that the chain $\mathcal{C}'_d$ cannot go from a state (x, ℓ, y) to a state (x', ℓ', y') with $\ell' < \ell$, without going through states $(0, \ell', 1)$, then $(0, \ell', 0)$).

Thus, if we define hitting times $t_X = \inf\{t \geq 0 : d_{I_{\min}}(X_t) = 0\}$ and $t_Y = \inf\{t \geq 0 : d(Y_t) = 0\}$, then we have $t_X \leq t_Y$, thus $T_{t_X} \leq t_Y$. But the expected value of T_{t_X} is the expected collision time of the chain $\mathcal{S}'_k$, while the expected

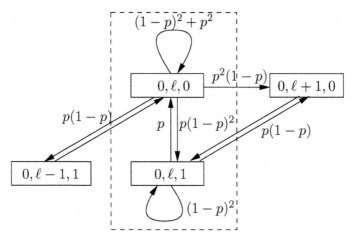

Fig. 3. Transition probabilities of chain $\mathcal{D}_d$.

value of t_Y is the expected hitting time of state $(0,0,1)$ for the chain $\mathcal{C}'_d$ (starting from states X_0 and Y_0, respectively), which ends the first part of the proof.

To give an upper bound on the hitting time of $(0,0,1)$ for $\mathcal{C}'_d$, we consider the simpler chain $\mathcal{D}_d$, which is exactly the chain $\mathcal{C}'_d$, stopped at each passage in a state of A; the transition probabilities of $\mathcal{D}_d$ are as illustrated in Figure 3. Note that, because, in $\mathcal{C}'_d$, states not in A have only states in A as their successors, a copy of $\mathcal{C}'_d$ will make at most twice as many steps as the corresponding (coupled) copy of $\mathcal{D}_d$; this ensures that the expected hitting time of state $(0,0,1)$ is at most twice as large in $\mathcal{C}'_d$ as it is in $\mathcal{D}_d$.

For convenience, we rename the states of $\mathcal{D}_d$ in the following way: $(0,\ell,0)$ will be denoted by 2ℓ, $(0,\ell,1)$ by $2\ell+1$ and δ by $2d+2$. For any $\ell \leq 2d+2$, let us upper bound $\mathbb{E}^1_\ell$ in chain $\mathcal{D}_d$. Since to go from state $j > i$ to state i, we should visit all the states from $j-1, j-2, \ldots, i+1$, we have in $\mathcal{D}_d$ that $\mathbb{E}^i_j = \sum_{k=i}^{j-1} \mathbb{E}^{k+1}_k$.

We make use of Theorem 1 to obtain, for $k < d$:

$$\mathbb{E}^{2k}_{2k+1} = \frac{1}{p} + (1-p)\mathbb{E}^{2k+1}_{2k+2}$$

$$\mathbb{E}^{2k-1}_{2k} = \frac{1}{p(1-p)} + \mathbb{E}^{2k}_{2k+1} + p\mathbb{E}^{2k+1}_{2k+2}$$

$$= \frac{2-p}{p(1-p)} + \mathbb{E}^{2k+1}_{2k+2}$$

It turns out that

$$\mathbb{E}^{2k-1}_{2k} = (d-k)\frac{2-p}{p(1-p)} + \mathbb{E}^{2d-1}_{2d}$$

$$\mathbb{E}^{2k}_{2k+1} = \frac{1}{p} + \frac{(d-k-1)(2-p)}{p} + (1-p)\mathbb{E}^{2d-1}_{2d}$$

The recurrence can be completed after the computation of $\mathbb{E}_\delta^{2d+1}$, $\mathbb{E}_{2d+1}^{2d}$ and $\mathbb{E}_{2d}^{2d-1}$:

$$\mathbb{E}_\delta^{2d+1} = 1$$
$$\mathbb{E}_{2d+1}^{2d} = 1 + (1-p)\mathbb{E}_\delta^{2d}$$
$$= \frac{2-p}{p}$$
$$\mathbb{E}_{2d}^{2d-1} = 1 + \left(p^2 + (1-p)^2\right)\mathbb{E}_{2d}^{2d-1} + p(1-p)\mathbb{E}_\delta^{2d-1}$$
$$= \frac{3-2p}{p(1-p)}$$

Since $\mathbb{E}_\ell^1 \le \mathbb{E}_\delta^1$, summing $\mathbb{E}_k^{k-1}$ for $k = 2 \ldots 2d$, we obtain that:

$$t_Y \le 2 \left(\mathbb{E}_\delta^{2d+1} + \sum_{k=2}^{2d+1} \mathbb{E}_k^{k-1} \right)$$
$$\le d^2 \left(\frac{2-p}{p} + \frac{p+2}{p(1-p)} \right) + d \left(\frac{4-3p}{p(1-p)} + \frac{2-p}{p} \right) + 2 + \frac{4-2p}{p} + \frac{6-4p}{p(1-p)}$$

Subsituying d by $\frac{n}{k}$ and summing t_Y's over all values of k from n downto 2, we obtain that the stabilization time is $O(n^2)$ for constant p.

4   Algorithms: With a Knowledge of n

We now consider the possibility that some particular processors have a different behavior from the others, with some probability. We call these processors *speed reducers*: each round, *normal* processors always transmit any token they are holding, while *speed reducers* do not transmit them.

4.1   SpeedReducer1 Protocol

Each processor i executes the following code: every n pulses, processor i randomly decides whether it must act as a speed reducer or not. Processor i acts as a speed reducer with probability $1/2n$.

Theorem 4. *In a n-sized ring containing an arbitrary number k of tokens ($k \ge 2$) in its initial state, the protocol **SpeedReducer1** has a stabilization time upper bounded by $(1 + 3e^{3/2})n$.*

Proof. Note that convergence is to occur as soon as, during a lapse of time of length n, a unique processor is a speed reducer. We estimate the average time before this situation happens in order to bound the expected convergence time.

A processor has two possible states: normal or speed reducer. At each round, the configuration of the ring (discounting token positions) can be described by a binary vector of n states. Let C_k be the configuration at time kn and let R_k its number of speed reducers. The probability $\Pr(R_k = 1)$ of the existence of a unique speed reducer in the configuration C_k is:

$$\Pr(R_k = 1) = \frac{1}{n} \left(1 - \frac{1}{2n}\right)^{n-1} \binom{n}{1}$$

$$= e^{(n-1)\ln(1-1/2n)}$$

$$\geq e^{\frac{(1-n)}{n}}.$$

For $x \in]0, 1/2]$, $\ln(1-x) \geq -2x$. This implies that for $n \geq 2$, $\Pr(R) \geq e^{-1/2}$. Similarly, we have $\Pr(R_k = 0)\left(1 - \frac{1}{2n}\right)^n \geq e^{-1/2}$.

Let us define $\mathcal{E}_k$ the event "$R_{k-1} = 0, R_k = 1$ and $R_{k+1} = 0$", and assume $\mathcal{E}_k$ occurs. Let i be the unique speed reducer node at time kn, and let t denote the last time before kn where it had to decide on its state; $(k-1)n < t \leq kn$. $\mathcal{E}_k$ implies that, from time $(k-1)n$ to time $(k+1)n$, all nodes other than i chose to be *normal* whenever they had to choose. Thus, i is the only speed reducer from time t to time $t+n-1$, and convergence occurs no later than time $t+n-1 < (k+1)n$.

From what has been written previously, $\Pr(\mathcal{E}_k) \geq e^{-3/2}$. If J is the smallest integer j such that $\mathcal{E}_{3i+1}$ occurs, J has an expected value no larger than $e^{3/2}$ (the events $(\mathcal{E}_{3i+1})_{i \geq 0}$ are independent, contrary to $(\mathcal{E}_i)_{i \geq 0}$). As a consequence, the expected stabilization time is less than $(1 + 3e^{3/2})n$.

In order to count n pulses, protocol **SpeedReducer1** requires logarithmic memory. The next protocol **SpeedReducer2** does not need that much space, and only uses a constant memory (that is independent of n).

4.2 SpeedReducer2 Protocol

Each processor i executes the following code: at each pulse, if the state of the processor is *normal*, it becomes a *speed reducer* with probability $q = \frac{1}{n(n-1)}$; otherwise (if the state of the processor is *speed reducer*), it becomes *normal* with probability $p = 1/n$.

Theorem 5. *In a n-sized ring containing an arbitrary number k of tokens ($k \geq 2$) in its initial state, the protocol **SpeedReducer2** has a stabilization time upper bounded by $n(1 + \frac{e^4}{e-1})$ and only needs one bit of memory.*

Proof. Let us show that after n rounds, we have a constant probability to have a unique speed reducer during n rounds.

The state of each node evolves independently from the other nodes like a two states Markov chain of transition probabilities $\alpha = \frac{1}{n(n-1)}$ and $\beta = \frac{1}{n}$. Let $\mathcal{E}_{x,t}$ be the event "processor x is in the normal state at time t". From Lemma 1,

$\Pr(\mathcal{E}_{x,t}) = 1 - \frac{1}{n} + \frac{1}{n}\left(1 - \frac{1}{n-1}\right)^t$. For $t \geq n-1$, $1 - 1/n \leq \Pr(\mathcal{E}_{x,t}) \leq 1 - 1/n +$

e^{-1}/n. Let R_t be the number of speed reducers at time t. The probability that there exists a unique speed reducer at time $t \geq n - 1$ is:

$$\Pr(R_t = 1) \geq \frac{1 - e^{-1}}{n} \left(1 - \frac{1}{n}\right)^{n-1} \binom{n}{1} \geq \frac{1 - e^{-1}}{e}.$$

The probability that a speed reducer stays in the same state during n rounds is $(1 - 1/n)^n = e^{-1} + o(1)$ and the probability that the $n - 1$ other nodes remain normal during n rounds is $(1 - \frac{1}{n(n-1)})^{n(n-1)} = e^{-1} + o(1)$.

Therefore, for any configuration of states at time 0, the probability that a node is a unique speed reducer during n rounds between $t = n$ and $t = 2n - 1$ (implying the total merger between tokens takes place before time $2n$) is asymptotically greater than $p = \frac{e-1}{e^4}$. The same is true every n rounds thereafter until stabilization occurs, so that the probability that stabilization fails to occur in the first $(k+1)n$ rounds is at most p^k; this, in turn, implies that the expected stabilization time is at most $n\left(1 + \frac{e^4}{e-1} + o(1)\right)$.

5   Conclusion

We propose several self-stabilizing protocols for synchronous, anonymous, uniform, and unidirectional ring networks, where processors communicate by exchanging messages. A common quality of all presented algorithm is that they are transparent to the upper layer application (that uses the token passing algorithm to perform *e.g.* critical sections of code). First, we provided tight complexity results about previously known self-stabilizing algorithm ([Her90,BCD95,DGT00]). Then, we provided original algorithms using the notion of a speed reducer. One algorithm, **SpeedReducer1**, is optimal in stabilization time and service time, but require $O(log(n))$ bits of memory per processor. The last algorithm, **SpeedReducer2**, is optimal with respect to all three complexity measures of self-stabilizing token passing algorithms: stabilization time, service time, and memory.

There remains the open question of having an optimal self-stabilizing algorithm for uniform and anonymous unidirectional rings of any size that is optimal in stabilization time, service time, and memory, but also that has a bounded service time on all possible executions.

References

[BCD95]   J. Beauquier, S. Cordier, and S. Delaët.   Optimum probabilistic self-stabilization on uniform rings.   In *WSS95 Second Workshop on Self-Stabilizing Systems*, pages 15.1–15.15, 1995.

[BGJ99]   J. Beauquier, M. Gradinariu, and C. Johnen. Memory space requirements for self-stabilizing leader election protocols. In *PODC99 18th Annual ACM Symposium on Principles of Distributed Computing*, pages 199–208, 1999.

[BP89]   J. E. Burns and J. Pachl. Uniform self-stabilizing rings. *ACM Transactions on Programming Languages and Systems*, 11(2):330–344, 1989.

[DFP01]   M. Duflot, L. Fribourg, and C. Picaronny. Finite-state distributed algorithms as markov chains. In *DISC01 Distributed Computing 15th International Symposium, Springer LNCS:2180*, pages 240–255, 2001.

[DGT00]   A. K. Datta, M. Gradinariu, and S. Tixeuil. Self-stabilizing mutual exclusion using unfair distributed scheduler. In *IPDPS00 14th International Parallel and Distributed Processing Symposium*, pages 465–470, 2000.

[Dij74]   E. W. Dijkstra. Self stabilizing systems in spite of distributed control. *Communications of the ACM*, 17(11):643–644, 1974.

[Dol00]   S. Dolev. *Self-stabilization*. The MIT Press, 2000.

[FMP04]   L. Fribourg, S. Messika, and C. Picaronny. Coupling and self-stabilization. In *DISC 2004, Amsterdam, The Nederlands*, October 2004. Also available as LSV Research Report 04-5.

[Her90]   T. Herman. Probabilistic self-stabilization. *Information Processing Letters*, 35(2):63–67, 1990.

[Joh02]   C. Johnen. Service time optimal self-stabilizing token circulation protocol on anonymous unidrectional rings. In *SRDS02 21th Symposium on Reliable Distributed Systems*, pages 80–89. IEEE Computer Society Press, 2002.

[KP93]   S. Katz and K. J. Perry. Self-stabilizing extensions for message-passing systems. *Distributed Computing*, 7(1):17–26, 1993.

[KY02]   H. Kakugawa and M. Yamashita. Uniform and self-stabilizing fair mutual exclusion on unidirectional rings under unfair distributed daemon. *Journal of Parallel and Distributed Computing*, 62(5):885–898, May 2002.

[Nor97]   J.R. Norris. *Markov Chains*. Cambridge University Press, 1997.

[Ros00]   L. Rosaz. Self-stabilizing token circulation on asynchronous uniform unidirectional rings. In *PODC00 19th Annual ACM Symposium on Principles of Distributed Computing*, pages 249–258, 2000.

Virtual Mobile Nodes
for Mobile *Ad Hoc* Networks[*]
(Extended Abstract)

Shlomi Dolev[1], Seth Gilbert[2], Nancy A. Lynch[2], Elad Schiller[1],
Alex A. Shvartsman[3,2], and Jennifer L. Welch[4]

[1] Dept. of Computer Science, Ben-Gurion University
{dolev,schiller}@cs.bgu.ac.il
[2] MIT CSAIL
{sethg,lynch}@theory.lcs.mit.edu
[3] Dept. of Computer Science & Eng., University of Connecticut
alex@theory.lcs.mit.edu
[4] Dept. of Computer Science, Texas A&M University
welch@cs.tamu.edu

Abstract. One of the most significant challenges introduced by mobile networks is coping with the *unpredictable* motion and the *unreliable* behavior of mobile nodes. In this paper, we define the *Virtual Mobile Node Abstraction*, which consists of robust virtual nodes that are both predictable and reliable. We present the *Mobile Point Emulator*, a new algorithm that implements the Virtual Mobile Node Abstraction. This algorithm replicates each virtual node at a constantly changing set of real nodes, modifying the set of replicas as the real nodes move in and out of the path of the virtual node. We show that the Mobile Point Emulator correctly implements a virtual mobile node, and that it is robust as long as the virtual node travels through well-populated areas of the network. The Virtual Mobile Node Abstraction significantly simplifies the design of efficient algorithms for highly dynamic mobile *ad hoc* networks.

1 Introduction

Devising algorithms for mobile networks is hard. In this paper we present the Virtual Mobile Node Abstraction, which can be used to make this process easier.

The key challenge in mobile networks is coping with the completely *unpredictable motion* of the nodes. This complication is unavoidable: the defining

---

[*] This work is supported in part by NSF grants CCR-0098305, ITR-0121277, 64961-CS, 9988304, 0311368, 9984774 and 0098305, AFOSR #F49620-00-1-0097, USAF–AFRL Award #FA9550-04-1-0121, DARPA #F33615-01-C-1896, NTT MIT9904-12,Texas Advanced Research Program 000512-0091-2001, an IBM faculty award, the Israeli Ministry of Defense, the Ministry of Trade and Industry, and the Rita Altura chair. Part of the work of the first and fourth authors has been done during visits to MIT and Texas A&M.

R. Guerraoui (Ed.): DISC 2004, LNCS 3274, pp. 230–244, 2004.

feature of a mobile network is that the nodes do, in fact, move. The other main difficulty is the *unpredictable availability* of nodes that continually join and leave the system: nodes may fail and recover, or be turned on and off by the user, or may sometimes choose to sleep and save power.

If mobile nodes were reliable and their motion were predictable, the task of designing algorithms for mobile networks would be significantly simplified. Moreover, if mobile nodes moved in a programmable way, algorithms could take advantage of the motion, performing even more efficiently than in static networks. This idea is illustrated by Hatzis et al. in [10], which defines the notion of a *compulsory* protocol, one that requires a subset of the mobile nodes to move in a pre-specified manner. They present an efficient compulsory protocol for leader election. The routing protocols of Chatzigiannakis et al. [4] and Li et al. [15] provide further evidence that compulsory protocols are simple and efficient.

Alas, users of mobile devices are not amenable to following instructions as to where their devices may travel. It may be difficult to ensure that mobile nodes move as desired, especially for highly dynamic systems where nodes may fail or be diverted from the prescribed path. Thus our objectives are (*a*) to retain the effectiveness of the compulsory protocols, and (*b*) to achieve this without imposing requirements on the motion of the nodes.

Our Contributions

In this paper we introduce the Virtual Mobile Node (VMN) Abstraction, and show how it can be used to design distributed algorithms for mobile *ad hoc* networks. We develop an algorithm, the *Mobile Point Emulator*, that implements the VMN abstraction, and show that it is correct and efficient.

Virtual Mobile Nodes. We propose executing algorithms on both *virtual mobile nodes* (VMNs), abstract nodes that move in a predetermined, predictable manner, and clients (i.e., real mobile nodes), which move in an unpredictable manner. The motion of a VMN is determined in advance, and is known to the programs executing on the mobile nodes. For example, a VMN may traverse the plane in a regular pattern, or it may perform a pseudorandom walk.

The motion of the virtual nodes may be completely uncorrelated with the motion of the real nodes: even if all the real nodes are moving in one direction, the virtual nodes may travel in the opposite direction. Consider, for example, an application to monitor traffic on a highway: even though all the cars are driving in one direction, a VMN could move in the opposite direction, notifying oncoming cars of the traffic ahead.

A virtual node is prone to "crash-reboot" failures. As long as the virtual node travels through dense areas of the network, the virtual node does not fail. However, if the VMN moves to an empty spot – where there are no mobile nodes to act as replicas – a failure may occur. The VMN can recover to its initial state when it reenters a dense area.

The virtual nodes and the clients communicate using only a local communication service; no long-distance communication is required.

Implementing Virtual Mobile Nodes. We present the *Mobile Point Emulator*, a new algorithm that implements robust VMNs. The main idea of the algorithm is to allow real nodes traveling near the location of a VMN to assist in emulating the VMN. In order to achieve robustness, the algorithm replicates the state of a virtual node at a number of real mobile nodes. As the execution proceeds, the algorithm continually modifies the set of replicas so that they always remain near the virtual node. We use a replicated state machine approach, augmented to support joins, leaves, and recovery, to maintain the consistency of the replicas.

Other Related Work

While the idea of executing algorithms on virtual mobile nodes was inspired by the development of compulsory protocols [10, 4, 15], many of the techniques used in the Mobile Point Emulator were developed as part of the GeoQuorums algorithm [6, 7], which defines a Focal Point Abstraction in which geographic regions of the network – *focal points* – simulate atomic objects. The Virtual Mobile Node Abstraction differs from the Focal Point Abstraction in four main ways. First, in the earlier work, the focal points are *static*: they are limited to fixed, predetermined locations. In this paper, we implement virtual mobile nodes that *move*, traveling on an arbitrary, predetermined path. Second, the Focal Point Abstraction includes only atomic objects, such as read/write registers. In this paper, the virtual mobile nodes can be arbitrary automata. Third, the focal points cannot recover, should they fail, whereas the VMN Abstraction supports recovery. Fourth, the Focal Point Abstraction uses a GeoCast service, a relatively expensive non-local service, to communicate with clients. In the VMN Abstraction, virtual nodes and clients communicate using only local communication.

This paper also generalizes the *PersistentNode* abstraction by Beal [1, 2]. A PersistentNode is a virtual entity that travels around a static (rather than mobile) sensor network. It can carry with it some state, but implements neither atomic objects (as in GeoQuorums), nor arbitrary automata (as in this paper).

The work of Nath and Niculescu [18] also takes advantage of precalculated paths to forward messages in dense networks. Messages are routed along trajectories, where nodes on the path forward the messages. Similarly, prior GeoCast work (for example, [19, 3]) attempts to route data geographically. In many ways, these strategies are *ad hoc* attempts to emulate some kind of traveling node. We provide a more general framework to take advantage of predictably dense areas of the network to perform arbitrary computation. A significant focus of these prior papers is *determining* good trajectories, a problem that we do not address.

Document Structure

We first describe the underlying system model in Section 2, and present the VMN Abstraction in Section 3. We present the Mobile Point Emulator and the implementation of the VMN Abstraction in Section 4, and sketch a proof of correctness in Section 5. In Section 6, we briefly discuss several simple algorithms that could execute on virtual nodes. Finally, in Section 7, we discuss open problems and future work. For more details, see [5].

2   Basic System Model

The underlying system model consists of real mobile nodes moving in a bounded region of a two-dimensional plane. Each mobile node is assigned a unique identifier from a finite set, I. The real mobile nodes may join and leave the system, and may fail at any time. (We treat leaves as failures.) The real mobile nodes can move on any continuous path, with speed bounded by a constant, v_{max}.

The *Geosensor* is a component of the environment that maintains the current location of each mobile node. It also maintains the current real time. A mobile node receives geo-update(t, ℓ) updates from the Geosensor, notifying it of the current time and its current location. Throughout this paper, we assume exact knowledge of the time and location; in fact, all the algorithms presented could be easily modified to tolerate approximately correct information. In an outdoor setting, the Geosensor can be implemented by a Global Positioning System (GPS) receiver. In an indoor environment, a Cricket [20] device may be a more effective Geosensor. In a static sensor network (for which GPS devices may be too expensive), synthetic coordinates (e.g., [17]) may be sufficient. We assume that each real mobile node receives an update from its Geosensor at least every t_{geo} units of time, where t_{geo} is a constant.

LocalCast Communication Service

The mobile nodes communicate using a local broadcast service, LocalCast, which is parameterized by a radius, R. When some node i performs a send$(m)_i$, the R-LocalCast service delivers the message – by a rcv$(m)_j$ – to every mobile node j within a radius R of the sender. We further assume that every message is delivered within d time, where d is a constant. The service has the following properties: (i) *Reliable Delivery*: Assume that the mobile node i performs a send$(m)_i$ action. Then for every mobile node j that is within distance R of the location of i when the message is sent, and remains within distance R of that location for d time and does not fail, a rcv$(m)_j$ event occurs within d time, delivering the message to node j. (ii) *Integrity*: For any LocalCast message m and mobile node i, if a rcv$(m)_i$ event occurs, then a send$(m)_j$ event precedes it, for some mobile node j. Intuitively, sending a message using this service should be thought of as making a single wireless broadcast (with a small number of retries, if necessary, to avoid collisions). We believe that for small R, this service is a reasonable (if simplistic) model of sending and receiving messages using wireless broadcast.

Formally, we assume that the LocalCast service has one or more sets of send/receive ports for each mobile node, and contains one or more message buffers. More specifically, we assume that the real nodes support an R_{RMN}-LocalCast service, for a constant R_{RMN}, which we call the RMN-LocalCast service. The RMN-LocalCast service has two sets of ports for each mobile node. The service contains two sets of message buffers, *messages*[i] and *mpe-messages*[i] for each $i \in I$, each of which temporarily hold messages destined for node i.

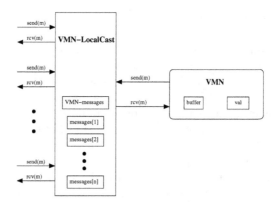

Fig. 1. Components of the VMN Abstraction. The VMN communicates with the clients using the VMN-LocalCast communication service.

3   Virtual Mobile Nodes

The *VMN Abstraction* consists of both client mobile nodes and virtual mobile nodes (VMNs, also referred to as "virtual nodes"), which communicate using a LocalCast service. Throughout this paper, the term *mobile node* refers to any node in the abstraction, a client or a VMN. Each mobile node is an arbitrary I/O automaton [16] (without tasks or fairness)[1]. A mobile node is prone to "crash-reboot" failures: a node may fail and recover. When a node recovers, it begins again in its initial state. A mobile node receives frequent updates from a Geosensor regarding the current time and its current location.

The key difference between clients and virtual nodes is that VMNs move in a predictable, predetermined path that is chosen in advance when the algorithm is specified. Clients, on the other hand, travel on an arbitrary path. Moreover, virtual nodes are robust. If the path of a VMN goes through a sparse region of the network, then the VMN fails during that interval of time; as soon as it reenters a dense region, it recovers.

For the rest of this paper, we assume that there is only a single VMN, communicating with several clients, as is depicted in Figure 1. Our results extend naturally to a model containing an arbitrary number of virtual nodes.

Formally, the VMN has two main state components: *VMN.val*, which represents the abstract state of the VMN I/O automaton, and *VMN.buffer*, a buffer that holds outgoing messages until they are ready to be sent.

Clients and virtual nodes communicate by sending messages using a Local-Cast service, as defined in Section 2[2]. Recall that the LocalCast service is parameterized by a radius, R. The VMN Abstraction implements an R_{VMN}-LocalCast

---

[1] We expect that it is a simple extension to support timed and hybrid virtual nodes, instead of just I/O automata.

[2] Formally, we restrict the I/O automata to only two possible input actions: geo-update(t, ℓ) and rcv(m), and one possible output action: send(m).

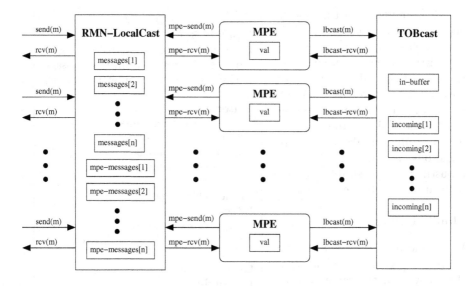

Fig. 2. Components of the VMN Abstraction implementation. The clients communicate with the *MPE* components using the RMN-LocalCast service; the *MPE* maintains consistent replicas using the TOBcast service.

service, for some fixed constant R_{VMN}, which we call VMN-LocalCast. We call the message buffers in the VMN-LocalCast service *messages*[i], for each $i \in I$, each of which holds messages destined for node i. If i is the identifier of the VMN, we refer to the *messages*[i] message buffer as *VMN-messages*.

4 Implementing the VMN Abstraction

In this section we present our implementation of the VMN abstraction. Recall that the VMN Abstraction consists of three components: virtual nodes, clients, and the VMN-LocalCast service. Our implementation consists of the Mobile Point Emulator (MPE) and the TOBcast service, which together implement the VMN and the VMN-LocalCast service. (The client automata, along with the automata to execute on the virtual node, are provided by the application developer, and hence no further discussion is necessary.) Formally, the MPE consists of one automaton, MPE_i, for every real node i. The relationship between these components is depicted in Figure 2.

Simple VMN Implementation

The simplest way to implement a VMN is by using a mobile "agent". An agent is a dynamic process that jumps from one real node to another, moving in the direction specified by the VMN path. An agent "hitches a ride" with a host that is near to the specified location of the VMN. This strategy has been used in the past to implement various services, such as group communication (see [8]). It can be generalized to support arbitrary I/O automata.

This simple algorithm meets one of the two goals of a VMN implementation: the movement of the virtual node is predictable. However, the host of the agent may fail, and therefore the VMN is not robust. For some applications, such as simple routing, this may be sufficient. For many applications, however, this lack of robustness is undesirable. We use replication to solve this problem.

Mobile Points

We define a *mobile point* to be a circular region, of radius R_{mp}, that moves on the same path as the VMN: at time t, the center of the mobile point coincides with the preplanned location of the VMN at time t. (Even if the VMN has "failed", the mobile point – and the defunct VMN – conceptually continue along the prespecified path.) Every real node that resides within a mobile point replicates the state of the virtual node.

Totally-Ordered Broadcast

Since the state of the VMN is replicated at multiple real nodes, the mobile point algorithm must maintain consistency among the replicas. We use the RMN-LocalCast communication service and the synchronized clocks to implement a totally-ordered broadcast service, which we call TOBcast, within the region defined by the mobile point[3].

We use a standard technique to implement the totally-ordered

```
                    TOBcastᵢ
Input TOBcast(m)ᵢ, m a message
Input rcv(m)ᵢ, m an internal message          2
Output TOBcast-rcv(m)ᵢ, m a message
Output send(m)ᵢ, m an internal message        4

State:                                        6
  clock, current real time
  location, current location
  incoming, initially ∅                       8
  outgoing, initially ∅                       10

Input TOBcast(m)ᵢ                             12
Effect:
  outgoing ← outgoing ∪                       14
          {⟨m, i, clock, location⟩}
                                              16
Output send(m)ᵢ
Precondition:                                 18
  m ∈ outgoing
Effect:                                       20
  outgoing ← outgoing / {m}
                                              22
Input rcv(⟨m, j, t, ℓ⟩)ᵢ
Effect:                                       24
  incoming ← incoming ∪ {⟨m, j, t, ℓ⟩}
                                              26
Output TOBcast-rcv(m)ᵢ
Precondition:                                 28
  ⟨m, j, t, ℓ⟩ ∈ incoming
  t+d+1 = clock                               30
  ∄ ⟨m', j', t', *⟩ ∈ incoming s.t. j' < j
Effect:                                       32
  incoming ← incoming \ {⟨m, j, t, ℓ⟩}
                                              34
Trajectories:
satisfies                                     36
  d(time) = 1
  d(location[i]) is arbitrary                 38
  constant incoming, outgoing
stops when                                    40
  ∃ ⟨m, j, t, ℓ⟩ ∈ incoming such that:
    t+d+1 = time                              42
  ∃ ⟨m, j, t, ℓ⟩ ∈ outgoing
```

Fig. 3. The TOBcast service implementation.

---

[3] The TOBcast service takes the place of the "LBcast" service used in [6].

mp-location, a location, continuously updated, defining the location of the VMN
status ∈ {idle, joining, listening, active}, initially active if $i ∈ mp\text{-}location$, else idle
val ∈ *states*, holds state of the simulated I/O automaton, initially start
anwered-joins, set of ids of answered join requests, initially ∅
join-id, a tuple of time and a node id, a unique id for a join request, initially $\langle 0, i_0 \rangle$
pending-actions, queue of actions waiting to be simulated, initially ∅
completed-actions, queue of actions that have been simulated, initially ∅
clock ∈ $R^{\geq 0}$, current time, initially 0, continuously updated by the Geosensor
location, current location, continuously updated by the Geosensor

Fig. 4. MPE State for Node i and VMN h for IOA $\tau = \langle sig, states, start, \delta \rangle$.

broadcast. A timestamp is affixed to each message, defining a total order. (Each
node only sends a single message for each real time, and ties are broken using
node identifiers.) Before delivering a message, the mobile node waits until at
least time $d + 1$ has elapsed since the message was sent, ensuring that all earlier
messages are received first. See Figure 3 for the pseudocode (using the TIOA
formalism [11]) that implements the totally-ordered broadcast service, which we
call TOBcast.

Theorem 1. *The TOBcast service guarantees that messages are delivered in the
order in which they are sent (according to real time), and if a real node within
a mobile point sends a message, then every other real node in the mobile point
(that resides in the mobile point for the duration of the broadcast) receives the
message.*

The Mobile Point Emulator

The Mobile Point Emulator is based on a replicated state machine technique
similar to that originally presented in [14], augmented to support joins, leaves,
and recovery. The MPE replicates the state of the VMN at every node within the
mobile point's region. It uses the total ordering of messages to ensure that the
replicas are updated consistently. The state of each MPE_i is given in Figure 4,
and the signature of each MPE_i is given in Figure 5. The algorithm itself is in
Figure 6. (All the line numbers in this section refer to Figure 6.)

MPE State. The *status* of the Mobile Point Emulator at node i transitions
between four *status* value: idle, indicating that the real node is not within the
mobile point, joining or listening, indicating that the real node is in the process
of joining the VMN, or active, indicating that the real node is participating in
the VMN emulation.

When a node is active in the mobile point, it maintains a replicated copy of
the state of the virtual node, *val*. The MPE maintains a queue of *pending-actions*,
which are processed in order. The TOBcast service is used to ensure that each
MPE processes the pending actions in the same order. The *completed-actions* and

answered-joins store information on which actions have already been processed, thus preventing a message from being processed twice. The *join-id* is used during the join protocol.

The *mp-location* variable maintains the current location of the center of the mobile point. This may be continually changing, however it is a predetermined function of time. The *location* variable maintains the current location of the real node on which the MPE is executnig. The *clock* maintains the current real time.

MPE Transitions. The MPE_i modifies the replicated state, *val* only when the real node receives a TOBcast message indicating that a particular action should be performed. Since all active nodes process the TOBcast messages in the same order, all nodes modify their state in the same way, thus maintaining consistent replicas.

> **Signature:**
>
> **Input**:
> $rcv(m)_i$, m a client message
> $lbcast\text{-}rcv(m)_i$, m a TOBcast message
> $geo\text{-}update(l, t)_i$, l a *location*, $t \in R^{>0}$
> $reset()_i$
>
> **Output**:
> $send(m)_i$, m a client message
> $lbcast(m)_i$ m a TOBcast message
>
> **Internal**:
> $join()_i$
> $init\text{-}action(act)_i$, $act \in sig$
> $simulate\text{-}action(act)_i$, $act \in sig$

Fig. 5. Mobile Point Emulator Signature for real node i and VMN h for IOA $\tau = \langle sig, states, start, \delta \rangle$.

When an active node, i, receives a message destined for the VMN – that is, a rcv_i occurs – it immediately resends it to the other replicas using the TOBcast service (lines 1–4). When the TOBcast service delivers the message, each node modifies its replica, performing a VMN rcv of that message (lines 65–69 and lines 48–61).

Sometimes, a VMN chooses to initiate an internal or output action. In this case, an active node determines that a certain action is enabled, and broadcasts a message to the other replicas (lines 12–20). As in the previous case, when the TOBcast service delivers the message, each node modifies the state of its replica, performing the specified VMN action (again, lines 65–69 followed by lines 48-61). In some cases, this causes the VMN itself to send a message (line 61).

Joining a Mobile Point. Whenever a real node is within the perimeter defined by the mobile point, it initiates the join protocol (lines 22–30); whenever a real node is outside of a mobile point, it executes the leave protocol, which reinitializes its states and sets its status to idle (lines 42–46). The maximum speed of the VMN is effectively determined by the speed of the join protocol and the speed of the real nodes: the mobile point must move slowly enough so that new nodes can enter and join the mobile point before the old nodes leave.

The join protocol for node i begins when i broadcasts a join-req, requesting a copy of the current state (line 30). When node i receives the TOBcast for its own join request, it enters the listening state (lines 71–72). This indicates that node i can begin to monitor the messages in the system. In particular, it saves any messages that it cannot yet process in *pending-actions*.

When some active node, j, receives a join request, it sends a join acknowledg-ment, join-ack (lines 73-78). This acknowledgment includes a copy of its replica of the virtual node, val_j. When i receives the join acknowledgment, it copies the replicated state (lines 79–78), and begins to process its *pending-actions*.

Recovery. The Mobile Point Emulator simulates VMNs that are quite robust: they fail only when they enter a depopulated region of the network. However, as soon as all the nodes leave a mobile point, the virtual node loses its state. The Mobile Point Emulator contains a recovery mechanism that restarts the virtual node in this case. When a real node enters the mobile point and cannot communicate with any other active nodes, it can choose to broadcast a reset message (lines 32–35). (Should it choose not to, the VMN may not recover.) When a node receives a reset message it reinitializes its state (lines 85-87). In particular, when the node that discovers the mobile point has failed receives its own reset message, it restarts the mobile point.

VMN-LocalCast

When a client sends a message to the VMN using the VMN-LocalCast service, three steps occur: first, the client uses the RMN-LocalCast service to send the message to a real node in the VMN; second, the real node in the VMN rebroad-casts the message using the TOBcast service; finally, each node in the mobile point processes the message, and the VMN receives the message. Therefore, if the underlying real nodes deliver messages within time d, then the VMN-LocalCast guarantees that messages are delivered within time $2d + 1$: it takes time d for the real node to receive the message from the client, and an additional time $d + 1$ for the TOBcast service to redeliver the message.

The same process occurs (partially in reverse) when the VMN sends a mes-sage to a client: first a real node in the VMN broadcasts the intent of the VMN to send a message using the TOBcast service; second, the real nodes in the VMN process the message (at which point the VMN has buffered the outgoing message); third, some real node uses the RMN-LocalCast service to send the message to the client.

Recall that the VMN-LocalCast service has a range of R_{VMN} and the RMN-LocalCast service has a range of R_{RMN}. In order for the algorithm to be correct we assume that:

$$R \geq 2R_{VMN} + 2t_{geo} \cdot v_{max} .$$

There are two reasons why the extra broadcast range is necessary. First, a real node that is at distance R_{VMN} from the center must be able to send a message to any client that is at distance R_{VMN} from (the center of) the VMN; thus a radius of $2R_{VMN}$ is necessary. Second, a real node only receives updates about its location every t_{geo} time units; therefore, a real node may be an additional $t_{geo} \cdot v_{max}$ distance outside the mobile point before detecting that it is no longer a part of the VMN emulation.

Input rcv$(m)_i$
2 **Effect:**
  $TOBcast\text{-}out \leftarrow TOBcast\text{-}out \cup$
4     $\{\langle simulate, \langle rcv, m \rangle, \perp \rangle\}$

6 **Output** send$(m)_{h,i}$
  Precondition:
8 $m \in local\text{-}out$
  Effect:
10 $local\text{-}out \leftarrow local\text{-}out \, / \, \{m\}$

12 **Internal** init-action$(act)_{h,i}$
  Precondition:
14 $status = $ active
  $|mp\text{-}location - location| < R$
16 $\delta(val, act) \neq \perp$
  Effect:
18 $temp\text{-}oid \leftarrow \langle clock, i \rangle$
  $TOBcast\text{-}out \leftarrow TOBcast\text{-}out \cup$
20     $\{\langle simulate, act, temp\text{-}oid \rangle\}$

22 **Internal** join$()_i$
  Precondition:
24 $|mp\text{-}location - location| < R$
  $status = idle$
26 **Effect:**
  $join\text{-}id \leftarrow \langle clock, i \rangle$
28 $status \leftarrow $ joining
  $TOBcast\text{-}out \leftarrow TOBcast\text{-}out \cup$
30     $\{\langle join\text{-}req, \perp, join\text{-}id \rangle\}$

32 **Input** reset$()_i$
  Effect:
34 $TOBcast\text{-}out \leftarrow TOBcast\text{-}out \cup$
     $\{\langle reset \rangle\}$
36 **Input** geo-update$(\ell, t)_i$
  Effect:
38 $location \leftarrow \ell$
  $clock \leftarrow t$
40 $val \leftarrow \delta(val,$
     $\langle geo\text{-}update, t, mp\text{-}location \rangle)$
42 **if** $(|mp\text{-}location - location| \geq R)$
     and $(status \neq idle)$ **then**
44 $status \leftarrow idle$
  $val \leftarrow start(\tau)$
46 $pending\text{-}actions \leftarrow \emptyset$

48 **Internal** simulate-action$(act)_i$
  Precondition:
50 $status = $ active
  $|mp\text{-}location - location| < R$
52 $head(pending\text{-}actions) = \langle simulate, act, oid \rangle$
  Effect:
54 Dequeue$(pending\text{-}actions)$
  if $(\langle simulate, act, oid \rangle \in completed\text{-}actions)$
56   **then continue;**
  if $(\delta(val, act) = \perp)$ **then continue;**
58 $val \leftarrow \delta(val, act)$
  $completed\text{-}actions \leftarrow completed\text{-}actions \cup$
60                  $\{\langle simulate, act, oid \rangle\}$
  if $(act = \langle send, m \rangle)$ **then** send(m)

62
  Input TOBcast-rcv$(\langle optype, param, oid \rangle)_i$
64 **Effect:**
  if $(optype = $ simulate$)$ **then**
66   **if** $(status \neq $ listening or active$)$ **then**
        continue;
68   **else** Enqueue$(pending\text{-}actions,$
                 $\langle simulate, param, oid \rangle)$
70 **else if** $(optype = $ join-req$)$ **then**
     if $((status = $ joining$)$ **and** $(oid = join\text{-}id))$
72   **then** $status \leftarrow $ listening
     if $((status = $ active$)$ **then**
74   **if** $(oid \in answered\text{-}joins)$ **then**
           continue;
76   **else if** $(|mp\text{-}location - location| < R)$
           then TOBcast$(\langle join\text{-}ack,$
78                 $\langle val, completed\text{-}actions \rangle, oid \rangle)$
  else if $(optype = $ join-ack$)$
80     $answered\text{-}joins \leftarrow answered\text{-}joins \cup \{oid\}$
     if $(status = $ listening$)$ **then**
82   **if** $(oid = join\text{-}id)$ **then**
           $status \leftarrow $ active
84           $\langle val, completed\text{-}actions \rangle \leftarrow param$
  else if $(optype = $ reset$)$ **then**
86     $status \leftarrow $ active
     $pending\text{-}actions \leftarrow \emptyset$

88 **Output** TOBcast$(m)_i$
  Precondition:
90 $m \in TOBcast\text{-}out$
  Effect:
92 $TOBcast\text{-}out \leftarrow TOBcast\text{-}out \, / \, \{m\}$

Fig. 6. Automaton $MPE_{h,i}$ running on node i implementing the VMN executing IOA $\tau = \langle sig, states, start, \delta \rangle$.

VMN Performance

Each step of the VMN automata requires at most one TOBcast message to be sent, which takes time $d + 1$; no other delay is incurred. Therefore, the Mobile Point Emulator ensures that a program executing on a VMN is slowed by at most a factor of $d + 1$.

Theorem 2. *The Mobile Point Emulator and the TOBcast service (and the trivial client implementation) correctly implement the VMN Abstraction. More formally: let A be the abstract VMN model, and let S be the implementation. Then timed-traces(S) $\subseteq$ timed-traces(A)*[4].

5   Correctness of the Mobile Point Emulator

In this section, we present a sketch of the proof that the Mobile Point Emulator correctly implements the VMN abstraction. We demonstrate a forward simulation relation [11] between the implementation described in Section 4 and the VMN Abstraction described in Section 3, which implies the correctness of our algorithm. For more details, see [5].

The simulation relation consists of five main conditions. The first two conditions relate messages in the RMN-LocalCast service and messages in the VMN-LocalCast service. Condition 1 relates incoming messages: if m is a message in *RMN-LocalCast.mpe-messages*[i] waiting to be delivered to some mobile node i, then message m is also waiting in *VMN-LocalCast. VMN-messages* to be delivered to the VMN. Condition 2 relates outgoing messages: if m is a message in *RMN-LocalCast.messages*[i] being sent by some Mobile Point automaton to node i, then message m is also in *VMN-LocalCast.messages*[i].

Condition 3 relates the replicated state of a Mobile Point Emulator to the state of the abstract VMN: for all active mobile nodes i that have completed the join protocol, if you start with the state represented by $MPE.val_i$, and process all the pending actions in $MPE.pending\text{-}actions_i$ in the order they are stored in the queue and all the messages waiting in the TOBcast queue $TOBcast.outgoing[i]$ (again, in the order they are stored in the queue), then the resulting value is equivalent to the state of the VMN, $VMN.val$.

Condition 4 is used to show that the join protocol works: if v is a state contained in a join acknowledgment message stored anywhere in the system, then if you start with the state represented by v and process all the messages in the $MPE.pending\text{-}actions_i$ queue that are sent after the associated join request, then the resulting value is equal to the state of the VMN, $VMN.val$.

Condition 5 ensures that if the implementation initiates a send, then the VMN can perform a send: if m is a message indicating that a send(x) is to occur, and m is either in a TOBcast queue (*TOBcast.messages*[i]) or waiting to be performed (in $MPE.pending\text{-}actions_i$), then the message x is in *VMN.buffer*.

---

[4] The *timed-traces* of a system capture the externally visible behavior and the times at which the external visible events occur.

We claim that the Mobile Point Emulator correctly implements the VMN abstraction, in that any service built on the VMN abstraction runs correctly on the Mobile Point Emulator:

Proof of Theorem 2 (sketch).   In the initial state, the five conditions described above hold: all the message queues and buffers are empty, and the *MPE.val* component of the replicated automata is set to the initial state, as is the *VMN.val* component.

We proceed by induction, examining all possible actions in the implementation, and determining a suitable sequence of actions in the abstract model. For example, assume that a client attempts to send a message to the VMN. In the implementation, this results in a message being added to the communication service's message queues; in the abstract model, this results in a message being added to the high-level communication service's VMN message queue, preserving Condition 1.

One interesting case occurs when a mobile node broadcasts a message using the TOBcast service indicating that a transition of the VMN automaton should occur. In the low-level implementation, a message is added to *TOBcast.messages*[i], for all nodes i. In order to maintain Condition 5, it is necessary to immediately perform the required transition in the VMN, updating *VMN.val*. If the required transition is an output action, the VMN sends a message, placing it in *VMN.buffer*, thus maintaining Condition 5. We omit the many remaining cases.

The conditions are also maintained when time passes: if a node is far enough away that it does not receive a LocalCast message, then it has left the focal point. We conclude that Conditions 1–5 are a forward simulation relation.   □

6   Algorithms for Virtual Mobile Nodes

To demonstrate the utility of the new approach, we briefly discuss several basic algorithms that use VMNs to solve interesting problems simply and efficiently. For more details, see [5].

Consider the problem of routing messages. The simplest algorithm to route message relies on a single virtual node traversing the network collecting messages and delivering them. It is possible to adapt the compulsory protocols of Chatzigiannakis et al. [4], yielding alternate message delivery services that can operate in a non-compulsory framework. Routing a message to a virtual node is even simpler: the current location of a virtual node is known in advance, so we can route messages directly to the predicted location of the virtual node.

Virtual nodes can also be used to collect sensor data, traversing the network. Instead of maintaining a complicated dynamic data structure of sensor readings, a virtual node can aggregate data as it is collected and process complex queries.

Finally, we suggest that VMNs may be useful for a number of common generic services. Group communication services (e.g., as in [9, 12, 13]) can be implemented by adapting the strategy in [8] to use a robust virtual node, instead of a fragile token, to collect and deliver group information. An atomic memory service can be constructed using the approach developed in [6]; in this case, however, the data can be programmed to travel around the network.

7   Discussion and Concluding Remarks

We have presented a new technique for implementing algorithms in mobile *ad hoc* networks. In general, it is difficult to devise algorithms for such chaotic, unpredictable environments. The VMN abstraction makes the task easier by providing robust virtual nodes that move in a predictable manner. Moreover, we have presented the Mobile Point Emulator, a new algorithm that allows real mobile nodes to emulate reliable virtual nodes, using location information and a basic (though powerful) local communication service.

We believe that the VMN abstraction and low-level algorithms similar to the Mobile Point Emulator can significantly simplify the development of application-level algorithms for mobile networks.

There are a number of limitations, however, to the Mobile Point Emulator. It depends on a powerful local communication service, and the correctness of the algorithm depends on both the reliability and timeliness of the service. Moreover, it assumes that the algorithm is executing in a trusted environment; it remains an open question to consider the security implications, and whether such a solution could work in a more hostile environment. Finally, the Mobile Point Emulator is an expensive algorithm, requiring significant amounts of communication and power consumption.

Engineering and Experimentation. There are many ways in which the Mobile Point Emulator can be optimized for implementation purposes. For example, if a (temporary) leader is elected within a mobile point, and the leader initiates all the transitions for the replica, conflicting requests are avoided and power is saved. As a second example, when a node leaves a mobile point, it need not wholly reset its replica state; on rejoining the mobile point, the join acknowledgment only needs to contain the changes in the state. It would be interesting to experiment with a real implementation of VMNs to determine the extent to which the algorithms can be optimized, and whether the utility outweighs the implementation overhead.

Self-Stabilizing VMNs. Long-term robustness of the VMN abstraction could be improved if the virtual nodes could tolerate transient faults, such as state-corruption or a violation of the broadcast assumptions. It is an interesting open question whether the Mobile Point Emulator can be made self-stabilizing.

Dynamic Virtual Mobile Nodes. We have assumed that the set of VMNs and their paths are fixed in advance. For some applications, this is sufficient; however, for others, it would be useful if the paths of the VMNs could be determined on-the-fly. For example, one can imagine using a VMN to follow a moving entity, either performing a service for that entity, or tracking the location of the entity. Dynamic paths can also be used to help VMNs avoid unpopulated areas of the mobile network, thus improving robustness. It may also be useful to generate virtual nodes dynamically; for example, a new VMN might be generated to track every entity that enters a certain geographical area.

References

1. J. Beal. Persistent nodes for reliable memory in geographically local networks. Tech Report AIM-2003-11, MIT, 2003.
2. J. Beal. A robust amorphous hierarchy from persistent nodes. In *Proc. of Communication Systems and Networks*, 2003.
3. T. Camp, Y. Liu. An adaptive mesh-based protocol for geocast routing. *Journal of Parallel and Distributed Computing: Special Issue on Mobile Ad-hoc Networking and Computing*, pp. 196–213, 2002.
4. I. Chatzigiannakis, S. Nikoletseas, P. Spirakis. An efficient communication strategy for ad-hoc mobile networks. In *Proc. 15th International Symp. on Distributed Computing*, 2001.
5. S. Dolev, S. Gilbert, N. A. Lynch, E. Schiller, A. A. Shvartsman, J. L. Welch. Virtual mobile nodes for mobile adhoc networks. Tech Report LCS-TR-937, MIT, 2004.
6. S. Dolev, S. Gilbert, N. A. Lynch, A. A. Shvartsman, J. Welch. Geoquorums: Implementing atomic memory in mobile ad hoc networks. In *Proceeding of the 17th International Conference on Distributed Computing*, 2003.
7. S. Dolev, S. Gilbert, N. A. Lynch, A. A. Shvartsman, J. L. Welch. Geoquorums: Implementing atomic memory in ad hoc networks. Tech Report LCS-TR-900, MIT, 2003.
8. S. Dolev, E. Schiller, J. Welch. Random walk for self-stabilizing group communication in ad-hoc networks. In *Proc. of the 21st IEEE Symp. on Reliable Distributed Systems*, 2002.
9. *Communications of the ACM, Special section on Group Communication Systems*, volume 39(4), 1996.
10. K. P. Hatzis, G. P. Pentaris, P. G. Spirakis, V. T. Tampakas, R. B. Tan. Fundamental control algorithms in mobile networks. In *Proc. of the 1st ACM Symp. on Parallel Algorithms and Architectures archive*, Saint Malo, France, 1999.
11. D. K. Kaynar, N. Lynch, R. Segala, F. Vaandrager. The theory of timed I/O automata. Tech Report MIT-LCS-TR-917a, MIT, 2004.
12. I. Keidar. A highly available paradigm for consistent object replication. Master's thesis, Hebrew University, Jerusalem, 1994.
    URL: http://www.cs.huji.ac.il/simtransis/publications.html.
13. I. Keidar, D. Dolev. Efficient message ordering in dynamic networks. In *Proc. of the 15th annual ACM Symp. on Principles of distributed computing*, 1996.
14. L. Lamport. Time, clocks, and the ordering of events in a distributed system. *Communications of the ACM*, 21(7):558–565, 1978.
15. Q. Li, D. Rus. Sending messages to mobile users in disconnected ad-hoc wireless networks. In *Proc. of the 6th MobiCom*, 2000.
16. N. A. Lynch. *Distributed Algorithms*. Morgan Kaufman, 1996.
17. R. Nagpal, H. Shrobe, J. Bachrach. Organizing a global coordinate system from local information on an ad hoc sensor network. In *2nd Workshop on Information Processing in Sensor Networks*, 2003.
18. B. Nath, D. Niculescu. Routing on a curve. *ACM SIGCOMM Computer Communication Review*, 33(1):150 – 160, 2003.
19. J. C. Navas, T. Imielinski. Geocast – geographic addressing and routing. In *Proc. of the 3rd MobiCom*, 1997.
20. N. B. Priyantha, A. Chakraborty, H. Balakrishnan. The cricket location-support system. In *Proc. of the 6th MobiCom*, 2000.

Contention-Free MAC Protocols
for Wireless Sensor Networks

Costas Busch, Malik Magdon-Ismail, Fikret Sivrikaya, and Bülent Yener

Department of Computer Science
Rensselaer Polytechnic Institute
Troy, NY 12180, USA
{buschc,magdon,sivrif,yener}@cs.rpi.edu

Abstract. A MAC protocol specifies how nodes in a sensor network access a shared communication channel. Desired properties of such MAC protocol are: it should be *distributed* and *contention-free* (avoid collisions); it should *self-stabilize* to changes in the network (such as arrival of new nodes), and these changes should be *contained*, i.e., affect only the nodes in the vicinity of the change; it should not assume that nodes have a global time reference, i.e., nodes may not be time-synchronized. We give the first MAC protocols that satisfy all of these requirements, i.e., we give distributed, contention-free, self-stabilizing MAC protocols which do not assume a global time reference. Our protocols self-stabilize from an arbitrary initial state, and if the network changes the changes are contained and the protocol adjusts to the local topology of the network. The communication complexity, number and size of messages, for the protocol to stabilize is small (logarithmic in network size).

1 Introduction

Sensor networks are the focus of significant research efforts on account of their diverse applications, that include disaster recovery, military surveillance, health administration and environmental monitoring. A sensor network is comprised of a large number of limited power sensor nodes which collect and process data from a target domain and transmit information back to specific sites (e.g., headquarters, disaster control centers). We consider wireless sensor networks which share the same wireless communication channel. A Medium Access Control (MAC) protocol specifies how nodes share the channel, and hence plays a central role in the performance of a sensor network.

Sensor networks contain many nodes, typically dispersed at high, possibly non-uniform, densities; sensors may turn on and off in order to conserve energy; and, the communication traffic is space and time correlated. *Contention* occurs when two nearby sensor nodes both attempt to access the communication channel at the same time. Contention causes message collisions, which are very likely to occur when traffic is frequent and correlated, and they decrease the lifetime of a sensor network. A MAC protocol is contention-free if it does not allow any collisions. All existing contention-free MAC protocols assume that the sensor nodes

R. Guerraoui (Ed.): DISC 2004, LNCS 3274, pp. 245–259, 2004.
© Springer-Verlag Berlin Heidelberg 2004

are time-synchronized in some way. This is usually not possible on account of the large scale of sensor networks.

The preceding discussion emphasizes the following desirable properties for a MAC protocol in sensor networks: it should be *distributed* and *contention-free*; it should *self-stabilize* to changes in the network (such as the arrival of new nodes into the network), and these changes should be *contained*, i.e., affect only the nodes in the vicinity of the change; it should not assume that nodes have access to a global time reference, i.e., nodes may not be time-synchronized. These properties are essential to the scalability of sensor networks and for keeping the sensor hardware simple. In this paper, we give the first MAC protocols that satisfy all of these requirements.

A contention-free MAC protocol should be able to bring the network from an arbitrary state to a collision-free stable state. Since the protocol is distributed, during this stabilization phase collisions are unavoidable. We measure the quality of the stabilization phase in terms of the time it takes to reach the stable state, and the amount of control messages exchanged. When the nodes reach the stable state, they use the contention-free MAC protocol to transmit messages without collisions. In the stable state, we measure the efficiency by a node's *throughput*, the inverse of the time interval between its transmissions.

Model. A sensor network with n nodes can be represented by a graph $G = (V, E)$, in which two sensor nodes are connected if they can communicate directly, i.e., if they are within each other's transmission range. We assume that all sensor nodes have the same transmission range, hence all links are bidirectional and the graph G is undirected.

A message sent by a node is received by all of its adjacent nodes. If two nodes are adjacent and send messages simultaneously, their messages collide. If two nodes u and w are not adjacent and have the same common adjacent node v, then when u and w transmit at the same time their messages collide in v (*hidden terminal problem*). We assume that nodes can detect such collisions.

The *k-neighborhood* of a node v, $\Delta_k(v)$, is the set of nodes whose shortest path to v has length at most k. We denote the number of nodes in the k-neighborhood by $\delta_k(v)$ (where $\delta_k(v) = |\Delta_k(v)|$), and the maximum k-neighborhood size by δ_k ($\delta_k = \max_v \delta_k(v)$). We refer to 1-neighbors as neighbors. We can also define the k-neighborhood of a set of nodes S: $\Delta_k(S)$ is the set of nodes that are at most a distance k away from *some* node in S. We assume that at the start of the algorithm, every node has been provided an upper bound on δ_1 and δ_2 (for example this information can be provided by the network administrator).

Contributions. We give a distributed, contention-free, self-stabilizing MAC protocol which does not assume a global time reference. The protocol has two parts. Starting from an arbitrary initial state, the protocol first enters a *loose* phase where nodes set up a preliminary MAC protocol. This phase is followed by a *tight* phase in which nodes make the MAC protocol more efficient. Both parts of the protocol are self-stabilizing. Since we make no assumptions about the initial state, the protocol will also re-stabilize after any network change.

During the *loose* phase, every node transmits at most $O(\log n)$ control messages, each of size at most $O(\log n)$ bits. The time duration of this phase is $O(\log n \cdot \min\{\delta_1^3, \delta_2^2\})$. The protocol has now reached a stable state in which the throughput of a node is $O(1/\min\{\delta_1^3, \delta_2^2\})$. The network may either remain in this protocol, or proceed to the next (tight) phase in which we improve the steady state throughput of the nodes. The tightening phase also requires at most $O(\log n)$ control messages per node of size at most $O(\log n)$ bits to reach the steady state. The time duration of this phase is $O(\log n \cdot \min\{\delta_1^5, \delta_1^2\delta_2^2\})$. During steady state, the throughput of node v is closely related to $1/\phi_v$, where ϕ_v is the maximum 2-neighborhood size among all nodes in v's 2-neighborhood. An important property of the tight phase is that the throughput of a node is related only to the local "density" of the graph in the vicinity of the node, and hence adapts to the varying topology of the network.

If the network changes, for example a set S of nodes suddenly power up after being powered down for some time, as already mentioned, the protocol will self-stabilize to the change. Further, the only nodes that are affected by the stabilization are nodes in $\Delta_2(S)$ for the loose phase, and $\Delta_6(S)$ for the tight phase.

Approach. Our approach is based on the concept of a *frame* (see Figure 1), which is the basis of TDMA MAC protocols. We adapt the frame approach so that it does not depend on any global time reference. Each node divides time into equal sized frames. Each frame is further divided into equal sized time *slots*; a time slot corresponds to the time duration of sending one message. Frames in the same node have the same size (number of slots). However, different nodes can have different frame sizes. The frames do not need to be aligned at the various nodes, and neither do the time slots.

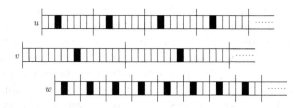

Fig. 1. Frames of three nodes. Frames at different nodes may not be aligned. Solid shaded time slots indicate the selected time slot of each node; longer vertical lines identify the frame boundaries.

The basic idea is that each node selects a slot in its own frame which it then uses to transmit messages. The selected slots of any 2-neighbor nodes must not overlap (they should be *conflict-free*), since otherwise collisions can occur. In order to guarantee that slots remain conflict-free in any frame repetitions, the frame sizes in the same neighborhood are chosen to be multiples of each other. In our algorithms the frame sizes are powers of 2. Thus, nodes need to select slots only once, and the slots remain conflict-free thereafter.

The MAC protocols (algorithms) we provide find conflict-free time slots. For the loose phase, we have developed algorithm LooseMAC in which all nodes have the same fixed frame size, which is proportional to $\min\{\delta_1^3, \delta_2^2\}$. For the tight phase we have developed algorithm TightMAC in which each node v has frame size proportional to ϕ_v, which depends only on the local area density of node v. Thus, in TightMAC different nodes in the network have different frame sizes that reflects the variation of the node density in different areas of the network.

Related Work. MAC protocols are either *contention-based* or *contention-free.* Contention-based MAC protocols are also known as *random access protocols*, requiring no coordination among the nodes accessing the channel. Colliding nodes back off for a random duration and try to access the channel again. Such protocols first appeared as Pure ALOHA [1] and Slotted ALOHA [21]. The throughput of Aloha-like protocols was significantly improved by the Carrier Sense Multiple Access (CSMA) protocol [14]. Recently, CSMA and its enhancements with collision avoidance (CA) and request to send (RTS) and clear to send (CTS) mechanisms have led to the IEEE 802.11 [29] standard for wireless ad-hoc networks. The performance of contention based MAC protocols is weak when traffic is frequent or correlated and these protocols suffer from stability problems [23]. As a result, contention-based protocols are not suitable for sensor networks.

Our work is most related to contention-free MAC protocols. In these protocols, the nodes are following some particular schedule which guarantees collision-free transmission times. Typical examples of such protocols are: Frequency Division Multiple Access (FDMA); Time Division Multiple Access (TDMA) [15]; Code Division Multiple Access (CDMA) [25]. In addition to TDMA, FDMA and CDMA, various reservation based [13] or token based schemes [7, 10] are proposed for distributed channel access control. Among these schemes, TDMA and its variants are most relevant to our work. Allocation of TDMA slots is well studied (e.g., in the context of packet radio networks) and there are many centralized [19, 24], and distributed [2, 8, 20] schemes for TDMA slot assignments. These existing protocols are either centralized or rely on a global time reference.

There is considerable work on multi-layered, integrated views in wireless networking. Power controlled MAC protocols have been considered in settings that are based on collision avoidance [17, 16, 27], transmission scheduling [9], and limited interference CDMA systems [18]. Some recent work on energy conservation by powering off some nodes is studied in [22, 28, 6, 5]. While GAF [28] and SPAN [6] are distributed approaches with coordination among neighbors, in ASCENT a node decides itself to be on or off [5]. S-MAC [30] proposes that nodes form virtual clusters based on common sleep schedules. Sleep and wake schedules are used in [12], but based on energy and traffic rate at the nodes in order to balance energy consumption. A different approach is used in [26], with an adaptive rate control mechanism to provide a fair and energy-efficient MAC protocol.

Paper Outline. In Section 2 we give Algorithm LooseMAC and an outline of its analysis (the detailed analysis can be found in [4]). We proceed with Algorithm TightMAC in Section 3, followed by some concluding discussion in Section 4.

2 Algorithm LooseMAC

Here we present Algorithm LooseMAC and an outline of its analysis. Each node selects the same frame size, which is proportional to $\min\{\delta_1^3, \delta_2^2\}$. The algorithm is randomized and guarantees that all nodes will find their slots quickly, with low communication complexity. Further, the algorithm is self-stabilizing with good containment properties.

For simplicity of the presentation, we will assume that slots are aligned (frames do not need to be aligned). All results hold immediately for when the slots are not aligned (with small constant factors, since each slot may overlap with at most two slots in a neighbor's frame). For notation convenience, given a set of nodes $V = \{v_1, v_2, \ldots, v_n\}$, we will denote node v_i simply as node i.

2.1 Description of LooseMAC

Algorithm 1 depicts the basic functionality of LooseMAC. Consider some node i. Node i divides time into frames of size Λ. The task for node i is to select a conflict-free slot. When this occurs we say that the node is "ready", and we set its local variable variable ready to TRUE.

Algorithm 1 LooseMAC(node i).

1: Divide time into frames of size Λ;
2: ready ← FALSE;
3: **while** not ready **do**
4:    Select a slot σ_i randomly in the frame;
5:    Send a "beacon" message in slot σ_i;
6:    Listen for a period of Λ time slots;
7:    **if** no collision is detected by i and no neighbor of i reports a conflict **then**
8:       ready ← TRUE;

Initially, when node i enters the network it is not ready. Node i selects randomly and uniformly a slot σ_i in its frame. In σ_i, node i sends a "beacon" message m_i to its neighborhood. Let Z denote the time period during the next Λ time slots. If σ_i doesn't create any slot conflicts in its neighbors during Z, then node i keeps slot σ_i and becomes ready. After the node becomes ready it remains ready and doesn't select a new slot (with the exception of when a new neighbor joins the network, which is described in Section 2.2). Below we explain how node i can detect that σ_i creates a conflict, and therefore, whether to keep or abandon the selected time slot (see also Figure 2).

If m_i creates slot conflicts in some neighbor j, then j responds by transmitting a message m_j reporting the conflict (this message simply says that j detected a conflict, without specifying which nodes are conflicting). Node j sends m_j during its currently selected slot σ_j. Since the frame length of j is also Λ, the message m_j is sent before the end of Z. If m_j is received by i without collisions, i decodes

m_j to note that j detected a conflict. For safety, i assumes that the conflict was with σ_i, and i abandons slot σ_i continuing by selecting another slot in its next frame. If m_j collides at node i, i does not know if m_j was reporting a conflict or not as i cannot decode two or more colliding messages. Again i assumes that the collided message was reporting a conflict, abandons slot σ_i and selects another slot in its next frame. The process repeats until i does not detect any message collisions or does not receive any conflict reports during Z. Note that a node will transmit at most twice during any arbitrary period of Λ slots, since the frame size is Λ and a node transmits at most once during every particular frame.

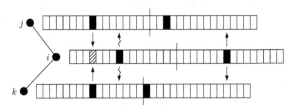

Fig. 2. Execution of the LooseMAC algorithm, where the shaded slot corresponds to a collision and the waived lines to a conflict report message.

To enable a node to detect slot conflicts, the node marks the time slots that are being used by its neighbors. Consider node j. Suppose that a neighbor i sends a message m_i to j at a slot π. If node j receives m_i without collisions, and π is unmarked, then j marks π as being used by i. If later i selects another slot, node j will mark the new slot position and unmark the previous position. Using the marking mechanism, node j can detect slot conflicts as follows. Suppose that a neighbor node k sends a message during slot π, which is already marked with i. Node j then detects a conflict between the time slots chosen by i and k. A conflict occurs also if nodes i and k transmit at the same time, which is observed as a message collision by j. Actually, in the LooseMAC algorithm (Algorithm 1, when a node picks a new slot in its frame it picks it among the unreserved slots. We obtain the following result.

Lemma 1. *For some constant c, if $\Lambda \geq c\min\{\delta_1^3, \delta_2^2\}$, all non-ready nodes become ready within $\Lambda \cdot \log n$ time slots, with probability at least $1 - \frac{1}{n}$.*

Sketch of proof: We sketch the case $\Lambda \geq c\delta_1^3$ (the case $\Lambda \geq c\delta_2^2$ is treated similarly). Let i be a non-ready node and let R_i denote the nodes that are ready in $\Delta_1(i)$. Suppose i selects a new slot σ_i, and let Z denote the following Λ slots, and Z' the preceding Λ slots. Let p_1 denote the probability that some neighbor node conflicts with σ_i (i.e. attempts to reserve the same slot), let p_2 be the probability that i hears a collision during Z, and let p_3 be the probability that i receives a conflict report during Z. Then the probability that i fails to become ready is at most $p_1 + p_2 + p_3$.

Node i selects a slot from among $\Lambda - R_i$ slots. σ_i can only conflict with a non-ready neighbor of i. Let j be one such neighbor. j chooses from among $\Lambda - R_j$ slots, therefore j selects the same slot σ_i with probability at most $1/(\Lambda - R_j) \leq 2/\Lambda$ for $\Lambda \geq 2\delta_1$ (since $R_j \leq \delta_1$). The union bound then gives $p_1 \leq 2(\delta_1 - R_i)/\Lambda \leq 2\delta_1/\Lambda$. Node i will hear a collision if two neighbors j, j' both transmit on the same slot σ_k. This occurs with probability at most $4/(\Lambda - R_j)(\Lambda - R_{j'}) \leq 16/\Lambda^2$, since a node may transmit at most twice during Z. Since there are at most Λ such slots hear a collision and at most $\delta_1^2/2$ different pairs of neighbors, the union bound gives $p_2 \leq 8\delta_1^2/\Lambda$.

A neighbor j will report a conflict in Z only if two of its neighbors collide in $Z \cup Z'$. A similar argument to the bound for p_2 bounds this probability by $16\delta_1^2/\Lambda$. Since there are at most δ_1 such neighbors, the union bound gives $p_3 \leq 16\delta_1^3/\Lambda$.

Thus, for some c, $p_1 + p_2 + p_3 \leq c\delta_1^3/\Lambda$. If $\Lambda \geq 4c\delta_1^3$, then the probability that i becomes ready is at least $\frac{1}{4}$. Consequently, after $\log n$ independent tries, i will not be ready with probability at most $4^{-\log n} = \frac{1}{n^2}$. Since there are at most n non-ready nodes, applying the union bound gives the result. ∎

2.2   Fresh Nodes

Algorithm LooseMAC adapts dynamically to nodes joining or leaving the network. When a node leaves, it informs its neighbors who can then unmark the slot they reserved for the departing node. If a node fails or crashes, it cannot inform its neighbors, and its slot will remain marked; the correctness of the algorithm and the rest of the network remain unaffected.

The situation is more complicated when a node joins the network, due to the hidden terminal problem. Suppose node i enters the network. Nodes j and k that were previously *not* 2-neighbors may now be 2-neighbors because they both become neighbors of i. In this case, j and k may be using the same slot and creating a conflict in i. Thus, j and k may need to reselect slots. To accomplish this, node i will force nodes j and k to become non-ready. In order to achieve this, when i joins the network, it is in a special status which is called *fresh*. Node i informs its neighbors about its special status by sending control messages. When a neighbor node j receives a control message from i indicating that i is fresh, then j becomes non-ready.

While i is fresh, it selects a random slot in its frame and transmits a message reporting that it is fresh. It continues to do so in the subsequent frames until it hears no collisions, nor any conflict reports. When this happens, it knows that every one of its neighbors has received its "I'm fresh" message, and so it switches to the non-fresh, non-ready status. At this point, every neighbor of i has become non-ready. i now continues with the original LooseMAC algorighm as a non-ready node. The analysis of the time for fresh nodes to become non-ready is similar to the proof of Lemma 1:

Lemma 2. *For some constant c, if $\Lambda \geq c\min\{\delta_1^3, \delta_2^2\}$, all fresh nodes become non-fresh within $\Lambda \cdot \log n$ slots with probability at least $1 - \frac{1}{n}$.*

2.3   Complexity of LooseMAC

A network is in a *stable* state when all nodes are ready. Once a network is stable, it remains so until a node joins the network. We show that from an arbitrary initial state I, the network will stabilize if no changes are made to the network. Suppose that $\Lambda \geq c \min\{\delta_1^3, \delta_2^2\}$, and let S be the set of non-ready nodes in state I. Let $S_f \subseteq S$ be the set of fresh nodes in state I.

Lemma 2 implies that, with probability at most $\frac{1}{n}$, after $\Lambda \cdot \log n$ slots, *some* node fails to become non-fresh. Similarily, after an additional $\Lambda \cdot \log n$ slots, Lemma 1 implies that, with probability at most $\frac{1}{n}$, after $\Lambda \cdot \log n$ slots, *some* node fails to become ready. Applying the union bound, we have that with probability at least $1 - \frac{2}{n}$, every node is ready after $2\Lambda \cdot \log n$ slots, i.e., w.h.p., the network has reached a stable state.

Containment. Nodes that send control messages until stabilization are *affected* nodes. Only nodes in $\Delta_1(S_f) \subseteq \Delta_1(S)$ become non-ready on account of the fresh nodes. Nodes that are neighbors of non-ready nodes may need to send control messages to report conflicts, thus the affected nodes are all in $\Delta_2(S)$.

Communication Complexity. Each affected node sends at most $O(\log n)$ control messages, since in every frame it sends at most 1 message. Each message has size $O(\log n)$ bits, since the message consists of the sender's id ($\log n$ bits), fresh status (1 bit), and conflict report (1 bit). We thus have the following theorem.

Theorem 1 (Complexity of LooseMAC). *From an arbitrary initial state I with non-ready nodes S, the network stabilizes within $2\Lambda \cdot \log n$ slots with probability at least $1 - \frac{1}{\Theta(n)}$. The affected area is $\Delta_2(S)$. Each affected node sends $O(\log n)$ messages, of size $O(\log n)$ bits.*

3   Algorithm TightMAC

We consider now the case where nodes have different frame sizes. We present the self-stabilizing Algorithm TightMAC in which each node i has a frame size proportional to ϕ_i; recall that $\phi_i = \max_{j \in \Delta_2(i)} \delta_2(j)$ is the maximum 2-neighborhood size among i's 2-neighbors. This algorithm runs on top of LooseMAC. (We refer to the frames of TightMAC as "tight", and the frames of LooseMAC as "loose".)

A node entering the network first runs LooseMAC. Once its 2-neighborhood is ready, it uses its selected slot in the loose frame (loose slot) to communicate with its neighbors. It can thus compute the size of the tight frame, and find a conflict-free tight slot (in the tight frame). Then the node starts using the tight frame's slots. The tight frames and the loose frames are interleaved so that a node can switch between them whenever necessary. This enables algorithm TightMAC to be self-stabilizing, due to the self-stabilizing nature of LooseMAC.

Ready Levels. After a node runs LooseMAC, the TightMAC algorithm requires that all nodes in its 2-neighborhood are ready (in order to compute ϕ_i). In order to make this possible, we modify the LooseMAC algorithm to incorporate

5 levels of "readiness": ready-0 (or ready); ready-1; ready-2; ready-3; and, ready-4. Further, we modify the loose frame size to be the smallest power of 2 that is at least the required loose frame size, i.e., $\Lambda = 2^{\lceil \log c \min\{\delta_1^3, \delta_2^2\} \rceil}$. A node becomes ready-0 as explained earlier in LooseMAC. A node becomes ready-K (for $K > 0$) if all nodes in its neighborhood are ready at level at least $K - 1$. We assume that when nodes send messages, they also include their ready status (fresh, not-ready, ready-0, ready-1, ready-2, ready-3 or ready-4). Thus, when a node becomes ready-K, it sends a message (in its loose slot) informing its neighbors. When a ready-K node has received ready-K messages from all of its neighbors it becomes ready-$(K+1)$ (if $K < 4$).

If a node is ready-K and hears that one of its neighbors is fresh, then it becomes not-ready. If a node hears that one of its neighbors drops down in ready level, it adjusts its ready level correspondingly. Any node that is not ready-4 is operating on the loose frame. A node starts executing the TightMAC algorithm when it is ready-4.

3.1   Description of TightMAC

Algorithm 2 gives an outline of TightMAC. A node first executes LooseMAC until it becomes ready-4. In the main loop of TightMAC, all the control messages are sent using loose slots, until the node switches to using tight frames.

Algorithm 2 TightMAC(node i).

1: **repeat**
2:     Execute LooseMAC(i)
3: **until** i becomes ready-4
4: Transmit neighborhood information and compute ϕ_i;
5: Choose a frame F_i with $|F_i| = 2^{\lceil \log 6\phi_i \rceil}$;
6: Inform neighbors for the relative position of F_i, with respect to i's loose slot;
7: Execute FindTightSlot();
8: Start using the tight frame;

The highest throughput is obtained by choosing ϕ to be the maximum 2-neighborhood size among a node's 2-neighbors, $\phi_i = \max_{j \in \Delta_2(i)} \delta_2(j)$. This means that nodes need to obtain their 2-neighborhood size, and each node needs to communicate to its 1-neighbors the actual IDs of the nodes in its 1-neighborhood, which is a message of size $O(\delta_1 \log n)$ bits. An alternative is to use an upper bound for ϕ_i, which is to take the maximum of an upper bound on the 2-neighborhood size over i's 2-neighborhood: $\overline{\phi}_i = \max_{j \in \Delta_2(i)} \overline{\delta}_2(j)$, where $\overline{\delta}_2(j) = \sum_{k \in \Delta_1(j)} \delta_1(k)$ is an upper bound on $\delta_2(j)$. Since the steady-state throughput is $1/\phi$, this results in lower throughput. However, the advantage is that only the 1-neighborhood size needs to be sent, which has a message length of $O(\log n)$ bits. In either event, only 1-neighborhood information needs to be exchanged (whether it is 1- neighborhood node IDs or 1-neighborhood size).

When a node becomes ready-1, it knows its 1-neighborhood (by examining the number of marked slots in its loose frame), so it can send the relevant information to its neighbors. When a node becomes ready-2, it will have received the 1-neighborhood information from all its neighbors. It processes this information to compute either δ_2 or $\overline{\delta_2}$, which it transmits. When a node becomes ready-3, it will have received the δ_2 or $\overline{\delta_2}$ information from all its neighbors and hence can take the maximum which it transmits. When a node becomes ready-4, it will have received maximums from all its neighbors, so it can take the maximum of these maximums to compute ϕ or $\overline{\phi}$. This entire process requires at most 3 control messages from each node. For simplicity we will present most of the results using ϕ_i and $\delta_2(i)$. The same results hold for $\overline{\phi}_i$ and $\overline{\delta}_2(i)$ with similar proofs.

Finally, node i chooses its tight frame size F_i to be the smallest power of 2 that is at least $6\phi_i$; i notifies its neighbors about the position of F_i relative to its loose slot (this information will be needed for the neighbor nodes to determine whether the tight slots conflict); and, node i executes FindTightSlot (described in Section 3.2) to compute its conflict-free tight slot in F_i. After the tight slot is computed, node i switches to using its tight frame F_i.

To ensure proper interleaving of the loose and tight frames, in F_i, in addition to the tight slot, node i also reserves slots for its loose slot and all other marked slots in its loose frame. This way, the slots used by LooseMAC are preserved and can be re-used even in the tight frame. This is useful when node i becomes non-ready, or some neighbor is non-ready, and i needs to execute the LooseMAC algorithm again.

3.2   Algorithm FindTightSlot

The heart of TightMAC is algorithm FindTightSlot, which obtains conflict-free slots in the tight frames. The tight frames have different sizes at various nodes which depends locally on ϕ_i. Different frame sizes can cause additional conflicts between the selected slots of neighbors. For example, consider nodes i and j with respective frames F_i and F_j. Let s_i be a slot of F_i. Every time that the frames repeat, s_i overlaps with the same slots in F_j. The *coincidence set* $C_{i,j}(s_i)$ is the set of time slots in F_j that overlap with s_i in any repetitions of the two frames. If $|F_i| \geq |F_j|$, then s_i overlaps with exactly one time slot of F_j. If on the other hand $|F_i| < |F_j|$, then $|C_{i,j}(s_i)| > 1$. Nodes i and j *conflict* if their selected slots s_i and s_j are chosen so that $s_j \in C_{i,j}(s_i)$ (or equivalently $s_i \in C_{j,i}(s_j)$); in other words, s_i and s_j overlap at some repetition of the frames F_i and F_j.

The task of algorithm FindTightSlot for node i is to find a conflict-free slot in F_i. In order to detect conflicts, node i uses a slot reservation mechanism, similar to the marking mechanism of LooseMAC. When frame F_i is created, node i reserves in each F_i as many slots as the marked slots in its loose frame. This way, when FindTightSlot selects slots, it will avoid using the slots of the loose frame, and thus, both frames can coexist.

Slot selection proceeds as follows. Node i attempts to select an unreserved conflict-free slot in the first $6\delta_2(i)$ slots of F_i. We will show that this is possible. Node i then notifies its neighbors of its choice using its loose slot. Each neighbor

---

Algorithm 3 FindTightSlot().

1: SlotFound ← FALSE;
2: **while** not SlotFound **do**
3:     Select ← FALSE;
4:     With probability $1/\phi_i$: Select ← TRUE;
5:     **if** Select **then**
6:         Let s_i be an randomly chosen unreserved slot in the first $6\delta_2(i)$ slots of F_i;
7:         Send the position of s_i (relative to its loose slot);
8:         Listen for a period of Λ time slots;
9:         **if** no conflict is reported by any neighbor **then**
10:             SlotFound ← TRUE;

---

j then checks if σ_i creates any conflicts in their own tight slots, by examining whether s_i conflicts with reserved slots in j's tight and loose frame. If conflicts occur, then j responds with a conflict report message (again in its loose slot). Node i listens for Λ time slots. During this period, if a neighbor detected a conflict, it reports it. Otherwise the neighbor marks this slot as belonging to i (deleting any previously marked tight slot for i). If i receives a conflict report, the process repeats, with i selecting another tight slot. If i does not receive a conflict report, then fixes this tight slot. Note that this communication between i and its neighbors can occur because all its neighbors are at least ready-2.

In the algorithm, a node chooses to select a new slot with probability $1/\phi_i$, so not many nodes attempt to select a slot at the same time, which increases the likelihood that the selection is succesful. This is what allows us to show stabilization with low message complexity, even with small frame sizes.

The intuition behind the frame size choice of approximately $6\phi_i$ is as follows. Take some node j which is a 2-neighbor of i. Node j chooses a slot in the first $Z = 6\delta_2(j)$ of its tight frame F_j. Node i has frame size larger than Z. Thus, node i cannot have more than one slot repetition in Z. This implies that i and j conflict at most once during Z in their tight frames, and so, the possible conflicting slots for j during Z are bounded by the 2-neighborhood size of j. This observation is the basis for the probabilistic analysis of the algorithm.

Lemma 3. *Let node $j \in \Delta_2(i)$ select tight slot s_j; s_j does not cause conflicts in any node of $\Delta_1(i)$ with probability at least $1/2$.*

Proof. The neighbors of j have reserved at most $2\delta_1(j)$ slots in j (one loose and one tight slot). Therefore, node j chooses its slot s_j from among $6\delta_2(j) - 2\delta_1(j) \geq 4\delta_2(j)$ unreserved slots in its frame F_j. This slot can cause conflicts only in neighbors of i that are in $S = \Delta_1(i) \cap \Delta_1(j) \subseteq \Delta_1(j)$. The only nodes that can reserve slots in members of S are therefore 2-neighbors of j. Each such node can mark at most two slots (one loose and one tight slot), and so at most $2\delta_2(j)$ (absolute) time slots which can possibly conflict with s_j are reserved in *all* the nodes in S. Therefore, there are at least $2\delta_2(j)$ slots available, of the $4\delta_2(j)$ chosen from, hence the probability of causing no conflict is at least $\frac{1}{2}$.

Lemma 4. *For node i, during a period of Λ time slots, no conflicts occur in $\Delta_1(i)$ with probability at least $1/2$.*

Proof. Let Z be the period of Λ time slots. A conflict is caused during Z in $\Delta_1(i)$ by any slot selection of nodes in $\Delta_2(i)$. A slot selection by node $j \in \Delta_2(i)$ occurs with probability $1/\phi_j$. From Lemma 3, a slot selection of j causes conflicts in $\Delta_1(i)$ with probability at most $1/2$. There are at most $\delta_2(i)$ nodes similar to j. Let q be the probability that any of them causes a conflict during Z in $\Delta_1(i)$, then $q \leq \delta_2(i)/(2\min_{\{j \in \Delta_2(i)\}} \phi_j)$. Since for any $j \in \Delta_2(i)$, $\phi_j \geq \delta_2(i)$, we have that $q \leq \frac{1}{2}$, hence the probability of no conflicts is $1 - q \geq \frac{1}{2}$.

Lemma 4 implies that every time i selects a slot in its tight frame, this slot is conflict-free with probability at least $1/2$. Since i selects a time slot with probability $1/\phi_i$ in every loose frame, in the expected case i will select a slot within $O(\phi_i)$ repetitions of the loose frame. We obtain the following result.

Corollary 1. *For some constant c, within $c \cdot \phi_i \cdot \Lambda \cdot \log n$ time slots, a ready-4 node successfully chooses a conflict-free tight time slot in F_i, with probability at least $1 - \frac{1}{n^2}$.*

3.3 Complexity of TightMAC

The network is *stable* if all nodes in the network have selected conflict-free tight slots. When a network stabilizes, it remains so until some node joins/leaves the network. We now show that starting from an arbitrary initial state I, if no changes occur in the network after I, the network reaches a stable state.

Let S be the non-ready nodes in state I. By Theorem 1, with high probability, LooseMAC requires $O(\Lambda \log n)$ time slots for all nodes to become ready. Then, $O(1)$ time is required for the nodes to become ready-4. Consider a node i. Suppose that the algorithm uses $\overline{\phi}_i$ and $\overline{\delta}_2(i)$ for practical considerations (smaller message sizes). Node i sends $O(1)$ messages of size $O(\log n)$ bits so that itself and its neighbors can compute $\overline{\phi}$. From Corollary 1, with high probability, node i then requires $O(\overline{\phi}_i \Lambda \log n)$ time slots to select a conflict-free tight slot. Since, $\delta_1^2 \geq \overline{\phi}_i$, the total time for stabilization is $O(\delta_1^2 \Lambda \log n)$. When a fresh node i arrives the nodes in $\Delta_5(i)$ drop in ready level, hence the affected area is at most $\Delta_6(i)$. Following an analysis similar to Corollary 1, we obtain the following theorem.

Theorem 2 (Complexity of TightMAC). *From an arbitrary initial state I, with non-ready nodes S, the network stabilizes within $O(\delta_1^2 \cdot \Lambda \cdot \log n)$ time slots, with probability at least $1 - \frac{1}{\Theta(n)}$. The affected area is $\Delta_6(S)$. Each affected node sends $O(\log n)$ messages, of size $O(\log n)$ bits.*

4   Discussion

We have introduced and presented the theoretical analysis of a distributed, contention-free MAC protocol. This protocol is frame based and has the desirable properties of self-stabilization and containment, i.e., changes to the network only affect the local area of the change, and the protocol automatically adapts to accommodate the change. Further, the efficiency of the protocol depends only on the local topology of the network, and so bottlenecks do not affect the entire network. In general, such frame based protocols tend to be preferable when traffic is constant (rather than bursty).

The time to stabilization and throughput are related to the maximum 1 or 2-neighborhood size. For unit disc graphs, the maximum k-neighborhood size δ_k grows at the same rate as the 1-neighborhood size, i.e., $\delta_1 = \Omega(\delta_k)$ for fixed k. Since the average 1-neighborhood size required to ensure connectivity in random graphs is $O(\log n)$, [11], it follows that throughput is inverse polylogarithmic and time to stabilization is polylogarithmic in the network size.

Practical Considerations. Our model assumes that a node detects a collision if and only if two or more nodes (including itself) within its transmission radius attempt to transmit. One way to distinguish a collision from random background noise is to place a threshold on the power of the incoming signal. Signals with sufficiently high power are collisions. Since wireless signals attenuate with distance rather than drop to zero at the transmission radius, it is then possible many nodes that are outside the transmission radius will transmit at the same time, resulting in a collision detected at the central node, even though none of the nodes are actually colliding. The correctness of the algorithm is not affected, however the required frame size or convergence time may get affected, because (for example) a spurious collision may prevent a node from taking a time slot. A natural next step is to investigate such issues using simulation techniques for real sensor networks.

We have assumed that the time slots of the nodes are aligned, even though the frames may not be aligned. This simplification is not necessary, because we can accommodate misaligned time slots by having a node become ready in its time slot only if there are no collisions detected in its time slot as well as neighboring time slots. This means that a node's time slot may block off at most 4 time slots at every one of its two neighbors, which means that the frame size will have to be at most a constant factor larger.

All our discussion applies when there is no relative drift between the local clocks of the nodes. In practice there can be a very small drift (clock skew). One approach to addressing this problem is to run a clock skew algorithm (for example [3]) on top of our protocol. Another solution which illustrates the value of the self stabilizing nature of our protocol is to allow the algorithm to automatically address the clock skew when it leads to a collision. In such an event, the algorithm will re-stabilize and the communication can continue from there. This second approach will be acceptable providing the clock skew results in collisions at a rate that is much slower than the rate of stabilization.

Future Research. Two natural directions are to improve the convergence properties or to obtain lower bounds on the stabilization time and/or the required frame size for any such distributed contention free algorithm which does not use global time synchronization. Many aspects of our protocol are hard to analyze theoretically and would benefit from experimental analysis, for example, how the performance varies with the rate at which the network topology is changing, or what the lifetime of the network will be. Further, we have made certain simplifying assumptions such as the graph is undirected, when in fact link quality may vary with time. Future directions would be to investigate how the choice of the power level would interact with such parameters as the performance of the protocol, the lifetime of the network and the connectivity of the network. It would also be useful to compare the performance of our algorithms with existing algorithms (such as IEEE 802.11 and TDMA) on real networks using simulation packages (such as OPNET and NS2).

References

1. Abramson, N.: The ALOHA System - Another Alternative for Computer Communications. Proceedings of the AFIPS Conference, vol. 37, pp. 295-298, 1970.
2. Ammar, M.H., Stevens, D. S.: A Distributed TDMA Rescheduling Procedure for Mobile Packet Radio Networks. Proceedings of IEEE International Conference on Communications (ICC), pp. 1609-1613, Denver, CO, June 1991.
3. Arvind, K.: Probabilistic Clock Synchronization in Distributed Systems. IEEE Trans. Parallel Distrib. Syst., vol. 5, no. 5, pp. 474–487, 1994.
4. Busch, C., Magdon-Ismail, M., Sivrikaya, F., Yener, B.: Contention-Free MAC protocols for Wireless Sensor Networks. Technical Report, Rensselaer Polytechnic Institute, 2004. Available at http://www.cs.rpi.edu/research/tr.html.
5. Cerpa, A., Estrin, D.: ASCENT: Adaptive Self-configuring Sensor Network Topologies. Proceedings of INFOCOM'02, 2002.
6. Chen, B., Jamieson, K., Balakrishnan, H., Morris, R.: Span: An Energy-efficient Coordination Algorithm for Topology Maintenance in Ad Hoc Wireless Networks. Proceedings of ACM International Conference On Mobile Computing And Networking (MOBICOM'01), 2001.
7. Chlamtac, I., Franta, W. R., Levin, K.: BRAM: The Broadcast Recognizing Access Method. IEEE Transactions on Communications, vol. 27, no. 8, August 1979.
8. Cidon, I., Sidi, M.: Distributed Assignment Algorithms for Multihop Packet Radio Networks. IEEE Transactions on Computers, vol. 38, no. 10, pp. 1353-1361, October 1989.
9. ElBatt, T., Ephremides, A.: Joint Scheduling and Power Control for Wireless Ad Hoc Networks. IEEE Computer and Communications Conference (INFOCOM), June 2002.
10. Farber, D., Feldman, J., Heinrich, F.R., Hopwood, M.D., Larson, K.C., Loomis, D.C., Rowe, L.A.: The Distributed Computing System. Proceedings of IEEE COMPCON, pp. 31-34, San Francisco, CA, February 1973.
11. P. Gupta and P. R. Kumar: Critical power for asymptotic connectivity in wireless networks. in Stochastic Analysis, Control, Optimization and Applications, A Volume in Honor of W.H. Fleming. Edited by W.M. McEneany, G. Yin, and Q. Zhang, pp 547–566. Birkhauser, 1998.
12. Kannan, R., Kalidindi, R., Iyengar, S.S., Kumar, V.: Energy and Rate based MAC Protocol for Wireless Sensor Networks. ACM SIGMOD Record, vol. 32 no. 4, pp. 60-65, 2003.

13. Kleinrock, L., Scholl, M.O.: Packet Switching in Radio Channels: New Conflict-free Multiple Access Schemes. IEEE Transactions on Communications, vol. 28, no. 7, pp. 1015-1029, July 1980.

14. Kleinrock, L., Tobagi, F.A.: Packet Switching in Radio Channels: Part I - Carrier Sense Multiple-Access Modes and their Throughput-Delay Characteristics. IEEE Transactions on Communications, vol. 23, no. 12, pp. 1400-1416, December 1975.

15. Martin, J.: Communication Satellite Systems. Prentice Hall, New Jersey, 1978.

16. Monks, J.P., Bharghavan, V., Hwu, W.: A Power Controlled Multiple Access Protocol for Wireless Packet Networks. Proceedings of the IEEE INFOCOM 2001, Anchorage, Alaska, April, 2001.

17. Muqattash A., Krunz, M.: Power Controlled Dual Channel (PCDC) Medium Access Protocol for Wireless Ad Hoc Networks. Proceedings of the IEEE INFOCOM 2003 Conference, San Francisco, April 2003.

18. Muqattash, A., Krunz, M.: CDMA-based MAC protocol for Wireless Ad Hoc Networks. Proceedings of the ACM MobiHoc 2003 Conference, Annapolis, Maryland, June 2003.

19. Nelson, R., Kleinrock, L.: Spatial TDMA: A Collision Free multihop Channel Access Protocol. IEEE Transactions on Communications, vol. 33, no. 9, pp. 934-944, September 1985.

20. Rajendran, V., Obraczka, K., Garcia-Luna-Aceves, J.J.: Energy-Efficient, Collision-Free Medium Access Control for Wireless Sensor Networks. Proceedings of ACM SenSys'03, pp. 181-192, 2003.

21. Roberts, L.G.: ALOHA Packet System with and without Slots and Capture. Computer Communications Review, vol. 5, no. 2, April 1975.

22. Singh, S., Raghavendra, C.S.: Power Efficient MAC Protocol for Multihop Radio Networks. Nineth IEEE International Personal, Indoor and Mobile Radio Communications Conference (PIMRC'98), pp:153-157, 1998.

23. Tobagi, F., Kleinrock, L.: Packet Switching in Radio Channels: Part IV - Stability Considerations and Dynamic Control in Carrier Sense Multiple-Access. IEEE Transactions on Communications, vol. 25, no. 10, pp. 1103-1119, October 1977.

24. Truong, T.V.: TDMA in Mobile Radio Networks: An Assessment of Certain Approaches. Proceedings of IEEE GLOBECOM, pp. 504-507, Atlanta, GA, Nov, 1984.

25. Viterbi, A.J.: CDMA: Principles of Spread Spectrum Communication. Addison-Wesley, Reading, MA, 1995.

26. Woo, A., Culler, D.: A Transmission Control Scheme for Media Access in Sensor Networks. In proceedings of Mobicom 2001, pp 221-235.

27. Wu, S.L., Tseng, Y.C., Sheu, J.P.: Intelligent Medium Access for Mobile Ad-hoc Networks with Busy Tones and Power Control. IEEE Journal on Selected Areas in Communications (JSAC), 18(9):1647–1657, 2000.

28. Xu, Y., Heidemann, J., Estrin, D.: Geography-informed Energy Conservation for Ad Hoc Routing. Proceedings of ACM International Conference On Mobile Computing And Networking (MOBICOM'01), 2001.

29. Wireless LAN Medium Access Control (MAC) and Physical Layer (PHY) Specifications. IEEE standards 802.11, January 1997.

30. Ye, W., Heidemann, J., Estrin, D.: Medium Access Control with Coordinated, Adaptive Sleeping for Wireless Sensor Networks. IEEE/ACM Transactions on Networking, vol. 12, no. 3, pp. 493-506, June 2004.

Relationships Between Broadcast and Shared Memory in Reliable Anonymous Distributed Systems

James Aspnes[1], Faith Fich[2], and Eric Ruppert[3]

[1] Yale University
[2] University of Toronto
[3] York University

Abstract. We study the power of reliable anonymous distributed systems, where processes do not fail, do not have identifiers, and run identical programmes. We are interested specifically in the relative powers of systems with different communication mechanisms: anonymous broadcast, read-write registers, or registers supplemented with additional shared-memory objects. We show that a system with anonymous broadcast can simulate a system of shared-memory objects if and only if the objects satisfy a property we call *idemdicence*; this result holds regardless of whether either system is synchronous or asynchronous. Conversely, the key to simulating anonymous broadcast in anonymous shared memory is the ability to count: broadcast can be simulated by an asynchronous shared-memory system that uses only counters, but registers by themselves are not enough. We further examine the relative power of different types and sizes of bounded counters and conclude with a non-robustness result.

1 Introduction

Consider a minimal reliable distributed system, perhaps a collection of particularly cheap wireless sensor nodes. The processes execute the same code, because it is too costly to program them individually. They lack identities, because identities require customization beyond the capabilities of mass production. And they communicate only by broadcast, because broadcast presupposes no infrastructure. Where fancier systems provide specialized roles, randomization, point-to-point routing, or sophisticated synchronization primitives, this system is just a big bag of deterministic clones shouting at one another. The processes' only saving grace is that their uniformity makes them absolutely reliable—no misplaced sense of individuality will tempt any of them to Byzantine behaviour, no obscure undebugged path through their common code will cause a crash, and no glitch in their nonexistent network will lose any messages. The processes may also have distinct inputs, which saves them from complete solipsism, even though processes with the same input cannot tell themselves apart. What can such a system do?

Although anonymous systems have been studied before (see Section 1.1), much of the work has focused on systems where processes communicate with

R. Guerraoui (Ed.): DISC 2004, LNCS 3274, pp. 260–274, 2004.

one another by passing point-to-point messages or by accessing shared read-write registers. In this paper, we start with simple broadcast systems, where processes transmit messages to all of the processes (including themselves), which are delivered serially but with no return addresses. We characterize the power of such systems by showing what classes of shared-memory objects they can simulate. In Section 3, we show that such a system can simulate a shared object if and only if the object can always return the same response whenever it is accessed twice in a row by identical operations, a property we call *idemdicence*; examples of such idemdicent objects include read-write registers, counters (with separate increment and read operations), and any object for which any operation that modifies the state returns only *ack*.

This characterization does not depend on whether either the underlying broadcast system or the simulated shared-memory system is synchronous or asynchronous. The equivalence of synchrony and asynchrony is partially the result of the lack of failures, because in an asynchronous system we can just wait until every process has taken a step before moving on to the next simulated synchonous round, but it also depends on the model's primitives providing enough power that detecting this condition is possible.

Characterizing the power of broadcast systems in terms of what shared-memory objects they can simulate leads us to consider the closely related question of what power is provided by different kinds of shared-memory objects. We show in Section 4 that counters of sufficient size relative to the number of processes, n, are enough to simulate an anonymous broadcast model, even if no other objects are available, which in turn means that they can simulate any reliable anonymous shared-memory system with idemdicent objects. In contrast, read-write registers by themselves cannot simulate broadcast, because they cannot distinguish between different numbers of processes with the same input value, while broadcasts can.

This leads us to consider further the relative power of different sizes of counters in an anonymous system. We show in Section 5 that mod-m counters are inherently limited if the number of processes, n, exceeds m by more than two, although they become more powerful when $n = m + 1$ if read-write registers are also available. Although these results hint at a hierarchy of increasingly powerful anonymous shared-memory objects, any such hierarchy is not *robust* [11, 12]; we show in Section 6 that mod-m counters with different values of m can simulate more objects together than they can alone. Previous non-robustness results typically use rather unusual object types, designed specifically for the non-robustness proofs (see [8] for a survey). The result given here is the first to use natural objects.

1.1   Related Work

Some early impossibility results in message-passing systems assumed that processes were anonymous [1]. This assumption makes symmetry-based arguments possible: all processes behave identically, so they cannot solve problems that require symmetry to be broken. A wide range of these results are surveyed in [8].

Typically, they assume that the underlying communication network is symmetric (often a ring or regular graph); our broadcast model is a complete graph. Some work has been done on characterizing the problems that are solvable in anonymous message-passing systems, depending on the initial knowledge of processes (see, for example, [4, 5, 15]).

With randomization, processes can choose identities at random from a large range, which solves the *naming problem* with high probability. Unfortunately, Buhrman *et al.* [6] show that no protocol allows processes to *detect* whether they have solved this problem in an asynchronous shared-memory model providing only read-write registers. Surprisingly, they show that wait-free consensus can nonetheless be solved in this model. The upper bound for consensus has since been extended to an anonymous model with infinitely many processes by Aspnes, Shah, and Shah [2].

Attiya, Gorbach and Moran [3] give a systematic study of the power of asynchronous, failure-free anonymous shared-memory systems that are equipped with read-write registers only. They characterize the agreement tasks that can be solved in this model if the number of processes is unknown. Drulă has shown the characterization is the same if the number of processes is known [7]. In particular, consensus is solvable, assuming the shared registers can be initialized. If they cannot, consensus is unsolvable [13]. Attiya *et al.* also give complexity lower bounds for solving consensus in their model.

The robustness question has been extensively studied in non-anonymous systems. It was first addressed by Jayanti [11, 12]. See [8] for a discussion of previous work on robustness.

2   Models

We consider *anonymous* models of distributed systems, where each process executes the same algorithm. Processes do not have identifiers, but they may begin with input values (depending on the problem being solved). We assume algorithms are deterministic and that systems are reliable (i.e. failures do not occur). Let $n \geq 2$ denote the number of processes in the system.

We assume throughout that the value of n is known to all processes. This assumption can be relaxed in some models even if new processes can join the system. In a shared-memory model with unbounded counters, it is easy to maintain the number of processes by having a process increment a size counter when it first joins the system. In a broadcast model, a new process can start by broadcasting an arrival message. Processes keep track of the number of arrival messages they have received and respond to each one by broadcasting this number. Processes use the largest number they have received as their current value for size. Algorithms will work correctly when started after this number has stabilized.

In the *asynchronous broadcast* model, each process may execute a *broadcast(msg)* command at any time. This command sends a copy of the message *msg* to each process in the system. The message is eventually delivered to all processes (including the process that sent it), but the delivery time may be different for different recipients and can be arbitrarily large. Thus, broadcasted messages are not globally ordered: they may arrive in different orders at different recipients.

A *synchronous broadcast model* is similar, but assumes that every process broadcasts one message per round, and that this message is received by all processes before the next round begins.

We also consider an anonymous shared-memory model, where processes can communicate with one another by accessing shared data structures, called *objects*. A process may invoke an operation on an object, and at some later time it will receive a response from the object. We assume that objects are linearizable [10], so that each operation performed on an object appears to take place instantaneously at some time between the operation's invocation and response (even though the object may in fact be accessed concurrently by several processes). The *type* of an object specifies what operations may be performed on it. Each object type has a set of possible states. We assume that a programmer may initialize a shared object to any state. An operation may change the state of the object and then return a result to the invoking process that may depend on the old state of the object. A *step* of an execution specifies an operation, the process that performs this operation, the object on which it is performed, and the result returned by the operation.

A *read-write register* is an example of an object. It has a *read* operation that returns the state of the object without changing the state. It also supports *write* operations that return *ack* and set the state of the object to a specified value.

Another example of an object is an *(unbounded) counter*. It has state set $\mathbf{N}$ and supports two operations: *read*, which returns the current state without changing it, and *increment*, which adds 1 to the current state and returns *ack*.

There are many ways to define a *bounded* counter, i.e., one that uses a bounded amount of space. For any positive integer m, a *mod-m counter* has state set $\{0, 1, 2, \ldots, m - 1\}$ and an increment changes the state from x to $(x + 1) \bmod m$. A *threshold-m counter* has state set $\{0, 1, 2, \ldots, m\}$. An increment adds 1 to the current state provided it is less than m and otherwise leaves it unchanged. A read of a mod-m or threshold-m counter returns the current state without changing it. An *m-valued counter* also has state set $\{0, 1, 2, \ldots, m\}$ and increment behaves the same as for a threshold-m counter. However, the behaviour of the read operation becomes unpredictable after m increments: in state m, a read operation may nondeterministically return any of the values $0, 1, 2, \ldots, m - 1$, or may even fail to terminate. Note that both mod-m counters and threshold-$(m - 1)$ counters are implementations of m-valued counters. Also, for $m' > m$, an m'-valued counter is an implementation of an m-valued counter.

In an *asynchronous* shared-memory system, processes run at arbitrarily varying speeds, and each operation on an object is completed in a finite but unbounded time. The scheduler is required to be fair in that it allocates an opportunity for each process to take a step infinitely often. In a *synchronous* shared-memory system, processes run at the same speed; the computation proceeds in rounds. During each round, each process can perform one access to shared memory. Several processes may access the same object during a round, but the order in which those accesses are linearized is determined by an adversarial scheduler.

An example of a synchronous shared-memory system is the anonymous AR-BITRARY PRAM. This is a CRCW PRAM model where all processes run the same code and the adversary chooses which of any set of simultaneous writes succeeds. It is equivalent to a synchronous shared-memory model in which all writes in a given round are linearized before all reads. PRAM models have been studied extensively for non-anonymous systems (e.g. [14]).

3   When Broadcast Can Simulate Shared Memory

In this section, we characterize the types of shared-memory systems that can be simulated by the broadcast model in the setting of failure-free, anonymous systems. We also consider the functions that can be computed in this model.

Definition 1. *An operation on a shared object is called* idemdicent[1] *if, for every starting state, two consecutive invocations of the operation on an object (with the same arguments) can return identical answers to the processes that invoked the operations.*

It follows by induction that any number of repetitions of the same idemdicent operation on an object can all return the same result. *Idempotent* operations are idemdicent operations that leave the object in the same state whether they are applied once or many times consecutively. Reads and writes are idempotent operations. Increment operations for the various counters defined in Section 2 are idemdicent, but are not idempotent. In fact, any operation that always returns *ack* is idemdicent.

An object is called idemdicent if every operation that can be performed on the object is idemdicent. Similarly, an object is called idempotent if every operation that can be performed on the object is idempotent. Examples of idempotent objects include registers, sticky bits, snapshots and resettable consensus objects.

Theorem 2. *A n-process asynchronous broadcast system can simulate an n-process synchronous shared-memory system that uses only idemdicent objects.*

Proof. Each process simulates a different process and maintains a local copy of the state of each simulated shared object. We now describe how a process P simulates the execution of the rth round of the shared-memory computation. Suppose P wants to perform an operation op on object X. It broadcasts the message (r, X, op). (If a process does not wish to perform a shared-memory operation during the round, it can broadcast the message (r, nil, nil) instead.) Then, P waits until it has received n messages of the form $(r, *, *)$, including the message it broadcast.

Process P orders all of the messages in lexicographic order and uses this as the order in which the round's shared-memory operations are linearized. Process P simulates this sequence of operations on its local copies of the shared objects to

---

[1] From Latin *idem* same + *dicens -entis* present participle of *dicere* say, by analogy with idempotent.

update the states of the objects and to determine the result of its own operation during that round. All identical operations on an object are grouped together in the lexicographic ordering, so they all return the same result, since the objects are idemdicent. This is the property that allows P to determine the result of its own operation if several processes perform the same operation during the round. □

Since a synchronous execution is possible in an asynchronous system, an asynchronous shared-memory system with only idemdicent objects can be simulated by a synchronous system with the same set of objects and, hence, by the asynchronous broadcast model. However, even an asynchronous system with one non-idemdicent object cannot be simulated by a synchronous broadcast system nor, hence, by an asynchronous broadcast system. The difficulty is that a non-idemdicent object can be used to break symmetry.

Theorem 3. *A synchronous broadcast system cannot simulate an asynchronous shared-memory system if any of the shared objects are non-idemdicent.*

Proof. Let X be an object that is not idemdicent. Consider the *k-election problem*, where processes receive no input, and exactly k processes must output 1 while the remaining processes output 0. We shall show that it is possible to solve k-election for some k, where $0 < k < n$, using X, but that there is no such election algorithm using broadcasts. The claim follows from these two facts.

Initialize object X to a state q where the next two invocations of some operation op will return different results r and r'. The election algorithm requires each process to perform op on X. Those processes that receive the result r output 1, and all others output 0. Let k be the number of operations that return r if op is performed n times on X, starting from state q. Clearly, this algorithm solves k-election. Furthermore, $k > 0$ since the first operation will return r, and $k < n$ since the second operation will return $r' \neq r$.

In a synchronous broadcast system, where processes receive no input, all processes will execute the same sequence of steps and be in identical states at the end of each round. Thus, k-election is impossible in such a system if $0 < k < n$. □

A function of n inputs is called *symmetric* if the function value does not change when the n inputs are permuted. We say an anonymous system *computes* a symmetric function of n inputs if each process begins with one input and eventually outputs the value of the function evaluated at those inputs. (It does not make sense to talk about computing non-symmetric functions in an anonymous system, since there is no ordering of the processes.)

Proposition 4. *Every symmetric function can be computed in the asynchronous broadcast model.*

Proof. Any symmetric function can be computed as follows. Each process broadcasts its input value. When a process has received n messages, it orders the n input values arbitrarily and computes the function at those values. □

4   When Counters Can Simulate Broadcast

In this section, we consider conditions under which unbounded and various types of bounded counters can be used to simulate broadcast. In the following section, we consider when different types of bounded counters can be used to simulate one another, which will show that some cannot be used to simulate broadcast.

We begin by proving that an asynchronous shared-memory system with mod-n counters can be used to simulate a synchronous broadcast system. Unbounded counters can simulate mod-n counters (and hence synchronous broadcast). Moreover, since counters are idemdicent, an asynchronous shared-memory system with counters can be simulated by an asynchronous broadcast system. Hence, shared-memory systems with mod-n counters, shared-memory systems with unbounded counters, and atomic broadcast systems are equivalent in power.

Theorem 5. *An n-process asynchronous shared-memory system with mod-n counters or unbounded counters can simulate the n-process synchronous broadcast system.*

Proof. The idea is to have each of the n asynchronous processes simulate a different synchronous process and have a mod-n counter for each possible message that can be sent in a given round. Each process that wants to send a message that round increments the corresponding counter. Another mod-n counter, *WriteCounter*, is used to keep track of how many processes have finished this first phase. After all processes have finished the first phase, they all read the message counters to find out which messages were sent that round. One additional mod-n counter, *ReadCounter*, is used to keep track of how many processes have finished the second phase. Simulation of the next round can begin when all processes have finished the second phase.

Let d denote the number of different possible messages that can be sent. The shared counter $M[i]$ corresponds to the i-th possible message (say, in lexicographic order) that can be sent in the current round. For $i = 1, \ldots, d$, the local variables $x_{0,i}$ and $x_{1,i}$, are used by a process to store the value of $M[i]$ in the most recent even- and odd-numbered round, respectively. The variables $x_{0,1}, \ldots, x_{0,d}$ are initialized to 0 at the beginning of the simulation. *WriteCounter* and *ReadCounter* are also initialized to 0.

The simulation of each round is carried out in two phases. In phase 1, a process that wants to broadcast the i-th possible message increments $M[i]$ and then increments *WriteCounter*. A process that does not want to broadcast in this round just increments *WriteCounter*. In either case, each process repeatedly reads *WriteCounter* until it has value 0, at which point it begins phase 2. Note that *WriteCounter* will have value 0 whenever a new round begins, because each of the n processes will increment it exactly once each round.

In phase 2, each process reads the values from $M[1], \ldots, M[d]$ and stores them in its local variables $x_{r,1}, \ldots, x_{r,d}$, where r is the parity of the current round. From these values and the values of $x_{1-r,1}, \ldots, x_{1-r,d}$, the process can determine the number of occurrences of each possible message that were supposed to be sent during that round. Specifically, the number of occurrences of the i-th possible message is $x_{r,i} - x_{1-r,i}$ mod n, except when this is the message that the process sent and $x_{r,i} = x_{1-r,i}$. In this one exceptional case, the number of occurrences of the i-th possible message is n rather than 0. Once the process knows the set of messages that were sent that round, it can simulate the rest of the round by doing any necessary local computation. Finally, the process increments *ReadCounter* and then repeatedly reads it until it has value 0. At this point, the process can begin simulation of the next phase.

Since an unbounded counter can be used to directly simulate a mod-n counter by taking the result of every read modulo n, the simulation will also work for unbounded counters. However, the values in the counters can get increasing large as the simulation of the execution proceeds.

The number of counters used by this algorithm is $\Theta(d)$. If d is very large (or unbounded), the space complexity of this algorithm is poor. The number of counters can be improved to $\Theta(n)$ by simulating the construction of a trie data structure [9] over the messages transmitted by the processes; up to $4n$ counters are used to transmit the trie level by level, with each group of 4 used to count the number of 0 children and 1 children of each node constructed so far.

In terms of messages, processes broadcast their messages one bit per round and wait until all other messages are finished before proceeding to their next message. However, it does not suffice to count the number of 0's and 1's sent during each of the rounds. For example, it is necessary to distinguish between when messages 00 and 11 are sent and when messages 01 and 10 are sent.

Each process uses the basic algorithm described above to broadcast the first bit of its message. Once processes know the first k bits of all messages that are k or more bits in length, they determine the next bit of each message or whether the message is complete. Four counters ($M[0]$, $M[1]$, *WriteCounter*, and *Read-Counter*) are allocated for each distinct k-bit prefix that has been seen. Since all processes have seen the same k-bit prefixes, they can agree on this allocation without any communication with one another. If a process has a message $s_1 s_2 \ldots s_\ell$, where $\ell > k$, it participates in an execution of the basic algorithm described above to broadcast s_{k+1}, using the four counters assigned to the prefix $s_1 s_2 \ldots s_k$. Each process also participates in executions of the basic algorithms for the other k-bit prefixes that have been seen, but does not send messages in them. This procedure to broadcast one more bit of the input of a message is continued until no process has these k bits as a proper prefix of its message. Because counters are reused for different bits of the messages, the number of counters needed is at most $4n$. $\square$

A similar algorithm can be used to simulate the n-process synchronous broadcast system using threshold-n or $(n+1)$-valued counters, provided the counters support a decrement operation or a reset operation. Decrement changes the state of such a counter from $x \in \{1, \ldots, n\}$ to $x - 1$. Decrement leaves a threshold-n counter in state 0 unchanged. In an $(n+1)$-valued counter, when decrement is performed in state 0 or $n+1$, the new state is $n+1$. Reset changes the state of a counter to 0. The only exception is that an $(n+1)$-valued counter in state $n+1$ does not change state. Both decrement and reset always return *ack*.

Theorem 6. *An n-process asynchronous shared-memory system with threshold-n or $(n+1)$-valued counters that also support a decrement or reset operation can simulate the n-process synchronous broadcast system.*

Proof. In this simulation, there is an additional counter, *ResetCounter*, and each round has a third phase. *ReadCounter* and *ResetCounter* are initialized to n. All other counters are initialized to 0.

In phase 1 of a round, a process that wants to broadcast the i-th possible message increments $M[i]$, then decrements or resets *ReadCounter*, and, finally increments *WriteCounter*. A process that does not want to broadcast in this round does not increment $M[i]$ for any i. In either case, each process then repeatedly reads *WriteCounter* until it has value n. Note that when *WriteCounter* first has value n, *ReadCounter* will have value 0.

In phase 2, each process first decrements or resets *ResetCounter*. Next, it reads the values from $M[1], \ldots, M[d]$ to obtain the number of occurrences of each possible message that were supposed to be sent during that round. Then it can simulate any necessary local computation. Finally, the process increments *ReadCounter* and then repeatedly reads it until it has value n. When *ReadCounter* first has value n, *ResetCounter* has value 0.

In phase 3, each process first decrements or resets *WriteCounter*. If it incremented $M[i]$ during phase 1, then it now decrements or resets it. Finally, the process increments *ResetCounter* and then repeatedly reads it until it has value n. When *ResetCounter* first has value n, *WriteCounter* has value 0.

The space complexity of this algorithm can be changed from $\Theta(d)$ to $\Theta(n)$ as described in the proof of Theorem 5.   □

5   When Counters Can Simulate Other Counters

We now consider the relationship between different types of bounded counters. A consequence of these results is that the asynchronous broadcast model is *strictly stronger* than some shared-memory models.

Definition 7. *Let m be a positive integer. An object is called m-idempotent if it is idemdicent and, for any initial state and for any operation op, the object state that results from applying op $m + 1$ times is identical to the state that results from applying op once.*

If an object is m-idempotent, then, by induction, it is km-idempotent for any positive integer k. Any idempotent object (e.g. a read-write register) is 1-idempotent. A mod-m counter is m-idempotent. An m-idempotent object has the property that the actions of $m + 1$ clones (i.e. processes behaving identically) are indistinguishable from the actions of one process.

Lemma 8 (Cloning Lemma). *Consider an algorithm for $n > m$ processes that uses only m-idempotent objects. Let γ be an execution of the algorithm in which processes $P_1, \ldots, P_m$ take no steps. Let $P \notin \{P_1, \ldots, P_m\}$. Let γ' be the execution that is constructed from γ by inserting, after each step by P, a sequence* *of steps in which each of processes $P_1, \ldots, P_m$ applies the same operation as P to the same object and gets the same result. If processes $P_1, \ldots, P_m$ have the same input as P, then γ' is a legal execution and no process outside $\{P_1, \ldots, P_m\}$ can distinguish γ from γ'.*

Proof. (Sketch) The state of the object that results from performing one operation is the same as the one that results from performing that operation $m + 1$ times. Also, the response to each of those $m + 1$ repetitions of the operation will be the same, since the object is idemdicent. Notice that P_i has the same input as P, and P_i is performing the same sequence of steps in γ' as P and receiving the same sequence of responses. Since the system is anonymous, this is a correct execution of P_i's code.   □

The n-ary threshold-2 function is a binary function of n inputs whose value is 1 if and only if at least two of its inputs are 1.

Proposition 9. *Let m be a positive integer and let $m \leq n - 2$. The n-ary threshold-2 function cannot be computed in an n-process synchronous shared-memory system if all shared objects are m-idempotent.*

Proof. Suppose there is an algorithm that computes the n-ary threshold-2 function in the shared-memory system. Let $P_1, \ldots, P_n$ be the processes of the system. Suppose the input to process P_n is 1, and the inputs to all other processes are 0. Let γ be an execution of the algorithm where processes $P_1, \ldots, P_m$ take no steps and all other processes run normally. (This is not a legal execution in a failure-free synchronous model, but we can still imagine running the algorithm in this way.)

Consider the execution α obtained by inserting into γ steps of $P_1, \ldots, P_m$ right after each step of P_{m+1}, as described in Lemma 8. This results in a legal execution of the algorithm where all processes must output 0.

Consider another execution, β, where the inputs of $P_1, \ldots, P_m$ are 1 instead, obtained from γ by inserting steps by processes $P_1, \ldots, P_m$ after each step of P_n, as described in Lemma 8. This results in a legal execution as well, but all processes must output 1.

Processes outside the set $\{P_1, \ldots, P_m\}$ cannot distinguish between α and γ, or between β and γ, so those processes must output the same result in both α and β, a contradiction.   □

Since the n-ary threshold-2 function is symmetric, it is computable in the asynchronous broadcast model, by Proposition 4. However, by Proposition 9, for $n - 2 \geq m \geq 1$, it cannot be computed in a synchronous (or asynchronous) shared-memory system, all of whose shared objects are m-idempotent. This implies that the n-process asynchronous broadcast model is strictly stronger than these shared-memory systems. In particular, it is stronger than the anonymous ARBITRARY PRAM and shared-memory systems with only read-write registers and mod-m counters for $m \leq n - 2$.

Corollary 10. *For $1 \leq m \leq n - 2$ and $t \geq 2$, a threshold-t counter cannot be simulated using registers and mod-m counters in an n-process synchronous shared-memory system.*

Proof. The n-ary threshold-2 function can be computed using a threshold-t object in an n-process synchronous system. The threshold-t object is initialized to 0. In the first round, each process with input 1 increments the threshold-t object. In the second round, all processes read the threshold-t object. They output 0 if their result is 0 or 1 and output 1 otherwise.

Since registers and mod-m counters are m-idempotent, it follows from Proposition 9 that the n-ary threshold-2 function cannot be computed in an n-process shared-memory system.   □

A similar result is true for simulating m-valued counters.

Proposition 11. *If $1 \leq n \leq m - 1$, than an m-valued counter cannot be simulated in an shared-memory system of n or more processes using only mod-$(n-1)$ counters and read-write registers.*

Proof. Suppose there was such a simulation. Let E be an execution of this simulation where the m'-valued counter is initialized to the value 0, and process P performs an increment on the m-valued counter and then performs a read operation. The simulated read operation must return the value 1.

Since $(n-1)$-counters and read-write registers are $(n-1)$-idempotent, Lemma 8, the Cloning Lemma, implies that there is a legal execution E' using n-processes which cannot be distinguished from E by P. Thus, P's read must return the value 1 in E'. However, there are n increments that have completed before P's read begins, so P's read should output n in E'. Notice that no non-deterministic behaviour can occur in the m-valued counter since $n \leq m - 1$.   □

Since an n-process broadcast system can simulate an m-valued counter, for any m, it follows that an n-process shared-memory system with mod-$(n - 1)$ counters and read-write registers cannot simulate an n-process broadcast system.

The requirement in Proposition 11 that $n \leq m - 1$ is necessary: In an n-process shared-memory system, it is possible to simulate an n-valued counter using only mod-$(n - 1)$ counters and read-write registers.

Proposition 12. *It is possible to simulate an $(m + 1)$-valued counter in an n-process shared-memory system with one mod-m counter and one read-write register.*

Proof. Consider the following implementation of an $(m+1)$-valued counter from a mod-m counter C and a register R. Assume C and R are both initialized to 0. The variables x and y are local variables.

```
                                   READ
INCREMENT                             y ← R
    increment C                       x ← C
    write 1 to R                      if y = 0 then return 0
end INCREMENT                         elsif x = 0 then return m
                                      else return x
                                   end READ
```

Linearize all INCREMENT operations whose accesses to C occur before the first write to R in the execution at the first write to R (in an arbitrary order). Linearize all remaining INCREMENT operations when they access C.

Linearize any READ that reads 0 in R at the moment it reads R. Since no INCREMENTS are linearized before this, the READ is correct to return 0. Linearize each other READ when it reads counter C. If at most m INCREMENTS are linearized before the READ, the result returned is clearly correct. If more than m INCREMENTS are linearized before the READ, the READ is allowed to return any result whatsoever.   □

The following result shows that the read-write register is essential for the simulation in Proposition 12.

Proposition 13. *It is impossible to simulate an n-valued counter in an n-process shared-memory system using only mod-$(n-1)$ counters.*

Proof. Suppose there was such a simulation. Consider an execution where $n-1$ clones each perform an INCREMENT operation, using a round-robin schedule. After each complete round of $n-1$ steps, all shared mod-$(n-1)$ counters will be in the same state as they were initially. So if the one remaining process P performs a READ after all the INCREMENTS are complete, it will not be able to distinguish this execution from the one where P runs by itself from the initial state. In the constructed execution, P must return $n-1$, but in the solo execution, it must return 0. This is a contradiction.   □

6   Counter Examples Demonstrating Non-robustness

This section proves that the reliable anonymous shared-memory model is not robust. Specifically, we show how to implement a 6-valued counter from mod-2 counters and mod-3 counters. Then we apply Proposition 11, which says that a 6-valued counter cannot be implemented from either only mod-2 counters and read-write registers or only mod-3 counters and read-write registers.

Let $m = \mathrm{lcm}(m_1, \ldots, m_r)$. We give a construction of an m-valued counter from the set of object types $\{\text{mod-}m_1 \text{ counter}, \ldots, \text{mod-}m_r \text{ counter}\}$. We shall make use of the following theorem, which is proved in introductory number theory textbooks (see, for example, Theorem 5.4.2 in [16]).

Theorem 14 (Generalized Chinese Remainder Theorem). *The system of equations $x \equiv b_j \pmod{m_j}$ for $1 \leq j \leq r$ has a solution for x if and only if $b_j \equiv b_k \pmod{\gcd(m_j, m_k)}$ for all $j \neq k$. If a solution exists, it is unique modulo $\mathrm{lcm}(m_1, m_2, \ldots, m_r)$.*

Proposition 15. *Let $m_1, \ldots, m_r$ be positive integers. Let $m = \mathrm{lcm}(m_1, \ldots, m_r)$. For any number of processes, there is an implementation of an m-valued counter from $\{\text{mod-}m_1 \text{ counter}, \ldots, \text{mod-}m_r \text{ counter}\}$.*

Proof. Let $q = 2m/m_1 + 1$. The implementation uses a shared array $A[1..q, 1..r]$ of base objects. The base object $A[i, j]$ is a mod-m_j counter, initialized to 0.

The array $B[1..q, 1..r]$ is a private variable used to store the results of reading A. (We assume the m-valued counter is initialized to 0. To implement a counter initialized to the value v, one could simply initialize $A[i, j]$ to $v \bmod m_j$, and the proof of correctness would be identical.)

The implementation is given in pseudocode below. A process INCREMENTS the m-valued counter by incrementing each counter in A. A process READS the m-valued counter by repeatedly reading the entire array A (in the opposite order) until the array appears consistent (i.e. the array looks as it would if no INCREMENTS were in progress). We shall linearize each operation when it accesses an element in the middle row of A, and show that each READ operation reliably computes (and outputs) the number of times that element has been incremented. Note that the second part of the loop's exit condition guarantees that the result to be returned by the last line of the READ operation exists and is unique, by Theorem 14.

```
                            READ
                              loop
                                for i ← 1..q
INCREMENT                         for j ← 1..r
  for i ← q downto 1                 B[i, j] ← A[i, j]
    for j ← r downto 1            end for
      increment A[i, j]          end for
    end for                      exit when B[i, j] ≡ B[1, j] (mod m_j) ∀i, j and
  end for                                  B[1, j] ≡ B[1, k] (mod gcd(m_j, m_k)) ∀j ≠ k
end INCREMENT                    end loop
                              return the value x ∈ {0, ..., m − 1} that satisfies
                                  x ≡ B[1, j] (mod m_j) for all j
                            end READ
```

Consider any execution of this implementation where there are at most $m - 1$ INCREMENTS. After sufficiently many steps, all INCREMENTS on the m-valued counter will be complete (due to the fairness of the scheduler). Let v_{final} be the number of increment operations on the m-valued counter that have occurred at that time. The collection of reads performed by any iteration of the main loop of the READ algorithm that begins afterwards will get the response $v_{final} \bmod m_j$ from each mod-m_j counter, and this will be a consistent collection of reads. Thus, every operation must eventually terminate. If more than $m - 1$ INCREMENTS occur in the execution, READS need not terminate.

Let $s = m/m_1 + 1$. Ordinarily, we linearize each operation when it last accesses $A[s, 1]$. However, if there is a time T when $A[q, r]$ is incremented for the mth time, then all INCREMENTS in progress at T that have not been linearized before T are linearized at T (with the INCREMENTS preceding the READS). Each operation that starts after T can be linearized at any moment during its execution. Note that m INCREMENTS are linearized at or before T, so any READ that is linearized at or after T is allowed to return an arbitrary response.

Consider any READ operation R that is linearized before T. Let x be the value R returns. We shall show that this return value is consistent with the linearization. Let $a_{i,j} \in \{0, \ldots, m-1\}$ be the number of times $A[i, j]$ was incremented before R read it for the last time. Then $a_{i,j} \equiv x (\bmod m_j)$ for all i and j. Because INCREMENTS and READS access the base objects in the opposite order, $a_{i,j} \leq a_{i,j+1}$ and $a_{i,r} \leq a_{i+1,1}$. From the exit condition of the main loop in the READ algorithm, we also know that $a_{i,j} \equiv a_{1,j} \pmod{m_j}$. We shall show that $x = a_{s,1}$, thereby proving that the result of R is consistent with the linearization.

We first prove by cases that, for $i \geq 1$, $a_{i+1,1} \geq \min(x, a_{i,1} + m_1)$.

Case I ($a_{i+1,1} = a_{i,1}$): Since $a_{i,1} \leq a_{i,2} \leq \cdots \leq a_{i,r} \leq a_{i+1,1} = a_{i,1}$, we have $a_{i,1} = a_{i,2} = \cdots = a_{i,r} = a_{i+1,1}$. Thus, for all j, $a_{i+1,1} = a_{i,j} \equiv a_{1,j} \pmod{m_j}$. By the uniqueness claim of Theorem 14, $a_{i+1,1} = x \geq \min(x, a_{i,1} + m_1)$.

Case II ($a_{i+1,1} > a_{i,1}$): Since $a_{i+1,1} \equiv a_{i,1} \pmod{m_1}$, it must be the case that $a_{i+1,1} \geq a_{i,1} + m_1 \geq \min(x, a_{i,1} + m_1)$.

It follows by induction that $a_{i,1} \geq \min(x, a_{1,1} + (i-1)m_1)$. Thus, $a_{s,1} \geq x$, since s was chosen so that $(s-1)m_1 = m > x$.

We now give a symmetric proof to establish that $a_{s,1} \leq x$. We can prove by cases that, for $i < q$, $a_{i,1} \leq \max(x, a_{i+1,1} - m_1)$.

Case I ($a_{i,1} = a_{i+1,1}$): Since $a_{i,1} \leq a_{i,2} \leq \cdots \leq a_{i,r} \leq a_{i+1,1} = a_{i,1}$, we have $a_{i,1} = a_{i,2} = \cdots = a_{i,r}$. Thus, for all j, $a_{i,1} = a_{i,j} \equiv a_{1,j} \pmod{m_j}$. By the uniqueness claim of Theorem 14, $a_{i,1} = x \leq \max(x, a_{i+1,1} - m_1)$.

Case II ($a_{i,1} < a_{i+1,1}$): Since $a_{i,1} \equiv a_{i+1,1} \pmod{m_1}$, it must be the case that $a_{i,1} \leq a_{i+1,1} - m_1 \leq \max(x, a_{i+1,1} - m_1)$.

It follows by induction that $a_{i,1} \leq \max(x, a_{q,1} - (q-i)m_1)$. Thus we have $a_{s,1} \leq x$, since s was chosen so that $(q-s)m_1 = m$ and $a_{q,1} - (q-s)m_1 = a_{q,1} - m < 0 \leq x$. So we have shown that $x = a_{s,1}$, and this completes the proof of correctness for the implementation of the m-valued counter.   □

Theorem 16. *The reliable, anonymous model of shared memory is non-robust. That is, there exist three object types A, B, and C such that an object of type A cannot be implemented from only read-write registers and objects of type B and an object of type A cannot be implemented from only read-write registers and objects of type C, but an object of type A can be implemented from objects of types B and C.*

Proof. Let A be a 6-valued counter, B be a mod-3 counter and C be a mod-2 counter. In a 4-process shared-memory system, an object of type A cannot be implemented from read-write registers and objects of type B, by Proposition 11. Similarly an object of type A cannot be implemented from read-write registers and objects of type C. However, by Proposition 15, an object of type A can be implemented using objects of type B and C.   □

Acknowledgements

James Aspnes was supported in part by NSF grants CCR-0098078 and CNS-0305258. Faith Fich was supported by Sun Microsystems. Faith Fich and Eric Ruppert were supported by the Natural Sciences and Engineering Research Council of Canada.

References

1. Dana Angluin. Local and global properties in networks of processors. In *Proceedings of the 12th ACM Symposium on Theory of Computing*, pages 82–93, 1980.
2. James Aspnes, Gauri Shah, and Jatin Shah. Wait-free consensus with infinite arrivals. In *Proceedings of the 34th ACM Symposium on Theory of Computing*, pages 524–533, 2002.
3. Hagit Attiya, Alla Gorbach, and Shlomo Moran. Computing in totally anonymous asynchronous shared memory systems. *Information and Computation*, 173(2):162–183, March 2002.
4. Paolo Boldi and Sebastiano Vigna. Computing anonymously with arbitrary knowledge. In *Proceedings of the 18th ACM Symposium on Principles of Distributed Computing*, pages 173–179, 1999.
5. Paolo Boldi and Sebastiano Vigna. An effective characterization of computability in anonymous networks. In *Distributed Computing, 15th International Conference*, volume 2180 of *LNCS*, pages 33–47, 2001.
6. Harry Buhrman, Alessandro Panconesi, Riccardo Silvestri, and Paul Vitanyi. On the importance of having an identity or, is consensus really universal? In *Distributed Computing, 14th International Conference*, volume 1914 of *LNCS*, pages 134–148, 2000.
7. Catalin Drulă. The totally anonymous shared memory model in which the number of processes is known. Personal communication.
8. Faith Fich and Eric Ruppert. Hundreds of impossibility results for distributed computing. *Distributed Computing*, 16(2-3):121–163, September 2003.
9. Edward Fredkin. Trie memory. *Communications of the ACM*, 3(9), August 1960.
10. Maurice P. Herlihy and Jeannette M. Wing. Linearizability: A correctness condition for concurrent objects. *ACM Transactions on Programming Languages and Systems*, 12(3):463–492, July 1990.
11. Prasad Jayanti. Robust wait-free hierarchies. *Journal of the ACM*, 44(4):592–614, July 1997.
12. Prasad Jayanti. Solvability of consensus: Composition breaks down for nondeterministic types. *SIAM Journal on Computing*, 28(3):782–797, September 1998.
13. Prasad Jayanti and Sam Toueg. Wakeup under read/write atomicity. In *Distributed Algorithms, 4th International Workshop*, volume 486 of *LNCS*, pages 277–288, 1990.
14. John H. Reif, editor. *Synthesis of Parallel Algorithms*. Morgan Kaufmann, 1993.
15. Naoshi Sakamoto. Comparison of initial conditions for distributed algorithms on anonymous networks. In *Proceedings of the 18th ACM Symposium on Principles of Distributed Computing*, pages 173–179, 1999.
16. Harold N. Shapiro. *Introduction to the Theory of Numbers*. John Wiley and Sons, 1983.

A Local Algorithm for Ad Hoc Majority Voting via Charge Fusion

Yitzhak Birk, Liran Liss, Assaf Schuster, and Ran Wolff*

Technion – Israel Institute of Technology, Haifa 32000, Isreal
{birk@ee,liranl@tx,assaf@cs,ranw@cs}.technion.ac.il

Abstract. We present a local distributed algorithm for a general Majority Vote problem: different and time-variable voting powers and vote splits, arbitrary and dynamic interconnection topologies and link delays, and any fixed majority threshold. The algorithm combines a novel, efficient anytime spanning forest algorithm, which may also have applications elsewhere, with a "charge fusion" algorithm that roots trees at nodes with excess "charge" (derived from a node's voting power and vote split), and subsequently transfers charges along tree links to oppositely charged roots for fusion. At any instant, every node has an ad hoc belief regarding the outcome. Once all changes have ceased, the correct majority decision is reached by all nodes, within a time that in many cases is independent of the graph size. The algorithm's correctness and salient properties have been proved, and experiments with up to a million nodes provide further validation and actual numbers. To our knowledge, this is the first locality-sensitive solution to the Majority Vote problem for arbitrary, dynamically changing communication graphs.

1   Introduction

1.1   Background

Emerging large-scale distributed systems, such as the Internet-based peer-to-peer systems, grid systems, ad hoc networks and sensor networks, impose uncompromising scalability requirements on (distributed) algorithms used for performing various functions. Clearly, for an algorithm to be perfectly scalable, i.e., O(1) complexity in problem size, it must be "local" in the sense that a node only exchanges information with nodes in its vicinity. Also, information must not need to flow across the graph. For some problems, there are local algorithms whose execution time is effectively independent of the graph size. Examples include Ring Coloring [1] and Maximal Independent Set [2].

Unfortunately, there are important problems for which there cannot be such perfectly-scalable solutions. Yet, locality is a highly desirable characteristic: locality decouples computation from the system size, thus enhancing scalability; also, handling the effects of input changes or failures of individual nodes locally

---

* The work of Liran Liss, Assaf Schuster, and Ran Wolff was supported by the Intel Corporation and the Mafat Institute for Research and Development.

R. Guerraoui (Ed.): DISC 2004, LNCS 3274, pp. 275–289, 2004.

cuts down resource usage and prevents hot spots; lastly, a node is usually able to communicate reliably and economically with nearby nodes, whereas communication with distant nodes, let alone global communication, is often costly and prone to failures.

With these motivations in mind, efficient local (or "locality sensitive") algorithms have also been developed for problems that do not lend themselves to solutions whose complexity is completely independent of the problem instance. One example is an efficient Minimum Spanning Tree algorithm [2]. Another example is fault-local mending algorithms [3, 4]. There, a problem is considered fault-locally mendable if the time it takes to mend a batch of transient faults depends only on the number of failed nodes, regardless of the size of the network. However, the time may still be proportional to the size of the network for a large number of faults.

The notion of locality that was proposed in [3, 4] for mending algorithms can be generalized as follows: an algorithm is local if its execution time does not depend directly on the system size, but rather on some other measure of the problem instance. The existence of such a measure for non-trivial instances of a problem suggests (but may not guarantee) the possibility of a solution with unbounded scalability (in graph size) for these instances. This observation encourages the search for local algorithms even for problem classes that are clearly global for some instances. In this paper, we apply this idea to the Majority Vote problem, which is a fundamental primitive in distributed algorithms for many common functions such as leader election, consensus and synchronization.

1.2 The Majority Vote Problem

Consider a system comprising an unbounded number of nodes, organized in a communication graph. Each node has a certain (possibly different) voting power on a proposed resolution, and may split its votes arbitrarily between "Yes" and "No". Nodes may change their connectivity (topology changes) at any moment, and both the voting power and the votes themselves may change over time[1]. In this dynamic setting, we want every node to decide whether the fraction of Yes votes is greater than a given threshold. Since the outcome is inherently ad hoc, it makes no sense to require that a node be aware of its having learned the "final" outcome, and we indeed do not impose this requirement. However, we do require eventual convergence in each connected component.

The time to determine the correct majority decision in a distributed vote may depend on the significance of the majority rather than on system size. In certain cases such as a tie, computing the majority would require collecting at least half of the the votes, which would indeed take time proportional to the size of the system. Yet, it appears possible that whenever the majority is evident throughout the graph, computation can be extremely fast by determining the correct majority decision based on local information alone.

---

[1] Nodes are assumed to trust one another. We do not address Byzantine faults in this paper.

Constantly adapting to the input in a local manner can also lead to efficient anytime algorithms: when the global majority changes slowly, every node can track the majority decision in a timely manner, without spending vast network resources; when a landslide majority decision flips abruptly due to an instant change in the majority of the votes, most of the nodes should be able to reach the new decision extremely fast as discussed above; and, after the algorithm has converged, it should be possible to react to a subsequent vote change that increases the majority with very little, local activity. A less obvious situation occurs when a vote change reduces the majority (but does not alter the outcome), because the change may create a local false perception that the outcome has changed as well. The challenge to the algorithm is to squelch the wave of erroneous perceived outcome fast, limiting both the number of affected nodes and the duration of this effect.

The Majority Vote problem thus has instances that require global communication, instances that appear to lend themselves trivially to efficient, local solutions, and challenging instances that lie in between.

The main contribution of this paper is a local algorithm for the Majority Vote problem. Our algorithm comprises two collaborating components: an efficient anytime spanning forest algorithm and a charge-fusion mechanism. A node's initial charge is derived from its voting power and vote split such that the majority decision is determined by the sign of the net charge in the system. Every node bases its ad-hoc belief of the majority decision on the sign of its charge or that of a charged node in its vicinity. The algorithm roots trees at charged nodes, and subsequently fuses opposite charges using these trees until only charges of one (the majority) sign are left, thus disseminating the correct decision to all nodes.

We provide proof sketches for key properties (for full proofs, which are omitted for brevity, see [5]) as well as simulation results that demonstrate actual performance and scalability. Offering a preview of our results, our experiments show that for a wide range of input instances, the majority decision can be computed "from scratch" in constant time. Even for a tight vote of 52% vs. 48%, each node usually communicates with only tens of nearby nodes, regardless of system size. In [6], similar behavior was demonstrated using an (unrelated) algorithm that was suited only for tree topologies. To our knowledge, the current paper offers, for the first time, a locality-sensitive solution to the Majority Vote problem for arbitrary, dynamically changing topologies.

The remainder of the paper is organized as follows: In Section 2 we provide an overview of our approach. In sections 3 and 4 we present our Spanning Forest (SF) and Majority Vote (MV) algorithms, respectively, along with formal statements of their properties. In section 5, we provide some empirical results to confirm our assumptions and demonstrate the performance of our algorithm. Section 6 describes at some length related work. We conclude the paper in Section 7.

2   Overview of Our Approach

Consider a vote on a proposition. The voting takes place at a set of *polls*, which are interconnected by communication links. We propose the following simple scheme for determining the global majority decision. For each unbalanced poll, transfer its excess votes to a nearby poll with an opposite majority, leaving the former one balanced. Every balanced poll bases its current belief regarding the majority decision on some unbalanced poll in its vicinity. We continue this poll consolidation process until all remaining unbalanced polls posses excess votes of the same type, thus determining the global majority decision. We next state the problem formally, and elaborate on our implementation of the foregoing approach, extending it to an arbitrary majority threshold.

Let $G(V,E)$ be a graph, and let $\lambda = \lambda_n/\lambda_d$ be a rational threshold between 0 and 1. Every node i is entitled to V_i votes; we denote the number of node i's Yes votes by Y_i. For each connected component X in G, the desired majority vote decision is Yes if and only if the fraction of Yes votes in X is greater than the threshold: $\dfrac{\sum_{i \in X} Y_i}{\sum_{i \in X} V_i} > \lambda$.

A node can change its current vote in any time. Therefore, we need to distinguish between a node's current vote and the votes or "tokens" that we transfer between nodes during the consolidation process. In order to prevent confusion, we introduce the notion of the *("electrical") charge* of a node, and base the majority decision on the sign of the net charge in the system. The following equivalent criterion for determining a Yes majority vote decision allows us to work with integers and only deal with linear operations (addition and subtraction) for an arbitrary majority threshold: $\lambda_d \sum_{i \in X} Y_i - \lambda_n \sum_{i \in X} V_i > 0$.

A node i's charge, C_i, is initially set to $\lambda_d Y_i - \lambda_n V_i$. Subsequent single-vote changes at a node from No to Yes (Yes to No) increase (decrease) its charge by λ_d. An addition of one vote to the voting power of a node reduces its charge by λ_n if the new vote is No, and increases it by $\lambda_d - \lambda_n$ if the vote is Yes. A reduction in a node's voting power has an opposite effect. Charge may also be transferred among nodes, affecting their charges accordingly but leaving the total charge in the system unchanged. Therefore, the desired majority vote decision is Yes if and only if the net charge in the system is non-negative: $\sum_{i \in X} C_i \geq 0$.

Our Majority Vote algorithm (MV) entails transferring charge among neighboring nodes, so as to "fuse" and thereby eliminate equal amounts of opposite-sign charges. So doing also relays ad hoc majority decision information. Eventually, all remaining charged nodes have an identical sign, which is the correct global majority decision. Therefore, if we could transfer charge such that *nearby* charged nodes with opposite signs canceled one another without introducing a livelock, and subsequently disseminate the resulting majority decision to neutral nodes locally, we would have a *local* algorithm for the Majority Vote problem.

We prevent livelock with the aid of a local spanning forest algorithm (SF) that we will introduce shortly. The interplay between SF and MV is as follows. The roots of SF's trees are set by MV at charged nodes. SF gradually constructs distinct trees over neutral nodes. MV then deterministically routes charges of one sign over directed edges of the forest constructed by SF towards roots containing opposite charge. The charges are fused, leaving only their combined net charge. Finally, MV unroots nodes that turned neutral, so SF guarantees that all neutral nodes will join trees rooted at remaining charged ones in their vicinity. Each node bases its (perceived global) majority decision on the sign of the charge of its tree's root. Therefore, dissemination of a majority decision to all nodes is inherently built into the algorithm.

We note that although the system is dynamic, we ensure that the total charge in any connected component of the graph always reflects the voting power and votes of its nodes. By so doing, we guarantee that the correct majority decision is eventually reached by every node in any given connected component, within finite time following the cessation of changes.

3   Spanning Forest Algorithm (SF)

In this section, we describe SF, an efficient algorithm for maintaining a spanning forest in dynamic graphs, and state its loop-freedom and convergence properties. In the next section, we will adapt this algorithm and utilize it as part of MV.

3.1   SF Algorithm Description

Overview. Given a (positive) weighted undirected graph and a set of nodes marked as *active* roots, the algorithm gradually builds trees from these nodes. At any instant, edges and nodes can be added or removed, edge weights can change, and nodes can be marked/unmarked as active roots on the fly. However, the graph is always loop-free and partitioned into distinct trees. Some of these trees have active roots, while others are either inactive singletons (the initial state of every node) or rooted at nodes that used to be active. We denote a tree as *active* or *inactive* based on the activity state of its root.

Whenever the system is static, each connected component converges to a forest in which every tree is active (if active roots exist). Loop freedom ensures that any node whose path to its root was cut off, or whose root became inactive, will be able to join an active tree in time proportional to the size of its previous tree. Unlike shortest path routing algorithms that create a single permanent tree that spans the entire graph (for each destination), SF is intended to create multiple trees that are data-dependent, short-lived, and local. Therefore, in order to reduce control traffic, an edge-weight change does not by itself trigger any action. Nevertheless, expanding trees do take into account the most recent edge weight information. So, although we do not always build a shortest path forest, our paths are short.

The Algorithm. Algorithm 1 presents SF. In addition to topological changes, the algorithm supports two operations to specify whether a node should be treated as an active root ($Root_i$ and $UnRoot_i$), and one query ($NextHop_i$) that returns the identity of a node's downtree neighbor, or $\perp$ if the node is a root. (We denote by downtree the direction from a node towards its root.)

Algorithm 1 Spanning Forest (SF).

Variables for node i:
- R_i, T_i, W_i, A_i, P_i - Root and tree activity states ($\{0,1\}$), path weight and Ack number (positive Int), and a next-hop pointer (a node identifier), respectively.
- $\forall j \in N^i : \lambda_i(T_j), \lambda_i(W_j), \lambda_i(A_j)$ - A neighbor j's tree state, weight and Ack number as known to i.

Macros:
$Inactive(i) \equiv (T_i = 0) \vee (P_i \neq \bot \wedge \lambda_i(T_{P_i}) = 0)$
$IsAck(i)$ - Evaluates to *true* iff i's neighbors have all acknowledged i's most recent (highest) Ack number. Nodes that become neighbors are considered to have sent and received all Acks that could have been pending to or from each other. (The details of Ack management are omitted for brevity, but are included in the running code.)

Events: /* trigger + event-specific action */
- $Init_i()$: $R_i = 0; T_i = 0; W_i = \infty; P_i = \bot; A_i = 0; \forall j \in N^i : LinkDown_i(j)$
- $LinkUp_i(j)$: send $Update(T_i, W_i, A_i)$ to j
- $LinkDown_i(j)$: $\lambda_i(T_j) = 0; \lambda_i(W_j) = \infty; \lambda_i(A_j) = \bot$; if $(P_i = j)$ $P_i = \bot$
- $Root_i$ operation: $R_i = 1$
- $UnRoot_i$ operation: $R_i = 0$
- receive $Update(T, W, A)$ from j: update $\lambda_i(T_j)$, $\lambda_i(W_j)$, and $\lambda_i(A_j)$
- receive $Ack(A)$ from j: record the value of i's Ack num as acknowledged by j

After every event also do: /* common actions*/
1. if $(R_i = 1)$ /* set i as an active root */
   (a) $T_i = 1, W_i = 0, P_i = \bot$
2. else /* $R_i = 0$ */
   (a) /* if i is inactive and all uptree nodes have acknowledged, update i's weight according to its next hop */
   $$\text{if } ((T_i = 0) \wedge (IsAck(i) = true)) \ W_i = \begin{cases} \infty, & P_i = \bot \vee \lambda_i(W_{P_i}) = \infty \\ \lambda_i(W_{P_i}) + d(i, P_i), & \text{otherwise} \end{cases}$$
   (b) /* improve i's path or join an active tree with the same weight if i is inactive or about to become inactive */
   let $j \in N^i$ s.t. $W(j)$ is minimal, where
   $$W(j) = \begin{cases} \lambda_i(W_j) + d(i, j), & \lambda_i(T_j) \neq 0 \\ \infty, & \text{otherwise} \end{cases}$$
   if $((W(j) < W_i) \vee (W(j) = W_i \wedge W(j) < \infty \wedge Inactive(i)))$
       $P_i = j, W_i = W(j), T_i = \lambda_i(T_j)$
   (c) /* if i is turning inactive, increment i's Ack */
   if $((T_i \neq 0) \wedge (P_i = \bot \vee \lambda_i(T_{P_i}) = 0))$ $T_i = 0, A_i = A_i + 1$
3. send $Update(T_i, W_i, A_i)$ to all neighbors if anything changed
4. send $Ack(\lambda_i(A_j))$ to each unacknowledged neighbor j, with the exception of P_i if $IsAck(i) = false$
The answer to the $NextHop_i$ query is P_i's current value

To its neighbors, a node i's state is represented by its perceived tree's activity state T_i, its current path weight W_i to some root, and an acknowledgement number A_i. The algorithm converges in a similar manner to Bellman-Ford algorithms [7]: after each event, node i considers changing its next hop pointer (P_i) to a neighbor that minimizes the weight of its path to an active root (step 2b).

More formally, to a neighbor j that is believed by i to be active ($\lambda_i(T_j) = 1$) and for which $\lambda_i(W_j) + d(i,j)$ is minimal.

Loops are prevented by ensuring that whenever a portion of a tree is inactivated due to an *UnRoot* operation or a link failure, a node will not point to a (still active) node that is uptree from it [8]. (Edge weight increases can also cause loops. However, we do not face this problem because such increases do not affect a node's current weight in our algorithm.) This is achieved both by limiting a node i's choice of its downtree node (next hop) to neighbors that reduce i's current weight, and by allowing i to increase its current weight only when i and all its uptree nodes are inactive (step 2a).

In order to relay such inactivity information, we use an acknowledgement mechanism as follows: a node i will not acknowledge the fact that the tree state of its downtree neighbor has become inactive (step 4), before i is itself inactivated (T_i is set to 0 and A_i is incremented in step 2c) and receives acknowledgements for its own inactivation from all its neighbors (*IsAck(i)* becomes *true*). Note that i will acknowledge immediately an inactivation of a neighbor that is not its downtree node. Therefore, if a node i is inactive and has received the last corresponding acknowledgement, all of i's uptree nodes must be inactive and their own neighbors are aware of this fact.

An active root expands and shrinks its tree at the fastest possible speed according to shortest path considerations. However, once a root is marked inactive, a three-phase process takes place to mark all nodes in the corresponding tree as inactive and reset their weight to ∞. First, the fact that the tree is inactive ($T_i = 0$) propagates to all the leaves. Next, Acks are aggregated from the leaves and returned to the root. (Note that node weights remain unchanged.) Finally, the root increases its weight to ∞. This weight increase propagates towards the leaves, resetting the weight of all nodes in the tree to ∞ on its way. It may seem that increasing the weight of the leaves only in the third phase is wasteful. However, this extra phase actually speeds up the process by ensuring that nodes in "shorter" branches do not choose as their next hop nodes in "longer" branches that haven't yet been notified that the tree is being inactivated. (This phase corresponds to the *wait* state in [8].)

3.2   Loop Freedom

For facility of exposition, given a node i we define $\widehat{W_i}$ to equal W_i if $T_i = 1$ and ∞ otherwise. In [5], we prove the following technical lemma by induction on all network events:

Lemma 1. *For every node i*

1. *if $IsAck(i) = true$ then, for every j uptree from i or $j = i$ and for every neighbor m of j: (a) $\lambda_m(\widehat{W_j}) \geq \widehat{W_i}$, and (b) for every in-transit update message u sent by j with weight $\widehat{W_u}: \widehat{W_u} \geq \widehat{W_i}$.*
2. *if $IsAck(i) = false$ then the same claims hold when replacing $\widehat{W_i}$ with W_i.*

Theorem 1. *There are no cycles in the graph at any instance.*

Proof. Let i be a node that closes a cycle at time t_0. Therefore, at t_o^+ we have $\lambda_i(\widehat{W_{P_i}}) = \lambda_i(W_{P_i}) < W_i = \widehat{W_i}$. According to 1) or 2) of Lemma 1, $\lambda_i(\widehat{W_{P_i}}) \geq \widehat{W_i}$, since P_i is also uptree from i. A contradiction. □

3.3   Convergence

We assume that the algorithm was converged at time 0, after which a finite number of topological and root changes occurred. Let t_0 be the time of the last change.

Theorem 2. *After all topological and root changes have stopped, SF converges in finite time.*

Proof. Based on the fact that the number of possible weights that a node can have at t_0 is finite, we show in [5] that there exists a time $t_1 > t_0$ such that for every $t > t_1$ *IsAck* = *true* for all nodes. After this time, every node that joins some active tree will remain in one. Since the graph is finite and loop-free, all nodes will either join some active tree (if there are any) or increase their weight to ∞. From this point onward, the algorithm behaves exactly like the standard Bellman-Ford algorithm, in which remaining active roots are simulated by zero weighted edges connected to a single destination node. Therefore, proofs for Bellman-Ford algorithms apply here [9]. □

4   Majority Vote Algorithm (MV)

In this section, we first describe the required adaptations to SF for use in our Majority Vote algorithm (MV). Next, we provide a detailed description of MV, discuss its correctness, and state its locality properties.

4.1   SF Adaptation

We augment SF as follows:

1. To enable each neutral node to determine its majority decision according to its tree's root, we expand the SF root and tree state binary variables (R_i and T_i) to include the value of -1 as well. While inactive nodes will still bear the value of $T = 0$, the tree state of an active node i will always equal the sign of its next hop (downtree neighbor) as known to i: $T_i = \lambda_i(T_{P_i})$ or the sign of R_i if i itself is an active root.
2. We attach a "Tree ID" variable to each node for symmetry breaking as explained next. It is assigned a value in every active root, and this value is propagated throughout its tree.
3. To enable controlled routing of charge from the root of one tree to that of an opposite-sign tree that collided with it, each node also maintains an *inverse hop*, which designates a weighted path to the other tree's root.

Node i considers a neighbor j as a candidate for its inverse hop in two cases: (a) i and j belong to different trees and have opposite signs $(T_i = -T_j)$; (b) i is j's next hop, both nodes have the same sign $(T_i = T_j)$, and j has an inverse hop. We further restrict i's candidates to those designating a path towards a root with a higher Tree ID. (Different IDs ensure that only one of the colliding trees will develop inverse hops.) If there are remaining candidates, i selects one that offers a path with minimal weight.

4. To guarantee that paths do not break while routing charges, we prevent an active node from changing its next hop[2]. However, as will be explained shortly, there are cases wherein new active roots should be able to take over nodes of neighboring active trees. Therefore, we extend the *Root* operation to include an *expansion flag*. Setting this flag creates a bounded one-shot expansion wave, by repeatedly allowing any neighboring nodes to join the tree. The wave will die down when it stops improving the shortest path of neighboring nodes or when the bound is reached.

The adaptations do not invalidate the correctness or the convergence of the SF algorithm [5]. The interface of the augmented SF algorithm exposed to MV is summarized in the following table:

Procedure	Function
$Root_i \, (sign, ID, expand)$	Mark i as an active root
$UnRoot_i$	Unmark i as an active root
$TreeSign_i$	Return i's tree state
$TreeID_i$	Return i's tree ID
$NextHop_i$	Return i's next hop, or $\perp$ if i is a root
$InvHop_i$	Returns i's preferred inverse hop, or $\perp$ if there is none

4.2   MV Algorithm Description

Overview. MV is an asynchronous reactive algorithm. It operates by expressing local vote changes as charge, relaying charge sign information among neighboring nodes using SF, and fusing opposite charges to determine the majority decision based on this information. Therefore, events that directly affect the current charge of a node, as well as ones that relay information on neighboring charges (via SF), cause an algorithm action.

Every distinct charge in the system is assigned an ID. The ID need not be unique, but positive and negative charges must have different IDs (e.g., by using the sign of a charge as the least significant bit of its ID). Whenever a node remains charged following an event, it will be marked as an active root (using the SF *Root* operation), with the corresponding sign and a charge ID. If the event was a vote change, we also set the root's expansion flag in order to balance tree sizes among the new tree and its neighbors. This improves overall tree locality, since a vote change has the potential of introducing a new distinct charge (and hence, a new tree) into the system.

---

[2] We apply similar restrictions to an active node that is marked as a new root [5].

When trees of opposite signs collide, one of them (the one with the lower ID) will develop inverse hops as explained above. Note that inverse hops are not created arbitrarily: they expand along a path leading directly to the root. Without loss of generality, assume that the negative tree develops inverse hops. Once the negative root identifies an inverse hop, it sends all its charge (along with its ID) to its inverse hop neighbor and subsequently unmarks itself as an active root (using the SF *UnRoot* operation). The algorithm will attempt to pass the charge along inverse hops of (still active) neutral nodes that belonged to the negative tree (using the SF *InvHop* query), and then along next hops of nodes that are part of the positive tree (using the SF *NextHop* query).

As long as the charge is in transit, no new roots are created. If it reaches the positive root, fusion takes place. The algorithm will either inactivate the root or update the root's sign and charge ID, according to the residual charge. In case the propagation was interrupted (due to topological changes, vote changes, expanding trees, etc.), the charge will be added to that of its current node, possibly creating a new active root.

The Algorithm. Algorithm 2 states MV formally. $C_i(j)$ keeps track of every charge transferred between a node and each of its neighbors. It is used to ensure that charges remain within the connected component in which they were generated. $GenID(charge)$ can be any function that returns a positive integer, as long as different IDs are generated for positive and a negative charges. However, we have found it beneficial to give higher IDs to charges with greater absolute values, as this causes them to "sit in place" as roots. This scheme results in faster fusion since charges with opposite signs and lower absolute values will be routed towards larger charges in parallel. It also discourages fusion of large same-sign charges. This situation could arise when multiple same-sign charges are sent concurrently to a common destination node that held an opposite-sign charge.

After updating a node i's charge information following an event, the algorithm performs two simple steps. In step 1, if i is charged, the algorithm attempts to transfer the charge according to i's tree sign and current next/inverse hop information obtained from SF. In step 2, i's root state is adjusted according to its remaining charge. The output of the algorithm, i.e., the estimated majority decision at every node, is simply the sign of the node's tree state (using SF's *TreeSign* query). For inactive nodes, we arbitrarily return *true*.

4.3   Correctness

Assume that all external events (link state changes, bit changes, etc.) stop at some time t_0. Because no new charges are introduced to the system and existing charges can only be fused together, the number of distinct charges after t_0 becomes constant after some finite time $t_1 > t_0$. By induction on charge IDs, we show in [5] that all remaining charges after t_1 must be of the same sign.

Theorem 3. *After all external events have ceased, MV stops in finite time with the correct output in every node.*

Algorithm 2 Majority Vote.

Variables for node i:
- Y_i, V_i, C_i, ID_i - "Yes" votes, total votes,charge and charge ID, respectively.
- $\forall j \in N^i : C_i(j)$ - total charge transferred **between** i and a neighbor j, from i's perspective.

Macros:
$GenID(charge)$ generates a new charge ID
$Charge(V,Y) \equiv \lambda_d \cdot Y - \lambda_n \cdot V$

Events: /* trigger + event specific action */
- $Init_i$: $V_i; Y_i; C_i = Charge(V_i, Y_i); ID_i = GenID(C_i); \forall j \in N(i) : C_i(j) = 0$
- $LinkUp_i(j)$: do nothing
- $LinkDown_i(j)$: $C_i = C_i + C_i(j); C_i(j) = 0$
- $ChangeVote_i(V,Y)$: $C_i = C_i + (Charge(V,Y) - Charge(V_i, Y_i))$;
  $V_i = V; Y_i = Y; ID_i = GenID(C_i)$
- Receive $Transfer(C, ID)$ from j:
  if $(C_i = 0)$ $ID_i = ID$ else $ID_i = GenID(C_i + C)$;
  $C_i = C_i + C; C_i(j) = C_i(j) - C$

After each of the events above or a change in SF's state do: /* common actions */
1. /* if i is charged, try to transfer the charge */
   if $((C_i \neq 0) \wedge (TreeID_i \geq ID_i))$
      if $(Sign(C_i) = -TreeSign_i)$ $temp = NextHop_i$ else $temp = InvHop_i$;
      if $(temp \neq \perp)$ send $Tansfer(C_i, ID_i)$ to $temp, C_i(j) = C_i(j) + C_i, C_i = 0$
2. /* Mark i as an active root if it remained charged. Otherwise, unmark it */
   if $(C_i = 0)$ $UnRoot_i$ else $Root_i(Sign(C_i), ID_i, f)$ where $f = true$ if invoked by a
   $ChangeVote_i$ operation

Output: $true$ if $TreeSign_i \geq 0$, and $false$ otherwise

Proof. Once all charges are identical, termination is guaranteed [5]. Let X be a connected component after the algorithm stopped. Assume that the majority decision for all nodes in X should be $true$, i.e., $\lambda_d \sum_{i \in X} Y_i - \lambda_n \sum_{i \in X} V_i \geq 0$. Hence, $\sum_{i \in X} C_i \geq 0$ [5]. Since all remaining charges have the same sign, it follows that $\forall i \in X : C_i \geq 0$. Therefore, all nodes in X decide $true$, as there are no negative trees in the graph. The situation when the majority decision should be $false$ is shown similarly.   □

4.4 Locality Properties

The locality of an execution depends on the input instance. In all cases in which the majority is evident throughout the graph, the algorithm takes advantage of this by locally fusing minority and majority charges in parallel. Many input instances follow this pattern, especially when the majority is significant.

The algorithm operates in a way that preserves the charge distribution because: 1) further vote changes create new roots uniformly, and 2) our charge ID scheme discourages fusion of charges of the same sign. Therefore, we conjecture that for many input instances, the size of remaining trees after the algorithm has converged will be determined by the majority percentile, rather than by the graph size. For example, consider a fully connected graph of size N for which each node has a single vote, a threshold of $1/2$, and a tight vote of 48% vs. 52%. After the algorithm converges, the absolute net charge is $4\% \cdot N$. Assuming that the remaining charge is spread uniformly so that every charge unit establishes an active root of its own, the number of nodes in each tree is about $\frac{N}{4\% \cdot N} = 25$, regardless of whether the graph contains a hundred or a million nodes.

From this conjecture it follows that, for these instances, there exists a non-trivial upper bound R on the radius of any tree in the graph. We initially prove that the algorithm is local for single vote changes and when several changes occur far from one another. We then show that the algorithm is local for any fixed number of changes. In the next section, we will use simulations to verify our conjecture empirically, and to demonstrate the local characteristics of our algorithm for arbitrary vote changes.

Theorem 4. *Assume that all vote and topological changes have stopped, and MV has converged. Let R be an upper bound on the radius of any tree in the graph. If some node changes a single vote, then the algorithm converges in $O(R)$ time, independent of the overall graph size.*

Proof (sketch). An increase in the majority can only result in establishing an additional local tree. A decrease in the majority can introduce a single opposite-sign charge of bounded size, and therefore will be covered by charges from a fixed-sized neighborhood. Note that an opposite-sign charge may still generate an opposite-sign tree. However, the growth rate of this tree is at most half the one-way propagation speed, because other trees have to be inactivated before their nodes can join it [5]. Therefore, an opposite-sign tree cannot expand too far before it is itself inactivated, and its nodes rejoin remaining trees. All these operations take $O(R)$ time. □

Corollary 1. *Theorem 4 also holds for multiple vote changes at different nodes, such that the resulting protocol actions do not coincide with one another.*

For an arbitrary number of vote changes, we do not give a bound on convergence time. However, we show that the algorithm remains local when the majority decision does not change, by proving finite convergence time even for infinite graphs.

Theorem 5. *Let G be an infinite graph, for which MV has converged. Assume G has infinitely many charged roots (of the same sign) such that there exists an upper bound R on the radius of any tree in the graph. If $m < \infty$ vote changes occur, then the algorithm converges in finite time.*

Proof (sketch). We show that the number of opposite-sign charges (with respect to charges before the vote changes) drops to zero in finite time, thereby reducing the problem to a finite region of the graph, which converges in finite time. □

5   Empirical Study

We simulated the algorithm's execution on large graphs. For simplicity, we only considered a 50% majority threshold and one vote per node. However, simulations were run for several Yes/No voting ratios, thereby checking the sensitivity of the results to the proximity of the vote to the decision threshold. Two representative graph topologies were used: a mesh for computing centers and sensor networks, and de Bruijn graphs for structured peer-to-peer systems [10]. For each, graph sizes varied from 256 to one million nodes. Finally, both bulk ("from scratch") voting and ongoing voting were simulated.

In bulk voting, all nodes voted simultaneously at $t = 0$ with the desired Yes/No ratio, and we measured the time until various fractions (90%, 95%, 100%, etc.) of the nodes decided on the correct outcome without subsequently retracting. Multiple experiments were carried out for a <graph type, size, Yes/No ratio> combination, with i.i.d drawings of the votes in the different experiments, and the results were averaged.

We found that the mean time to achieve any convergence percentile under 100% only depends on the Yes/No ratio and is independent of graph size. The algorithm's communication costs follow a similar pattern [5]. This is evidence of the algorithm's local behavior. Figure 1 (a) depicts the results for a convergence percentile of 100%, i.e, the time until the last node reaches the correct outcome. We observe that for de Bruijn graphs, the time to 100% convergence is nearly constant regardless of graph size. For mesh graphs, the time appears proportional to the logarithm of graph size as the Yes/No ratio approaches the threshold. Nevertheless, this time is sub-linear in the graph diameter.

Figure 1 (b) focuses on the convergence percentile, providing the probability distribution of converged nodes over time. Two things are readily evident from the figure: 1) beyond the mean time to convergence, the number of unconverged nodes declines exponentially with time; 2) this distribution is independent of graph size. In fact, the distributions for different graph sizes are barely distinguishable. This strongly suggests that locality and scalability hold for virtually every convergence percentile except 100%.

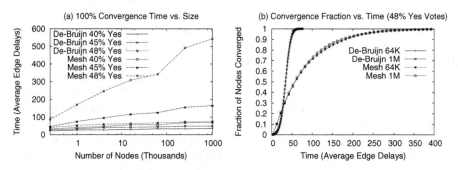

Fig. 1. Bulk voting convergence and locality.

In ongoing voting, a given fraction (0.1%) of the nodes changes its vote once every mean edge delay, while the overall Yes/No ratio remains constant. We view this operation mode as the closest to real-life. In this setting we wish to evaluate the time it takes for the effects of dispersed vote changes to subside and to validate that our algorithm does not converge to some pathological situation (e.g., all remaining charge converges to a single node, whose tree spans the entire graph). Therefore, we ran the system for some time reaching a steady state. Subsequently, we stopped all changes and measured the convergence time and the number of nodes in each tree upon convergence.

As expected, convergence time in on-going voting only depended on the Yes/No ratio. Furthermore, it was substantially shorter compared to bulk voting. For example, the time for 95% convergence in on-going voting took half that of bulk voting for 45% Yes votes, and a tenth for 40%. In addition, tree sizes where tightly distributed about their mean, which was less than twice the ideal size according to a given Yes/No ratio. These experiments thus confirm our conjecture that tree sizes are small, and demonstrate that locality is maintained in on-going voting as well.

6   Related Work

Our work bears some resemblance to Directed Diffusion [11], a technique to collect aggregate information in sensor networks. As in their work, our routing is data-centric and based on local decisions. However, our induced routing tables are relatively short-lived, and do not require refreshments or enforcements. The SF algorithm we present, builds upon previous research in distributed Bellman-Ford routing algorithms which avoid loops such as [8] and [9].

Several alternative approaches can be used to conduct majority voting such as sampling, pseudo-static computation, and flooding. With sampling, the idea is to collect data from a small number of nodes selected with uniform probability from the system, and compute the majority based on that sample. One such algorithm is the gossip based work of Kempe et al. [12]. Unfortunately, sampling cannot guarantee correctness and is sensitive to biased input distributions. Moreover, gossip based algorithms make assumptions on the mixing properties of the graph which do not hold for any graph. Pseudo-static computation suggests to perform a straightforward algorithm that would have computed the correct result had the system been static, and then bound the error due to possible changes. Such is the work by Bawa et. al. [13]. In flooding, input changes of each node are flooded over the whole graph, so every node can compute the majority decision directly. While flooding guarantees convergence, its communication costs are immense and it requires memory proportional to the system size in each node.

One related problem that has been addressed by local algorithms is the problem of local mending or persistent bit. In this problem all nodes have a state bit that is initially the same. A fault changes a minority of the bits and the task of the algorithm is to restore the bits to their initial value. Local solutions for this problem were given in [3, 4]. However, these solutions assume a static topology and synchronous communication.

Finally, [6] also conducts majority votes in dynamic settings. However, their algorithm assumes the underlying topology is a spanning tree. Although this algorithm can be layered on top of another distributed algorithm that provides a tree abstraction, a tree overlay does not make use of all available links as we do, and its costs must be taken into account. Even when assuming that once a tree is constructed its links do not break, simulations have shown that while [6] is faster in cases of a large majority, our algorithm is much faster as the majority is closer to the threshold.

7 Conclusions

We presented a local Majority Vote algorithm intended for dynamic, large-scale asynchronous systems. It uses an efficient, anytime spanning forest algorithm as a subroutine, which may also have other applications. The Majority Vote algorithm closely tracks the ad hoc solution, and rapidly converges to the correct solution upon cessation of changes. Detailed analysis revealed that if the occurrences of voting changes are uniformly spread across the system, the performance of the algorithm depends only on the number of changed votes and the current majority size, rather than the system size. A thorough empirical study demonstrated the excellent scalability of the algorithm for up to millions of nodes – the kind of scalability that is required by contemporary distributed systems.

References

1. Linial, N.: Locality in distributed graph algorithms. SIAM J. Comp. **21** (1992) 193–201
2. Awerbuch, B., Bar-Noy, A., Linial, N., Peleg, D.: Compact distributed data structures for adaptive network routing. Proc. 21st ACM STOC (1989)
3. Kutten, S., Peleg, D.: Fault-local distributed mending. Proceedings of the 14th Annual ACM Symposium on Principles of Distributed Computing (1995)
4. Kutten, S., Patt-Shamir, B.: Time-adaptive self-stabilization. Proc. of the 16th Annual ACM Symp. on Principles of Distributed Computing (1997) 149–158
5. Birk, Y., Liss, L., Schuster, A., Wolff, R.: A local algorithm for ad hoc majority voting via charge fusion. Technical Report EE1445 (CCIT497), Technion (2004)
6. Wolff, R., Schuster, A.: Association rule mining in peer-to-peer systems. In Proc. of the IEEE Conference on Data Mining (ICDM) (2003)
7. Ford, L., Fulkerson, D. In: Flows in Networks. Princton University Press (1962)
8. Jaffe, J., Moss, F.: A responsive routing algorithm for computer networks. IEEE Transactions on Communications (1982) 1758–1762
9. Garcia-Luna-Aceves, J.: A distributed, loop-free, shortest-path routing algorithm. Proceedings of IEEE INFOCOM (1988) 1125–1137
10. Kaashoek, F., Karger, D.: Koorde: A simple degree-optimal distributed hash table. In Proc. of the Second Intl. Workshop on Peer-to-Peer Systems (IPTPS) (2003)
11. C. Intanagonwiwat, R.G., Estrin, D.: Directed diffusion: A scalable and robust communication paradigm for sensor networks. In Proceedings of the Sixth Annual Intl. Conf. on Mobile Computing and Networking (2000)
12. Kempe, D., Dobra, A., Gehrke, J.: Computing aggregate information using gossip. Proceedings of Foundations of Computer Science (FOCS) (2003)
13. Bawa, M., Garcia-Molina, H., Gionis, A., Motwani, R.: Estimating aggregates on a peer-to-peer network. Technical report, Stanford University, DB group (2003)

Message-Optimal and Latency-Optimal Termination Detection Algorithms for Arbitrary Topologies

Neeraj Mittal, Subbarayan Venkatesan, and Sathya Peri

Department of Computer Science
The University of Texas at Dallas, Richardson, TX 75083
{neerajm,venky}@utdallas.edu
sathya.p@student.utdallas.edu

Abstract. Detecting termination of a distributed computation is a fundamental problem in distributed systems. We present two optimal algorithms for detecting termination of a non-diffusing distributed computation for an arbitrary topology. Both algorithms are *optimal* in terms of message complexity and detection latency. The first termination detection algorithm has to be initiated along with the underlying computation. The message complexity of this algorithm is $\Theta(N + M)$ and its detection latency is $\Theta(D)$, where N is the number of processes in the system, M is the number of application messages exchanged by the underlying computation, and D is the diameter of the communication topology. The second termination detection algorithm can be initiated at any time *after* the underlying computation has started. The message complexity of this algorithm is $\Theta(E + M)$ and its detection latency is $\Theta(D)$, where E is the number of channels in the communication topology.

Keywords: termination detection, quiescence detection, optimal message complexity, optimal detection latency

1 Introduction

One of the fundamental problems in distributed systems is to detect termination of an ongoing distributed computation. The termination detection problem was independently proposed by Dijkstra and Scholten [1] and Francez [2] more than two decades ago. Since then, many researchers have studied this problem and, as a result, a large number of algorithms have been developed for termination detection (*e.g.,* [3–15]). Although most of the research work on termination detection was conducted in 1980s and early 1990s, a few papers on termination detection still appear every year (*e.g.,* [13–15]).

Most termination detection algorithms can be broadly classified into three categories, namely *computation tree based, invigilator based,* and *wave based.* (A more detailed survey of termination detection algorithms can be found in [16].)

In the computation tree based approach, a dynamic tree is maintained based on messages exchanged by the underlying computation. A process not currently "participating" in the computation, on receiving an application message, remembers the process that sent the message (and joins the dynamic tree) until it

R. Guerraoui (Ed.): DISC 2004, LNCS 3274, pp. 290–304, 2004.

"leaves" the computation. This creates a parent-child relationship among processes that are currently "part" of the computation. A process may join and leave the tree many times. Example of algorithms based on this idea can be found in [1, 4, 10].

In the invigilator based approach, a distinguished process, called the *coordinator*, is responsible for maintaining current status of all processes. The coordinator may either explicitly maintain the number of processes that are currently "participating" in the computation [14] or may only know whether there exists at least one process that is currently "participating" in the computation (ascertained via missing credit or weight) [7, 9]. Algorithms in this class typically assume that the topology contains a star and the coordinator is directly connected to every process. These algorithms can be generalized to work for any communication topology at the expense of increased message complexity.

In the wave based approach, repeated snapshots of the underlying computation are taken and tested for termination condition. The testing procedure for termination takes into consideration the possibility that the snapshot may not be consistent. Examples of algorithms based on this approach can be found in [3, 5, 6, 8, 17].

Termination detection algorithms can also be classified based on two other attributes: (1) whether the distributed computation starts from a single process or from multiple processes: *diffusing computation* versus *non-diffusing computation*, and (2) whether the detection algorithm should be initiated along with the computation or can be initiated anytime after the computation has started: *simultaneous initiation* versus *delayed initiation*. Delayed initiation is useful when the underlying computation is message-intensive and therefore it is preferable to start the termination detection algorithm later when the computation is "close" to termination.

A termination detection algorithm should have low message-complexity (that is, it should exchange as few control messages as possible) and low detection latency (that is, it should detect termination as soon as possible). The former is desirable because it minimizes the overhead incurred on executing the termination detection algorithm. The latter is desirable in situations when the results of the computation can be used only after the computation has terminated.

Chandy and Misra [18] prove that any termination detection algorithm, in the worst case, must exchange at least M control messages, where M is the number of application messages exchanged by the underlying computation. Further, for a general non-diffusing computation (when an arbitrary subset of processes can be active initially), any termination detection algorithm must exchange at least $N - 1$ control messages in the worst-case, where N is the number of processes in the system. Chandrasekaran and Venkatesan [10] prove another lower bound that if the termination detection algorithm is initiated after the computation has started, then the algorithm, in the worst case, must exchange at least E control messages, where E is the number of communication channels in the topology. They also show that delayed initiation is not possible unless all channels are first-in-first-out (FIFO). Finally, note that, in the worst-case, the detection latency of any termination detection algorithm measured in terms of message hops is D, where D is the diameter of the communication topology.

Table 1. Comparison of various termination detection algorithms (assume diffusing computation and simultaneous initiation unless indicated otherwise).

Category	Message Complexity	Detection Latency	Communication Topology	Representative References
Computation Tree Based	$O(M)$	$O(N)$	any	[1, 4, 10]
Invigilator Based	$O(M)$	$O(1)$	contains a star	[14, 7, 9]
Modified Invigilator Based*	$O(MD)$	$O(D)$	any	
Wave Based	$O(NM)$	$O(D)$	any	[3, 5, 6, 8, 17]
Our Algorithm	$O(M)$	$O(D)$	any	[this paper]
Our Algorithm (non-diffusing computation)	$O(M + N)$	$O(D)$	any	[this paper]
Our Algorithm (non-diffusing computation and delayed initiation)	$O(M + E)$	$O(D)$	any	[this paper]

N: number of processes in the system
M: number of (application) messages exchanged by the underlying computation
D: diameter of the communication topology
E: number of channels in the communication topology
*: invigilator based adapted for arbitrary communication topology

Table 1 shows the (worst-case) message complexity and detection latency for the best algorithm in each of the three classes and for our algorithms. (For the wave based approach, we assume that a spanning tree is used to collect a snapshot of the system.) The table also indicates assumption, if any, made about the communication topology. Algorithms based on the computation tree based approach have optimal message complexity but non-optimal detection latency. On the other hand, algorithms that use the invigilator based approach have optimal detection latency but non-optimal message complexity. (The message-complexity is optimal only when the topology contains a star.)

To our knowledge, at present, there is no termination detection algorithm that has optimal message complexity as well as optimal detection latency for *all* communication topologies. We present two message-optimal and latency-optimal termination detection algorithms, which do not make any assumptions about the underlying communication topology. Furthermore, the amount of control information carried by each message is small ($\approx O(\log D)$). The first algorithm has to be started along with the computation. The second algorithm can be started anytime after the commencement of the computation. Our approach is a combination of computation tree based and invigilator based approaches.

2   System Model and Problem Description

2.1   System Model

We assume an asynchronous distributed system consisting of N processes $P = \{p_1, p_2, \ldots, p_N\}$, which communicate with each other by sending messages over a set of bidirectional channels. There is no common clock or shared memory. Processes are non-faulty and channels are reliable. Message delays are finite but may be unbounded. Processes change their states by executing events.

2.2   The Termination Detection Problem

The termination detection problem involves detecting when an ongoing distributed computation has terminated. The distributed computation is modeled as follows. A process can be either in an *active* state or a *passive* state. A process can send a message only when it is active. An active process can become passive at anytime. A passive process becomes active on receiving a message. The computation is said to have *terminated* when all processes have become passive and all channels have become empty.

A computation is *diffusing* if only one process is active initially; otherwise it is *non-diffusing*. If the termination detection algorithm is initiated along with the computation, then we refer to it as *simultaneous initiation*. On the other hand, if the termination detection algorithm is initiated after the computation has started, then we refer to it as *delayed initiation*.

To avoid confusion, we refer to the messages exchanged by the underlying computation as *application messages*, and the messages exchanged by the termination detection algorithm as *control messages*.

3   An Optimal Algorithm for Simultaneous Initiation

3.1   The Main Idea

We first describe the main idea behind the algorithm assuming that the underlying computation is a diffusing computation. We relax this assumption later.

Detecting Termination of a Diffusing Computation: First, we explain the main idea behind computation tree based and invigilator based approaches. Then we discuss how to combine them to obtain the optimal algorithm.

Computation Tree Based Approach: Consider a termination detection algorithm using computation tree based approach [1, 10]. Initially, only one process, referred to as the *initiator*, is active and all other processes are passive. A process, on receiving an application message, sends an *acknowledgment* message to the sender as soon as it knows that all activities triggered by the application message have ceased. The initiator announces termination as soon as it has received an *acknowledgment* message for every application message it has sent so far and is itself passive. The algorithm has optimal message complexity because it exchanges exactly one control message, namely the *acknowledgment* message, for every application message exchanged by the underlying computation. The detection latency, however, is far from optimal. Specifically, a chain of pending *acknowledgment* messages (sometimes referred to as an *acknowledgment* chain) may grow to a length as long as M, where M is the number of application messages exchanged. (The reason is that a process may appear multiple times on an *acknowledgment* chain as is the case with the algorithm of [10].)

The detection latency of the algorithm can be reduced from $O(M)$ to $O(N)$ (assuming $M = \Omega(N)$) as follows. Suppose a process has not yet sent an *acknowledgment* message for an application message it received earlier. In case the process receives another application message, it can immediately send an *acknowledgment* message for the latter application message. For termination detection purposes, it is sufficient to assume that all computation activities triggered by the receipt of the latter application message are triggered by the former application message. We refer to the former application message as an engaging application message and to the latter as a non-engaging application message.

Observe that the set of engaging application messages imposes a parent-child relationship among processes "currently participating" in the computation. Specifically, if a process has not yet sent an *acknowledgment* message for every application message it has received so far, then it is "currently a part" of the computation and is referred to as a nonquiescent process. Otherwise, it is "not currently a part" of the computation and is referred to as a quiescent process. At any time, the computation tree, which is dynamic, consists of the set of processes that are nonquiescent at that time.

Invigilator Based Approach: Now, consider a termination detection algorithm using the invigilator based approach [14]. One process is chosen to act as the coordinator. The coordinator is responsible for maintaining the current status of every process in the system. Suppose a process receives an application message. In case the coordinator does not already know that it (the process) is currently active, it sends a control message indicating "I am now active" to the coordinator. Once the process knows that the coordinator has received the control message, it sends an *acknowledgment* message to the sender of the application message. On the other hand, in case the coordinator already knows that it (the process) is currently active, it immediately acknowledges the application message. Once a process becomes passive and has received an *acknowledgment* message for every application message it has sent so far, it sends a control message indicating "I am now passive" to the coordinator. Intuitively, if the underlying computation has not terminated, then, as per the coordinator, at least one process is currently active. When the coordinator is directly connected to every other process in the system, the algorithm has optimal message complexity (at most three control message for every application message) and optimal detection latency (which is $O(1)$). When the topology is arbitrary, however, for communication between the coordinator and other processes, a static breadth-first-search (BFS) spanning tree rooted at the coordinator has to be constructed. Every control message that a process sends to the coordinator (along the spanning tree) may generate up to D additional messages, thereby increasing the message complexity to $O(MD)$.

Achieving the Best of the Two Approaches: As explained above, in the computation tree based approach, a process reports its status, when it becomes quiescent, to its parent. On the other hand, in the invigilator based approach, a process reports its status, when it becomes quiescent, to the coordinator. The main idea is to restrict the number of times processes report their status to the coordinator—to achieve optimal message complexity—and, at the same time, restrict the length of an *acknowledgment* chain—to achieve optimal detection latency.

Whenever a process reports its status to the coordinator, as many as D control messages may have to be exchanged. As a result, the number of times when

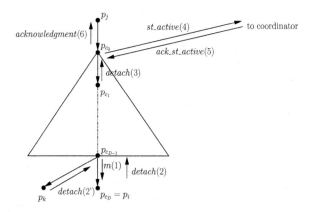

Fig. 1. An Illustration of the Termination Detection Algorithm.

processes report their quiescent status to the coordinator should be bounded by $O(M/D)$. The rest of the times processes should report their quiescent status to their respective parents in the computation tree. To ensure optimal detection latency, the length of an *acknowledgment* chain should be bounded by $O(D)$. The main problem is to determine, while the computation is executing, when a process should choose the former over the latter. In our algorithm, a process, by default, is supposed to report its status to its parent until it learns that the length of a chain of pending *acknowledgment* messages, starting from it, has become sufficiently long, that is, its length has become $\Theta(D)$. At that time, it starts reporting its status to the coordinator. Specifically, it first sends an *st_active* message signifying that "my computation subtree is currently active" to the coordinator. It waits until it has received an acknowledgment from the coordinator in the form of an *ack_st_active* message. The receipt of the *ack_st_active* message implies that the coordinator is aware of some activity in the system and therefore will now announce termination as yet. It then sends an *acknowledgment* message to its parent, thereby breaking its link with its parent and shortening the *acknowledgment* chain. Later, when it becomes quiescent, it sends an *st_passive* message indicating "my computation subtree has now become passive" to the coordinator.

To measure the length of an *acknowledgment* chain, we piggyback an integer on every application message that refers to the current length of an *acknowledgment* chain. On receiving an application message, if a process learns that the length of the *acknowledgment* chain has become at least D, then it resets the value of the integer to zero. Further, it sends a special control message, referred to as a *detach* message, to the process at a distance of D from it along the *acknowledgment* chain but in the reverse direction. The objective of a *detach* message is to instruct its intended recipient that it should become the head of the chain and report its status to the coordinator instead of its parent (the details of how it happens are discussed in the previous paragraph). The reason is that the overhead incurred on exchanging control messages with the coordinator, namely *st_active*, *ack_st_active* and *st_passive*, can now be amortized over enough number of processes so as not to affect the message complexity adversely. Note that a process may have multiple chains of *acknowledgment* messages emanating from it. As a result, there may be multiple processes that are at a distance of D from it, all of which will send *detach* messages destined for it. This may increase the message complexity significantly. To that end, we propagate *detach* messages upward along an *acknowledgment* chain in a modified convergecast fashion. If a process has already propagated a *detach* message to its parent, then it ignores any subsequent *detach* messages it receives.

Example 1. Figure 1 illustrates the main idea behind our termination detection algorithm. Suppose process p_i, on receiving an engaging application message m, learns that the length of the *acknowledgment* chain has become at least D. Let the last $D + 1$ processes along the chain be denoted by $p_{c_0}, p_{c_1}, \ldots, p_{c_D} = p_i$. As per our algorithm, p_i sends a *detach* message to its parent $p_{c_{D-1}}$. The *detach* message is propagated upward all the way to p_{c_0}, which is at a distance of D from p_i. Process p_{c_0}, on receiving the *detach* message, sends an *st_active* message to the coordinator. The coordinator, on receiving the *st_active* message, sends an *ack_st_active* message to p_{c_0}. On receiving the *ack_st_active* message, p_{c_0} sends an *acknowledgment* message to its parent, denoted by process p_j, thereby breaking the chain. Numbers in the brackets show the sequence in which various control messages are exchanged. It is possible that $p_{c_{D-1}}$ has another child, namely process p_k, which also sends a *detach* message to it destined for p_{c_0}. On receiving the second *detach* message, $p_{c_{D-1}}$ simply ignores it and does not forward it to its parent $p_{c_{D-2}}$. ☐

Message-complexity: Our algorithm exchanges five different types of control messages, namely *acknowledgment*, *detach*, *st_active*, *st_passive* and *ack_st_active*. One *acknowledgment* message is exchanged for every application message. Also, a process sends at most one *detach* message for every application message it receives. Therefore the total number of *acknowledgment* and *detach* messages is bounded by $2M$. The number of *st_active* messages generated by all processes combined is given by $O(M/D)$. This is because a process sends an *st_active* message only when it knows that there are at least $O(D)$ processes in its computation subtree. Each *st_active* message is sent on the BFS spanning tree, which may generate at most D additional messages. Finally, the number of *st_passive* messages as well as the number of *ack_st_active* messages is equal to the number of *st_active* messages. Thus the message complexity of our algorithm is $O(M)$.

Detection-latency: Our algorithm ensures that whenever the length of an *acknowledgment* chain grows beyond $2D$, within $3D + 1$ message hops (consisting of *detach*, *st_active* and *ack_st_active* messages), the chain is reduced to length smaller than D. Thus the detection latency of our algorithm is $O(D)$.

Generalizing for a Non-diffusing Computation: Assume that there may be multiple initiators of the computation. Intuitively, the coordinator should announce termination only after every initiator has informed it that the computation triggered by it has terminated. The coordinator, however, does not know how many initiators of the computation are there. Therefore, every process, on becoming quiescent for the first time (including the case when it is quiescent to begin with), sends an *initialize* message to the coordinator. The coordinator announces termination only after it has received an *initialize* message from every process (and, of course, a matching *st_passive* message for every *st_active* message). The *initialize* messages are propagated to the coordinator in a convergecast fashion, thereby resulting in only $O(N)$ more messages.

3.2   Formal Description

A formal description of the termination detection algorithm TDA-SI for simultaneous initiation is given in Fig. 2 and Fig. 3. Actions A0-A8 described in the two figures capture the behavior of a process as part of the computation tree. Due to lack of space, actions of processes as part of the BFS spanning tree have been omitted and can be found in [19]. The main function of a process as part of the spanning tree is to propagate messages, namely *initialize*, *st_active*, *ack_st_active* and *st_passive*, back and forth between the coordinator and its descendants in the spanning tree.

3.3   Proof of Correctness and Optimality

A process, on sending an *st_active* message to the coordinator, expects to receive an *ack_st_active* message eventually. Note that it is easy to route an *st_active* (or *st_passive*) message from a non-coordinator process to the coordinator. However, routing an *ack_st_active* message from the coordinator to the process that generated the corresponding *st_active* message is non-trivial. One approach to achieve this is by piggybacking the identity of the generating process on the *st_active* message which can then be used to appropriately route the corresponding *ack_st_active* message. This, however, increases the message overhead to $O(\log N)$, and also requires each process to know all its descendants. Instead, we employ the following mechanism. Every process on the BFS spanning tree sends the kth *ack_st_active* message to the sender of the kth *st_active* message. This can be accomplished by maintaining a FIFO queue that records the sender of every *st_active* message that a process receives. Later, on receiving an *ack_st_active* message, the process uses the queue to forward the *ack_st_active* message to the appropriate process, which is either itself or one of its children. We have,

Lemma 1. *A process eventually receives an ack_st_active message for every st_active message it sends.*

Due to lack of space, proofs of lemmas and some theorems have been omitted, and can be found in [19]. The second lemma states that if a process receives a matching *ack_st_active* message for its *st_active* message, then the coordinator "knows" that its subtree is "active"

Lemma 2. *A process receives a matching ack_st_active message for its st_active message only after the st_active message has been received by the coordinator.*

Termination detection algorithm for process p_i:

Variables:
    D: diameter of the topology;
    $state_i :=$ my initial state;   // whether I am active or passive
    $missing_i := 0$;   // number of unacknowledged application messages
    $hops_i := 0$;   // hop count: my distance from a root process
    $parent_i := \perp$;   // process which made me nonquiescent
    $independent_i :=$ true;   // if root, can I detach myself from my parent?
    $pending_i := 0$;   // the number of unacknowledged st_active messages

// Actions of process p_i as part of the computation tree

Useful expressions:
    $quiescent_i \triangleq (state_i = passive) \wedge (missing_i = 0)$;
    $root_i \triangleq (hops_i = 0)$

(A0) Initial action:
    call sendIfQuiescent( );   // send an initialize message if passive

(A1) On sending an application message m to process p_j:
    send $\langle m, hops_i \rangle$ to process p_j;
    $missing_i := missing_i + 1$;   // one more application message to be acknowledged

(A2) On receiving an application message $\langle m, count \rangle$ from process p_j:
    if not($quiescent_i$) then   // a non-engaging application message
        send $\langle acknowledgment \rangle$ message to process p_j;
    else   // an engaging application message
        $parent_i := p_j$;
        $hops_i := (count + 1)$ mod D;
        if $root_i$ then
            send $\langle detach \rangle$ message to $parent_i$; // instruct root of my parent's subtree to detach
            $independent_i :=$ false;   // but I am still attached to my parent
        endif;
    endif;
    $state_i := active$;
    deliver m to the application;

(A3) On receiving $\langle acknowledgment \rangle$ message from process p_j:
    $missing_i := missing_i - 1$;   // one more application message has been acknowledged
    call acknowledgeParent( );   // send acknowledgment to my parent if quiescent
    call sendIfQuiescent( );   // send initialize/st_passive message if quiescent

(A4) On changing state from active to passive:
    call acknowledgeParent( );   // send acknowledgment to my parent if quiescent
    call sendIfQuiescent( );   // send initialize/st_passive message if quiescent

Fig. 2. Termination detection algorithm TDA-SI for simultaneous initiation.

We say that a process is *quiescent* if it is passive and has received an *acknowledgment* message for every application message it has sent so far. We partition the events on a process into two categories: *quiescent* and *nonquiescent*. An event is said to be quiescent if the process becomes quiescent immediately after executing the event; otherwise it is nonquiescent. A maximal sequence of contiguous quiescent events on a process is called a *quiescent interval*. The notion of *nonquiescent interval* can be similarly defined. We also partition the set of application messages into two categories: *engaging* and *non-engaging*. An ap-

---

Termination detection algorithm for process p_i (continued):

(A5) On receiving $\langle detach \rangle$ message from process p_j:
    if $(root_i \wedge \textbf{not}(independent_i))$ **then**   // should I handle detach message myself?
        $independent_i :=$ true;   // I can now detach myself from my parent
        send $\langle st\_active \rangle$ to the coordinator (via the BFS spanning tree);
        $pending_i := pending_i + 1;$
    else if not$(root_i)$ **then**   // detach message is meant for the root of my subtree
        if (have not yet forwarded a detach message
            to $parent_i$ since last becoming nonquiescent) **then**
            send $\langle detach \rangle$ message to $parent_i$;
        endif;
    endif;

(A6) On receiving $\langle ack\_st\_active \rangle$ message from the coordinator (via the BFS spanning tree);
    $pending_i := pending_i - 1;$ // one more st_active message has been acknowledged
    call acknowledgeParent( );   // may need to send acknowledgment to my parent

(A7) On invocation of acknowledgeParent( ):
    if $(quiescent_i$ **or**
        $(root_i \wedge independent_i \wedge (pending_i = 0)))$ **then**
        if $(parent_i \neq \bot)$ **then**   // do I have a parent?
            send $\langle acknowledgment \rangle$ message to $parent_i$;
            $parent_i := \bot;$
        endif;
    endif;

(A8) On invocation of sendIfQuiescent( ):
    if $(root_i \wedge independent_i \wedge quiescent_i)$ **then**   // should I send initialize/st_passive message?
        if (have not yet sent an initialize message) **then**
            send $\langle initialize \rangle$ message to the coordinator (via the BFS spanning tree);
        else send $\langle st\_passive \rangle$ to the coordinator (via the BFS spanning tree); **endif**;
    endif:

Fig. 3. Termination detection algorithm TDA-SI for simultaneous initiation (contd.).

plication message is said to be *engaging* if its destination process, on receiving the message, changes its status from quiescent to nonquiescent; otherwise it is non-engaging. We have,

Lemma 3. *Assume that the underlying computation eventually terminates. Then, every nonquiescent process eventually becomes quiescent.*

From the algorithm, a process sends an *initialize* message when it becomes quiescent for the first time (including the case when it is quiescent to begin with). The following proposition can be easily verified:

Proposition 4. *Assume that the underlying computation eventually terminates. Then, every process eventually sends an initialize message. Moreover, a process sends an initialize message only when it is quiescent for the first time.*

The following lemma establishes that if the computation terminates then every process sends an equal number of *st_active* and *st_passive* messages in alternate order.

Lemma 5. *Every process sends a (possibly empty) sequence of st_active and st_passive messages in an alternate fashion, starting with an st_active message. Furthermore, if the underlying computation eventually terminates, then every st_active message is eventually followed by an st_passive message.*

It is important for the correctness of our algorithm that the coordinator receives *st_active* and *st_passive* messages in correct order. If channels are FIFO, then this can be achieved easily. If one or more channels are non-FIFO, then the algorithm has to be slightly modified. Details of the modification are described in [19]. For now, assume that all channels are FIFO. We are now ready to prove the correctness of our algorithm. First, we prove that our algorithm is live.

Theorem 6 (TDA-SI is live). *Assume that the underlying computation eventually terminates. Then, the coordinator eventually announces termination.*

Proof. To establish the liveness property, it suffices to show that the following two conditions hold eventually. First, the coordinator receives all *initialize* messages it is waiting for. Second, the activity counter at the coordinator, given by *"number of st_active messages received - number of st_passive messages received"*, becomes zero permanently.

Note that *initialize* messages are propagated to the coordinator in a convergecast fashion. From Proposition 4, eventually every process sends an *initialize* message. It can be easily verified that every process on the BFS spanning tree will eventually send an *initialize* message to its parent on the (spanning) tree. As a result, the first condition holds eventually.

For the second condition, assume that the underlying computation has terminated. Then, from Lemma 3, every process eventually becomes quiescent and stays quiescent thereafter. This implies that every process sends only a finite number of *st_active* and *st_passive* messages. Therefore the coordinator also receives only a finite number of *st_active* and *st_passive* messages. Furthermore, from Lemma 5, the coordinator receives an equal number of *st_active* and *st_passive* messages.   □

Now, we prove that our algorithm is safe, that is, it never announces false termination. The proof uses the well-known Lamport's happened-before relation, which we denote by →.

Theorem 7 (TDA-SI is safe). *The coordinator announces termination only after the underlying computation has terminated.*

Proof. Consider only those processes that become active at least once. Let *announce* denote the event on executing which the coordinator announces termination, and let d_i denote the *last* quiescent event on process p_i that happened-before *announce*. Such an event exists for every process. This is because the coordinator announces termination only after it has received all *initialize* messages it is waiting for. This, in turn, happens only after every process has sent an *initialize* message, which a process does only when it is quiescent.

Consider the snapshot S of the computation passing through all d_is. Assume, on the contrary, that the computation has not terminated for S and that some

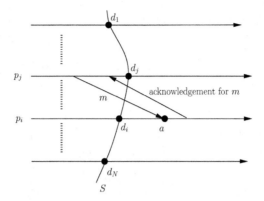

Fig. 4. Proving the safety of TDA-SI.

process becomes active after S. Let NQE denote the set of nonquiescent events executed in the future of S. Consider a *minimal* event a in NQE—minimal with respect to the happened-before relation. Formally,

$$\langle \forall x : x \in NQE : x \nrightarrow a \rangle$$

Clearly, a occurred on receiving an engaging application message, say m. Moreover, m is a message sent from the past of S to the future of S. Otherwise, it can be shown that a is not a minimal event in NQE—a contradiction. Let m be sent by process p_j to process p_i. Also, let $snd(m)$ and $rcv(m)$ correspond to the send and receive events of m, respectively. Then, $snd(m) \rightarrow d_j$. This implies that p_j becomes quiescent after sending m. Therefore it receives the *acknowledgment* message for m before executing d_j. This is depicted in Fig. 4. There are two cases to consider:

Case 1: Process p_i sends an *acknowledgment* message for m on executing a quiescent event, say b. Clearly, the *acknowledgment* message creates a causal path from b to d_j. We have,

$$(b \text{ is a quiescent event on } p_i) \wedge (d_i \rightarrow b) \wedge (b \rightarrow d_j) \wedge (d_j \rightarrow announce)$$

In other words, b is a quiescent event on p_i that happened-before *announce* and is executed after d_i. This contradicts our choice of d_i.

Case 2: Process p_i sends an *acknowledgment* message for m before becoming quiescent. This happens only when p_i receives an *ack_st_active* message for the *st_active* message it sends in the current nonquiescent interval (which starts with a). Let the receive event of the *st_active* message on the coordinator be denoted by r. Using Lemma 2, $r \rightarrow d_j$. Since $d_j \rightarrow announce$, $r \rightarrow announce$. For the coordinator to announce termination, it should receive a matching *st_passive* message from p_i later but before announcing termination. Clearly, p_i sends this *st_passive* message only on executing some quiescent event after a. This again contradicts our choice of d_i. □

We next show that our termination detection algorithm is optimal in terms of message complexity and detection latency.

Theorem 8 (TDA-SI is message-optimal). *Assume that the underlying computation eventually terminates. Then, the number of control messages exchanged by the algorithm is $\Theta(M + N)$, where N is the number of processes in the system and M is the number of application messages exchanged by the underlying computation.*

Also, we have,

Theorem 9 (TDA-SI is latency-optimal). *Once the underlying computation terminates, the coordinator announces termination within $O(D)$ message hops.*

We now show how to modify our termination detection algorithm so that it can be started later anytime after the computation has begun.

4   An Optimal Algorithm for Delayed Initiation

If the underlying computation is message-intensive, then it is desirable not to initiate the termination detection algorithm along with the computation. It is preferable, instead, to initiate it later, when the underlying computation is "close" to termination. This is because, in the latter case, the (worst-case) message-complexity of the termination detection algorithm would depend on the number of application messages exchanged by the computation *after* the termination detection algorithm has commenced. As a result, with delayed initiation, the termination detection algorithm generally exchanges a fewer number of control messages than with simultaneous initiation.

To correctly detect termination with delayed initiation, we use the scheme proposed in [10]. The main idea is to distinguish between application messages sent by a process *before* it started *termination detection* and messages sent by it *after* it started *termination detection*. Clearly, the former messages should not be "tracked" by the termination detection algorithm and the latter messages should be "tracked" by the termination detection algorithm. Note that delayed initiation is not possible unless all channels are FIFO. This is because if one or more channels are non-FIFO then an application message may be delayed arbitrarily on a channel, no process would be aware of its existence, and this message may arrive at the destination after termination has been announced. Henceforth, we assume that all channels are FIFO.

In order to distinguish between the two kinds of application messages, we use a *marker* message. Specifically, as soon as a process starts the termination detection algorithm, it sends a *marker* message along all its outgoing channels. Therefore, when a process receives a *marker* message along an incoming channel, it knows that any application message received along that channel from now on has to be acknowledged as per the termination detection algorithm. On the other hand, if a process receives an application message on an incoming channel along which it has not yet received a *marker* message, then that message should not be acknowledged and should be simply delivered to the application. Intuitively, a *marker* message sent along a channel "flushes" any in-transit application messages on that channel. For ease of exposition, we assume that initially all incoming channels are *uncolored*. Further, a process, on receiving a *marker* message along an incoming channel, *colors* the channel along which it has received the *marker* message.

To initiate the termination detection algorithm, the coordinator sends a *marker* message to itself. When a process receives a *marker* message, as explained before, it colors the incoming channel along which the *marker* message is received. Additionally, if it is the first *marker* message to be received, the process starts executing the termination detection algorithm and also sends a *marker* message along all its outgoing channels. Note that the coordinator should not announce termination at least until every process has received a *marker* message along all its incoming channels and therefore has colored all its incoming channels. To enable delayed initiation, we just redefine the notion of quiescence as follows: a process is quiescent if it is passive, has received an *acknowledgment* message for every application message it has sent so far, and *all its incoming channels have been colored*. A formal description of the termination detection algorithm for delayed initiation, which we refer to as TDA-DI, is given in [19].

The correctness and optimality proof of TDA-DI is similar to that of TDA-SI. Intuitively, it can be verified that once the underlying computation terminates, TDA-DI eventually announces termination after all incoming channels have been colored (that is, TDA-DI is live). Also, TDA-DI announces termination only after all processes have become quiescent. This in turn implies that the underlying computation has terminated (that is, TDA-DI is safe). The message-complexity of TDA-DI is at most E more than the message complexity of TDA-SI, where E is the number of channels in the communication topology. Also, assuming that the termination detection algorithm is started before the underlying computation terminates, the detection latency of TDA-DI is $O(D)$.

5   Conclusion and Future Work

In this paper, we present two optimal algorithms for termination detection when processes and channels are reliable, and all channels are bidirectional. Both our algorithms have optimal message complexity and optimal detection latency. The first termination detection algorithm has to be initiated along with the computation. The second termination detection algorithm can be initiated at any time after the computation has started. However, in this case, all channels are required to be FIFO. Our algorithms do not make any assumptions about the communication topology (whether it contains a star or is fully connected) or the distributed computation (which processes are active initially).

Our termination detection algorithms have the following limitations. First, we assume that every process knows the diameter D of the communication topology. Second, each application message carries an integer whose maximum value is D. As a result, the bit-message complexity of our algorithms is given by $O(M \log D + N)$ and $O(M \log D + E)$, respectively, which is sub-optimal. Third, we use a coordinator, which is responsible for processing *st_passive* and *st_active* messages sent by other processes. The coordinator may become a bottleneck. As future work, we plan to develop a termination detection algorithm that does not suffer from the above-mentioned limitations.

References

1. Dijkstra, E.W., Scholten, C.S.: Termination Detection for Diffusing Computations. Information Processing Letters (IPL) **11** (1980) 1–4
2. Francez, N.: Distributed Termination. ACM Transactions on Programming Languages and Systems (TOPLAS) **2** (1980) 42–55
3. Rana, S.P.: A Distributed Solution of the Distributed Termination Problem. Information Processing Letters (IPL) **17** (1983) 43–46
4. Shavit, N., Francez, N.: A New Approach to Detection of Locally Indicative Stability. In: Proceedings of the International Colloquium on Automata, Languages and Systems (ICALP), Rennes, France (1986) 344–358
5. Mattern, F.: Algorithms for Distributed Termination Detection. Distributed Computing (DC) **2** (1987) 161–175
6. Dijkstra, E.W.: Shmuel Safra's Version of Termination Detection. EWD Manuscript 998. Available at http://www.cs.utexas.edu/users/EWD (1987)
7. Mattern, F.: Global Quiescence Detection based on Credit Distribution and Recovery. Information Processing Letters (IPL) **30** (1989) 195–200
8. Huang, S.T.: Termination Detection by using Distributed Snapshots. Information Processing Letters (IPL) **32** (1989) 113–119
9. Huang, S.T.: Detecting Termination of Distributed Computations by External Agents. In: Proceedings of the IEEE International Conference on Distributed Computing Systems (ICDCS). (1989) 79–84
10. Chandrasekaran, S., Venkatesan, S.: A Message-Optimal Algorithm for Distributed Termination Detection. Journal of Parallel and Distributed Computing (JPDC) **8** (1990) 245–252
11. Tel, G., Mattern, F.: The Derivation of Distributed Termination Detection Algorithms from Garbage Collection Schemes. ACM Transactions on Programming Languages and Systems (TOPLAS) **15** (1993) 1–35
12. Stupp, G.: Stateless Termination Detection. In: Proceedings of the 16th Symposium on Distributed Computing (DISC), Toulouse, France (2002) 163–172
13. Khokhar, A.A., Hambrusch, S.E., Kocalar, E.: Termination Detection in Data-Driven Parallel Computations/Applications. Journal of Parallel and Distributed Computing (JPDC) **63** (2003) 312–326
14. Mahapatra, N.R., Dutt, S.: An Efficient Delay-Optimal Distributed Termination Detection Algorithm. To Appear in Journal of Parallel and Distributed Computing (JPDC) (2004)
15. Wang, X., Mayo, J.: A General Model for Detecting Termination in Dynamic Systems. In: Proceedings of the 18th International Parallel and Distributed Processing Symposium (IPDPS), Santa Fe, New Mexico (2004)
16. Matocha, J., Camp, T.: A Taxonomy of Distributed Termination Detection Algorithms. The Journal of Systems and Software **43** (1999) 207–221
17. Atreya, R., Mittal, N., Garg, V.K.: Detecting Locally Stable Predicates without Modifying Application Messages. In: Proceedings of the 7th International Conference on Principles of Distributed Systems (OPODIS), La Martinique, France (2003)
18. Chandy, K.M., Misra, J.: How Processes Learn. Distributed Computing (DC) **1** (1986) 40–52
19. Mittal, N., Venkatesan, S., Peri, S.: Message-Optimal and Latency-Optimal Termination Detection Algorithms for Arbitrary Topologies. Technical Report UTDCS-08-04, The University of Texas at Dallas (2004) Available at http://www.utdallas.edu/~neerajm/.

Routing with Improved Communication-Space Trade-Off
(Extended Abstract[*])

Ittai Abraham[1], Cyril Gavoille[2], and Dahlia Malkhi[1]

[1] School of Computer Science and Engineering,
The Hebrew University of Jerusalem, Jerusalem, Israel
{ittaia,dalia}@cs.huji.ac.il
[2] Laboratoire Bordelais de Recherche en Informatique,
University of Bordeaux, Bordeaux, France
gavoille@labri.fr

Abstract. Given a weighted undirected network with arbitrary node names, we present a family of routing schemes characterized by an integral parameter $\kappa \geq 1$. The scheme uses $\widetilde{O}(n^{1/\kappa} \log D)$ space routing table at each node, and routes along paths of linear stretch $O(\kappa)$, where D is the normalized diameter of the network. When D is polynomial in n, the scheme has asymptotically optimal stretch factor. With the same memory bound, the best previous results obtained stretch $O(\kappa^2)$.

Of independent interest, we also construct a single-source name-independent routing scheme for uniform weighted graphs with $O(1)$ stretch and $\widetilde{O}(1)$ bits of storage. With the same stretch, the best previous results obtained memory $\widetilde{O}(n^{1/9})$.

1 Introduction

The ability to route messages to specific destinations is one of the basic building blocks of any networked distributed system. Consider a weighted undirected network $G = (V, E, \omega)$ with n nodes having arbitrary unique network identifiers in $\{1, \ldots, n\}$. A *name-independent routing scheme* is a distributed algorithm that allows any source node to route messages to any destination node, given the destination's network identifier.

Several measures characterize the efficiency and feasibility of a routing scheme.

Memory: The amount of memory bits stored by each node for purposes of routing.

Headers: The size of message headers that are written by nodes along the route.

Stretch: The maximum ratio, over all pairs, of the length of the routing path produced by the routing scheme by routing from s to t and the shortest path distance from s to t in G.

---

[*] Full version appears as Technical Report #RR-1330-04 of Bordeaux University [1].

R. Guerraoui (Ed.): DISC 2004, LNCS 3274, pp. 305–319, 2004.
© Springer-Verlag Berlin Heidelberg 2004

Our aim is to devise *compact* routing schemes with poly-logarithmic headers that have improved tradeoffs between the memory consumption and the stretch factor.

Our contributions. We first present in **Section 3** a family of routing schemes parameterized by an integer $\kappa > 0$, that has the complexity measures below. The $\widetilde{O}()$ notation denotes complexity similar to $O()$ up to poly-logarithmic factors. Concrete constants are provided in the body of the paper.

Each node keeps $\widetilde{O}(n^{1/\kappa} \log D)$ bits of storage, where D is the normalized diameter of the graph. Message headers are of size $\widetilde{O}(1)$, and each route has stretch $O(\kappa)$

When D is polynomial in n, the scheme has asymptotically optimal stretch factor, as proven by [17]. With the same memory bound, the best previous results obtained stretch $O(\kappa^2)$ [6,3].

Then, in **Section 4**, we consider the problem of routing messages from a distinguished node, the *source*, to all the other nodes. Single source routing problem with small local storage can also be seen as a searching problem through DHT or distributed dictionaries, or as locating keys in peer-to-peer systems. Efficient solution to these problems is interesting on its own right, and might be of practical interests. We show prove that uniform weighted graphs have a single-source name-independent routing scheme with $O(1)$ stretch and $\widetilde{O}(1)$ bits of storage, the first constant stretch routing scheme with poly-logarithmic memory. The best previous bound with similar stretch was $\widetilde{O}(n^{1/9})$ bits of storage [14].

Previous results. There is a subtle distinction between a *designer port* model and a *fixed port* model. In the *fixed port* model (also known as the adversarial port model) the names of outgoing links, or ports, from each node may be arbitrarily chosen by an adversary from the set $\{1, \ldots, n\}$. In the *designer port* model they may be determined by the designer of the routing scheme. In particular, Gavoille and Gengler [12] indicate at least stretch-3 when each node has memory $o(n)$. For stretch-k routing scheme Peleg and Upfal [17] prove that a total of $\Omega(n^{1+1/(2k+4)})$ routing information bits is required. Thorup and Zwick refine this bound and show in [20] that the stretch is at least $2k + 1$ when each node has memory $o(n^{1/k})$, proved for $k = 1, 2, 3, 5$ and conjectured for other values of k. For comprehensive surveys on compact routing and compact network data structures, see [11,13].

Initial results in [5] provide name-independent routing with $\widetilde{O}(n^{3/2})$ total memory. Awerbuch and Peleg [6] presented a scheme that for any k, requires $\widetilde{O}(k^2 n^{1/k} \log D)$ bits per node and routes on paths of stretch $O(k^2)$. Arias et al. [3] present a slight improvement that uses the same memory bounds but improves the constant in the $O(k^2)$ stretch by a factor of 4.

All known name-independent schemes that are "combinatorial" and do not rely on the normalized diameter, D, in their storage bound have exponential stretch factor. Awerbuch et al. [4] achieve with $\widetilde{O}(n^{1/k})$ memory stretch $O(9^k)$, and [3] improved to stretch $O(2^k)$ with the same memory bound. For $\widetilde{O}(\sqrt{n})$

memory Arias et al. provide stretch 5. Recently, Abraham et al. [2], achieve optimal stretch 3 with $\widetilde{O}(\sqrt{n})$.

A weaker variant of the routing problem, *labeled routing*, was initiated in [4]. In this problem model, the algorithm's designer can choose the network addresses of nodes (and of course, use node names to store information about their location in the graph). This paradigm does not provide for a realistic network design, however, the tools devised for its solution have proven useful as building blocks of full routing schemes (in fact, we make use here of certain building blocks devised in the context of labeled routing schemes).

Indeed, optimal compact schemes for labeled routing are known. The first non trivial stretch-3 scheme was given by Cowen [9] with $\widetilde{O}(n^{2/3})$ memory. Later, Thorup and Zwick [19,20] improved the memory bound to only $\widetilde{O}(\sqrt{n})$ bits. They also gave an elegant generalization of their scheme, achieving stretch $4k - 5$ (and even $2k - 1$ with handshaking) using only $\widetilde{O}(n^{1/k})$ bits. Additionally, there exist various labeled routing schemes suitable only for certain restricted forms of graphs. For example, routing in a tree is explored, e.g., in [10,20], achieving optimal routing. It requires $\widetilde{O}(1)$ bits for local tables and $\widetilde{O}(1)$ bits for headers.

Due to space limitation, some proofs have been moved in [1].

2   Preliminaries

We denote an undirected weighted graph by $G = (V, E, \omega)$, where V is the set of nodes, E the set of links, and $\omega : E \to \mathbb{R}^+$ a link-cost function. For any two nodes $u, v \in V$ let $d_G(u, v)$ be the cost of a minimum cost path from u to v, where a cost of a path is the sum of weights of its edges. Define the *normalized diameter* of G, $D = \frac{\max_{u,v} d_G(u,v)}{\min_{u \neq v} d_G(u,v)}$. Let $B(v, r) = \{u \in V \mid d_G(v, u) \leq r\}$.

We denote a rooted weighted tree by $T = (V, r, E, \omega)$, and define for every node $u \in V$ its *parent* $p(u)$ and for the root $p(r) = r$. The *children* of a node u are defined as $\text{child}(u) = \{v \mid p(v) = u\}$. The *weight* of a node u denoted $w(u)$ is the number of nodes in u's subtree not including u itself. Define the *radius* of T as maximum distance from the root, $\text{rad}(T) = \max_u \{d_T(r, u)\}$.

Define the *maximum edge weight* of a weighted tree $T = (V, E, \omega)$ as $\text{maxE}(T) = \max_{e \in E} \{\omega(e)\}$.

For $u \in V$, let $N(u) = \{v \mid (u, v) \in E\}$ denote u's neighbors. For every node u, let $\text{port}(u, v)$ for every $v \in N(u)$ be a unique port name in $\{1, \ldots, n\}$. If node u wants to forward a message to node $v \in N(u)$ it does so by sending the message on port $\text{port}(u, v)$. In the *fixed port* model (also known as the adversarial port model) the values $\{\text{port}(u, v) \mid v \in N(u)\} \subseteq \{1, \ldots, n\}$ are arbitrarily chosen.

3   Linear Communication-Space Trade-Off

Let $G = (V, E, \omega)$ be a graph, where $|V| = n$. In this section, we provide a family of name-independent routing schemes for G parameterized by κ, in which each node keeps $\widetilde{O}(n^{1/\kappa} \log D)$ storage, where D is the normalized diameter of the graph, and each route has stretch $O(\kappa)$. When D is polynomial in n, the scheme has asymptotically optimal stretch factor, as proven by [17].

The construction makes use of two building blocks. The first one is a new tree cover based on Sparse Partitions, the second is a novel tree-routing scheme we devise. Below, we first state these building blocks, then make a black-box use of them for our full solution, and finally go back to provide the details of our novel tree-routing scheme.

3.1 Tree Cover Based on Sparse Partitions

Lemma 1. [6,7,16] *For every weighted graph $G = (V, E, \omega)$, $|V| = n$ and integers $\kappa, \rho \geq 1$, there exists a polynomial algorithm that constructs a collection of rooted trees $\mathcal{TC}_{\kappa,\rho}$ such that:*

1. *(Cover) For all $v \in V$, there exists $T \in \mathcal{TC}_{\kappa,\rho}$ such that $B(v, \rho) \subseteq T$.*
2. *(Sparse) For all $v \in V$, $|\{T \in \mathcal{TC}_{\kappa,\rho} \mid v \in T\}| \leq 2\kappa n^{1/\kappa}$.*
3. *(Small radius) For all $T \in \mathcal{TC}_{\kappa,\rho}$, $\mathrm{rad}(T) \leq (2\kappa - 1)\rho$.*
4. *(Small edges) For all $T \in \mathcal{TC}_{\kappa,\rho}$, $\mathrm{maxE}(T) \leq 2\rho$.*

Note that property (4) is a novel property that does to appear in the tree covers of [6,7,16]. However, it is crucial for our construction and its proof is a simple consequence of the manner in which the cover algorithm works: in each iteration, any cluster S added to a cover Y has $\mathrm{rad}(S) \leq \rho$. The end result is a set of covers $\mathcal{R}$ that has properties (1),(2), and (3). For every cover $Y \in \mathcal{R}$ define $r(Y)$ as the initial node that started that cover, and $G[Y]$ as the subgraph containing Y and all the edges connecting nodes in Y whose cost is at most 2ρ. $G[Y]$ spans Y because Y is formed by a connected union of clusters whose radius is at most ρ. The set $\mathcal{TC}_{\kappa,\rho}$ is defined by taking every $Y \in \mathcal{R}$ and setting $T_Y \in \mathcal{TC}_{\kappa,\rho}$ to be a minimum cost path tree spanning $G[Y]$ whose root is $r(Y)$.

W.l.o.g. assume that the minimum cost edge is 1. We define an index set $I = \{1, \ldots, \lceil \log D \rceil\}$. For all $i \in I$, we build a tree cover $\mathcal{TC}_{\kappa,2^i}$ according to **Lemma 1** above. For all $v \in V$ and $i \in I$, let $\mathrm{Tree}_v[i]$ be a tree $T \in \mathcal{TC}_{\kappa,2^i}$ such that $B(v, 2^i) \subseteq T$.

3.2 Bounded Cost Name-Independent Tree-Routing

Having built a hierarchy of tree covers, any source v would like to perform name-independent routing on $\mathrm{Tree}_v[i]$, for $i \in I$ in increasing order, until the target is found. Our second building block addresses this need using a novel and efficient construction. This construction provides a name-independent *error-reporting* routing scheme in which the cost of routing to a destination in the tree or learning that the name does not exist is bounded by a function of the tree's radius, the maximum edge cost, and a parameter κ.

Theorem 1. *For every tree $T = (U, E, \omega)$, $|U| = m$, $U \subset V$, $|V| = n$, and integer κ there exists a name-independent routing scheme on T with error-reporting that routes on paths of length bounded by $4\mathrm{rad}(T) + 2\kappa\mathrm{maxE}(T)$, each* node requires $O(\kappa n^{1/\kappa} \log^2 n)$ memory, and headers are of length $O(\log^2 n)$. (And routing for a non-existent name in T also incurs a path of length $4\mathrm{rad}(T) + 2\kappa \mathrm{maxE}(T)$ until a negative result is reported back to the source.)

The proof of **Theorem 1** is deferred until **Section 3.4**.

For a tree T containing a node v, we let $\phi(T, v)$ denote the routing information of node v as required from **Theorem 1**.

3.3   The Name-Independent Routing Scheme

We now combine **Theorem 1** with **Lemma 1** in a manner similar to the hierarchical routing scheme of Awerbuch and Peleg [7].

Storage. For all $v \in V$, $i \in I$, and $T \in TC_{\kappa,2^i}$ such that $v \in T$ node v stores $\phi(T, v)$. According to **Lemma 1** and **Theorem 1** above, the total storage of each node is $O(\kappa^2 n^{2/\kappa} \log D \log^2 n)$.

Routing. The sender s looks for destination t in the tree $\mathrm{Tree}_s[i]$ successively for $i = 1, 2, \ldots, \lceil \log D \rceil$ using the construction in **Theorem 1**.

Stretch analysis. From **Lemma 1** for $T \in TC_{\kappa,\rho}$ we have that the cost $4\mathrm{rad}(T) + 2\kappa \mathrm{maxE}(T)$ is bounded by $4(2\kappa - 1)\rho + 2\kappa 2\rho \le 12\kappa\rho$. Hence, for any source s, integer $i \in I$, the cost of searching for any target t in $\mathrm{Tree}_s[i]$ is at most $12\kappa 2^i$.

For the index $j \in I$ such that $2^{j-1} < d(s,t) \le 2^j$ we have $t \in B(v, 2^j) \subseteq \mathrm{Tree}_v[j]$ and therefore t will be found in the jth phase. The total cost will be $\sum_{1 \le i \le j} 12\kappa 2^i \le 12\kappa 2^{j+1} < 48\kappa d(s,t)$. Hence, using $\hat{\kappa} = 2\kappa$ instead of κ in the above construction, we proved the following.

Theorem 2. *For every weighted graph $G = (V, E, \omega)$ whose normalized diameter is D and integer $\kappa \ge 1$, there is a polynomial time constructible name-independent routing scheme with stretch $O(\kappa)$ and memory $O(\kappa^2 n^{1/\kappa} \log D \log^2 n)$.*

In the remainder of this section, we provide the construction that proves **Theorem 1** above.

3.4   Bounded-Cost Name-Independent Tree-Routing

Consider a set V of n nodes in which every node $u \in V$ has a unique name $n(u) \in \{1, \ldots, n\}$. (We can remove this assumption using hash functions given by **Lemma 6**. Let $T = (U, r, E, \omega)$ be a rooted tree with $r \in U \subseteq V$ and $|U| = m$.

Sorting the nodes in U by their unique name $n()$, we denote $U[i]$ as the ith largest node in U, $U[1] = \max_{v \in U}\{n(v)\}$ and for $1 < i \le m$ define $U[i] = \max_{v \in U}\{n(v) \mid n(v) < U[i-1]\}$.

In addition to their given name $n(v)$, we give each node $v \in T$ three more names.

First, we give v its name in the labeled tree-routing of Thorup & Zwick [20] and Fraigniaud & Gavoille [10]:

Lemma 2. [10,20] *For every weighted tree T with n nodes there exists a labeled routing scheme that, given any destination label, routes optimally on T from any source to the destination. The storage per node in T, the label size, and the header size are $O(\log^2 n/\log\log n)$ bits. Given the information of a node and the label of the destination, routing decisions take constant time.*

For a tree T containing a node v, we let $\mu(T, v)$ denote the routing information of node v and $\lambda(T, v)$ denote the destination label of v in T as required from **Lemma 2**. Thus, the first name we assign with v is $\ell(v) = \lambda(T, v)$.

Secondly, $d(v)$ denotes the depth-first-search (DFS) preorder enumeration of the rooted tree, note that $\{d(u)|u \in U\} = \{1, \ldots, m\}$. Finally every node has a name $s(v)$ which will be defined as a function of its own subtree size relative to its siblings' subtree sizes. In some sense this reflects its rank among its siblings. The formal value of $s(v)$ will be defined later.

In our construction a node whose DFS enumeration is i is responsible to the ith largest node in U. Formally, for any $x \in T$ we define its *responsibility* as $o(x) = U[d(x)]$. Given a target u the idea is first to route to the node y such that $o(y) = n(u)$ and then use labeled tree-routing to reach u.

We begin by presenting a simple name-independent scheme in which the storage requirements on any node v is $\widetilde{O}(|\text{child}(v)| + 1)$ and the total cost of routing will be at most $4\text{rad}(T)$.

Storage. Every node $x \in T$ stores the following:

1. Let $y \in T$ be such that $o(x) = n(y)$. Node x stores the tuple $(y,\ n(y),\ \ell(y))$.
2. Node x stores $A(x) = \{o(y) \mid y \in \text{child}(x)\}$ together with a map from any $o(y) \in A(x)$ to the corresponding port name $\text{port}(x, y)$ to reach the child y.
3. x stores $\mu(T, x)$, its tree-routing label as required from **Lemma 2**.

Routing. Given a target $u \in U$, first route to the root r.

1. On a node x
   (a) If $o(x) = n(u)$ then use $\ell(u)$ to reach u.
   (b) If there is no child $y \in \text{child}(x)$ such that $o(y) \leq n(u)$ then report back that $u \notin T$.
   (c) Route to the child $y \in \text{child}(x)$ with the maximum $o(y)$ such that $o(y) \leq n(u)$. Set $x := y$ and goto 1.

This procedure is similar to the interval routing of [18,22]. If the label $\ell(u)$ is found, routing proceeds using the labeled tree-routing scheme of **Lemma 2**. In the simple scheme presented above, the cost of reaching root is at most $\text{rad}(T)$, cost of reaching the node storing the required label is bounded by $\text{rad}(T)$ and reaching the target (or reporting an error to the source) requires at most another $2\text{rad}(T)$. In the fixed port model the storage per node is $\widetilde{O}(|\text{child}(v)|+1) = \widetilde{O}(n)$.

Bounding storage. We proceed to show how, at the cost of adding at most κ length-2 cycles to the routing path, we can reduce the storage of each node to only $\widetilde{O}(n^{1/\kappa})$ bits even in the fixed port model. The idea is to spread the information about v's children in a directory among v and its children child(v) in a load balanced manner that will ensure that at most κ probes to directories are performed in the whole routing path until the target is found.

First, for determining $d(v)$ we use a DFS enumeration that always prefers heavy children first (when faced with a choice, it explores a child with the maximum weight among the unexplored children).

Second, for every node u, we now define its child name $s(u)$. For any node v, we enumerate its children child(v) in their weighted order from large to small using words of the alphabet $\Sigma = \{0, 1, 2, \ldots n^{1/\kappa} - 1\}$. Specifically, for any node, given a list of its children sorted by their weight (from large to small), we name each of the first $n^{1/\kappa}$ nodes in non-increasing order of their weights by a child name which consists of one digit in Σ in increasing order $(0), (1), \ldots, (n^{1/\kappa} - 1)$. Then we name each of the next $n^{2/\kappa}$ nodes in order of their weights by a child name in Σ^2 in increasing lexicographic order, $(0, 0), (0, 1), \ldots, (0, n^{1/\kappa} - 1), (1, 0), (1, 1), \ldots, (1, n^{1/\kappa} - 1), \ldots, (n^{1/\kappa} - 1, 0), \ldots, (n^{1/\kappa} - 1, n^{1/\kappa} - 1)$. We continue this naming process until all nodes in child(v) are exhausted, up to at most a κ-digit child name in Σ^κ.

The central property of our naming is as follows. Let u be a child of v with a child name $s(u)$ consisting of $j > 1$ digits. Then $w(u) \leq w(v)/n^{(j-1)/\kappa}$. The reason this property holds is that v must have $n^{(j-1)/\kappa}$ children that are at least as heavy as u. Since each one weights at least $w(u)$ their total weight would be larger than $w(v)$, a contradiction.

Storage. For every $x \in T$, we define $S(x)$ as follows:

$$S(x) = \left\{ \begin{array}{cccc} (0) & (1) & \cdots & (n^{1/\kappa} - 1) \\ (0,0) & (1,0) & \cdots & (n^{1/\kappa} - 1, 0) \\ \vdots & & & \vdots \\ (\underbrace{0,0,\ldots,0}_{\kappa-1}) & (\underbrace{1,0,\ldots,0}_{\kappa-1}) & \cdots & (n^{1/\kappa} - 1, \underbrace{0,\ldots,0}_{\kappa-1}) \end{array} \right\}$$

For each child y of x such that $s(y) \in S(x)$, node x stores $o(y)$ and a map from $o(y)$ to the corresponding port name port(x, y) to reach child y.

We now define the storage held by x's children to assist in lookup. Let y be in child(x) and assume y has a length-j child name, $s(y)$, with with $j - i$ trailing zeros, $s(y) = (a_1, \ldots, a_i, \underbrace{0, \ldots, 0}_{j-i})$ for some $i \leq j$. We define a subset $S'(y)$ of the enumerated set of v's children as follows:

$$S'(y) = \left\{ \begin{array}{ccc} (a_1, \ldots, a_i, \underbrace{0, \ldots, 0}_{j-i-1}, 0) & \cdots & (a_1, \ldots, a_i, \underbrace{0, \ldots, 0}_{j-i-1}, n^{1/\kappa} - 1) \\ (a_1, \ldots, a_i, \underbrace{0, \ldots, 0}_{j-i-2}, 0, 0) & \cdots & (a_1, \ldots, a_i, \underbrace{0, \ldots, 0}_{j-i-2}, n^{1/\kappa} - 1, 0) \\ \vdots & & \vdots \\ (a_1, \ldots, a_i, 0, 0, \underbrace{\ldots, 0}_{j-i-1}) & \cdots & (a_1, \ldots, a_i, n^{1/\kappa} - 1, \underbrace{0, \ldots, 0}_{j-i-1}) \end{array} \right\}$$

The child node y of x stores the following information. For each $z \in \text{child}(x)$ such that $s(z) \in S'(y)$, y stores $o(z)$ and a map from $o(z)$ to the corresponding port name $\text{port}(x,z)$ to reach child z from parent x.

Intuitively, here is how this directory scheme works. Suppose the current node is x and the target node is u. The child-name enumeration of x's children is consistent with their responsibility enumeration order. That is, let v be the child of x whose sub-tree has responsibility for the value $n(u)$. Denote the child name of v by $s(v) = (a_1, \ldots, a_j)$. Then because of our DFS ordering, given any child $y \in \text{child}(x)$:

- If $s(y)$ has more than j digits then $o(v) \le n(u) < o(y)$;
- If $s(y)$ has less than j digits then $o(y) < o(v) \le n(u)$;
- If $s(y)$ has j digits, and according to lexicographical order $s(y) < s(v)$, then $o(y) < o(v) \le n(u)$;
- If $s(y)$ has j digits, and according to lexicographical order $s(v) < s(y)$, then $o(v) \le n(u) < o(y)$;

Given a target u, node x would like to find the appropriate child v such that $o(v)$ is the maximum value out of all $\{o(y) \le n(u) \mid y \in \text{child}(x)\}$. Since x does not maintain $o(y)$ of all of its children $y \in \text{child}(x)$, the highest $o()$ value it maintains that is no greater than the target $n(u)$ belongs to the node y_1 with child name $s(y_1) = (a_1, \underbrace{0, \ldots, 0}_{j-1})$. Continuing from y_1, it too maintains only partial information about x's children. Here, the highest $o()$ value it maintains that is no greater than the target $n(u)$ belongs to the node y_2 with child name $s(y_2) = (a_1, \underbrace{0, \ldots, 0}_{i}, a_{i+2}, \underbrace{0, \ldots, 0}_{j-i-2})$ where $i \ge 0$ is the number of consecutive zeros that $s(v)$ has starting from its second digit a_2. And so on. With each such step, we reach a child of x whose child name matches the target's child name $s(v)$ in one more digit at least (and zero's in v's child name are matched without further steps). After at most j such steps, we reach v, and continue to search for u within the sub-tree it roots.

More precisely, the routing algorithm is as follows.

Routing algorithm. Given a target $u \in U$, first route to the root r. Then, on any node x there are three cases:

1. if $o(x) = n(u)$ then use $\ell(u)$ to reach u.
2. if x is a leaf or if $n(u) < o(y)$ for all y such that $s(y) \in S(x)$, then report back that $u \notin T$.
3. Otherwise, we would like to route to the child $y \in \text{child}(x)$ with the maximum $o(y)$ value out of all y such that $o(y) \le n(u)$. Since x does not store $o(y)$ for all $y \in \text{child}(x)$ performing this case is done using the following directory algorithm.

Directory algorithm.

1. Route to the child y with maximum $o(y)$ value out of all y such that $o(y) \le n(u)$ and $s(y) \in S(x)$.

2. On node y,
   (a) If $n(u) < o(z)$ for all z such that $s(z) \in S'(y)$ then the directory algorithm has reached the required child and the routing algorithm can proceed from node y.
   (b) Otherwise, route to the sibling z such that $o(z)$ has maximum value out of all z such that $o(z) \leq n(u)$ and $s(z) \in S'(y)$.
       Set $y := z$ and goto 2.

3.5   Analysis

Lemma 3. *Given a parameter κ, the name-independent error-reporting tree-routing scheme requires $O(\kappa n^{1/\kappa} \log^2 n)$ bits of storage per node in the tree.*

Lemma 4. *Given a parameter κ, the name-independent error-reporting tree-routing scheme routs on paths whose cost is at most $4\mathrm{rad}(T) + 2\kappa \mathrm{maxE}(T)$ until either the destination is reached or the source receives notification that the destination does not exists in the tree*

Proof. We now bound the total cost of searching for a target u on a tree T. Reaching the root takes at most $\mathrm{rad}(T)$, reaching the node v such that $o(v) = n(u)$ (or getting a negative result) takes $\mathrm{rad}(T) + 2j\mathrm{maxE}(T)$ where j is the number of times the directory service had to probe other children along the path to node u. Once node u is reached, routing to t or reporting a negative result back to the source takes at most $2\mathrm{rad}(T)$.

Therefore, we are left to show that $j \leq \kappa$. The directory structure above guarantees that if appropriate next hop child has a length-i child name then it will reached in at most $i - 1$ intermediate queries. Specifically, let $s(y)$ denote a length-i child name of x's child, whose sub-tree stores information on a target $n(u)$. Given a target name $n(u)$, node v finds $o(u_1)$, the maximum name stored by v that is at most $n(u)$. Then v routes to u_1, a child with length-i child-name whose first digit is the same as the child covering $n(u)$. Node u_1 is either the actual child y, or it finds $o(u_2)$, the maximum name stored in u_1 that is at most $n(u)$. Then u_1 routes up to v and down to u_2, which has a length-i child name that matches $s(y)$ in at least the first two digits. This process continues until the correct child y is reached after at most $i - 1$ intermediate steps from v to a child and back.

A crucial property maintained by the storage hierarchy is that if v has weight $w(v)$, then a child with a length-i child name with $i > 1$ has weight at most $w(v)/n^{(i-1)/\kappa}$. This is due to the weighted sorting: Otherwise the $n^{(i-1)/\kappa}$ children with length $i - 1$ child names would each have at least $w(v)/n^{(i-1)/\kappa}$ children, and their total weight would be larger than $w(v)$ which is a contradiction.

Following a path from the root r to the node containing the label takes at most distance $\mathrm{rad}(T)$. Along the path, every node with child name of length $i > 1$ may cost additional $i - 1$ double-steps from its parent to a child and back to the parent. Since every node with a length-i id reduces the weight of the tree by a factor of at least $n^{(i-1)/\kappa}$, there are at most $j \leq \kappa$ such extra double-steps along the whole path. Each double-step costs at most $2\mathrm{maxE}(T)$. Therefore, the total distance of the path is bounded by $4\mathrm{rad}(T) + 2\kappa\mathrm{maxE}(T)$.   □

4   Single-Source Name-Independent Routing Scheme

In this part we consider the problem of routing messages from a distinguished node, the *source*, to all the other nodes, while keeping the name-independent constraint. The Single-source routing problem with small local storage can also be seen as a searching problem through a distributed information system, e.g., a distributed dictionary or a hash table. Efficient solutions to these problems are interesting in their own right.

We restrict our attention to single-source routing schemes in trees rooted at the source, i.e., the single-source shortest path tree rooted at the source in the graph. We assume that node names of the tree are taken from some universe $\mathcal{U}$ with $|\mathcal{U}| \geq n$, the number of nodes of the tree. The names and the port numbers are assumed to be fixed by an adversary (fixed port model) after the given tree and before the design of the routing scheme.

A single-source routing scheme on a tree T with source s is *L-reporting* if, for every $v \in \mathcal{U}$, the routing from s to v reports to s a *failure* mark in the header if $v \notin T$ after a loop of cost at most L. And, if $v \in T$, then the route from s to v has cost at most $L + d_T(s,v)$. Note that the stretch constraint of an L-reporting routing scheme concerns restriction on route length to destinations $v \in T$ only. In the following $d(T)$ denotes the *depth* of the tree T, i.e., $d(T) = \max_{v \in T} d_T(s,v)$.

Theorem 3. *Every unweighted rooted tree T with n nodes taken from $\mathcal{U}$ has a single-source name-independent routing scheme of stretch 17 that is $12d(T)$-reporting, and using $O(\log^5 n/(\log \log n)^2 + \log |\mathcal{U}| \log^3 n/\log \log n)$ bits per node, that is $o(\log^5 n)$ if $|\mathcal{U}| \leq n^{o(\log n \log \log n)}$.*

The best previous scheme, due to [14] and for $|\mathcal{U}| = n$, was using $\widetilde{O}(n^{1/k})$ bits for a stretch factor of $2k - 1$, i.e., $\widetilde{O}(n^{1/9})$ bits for stretch 17. However our scheme works only for uniform weights.

The next lemma reduces the problem to one of designing efficient L-reporting schemes on trees without any specification of the stretch. Observe that there is no straightforward relationship between the L-reporting property and the stretch factor property of a routing scheme. This reduction can be seen as the specialization of the Awerbuch-Peleg's sparse cover for trees [6,16].

Lemma 5. *Assume that there exists $\alpha \geq 1$ such that every unweighted rooted tree T with at most n nodes has (in the fixed port model) a single-source name-independent routing scheme that is $\alpha d(T)$-reporting and that uses at most M bits per node. Then, every rooted tree T with n nodes has a single-source name-independent routing scheme (also in the fixed port model) of stretch $4\alpha + 1$ that is $3\alpha d(T)$-reporting, and using at most $M(\lceil \log d(T) \rceil + 1)$ bits per node.*

According **Lemma 5**, to prove **Theorem 3** it suffices to prove that we can set $\alpha = 4$ with a suitable memory bound M. More precisely:

Theorem 4. *Every unweighted rooted tree with n nodes taken from $\mathcal{U}$ has a single-source name-independent routing scheme (in the fixed port model) that is $4d(T)$-reporting, and using $O(\log^4 n/(\log \log n)^2 + \log |\mathcal{U}| \log^2 n/ \log \log n)$ bits per node. Moreover, the first header construction takes $O(\log n)$ time at the source, and all the other routing decisions $O(\log \log n)$ time.*

Before proving **Theorem 4** we need some basic results about hash functions (see [8,15]). W.l.o.g. we assume that $\mathcal{U} = \{0, \ldots, |\mathcal{U}| - 1\}$.

Lemma 6. **[8]** *Let $\mathcal{P} = \{0, \ldots, p-1\}$ for some prime number $p = \Theta(n)$. There exists a family of hash functions $\mathcal{H} = \{h : \mathcal{U} \to \mathcal{P}\}$ such that for every set $V \subseteq \mathcal{U}$ with $|V| = n$, there exists a function $h \in \mathcal{H}$ such that:*

1. *h is a degree-$O(\log n)$ polynomial of the field $\mathbb{Z}_p$;*
2. *$|\{v \in V \mid h(v) = k\}| = O(\log n)$ for every $k \in \mathcal{P}$;*

The first point of **Lemma 6** implies that each function h can be stored with $O(\log^2 n)$ bits and have time complexity $O(\log n)$, whereas the second point states that there are at most $O(\log n)$ collisions for each $v \in V$.

The proof of Theorem 4. From now, we consider a tree T with source s. The node set of T is denoted by V, $n = |V|$, and p is a prime number such that $n \leq p < 2n$. Let $\mathcal{P} = \{0, \ldots, p-1\}$. Each value $k \in \mathcal{P}$ is called hereafter a *key*. We consider the hash function $h \in \mathcal{H}$ for V as given by **Lemma 6**.

For every $v \in V$, we denote by $\ell_T(v)$ the tree-routing label of v in T, which is used for the routing in T from source s to destination v. The length of each of these labels is $O(\log^2 n/ \log \log n)$ bits [20,10].

Overview of the scheme. The basic idea of the scheme is to use *indirection*: the keys of $\mathcal{P}$ are mapped to the nodes of T in a balanced way, typically with no more than $\widetilde{O}(1)$ keys per node. Then the node on which the key k is mapped is in charge of the tree-routing label of all names $u \in \mathcal{U}$ such that $h(u) = k$. First we route from s to the node in charge of k, and then to the destination.

More precisely, consider the routing from the source s to an arbitrary name $v \in \mathcal{U}$. First s hashes v into the key $k = h(v) \in \mathcal{P}$. Then we use a label-based routing scheme (i.e., a name-dependant routing scheme) to find a route in T from s to the node labeled k in this routing scheme, say node w. Roughly speaking, this labeled scheme is similar to Interval Routing Scheme [18,22] which is based on a DFS numbering of the nodes. Locally w is aware of the tree-routing labels $\ell_T(s)$, $\ell_T(w)$, and $\ell_T(u)$ for all $u \in V$ such that $h(u) = k$. Node w also stores the corresponding list of names, i.e., the u's of V with $h(u) = k$. Our scheme ensures that each possible key of $\mathcal{P}$ is mapped to exactly one node of T. So that once node w is attained, we only need to check whether v belongs or not to the list of names stored by w. If it does not belong to, then we can conclude that $v \notin V$, and then w reports to s a failure mark thanks to the tree-routing labels $\ell_T(s)$ and $\ell_T(w)$. If v is found in the w's name list, then w directly routes to v thanks to $\ell_T(v)$ and $\ell_T(w)$. Such a scheme is therefore $2d(T)$-reporting.

However, in the scheme sketched above, the routing from s to k cannot be done via a standard implementation of Interval Routing Scheme for several reasons: 1) the set of keys, $\mathcal{P}$, is in general larger than V; 2) the memory requirements of node w for interval routing is $O(\deg(w)\log n)$ bits whereas we expect $\widetilde{O}(1)$ bits of storage for every node.

The remainder of the proof consists in constructing the mapping from $\mathcal{P}$ to V, and the compact encoding of routing information.

The header of the message at any step of the routing from s to v is composed at most of the following fields: a type of message on a constant number of bits, a key of $\mathcal{P}$, a name of $\mathcal{U}$, and possibly a tree-routing label. The second and the third fields never change and are initialized to $h(v)$ and v respectively. The length of the header is no more than $O(\log n + \log |\mathcal{U}|)$ bits.

Simulating designer port model via double-step routing. An important hypothesis to apply **Lemma 5** is that the ports of each node x of the tree are arbitrarily permuted (the fixed port model). However, according to the next remark we will assume that the routing from s to the key k is done in the designer port model (i.e., the ports of each node have been permuted with a desirable permutation). Nevertheless it should be clear that once k is attained, then the routing to v (if $v \in V$) or to s (if $v \notin V$) is done thanks to the label $\ell_T(v)$ or $\ell_T(s)$ that have been computed in the fixed port model.

Indeed, during the routing from s to the key of v, one can apply the following *routing simulation*: Let $\mathrm{port}_d(x, y)$ (resp. $\mathrm{port}_f(x, y)$) be the port number between x and y in the designer port model (resp. in the fixed port model). For the simulation, every node y with parent x stores the numbers $p_1 = \mathrm{port}_d(y, x)$, $p_2 = \mathrm{port}_f(y, x)$, and $p_3 = \mathrm{port}_f(x, z)$ where z is the child of x such that $\mathrm{port}_d(x, z) = \mathrm{port}_f(x, y)$. In y, if the routing scheme outputs p_1, then the answer is converted to port p_2. If in x, the answer p of the routing scheme is different from port number of its parent (x knows it), x sends the message on port number p with a mark m_1 attached to the header. If y receives a message with mark m_1, it forwards to its parent, on port p_2, the message with mark m_2 and the value p_3 attached to its header. Finally, in x, if the routing scheme receives a header with a m_2 mark, then it extracts from the header the value p, and forward the message on port number p. To summarize the routing from y toward its parent is done as previously, whereas the routing from x toward its child z is done by a route of length 3. So if $v \notin V$, the routing will report to s a fail mark after a route of length $3d(T) + d(T) = 4d(T)$ instead of $2d(T)$. And if $v \in V$, the route length is at most $3d(T) + d_T(k, v) \le 4d(T) + d_T(s, v)$. This leads to a $4d(T)$-reporting scheme with an $O(\log n)$ additive factor on the memory requirements and on the header size. So, simulating and superposing the $O(\log d(T)) = O(\log n)$ designer port schemes raise the overall memory requirement of a node to an $O(\log^2 n)$ additive factor, for headers the overhead is only $O(\log \log n)$ bits.

Routing in the designer port model. So we restrict our attention to the routing from s to the key of v in the designer port model. From now we assume that the children x_i's of every node x are ordered according to their increasing number of descendants and that $\text{port}_d(x, x_i) = i$. (We fix $\text{port}_d(x_i, x) = 0$.) Let $w(x)$ be the *weight* of x defined by the number of descendents of x in T (x included).

The scheme is parametrized by $t = \lceil \log n \rceil$. We partition the nodes of T in *heavy* and *light*. The t heaviest children of x are heavy and the others (if any) are light. The root is heavy. Clearly, if the child x_i of x is light, then $w(x_i) < w(x)/t$, so that the number of light ancestors of x_i is at most $O(\log_t n)$.

The routing scheme is based on two numbers, $c(x)$ and $q(x)$, we assign to each node x. The first, called the *charge of x*, represents the total number of keys that must be mapped on the nodes of T_x, the subtree of root x. (So for the root, $c(s) = p$). The second one denotes the number of keys assigned to x. These two numbers must satisfy that, for every x,

$$c(x) \;=\; \sum_{y \in T_x} q(y) \,. \tag{1}$$

The heart of our scheme is the way we compute and encode $c(x)$ while balancing the charge of x over its descendants, i.e., guaranteeing $q(y) = \widetilde{O}(1)$ for every y. Given the numbers $c(x)$ and $q(x)$ one can then route through a *modified* DFS number $f(x)$ associated with each x and defined by: $f(s) := 0$, and $f(x_i) := f(x) + q(x) + \sum_{j<i} c(x_j)$, where x_i is the ith child of x. (This matches to the standard definition if $q(x) = 1$ for every x.)

Now the routing is done similarly to Interval Routing Scheme. Let w be the node in charge of $h(v)$, the key of v. Assume that w is a descendant of some node x, initially $x = s$. It is easy to see that:

1. either $h(v) \in [f(x), f(x) + q(x))$, and $w = x$, i.e., the key of v is stored by x;
2. or w is a descendant of x_i where $h(v) \in [f(x_i), f(x_{i+1}))$, and thus the routing in x must answer port i.

So the routing from x to $h(v)$ is well defined if x is aware of $f(x)$, $q(x)$, and of the vector $\vec{c}(x) = (c(x_1), c(x_2), \ldots)$ of charges of x's children. Indeed the numbers $f(x_i)$ and $f(x_{i+1})$ can be computed from $f(x)$, $q(x)$, and from $\vec{c}(x)$. We are now left with the description of $c(x)$, $q(x)$, and the compact encoding of $\vec{c}(x)$.

For that, let W be the function $W(k, q, m) = 2^k \cdot (1 + 1/q)^m$, where $k, m \geq 0$ and $q \geq 1$ are all integers. Function W satisfies the following properties:

1. $q \cdot W(k, q, m + 1) = (q + 1) \cdot W(k, q, m)$.
2. $W(k, q, m) < W(k, q, m + 1)$, since $1 + 1/q > 1$.
3. $W(k, q, q) \geq W(k + 1, q, 0)$, because $(1 + 1/q)^q \geq 2$ for $q \geq 1$.

Computing $c(x)$ and $q(x)$. The numbers $c(x)$ and $q(x)$ are computed through a DFS with priority to lightest children. We start from the source by setting: $c(s) := p$ and $q(s) := \lceil p/n \rceil \leq 2$. Then, for the ith child of x such that $c(x) > 0$:

1. Let $q = q(x)$ and $k = \lfloor \log w(x_i) \rfloor$.
2. If x_i is heavy, then $c(x_i) := q \cdot w(x_i)$ and $q(x_i) := q$.

3. If x_i is light, then $c(x_i) := \lceil (q+1) \cdot W(k,q,m) \rceil$ and $q(x_i) := q+1$ where m is such that $w(x_i) \in [W(k,q,m), W(k,q,m+1))$.
4. If $\sum_{j \leq i} c(x_j) > c(x) - q(x)$ then set $c(x_i) := \max\{c(x) - q(x) - \sum_{j<i} c(x_j), 0\}$.
5. If $q(x_i) > c(x_i)$, then correct $q(x_i) := c(x_i)$.

By induction on the depth of x, $q(x) = O(\log_t n) = O(\log n / \log\log n)$.

In order to validate our routing algorithm, based on $f(x)$, $q(x)$ and $\vec{c}(x)$, we need to show that $c(x)$ and $q(x)$ numbers satisfy Eq. (1), i.e.,

Lemma 7. *For every x, $c(x) = \sum_{y \in T_x} q(y)$.*

A *range query* on a sequence of integers $(c_1, \ldots, c_r)$ consists in finding, for every input z, the index i such that $z \in [\sum_{j \leq i} c_j, \sum_{j \leq i+1} c_j)$. Clearly, the routing algorithm as described above reduces to the range query $z = h(v) - f(x) - q(x)$ on the sequence $\vec{c}(x)$. Remark: range queries can be solved in $O(\log\log n)$ time with the $O(r)$ space van Emde Boas's data structure [21]. We show here that one can obtain the same time complexity while working on a very compact representation of the sequence. Compact representation of $\vec{c}(x)$ is possible because of the special choice of $c(x_i)$ values.

Lemma 8. *For every x, $\vec{c}(x)$ can be coded with a data structure of $O(\log^3 n / \log\log n)$ bits supporting range queries in $O(\log\log n)$ worst-case time.*

The time complexity of the routing in $x \neq s$ is bounded by a range query in $\vec{c}(x)$, since the other tasks consist in search in tables of size $O(\log n)$ (so in $O(\log\log n)$ time using binary search), or consist in routing with tree-routing label that takes constant time. The source however spends $O(\log n)$ time to initialize the header with $h(v)$. To complete the proof of **Theorem 4**, we show:

Lemma 9. *The memory requirement for x is $O(\log^4 n / (\log\log n)^2 + \log |\mathcal{U}| \log^2 n / \log\log n)$ bits.*

Acknowledgements

The authors would like to thank the anonymous reviewers for their comments.

References

1. I. ABRAHAM, C. GAVOILLE, AND D. MALKHI, *Routing with improved communication-space trade-off*, Tech. Report RR-1330-04, LaBRI, University of Bordeaux 1, 351, cours de la Libération, 33405 Talence Cedex, France, July 2004.
2. I. ABRAHAM, C. GAVOILLE, D. MALKHI, N. NISAN, AND M. THORUP, *Compact name-independent routing with minimum stretch*, in 16th Annual ACM Symposium on Parallel Algorithms and Architecture (SPAA), ACM Press, 2004, pp. 20–24.
3. M. ARIAS, L. COWEN, K. LAING, R. RAJARAMAN, AND O. TAKA, *Compact routing with name independence*, in 15th Annual ACM Symposium on Parallel Algorithms and Architectures (SPAA), ACM Press, June 2003, pp. 184–192.

4. B. AWERBUCH, A. BAR-NOY, N. LINIAL, AND D. PELEG, *Compact distributed data structures for adaptive routing*, in 21st Annual ACM Symposium on Theory of Computing (STOC), ACM Press, May 1989, pp. 479–489.

5. B. AWERBUCH, A. B. NOY, N. LINIAL, AND D. PELEG, *Improved routing strategies with succinct tables*, Journal of Algorithms, 11 (1990), pp. 307–341.

6. B. AWERBUCH AND D. PELEG, *Sparse partitions*, in 31th Annual IEEE Symposium on Foundations of Computer Science (FOCS), Oct. 1990, pp. 503–513.

7. B. AWERBUCH AND D. PELEG, *Routing with polynomial communication-space trade-off*, SIAM J. Discret. Math., 5 (1992), pp. 151–162.

8. J. L. CARTER AND M. N. WEGMAN, *Universal hash functions*, Journal of Computer and System Sciences, 18 (1979), pp. 143–154.

9. L. J. COWEN, *Compact routing with minimum stretch*, Journal of Algorithms, 38 (2001), pp. 170–183.

10. P. FRAIGNIAUD AND C. GAVOILLE, *Routing in trees*, in 28th International Colloquium on Automata, Languages and Programming (ICALP), vol. 2076 of Lecture Notes in Computer Science, Springer, July 2001, pp. 757–772.

11. C. GAVOILLE, *Routing in distributed networks: Overview and open problems*, ACM SIGACT News - Distributed Computing Column, 32 (2001), pp. 36–52.

12. C. GAVOILLE AND M. GENGLER, *Space-efficiency of routing schemes of stretch factor three*, J. of Parallel and Distributed Computing, 61 (2001), pp. 679–687.

13. C. GAVOILLE AND D. PELEG, *Compact and localized distributed data structures*, J. of Distributed Computing, 16 (2003), pp. 111–120. PODC 20-Year Special Issue.

14. K. LAING, *Name-independent compact routing in trees*, Tech. Report 2003-02, Tufts Univ. Dep. of Comp. Science, Nov. 2003. Also in PODC '04 as brief announcements.

15. R. MOTWANI AND P. RAGHAVAN, *Randomized Algorithms*, Camb Univ Press, 1995.

16. D. PELEG, *Distributed Computing: A Locality-Sensitive Approach*, SIAM Monographs on Discrete Mathematics and Applications, 2000.

17. D. PELEG AND E. UPFAL, *A trade-off between space and efficiency for routing tables*, Journal of the ACM, 36 (1989), pp. 510–530.

18. N. SANTORO AND R. KHATIB, *Labelling and implicit routing in networks*, The Computer Journal, 28 (1985), pp. 5–8.

19. M. THORUP AND U. ZWICK, *Approximate distance oracles*, in 33rd Annual ACM Symposium on Theory of Computing (STOC), July 2001, pp. 183–192.

20. ———, *Compact routing schemes*, in 13th Annual ACM Symposium on Parallel Algorithms and Architectures (SPAA), ACM Press, July 2001, pp. 1–10.

21. P. VAN EMDE BOAS, *Preserving order in a forest in less than logarithmic time and linear space*, Information Processing Letters, 6 (1977), pp. 80–82.

22. J. VAN LEEUWEN AND R. B. TAN, *Computer networks with compact routing tables*, in The Book of L, Springer-Verlag, 1986, pp. 259–273.

Active and Concurrent Topology Maintenance

Xiaozhou Li*, Jayadev Misra**, and C. Greg Plaxton*

Department of Computer Science, University of Texas at Austin,
1 University Station C0500, Austin, Texas 78712–0233
{xli,misra,plaxton}@cs.utexas.edu

Abstract. A central problem for structured peer-to-peer networks is topology maintenance, that is, how to properly update neighbor variables when nodes join and leave the network, possibly concurrently. In this paper, we first present a protocol that maintains a ring, the basis of several structured peer-to-peer networks. We then present a protocol that maintains Ranch, a topology consisting of multiple rings. The protocols handle both joins and leaves concurrently and actively (i.e., neighbor variables are updated once a join or a leave occurs). We use an assertional method to prove the correctness of the protocols, that is, we first identify a global invariant for a protocol and then show that every action of the protocol preserves the invariant. The protocols are simple and the proofs are rigorous and explicit.

1   Introduction

In a structured peer-to-peer network, nodes (i.e., processes) maintain some neighbor variables. The neighbor variables of all the nodes in the network collectively form a certain topology (e.g., a ring). Over time, membership may change: nodes may wish to join or leave the network, possibly concurrently. When membership changes, the neighbor variables should be properly updated to maintain the designated topology. This problem, known as topology maintenance, is a central problem for structured peer-to-peer networks.

Depending on whether the neighbor variables are immediately updated once a membership change occurs, there are two general approaches to topology maintenance: the *passive* approach and the *active* approach. In the passive approach, a repair protocol runs in the background to periodically restore the topology. Joins and leaves may be treated using the same approach or using different approaches (e.g., passive join and passive leave [12], active join and passive leave [6, 13], active join and active leave [2, 14]).

Existing work on topology maintenance has certain shortcomings. For the passive approach, since the neighbor variables are not immediately updated, the network may diverge significantly from its designated topology. And the passive approach is not as responsive to membership changes and requires considerable background traffic (i.e., the repair protocol). On the other hand, active topology

---

* Supported by NSF Grant CCR–0310970.
** Supported by NSF Grant CCR–0204323.

R. Guerraoui (Ed.): DISC 2004, LNCS 3274, pp. 320–334, 2004.
© Springer-Verlag Berlin Heidelberg 2004

maintenance is a rather complicated task. Some existing work gives protocols without proofs [14], some handle joins actively but leaves passively [6, 13], and some uses a protocol that only handles joins and a separate protocol that only handles leaves [2]. It is not true, however, that an arbitrary join protocol and an arbitrary leave protocol, if put together, can handle both joins and leaves (e.g., the protocols in [2] cannot; see a detailed discussion in Section 5). Finally, existing protocols are complicated and their correctness proofs are operational and sketchy. It is well known, however, that concurrent programs often contain subtle errors and operational reasoning is unreliable for proving their correctness.

In this paper, we first present a topology maintenance protocol for the ring topology, the basis of several structured peer-to-peer networks (e.g., [5, 11, 16, 22]). We then present a topology maintenance protocol for Ranch, a structured peer-to-peer network topology consisting of multiple rings. Our protocols handle both joins and leaves concurrently and actively. To the best of our knowledge, our protocols are the first to handle both joins and leaves actively. Our protocols are simple. For example, the join protocol for Ranch, discussed in Section 4.2, is much simpler than the join protocols for other topologies (e.g., [2, 6, 13]). Our protocols are based on an asynchronous communication model where only reliable delivery is assumed.

As operational reasoning is unreliable, we use an assertional method to prove the correctness of the protocols, that is, we first identify a global invariant for a protocol and then show that every action of the protocol preserves the invariant. We show that, although a topology may be tentatively disrupted during membership changes, the protocols restore the topology once the messages associated with each pending membership change are delivered, assuming that no new changes are initiated. In practice, it is likely that message delivery time is much shorter than the mean time between membership changes. Hence, in practice, our protocols maintain the topology most of the time.

Unlike the passive approach, which handles leaves as fail-stop faults, we handle leaves actively (i.e., we handle leaves and faults differently). Although treating leaves and faults the same is simpler, we have several reasons to believe that handling leaves actively is worth investigating. Firstly, leaves may occur more frequent than faults. In such situations, handling leaves and faults in the same way may lead to some drawbacks in terms of performance (e.g., delay in response, substantial background traffic). To see this, note that only four messages is needed to handle an active leave (see Section 3.2), while a linear number of messages is needed to detect a passive leave. Secondly, while a node can leave the network silently, we consider it reasonable to assume that a node will execute a leave protocol, because nodes in peer-to-peer networks cooperate with each other all the time, by forwarding messages or storing contents. Thirdly, as an analogy, communication protocols like TCP have "open connection" and "close connection" phases, even though they handle faults as well.

Our work is only a first step towards designing topology maintenance protocols that have rigorous foundations. For example, a shortcoming of our protocols is that some of them may cause livelocks; see a detailed discussion in Section 4.4. We outline some future work in Section 6.

The rest of this paper is organized as follows. Section 2 provides some preliminaries. Section 3 discusses how to maintain a single ring. Section 4 discusses how to maintain the Ranch topology. Section 5 discusses related work. Section 6 provides some concluding remarks.

2 Preliminaries

We consider a fixed and finite set of processes denoted by V. Let V' denote $V \cup \{\mathbf{nil}\}$, where $\mathbf{nil}$ is a special process that does not belong to V. In what follows, symbols u, v, w are of type V, and symbols x, y, z are of type V'. We use $u.a$ to denote variable a of process u, and we use $u.a.b$ to stand for $(u.a).b$. By definition, the $\mathbf{nil}$ process does not have any variable (i.e., $\mathbf{nil}.a$ is undefined). We call a variable x of type V' a *neighbor variable*. We assume that there are two reliable and unbounded communication channels between every two distinct processes in V, one in each direction. We also assume that there is one channel from a process to itself, and there is no channel from or to process $\mathbf{nil}$. Message transmission in any channel takes a finite, but otherwise arbitrary, amount of time.

A set of processes S form a (unidirectional) ring via their x neighbors if for all $u, v \in S$ (which may be equal to each other), there is an x-path of positive length from u to v and $u.x \in S$. Formally,

$$ring(S, x) = \langle \forall u, v : u, v \in S : u.x \in S \wedge path^+(u, v, x) \rangle,$$

where $path^+(u, v, x)$ means $\langle \exists i : i > 0 : u.x^i = v \rangle$ and where $u.x^i$ means $u.x.x \dots x$ with x repeated i times. We use $biring(S, x, y)$ to mean that a set of processes S form a bidirectional ring via their x and y neighbors, formally,

$$biring(S, x, y) = ring(S, x) \wedge ring(S, y) \wedge \langle \forall u : u \in S : u.x.y = u \wedge u.y.x = u \rangle.$$

We sometimes omit writing S in the $ring(S, x)$ notation when $S = \{u : u.x \neq \mathbf{nil}\}$, and we omit S in $biring(S, x, y)$ when $S = \{u : u.x \neq \mathbf{nil}\} = \{v : v.y \neq \mathbf{nil}\}$. Below are some other notations used in the paper.

$m(msg, u, v)$: The number of messages of type msg in the channel from u to v. We sometimes include the parameter of a message type. For example, $m(grant(x), u, v)$ denotes the number of $grant$ messages with parameter x in the channel from u to v.

$m^+(msg, u)$, $m^-(msg, u)$: The number of outgoing and incoming messages of type msg from and to u, respectively. A message from u to itself is considered both an outgoing message and an incoming message of u.

$\#msg$: The total number of messages of type msg in all the channels.

$\uparrow, \downarrow, \updownarrow$: Shorthands for "before this action", "after this action", and "before and after this action", respectively.

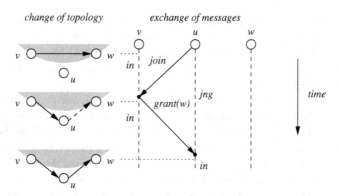

change of topology   *exchange of messages*

Fig. 1. Joining a unidirectional ring. A solid edge from u to v means $u.r = v$, and a dashed edge from u to v means that a $grant(v)$ message is in transmission to u, eventually causing u to set $u.r$ to v.

```
        process p
        var  s : {in, out, jng};  r : V';  a : V'
        init s = out ∧ r = nil
        begin
T₁         s = out → a := contact();
               if a = p → r, s := p, in [] a ≠ p → s := jng; send join() to a fi
T₂      [] rcv join() from q →
               if s = in → send grant(r) to q;  r := q
               [] s ≠ in → send retry() to q fi
T₃      [] rcv grant(a) from q → r, s := a, in
T₄      [] rcv retry() from q → s := out
        end
```

Fig. 2. The join protocol for a unidirectional ring. The states *in*, *out*, and *jng* stand for in, out of, and joining the network, respectively.

3   Maintaining a Single Ring

We discuss the maintenance of a single ring for two reasons. Firstly, we use the protocol for maintaining a single ring as a building block to maintain Ranch, a multi-ring topology. Secondly, the ring topology is the basis of several peer-to-peer networks (e.g., [5, 11, 16, 22]) and hence its maintenance is of independent interest.

3.1   Joins for a Unidirectional Ring

We begin by considering joins for a unidirectional ring. We discuss this seemingly simple problem to exemplify our techniques for solving the harder problems discussed later in this paper. The join protocol for a unidirectional ring is quite simple. Let r (the right neighbor) be a neighbor variable. When process u wishes to join the ring, we assume that u is able to find a member v of the ring (if there is no such process, then u creates a ring consisting of only u itself). Process u then sends a *join* message to v. Upon receiving the *join* message, v places u between v and its right neighbor w (which can be equal to v), by setting $v.r$ to u and sending a *grant*(w) message back to u. Upon receiving the *grant*(w) message, u sets $u.r$ to w.

Figure 2 describes the join protocol. We have written our protocol as a collection of actions, using a notation similar to Gouda's abstract protocol notation [4]. An execution of a protocol consists of an infinite sequence of actions. We assume a weak fairness model where each action is executed infinitely often; execution of an action with a false guard has no effect on the system. We assume, without loss of generality, that each action is atomic, and we reason about the system state in between actions. We assume that the *contact*() function in action T_1 returns a non-*out* process if there is one, and it returns the calling process otherwise[1]. A brief justification of the assumption on the atomicity of actions and on the behavior of the *contact*() function can be found in [9]. A more complete treatment of the issue of atomicity of actions can be found in [17]. Figure 1 shows an execution of the protocol where a join request is granted.

We now prove the correctness of the join protocol. We begin with safety properties. Proving safety properties often amounts to proving invariants. What is an invariant of this protocol? It is tempting to think that this protocol maintains $ring(r)$ at all times. This, however, is not true. For example, consider the moment when v has set $v.r$ to u but u has yet to receive the *grant* message. At this moment, $v.r = u$ but $u.r = \textbf{nil}$ (i.e., the ring is broken). In fact, no protocol can maintain $ring(r)$ at all times, simply because the joining of a process requires the modification of two variables (e.g., $v.r$ and $u.r$) located at different processes. This observation leads us to consider an extended ring topology, defined as follows. Let $u.r'$, an imaginary variable, be

$$u.r' = \begin{cases} x & \text{if } m^-(grant, u) = 1 \wedge m^-(grant(x), u) = 1 \\ u.r \text{ otherwise.} \end{cases}$$

In effect, a process with a non-**nil** r' value is either a member or a non-member for which the join request has been acknowledged with a *grant* message, although the *grant* message has yet to arrive. This definition of r' allows a single action to change the r' values of two different processes, solving the aforementioned problem. We now claim that $ring(r')$ holds at all times. To prove this claim, we find it useful to introduce a function $f : V \rightarrow \mathbf{N}$, where $\mathbf{N}$ denotes the nonnegative integers, defined as:

$$f(u) = m^+(join, u) + m^-(grant, u) + m^-(retry, u).$$

---

[1] Alternatively, we can assume that the *contact*() function returns an *in* process if there is one, and returns the calling process otherwise. For this protocol, this alternative assumption eliminates the need for the *retry* message. For subsequent protocols, however, this alternative assumption has to be modified. We keep the current assumption in order to maintain a consistent definition of the *contact*() function.

We define I as $I = A \wedge B \wedge C \wedge ring(r')$, where

$$A = \langle \forall u :: (u.s = jng \equiv f(u) = 1) \wedge f(u) \le 1 \rangle,$$
$$B = \langle \forall u :: u.s = in \equiv u.r \ne \mathbf{nil} \rangle,$$
$$C = (\#grant(\mathbf{nil}) = 0).$$

Theorem 1. invariant I.

Proof. It can be easily verified that I is true initially. It thus suffices to check that every action preserves I. We first observe that C is preserved by every action, simply because T_2 is the only action that sends a *grant* message and B implies that $p.r \ne \mathbf{nil}$. We itemize below the reasons why each action preserves the other conjuncts of I.

- $\{I\}\ T_1\ \{I\}$: Suppose T_1 takes the first branch (i.e., $a = p$). This action preserves $A \wedge B$ because it changes $p.s$ from *out* to *in* and changes $p.r$ from **nil** to p. This action preserves $ring(r')$ because

$$\quad contact() \text{ returns } p$$
$$\Rightarrow \quad \{\text{def. of } contact(); A; B; \text{def. of } r'\}$$
$$\quad \uparrow \langle \forall u :: u.s = out \wedge u.r' = \mathbf{nil} \rangle \wedge \#grant = 0$$
$$\Rightarrow \quad \{\text{action}\}$$
$$\quad \downarrow p.r' = p \wedge \langle \forall u : u \ne p : u.r' = \mathbf{nil} \rangle.$$

- $\{I\}\ T_1\ \{I\}$: Suppose T_1 takes the second branch (i.e., $a \ne p$). This action changes $p.s$ from *out* to *jng* and increases $f(p)$ from 0 to 1.
- $\{I\}\ T_2\ \{I\}$: Suppose T_2 takes the first branch (i.e., $s = in$). This action preserves $A \wedge B$ because it preserves $f(q)$ and $p.r \ne \mathbf{nil}$. Let w be the old $p.r$; B thus implies $w \ne \mathbf{nil}$. This action changes $p.r'$ from w to q and $q.r'$ from **nil** to w because

$$\quad \uparrow p.r = w \wedge p.s = in \wedge m(join, q, p) > 0$$
$$\Rightarrow \quad \{A; B; \text{def. of } r'\}$$
$$\quad \uparrow p.r' = w \wedge m^-(grant, p) = 0 \wedge q.r' = \mathbf{nil} \wedge m^-(grant, q) = 0$$
$$\Rightarrow \quad \{\text{action}; p \ne q \text{ because } p.r' \ne q.r'; \text{def. of } r'\}$$
$$\quad \downarrow p.r' = q \wedge q.r' = w.$$

  Hence, $ring(r')$ is preserved.
- $\{I\}\ T_2\ \{I\}$: Suppose T_2 takes the second branch (i.e., $s \ne in$). This action preserves $f(q)$.
- $\{I\}\ T_3\ \{I\}$: This action changes $p.s$ from *jng* to *in*, decreases $f(p)$ from 1 to 0, and truthifies $p.r \ne \mathbf{nil}$. It preserves $p.r'$ because $\uparrow p.r' = x$.
- $\{I\}\ T_4\ \{I\}$: This action changes $p.s$ from *jng* to *out* and decreases $f(p)$ from 1 to 0.

Therefore, **invariant I**. $\square$

Given the simplicity of this protocol, the reader may wonder if it is necessary to use assertional reasoning; instead, an argument based on operational reasoning might suffice. The effectiveness of operational reasoning, however, tends to

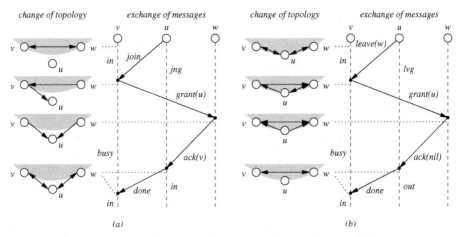

Fig. 3. Joining and leaving a bidirectional ring: (a) join, (b) leave.

diminish as the number of messages and actions of the protocol increase. Since our ultimate goal is to prove the correctness of the more involved protocols discussed later in this paper, we use assertional reasoning from the beginning.

As discussed above, although $ring(r')$ always holds, $ring(r)$ may sometimes be false. In fact, if processes keep joining the network, the protocol may never be able to establish $ring(r)$. However, by the definition of r', once all the *grant* messages are delivered, then $u.r' = u.r$ for all u and consequently, $ring(r)$ holds. A similar property is shared by all the protocols presented in this paper.

In addition, the join protocol in Figure 2 is livelock-free, and it does not cause starvation for an individual process. To see this, simply observe that a *retry* is sent by a *jng* node. Hence, although the *join* message of some node may be declined, some other node succeeds in joining. Furthermore, the ring cannot keep growing forever because there are only a finite number of processes. Hence, if a process keeps trying to join, it eventually succeeds.

3.2   Joins and Leaves for a Bidirectional Ring

We design the maintenance protocol for a bidirectional ring by first designing a join protocol and a symmetric leave protocol and then combining them. Figure 3 depicts how a process joins or leaves a ring. Converting this figure to protocols are straightforward. Hence, the join protocol and the leave protocol are omitted here, but they can be found in [10]. The resulting combined protocol is shown in Figure 4. Proofs of correctness of these protocols are given in [10].

We refer the interested reader to [8, 10] for a number of additional results on rings. For example, we show in [10] a join protocol for a bidirectional ring that does not have the *busy* state, but assumes FIFO channels. We show in [10] how a simple extension to the combined protocol in Figure 4 ensures that an *out* process does not have any incoming messages. We show in [8] that a simple extension of the protocol in Figure 3 maintains the Chord ring; the main idea is

process p
    var $s : \{in, out, jng, lvg, busy\};\ r, l : V';\ t, a : V'$
    init $s = out \wedge r = l = t = \textbf{nil}$
    begin
T_1^j $s = out \rightarrow a := contact();$
            if $a = p \rightarrow r, l, s := p, p, in \ [\!] \ a \neq p \rightarrow s := jng;$ **send** $join()$ **to** a **fi**
T_1^l $[\!] \ s = in \rightarrow$
            if $l = p \rightarrow r, l, s := \textbf{nil}, \textbf{nil}, out$
            $[\!] \ l \neq p \rightarrow s := lvg;$ **send** $leave(r)$ **to** l **fi**
T_2^j $[\!]$ **rcv** $join()$ **from** $q \rightarrow$
            if $s = in \rightarrow$ **send** $grant(q)$ **to** $r;\ r, s, t := q, busy, r$
            $[\!] \ s \neq in \rightarrow$ **send** $retry()$ **to** q **fi**
T_2^l $[\!]$ **rcv** $leave(a)$ **from** $q \rightarrow$
            if $s = in \wedge r = q \rightarrow$ **send** $grant(q)$ **to** $a;\ r, s, t := a, busy, r$
            $[\!] \ s \neq in \vee r \neq q \rightarrow$ **send** $retry()$ **to** q **fi**
T_3 $[\!]$ **rcv** $grant(a)$ **from** $q \rightarrow$
            if $l = q \rightarrow$ **send** $ack(l)$ **to** $a;\ l := a$
            $[\!] \ l \neq q \rightarrow$ **send** $ack(\textbf{nil})$ **to** $a;\ l := q$ **fi**
T_4 $[\!]$ **rcv** $ack(a)$ **from** $q \rightarrow$
            if $s = jng \rightarrow r, l, s := q, a, in;$ **send** $done()$ **to** l
            $[\!] \ s = lvg \rightarrow$ **send** $done()$ **to** $l;\ r, l, s := \textbf{nil}, \textbf{nil}, out$ **fi**
T_5 $[\!]$ **rcv** $done()$ **from** $q \rightarrow s, t := in, \textbf{nil}$
T_6 $[\!]$ **rcv** $retry()$ **from** $q \rightarrow$ **if** $s = jng \rightarrow s := out \ [\!] \ s = lvg \rightarrow s := in$ **fi**
    end

Fig. 4. The combined protocol for a bidirectional ring. The auxiliary variable t is for the purpose of the correctness proofs.

to forward a *join* message via the finger pointers until a node with an appropriate identifier is found.

4   Maintaining the Ranch Topology

The Ranch (*random cyclic hypercube*) topology, proposed in [11], is a structured peer-to-peer network topology with a number of nice properties, including scalability, locality awareness, and fault tolerance. The presentation of Ranch in this paper is self-contained.

4.1   The Ranch Topology

In Ranch, every process u has a binary string, denoted by $u.id$, as its *identifier*. Identifiers need not be unique or have the same length. We use ϵ to denote the empty string. For a set of processes S, we use S_α to denote the set of processes in S that are prefixed by α. Every process u uses two dynamic arrays of type V', $u.r$ and $u.l$, to be their right neighbors and left neighbors. A set of processes S form a Ranch topology if for every bit string α, all the processes in S prefixed by α form a ring. The rings in Ranch can be either unidirectional or bidirectional.

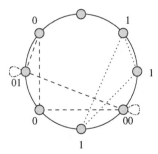

Fig. 5. An example of the Ranch topology. Bits in identifiers are numbered from left to right. For example, if $id = 01$, then $id[0] = 0$ and $id[1] = 1$.

Formally, S form a unidirectional Ranch if $\langle \forall \alpha : ring(S_\alpha, r[|\alpha|]) \rangle$ holds, and they form a bidirectional Ranch if $\langle \forall \alpha : biring(S_\alpha, r[|\alpha|], l[|\alpha|]) \rangle$ holds. Hence, the key to maintaining Ranch is the joining or leaving of a single ring. We call the ring consisting of all the processes prefixed by α simply *the α-ring*. Figure 5 shows an example of the Ranch topology.

At a high level, Ranch and skip graphs [2] share some similarities. But as far as topology maintenance is concerned, they have two key differences: (1) in Ranch, a new process can be added to an arbitrary position in the base ring (i.e., the ϵ-ring), while in skip graphs, a new process has to be added to an appropriate position; (2) in Ranch, the order in which the processes appear in, say the $\alpha 0$-ring, need not be the same as the order in which they appear in the α-ring, while in skip graphs, the orders need to be the same. For example, in Figure 5, the order in which the processes appear in the 0-ring is different from the order in which they appear in the ϵ-ring. This flexibility allows us to design simple maintenance protocols for Ranch.

4.2   Joins for Unidirectional Ranch

A process joins Ranch ring by ring. It first calls the *contact*() function to join the ϵ-ring, then after it has joined the α-ring, for some α, if it intends to join one more ring, it generates the next bit d of its identifier and joins the αd-ring. But how does the process find an existing process in the αd-ring? Note that we can no longer use the *contact*() function for this purpose.

The idea to overcome this difficulty is as follows. Suppose that process u intends to join the $\alpha 0$-ring, where $|\alpha 0| = i$. Process u sends a $join(u, i, 0)$ message to $u.r[i-1]$. This *join* message is forwarded around the α-ring. Upon receiving the *join* message, a process p makes one of the following decisions: (1) if $a = p$ (i.e., the *join* message originates from p and comes back), then the $\alpha 0$-ring is empty and p creates the $\alpha 0$-ring by setting $p.r[i] = p$; (2) if p is in the α-ring but is not in the $\alpha 0$-ring, then p forwards the *join* message to $p.r[i-1]$; (3) if p is not in the α-ring, or p itself is also trying to join the $\alpha 0$-ring, then p sends a *retry* message to a; (4) if p is in the $\alpha 0$-ring, then p sends a *grant* message

process p
   var id : dynamic bit string; s : dynamic array of $\{out, in, jng\}$;
      r : dynamic array of V'; $a : V'$; i : integer; $d : [0..1]$
   init $id = \epsilon \wedge s[0] = out$
   begin
T_1 $s[k] = out \vee s[k] = in \rightarrow$
         if $s[k] = out \rightarrow a, d := contact(), any$
         $[] \; s[k] = in \rightarrow a, d := r[k], random; \; id := grow(id, d)$ **fi**;
         if $a = p \rightarrow s[k] := in; \; r[k] := p$
         $[] \; a \neq p \rightarrow s[k] := jng; \; \textbf{send } join(p, k, d) \textbf{ to } a$ **fi**
T_2 $[]$ **rcv** $join(a, i, d)$ **from** $q \rightarrow$
         if $a = p \rightarrow r[k], s[k] := p, in$
         $[] \; a \neq p \wedge i > 0 \wedge s[i'] = in \wedge (k < i \vee id[i'] \neq d) \rightarrow$
               send $join(a, i, d)$ **to** $r[i']$
         $[] \; a \neq p \wedge ((i = 0 \wedge s[i] \neq in) \vee (i > 0 \wedge (s[i'] \neq in$
               $\vee (k \geq i \wedge id[i'] = d \wedge s[i] \neq in)))) \rightarrow \textbf{send } retry() \textbf{ to } a$
         $[] \; a \neq p \wedge (i = 0 \vee (s[i'] = in \wedge k \geq i \wedge id[i'] = d)) \wedge s[i] = in \rightarrow$
               send $grant(r[i])$ **to** $a; \; r[i] := a$ **fi**
T_3 $[]$ **rcv** $grant(a)$ **from** $q \rightarrow r[k], s[k] := a, in$
T_4 $[]$ **rcv** $retry()$ **from** $q \rightarrow s[k] := out;$
         if $k > 0 \rightarrow id := shrink(id)$ $[]$ $k = 0 \rightarrow$ **skip fi**
   end

Fig. 6. The join protocol for unidirectional Ranch. A call to $grow(id, d)$ appends bit d to id; a call to $shrink(id)$ removes the last bit from id. We use k and i' as shorthands for $|id|$ and $i - 1$, respectively. The array s has range $[0..k]$. If $s[0] = out$, then r is empty; otherwise, r has range $[0..k]$. When s and r grow, their new elements are initialized to out and **nil**, respectively.

to a, informing a that p is its $r[i]$ neighbor. Figure 6 shows the join protocol for unidirectional Ranch[2]. This protocol, however, is not livelock-free: when two processes attempt to join the same empty ring, they may reject each other. We show in [9] that, assuming a total order on the processes, we can use a leader election algorithm to obtain a livelock-free join protocol.

4.3   Joins and Leaves for Bidirectional Ranch

The join protocol for bidirectional Ranch is a simple combination of the ideas in Sections 3.1 and 4.2. A process leaves Ranch ring by ring, starting from the "highest" ring in which it participates. The leave protocol for bidirectional Ranch is a straightforward extension of the leave protocol in [10]. We omit presenting these two protocols here but they can be found in [9]. Designing a protocol that handles both joins and leaves is a much more challenging problem than designing two that handle them respectively. In particular, there are two subtleties.

---

[2] For the protocol in Figure 6, a single state, instead of an array of states, suffices. We keep an array of states so that the protocols in Figures 6 and 7 are more similar.

The first subtlety is as follows. Suppose that there is a $join(a, |\alpha 0|, 0)$ message in transmission from u to v, both of which are in the α-ring. Since we only assume reliable delivery, when this $join$ message is in transmission, v may leave the α-ring, and even worse, v may join the α-ring again, but at a different location. If this happens, then the $join$ message may "skip" part of the α-ring, which may contain some processes in the $\alpha 0$-ring. Therefore, if the $join$ message comes back to process a, it causes a to form a singleton ring, resulting in two $\alpha 0$-rings, which violates the definition of Ranch.

The second subtlety is as follows. Suppose that u and v belong to the α-ring and w is the only process in the $\alpha 0$-ring. Then u decides to join the $\alpha 0$-ring and sends out a $join(u, |\alpha 0|, 0)$ message. But when this message has passed v but has not reached w, v also decides to join the $\alpha 0$-ring and sends out a $join(v, |\alpha 0|, 0)$ message. Since we only assume reliable delivery, the $join(v)$ message may reach w earlier than the $join(u)$ message does. Hence, v is granted admission to the $\alpha 0$-ring, but then w may leave the $\alpha 0$-ring. Therefore, the $join(u)$ message does not encounter any process in the $\alpha 0$-ring before it comes back to u, causing u to create an $\alpha 0$-ring. This violates the Ranch definition, because the $\alpha 0$-ring already exists and consists of v.

We use the following idea to overcome these two subtleties. When u decides to join, say the $\alpha 0$-ring, it changes $u.s[|\alpha|]$ (from in) to wtg (waiting), a new state. Upon receiving a $join(u, i, 0)$ message, process v first checks if $v.s[i-1] = in$. If so, v takes a decision as before, and if it needs to forward the $join$ message, v changes $v.s[i-1]$ to wtg. If not, v sends a $retry$ message to u. After u receives either a $grant$ or a $retry$ message, it sends an end message to change the state of those processes which has been set to wtg by its $join$ message back to in. Intuitively, changing a state to wtg prevents a process from performing certain join or leave operation that may jeopardize an ongoing join operation. The combined protocol that realizes this idea is shown in Figure 7.

4.4   Discussion

A desirable property for a topology maintenance protocol is that a process that has left the network does not have any incoming messages related to the network. This property, however, is not provided by the protocol in Figure 7 if we only assume reliable, but not ordered delivery. On the other hand, if we assume reliable and ordered delivery of messages and we extend the protocol using a method similar to the one suggested in [10], then the extended combined protocol provides this property.

This combined protocol in Figure 7 is not livelock-free. In fact, as pointed out in [10], the leave protocol for a single ring is not livelock-free. We remark that this property is not provided by existing work either; see a detailed discussion in Section 5 and in [10]. Lynch et al. [14] have noted the similarity between this problem and the classical dining philosophers problem, for which there is no deterministic symmetric solution that avoids starvation [7]. However, one may use a probabilistic algorithm similar to the one in [7] to provide this property,

process p

    var id : dynamic bit string; s : dynamic array of $\{in, out, jng, lvg, busy, wtg\}$;
        r, l, t : dynamic array of V'; $a : V'$; i : integer; $d : [0..1]$
    init $id = \epsilon \wedge s[0] = out$
    begin

T_1^j $s[k] = out \vee s[k] = in \rightarrow$
         if $s[k] = out \rightarrow a, d := contact(), $ **any**
         $[]\ s[k] = in \rightarrow a, d := r[k], $ **random**; $id := grow(id, d)$ **fi**;
         if $a = p \rightarrow s[k] := in;\ r[k], l[k] := p, p$
         $[]\ a \neq p \rightarrow s[k] := jng;$ **send** $join(p, k, d)$ **to** a;
             if $k > 0 \rightarrow s[k'] := wtg\ []\ k = 0 \rightarrow$ **skip fi fi**

T_1^l $[]\ s[k] = in \rightarrow$
         if $l[k] = p \rightarrow r[k], l[k] := \mathbf{nil}, \mathbf{nil};\ s[k] := out;$
             if $k > 0 \rightarrow id := shrink(id)\ []\ k = 0 \rightarrow$ **skip fi**
         $[]\ l[k] \neq p \rightarrow s[k] := lvg;$ **send** $leave(r[k], k)$ **to** $l[k]$ **fi**

T_2^j $[]$ **rcv** $join(a, i, d)$ **from** $q \rightarrow$
         if $a = p \rightarrow r[i], l[i], s[i] := p, p, in;$
             if $i > 0 \rightarrow s[i'] := in;$ **send** $end(p, i')$ **to** $r[i']\ []\ i = 0 \rightarrow$ **skip fi**
         $[]\ a \neq p \wedge i > 0 \wedge s[i'] = in \wedge (k < i \vee id[i'] \neq d) \rightarrow$
             $s[i'] := wtg;$ **send** $join(a, i, d)$ **to** $r[i']$
         $[]\ a \neq p \wedge ((i = 0 \wedge s[i] \neq in) \vee (i > 0 \wedge (s[i'] \neq in$
             $\vee (k \geq i \wedge id[i'] = d \wedge s[i] \neq in)))) \rightarrow$ **send** $retry()$ **to** a
         $[]\ a \neq p \wedge (i = 0 \vee (s[i'] = in \wedge k \geq i \wedge id[i'] = d)) \wedge s[i] = in \rightarrow$
             send $grant(a, i)$ **to** $r[i];\ r[i], s[i], t[i] := a, busy, r[i]$ **fi**

T_2^l $[]$ **rcv** $leave(a, i)$ **from** $q \rightarrow$
         if $s[i] = in \wedge r[i] = q \rightarrow$ **send** $grant(q, i)$ **to** $a;\ r[i], s[i], t[i] := a, busy, r[i]$
         $[]\ s[i] \neq in \vee r[i] \neq q \rightarrow$ **send** $retry()$ **to** q **fi**

T_3 $[]$ **rcv** $grant(a, i)$ **from** $q \rightarrow$
         if $l[i] = q \rightarrow$ **send** $ack(l[i])$ **to** $a;\ l[i] := a$
         $[]\ l[i] \neq q \rightarrow$ **send** $ack(\mathbf{nil})$ **to** $a;\ l[i] := q$ **fi**

T_4 $[]$ **rcv** $ack(a)$ **from** $q \rightarrow$
         if $s[k] = jng \rightarrow r[k], l[k], s[k] := q, a, in;$ **send** $done(k)$ **to** $l[k];$
             if $k > 0 \rightarrow s[k'] := in;$ **send** $end(a, k')$ **to** $r[k']\ []\ k = 0 \rightarrow$ **skip fi**
         $[]\ s[k] = lvg \rightarrow$ **send** $done(k)$ **to** $l[k];\ r[k], l[k] := \mathbf{nil}, \mathbf{nil};\ s[k] := out;$
             if $k > 0 \rightarrow id := shrink(id)\ []\ k = 0 \rightarrow$ **skip fi fi**

T_5 $[]$ **rcv** $done(i)$ **from** $q \rightarrow s[i], t[i] := in, \mathbf{nil}$

T_6 $[]$ **rcv** $retry()$ **from** $q \rightarrow$
         if $s[k] = jng \wedge k > 0 \rightarrow s[k], s[k'] := out, in;\ id := shrink(id);$
             send $end(q, k)$ **to** $r[k]$
         $[]\ s[k] = jng \wedge k = 0 \rightarrow s[k] := out\ []\ s[k] = lvg \rightarrow s[k] := in$ **fi**

T_7 $[]$ **rcv** $end(a, i)$ **from** $q \rightarrow$
         if $p \neq a \rightarrow s[i] := in;$ **send** $end(a, i)$ **to** $r[i]\ []\ p = a \rightarrow$ **skip fi**
    end

Fig. 7. The combined protocol for bidirectional Ranch. We use k, k', and i' as shorthands for $|id|$, $k - 1$, and $i - 1$, respectively. The array s has range $[0..k]$. When $s[0] = out$, r, l, t are empty; otherwise, r, l, t have range $[0..k]$. When s grows, the new element is initialized to out; when r, l, t grow, the new elements are initialized to $\mathbf{nil}$.

or, as in the Ethernet protocol, a process may delay a random amount of time before sending out another leave request.

5   Related Work

Peer-to-peer networks belong in two categories, structured and unstructured, depending on whether they have stringent neighbor relationships to be maintained by their members. While unstructured networks do not maintain topologies as stringent as structured networks, it is still desirable to maintain a topology with certain properties (e.g., connectivity). For example, Pandurangan *et al.* [18] propose how to build a connected network with constant degree and logarithmic diameter. In recent years, numerous topologies have been proposed for structured peer-to-peer networks (e.g., [2, 5, 11, 15, 16, 19, 22, 20, 21, 23]). Many of them, however, assume that concurrent membership changes only affect disjoint sets of the neighbor variables. Clearly, this assumption does not always hold.

Chord [22] takes the passive approach to topology maintenance. Liben-Nowell *et al.* [12] investigate the bandwidth consumed by repair protocols and show that Chord is nearly optimal in this regard. Hildrum *et al.* [6] focus on choosing nearby neighbors for Tapestry [23], a topology based on PRR [19]. In addition, they propose a join protocol for Tapestry, together with a correctness proof. Furthermore, they describe how to handle leaves (both voluntary and involuntary) in Tapestry. However, the description of voluntary (i.e., active) leaves is high-level and is mainly concerned with individual leaves. Liu and Lam [13] have also proposed an active join protocol for a topology based on PRR. Their focus, however, is on constructing a topology that satisfies the bit-correcting property of PRR; in contrast with the work of Hildrum *et al.*, proximity considerations are not taken into account.

The work of Aspnes and Shah [2] is closely related to ours. They give a join protocol and a leave protocol, but their work has some shortcomings. Firstly, concurrency issues are addressed at a high level; for example, the analysis does not capture the system state when messages are in transmission. Secondly, the join protocol and the leave protocol of [2], if put together, do not handle both joins and leaves. (To see this, consider the scenario where a join occurs between a leaving process and its right neighbor.) Thirdly, for the leave protocol, a process may send a leave request to a process that has already left the network; the problem persists even if ordered delivery of messages is assumed. Fourthly, the protocols rely on the search operation, the correctness of which under topology change is not established.

In their position paper, Lynch *et al.* [14] outline an approach to providing atomic data access in peer-to-peer networks and give the pseudocode of the approach for the Chord ring. The pseudocode, excluding the part for transferring data, gives a topology maintenance protocol for the Chord ring. While [14] provides some interesting observations and remarks, no proof of correctness is given, and the proposed protocol has several shortcomings, some of which are similar to those of [2] (e.g., it does not work for both joins and leaves and a message may be sent to a process that has already left the network).

Assertional proofs of distributed algorithms appear in, e.g., Chandy and Misra [3]. It is not uncommon for a concurrent algorithm to have an invariant consisting of a number of conjuncts. Our work can be described by the closure and convergence framework of Arora and Gouda [1]: the protocols operate under the closure of the invariants, and the topology converges to a ring once the messages related to membership changes are delivered.

6 Concluding Remarks

We have shown in this paper simple protocols that actively maintain a single ring and the Ranch topology under both joins and leaves. Numerous issues merit further investigation. For example, it would be interesting to develop machine-checked proofs for the protocols, investigate techniques that may help reduce the proof lengths, design simple protocols that provide certain progress properties, and extend the protocols to faulty environments.

References

1. A. Arora and M. G. Gouda. Closure and convergence: A foundation for fault-tolerant computing. *IEEE Transactions on Software Engineering*, 19:1015–1027, 1993.
2. J. Aspnes and G. Shah. Skip graphs. In *Proceedings of the 14th Annual ACM-SIAM Symposium on Discrete Algorithms*, pages 384–393, January 2003. See also Shah's Ph.D. dissertation, Yale University, 2003.
3. K. M. Chandy and J. Misra. *Parallel Program Design: A Foundation*. Addison-Wesley, Reading, MA, 1988.
4. M. G. Gouda. *Elements of Network Protocol Design*. John Wiley & Sons, 1998.
5. N. J. A. Harvey, M. B. Jones, S. Saroiu, M. Theimer, and A. Wolman. Skipnet: A scalable overlay network with practical locality properties. In *Proceedings of the 4th USENIX Symposium on Internet Technologies and Systems*, pages 113–126, March 2003.
6. K. Hildrum, J. Kubiatowicz, S. Rao, and B. Y. Zhao. Distributed data location in a dynamic network. In *Proceedings of the 14th Annual ACM Symposium on Parallel Algorithms and Architectures*, pages 41–52, August 2002.
7. D. Lehmann and M. Rabin. On the advantages of free choice: A symmetric and fully distributed solution to the dining philosophers problem. In *Proceedings of 8th ACM Symposium on Principles of Programming Languages*, pages 133–138, January 1981.
8. X. Li. Maintaining the Chord ring. Technical Report TR–04–30, Department of Computer Science, University of Texas at Austin, July 2004.
9. X. Li, J. Misra, and C. G. Plaxton. Active and concurrent topology maintenance for a structured peer-to-peer network topology. Technical Report TR–04–21, Department of Computer Science, University of Texas at Austin, May 2004.

10. X. Li, J. Misra, and C. G. Plaxton. Brief announcement: Concurrent maintenance of rings. In *Proceedings of the 23rd ACM Symposium on Principles of Distributed Computing*, pages 376–376, July 2004. Full paper available as TR–04–03, Department of Computer Science, University of Texas at Austin, February 2004.

11. X. Li and C. G. Plaxton. On name resolution in peer-to-peer networks. In *Proceedings of the 2nd Workshop on Principles of Mobile Computing*, pages 82–89, October 2002.

12. D. Liben-Nowell, H. Balakrishnan, and D. Karger. Analysis of the evolution of peer-to-peer systems. In *Proceedings of the 21st ACM Symposium on Principles of Distributed Computing*, pages 233–242, July 2002.

13. H. Liu and S. S. Lam. Neighbor table construction and update in a dynamic peer-to-peer network. In *Proceedings of the 23rd International Conference on Distributed Computing Systems*, pages 509–519, May 2003.

14. N. Lynch, D. Malkhi, and D. Ratajczak. Atomic data access in content addressable networks. In *Proceedings of the 1st International Workshop on Peer-to-Peer Systems*, pages 295–305, March 2002.

15. D. Malkhi, M. Naor, and D. Ratajczak. Viceroy: A scalable and dynamic emulation of the butterfly. In *Proceedings of the 21st ACM Symposium on Principles of Distributed Computing*, pages 183–192, June 2002.

16. G. S. Manku, M. Bawa, and P. Raghavan. Symphony: Distributed hashing in a small world. In *Proceedings of the 4th USENIX Symposium on Internet Technologies and Systems*, pages 127–140, March 2003.

17. T. M. McGuire. *Correct Implementation of Network Protocols*. PhD thesis, Department of Computer Science, University of Texas at Austin, April 2004.

18. G. Pandurangan, P. Raghavan, and E. Upfal. Building low-diameter peer-to-peer networks. *IEEE Journal on Selected Areas in Communications*, 21:995–1002, August 2003.

19. C. G. Plaxton, R. Rajaraman, and A. W. Richa. Accessing nearby copies of replicated objects in a distributed environment. *Theory of Computing Systems*, 32:241–280, 1999.

20. S. Ratnasamy, P. Francis, M. Handley, R. Karp, and S. Shenker. A scalable content addressable network. In *Proceedings of the 2001 ACM SIGCOMM Conference on Applications, Technologies, Architectures, and Protocols for Computer Communication*, pages 161–172, 2001.

21. A. Rowstron and P. Druschel. Pastry: Scalable, decentralized object location and routing for large-scale peer-to-peer systems. In *Proceedings of the 18th IFIP/ACM International Conference on Distributed Systems Platforms*, pages 329–350, November 2001.

22. I. Stoica, R. Morris, D. Liben-Nowell, D. Karger, F. Kaashoek, F. Dabek, and H. Balakrishnan. Chord: A scalable peer-to-peer lookup service for Internet applications. *IEEE/ACM Transactions on Networking*, 11:17–32, February 2003.

23. B. Y. Zhao, L. Huang, J. Stribling, S. C. Rhea, A. D. Joseph, and J. Kubiatowicz. Tapestry: A resilient global-scale overlay for service deployment. *IEEE Journal on Selected Areas in Communications*, 22:41–53, January 2003.

Distributed Weighted Matching

Mirjam Wattenhofer and Roger Wattenhofer

Department of Computer Science, ETH Zurich, 8092 Zurich, Switzerland
{mirjam.wattenhofer,wattenhofer}@inf.ethz.ch

Abstract. In this paper, we present fast and fully distributed algorithms for matching in weighted trees and general weighted graphs. The time complexity as well as the approximation ratio of the tree algorithm is constant. In particular, the approximation ratio is 4. For the general graph algorithm we prove a constant ratio bound of 5 and a polylogarithmic time complexity of $O(\log^2 n)$.

1 Introduction and Related Work

In a weighted graph $G = (V, E)$, a maximum weighted matching is a subset $E' \subseteq E$ of edges such that no two edges in E' share a common vertex, every edge in $E - E'$ shares a common vertex with some edge in E' and the weight of the matching is maximized. Matching is one of the most fundamental problems studied in graph theory and computer science. A plethora of algorithms and heuristics for different matching variants have been proposed, culminating in the breakthrough work of Edmonds [Edm65] who has shown that the maximum weighted matching problem can be computed in polynomial time for general graphs.

The increasing importance of large-scale networks (e.g. Internet, ad-hoc and sensor networks) has shifted the focus of distributed computing research away from tightly-coupled multiprocessors towards loosely-coupled message passing systems. Solving a basic network problem such as matching by first collecting the graph topology of the network and then computing an optimal solution using Edmonds' algorithm is not economical because this approach leads to an immense data flow which is expensive in time and resources. Moreover, by the time the solution is computed, the network topology may already have changed.

In this paper we adopt the model of so-called *local graph (or network) algorithms*. Instead of sending the input (the network topology as a weighted graph) to a central processor, we let all the vertices of the network participate in the computation themselves. By only allowing the vertices to communicate with their direct neighbors in the graph, we keep the locality of the original problem[1].

Related Work. The general distributed graph network model and the objective to have algorithms that are as "local" as possible has long been an important area of research. Among the first results on this topic we would like to mention the ingenious $O(\log^* n)$

---

[1] In contrast, the widely studied parallel random access machine (PRAM) model does not preserve locality. In essence, a local graph algorithm is also a PRAM algorithm, but not vice versa.

R. Guerraoui (Ed.): DISC 2004, LNCS 3274, pp. 335–348, 2004.

coloring algorithm of Cole and Vishkin [CV86]. The matching lower bound was proven by Linial [Lin92]. Thanks to the applications for ad-hoc and sensor networks local graph algorithms recently experienced a second wind and are a field of intensive study ([JRS01], [KW03]). The model will be presented in detail in Sect. 2; for a proficient introduction to local distributed computing, we refer to [Pel00].

Up to now, only a small number of distributed algorithms for matching have been proposed. Indeed, we are not aware of any distributed algorithm that solves the maximum weighted matching problem optimally. Distributed computing researchers often cherish time more than quality, and consequently prefer approximation algorithms that only need polylogarithmic time over optimal linear time algorithms. To our knowledge, there exists just one maximum weighted matching approximation: Uehara and Chen [UC00] present a constant-time algorithm that achieves a $O(\Delta)$ approximation, Δ being the maximum degree in the graph. In this paper we significantly improve the approximation ratio while staying polylogarithmic in time.

In contrast, there is a whole selection of algorithms studying the special case of nonweighted graphs. For non-weighted graphs Karaata and Saleh [KS00] give a $O(n^4)$ algorithm that solves the maximum matching problem for trees. In bipartite graphs where the vertices know their partition Chattopadhyay et al. [CHS02] give an algorithm for the same problem with time complexity $O(n^2)$. In the same paper Chattopadhyay et al. study the maximal matching problem for general non-weighted graphs, presenting a linear-time algorithm. In [II86] Israeli and Itai give a randomized[2] $O(\log n)$ time algorithm for the maximal matching problem[3]. The methods Israeli and Itai use are similar to those used by Luby [Lub86] for the related maximal independent set problem. In Sect. 4 we will use methods inspired by [Lub86] and [II86] to achieve our results.

Outline. After this excursion to non-weighted graphs let us now return to weighted graphs. In our paper we present two randomized algorithms for approximating a maximum weighted matching, first one for trees, then one for general weighted graphs. The tree algorithm in Sect. 3 finds a 4-approximation in $O(1)$ time. The graph algorithm in Sect. 4 computes a 5-approximation in $O(\log^2 n)$-time. Beforehand—in Sect. 2—we formally introduce the model. Finally, in Sect. 5, we put our work into perspective.

2 Notation and Preliminaries

In this section we introduce the notation as well as some basic theorems we will use throughout the paper.

Let $G = (V, E)$ be an undirected simple graph, where V denotes the set of vertices, $|V| = n$, and E the set of edges. With each edge $e \in E$ we associate a positive weight $w(e) \in \mathbf{R}^+$. For a subset S of E, $w(S)$ denotes the total weight of the edges in S, that is $w(S) = \sum_{e \in S} w(e)$. A set $M \subseteq E$ is a *matching* if no two edges in M have a common vertex. A matching is *maximal* if it is not properly contained in any other matching, it is a *maximum (cardinality)* matching if its *size* is maximized over all matchings in G. A

---

[2] It is worth noting that Hanckowiak et al. [HKP01] manage to give a $O(\log^4)$ time deterministic algorithm for the same model.

[3] Note, that [KS00] and [CHS02] focus on self-stabilization, whereas [II86] does not.

matching is a *maximum weighted* or *optimal* matching of G if its *weight* is maximized over all matchings in G. Throughout the paper M_G^* will denote a maximum weighted matching in a graph G. Following the standard notation we say that our algorithm has a *approximation ratio* of ρ if $w(M_G)$ is within a factor of ρ of $w(M_G^*)$. Let $d_G(u)$ denote the degree of vertex u in G. We will make use of the maximum weight in the entire graph G, respectively in the neighborhood of a vertex u. For this purpose we define $w_{\max}(G)$ and $w_{\max}(u)_E$:

$$w_{\max}(G) := \max_{e \in E} w(e),$$

$$w_{\max}(u)_E := \max_{e \in E; e = \{u, x\}} w(e).$$

Whenever a vertex has to choose an edge with weight $w_{\max}(u)_E$ and there is more than one candidate, ties are broken lexicographically by choosing the edge with highest rank in a given ordering.

Though our tree-algorithm works for non-rooted trees, it simplifies some proofs to assume that there is a root. In this case, the terms *parent, child* and *sibling* have their *familiar* meaning. We define $n_{in}(T)$ for a tree $T = (V, E)$ as the number of interior (non-leaf) vertices:

$$n_{in}(T) := |\{u \mid u \in V, d_T(u) > 1\}|.$$

We use a purely synchronous model for communication. That is, in every communication round, each vertex is allowed to send a message to each of its direct neighbors. In our algorithms all messages need a constant number of bits only. The *time complexity* is the number of rounds the algorithms needs to solve the problem.

The section is concluded by giving four facts which will be used in subsequent sections. For a proof, we refer the reader to standard mathematical text books.

Fact 1. *For $n \geq x \geq 1$, we have*

$$\left(1 - \frac{x}{n}\right)^n \leq e^{-x}.$$

Fact 2. *In a graph $G = (V, E)$, we have*

$$|E| = \frac{1}{2} \cdot \sum_{u \in V} d_G(u).$$

Fact 3. *For any matching M on a graph $G = (V, E)$, it holds that $|M| \leq \frac{1}{2} \cdot |V|$.*

Fact 4. *If M^* is a maximum (cardinality) matching and M is a maximal matching then $|M^*| \leq 2 \cdot |M|$.*

3   Matching in Trees

3.1   The Algorithm

In this section we present a distributed algorithm for approximating a maximum weighted matching in (non-rooted) trees. The time complexity as well as the approximation ratio of this algorithm are shown to be constant. For the sake of clarity and simplicity the algorithm is divided into two procedures, which are to be executed one by one. Before we present the algorithm in detail we give a general overview.

Outline of the algorithm: To find a matching M_T in a weighted tree $T = (V, E)$ we foremost reduce the degree of the vertices without losing too much weight. Towards this goal, in the first procedure, each vertex u *requests* its heaviest incident edge e_u by sending a message through it. Thereafter, u *confirms* the heaviest edge e_v, $e_v \neq e_u$, on which it received a request. If u received a request through e_u, it additionally confirms e_u. All unconfirmed edges are deleted and the result is a set of vertex disjoint paths P. On this set of paths a matching is computed in the second procedure. As input for the second procedure we have an additional parameter k, which controls how often a vertex tries to become incident to the matching and consequently how large the matching will be. The given approximation ratios hold for $k = 1$. For details see the Tree-Matching Algorithm in Sect. 3.2.

3.2 Tree-Matching Algorithm

In order to compute a matching on a weighted tree $T = (V, E)$ with parameter k, each vertex u executes the following algorithms[4].

On input $T = (V, E)$, k each vertex u executes the following algorithm.
($*$ See Footnote 4 $*$)

procedure Tree-Matching (T, k):M
1: $P, M_T := \emptyset$
2: $P := $ Paths (T);
3: $M_T := $ Matching (P, k);
4: **return** M_T

procedure Paths (T):P
1: $R := \emptyset$
2: choose heaviest incident edge $e = \{u, v\}$, $e \in E$, i.e. $w(e) = w_{\max}(u)_E$
3: **send** message "requested" to v
4: **receive** message from all neighbors and add x to R if received message from x
5: **if** $(v \in R)$ **then**
6:     **send** message "confirmed" to v
7: **fi**
8: $w = \arg\max_{x \in R \setminus v} w(x)$
9: **send** message "confirmed" to w
10: **receive** message from all neighbors
11: **return** all confirmed edges
12: ($*$ Each node has degree at most 2 and hence the returned edges are a set of paths $*$)

---

[4] For the sake of readability, in all our algorithms we omit the subscripts, which should indicate, that a vertex only knows its direct neighborhood, not the entire graph/matching.

procedure Matching $(P, k){:}M$

1: $M_T := \emptyset, i := 0;$

2: **while** $i < k$ **do**

3:     choose uniformly at random one incident edge $e = \{u, v\}$ in P

4:     **send** message "you are my matching partner" to v

5:     **receive** message from all neighbors

6:     **if** (received message from v) **then**

7:         $M_T := M_T \cup \{e\}$

8:         delete e from P

9:         **return** M_T

10:    **fi**

11:    $i := i + 1$

12: **end while**;

13: ($*$ An edge is part of the matching M_T if both its incident vertices have chosen it. Therefore, M_T is a valid matching. $*$)

3.3 Analysis

Let us call a confirmed edge which was confirmed by both its endpoints *doubly confirmed*. Otherwise it is *singly confirmed*. Then for an edge $e = \{u, v\}$ the following three statements are equivalent:

1. e is doubly confirmed
2. e was u as well as v's heaviest incident edge
3. e was confirmed by a node that requested it.

Also note, that if e was requested by u and not confirmed by v, then v must have confirmed some other heavier edge.

In a first step we will prove that the weight of P is at least as large as the weight of an optimal matching M_T^* on T.

Lemma 5. $w(M_T^*) \le w(P)$.

Proof. In order to prove the lemma we will show that to each edge e in $M_T^* \backslash P$ we can assign one-to-one an edge e' in $P \backslash M_T^*$ with $w(e') \ge w(e)$. Towards this goal, we construct a 1:1 mapping $f : M_T^* \backslash P \rightarrow P \backslash M_T^*$, such that $w(f(e)) \ge w(e)$, which immediately implies $w(M_T^*) \le w(P)$.

To set up the mapping we root T at an arbitrary node and orient its edges away from the root (note, that we need a root just for the analysis of the algorithm, not for the algorithm itself). Thus, every edge has a *tail* (the parent) and a *head* (the child). There can be at most two types of edges in $M_T^* \backslash P$. Either edge $e = \{u, v\}$ was requested solely by its head v (*type 1*), or it was not requested by its head v (*type 2*). (Note, that if e is requested by both its head and its tail, it is in P.) We will first show how f maps type 1 edges and afterwards how type 2 edges are processed.

$e = \{u, v\}$ *is of type 1*: Since u did not confirm e, it must have singly confirmed a heavier edge $e' \in P$. Map e to e'. This mapping has the desired properties, since e' is adjacent to e and hence not in M_T^* and $w(e') \ge w(e)$. Furthermore, the mapping is one-to-one since e' is either a parent edge of e, singly confirmed by its head, or a sibling of e, singly confirmed by its tail. If we would map another type 1 edge e'' to e' then either e'' would be adjacent to e - contradicting its being in M_T^* - or e' would be singly confirmed by both endpoints - an oxymoron.

$e = \{u, v\}$ *is of type* 2: Vertex v is adjacent to an edge in M_T^* (namely, e) that it has not requested. Since v did not request its parent edge e, it must have requested a heavier child edge. Descend the tree, starting with $x := v$, in the following manner. While x is adjacent to an edge in M_T^* that it did not request, and the edge x did request is a child edge, set $x := y$, where y is the head of the edge requested by x. Let the path thus traversed in the tree be $v = v_0, v_1, \ldots, v_k$. Clearly, $k \geq 1$. It is easy to see that the path contains no edges of M_T^*, and that every v_i, except possibly v_k, is adjacent to an edge in M_T^*. Furthermore, the edges in the path are oriented from v_i to v_{i+1} and each was requested by its tail. Additionally, the weights along the path are monotone nondecreasing and at least as heavy as e.

Let e' be the last edge on this path. Then $e' \notin M_T^*$. If v_k requested e', then e' is doubly confirmed and therefore cannot have been mapped to by a type 1 edge. Map e to e'. Otherwise, v_k must have *singly* confirmed an edge e'' (possibly, $e'' = e'$) such that $w(e'') \geq w(e')$. Map e to e''. In this case we must show that e'' is not in M_T^* and has not been mapped to by a type 1 edge. Any edge in M_T^* incident to v_k must be a child edge of v_k (because v_k's parent edge is on the path) and it must have been requested by its tail, namely, v_k (otherwise v_k would not be last on the path). Thus e'' cannot be such an edge, for then it would be doubly confirmed. Also, such an edge cannot by of type 1, so it cannot be mapped to e''. It follows that if some type 1 edge is mapped to e'', then either e'' is a child edge of v_k and the type 1 edge mapped to it is a child edge of e'', or $e'' = e'$ and the type 1 edge mapped to it is a child edge of v_{k-1}. In both cases e'' is doubly confirmed - a contradiction.

Finally, no two type 2 edges may be mapped to the same edge, because every type 2 edge is mapped to a descendent edge such that the path connecting them contains no edges in M_T^* (and in particular, no type 2 edges). □

Lemma 6. *If every vertex in T executes the Matching Procedure with input parameter k and P and the output is denoted M_P, then $E[w(M_P)] \geq (1 - (3/4)^k)w(P)$.*

Proof. A vertex chooses an incident edge in P with probability at least $1/2$. Since the vertices choose independently of each other, an edge in P is chosen with probability at least $1/4$. Hence, if we denote by M_P the the chosen edges after k trials we have

$$E[X] \geq w(P) \sum_{i=1}^{k} (3/4)^i \cdot 1/4 = (1 - (3/4)^k)w(P).$$

□

Theorem 7. *In a tree T and for $k = 1$ we have that $E[w(M_T)] \geq \frac{1}{4}w(M_T^*)$. That is, the Tree-Matching Algorithm finds a matching which is on average a four approximation of a maximum weighted matching in T.*

Proof.

$$E[w(M_T)] \geq \frac{1}{4}w(P) \qquad\qquad \text{(Lemma 6)}$$

$$\geq \frac{1}{4}w(M_T^*) \qquad\qquad \text{(Lemma 5)}$$

$\square$

We conclude this section with the analysis of the time and message complexity.

Theorem 8. *The Tree-Matching Algorithm of Sect. 3.2* (Tree-Matching) *needs a constant number of time steps and a constant number of messages per edge with constant bit size.*

Proof. The theorem follows immediately from the description of the algorithm. $\square$

Corollary 9. *For any tree T we have that if the vertices synchronously execute the Tree-Matching Algorithm of Sect. 3.2 they find a matching in T with on average an approximation ratio of 4 and linear message complexity in constant time.*

4   Matching in General Graphs

4.1   The Algorithm

In this section we present a distributed algorithm which finds a matching on a weighed graph G with a constant approximation ratio of 5 in polylogarithmic time. Conceptually, the algorithm consists of several rounds in each of which it tries to thin out the input graph according to the edge-weights. On this thinned out graph a maximal matching is computed. After logarithmic many of such rounds, we can guarantee that the union of the maximal matchings on the thinned out graphs is a constant approximation of an optimal matching on the original graph. In the following we give a more detailed overview of the algorithm before we provide in Sect. 4.2 the algorithm itself.

Outline of the algorithm: The algorithm consist of $\log n$ *phases* Φ_i. Let us denote the input graph of phase Φ_i by $G^{(i)}$, where $G^{(1)} = G$. Then, in each phase, the algorithm first computes a subgraph $H_i^{(1)}$ of $G^{(i)}$, where for each node u the weight of its incident edges in $H_i^{(1)}$ is at least $1/2 \cdot w_{max}(u)_{E_G^{(i)}}$ (*"validation of edges phase"*). Secondly, it computes in $O(\log n)$ *rounds* $\mathcal{R}_j$ a maximal matching on $H_i^{(1)}$ (*"maximal matching phase"*). The two phases are described in the following.

"validation of edges phase": A vertex $u \in V$ calls an edge $e = \{u,v\}$ a *candidate* if $w(e) \geq \frac{1}{2} \cdot w_{\max}(u)_E$. Edge e is a *valid candidate* if it is a candidate for u and v. Each vertex u computes in phase Φ_i all its incident valid candidates (Procedure Valid). The set of all valid candidates induce the graph $H_i^{(1)}$ on $G^{(i)}$.

"maximal matching phase": A maximal matching on $H_i^{(1)}$ is computed in several rounds, where in each round $\mathcal{R}_j$ a sparse subgraph of a subgraph $H_i^{(j)}$ of $H_i^{(1)}$ is computed by the Select and Eliminate Procedure. In the Select Procedure, each vertex chooses randomly one incident edge and thus induces a graph $H_{S_i}^{(j)}$ on $H_i^{(j)}$. A

vertex $u \in V$ calls the edge it has chosen in the Select Procedure *chosen*. The other incident edges in $H_{Si}^{(j)}$ it calls *imposed*. In the Eliminate Procedure the vertices bound their degree in $H_{Si}^{(j)}$ by randomly choosing one imposed edge and deleting all the others, except the chosen one. The subgraph induced by this step is a collection of cycles and paths on which we find a matching in the Matching Procedure. After having removed all edges of the matching with all their adjacent edges from $H_i^{(j)}$ in the Cleanup Procedure the Uniform-Matching Procedure is repeated.

4.2 Graph-Matching

On input $G = (V, E)$ each vertex u executes the following algorithm.
($*$ See Footnote 4 $*$)
Procedure Graph-Matching $(G) : M$
1: $G^{(1)} := G,\ M_G := \emptyset$;
2: **for** (i from 1 to $\log n$ by 1) **do**
3:    ($*$ start of phase Φ_i $*$)
4:    $H_i^{(1)} := \text{Valid}(G^{(i)}$;
5:    $G^{(i+1)} := G^{(i)} \backslash H_i^{(1)}$;
6:    $j := 1$;
7:    **while** ($d_{H^{(j)}}(u) > 0$) **do**
8:       ($*$ start of round $\mathcal{R}_j$ $*$)
9:       $(H_i^{(j+1)}, M_H^{(j)}) := \text{Uniform-Matching}(H_i^{(j)})$;
10:       $M_G := M_G \cup M_H^{(j)}$;
11:       $j := j + 1$;
12:    **end while**;
13:    remove all edges adjacent to M_G from $G^{(i+1)}$
14: **od**;
15: **return** M_G

Procedure Valid $(G^{(i)}) : H$
1: $V_H := V_G^{(i)}; E_H = \emptyset$;
2: $S := \{v \mid e = \{u, v\} \in G^{(i)}, w(e) \geq \frac{1}{2} \cdot w_{\max}(u)_{E_G^{(i)}}\}$;
3: **for all** $v \in S$ **do**
4:    **send** message "you are a candidate" to v;
5: **od**;
6: **receive** message from all neighbors v in $G^{(i)}$;
7: ($*$ u waits until it received *all* messages $*$)
8: **if** (received message "you are a candidate" from $v \in S$) **then**
9:    $E_H := E_H \cup \{u, v\}$
10: **fi**;
11: **return** H
12: ($*$ H is the subgraph of $G^{(i)}$ which contains all *valid* candidates. The weight of the incident edges of u in H is at least $\frac{1}{2} \cdot w_{\max}(u)_{E_G^{(i)}}$. The degree of u in H may vary between zero and $d_{G^{(i)}}(u)$. $*$)

The Uniform-Matching subroutine computes a maximal matching on an input graph $H^{(j)}$. Each vertex u executes the following algorithm.

Procedure Uniform-Matching $(H^{(j)})$: $(H^{(j+1)}, M_H)$
1: $H_S^{(j)}$:= Procedure Select$(H^{(j)})$
2: $P^{(j)}$:= Eliminate$(H_S^{(j)})$;
3: $M_H^{(j)}$:= Matching$(P^{(j)})$;
4: $M_H := M_H \cup M_H^{(j)}$;
5: $H^{(j+1)}$:= Cleanup$((H^{(j)}, M_H^{(j)}))$;
6: **return** $(H^{(j+1)}, M_H)$

Procedure Select $(H^{(j)})$: $H_S^{(j)}$
1: $V_{H_S}^{(j)} := V_H^{(j)}; E_{H_S}^{(j)} := \emptyset$;
2: choose uniform at random one edge $e = \{u, v\}, e \in E_H^{(j)}$, call e *chosen*;
3: $E_{H_S}^{(j)} := E_{H_S}^{(j)} \cup \{e\}$;
4: **send** message "you are chosen" to v;
5: **receive** message from all neighbors w in $H^{(j)}$;
6: **if** (received message from w) **then**
7:     $E_{H_S}^{(j)} := E_{H_S}^{(j)} \cup \{u, w\}$; call $\{u, w\}$ *imposed*;
8: **fi**;
9: **return** $H_S^{(j)}$
10: (* If u has positive degree in $H^{(j)}$, it has positive degree in $H_S^{(j)}$. *)

Procedure Eliminate $(H_S^{(j)})$: $P^{(j)}$
1: $V_P^{(j)} := V_{H_S}^{(j)}, E_P^{(j)} := \emptyset$
2: choose uniform at random one *imposed* edge $e = \{u, v\}$;
3: **send** message "this edge is in $P^{(j)}$" to v;
4: $E_P^{(j)} := E_P^{(j)} \cup \{e\}$;
5: **receive** message from all neighbors w in $H_S^{(j)}$;
6: **if** (received message from w) **then**
7:     $E_P^{(j)} := E_P^{(j)} \cup \{u, w\}$;
8: **fi**;
9: **return** $P^{(j)}$
10: (* If u has at least one *imposed* edge, $d_{P^{(j)}}(u) \geq 1$. In general, $d_{P^{(j)}}(u) \leq 2$. *)

Procedure Matching $(P^{(j)})$: $M_G^{(j)}$
1: $M_G^{(j)} := \emptyset$;
2: choose uniformly at random one incident edge $e = \{u, v\}$ in $P^{(j)}$;
3: **send** message "you are my matching partner" to v;
4: **receive** message from all neighbors w in $P^{(j)}$;

5: **if** (received message from v) **then**

6:     $M_G^{(j)} := M_G^{(j)} \cup \{e\}$;

7: **fi**;

8: **return** $M_G^{(j)}$

9: (∗ An edge is part of the matching $M_G^{(j)}$ if both its endpoints have chosen it, therefore $M_G^{(j)}$ is a valid matching. ∗)

Procedure Cleanup $(H^{(j)}) : H^{(j+1)}$

1: $H^{(j+1)} := H^{(j)}$

2: remove all edges $e \in M_H^{(j)}$ from $H^{(j+1)}$, $E_{H^{(j+1)}} := E_H^{(j)} \backslash E_{M_H^{(j)}}$;

3: remove all edges adjacent to an edge in $M_H^{(j)}$ from $H^{(j+1)}$,

  $E_{H^{(j+1)}} := E_{H^{(j+1)}} \backslash \{e \mid e \text{ adjacent to } M_H^{(j)}\}$;

4: **return** $H^{(j+1)}$

4.3   Analysis

In this subsection we analyze the behavior of the Graph-Matching Algorithm given above. As in Sect. 3 we first study the quality of the computed matching, then the time and message complexity. If not stated otherwise, $G = (V, E)$ denotes the graph on which the matching is to be computed, with $|V| = n$. $G^{(i)} \in G$ is the graph in phase Φ_i containing all edges not yet adjacent to or in the matching M_G. $H_i^{(1)}$ is the graph of all valid candidates of $G^{(i)}$. Let $w_{\max}(G)$ be abbreviated $w_{\max}$.

We first present several lemmas which simplify the proof of the constant approximation ratio.

Lemma 10. *For each vertex u and each phase Φ_i it holds that after $O(\log n)$ rounds the condition in line 7 of Procedure Graph-Matching is false with high probability. That is, after $O(\log n)$ rounds all vertices in $H_i^{(1)}$ are incident to or in the matching and hence a maximal matching in $H_i^{(1)}$ was found with high probability.*

Proof. In the Select Procedure a vertex u chooses uniformly at random one incident edge. If u itself has at least one imposed edge after the Select Procedure, it has positive degree after the Eliminate Procedure and is further incident to the matching computed in the Matching Procedure with probability at least $\frac{1}{2}$. (This is apparent, since with probability $1/4$ an edge is in the matching itself and if it is not, with probability at least $1/4$ one of its incident edges is in the matching.) According to the terminology given in [II86] we call a vertex *good* if more than $1/3$ of its neighbors do not have a larger degree than itself. An edge e is *good* if at least one incident vertex is good. Then at least half of the edges are good[5]. Suppose, u is a good vertex and let $v_1, \ldots, v_d$ be u's neighbors. A neighbor v_j has degree d_j. The probability that u has at least one imposed edge after the Select Procedure can be computed using the following standard trick:

---

[5] For a proof see e.g. [KVY94].

$$\Pr(u \text{ has no imposed edge}) = \prod_{i=1}^{d}\left(1 - \frac{1}{d_i}\right)$$

$$\leq \left(1 - \frac{1}{d}\right)^{d/3}$$

$$\leq e^{-1/3} \quad \text{(Fact 1)}.$$

where the second equation follows since at least $d/3$ neighbors have smaller or equal degree. All together we may conclude that the probability that a good edge is removed in the Cleanup Procedure is constant. Since at least half of the edges of any graph are good, after logarithmic many rounds *all* edges are removed and a maximal matching is found with high probability[6]. □

Observation 11. *All edges $e \in E$ with weight $w(e) \geq \frac{1}{2} \cdot w_{\max}$ are valid candidates in phase Φ_1, that is e is an edge in $H_1^{(1)}$.*

Proof. For contradiction assume that $w(e) \geq \frac{1}{2} \cdot w_{\max}$ and $e = \{u, v\}$ is not an edge in $H_i^{(1)}$ of phase Φ_1. Then e was not a candidate for at least one incident vertex. W.l.o.g. let this vertex be u. Then $w_{\max}(u)_E > 2 \cdot w(e) \geq w_{\max}$, which is a contradiction. □

Corollary 12. *In phase Φ_1 and after $O(\log n)$ rounds all edges e with weight $w(e) \geq \frac{1}{2} \cdot w_{\max}$ are either adjacent to or in the matching M_G with high probability.*

Proof. The corollary follows immediately from Lemma 10 and Observation 11. □

Definition 13. *We say that an edge $e \in E$ is* heavy *if $w(e) \geq w_{\max}/n$, else it is* light.

Lemma 14. *After $\log n$ phases all heavy edges are either adjacent to or in the matching M_G with high probability.*

Proof. By Observation 11 all edges e with weight $w(e) \geq \frac{1}{2} \cdot w_{\max}$ are valid candidates in phase Φ_1 and therefore in $H_1^{(1)}$. After a maximal matching on $H_1^{(1)}$ was computed the vertices enter the next phase Φ_2. In $G^{(2)}$ the heaviest edge has weight less than $1/2 \cdot w_{\max}$ and following the argument of Corollary 12 all edges e with weight $w(e) \geq 1/4 \cdot w_{\max}$ are adjacent to or in the matching M_G with high probability after another $O(\log n)$ rounds. We repeat this argument $\log n$ times. In the graph $G^{(\log n+1)}$ the heaviest edge has weight less than $w_{\max}/2^{\log n} = w_{\max}/n$ with high probability and all heavier edges are either adjacent to or in the matching M_G. □

Observation 15. *We can partition the edge-set of a graph G in the following way:*

$$E = \dot{\bigcup_i} E_i, where$$

$$E_i = \{e \mid e \in E, \frac{w_{\max}}{2^{i+1}} < w(e) \leq \frac{w_{\max}}{2^i}\}.$$

---

[6] A standard probabilistic argument can be applied to derive constant fraction and high probability from constant fraction and constant probability.

Observation 16. *Let E' be the union of all heavy edges, $E' = \bigcup_{i=0}^{\log n} E_i$. The weight of a matching M_G^* can be decomposed by*

$$w(M_G^*) = w(M_G^* \cap E') + \sum_{i > \log n} w(M_G^* \cap E_i).$$

Lemma 17. *The sum of weights of all light edges in M_G^* is less than half of the weight of the heaviest edge:*

$$\sum_{i > \log n} w(M_G^* \cap E_i) < 1/2 \cdot w_{\max}.$$

Proof. Edges in E_i, $i > \log n$, have weight less than $w_{\max}/n$. Together with Fact 3 we have

$$\sum_{i > \log n} w(M_G^* \cap E_i) < |M_G^*| \cdot w_{\max}/n$$
$$\leq 1/2 \cdot |V| \cdot w_{\max}/n = 1/2 \cdot w_{\max}.$$

$\square$

Lemma 18. *The sum of weights of all heavy edges in M_G^* is at most four times the weight of the matching computed by the Graph-Matching Algorithm, formally:*

$$w(M_G^* \cap E') \leq 4 \cdot w(M_G).$$

Proof. We will define a mapping $f : (M_G^* \cap E') \rightarrow M_G$ with the property that if $f : e \mapsto e'$ then $w(e) \leq 2 \cdot w(e')$. Furthermore, at most two elements of $(M_G^* \cap E')$ are mapped to the same element of M_G. Obviously, if f is well-defined, the lemma follows.

Let $e \in E$ be a heavy edge in M_G^*, that is $e \in (M_G^* \cap E')$. If $e \in M_G$ then $f : e \mapsto e$. Else, by Lemma 14 there must be an edge $e' \in M_G$, $e' \notin M_G^*$. This edge has weight at least $w(e') \geq 1/2 \cdot w(e)$, otherwise it would not have been a valid candidate and hence not in the matching. We let $f : e \mapsto e'$. Since each edge in M_G is adjacent to at most two edges in M_G^*, at most two elements of $(M_G^* \cap E')$ are mapped to the same element of M_G and f is well-defined. $\square$

Lemma 19. *The weight of the matching M_G is at least half of the weight of the heaviest edge in G:*

$$w(M_G) \geq 1/2 \cdot w_{\max}.$$

Proof. Let $e = \{u, v\} \in E$ be an edge with maximal weight, $w(e) = w_{\max}$. According to Observation 11, edge e is a valid candidate in phase Φ_1. All other valid candidates of phase Φ_1 incident to u and v must have weight at least $1/2 \cdot w_{\max}$. By Lemma 10 we have found a maximal matching on the valid candidates of phase Φ_1 after $O(\log n)$ rounds. Therefore, either e or an adjacent edge to e must be in the matching M_G after phase Φ_1. $\square$

Theorem 20. *After $O(\log^2 n)$ time we have, $w(M_G) > 1/5 \cdot w(M_G^*)$ with high probability.*

Proof.

$$w(M_G^*) = w(M_G^* \cap E') + \sum_{i > \log n} w(M_G^* \cap E_i) \qquad \text{(Observation 16)}$$

$$< w(M_G^* \cap E') + \frac{1}{2} \cdot w_{\max} \qquad \text{(Lemma 17)}$$

$$\leq 4 \cdot w(M_G) + \frac{1}{2} \cdot w_{\max} \qquad \text{(Lemma 18)}$$

$$\leq 5 \cdot w(M_G) \qquad \text{(Lemma 19)}.$$

$\square$

We conclude this section with the analysis of the time and message complexity.

Theorem 21. *The Graph-Matching Algorithm of Sect. 4.2 has time complexity $O(\log^2 n)$ and message complexity $O(n^2 \log^2 n)$.*

Proof. It follows immediately from the description of the algorithm that each of the Procedures Valid, Uniform-Matching, Select, Eliminate, Matching and Cleanup needs a constant number of time steps and a constant number of messages per edge with constant bit size. By Lemma 10 the while-loop of the Graph-Matching Algorithm is executed $O(\log n)$ times and therefore the claimed time and message complexity can be derived. $\square$

Corollary 22. *For any graph G we have that if the vertices synchronously execute the Graph-Matching Algorithm of Sect. 4.2 they find with high probability a matching in G with approximation ratio 5 and polylogarithmic message complexity per edge in polylogarithmic time.*

5   Conclusions

In this paper we presented two distributed constant-approximation algorithms for weighted matching, one for trees which runs in constant time, and one for general graphs which runs in time $O(\log^2 n)$, where n denotes the number of nodes in the graph. Recently, Kuhn et al. [KMW04] showed that in general (non-weighted) graphs matching cannot be approximated constantly without spending at least $\Omega(\log \Delta / \log \log \Delta + \sqrt{\log n / \log \log n})$ communication rounds, where Δ denotes the maximum degree in the graph. This result bounds the running time of our algorithm from below. Furthermore, in light of our result for trees, an interesting area of future research is to investigate which classes of graphs allow constant distributed approximations in constant time, and for which classes of graphs constant-time algorithms experience the lower bound of [KMW04].

We believe that a deeper general knowledge of local algorithms leads to a better understanding of a variety of problems in distributed computing and/or networking. Many *en vogue* research areas, such as ad-hoc and sensor networks, or peer-to-peer computing, essentially boil down to local algorithms, since local algorithms produce solutions with a low communication overhead, or work well in a highly dynamic environment. We believe that classic graph problems will be beneficial when building such systems. For matching in particular, we envision applications in the distributed match-making process of massive multiplayer online games. How our algorithms can be turned into practical match-making solutions, where the problems of self-stabilization and fault-tolerance also need to be addressed, is one of the goals of our future research.

References

[CHS02]   S. Chattopadhyay, L. Higham, and K. Seyffarth. Dynamic and self-stabilizing distributed matching. In *Proceedings of the Annual ACM Symposium on Principles of Distributed Computing (PODC)*, pages 290–297. ACM Press, 2002.

[CV86]   R. Cole and U. Vishkin. Deterministic coin tossing with applications to optimal parallel list ranking. *Information and Control*, 70(1):32–53, 1986.

[Edm65]   J. Edmonds. Paths, trees and flowers. *Canadian Journal of Mathematics*, 17:449–467, 1965.

[HKP01]   M. Hanckowiak, M. Karonski, and A. Panconesi. On the distributed complexity of computing maximal matchings. *SIAM Journal on Discrete Mathematics*, 15(1):41–57, 2001.

[II86]   A. Israeli and A. Itai. A fast and simple randomized parallel algorithm for maximal matching. *Information Processing Letters*, 22:77–80, 1986.

[JRS01]   L. Jia, R. Rajaraman, and T. Suel. An efficient distributed algorithm for constructing small dominating sets. *Proceedings of the Annual ACM Symposium on Principles of Distributed Computing (PODC)*, pages 33–42, 2001.

[KMW04]   F. Kuhn, T. Moscibroda, and R. Wattenhofer. Lower and upper bounds for distributed packing and covering. Technical report, ETH Zurich, Dept. of Computer Science, 2004.

[KS00]   M. Karaata and K. Saleh. A distributed self-stabilizing algorithm for finding maximal matching. *Computer Systems Science and Engineering*, 3:175–180, 2000.

[KVY94]   S. Khuller, U. Vishkin, and N. Young. A primal-dual parallel approximation technique applied to weighted set and vertex covers. *Journal of Algorithms*, 17(2):280–289, 1994.

[KW03]   F. Kuhn and R. Wattenhofer. Constant-time distributed dominating set approximation. *Proceedings of the Annual ACM Symposium on Principles of Distributed Computing (PODC)*, 2003.

[Lin92]   N. Linial. Locality in distributed graph algorithms. *SIAM Journal on Computing*, 21:193–201, 1992.

[Lub86]   M. Luby. A simple parallel algorithm for the maximal independent set problem. *SIAM Journal on Computing*, 15:1036–1053, 1986.

[Pel00]   D. Peleg. *Distributed Computing, A Locality-Sensitive Approach*. SIAM, 2000.

[UC00]   R. Uehara and Z. Chen. Parallel approximation algorithms for maximum weighted matching in general graphs. *Information Processing Letters*, 76:13–17, 2000.

Exploiting Content Localities for Efficient Search in P2P Systems⋆

Lei Guo[1], Song Jiang[2], Li Xiao[3], and Xiaodong Zhang[1]

[1] College of William and Mary, Williamsburg, VA 23187, USA
{lguo,zhang}@cs.wm.edu
[2] Los Alamos National Laboratory, NM, 87545, USA
sjiang@lanl.gov
[3] Michigan State University, East Lansing, MI 48824, USA
lxiao@cse.msu.edu

Abstract. Existing P2P search algorithms generally target either the performance objective of improving search quality from a client's perspective, or the objective of reducing search cost from an Internet management perspective. We believe that the essential issue to be considered for designing and optimizing search algorithms in unstructured P2P networks is the trade-off between the two performance objectives. Motivated by our observations, the locality of content serving in the peer community and the localities of search interests of individual peers, we propose *CAC-SPIRP*, a fast and low cost P2P searching algorithm. Our algorithm consists of two components. The first component aims to reduce the search cost by constructing a *CAC* (**C**ontent **A**bundant **C**luster), where content-abundant peers self-identify, and self-organize themselves into an inter-connected cluster providing a pool of popular objects to be frequently accessed by the peer community. A query will be first routed to the CAC, and most likely to be satisfied there, significantly reducing the amount of network traffic and the search scope. The second component in our algorithm is client oriented and aims to improve the quality of P2P search, called *SPIRP* (Selectively Prefetching Indices from Responding Peers). A client individually identifies a small group of peers who have the same interests as itself to prefetch their entire file indices of the related interests, minimizing unnecessary outgoing queries and significantly reducing query response time. Building SPIRP on the CAC Internet infrastructure, our algorithm combines both merits of the two components and balances the trade-off between the two performance objectives. Our trace-driven simulations show that CAC-SPIRP significantly improves the overall performance from both client's perspective and Internet management perspective.

1 Introduction

The effectiveness of content search in unstructured P2P networks such as Gnutella [6] and Kazaa [8] can be measured by two performance objectives that

---

⋆ This work is supported in part by the U.S. National Science Foundation under grants CNS-0098055 and CCF-0129883.

R. Guerraoui (Ed.): DISC 2004, LNCS 3274, pp. 349–364, 2004.

may have conflicting interests. The first objective coming from each *individual peer*'s perspective is to improve its *search quality*, i.e., to increase the number of effective results and to minimize the response time of each query. The second objective coming from the Internet management perspective is to reduce the total *search cost* of the *peer community* (all peers in the system), i.e., to minimize the network bandwidth consumptions and other related overheads, such as CPU and storage demands. Existing search algorithms generally aim at one of the objectives and have performance limits on the other. For example, flooding search targets to maximize the number of search results for each peer but results in too much traffic in the system, while random walking [11] target to reduce the search traffic for the system but can lead to long response time for individual peers.

We believe that the essential issue of designing and optimizing search algorithms in unstructured P2P networks is the trade-off between the two performance objectives. In this paper, we analyze the content serving regularities in the peer community and the search patterns of individual peers, and show there exist two kinds of localities in P2P content search. (1) The *locality of content serving* in the peer community: most search results are served by a small number of content-abundant peers. (2) The *localities of search interests* of individual peers: peers generally target contents on a few topics of interests, and can get most requested objects from a small number of peers with the same interests as themselves. Motivated by these two observations and the trade-off between the two performance objectives, we propose *CAC-SPIRP*, a fast and low cost P2P searching algorithm.

CAC-SPIRP algorithm comprises two complementary techniques, *CAC* and *SPIRP*. CAC technique aims to reduce the search cost by exploiting the content serving locality among the peer community. In this technique, a small number of content-abundant peers are self-identified based on their query-answering histories, and self-organized into a cluster called *CAC* (**C**ontent **A**bundant **C**luster), which serves as a pool of popular objects to be frequently requested. SPIRP technique is client oriented. By **S**electively **P**refetching **I**ndices from **R**esponding **P**eers, the search interest localities of individual peers can be well exploited to speedup query processing. By combining both techniques, CAC-SPIRP algorithm is highly effective in addressing the trade-off between the two performance objectives, and does not produce additional overheads in P2P networks, where the content-abundant cluster is constructed, and the SPIRP technique is facilitated in each peer, retaining the merits of both CAC and SPIRP.

Current unstructured P2P systems have been evolved from a Gnutella-like structure to a super-node [10] based system where high bandwidth peers serve as super-nodes to maintain the indices of their leaf nodes, such as Morpheus [12] and Kazaa [8]. Although the super-node structure has effectively reduced the overall network bandwidth usage of P2P search, it does not consider the trade-off between *search quality* and *search cost*. We have the following three reasons why our CAC-SPRIP solution effectively addresses the three major limits of super-node based systems.

1. *Index based super-nodes limit search ability to certain applications.* Since the index service is file name based, the search scope can be seriously limited in comparison with a full-text content-based search. Another example of the super-node limit is related to the content search for encrypted files. When a peer searches the content of an encrypted file (or a media file with a private decoder, such as DVD video), a secrete key (or a specific codec) in the query is required, however, an index server will not be able to support this kind of search. In contrast, our CAC-SPIRP is content-based, where the content abundant cluster directly provides search service to peers, thus can support a generic search in P2P systems.
2. *A super-node server is not responsible for the content quality of its leaf nodes.* Thus, a super-node service does not guarantee the search quality. In contrast, our content abundant cluster with a prefetching support aims at providing high quality search results to peers.
3. *Super-node structure is becoming inefficient.* In order to address the potential single-point-failure problem, in existing super-node based P2P systems, a peer has to connect to multiple super-nodes, which creates an increasingly large number of super-nodes on the Internet, significantly adding the maintenance costs of super-nodes. In contrast, our content abundant cluster is highly resilient by hosting a large number of powerful peers, where the single point of failure problem does not exist.

The remainder of the paper is organized as follows. Section 2 discusses some existing P2P searching algorithms. Section 3 presents our measurement observations. Sections 4 and 5 present the two searching techniques we proposed, CAC and SPIRP, respectively. Section 6 describes the CAC-SPIRP algorithm. Section 7 evaluates the two techniques and our proposed algorithm. We summarize our work in Section 8.

2   Related Work

Other solutions have been proposed for efficient search in unstructured P2P systems. *Directed BFS* [15] attempts to take advantage of the irregular content distribution by using very limited local information of the search history instead of fully exploiting the skewness of content distributions like CAC. *Random walk* search such as [11] and [3] can reduce search traffic effectively but can only give a small number of results and have long response time. *LightFlood* [7] aims to reduce the redundant messages of broadcast operations in P2P systems. *Interest-based locality* approach [14] shares the similar principle of SPIRP by exploiting the common interests among different peers. However, in this approach, a requesting peer connects to a small number of peers with same interests directly, limiting the locality of interests that can be exploited. Further more, the time for building interest groups is non-trivial, and these interest groups are not useful when the peer offline and online again, due to the transient nature of P2P networks. In contrast, our CAC scheme provides a persistent public service for all peers in the system.

3   Characterizing the Localities in the Peer Community and Individual Peers

Existing measurement studies such as [1] and [13] investigated the file distributions in P2P systems and show a small percentage of peers share much more number of files than other peers in P2P systems. Study [4] investigated the locality of files stored and transferred in P2P systems and found that a small percentage of popular files account for most shared storage and transmissions in P2P systems. However, a peer with many files does not necessarily mean that it can provide corresponding content service: some of files may be never accessed, or accessed rarely. In this section, we present our experimental observations on the P2P search patterns and content distributions, and characterize the content serving locality in the peer community and the search interest localities of individual peers.

3.1   Data Preparation

We built Gnutella crawlers based on the open source code of LimeWire Gnutella [9] and conducted a 4-day crawling to collect traces. We monitored the query sending of 25,764 different peers during their life time, and collected 409,129 queries. We randomly selected 1,600 peers and their corresponding queries (total 25,093) as the *P2P client set* for our study. We also collected the entire indices of 18,255 different peers and estimated that there are 37% free-riders in Gnutella networks. We used all index traces as well as the corresponding free-riders as the *P2P server set* (total 29,050 different peers) for our study. Finally, we matched all queries sent by peers in the P2P client set with all indices of peers in the P2P server set to complete the data preparation.

3.2   The Locality of Content Serving in the Peer Community

In our study, we ranked all peers in the P2P server set by the total number of queries they can reply and by the total number of results they can provide respectively, since a peer can reply a query with multiple results. Figure 1(a) shows the distribution of the number of queries that peers can respond. We can see a significant heterogeneity of the ability to reply queries among Gnutella peers: there are only about 6% peers that can reply more than 1,000 queries (4% of all queries) each, while there are more than 50% peers that can only reply less than 100 queries (0.4% of all queries) each. Figure 1(b) shows the distribution of the number of results that peers can provide. We can see that similar heterogeneity exists in this case as well: there are only about 10% peers that can provide more than 2,500 results (0.1 results per query on average) each, while there are more than 60% of peers that can only provide less than 500 results (0.02 results per query on average) each. We call those peers who can reply significantly more queries than other peers as *top query responders*, and call those peers who can provide significantly more results than other peers

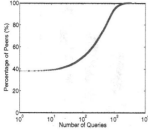

(a) The CDF of queries that peers can reply.

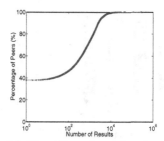

(b) The CDF of results that peers can provide.

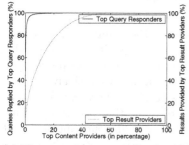

(c) The cumulative contributions of top content providers.

Fig. 1. The skewness of Gnutella peers' abilities to reply queries and to provide results.

as *top result providers*. We observed in most cases that a top query responder of the peer community is also a top result provider of the peer community, and vice versa. For example, 84% of peers in the top 10% query responder set are in the top 10% result provider set as well. Therefore, we call both of them as *top content providers*.

Next we study the cumulative contribution of these top content providers. We computed the union set of queries replied by top query responders and the cumulative number of results provided by top result providers, shown in Figure 1(c). We can see that the top 5% query responders can reply more than 98% of all queries altogether while the top 10% result providers can provide about 55% of all results in the system altogether.

The experiments above show strong *locality of content serving* in the peer community: a small percentage of peers (top content providers) account for most content contributions in the system.

3.3   The Localities of Search Interests of Individual Peers

The access patterns of individual peers differ from that of the peer community as a whole. In the following experiments, we try to get insight of the search behaviors of individual peers. We only consider queries that have been replied by other peers, and simply call them *replied queries*. We selected peers having at least 10 replied queries in the P2P client set as *requesting peers*. For a requesting peer, we

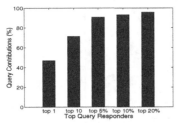
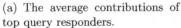
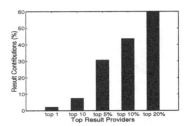

(a) The average contributions of   (b) The average contributions of
top query responders.   top result providers.

Fig. 2. The average contributions (in percentage) of top query responders and top result providers for peers having at least 10 replied queries.

define the *query contribution* of its each responder as the number of queries the responder has replied, and define the *result contribution* of its each responder as the number of results it has provided. We ranked each peer's responders by their query contributions and by their result contributions respectively.

Figure 2 shows the average query contributions of requesting peers' top query responders and the average result contributions of requesting peers' top result responders. The contributions are normalized by the overall contributions of all responders of the corresponding requesting peers. In Figure 2(a), the 5 bars represent the average contributions of the top 1, top 10, top 5%, top 10%, and top 20% query responders of requesting peers, respectively. The top 1 query responder of a requesting peer is a single peer who responds the highest number of queries. This responder can respond 47% of all replied queries on average. The top 5% query responders together can respond about 91% of all replied queries. Figure 2(b) shows that the top 10% result responders of the requesting peers account for about 31% of all results they receive on average, and that the top 20% result responders account for about 60% of all results on average. Figure 2(a) and 2(b) also show the top 10 query responders of requesting peers can reply 71% of all replied queries on average, and the top 10 result responders of requesting peers can provide about 7.5% of all results on average. Further studies show that the top content providers of individual requesting peers are their top query responders, because a peer answering a query with many results is not necessarily able to answer other queries. Our studies also show that the top query/result providers of an individual peer are not necessarily the top content providers of the peer community, because the former depends on the search interests of the requesting peer, while the latter depends on the group behaviors of the whole community.

The experiments above show a small number of top query responders of individual requesting peers account for most content contributions of these peers. This fact indicates that the requesting peers and their top query responders have the same interests in content searching and content sharing respectively. From the aspect of clients, there exist strong *localities of search interests* for individual peers: a peer's requests generally focus on a few interest topics, and it can be satisfied by a small number of peers with the same interests.

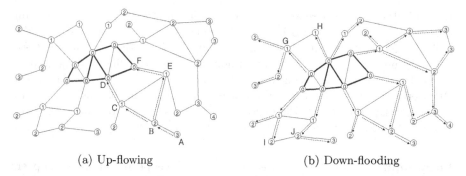

(a) Up-flowing   (b) Down-flooding

Fig. 3. The up-flowing and down-flooding operations. Each circle denotes a peer in the P2P network, and the number in the circle is the level of this peer. The bold lines denote the CAC links and the thin lines denote the original P2P links. (a) shows the routing paths of a query sent by peer A at level 3. The query is routed along the dash lines, passing through B, C, D and B, E, F until reaching the CAC. A query may have multiple paths to reach the CAC, improving the robustness of query routing. (b) shows the routing paths of down-flooding. The query is concurrently routed from all CAC peers to level 1 peers, then level 2 peers, until reaching peers with the maximal level. Only links from lower level peers to higher level peers are used to route messages; links such as GH and IJ are not used for query routing.

4   Constructing Content-Abundant Cluster (CAC)

The basic idea of CAC technique is to have a number of content-abundant peers in the peer community self-organized into a *content-abundant cluster* (CAC) to actively serve contents for the entire system. By being directed into the cluster for an efficient search first, most queries can be satisfactorily answered without meaninglessly bothering those content-scarce peers. Because these content-scarce peers account for a significant portion of the peer community, a large amount of network traffic and computational cost can be saved. For a small number of queries that can not be satisfied in the cluster, we relay them out of the cluster in an efficient fashion. The key components of the CAC technique are presented as follows.

System Structure. The content-abundant peers are those top content providers of the peer community. In CAC technique, we allow peers self-evaluate the quality of content service they can provide based on the history of their query-answering. The criterion of *content service quality* is the percentage of queries a peer can reply. Peers whose content service qualities reach a threshold are CAC member candidates and have the same possibility to join the CAC. Both the quality threshold for CAC members and the CAC size can be predefined or updated periodically by some mechanism to adapt to the dynamics in P2P systems. Our simulations show that CAC has no strict requirements on these two parameters (see Section 7.3).

CAC technique is modular and can be easily deployed on top of any P2P overlays. The content-abundant cluster is a connected overlay independent of the original P2P overlay. There are two types of links in P2P systems implementing CAC technique: one is the original P2P overlay links, the other is the CAC overlay links. Each peer in the system is assigned a *level*: the level of each CAC peer is defined as 0, and the level of an non-CAC peer is defined as the number of hops from this peer to the nearest CAC peer. When the CAC overlay or the P2P overlay changes, the level values of relevant peers can be updated one by one quickly. By using levels, the unstructured P2P system is organized logically for efficient and robust query routing without changing the original P2P overlay.

Query Routing. A query is routed from higher level peers to lower level peers until reaching the CAC, shown in Figure 3(a). We call this operation *up-flowing*. As soon as a query enters the CAC, it is flooded in the CAC to search contents.

The responses of a query are routed back to the requester along the same path that it comes. The requester waits a period of time for the arrival of responses from the CAC, called the *response waiting time*. If the requester does not get enough number of results during the waiting time, the query will be routed in the entire system for a global search as follows. First, the query is up-flowed to and then flooded in the CAC again. Upon receiving the query, each CAC peer propagates it to level 1 peers immediately. Then the query is propagated from lower level peers to higher level peers in the P2P overlay. We call this operation *down-flooding*, shown in Figure 3(b). Down-flooding is much more efficient than simply flooding the query in the P2P overlay because only links between two successive levels of peers are used for propagating queries, reducing a great amount of unnecessary traffic.

Different from having each non-CAC peer directly connect to a CAC peer like super-node approach, CAC technique is more robust in query routing, because the failures of individual CAC peers have little effects on those non-CAC peers.

System Maintenance. The content-abundant cluster is maintained in a proper size. Each CAC peer holds the value of the CAC size locally and updates the value periodically by broadcasting ping messages and receiving corresponding pong messages in the CAC.

Each self-identified content-abundant peer, p, tries to join the CAC by up-flowing *join* requests periodically until success. Upon receiving a join request message, a CAC peer, P, accepts or denies the request based on the CAC size value it holds. If P believes the CAC needs more members, it accepts the request and sends a list of randomly chosen CAC members back to p. Then p randomly selects several of them as its neighbors to join the CAC. These CAC members can still reject the connection request based on their local values of the CAC size, preventing malicious attacks such as adding members to the CAC repeatedly.

CAC peers who can not provide qualified services for some period of time and overloaded peers leave the CAC to become a normal peer. Before leaving the CAC, a peer broadcasts a *leave* message to let other CAC peers update the CAC size values they hold. Even if a CAC peer disconnects abnormally, other CAC peers can still update the size values when broadcasting the next ping.

5   Selectively Prefetching Indices from Responding Peers

SPIRP technique is client oriented and motivated by the search interest localities of individual peers. Although the contents in a typical P2P network are huge and highly diverse, each peer's interests are limited and generally focused on a few topics. Queries from a requesting peer can be frequently answered by a small number of serving peers, as Section 3.3 shows. In SPIRP, after receiving answers to its initial queries, a client selectively identifies a small group of responders who have the same interests as itself, and asks them to send their entire file indices of the related interests to this client. With SPIRP, the number of outgoing queries is minimized in the client side by exploiting the common interests between the requesting peer and its responders, reducing both the response time and bandwidth consumptions. In addition, since each requesting peer only prefetches and maintains the file indices of a limited number of peers, the index transmission overheads and the storage requirement are small.

5.1   Data Structure

The basic data structure of SPIRP in each peer consists of several key components. Each peer maintains a set of indices of files to be shared in the P2P network, called the *outgoing index set*. It also maintains a set of indices selectively prefetched from its responders, called the *incoming index set*. In addition, each peer maintains a set of responders who have replied to it, called the *responder set*. This set is organized as a hash table in which the key is the responder's GUID (Globally Unique Identifier) and the value is the responder's meta data. The major fields of a responder's meta data are shown in Table 1. The responder set is also ranked as a *priority queue*, where the *priority* is defined as the number of queries a responder has responded so far.

Table 1. The data structure of responder's meta data.

Field	IP addr.	port	is cached	priority	index size	timestamp	expire time	update time
Bytes	4	2	2	4	4	4	4	4

A peer does not keep any information for other peers prefetching its indices. To help these peers refresh the indices they prefetched, each responding peer averages its previous on-line session durations as the estimated duration of its current session, and averages its previous update intervals as the estimated update interval. When indices in a responding peer are prefetched, the estimated expire time, update time, and current timestamp of the peer are piggybacked to the requesting peer.

5.2   SPIRP Operations

With the support of the above data structure, several key SPIRP operations are defined as follows.

Sending Queries. Initially the incoming index set and the responder set are both empty. As a requesting peer sends a query, it searches the incoming index set first. If any indices match the query, the requesting peer checks if the corresponding responders are still alive (see the *Checking Index Expiration* operation) and then returns the available matched results to the user. If the query cannot be satisfied locally, the peer sends the query to the P2P network in a normal way (e.g., flooding search), and then returns the corresponding results to the user. Then the peer updates the responder set and the priority queue.

Prefetching and Replacing Indices. The requesting peer asks those high priority responders, which are not in the incoming index set currently, to send their related indices until the incoming index set is full. When the priority queue changes, a simple replacement policy is used. The peer removes the indices of low priority responders from the incoming index set and prefetches the indices of high priority responders that are not in the incoming index set currently.

Checking Index Expiration. When the estimated expiration time of a responder reaches, or a query hits its incoming index set, the peer checks if the responder is still alive. If not, the peer deletes its indices from the incoming index set and its meta data from the responder set, then updates the priority queue.

Checking Index Update. When the estimated update time of a responder reaches, the peer sends the responder the timestamp of the prefetched indices to check if update happens. If yes, the responder sends the difference set of the indices or simply resends the whole index set.

6 CAC-SPIRP: Combining CAC and SPIRP Techniques

The CAC technique has its strong merits on reducing both bandwidth consumption and client response time when the requests success in the CAC, while the SPIRP technique shares the same advantage when the search interests is well exploited by the selective prefetching. However, each technique has its limits. Although the percentage of requests that fail in the CAC is small, the miss penalty can be non-trivial, negatively affecting the average latency. On the other hand, the flooding operations of outgoing queries in SPIRP produce a great amount of traffic. The motivation of CAC-SPIRP algorithm is to combine the merits of these two complementary techniques and tune the trade-off between the two performance objectives to improve the overall performance of P2P search.

SPIRP is client-oriented and overlay independent. On the other hand, CAC is an application-level infrastructure for unstructured P2P systems. Applying SPIRP technique on the CAC infrastructure, we have the CAC-SPIRP algorithm. The algorithm is simply to combine both CAC and SPIRP: the peers use SPIRP to prefetch file indices, and use CAC to route outgoing queries.

7 Experiments and Performance Evaluation

7.1 Simulation Methodology

In P2P systems, peers join and leave P2P network from time to time. A measurement study in Gnutella and Napster presented in [13] shows that the session duration of peers follows heavy tail distribution, where the duration median is about 60 minutes. This study is consistent with our observations about the connection durations between the query collection crawler and Gnutella peers in Section 3.1. Study [2] further shows the lifespan of peers follows the Pareto distribution. Different from the simulations of existing studies such as [14], we considered the population dynamics in our evaluation, since the performance of SPIRP can be affected by the lifespan of responders. We assigned each peer in the P2P server set a random value of session duration following the Pareto distribution $P(x) = 14.5311 * x^{-1.8598}$ based on the statistics in [13] and our trace. We use the topology traces provided by Clip2 Distributed Search Solutions [5] and University of Chicago in our simulations. Due to page limit, we only present the simulation on a Gnutella snapshot of 6,946 nodes. Experiments on other topologies have similar results.

7.2 Performance Metrics

In P2P systems, the satisfaction of a content search depends on the number of results the user needs (10-50 results are in the normal range covering both low and high ends). In our simulations, we choose 1, 10, and 50 as the criteria of *query satisfaction* to show the search performances under different user requirements.

The metrics we used for content search in P2P systems are the *overall network traffic* in the system, the *average response time per query*, and the *query success rate*. The overall network traffic is a major concern of system designers and administrators, while the average response time and query success rate are major concerns of end users.

The overall traffic in our simulation comes from the accumulated communications of all queries, responses, and indices transferred in the network. Instead of modeling the actual network latency, we use the number of hops to measure the response time. The response time of a single result is measured by the number of a round trip hops from the requester to the responder, plus the response waiting time for CAC technique when the responder is not in CAC. For SPIRP technique, the response time of a result found in local index set is zero. The response time of a successful query is defined as the average response time of the first N results the requester receives, where N is the query satisfaction.

Both the flooding search and our CAC/SPIRP techniques can cover almost all peers in the system if necessary. What we are really concerned is not the absolute success rate of queries, but the *cluster relative success rate* for CAC technique, which is defined as the number of queries that can be satisfied in the cluster over the number of queries that can be satisfied by flooding search, and the *local relative success rate* for SPIRP technique, which is defined as the number of queries that can be satisfied in the incoming index set over the number of queries that can be satisfied by flooding search, respectively.

7.3 Performance Evaluation

In this section, we first evaluate the effectiveness of CAC infrastructure, and then present the performance of CAC-SPIRP algorithm. We do not present the

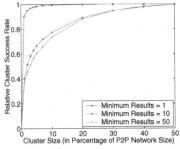

(a) The cluster relative success rate.

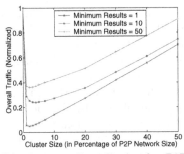

(b) The overall traffic in the P2P network.

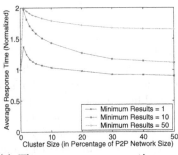

(c) The average response time per query.

Fig. 4. The performance of CAC technique under different query satisfactions and different sizes of clusters in which the cluster peers are those top query responders. The overall traffic and average response time are both normalized by the corresponding values of flooding search.

performance of SPIRP algorithm separately due to page limits. We chose the 1,600 peers in the P2P client set as requesting peers, and randomly placed these requesting peers on the simulated P2P network. Each requesting peer sends queries according to the corresponding timestamps in the query records.

Performance Evaluation of CAC Technique. The effectiveness of CAC technique depends on both the cluster size and the capacities of cluster peers. Our first experiment evaluated the performance of CAC with different sizes of clusters to find a good cluster size. We chose the "best" content-abundant peers, those top N query responders, where N is the cluster size, as the cluster peers. We set the response waiting time as 12 hops. Changing the size of cluster, we have measured the cluster relative success rate, the overall network traffic, and the average response time per query for different query satisfactions.

Figure 4(a) shows the cluster relative success rates in clusters of different sizes for different query satisfactions. The cluster relative success rate increases with the increase of the cluster size, and decreases as the query satisfaction value increases. However, the curves of cluster relative success rates under 10 and 50 query satisfactions are quite close, indicating a high quality of content service of CAC. The cluster relative success rates are more than 55% for the cluster consisting of top 5% content providers, and more than 70% for the cluster consisting of top 10% content providers.

Although a large cluster helps to increase the cluster success rate, it increases the intra-cluster traffic as well. Figure 4(b) shows the overall traffic of CAC technique. We can see the cluster of top 5% content providers is effective enough in traffic reduction for all query satisfactions from 1 to 50. For example, compared with flooding search, CAC technique under this condition can reduce more than 90% traffic for queries that need only one result, more than 75% traffic for queries that need 10 results, and more than 60% traffic for queries that need 50 results.

The response time of CAC technique is not so good. Figure 4(c) shows the response time under different cluster sizes and query satisfactions. We can see the response time is higher than that of flooding algorithm unless the cluster size is very large and the query satisfaction is very small. This is because the flooding search can always find the shortest and fastest paths in the P2P network, while in CAC technique, both flooding in the cluster and up-flowing to the cluster consume time, and the response waiting time is a big penalty for queries not satisfied in the cluster.

CAC technique randomly selects cluster peers from content-abundant peers instead of ranking them and selecting the best ones, which is not realistic in practice. Our second experiment evaluated the performances of CAC with different qualities of cluster peers in order to find a proper threshold for content-abundant peers. We set the cluster size as 5% of the community population size, measured the cluster relative success rate, overall traffic, and average response time under different thresholds for content-abundant peers. The results are presented as follows.

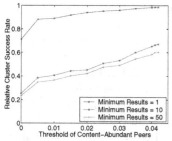

(a) The cluster relative success rate.

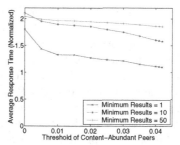

(b) The overall traffic in the P2P network.

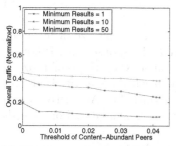

(c) The average response time per query.

Fig. 5. The performance of CAC technique under different query satisfactions and different quality thresholds of content-abundant peers. The cluster size is set to 5% of the P2P network size. The overall traffic and average response time are both normalized by the corresponding values of flooding search.

Figure 5 shows that a high quality threshold of content-abundant peers helps to improve all performance metrics. However, the overall network traffic is not sensitive to the quality threshold, and the traffic can still be significantly reduced even the quality threshold is set to 0 (meaning the cluster peers are randomly selected from the peer community) due to the high efficiency of down-flooding. In the following experiments of this paper, we chose the threshold of content-abundant peers as 0.035, corresponding to peers who can respond 3.5% of all queries it receives. Under such a threshold, the overall traffic and the average response time are only 1.10 and 1.06 times of the corresponding performances of the ideal CAC systems. Meanwhile, the number of cluster peer candidates is about 1.7 times of the cluster size, indicating moderate population dynamics can not affect the system performance seriously.

We have also compared the performance of CAC with iterative deepening [15] and expanding ring [11] algorithms. Our experiments show that the overall traffic of CAC technique is less than half of both algorithms, and the response time of CAC is lower than that of both algorithms under the same conditions. We do not present the figures due to page limit.

Performance Evaluation of CAC-SPIRP. CAC significantly reduces the overall network traffic at the expense of performance degradation in response time. SPIRP aims to reduce the response time though it can also decrease some network traffic as well. Both techniques only target one performance objective either from the perspective of system management or from the aspect of user experience. Our CAC-SPIRP algorithm considers the trade-off between these two performance objectives. Under certain conditions, the performance of CAC-SPIRP is nearly as good as that of SPIRP in terms of average response time reduction, and outperforms CAC in terms of the overall traffic reduction. The average response time, local relative success rate in the incoming index set buffer, and overall traffic of CAC-SPIRP algorithm are presented in Figure 6.

Figure 6(a) shows that CAC-SPIRP can significantly decrease the average response time of requesting peers. The response time reduction increases with the increase of the number of queries that are satisfied, because the interest localities of peers can be better exploited with an improved accuracy by gaining more experiences of content search. Figure 6(b) shows that the local relative success rate of SPIRP increases with the number of queries satisfied. For peers with more than 50 queries satisfied, the local relative success rate and the reduction of response time can be as high as about 95%.

Figure 6(a) and Figure 6(b) also show that increasing the size of incoming index set buffer helps to improve local success rate and response time. However, the local success rate and response time improve little when the buffer size is greater than 6 megabytes; and have no improvements when buffer size is greater than 10 megabytes. There are two implications for this: (1) CAC-SPIRP has a small storage requirement; (2) the locality of interests is limited and only needs a small buffer to hold.

Figure 6(c) shows that the traffic reduction of CAC-SPIRP is greater than that of CAC. The reason is that CAC can reduce network traffic by limiting the

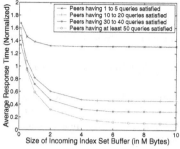

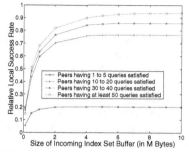

(a) The average response time per query (the query satisfaction is 50).

(b) The local relative success rate (query satisfaction is 50).

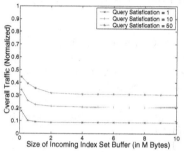

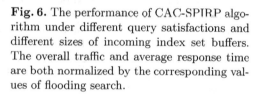

Fig. 6. The performance of CAC-SPIRP algorithm under different query satisfactions and different sizes of incoming index set buffers. The overall traffic and average response time are both normalized by the corresponding values of flooding search.

(c) The overall traffic in the P2P network.

scope of peers processing queries, and SPIRP can reduce traffic by limiting the number of outgoing queries. These two joint efforts are highly effective to reduce the overall traffic. The overall traffic reductions of CAC-SPIRP for different query satisfactions can be as high as 70% to 90%.

8 Summary

Efficient content locating in unstructured P2P networks is a challenging issue because searching algorithm designers need to consider the objectives of both improving search quality and reducing search cost, which may have conflicting interests. Existing search algorithms generally target one or the other objective. In this study, we propose CAC-SPIRP, a P2P searching algorithm aiming at both low traffic and low latency. By exploiting both the search interest localities of individual peers and the content serving locality in the peer community, our algorithm tunes the trade-off between the two objectives and achieves significant performance improvements.

Acknowledgment. We thank Beverley Yang at Stanford University, Matei Ripeanu and Adriana Iamnitchi at University of Chicago for providing their traces to us, and thank Theresa Long for proofreading this paper.

References

1. E. Adar and B.Huberman. Free Riding on Gnutella. Technical Report, Xerox PARC, August 2000.
2. F. Bustamante and Y. Qiao. Friendships that Last: Peer Lifespan and Its Role in P2P Protocols. in *Proceedings of WCW*, 2003.
3. Y. Chawathe, S. Ratnasamy, L. Breslau, N. Lanham and S. Shenker. Making Gnutella-like P2P Systems Scalable. in *Proceedings of ACM SIGCOMM*, 2003.
4. J. Chu, K. Labonte, and B. N. Levine. Availability and locality measurement of peer-to-peer file systems. In *Proceedings of SPIE*, 2002.
5. Clip2 Distributed Search Solutions, http://www.clip2.com
6. Gnutella, http://www.gnutella.com
7. S. Jiang, L. Guo, and X. Zhang. LightFlood: an Efficient Flooding Scheme for File Search in Unstructured Peer-to-Peer System. in *Proceedings of ICPP*, 2003.
8. KaZaA, http://www.kazaa.com
9. LimeWire, http://www.limewire.org
10. LimeWire LLC, Ultrapeers: Another Step Towards Gnutella Scalability. http://www.limewire.com/developer/Ultrapeers.html
11. Q. Lv, P. Cao, E. Cohen, K. Li, and S. Shenker. Search and Replication in Unstructured Peer-to-Peer Networks. In *Proceedings of ICS*, 2002.
12. Morpheus, http://www.musiccity.com
13. S. Saroiu, P. K. Gummadi, and S. D. Gribble, A Measurement Study of Peer-to-Peer File Sharing Systems. In *Proceedings of MMCN*, 2002.
14. K. Sripanidkulchai, B. Maggs, and H. Zhang. Efficient Content Location Using Interest-Based Locality in Peer-to-Peer Systems. in *Proceedings of INFOCOM*, 2003.
15. B. Yang and H. Garcia-Molina. Improving Search in Peer-to-Peer Networks. In *Proceedings of ICDCS*, 2002.

Compact Routing Schemes
for Bounded Tree-Length Graphs
and for k-Chordal Graphs

Yon Dourisboure

LaBRI, Bordeaux 1 University
yon.dourisboure@labri.fr

Abstract. In this paper we show how to use the notion of layering-tree introduced in [5], in order to construct efficient routing schemes. We obtain a routing scheme polynomial time constructible for tree-length δ graphs, i.e., graphs admitting a tree-decomposition with small diameter bags. This routing scheme uses address and local memory of size $O(\delta \log^2 n)$ bits, and for all pairs of nodes, the length of the route never exceed their distance plus $6\delta - 2$ (deviation at most $6\delta - 2$). Then we adapt our routing scheme for k-chordal graphs. In this later case, we obtain a deviation $k + 1$, with addresses and local memories of size $O(\log^2 n)$ bits per node, an improvement on the best previous to date. Observe that for chordal graphs, for which $\delta = 1$ and $k = 3$, the both schemes produce a deviation 4, with addresses and local memories of size $O(\log^2 n)$ bits per node, also an improvement on the best previous.

Keywords: tree-decomposition, tree-length, chordality, compact routing.

1 Introduction

Delivering messages between pairs of processors is a basic activity of any distributed communication network. This task is performed using a routing scheme, which is a mechanism for routing messages in the network. The routing mechanism can be invoked at any origin node and be required to deliver a message to any destination node.

It is naturally desirable to route messages along paths that are as short as possible. Routing scheme design is a well-studied subject. The efficiency of a routing scheme is measured in terms of its *multiplicative stretch* (or *additive stretch*), namely, the maximum ratio (or surplus) between the length of a route produced by the scheme for some pair of nodes, and their distance. A straightforward approach to achieving the goal of guarantees optimal routes is to store a *complete routing table* in each node u in the network, specifying for each destination v the first edge (or an identifier of that edge, indicating the output port) along some shortest path from u to v. However, this approach may be too expensive for large systems since it requires $O(n \log d)$ memory bits for a node of degree d in an n-node network. Thus, an important problem in large scale communication networks is the design of routing schemes that produce efficient routes and have relatively low *memory requirements*.

R. Guerraoui (Ed.): DISC 2004, LNCS 3274, pp. 365–378, 2004.
© Springer-Verlag Berlin Heidelberg 2004

The routing problem can be presented as requiring to assign two kinds of labels to every node of a graph. The first is the *address* of the node, whereas the second label is a data structure called the *local routing table*. The labels are assigned in such a way that at every source node u and given the address of any destination node v, one can decide the output port of an edge outgoing from u that leads to v. The decision must be taken locally at u, based solely on the two labels of u and with the address label of v. In order to allow each intermediate node to proceed similarly, a *header* is attached to the message to v. This header consists either of the destination label, or of a new label created by the current node.

It was shown in a series of papers (see, e.g., [25, 1–4, 29]) that there is a tradeoff between the memory requirements of a routing scheme and the worst-case stretch factor it guarantees. In [25] it is shown that every routing strategy that guarantees a multiplicative s stretched routing scheme for every n-node graph requires $\Omega(n^{1+1/(2s+4)})$ bits in total, so $\Omega(n^{1/(2s+4)})$ for local routing tables, for some worst-case graphs. Stronger lower bounds hold for small stretch factors. In particular, any multiplicative s stretched routing scheme must use $\Omega(\sqrt{n})$ bits for some nodes in some graphs for $s < 5$ [28], $\Omega(n)$ bits for $s < 3$ [12, 17], and $\Omega(n \log n)$ bits for $s < 1.4$ [21]. More precisely, for $s = 1$ [21] showed that for every shortest path routing strategy and for all d and fixed $\epsilon > 0$ such that $3 \leqslant d \leqslant (1-\epsilon)n$, there exists a graph of degree bounded by d for which $\Omega(n \log d)$ bit routing tables are required simultaneously on $\Theta(n)$ nodes, matching with the memory requirements of complete routing tables. All the lower bounds presented above assume that routes and addresses can be computed and optimized by the routing strategy in order to decrease the memory requirement.

These lower bounds are motivations for the design of routing strategies with compact tables on more specific class of graphs. Here we non exhaustively list some of them. Regular topologies (as hypercubes, tori, cycles, complete graphs, etc.) have specific routing schemes using $O(\log n)$ bit for addresses and for routing tables (cf. [22]). For non-regular topologies and wider class of graphs, several trade-offs between the stretch and the size of the routing tables have been achieved. In particular, for c-decomposable graphs [15] (including bounded tree-width graphs), planar graphs [14, 23], and bounded pagenumber graphs and bounded genus graphs [18]. More recently, a multiplicative $1 + \epsilon$ stretched routing scheme for every planar graph, for every $\epsilon > 0$, with only $(\log n)^{O(1)}$ bit addresses and routing tables, has been announced in [27]. For more detailed presentation of these schemes and for an overview of the other strategies and techniques, see [16] and [24].

Previous and New Results

Tree-decomposition is a rich concept introduced by Robertson and Seymour [26] and is widely used to solve various graph problems. In particular efficient algorithms exist for graphs having a tree-decomposition into subgraphs (or *bags*) of bounded size: for bounded *tree-width* graphs.

The *tree-length* of a graph G is the smallest integer δ for which G admits a tree-decomposition into bags of diameter at most δ. It has been formally in-

troduced in [10], and extensively studied in [8]. Chordal graphs are exactly
the graphs of tree-length 1, since a graph is chordal if and only if it has a
tree-decomposition in cliques (cf. [7]). AT-free graphs, permutation graphs, and
distance-hereditary graphs are of tree-length 2. More generally, [20] showed that
k-chordal graphs have tree-length at most $k/2$. However, there are graphs with
bounded tree-length and unbounded chordality[1], like the wheel. So, bounded
tree-length graphs is a larger class than bounded chordality graphs.

   For chordal graphs, the best known result produces a routing scheme of *deviation* 2, i.e., for all vertices, the length of the route never exceed their distance plus
2, with labels of size $O(\log^3 n/\log\log n)$ bits per node [9]. Tree-length δ graphs
are a natural generalization of chordal graphs, and their tree-decomposition induced can be successfully used. Indeed the last result can be generalized in case
of tree-length δ graphs, in order to obtain a routing scheme of deviation 2δ with
labels of size $O(\delta \log^3 n)$ bits per node [8]. But this generalization requires a
tree-decomposition of length minimum, which is probably NP-complete in general. In this paper we propose a routing scheme, polynomial time constructible
of deviation $6\delta - 2$ with shorter labels of size $O(\delta \log^2 n)$ bits per node.

   In the case where the chordality is at most k, our scheme can be adapted.
For such graphs we obtain a deviation of $k + 1$ with labels of size $O(\log^2 n)$ bits
per node and the routing decision is performed in constant time at every node.
The last known result in such graphs was of deviation $2\lfloor k/2 \rfloor$ with labels of size
$O(\log^3 n/\log\log n)$ bit per node, and the initial sender required $O(\log n)$ time
to compute the header of the message [11].

   Observe that for chordal graphs, the both schemes produce a deviation 4,
with addresses and local memories of size $O(\log^2 n)$ bits per node.

2   Preliminaries

Let G be a graph with a distinguished vertex s and we decompose $V(G)$ into
layers : for every integer $i \geqslant 0$, $L^i = \{u \in V(G) \mid d_G(s, u) = i\}$. Then, each layer
L^i is partitioned into $L_1^i, \dots, L_{p_i}^i$ such that two vertices stay in a same part if
and only if they are connected by a path visiting only vertices at distance at
least i from s.

   Let LT be the graph whose vertex set is the collection of all the parts L_j^i. In
LT, two vertices L_j^i and $L_{j'}^{i'}$ are adjacent if and only if there exists $u \in L_j^i$ and
$v \in L_{j'}^{i'}$ such that u and v are adjacent in G (see Fig. 1 for an example). The
vertex s is called the *source* of LT.

Lemma 1. [5] *The graph* LT, *called* layering-tree *of* G, *is a tree and is computable in linear time.*

   From now, LT denotes a layering-tree of a graph G and S denotes a shortest
path spanning tree of G rooted at the source of LT.

---

[1] The *chordality* is the smallest k such that the graph is k-chordal.

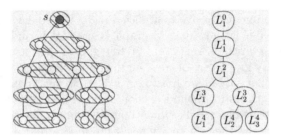

Fig. 1. A graph G and a layering-tree of it.

In the following we will use the standard notions of *parent, children, ancestor, descendant* and *depth* in trees. The *nearest common ancestor* between two vertices u, v in a tree T is: $nca_T(u, v)$. Moreover, given a layering-tree LT of a graph G, for every vertex u, $part(u)$ denotes the part of LT which contains u.

By construction of LT, one can prove the following property:

Property 1. Let u, v be two vertices of G, and let $X = nca_{LT}(part(u), part(v))$. Any path from u to v has to use at least one vertex of X. Moreover $d_G(u, v) \geqslant d_{LT}(part(u), part(v)) = d_S(u, X) + d_S(v, X)$

It is well known that every tree T has a vertex u, called *median*, such that each connected component of $T \backslash \{u\}$ has at most $\frac{1}{2}|V(T)|$ vertices. A *hierarchical tree* of T is then a rooted tree H defined as follows: the root of H is the median of T, u, and its children are the roots of the hierarchical trees of the connected components of $T \backslash \{u\}$. Observe that T and H share the same vertex set, and that the depth of H is at most[2] $\log |V(T)|$.

From now, H denotes a hierarchical tree of LT.

By construction of H, one can prove the following property:

Property 2. Let U, V be two parts of LT, $nca_H(U, V)$ separates U and V in LT.

3   The Main Routing Scheme

Let us outline the routing scheme. Each vertex u, contains in its address the information needed to route in S. Every part of LT has a special vertex, r_X, chosed arbitrarily. For every part X which is an ancestor of $part(u)$ in H ($part(u)$ included), the address of u contains all the information of a shortest path in G defined as follows: • if X is also an ancestor of $part(u)$ in LT, then the path is between r_X and the ancestor of u in S which belongs to X; • otherwise let $Y = nca_{LT}(part(u), X)$, the path is between the ancestor of r_X in S which belongs to Y and the ancestor of u in S which belongs to Y. Observe that u contains the information of at most $\log n$ paths.

To send a message from any vertex u to any other v, the solution we propose consists on first finding the nearest common ancestor in H between $part(u)$ and

---

[2] All the logs are in base two.

$part(v)$: $X = nca_H(part(u), part(v))$. By Property 2, X belongs to the path in LT from $part(u)$, and $part(v)$, so $nca_{LT}(part(u), part(v))$, is either $nca_{LT}(part(u), X)$ or $nca_{LT}(part(v), X)$. Thus $Y = nca_{LT}(part(u), part(v))$ is contained either in the address of u or in the address of v. Moreover by Property 1 any path from u to v has to use at least one vertex of $Y =$. Thus the message will follow the route depicted in figure 2.

3.1   Description of Labels

We assume that the outgoing edges of every vertex u of G are numbered arbitrarily by distinct integers, called *output port numbers*, and taken from $[1, \deg(u)]$.

Our scheme associate to every vertex u of G two labels: its *address*, denoted by address(u) and a *local routing table*, denoted by table(u).

• The local routing table of u in G, table(u), is set to $<$ $id(u), route(u)$ $>$ (defined hereafter);

• The address of u in G, is set to $<$ $id(u), route(u), path(u), help(u)$ $>$, where:

- $id(u)$ is the identifiant of u (an integer in $\{1, \ldots, n\}$);
- $route(u)$ is a binary label depending on the tree S and on u such that the route from u to any vertex v in S can be determined from the labels $route(u)$ and $route(v)$ only. More precisely, for a suitable computable function f (so independent of the tree), $f(route(u), route(v))$, for every $v \neq u$, returns the output port number of the first edge of the path from u to v in S. An implementation of these labels is discussed in Lemma 3.
- $path(u)$ is a binary label allowing to determine, given $path(u)$ and $path(v)$, the depth of the nearest common ancestor between $part(u)$ and $part(v)$ in H;
- $help(u)$ is a table with $1 + depth_H(part(u))$ entries. Let X be an ancestor of $part(u)$ in H ($X = part(u)$ is possible), $help(u)[depth_H(X)] =$ $<$ $route(r_X), rescue >$, defined as follows (see Fig. 2 for an example). Let $Y = nca_{LT}(part(u), X)$:
  • If $X = Y$ then $route(r_X) = \varnothing$, else $route(r_X)$ is the routing label in S of r_X: a special vertex of X defined arbitrarily in advance.
  • Let u' be the ancestor of u which belongs to Y, and r'_X be the one of r_X. $rescue$ contains all the port numbers and the identifiants of a shortest path in G between u' and r'_X.

3.2   The Routing Algorithm

Consider u, v two vertices of G, u the sender and v the receiver. Procedure $init(u, v)$ is in charge of initializing the header attached to the message sent by u. This header, denoted by h_{uv}, is $h_{uv} =$ $<$ $direction, route(v), route(r_X), rescue_1,$ $rescue_2 >$, computed as follows:

Algorithm *init*
Input: Two addresses: address(u) and address(v)
Result: h_{uv}, the header of a message to v
begin

 $h_X \leftarrow depth(nca_H(part(u), part(v)))$;
 $rescue_1 \leftarrow help(u)[h_X].rescue$;
 $rescue_2 \leftarrow help(v)[h_X].rescue$;
 if $help(u)[h_X].route(r_X) = \varnothing$ **then**
  $direction \leftarrow up$;
  $route(r_X) \leftarrow help(v)[h_X].route(r_X)$;
 else
  $direction \leftarrow down$;
  $route(r_X) \leftarrow help(u)[h_X].route(r_X)$;
 end

end

Consider any node w of G that receives a message with a header h_{uv}, the header computed from $init(u, v)$ (possibly, $w = u$). The output port number of the edge on which the message to v has to be sent from w is defined by the function $send(w, h_{uv})$ described below. Observe that once h_{uv} is initialized by the sender, h_{uv} is never changed along the route.

Algorithm *send*
Input: The address of a vertex w, a header h_{uv}
Result: The port number of an outgoing edge from w
begin

 if w *is an ancestor of* v **then**
  return $(f(route(w), route(v)))$;
 if $id(w) \in rescue_2$ **then**
  return (the port number associate to w);
 if w *is an ancestor of* r_X **then**
  if $direction = down$ **then**
   return $(f(route(w), route(r_X)))$;
  else return (the port number between w and its parent);
 if $id(w) \in rescue_1$ **then**
  return (the port number associate to w);
 return (the port number between w and its parent);

end

3.3   Correctness and Performances of the Routing Algorithm

We now give the correctness of the routing algorithm. Let $\rho(u, v)$ denote the length of the route produced by *init* and *send* from u to v. We denote by $d_G(u, v)$ the distance between u and v in G. The correctness of our scheme is done proving that $\rho(u, v)$ is bounded. More precisely:

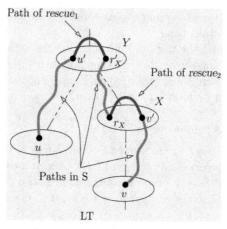

Path of rescue₁

Fig. 2. Example of the route induced by the scheme.

Lemma 2. *Let u, v be two vertices of G and let λ be the maximum distance between two vertices of a part of* LT, $\rho(u,v) \leqslant d_G(u,v) + 2\lambda$.

Proof. Clearly the route induced by the routing scheme is the path depicted in figure 2.

Moreover by Property 1, $d_G(u,v) \leqslant d_G(u,Y) + d_G(Y,v) = d_S(u,u') + d_S(r'_X, r_X) + d_S(v',v)$.

Thus in the worst case $\rho(u,v) \leqslant d_G(u,v) + d_G(u',r'_X) + d_G(r_X, v')$.   □

3.4   Implementation of the Scheme

We assume that the standard bitwise operations (like addition, xor, shift, etc.) on $O(\log n)$ bit words run in constant time.

Lemma 3. *For every vertex u,* address(u) *can be implemented with a binary string of size $O(\lambda \log^2 n)$ bits, such that* init(u,v) *runs in constant time. Moreover headers can be implemented with a binary string of size $O(\lambda \log n)$ bits such that for all vertex w,* send(w, h_{uv}) *runs in $O(\log \lambda)$ time.*

Proof. Let u be an arbitrary vertex of G.

To implement the routing in the tree S, we use the shortest path routing scheme proposed by [13] which produces binary labels of size $O(\log n)$ bits per vertex and such that for every u, v, the routing function $f(route(u), route(v))$ is computable in constant time. Thus the size of $route(u)$ is $O(\log n)$ bits.

To implement $path(u)$ we use an other known result, which produces labels of size $O(\log n)$, and a decodable function running in constant time [19].

Then, for every ancestor of $part(u)$ in H, $help(u)[h_X].rescue$ contains $O(\lambda)$ entries, and each entry contains three integers between 0 and n. Since the depth of H is $O(\log n)$, $help(u)$ contains $O(\lambda \log^2 n)$ bits.

In the function *init*, we only make some constant number of copies of pointers. Thus *init* runs in constant time.

In the function *send*, the tests to known if w is an ancestor of v or of r_X can be done in constant time using the routing function f. If we assume that the tables $rescue_1$ and $rescue_2$ are sorted, then by a dichotomic procedure, all the other information can be found in $O(\log \lambda)$ time.   □

From the previous lemmas, it follows that:

Theorem 1. *Every n-vertex graph admits a loop-free routing scheme of deviation 2λ such that the address and the local table have at most $O(\lambda \log^2 n)$ bits size per vertex, where λ is the maximum distance between two vertices of a same part of a layering-tree of G. Once computed by the sender, headers of size $O(\lambda \log n)$ never change. Moreover the scheme is polynomial time constructible and the routing decision is performed in $O(\log \lambda)$ time at every vertex.*

4   Routing Scheme for Tree-Length δ Graphs

We need the notion of *tree-decomposition* introduced by Robertson and Seymour in their work on graph minors [26]. A tree-decomposition of a graph G is a tree T whose nodes, called *bags*, are subsets of $V(G)$ such that:

1. $\bigcup_{X \in V(T)} X = V(G)$;
2. for all $\{u, v\} \in E(G)$, there exists $X \in V(T)$ such that $u, v \in X$; and
3. for all $X, Y, Z \in V(T)$, if Y is on the path from X to Z in T then $X \cap Z \subseteq Y$.

The *length* of a tree-decomposition T of a graph G is $\max_{X \in V(T)} \max_{u,v \in X} d_G(u, v)$, and the *tree-length of G* is the minimum of the length, over all tree-decompositions of G.

A well-known invariant related to tree-decompositions of a graph G is the *tree-width*, defined as minimum of $\max_{X \in V(T)} |X| - 1$ over all tree-decompositions T of G. We stress that the tree-width of a graph is not related to its tree-length. For instance cliques have unbounded tree-width and tree-length 1, whereas cycles have tree-width 2 and unbounded tree-length.

Now let us show the relation between tree-length and distances in a part of a layering-tree:

Lemma 4. *Let LT be a layering-tree of a tree-length δ graph G. For every part W of LT, there is a vertex c of G, called the center of W, s.t., $\forall u, v \in W$, $d_G(u, v) \leqslant 3\delta$ and $d_G(u, c) \leqslant 2\delta$.*

Proof. Let T be a tree-decomposition of G of length δ, w.l.o.g. T is supposed rooted at a bag containing s, the source of LT (see figure 3(a)). Let S be a shortest path spanning tree of G rooted at s.

Now let W be a part of LT at distance i of s. Let X be the bag of T that is the nearest common ancestor in T of all the bags containing a vertex of W, and let $d_X = \max_{u,v \in X} d_G(u, v)$ be its diameter. Let us prove that for every $u \in W$, $d_G(u, X) \leqslant \delta$. In this way, we obtain:

 - $\forall u, v \in W$, $d_G(u, v) \leqslant d_G(u, X) + d_X + d_G(v, X) \leqslant 3\delta$;
 - $\forall u \in W$ and $\forall c \in X$, $d_G(u, c) \leqslant d_G(u, X) + d_X \leqslant 2\delta$.

Let u be an arbitrary vertex of W, and let v be a vertex of W such that $X = nca_T(B(u), B(v))$ (observe that v is well defined). Let P be the path is S from s to u, P must intersect X at a vertex x. Since u, v are both in W, there exists a path Q from u to v in which every vertex w is such that $d_G(s, w) \geqslant i$. Q intersects X at a vertex r (see Fig. 3(a)).

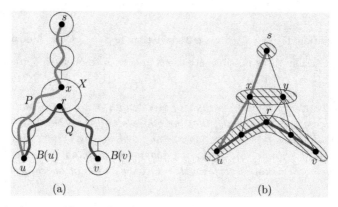

(a)   (b)

Fig. 3. A part of LT is of diameter at most 3δ and of radius at most 2δ.

Note that $d_G(s, u) = i = d_G(s, x) + d_G(x, u)$ and $d_G(s, r) \leqslant d_G(s, x) + \delta$. So, $d_G(s, r) \leqslant i + \delta - d_G(x, u)$. If $d_G(x, u) \geqslant \delta + 1$ then $d_G(s, r) \leqslant i - 1$: a contradiction since $r \in Q$. So, $d_G(u, X) \leqslant d_G(u, x) \leqslant \delta$ as claimed.   □

Observation 1 *Note that the center of W can be set to any vertex c which belongs to X and is an ancestor in S of a vertex of W. Thus let $u \in W$ such that for all $v \in W$, $d_S(u, X) \geqslant d_S(v, X)$. Let $c \in X$ such that $d_S(u, c) = d_S(u, X)$, we obtain : $\forall v \in W$, $d_G(v, c) \leqslant \delta + d_S(u, c) \leqslant 2\delta$.*

Lemma 4 and Theorem 1 imply the following corollary:

Corollary 1. *Every n-vertex graph of tree-length δ admits a loop-free routing scheme of deviation 6δ such that the address and the local table have at most $O(\delta \log^2 n)$ bits size per vertex. Once computed by the sender, headers of size $O(\delta \log n)$ never change. Moreover the scheme is polynomial time constructible and the routing decision is performed in $O(\log \delta)$ time at every vertex.*

This result can be improved because for every part X of LT the special vertex r_X can be set to the center of X which satisfies Observation 1. In this way the deviation is reduced to $6\delta - 2$. The formal proof is given in the full version of this paper, but an idea of it is given by figure 4.

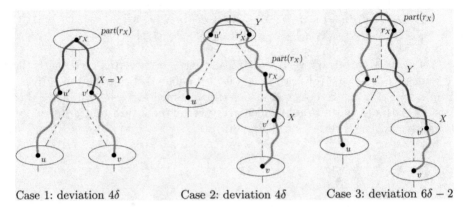

Case 1: deviation 4δ Case 2: deviation 4δ Case 3: deviation $6\delta - 2$

Fig. 4. The three possible situations in case of tree-length δ graphs.

Theorem 2. *Every n-vertex graph of tree-length δ admits a loop-free routing scheme of deviation $6\delta - 2$ such that the address and the local table have at most $O(\delta \log^2 n)$ bits size per vertex. Once computed by the sender, headers of size $O(\delta \log n)$ never change. Moreover the scheme is polynomial time constructible and the routing decision is performed in $O(\log \delta)$ time at every vertex.*

5   Routing Scheme for k-Chordal Graphs

A graph is k-chordal if the length of the longest induced cycle is at most k. The *chordality of G* is the smallest integer k such that G is k-chordal. Trees are, by convention, of chordality 2. Chordal graphs are 3-chordal graphs.

Now let us show the relation between chordality and distances in a part of a layering-tree. The first point of this lemma is already proved in [5] and the second one in [6].

Lemma 5. *Let LT be a layering-tree of a k-chordal graph G and S be a shortest path spanning tree of G rooted at s. Let L_j^i be an arbitrary part of LT and L_k^{i-1} be the parent of L_j^i in LT. For all vertices u, v of L_j^i we have:*

1. *$d_G(u, v) \leqslant \lfloor k/2 \rfloor + 2$;*
2. *there exists a path of length at most k from u to v wich contains ancestors of u then ancestors of v.*

Proof. Let G be a k-chordal graph, let LT be a layering-tree of G and let u, v be two vertices of G which belong to a same part of H: L_j^i.

By definition of L_j^i, there exists a path from u to v using only vertices which are at distance is at most i from s. Let P_1 be a such chordless path. Moreover there exists a path in S from u to s and from v to s. Let P_u, P_v be such paths and let $\langle x, y \rangle$ be the first edge between P_u, P_v, in the extreme case, $y = s$ (see Fig. 5).

If there is no chord between P_1 and P_u or between P_1 and P_v, then $P_1, u', \cdots,$ $x, y, \cdots, v'$ is an induced cycle containing both u and v, and thus $d_G(u, v) \leqslant k/2$.

Otherwise, by definition of S and as shown in Fig. 5, chords can exist only between the parent of u: u' (or the parent of v: v') and a vertex of P_1.

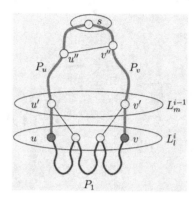

Fig. 5. Relation between chordality and distances in a part LT.

In the extreme case, there is a chord from both u' and v'. Nevertheless there is an induced cycle containing u' and v'. Thus $d_G(u', v') \leqslant k/2$ and $d_G(u, v) \leqslant k/2 + 2$.

The path claimed by the second point of Lemma 5 is the subpath of P_u (from u to u''), the edge $\langle u'', v'' \rangle$, and the subpath of P_v (from v'' to v).   □

Here again we obtain a corollary of Theorem 1:

Corollary 2. *Every k-chordal graph with n vertices admits a loop-free routing scheme of deviation $2 \lceil k/2 \rceil + 4$ such that the addresses and the local tables have at most $O(k \log^2 n)$ bits size per vertex. Once computed by the sender, headers of size $O(k \log n)$ never change. Moreover the scheme is computable in polynomial time and the routing decision is performed in $O(\log k)$ time at every vertex.*

This result can again be improved thanks to the second point of Lemma 5. Indeed paths of $rescue_1$ and $rescue_2$ can be reduced to one edge, thus the memory requirement and the decision time become independent of k. Moreover the deviation is also improved: $k + 1$. The formal proof is given in the full version of this paper, but an idea of it is given by figure 6.

Theorem 3. *Every k-chordal graph with n vertices admits a loop-free routing scheme of deviation $k + 1$ such that the addresses and the local tables have at most $O(\log^2 n)$ bits size per vertex. Once computed by the sender, headers of size $O(\log n)$ never change. Moreover the scheme is computable in polynomial time and the routing decision is performed in constant time at every vertex.*

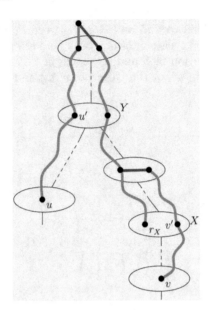

Fig. 6. The route induced by our scheme in case of k-chordal graphs.

6 Conclusion

In this paper we show how to use the notion of layering-tree to construct efficient compact routing schemes for tree-length δ graphs and for k-chordal graphs. It would be interesting to find other classes of graphs for which distances in parts of a layering-tree are related to some parameters of the class. In this way we would be able to obtain a very fast constructible and efficient routing scheme, even if the class of graph is hard to construct. Indeed, producing a tree-decomposition of length minimum is probably NP-complete for general graphs. Nevertheless, we propose an efficient routing scheme, constructible in very short time.

Acknowledgements

This work has been done during the author's stay at Kent State University. The author is thankful to Feodor Dragan and Chenyu Yan for helpful discussions, specifically about Theorem 3.

References

1. B. AWERBUCH, A. BAR-NOY, N. LINIAL, AND D. PELEG, *Compact distributed data structures for adaptive routing*, in 21st Symposium on Theory of Computing (STOC), vol. 2, May 1989, pp. 230–240.
2. ——, *Improved routing strategies with succinct tables*, Journal of Algorithms, 11 (1990), pp. 307–341.

3. B. AWERBUCH AND D. PELEG, *Sparse partitions*, in 31th Symposium on Foundations of Computer Science (FOCS), IEEE Computer Society Press, 1990, pp. 503–513.

4. ——, *Routing with polynomial communication-space trade-off*, SIAM Journal on Discrete Mathematics, 5 (1992), pp. 151–162.

5. V. D. CHEPOI AND F. F. DRAGAN, *A note on distance approximating trees in graphs*, Europ. J. Combinatorics, 21 (2000), pp. 761–768.

6. V. D. CHEPOI, F. F. DRAGAN, AND C. YAN, *Additive spanner for k-chordal graphs*, in Algorithms and Complexity: 5th Italian Conference (CIAC 2003), vol. 2653 of Lecture Notes in Computer Science, Springer-Verlag Heidelberg, May 2003, pp. 96–107.

7. R. DIESTEL, *Graph Theory (second edition)*, vol. 173 of Graduate Texts in Mathematics, Springer, Feb. 2000.

8. Y. DOURISBOURE, *Routage compact et longueur arborescente*, 2003. PhD Thesis, LaBRI, University of Bordeaux 1.

9. Y. DOURISBOURE AND C. GAVOILLE, *Improved compact routing scheme for chordal graphs*, in 16-th International Symposium on DIStributed Computing (DISC 2002), vol. 2508 of Lecture Notes in Computer Science, Springer-Verlag, Oct. 2002, pp. 252–264.

10. ——, *Tree-decomposition of graphs with small diameter bags*, in European conference on Combinatorics, Graph Theory and Applications (EUROCOMB 2003), ITI, Sept. 2003, pp. 100–104.

11. F. F. DRAGAN, C. YAN, AND I. LOMONOSOV, *Collective tree spanners of graphs*, in 9th Scandinavian Workshop on Algorithm Theory (SWAT), 2004. To appear.

12. P. FRAIGNIAUD AND C. GAVOILLE, *Universal routing schemes*, Journal of Distributed Computing, 10 (1997), pp. 65–78.

13. ——, *Routing in trees*, Research Report RR-1252-01, LaBRI, University of Bordeaux, 351, cours de la Libération, 33405 Talence Cedex, France, Jan. 2001. Sumitted.

14. G. N. FREDERICKSON AND R. JANARDAN, *Efficient message routing in planar networks*, SIAM Journal on Computing, 18 (1989), pp. 843–857.

15. ——, *Space-efficient message routing in c-decomposable networks*, SIAM Journal on Computing, 19 (1990), pp. 164–181.

16. C. GAVOILLE, *Routing in distributed networks: Overview and open problems*, ACM SIGACT News - Distributed Computing Column, 32 (2001), pp. 36–52.

17. C. GAVOILLE AND M. GENGLER, *Space-efficiency of routing schemes of stretch factor three*, Journal of Parallel and Distributed Computing, 61 (2001), pp. 679–687.

18. C. GAVOILLE AND N. HANUSSE, *Compact routing tables for graphs of bounded genus*, in 26th International Colloquium on Automata, Languages and Programming (ICALP), J. Wiedermann, P. van Emde Boas, and M. Nielsen, eds., vol. 1644 of Lecture Notes in Computer Science, Springer, July 1999, pp. 351–360.

19. C. GAVOILLE, M. KATZ, N. A. KATZ, C. PAUL, AND D. PELEG, *Approximate distance labeling schemes*, Research Report RR-1250-00, LaBRI, University of Bordeaux, 351, cours de la Libération, 33405 Talence Cedex, France, Dec. 2000.

20. ——, *Approximate distance labeling schemes*, in 9th Annual European Symposium on Algorithms (ESA), F. M. auf der Heide, ed., vol. 2161 of Lecture Notes in Computer Science, Springer, Aug. 2001, pp. 476–488.

21. C. GAVOILLE AND S. PÉRENNÈS, *Memory requirement for routing in distributed networks*, in 15th Annual ACM Symposium on Principles of Distributed Computing (PODC), ACM PRESS, May 1996, pp. 125–133.

22. F. T. LEIGHTON, *Introduction to Parallel Algorithms and Architectures: Arrays - Trees - Hypercubes*, Morgan Kaufmann, 1992.

23. H.-I. LU, *Improved compact routing tables for planar networks via orderly spanning trees*, in 8th Annual International Computing & Combinatorics Conference (CO-COON), vol. 2387 of Lecture Notes in Computer Science, Springer, Aug. 2002, pp. 57–66.

24. D. PELEG, *Distributed Computing: A Locality-Sensitive Approach*, SIAM Monographs on Discrete Mathematics and Applications, 2000.

25. D. PELEG AND E. UPFAL, *A trade-off between space and efficiency for routing tables*, Journal of the ACM, 36 (1989), pp. 510–530.

26. N. ROBERTSON AND P. D. SEYMOUR, *Graph minors. II. Algorithmic aspects of tree-width*, Journal of Algorithms, 7 (1986), pp. 309–322.

27. M. THORUP, *Compact oracles for reachability and approximate distances in planar digraphs*, in 42th Annual IEEE Symposium on Foundations of Computer Science (FOCS), IEEE Computer Society Press, Oct. 2001.

28. M. THORUP AND U. ZWICK, *Approximate distance oracles*, in 33rd Annual ACM Symposium on Theory of Computing (STOC), Hersonissos, Crete, Greece, July 2001, pp. 183–192.

29. ——, *Compact routing schemes*, in 13th Annual ACM Symposium on Parallel Algorithms and Architectures (SPAA), Hersonissos, Crete, Greece, July 2001, ACM PRESS, pp. 1–10.

Towards a Theory of Consistency Primitives

(Extended Abstract)

Ueli Maurer*

Department of Computer Science
ETH Zurich
CH-8092 Zurich, Switzerland
`maurer@inf.ethz.ch`

Abstract. One of the classical results in the theory of distributed systems is the theorem by Lamport, Shostak, and Pease stating that among n parties, any t of which may be cheaters, one of the parties (the sender) can consistently broadcast a value to the other parties if and only if $t \leq n/3$. This is achieved by use of a protocol among the players, using bilateral channels.

The purpose of this paper is to look at various generalizations of this result and to propose a new concept, called consistency specification, a very general type of consistency guarantee a protocol among n parties $P_1, \ldots, P_n$ can provide. A consistency specification specifies, for every possible set $H \subseteq \{P_1, \ldots, P_n\}$ of honest players and for every choice of their inputs, a certain security guarantee, i.e., a consistency condition on their outputs. This models that security can degrade smoothly with an increasing number of cheaters rather than abruptly when a certain threshold is exceeded, as is the case in the previous literature.

1 Introduction

1.1 Security in Distributed Systems

Distributed systems generally involve a number of entities (for instance called servers, parties, or players), connected by some communication channels, who are supposed to perform a certain task, using a well-defined protocol between the entities. The task can range from (apparently) simple problems like the synchronization of the entities' clocks to highly complex tasks like a distributed on-line auction among the entities. Typically, performing this task is in their mutual interest, but the entities cannot be assumed to perform the protocol correctly since some of them might gain an advantage by cheating.

A key problem in the design of protocols for distributed systems, and more generally for cryptographic applications, is to achieve security against the malicious behavior of some of the involved parties. In other words, there must be a certain security guarantee for the honest parties, even if the remaining parties cheat. Security can mean secrecy of certain data (e.g. the parties' inputs) and/or correctness of the parties' outputs.

---

* Supported in part by the Swiss National Science Foundation.

R. Guerraoui (Ed.): DISC 2004, LNCS 3274, pp. 379–389, 2004.

1.2   The General Setting

Throughout the paper, let $\mathcal{P} = \{P_1, \ldots, P_n\}$ be the set of n parties, also called players. Each player can either be honest or malicious. An honest player performs the prescribed protocol, whereas a malicious player can deviate arbitrarily from the protocol[1]. In order to model the coordinated cheating by several players, one often considers a central adversary who can corrupt some of the players and take full control of their actions. The non-corrupted players are called *honest*. An adversary is hence characterized by the set of corrupted players.

Typical results in the literature on secure distributed protocols provide a security guarantee as long as the number of cheating parties is bounded by some threshold t, accepting complete failure when this bound is exceeded. This threshold-type model can be generalized in many ways. In particular, we propose a more general concept of security where for each set H of honest players (or, equivalently, for any set of cheating players), the achieved level of security is specified. Of course, the achieved security level degrades monotonically when more parties cheat, but it can degrade smoothly rather than abruptly with an increasing set of cheating parties.

1.3   The Broadcast Problem

A classical problem in distributed systems is for one player $P_i \in \mathcal{P}$ (the sender) to broadcast a value (from a certain domain, e.g. $\{0, 1\}$) consistently to the other players, using only (authenticated) bilateral communication channels, with the following security requirements:

1. *Consistency:* All honest players decide on the same value v.
2. *Correctness:* If P_i is honest, then v is the value sent by P_i.

A third requirement, often tacitly assumed, is that the protocol must terminate.

The broadcast problem is a prototypical problem in which a protocol among the players guarantees some form of consistency of their output values. It is used as a subprotocol in many other secure distributed protocols, in particular also in secure multi-party computation (see Section 1.4).

A different variant of the broadcast problem is the so-called *consensus* problem, where each player has an input and the goal is that the players decide on the same value which, if the majority of the players entered the same value, must be equal to this value.

One of the most classical results in the theory of distributed systems is the theorem by Lamport, Shostak, and Pease [LSP82], stating that broadcast and consensus among n parties is possible if and only if strictly fewer than $n/3$ of the players cheat (i.e., $t < n/3$).

---

[1] More generally, there could be several levels of cheating. For example, in secure multi-party computation one often considers *passive* cheating which mans that such a cheater performs the protocol correctly but might pool his information with other cheaters to violate secrecy.

One can consider more general consistency guarantees for the output values of the honest players, not only the special type of guarantee that they be equal. To explore this space of possible consistency guarantees is the subject of this paper.

1.4   Secure Multi-party Computation

The purpose of this paper is to discuss consistency at a very general level, but to discard secrecy requirements relevant in a more general type of secure cooperation of parties. The reasons for restricting ourselves to consistency in this paper are that the definitions are simpler and cleaner, that understanding consistency appears to be an important goal on the way to understanding more general settings, and that consistency primitives are important building blocks in protocols achieving more general security goals.

But it is worthwhile to briefly discuss the more general setting because it sheds light on how one can view results on consistency and because many results in the literature have been derived for this more general setting (and hence also apply in our consistency setting).

One can view a broadcast protocol as the simulation of a trusted party whose task it is to accept an input value from the sender and to send this value to each other player. The simulation works correctly under the condition $t < n/3$. More generally, one can simulate a trusted party who performs more complicated tasks, including the secret storage of information and the computation of functions on the players' inputs. Broadcast is a special case, involving no secrecy requirement.

The general paradigm of simulating a trusted party is called *secure multi-party computation*. A typical example is a voting protocol which allows a set of voters to add their votes correctly while nevertheless keeping their votes secret from the other players, even if some of them cheat. In this case the simulated trusted party takes as inputs all votes of the players, adds them up, and sends the result to each player.

Some classical results on secure multi-party computation are as follows. Goldreich, Micali, and Wigderson [GMW87] proved that, based on cryptographic intractability assumptions, secure multi-party computation is possible if and only if the number t of corrupted players satisfies $t < n/2$. In the information-theoretic model, where bilateral secure channels between every pair of players are assumed and the adversary is assumed to be computationally unrestricted, Ben-Or, Goldwasser, and Wigderson [BGW88] (and independently Chaum, Crépeau, and Damgård [CCD88]) proved that perfect security is possible if and only if $t < n/3$. In a model in which a broadcast channel among the players is assumed, unconditional security (with exponentially small failure probability) is achievable if and only if $t < n/2$ [RB89]. We refer to [Mau02] for a discussion of known results on secure multi-party computation and for a conceptually very simple protocol.

Let us briefly discuss the relation between the two results for threshold $t < n/3$ mentioned above. The result on broadcast [LSP82] is a special case of the result on secure multi-party computation [BGW88], but a broadcast protocol tolerating up to $n/3$ cheaters (and hence the Lamport-Shostak-Pease theorem) is used as a crucial primitive within the secure multi-party computation protocol of [BGW88]. What is surprising is that the same threshold as for broadcast applies for a much more general problem.

1.5   Scope and Limitations of This Paper

In this paper we consider only consistency but not secrecy requirements. In terms of the simulation of a trusted party discussed above, this means that the simulated trusted party is allowed to be transparent in the sense that an adversary can learn the entire internal information. (But it is not transparent for the honest parties.)

The purpose of this extended abstract is to briefly review several types of recently proposed generalizations of the classical theorem by Lamport, Shostak, and Pease, and then to propose a new generalization. The goal of this generalization is to allow for the security (i.e., consistency) guarantee to degrade slowly with an increasing number of cheaters rather than abruptly and completely when a certain threshold is exceeded, as is the case in the previous literature. In other words, for every possible set of players the adversary might corrupt, there is a certain security (consistency) guarantee.

This extended abstract introduces the general concept of a consistency specification, gives a few examples, and discusses the reduction of one consistency specification to some other consistency specifications by use of a protocol. This calls for a general theory explaining which reductions are possible and which are not. However, such a theory is not developed in this paper.

We consider a synchronous setting in which the players are assumed to have synchronized clocks. Moreover, we consider a setting with zero failure probability. Both these points could be generalized to an asynchronous setting and to tolerating a small failure probability.

2   Generalizations of the Classical Results

As mentioned above, results for broadcast and for secure multi-party computation among n players are usually derived for a setting with at most t corrupted players, with no security guarantee if this threshold is exceeded.

This model and result can be generalized in various ways, discussed in this section, both for the case of general secure multi-party computation as well as for the case of broadcast and more general consistency protocols.

2.1   From Thresholds to General Adversary Structures

A first generalization was proposed in [HM97] where the adversary's corruption capability is modeled by a general so-called *adversary structure* rather than a threshold t.

Definition 1. Consider a finite set $\mathcal{P}$. We call a subset Π of the power set $2^{\mathcal{P}}$ of $\mathcal{P}$ a *(monotone) structure* for $\mathcal{P}$ if Π is closed under taking subsets, i.e.,

$$S \in \Pi \wedge S' \subseteq S \implies S' \in \Pi.$$

Example 1. The most common example of a structure is the threshold structure $\Pi = \{S : S \subseteq \mathcal{P}, |S| \le t\}$ for some t.

Informally, a protocol is secure against an adversary structure Π if it remains secure as long as the set of players corrupted by the adversary is within Π.

Definition 2. *Let $\sqcup$ be a (commutative and associative) operation on structures, defined as follows: $\Pi_1 \sqcup \Pi_2$ is the structure consisting of all unions of one element of Π_1 and one element of Π_2, i.e.,*

$$\Pi_1 \sqcup \Pi_2 := \{S_1 \cup S_2 : S_1 \in \Pi_1, S_2 \in \Pi_2\}.$$

It was proved in [HM97] that secure multi-party computation in the information-theoretic setting for a general adversary structure Π is possible if and only if no three sets in Π cover the full player set, i.e., if and only if

$$\mathcal{P} \notin \Pi \sqcup \Pi \sqcup \Pi.$$

This is a strict generalization of the threshold condition $(t < n/3)$.

Example 2. For instance, in the case of $n = 6$ players, with $\mathcal{P} = \{P_1, P_2, P_3, P_4, P_5, P_6\}$, one can obtain a protocol secure against the structure

$$\Pi = \{\{P_1\}, \{P_2, P_4\}, \{P_2, P_5, P_6\}, \{P_3, P_5\}, \{P_3, P_6\}, \{P_4, P_5, P_6\}\},$$

whereas in the threshold model one can tolerate only a single cheater, i.e., the adversary structure $\Pi' = \{\{P_1\}, \{P_2\}, \{P_3\}, \{P_4\}, \{P_5\}, \{P_6\}\}$.

The above mentioned result also implies the same generalization for broadcast, but the resulting protocol would not be efficient if there is no short description of the structure Π. An efficient secure broadcast protocol for all adversary structures satisfying $\mathcal{P} \notin \Pi \sqcup \Pi \sqcup \Pi$ was given in [FM98].

2.2   Available Primitives

In most secure distributed protocols in the literature (e.g. for the broadcast result of [LSP82]) it is assumed that authenticated bilateral channels between any pair of players are available. More generally, one can assume other primitives as being available. Such primitives can be stronger than authenticated channels, or they can be weaker when authenticated channels are not assumed to be available. A general problem is to understand reductions between such primitives, i.e., to construct a stronger primitive by application of a protocol involving the given weaker primitives. A natural interesting question is which reductions are possible, and if so, by how many invocations of the given primitives.

For example, the Lamport-Shostak-Pease result states that a broadcast channel among n players can be reduced to authenticated bilateral channels under the condition that the number of cheaters is less than $n/3$. As a more general example, a setting is considered in [FM00] where a broadcast channel is available for any three players, allowing a sender to consistently send a value to (any) two receivers. Under this stronger assumption about the available communication primitive one can prove that broadcast among n players is possible if and only if $t < n/2$, improving on the $t < n/3$ threshold. One can also consider broadcast channels among more than three players as being given, in which case the threshold can be increased even beyond $n/2$ (see [CFF^{+}04]).

2.3   Smooth Security Degradation

Typical results in the literature on secure distributed protocols provide a security guarantee only as long as the set of cheating parties is restricted (by a threshold or a general adversary structure), accepting complete failure when more players are corrupted.

However, this approach ignores the possibility that even if the set of cheaters is outside the adversary structure, there can still be some remaining security guarantee for the honest players, for instance that most (rather than all) honest players receive the same value [KS01]. One may even be willing to sacrifice some security guarantee below a given threshold for the sake of being able to achieve some level of security above the threshold.

In full generality, one need not even consider a threshold or an adversary structure. To fully characterize a primitive, one must specify the achieved security guarantee for every set of honest players. In other words, one must specify for every potential set of corrupted players what they can achieve in the worst case.

In the next section we consider the formalization of such primitives, referring to them as consistency specifications.

3   Consistency Specifications

3.1   Definition of Consistency Specifications

Let again $\mathcal{P} = \{P_1, \ldots, P_n\}$ be the set of players. For convenience, we sometimes also use i instead of P_i. We investigate protocols in which every player P_i has an input from a finite input domain $\mathcal{D}_i$ and receives an output from a finite output domain $\mathcal{R}_i$. The special case where some players have no input and/or no output can be modeled by letting the corresponding input and/or output domain be a singleton set with a default symbol (e.g. $\perp$). For example, for a broadcast channel only one player (the sender) has an input.

Let $\mathcal{D}_\mathcal{P} := \underset{i=1}{\overset{n}{\times}} \mathcal{D}_i$ be the Cartesian product of the input domains, and for a player set $S \subseteq \mathcal{P}$, let

$$\mathcal{D}_S := \times_{i \in S} \mathcal{D}_i$$

be the Cartesian product of the $\mathcal{D}_i$ with $i \in S$. For $S' \subseteq S$ and $\boldsymbol{x} \in \mathcal{D}_S$, let $\boldsymbol{x}_{|S'} \in \mathcal{D}_{S'}$ be the list $\boldsymbol{x}$ restricted to indices in S'. Similarly, for a set $L \subseteq \mathcal{D}_S$ of lists, let $L_{|S'} \subseteq \mathcal{D}_{S'}$ be the set of lists resulting by restricting each of them to S'. Analogous notation is used for the output domains $\mathcal{R}_i$. We also write $\boldsymbol{x}_{|i}$ instead of $\boldsymbol{x}_{|\{P_i\}}$ to denote the entry in $\boldsymbol{x}$ for player P_i.

The following definition captures the most general type of consistency guarantee that a protocol or primitive can give, if the failure probability is required to be zero. It was first proposed by the author and then investigated in [Asc01] and [KS01]. Special cases were then investigated in [FGH+02] and [FHHW03].

Definition 3. A *consistency specification* $\mathcal{C}$ for player set $\mathcal{P} = \{P_1, \ldots, P_n\}$, input domains $\mathcal{D}_1, \ldots, \mathcal{D}_n$, and output domains $\mathcal{R}_1, \ldots, \mathcal{R}_n$ is a function assigning to every set $H \subseteq \mathcal{P}$ (the honest players) and every list $\boldsymbol{x}_H \in \mathcal{D}_H$ (their input values) a set $\mathcal{C}(H, \boldsymbol{x}_H) \subseteq \mathcal{R}_H$ (of lists of possible output values), satisfying the following monotonicity constraint: For any H' and H with $H' \subseteq H$,

$$\mathcal{C}(H, \boldsymbol{x}_H)_{|H'} \subseteq \mathcal{C}(H', \boldsymbol{x}_{H|H'}).$$

Let us explain this definition in more detail. For every set H of honest players (where the remaining players $\mathcal{P} \setminus H$ are assumed to be potentially cheating), and for every choice of inputs of these honest players, a consistency condition satisfied by the outputs of these players is specified. Such a condition excludes certain combinations of output values or, equivalently, specifies the set $\mathcal{C}(H, \boldsymbol{x}_H)$ of admissible lists of output values. For any honest set H it is only guaranteed that the outputs of the players in H form some list in $\mathcal{C}(H, \boldsymbol{x}_H)$, with no further guarantee as to which of these lists is chosen. The smaller the set $\mathcal{C}(H, \boldsymbol{x}_H)$, the stronger is the consistency guarantee of the specification.

The monotonicity condition states that if one considers two settings with honest set H' and a larger honest set H, respectively, then the consistency guarantee for the players in H' cannot become worse by having more honest players. This is justified by the fact that in a (typical) protocol context, one of the options of a cheating player is to behave as if he were honest.

There are two ways of looking at consistency specifications. On one hand, one can assume one or several primitives satisfying certain consistency specifications as being given, defining a specific communication setting. A very common communication setting is the assumed availability of bilateral communication channels. On the other hand, one can consider a consistency specification as the goal of a protocol construction.

3.2 Some Examples

We give a few examples of consistency specifications.

Example 3. The weakest possible consistency specification is when no consistency guarantee is given, i.e., when $\mathcal{C}(H, \boldsymbol{x}_H) = \mathcal{R}_H$ for all H and $\boldsymbol{x}_H \in \mathcal{D}_H$. Obviously, a primitive satisfying only this trivial specification is useless.

Example 4. A bilateral authenticated channel from P_i to P_j, denoted $\text{AUTH}_{i,j}$, is a consistency specification (for the n players under consideration), where only P_i has an input (i.e., $\mathcal{R}_k = \{\bot\}$ for $k \neq i$) and where the only consistency constraint on the outputs is that P_j's output is equal to P_i's input, for any set H containing P_i and P_j. No guarantee is given for the honest players' outputs except for P_j (if he is honest). More formally, we have

$$\text{AUTH}_{i,j}(H, \boldsymbol{x}_H) = \left\{ \boldsymbol{y} \in \mathcal{R}_H \,\middle|\, i \in H \Rightarrow \boldsymbol{y}_{|j} = \boldsymbol{x}_{H|i} \right\}$$

for all $H \subseteq \mathcal{P}$.

Let AUTH denote the set of consistency specifications consisting of all $n(n-1)$ bilateral authenticated channels from any player to any other player. Note that AUTH could also be interpreted as a single consistency specification with a separate selection input for choosing the particular channel $\text{AUTH}_{i,j}$ to be used.

Example 5. A weaker primitive than $\text{AUTH}_{i,j}$ is a channel for which the ouput is not guaranteed to be equal to the input. For example, some error could be added to the input. Another example is a binary channel for which when the input is 0, then the output is also guaranteed to be 0, but if the input is 1, then the output can be 0 or 1.

Example 6. A broadcast channel from a sender $P_i \in \mathcal{P}$ to the remaining players $\mathcal{P} \setminus P_i$, secure for up to t cheaters among them, is denoted as BC_i^t and can be formalized as follows:

$$\text{BC}_i^t(H, \boldsymbol{x}_H) = \left\{ \boldsymbol{y} \in \mathcal{R}_H \,\middle|\, \exists v \left((\forall j \in H : \boldsymbol{y}_{|j} = v) \wedge (P_i \in H \Rightarrow v = \boldsymbol{x}_{H|i}) \right) \right\}$$

if $|H| \leq t$ and

$$\text{BC}_i^t(H, \boldsymbol{x}_H) = \mathcal{R}_H$$

if $|H| > t$.

Example 7. Detectable broadcast [FGH+02] among n players is a consistency specification where, again, only one player P_i has an input. If all players are honest ($H = \mathcal{P}$), then all players receive the sender's input, but if one or more players cheat, then all player either output the sender's input or a special failure symbol $\bot$. It is obvious how this specification can be formalized

Example 8. Two-threshold broadcast [FHHW03] is a consistency specification with two thresholds, t and T, satisfying $1 \leq t < T \leq n$. If the number of cheaters is at most t, then broadcast is achieved. In one of the flavors of two-threshold broadcast, consistency (but not correctness) is guaranteed even if the number of cheaters is between $t + 1$ and T. This means that all honest players receive the same value v, but even if the sender is honest, v need not be equal to the sender's input. It was proved in [FHHW03] that this is achievable if and only if $t + 2T < n$. Note that this is a strict generalization of the $t < n/3$ bound (when $t = T$).

Example 9. Consider a setting where a value in the domain $[1, \ldots, d]$ should be broadcast by a sender P_i. A less demanding goal is that all honest players' outputs lie in a certain (small) interval of length at most m, say, where m can depend on the number of cheaters. In other words, the fewer cheaters there are, the more accurate are the received values, capturing the idea of smooth security degradation. If the sender is honest, then the interval must contain his input value. It is an open problem to determine for which choices of parameters this consistency specification can be achieved.

3.3   A Partial Order on Consistency Specifications

It is natural to define the following relation between consistency specifications.

Definition 4. Consider two consistency specifications $\mathcal{C}$ and $\mathcal{C}'$ for the same player set $\mathcal{P}$, input domains $\mathcal{D}_1, \ldots, \mathcal{D}_n$ and output domains $\mathcal{R}_1, \ldots, \mathcal{R}_n$. Then $\mathcal{C}$ is *stronger* than $\mathcal{C}'$, denoted $\mathcal{C} \geq \mathcal{C}'$, if

$$\mathcal{C}(H, \boldsymbol{x}_H) \subseteq \mathcal{C}'(H, \boldsymbol{x}_H)$$

for all $H \subseteq \mathcal{P}$.

Note that this is only a partial order relation, i.e., two consistency specifications are generally incomparable.

4   Protocols and Reductions Among Consistency Specifications

A fundamental principle in computer science is to construct a complex system from simpler subsystems with well-defined interfaces and specifications. In our context, the basic question is if and how one can achieve a certain consistency primitive by invoking some weaker primitives.

Example 10. A trivial example is that one can use a broadcast primitive for a certain input (and output) domain $\mathcal{D}$ directly as the corresponding primitive for an input domain $\mathcal{D}' \subseteq \mathcal{D}$. For this purpose, the players must reject the output (and take as output a fixed default value in $\mathcal{D}'$, e.g. 0) if the actual received value is outside of $\mathcal{D}'$.

Example 11. Conversely, one can use a broadcast primitive multiple times to enlarge the domain. For example, one can directly use a binary ($\mathcal{D}_i = \{0, 1\}$) broadcast primitive k times to obtain the corresponding broadcast primitive for k-bit strings ($\mathcal{D}_i = \{0, 1\}^k$).

If a consistency primitive, described by consistency specification $\mathcal{C}$, can be achieved by some protocol invoking some weaker primitives described by consistency specifications $\mathcal{C}_1, \ldots, \mathcal{C}_m$ (for some m), one can say that $\mathcal{C}$ is *reduceable* to $\mathcal{C}_1, \ldots, \mathcal{C}_m$, denoted

$$\{\mathcal{C}_1, \ldots, \mathcal{C}_m\} \to \mathcal{C}.$$

As mentioned before, the main result of [LSP82] can be stated as

$$\text{AUTH} \to \text{BC}_i^{\lfloor n/3 \rfloor}$$

for any i. Similarly, the main result of [FM00] can be rephrased as

$$\text{BC}(3) \to \text{BC}_i^{\lfloor n/2 \rfloor}$$

for any i, where $\text{BC}(3)$ denotes the set of all broadcast channels from one sender to two other receivers. Note that, trivially, $\text{BC}(3) \to \text{AUTH}$ and hence authenticated channels need not explicitly be mentioned on the left side of the above formula. Note also that $\mathcal{C}_1 \geq \mathcal{C}_2$ trivially implies $\mathcal{C}_1 \to \mathcal{C}_2$.

A general protocol for achieving a consistency specification $\mathcal{C}$ with input domains $\mathcal{D}_1, \ldots, \mathcal{D}_n$ and output domains $\mathcal{R}_1, \ldots, \mathcal{R}_n$, based on some available consistency specifications $\mathcal{C}_1, \ldots, \mathcal{C}_m$, can be described as follows. The protocol consists of some ℓ rounds, where in each round one of the given primitives $\mathcal{C}_1, \ldots, \mathcal{C}_m$ is invoked. Let $\mathcal{C}^{(j)}$ be the primitive invoked in the jth round. In this round, each player computes the input to $\mathcal{C}^{(j)}$ as a function of his current state, which consists of the input to $\mathcal{C}$ as well as all the outputs of the previous calls to primitives $\mathcal{C}^{(1)}, \ldots, \mathcal{C}^{(j-1)}$. At the end of the protocol, each player computes the output (of $\mathcal{C}$) as a function of the final state.

Let us give a more formal description of a protocol π. Let the sequence of ℓ primitives $\mathcal{C}^{(1)}, \ldots, \mathcal{C}^{(\ell)}$ to be called in the protocol be fixed, and let the input and output domains of $\mathcal{C}^{(j)}$ be $\mathcal{D}_1^{(j)}, \ldots, \mathcal{D}_n^{(j)}$ and $\mathcal{R}_1^{(j)}, \ldots, \mathcal{R}_n^{(j)}$, respectively.

Definition 5. An ℓ-round protocol π for input domains $\mathcal{D}_1^{(j)}, \ldots, \mathcal{D}_n^{(j)}$ and output domains $\mathcal{R}_1^{(j)}, \ldots, \mathcal{R}_n^{(j)}$ consists of a list of functions $f_i^{(j)}$ for $1 \leq j \leq \ell$ and $1 \leq i \leq n$ as well as a list of functions g_i for $1 \leq i \leq n$, where

$$f_i^{(j)} : \mathcal{D}_i \times \mathcal{R}_i^{(1)} \times \cdots \times \mathcal{R}_i^{(j-1)} \to \mathcal{D}_i^{(j)}$$

and

$$g_i : \mathcal{D}_i \times \mathcal{R}_i^{(1)} \times \cdots \times \mathcal{R}_i^{(\ell)} \to \mathcal{R}_i.$$

Note that this definition refers only to the domains, but not to the primitives called in the protocol. The following definition captures when a certain protocol achieves a certain consistency specification when a given list of (domain-compatible) primitives is invoked.

Definition 6. Protocol π with a given schedule for calling primitives in the set $\{\mathcal{C}_1, \ldots, \mathcal{C}_m\}$ *reduces* $\mathcal{C}$ to $\{\mathcal{C}_1, \ldots, \mathcal{C}_m\}$, denoted

$$\{\mathcal{C}_1, \ldots, \mathcal{C}_m\} \xrightarrow{\pi} \mathcal{C},$$

if for all $H \subseteq \mathcal{P}$, for all $\boldsymbol{x}_H \in \mathcal{D}_H$, and for all choices of functions $f_i'^{(j)}$ and g_i' for replacing $f_i^{(j)}$ and g_i in π, for indices i with $P_i \notin H$, the list of output values of the players in H, when executing the modified protocol, is in $\mathcal{C}(H, \boldsymbol{x}_H)$.

The quantification over all functions $f_i'^{(j)}$ and g_i' for i with $P_i \notin H$ is needed because the cheating players can use arbitrary cheating strategies.

Acknowledgments. I would like to thank Reto Aschwanden, Matthias Fitzi, Martin Hirt, Fabian Kuhn, Renato Renner, Reto Strobl, and Jürg Wullschleger for interesting discussions.

References

[Asc01]   R. Aschwanden. Diploma Thesis, Dept. of Computer Science, ETH Zurich, May 2001.

[BGW88]   M. Ben-Or, S. Goldwasser, and A. Wigderson. Completeness theorems for non-cryptographic fault-tolerant distributed computation. In *Proc. 20th ACM Symposium on the Theory of Computing (STOC)*, pp. 1–10, 1988.

[CCD88]   D. Chaum, C. Crépeau, and I. Damgård. Multi-party unconditionally secure protocols (extended abstract). In *Proc. 20th ACM Symposium on the Theory of Computing (STOC)*, pp. 11–19, 1988.

[CFF+04] J. Considine, M. Fitzi, M. Franklin, L. A. Levin, U. Maurer, and D. Metcalf. Byzantine agreement in the partial broadcast model. Manuscript, July 2004.

[FGH+02] M. Fitzi, D. Gottesman, M. Hirt, T. Holenstein, and A. Smith. Detectable Byzantine agreement secure against faulty majorities. In *Proc. 21st ACM Symposium on Principles of Distributed Computing (PODC)*, July 2002.

[FHHW03] M. Fitzi, M. Hirt, T. Holenstein, and J. Wullschleger. Two-threshold broadcast and detectable multi-party computation. In *Advances in Cryptology — EUROCRYPT '03*, Lecture Notes in Computer Science, Springer-Verlag, vol. 2656, pp. 51-67, 2003.

[FHM99]   M. Fitzi, M. Hirt, and U. Maurer. General adversaries in unconditional multi-party computation, In *Advances in Cryptology – ASIACRYPT '99*, K.Y. Lam et al. (Eds.), Lecture Notes in Computer Science, Springer-Verlag, vol. 1716, pp. 232–246, 1999.

[FM98]   M. Fitzi and U. Maurer. Efficient Byzantine agreement secure against general adversaries. In *Distributed Computing — DISC '98*, Lecture Notes in Computer Science, Springer-Verlag, vol. 1499, pp. 134–148, 1998.

[FM00]   M. Fitzi and U. Maurer. From partial consistency to global broadcast. In *Proc. 32nd Annual ACM Symposium on Theory of Computing (STOC '00)*, pp. 494–503. ACM Press, 2000.

[GMW87]   O. Goldreich, S. Micali, and A. Wigderson. How to play any mental game — a completeness theorem for protocols with honest majority. In *Proc. 19th ACM Symposium on the Theory of Computing (STOC)*, pp. 218–229, 1987.

[HM97]   M. Hirt and U. Maurer. Complete characterization of adversaries tolerable in secure multi-party computation. *Proc. 16th ACM Symposium on Principles of Distributed Computing (PODC)*, pp. 25–34, Aug. 1997.

[LSP82]   L. Lamport, R. Shostak, and M. Pease. The Byzantine generals problem. *ACM Transactions on Programming Languages and Systems*, vol. 4, pp. 382–401, July 1982.

[KS01]   F. Kuhn and R. Strobl. Towards a general theory for consistency primitives. Term project report, Dept. of Computer Science, ETH Zurich, Nov. 2000.

[Mau02]   U. Maurer. Secure multi-party computation made simple. In *Security in Communication Networks (SCN'02)*, G. Persiano (Ed.), Lecture Notes in Computer Science, Springer-Verlag, vol. 2576, pp. 14–28, 2003.

[RB89]   T. Rabin and M. Ben-Or. Verifiable secret-sharing and multiparty protocols with honest majority. In *Proc. 21st ACM Symposium on the Theory of Computing (STOC)*, pp. 73–85, 1989.

Fault-Tolerant Storage
in a Dynamic Environment*

Uri Nadav and Moni Naor

Dept. of Computer Science and Applied Mathematics,
The Weizmann Institute of Science
{uri.nadav,moni.naor}@weizmann.ac.il

Abstract. We suggest a file storage system for a dynamic environment
where servers may join and leave the system. Our construction has a
$O(\sqrt{n})$ write complexity, $O(\sqrt{n}\log n)$ read complexity and a *constant*
data blowup-ratio, where n represents the number of processors in the
network. Our construction is fault-tolerant against an adversary that can
crash $\theta(n)$ processors of her choice while having slightly less *adaptive*
queries than the reader.
When both the reader and the adversary are nonadaptive we derive lower
bounds on the read complexity, write complexity and data blowup ratio.
We show these bounds are tight using a simple storage system construction, based on an ϵ-intersecting quorum system.

1 Introduction

We deal with methods for constructing distributed storage systems over peer-
to-peer networks, i.e. loosely coupled environments where servers join and leave
the system dynamically. Such networks are subject to various types of faults and
malicious attacks and hence providing even simple functionalities is a challenge.
Such a *'storage system'* should provide a distributed file system on a set of
processors (computers with storage capabilities), intended to store multiple files
and to be accessed by many users. The two natural components of such a system
are the *storage* mechanism that indicates how to distribute files on processors
and the *retrieval* mechanism that allows file retrieval.

The storage process is composed of two steps. First, selecting processors that
store data, and second, encoding a file into bits, which are then written to the
selected processors. The retrieval consists of reading bits from processors and
decoding them, so as to obtain the stored files. The procedures for selecting the
processors to which data is written and from which data is read are referred to
as *'write strategy'* and *'read strategy'* respectively. We distinguish between nonadaptive and adaptive strategies. In a nonadaptive strategy the set of processors
is determined prior to any access, whereas in an adaptive strategy, some queries
are allowed before the set is determined. A storage system is considered resilient
to an adversarial attack, if each file stored can be retrieved after the attack.

---

* Research supported by a grant from the Israel Science Foundation

R. Guerraoui (Ed.): DISC 2004, LNCS 3274, pp. 390–404, 2004.
© Springer-Verlag Berlin Heidelberg 2004

This paper deals with the fault-tolerance of storage systems in an adversarial model. The failing processors are chosen maliciously as opposed to a random fault model, where each processor independently fails with some constant probability. The adversary can be characterized by the amount of control it has over choosing the faulty processors and the amount of control it has over their behavior(fail-stop, Byzantine). Note that the ability to choose the faulty processors does not imply total control over their behavior. The type of faults considered here are fail-stop (or data deletion). A major issue in the adversarial fault model is the degree of adaptiveness the adversary has in selecting which processors to delete and query. One can consider a whole spectrum of adaptive behaviors. Most of our results consider an adversary who is allowed to delete the storage of up to t processors of her choice, selected in a nonadaptive manner.

We define a storage system as fault-tolerant if each file can be reconstructed with high probability (w.h.p.) after faults have been caused. This model characterizes better tolerance against a *censor*, because a censor may wish to target a small number of files and not only eliminate access to files on average.

We first consider storage systems in a static network model, for which the set of processors is fixed. We then proceed to discuss dynamic networks, where a major problem is finding processors that currently are in the network. Several designs [6, 11, 15, 17, 18] deal with this problem.

1.1   Definitions and Preliminaries

A *quorum system (QS)* $\mathcal{Q}$ over a universe U of processors, is a collection of subsets of U, every two of which intersect. The subsets in the collection are often referred to as quorums. An *access strategy* μ, for a quorum system $\mathcal{Q}$, is a probability distribution over the quorums in $\mathcal{Q}$, i.e. $\sum_{Q \in \mathcal{Q}} \mu(Q) = 1$. An access strategy can be thought of as a method for choosing a quorum. An *ϵ-intersecting quorum system*, as defined by Malkhi et al.[8], is a tuple $(\mathcal{Q}, \mu)$ of a set system and an access strategy μ, such that $Pr[Q \cap Q' \neq \emptyset] > 1 - \epsilon$, where the probability is taken with respect to μ.

Quorum systems are often used in distributed computation. A distributed storage system can be trivially constructed using any quorum system $\mathcal{Q}$ with an access strategy μ: To store a file, a quorum is selected in accordance with μ and a copy of the file is written to each of the processors in the chosen quorum. The retrieval scheme consists of selecting a quorum in accordance with μ and querying each of the processors in the chosen quorum for the file which is being retrieved. By the intersection property of quorum systems, the reconstruction of a file is then guaranteed. Notice that the same construction holds for any ϵ-intersecting quorum system $(\mathcal{Q}, \mu)$, in which case the reconstruction is guaranteed with probability at least $1 - \epsilon$. The reverse claim is also true in the sense that every storage system can serve as a quorum system, since a set of processors which is used for writing a file must intersect every set of processors that is used for reading that file. In Section 2 we show that no storage system can do better than this simple construction, in a nonadaptive model. In Section 3 we present a storage system that outperforms this quorum based solution, in terms of data blowup ratio, in a slightly modified model. This is the reason we define and investigate storage systems rather than just deal with QS.

The *load* on a system of processors induced by a strategy μ, defined in [14], captures the probability of accessing the busiest processor by μ. The load $\mathcal{L}(i)$ induced by a strategy on a processor $i \in U$ is the probability that processor i is chosen by the strategy, i.e. $\mathcal{L}(i) = Pr_\mu[i \in Q]$. The load induced by the strategy μ is $\mathcal{L}(\mu) = \max_{i \in U} \mathcal{L}(i)$. For a quorum system $\mathcal{S}$, the load $\mathcal{L}(\mathcal{S})$ is the minimum load induced by a strategy, over all strategies.

Storage systems are measured by the following parameters:

Write/Read Complexity: The average number of processors accessed by the write/read strategies of the storage system, in a write/read operation of a single file.

Blowup-Ratio: The ratio between the total number of bits used in the storage of a a file, and its size.

Resiliency: The strongest fault model in which the system is resilient.

A design goal of storage systems is to minimize the write/read complexity and the blowup-ratio. However, as we shall see, these goals are somewhat contradictory when the resiliency of the system is taken into considerations.

1.2   A Simple Example of a Fault-Tolerant Storage System

Malkhi et al. give in [8] an explicit construction for an ϵ- intersecting quorum system. The quorums are all the subsets of U of size $\ell\sqrt{n}$, where ℓ depends only on ϵ. The access strategy is the uniform distribution over all quorums. The storage system constructed using this quorum system has a $\ell\sqrt{n}$ blowup-ratio and write/read complexity.

Suppose a nonadaptive adversary can delete a set of processors T of size δn of her choice, where $0 < \delta < 1$ is a constant. Because of the independence between the faulty set T, and the quorums chosen for storage and retrieval, w.h.p. no more than δ fraction of a quorum is deleted. It is then possible to select ℓ in accordance with δ so as to maintain the ϵ-intersection property in the presence of such faults. In [1] Abraham et al. show how to adapt a quorum in this construction to a dynamic environment as processors join and leave, guaranteeing an ϵ-intersection property.

Another virtue of this storage system is that it is resilient even against an adaptive adversary. An adversary that reads the memory of some processors and knows what files they store, gains no information on the distribution of a file among the remaining processors.

1.3   Related Work

There are many models for the problem of fault-tolerant data networks. The works of [12, 17, 18] yield fault-tolerant storage systems for a dynamic environment, In a random fault model. In a much more powerful adversarial model, the adversary knows the memory content of each processor and may corrupt a constant fraction of the processors. In this case the storage system can be thought of as an error correcting code, where the message is made of the all files stored in the system concatenated together. The write complexity of such a scheme which is fault-tolerant to $\Omega(n)$ faults is $\Omega(n)$, from properties of error correcting codes. For this reason this approach is less appropriate in a dynamic environment.

Rabin defines an Information Dispersal Algorithm [16] as a storage scheme of a file over n processors, such that every m of them can recover the file. This scheme seems wasteful in our case since the dispersed information is made of all the files stored in the system. A single file cannot generally be retrieved from fewer than m processors.

There exist error correcting codes that enable the reconstruction of a single symbol of a message by looking at a limited number of bits of a (possibly) corrupted encoding. Katz and Trevisan [5] show that a code which is locally decodable from a constant number of queries, cannot have a constant rate.

In [3] a content addressable network is proposed in which after an adversarial removal of a constant fraction of the processors only a small fraction of the files are not accessible. However, a censor that wishes to eliminate access to a specific file can do it by crashing $\log n$ processors. In contrast we are concerned with a model in which each file can be recovered w.h.p. after adversarial deletions.

1.4 Results and Paper Organization

Our results split under two categories:

Good news: When the read strategy is slightly more powerful than the adversary (for example by using adaptive queries), a construction of a fault-tolerant storage system with constant blowup-ratio, write complexity $O(\sqrt{n})$ and read complexity $O(\sqrt{n}\log n)$ is given. We also present a storage system where the read complexity is dynamically adjusted to the number of faults so as to allow early stopping of the read process in the case less faults occur. These constructions are implemented in a dynamic environment(peer-to-peer like), yielding a fault-tolerant storage system with constant blowup-ratio.

Bad news: No fault-tolerant storage system with nonadaptive read strategy can do better than the construction discussed in Section 1.2. In particular, it will be shown that there exists a tradeoff between write complexity and read complexity, and that the above construction is optimal in this case. It is further shown that there exists a tradeoff between the blowup-ratio and the read complexity. Specifically, nonadaptive storage systems that are fault-tolerant against t nonadaptive deletions and have a blowup-ratio ρ, must have read complexity $\Omega(\frac{t}{\rho})$.

The remainder of this paper is organized in the following way. Section 2 discusses fault-tolerant storage system for nonadaptive retrieval model. In Section 3 we present a fault-tolerant storage system, with an adaptive read strategy that maintains a constant blowup-ratio. Both these sections deal with the storage of a single file in a static network. In Section 4 we discuss an adaptation of the above scheme to a dynamic model. We note that all proofs are omitted from this version due to lack of space[1].

2   Storage Systems with Nonadaptive Retrieval

This section deals with the analysis of storage systems with nonadaptive retrieval schemes. A nonadaptive read strategy determines which processors to probe prior to accessing any processor. A tradeoff between write complexity and read complexity is shown, and a lower bound on the blowup ratio is given.

2.1   The Nonadaptive Retrieval Model

We begin by giving a formal definition of a storage system with nonadaptive retrieval, and of fault-tolerance in the nonadaptive adversary model. The storage of a file is done in accordance with some *write strategy*, which defines the number of bits that are stored in each processor. Similarly, the retrieval of a file is done in accordance with some *read strategy*, which defines the set of processors from which data is read in the retrieval process.

Definition 1 (Write/Read Strategy). *A write strategy μ_w for a universe U of size n is a probability distribution on $\mathbb{N}^n$. A read strategy μ_r for U is a probability distribution on $\{0,1\}^n$.*

Let q_w, q_r be the vectors generated by write and read strategies respectively. The inner product of q_w and q_r, denoted by $\langle q_r, q_w \rangle$ represents the total number of bits read during the retrieval process. The support set of a vector is the set of processors involved in a write/read operation represented by it. We sometimes abuse notation by alternating between a vector and its support set, and denote by $|q|$ the size of the support set. We define the *read/write complexity* of a system as the expected number of processors accessed during a read/write operation.

The storage of a file includes memory allocation in a set of selected processors, and encoding of the file into the allocated storage space. The retrieval of a file f includes reading encoded data from the memories of a selected set of processors and decoding this information to retrieve f. A processor that holds no data about f can also be a member of the probed set. In this case it returns *null*.

Definition 2 (Nonadaptive Storage System). *A k-storage system is a 4-tuple $(\mu_w, \mu_r, \mathcal{E}, \mathcal{D})$ consisting of*

- *A write strategy μ_w and a read strategy μ_r.*
- *Encoding mapping: $\mathcal{E}(f, q_w) \mapsto (x_1, \ldots, x_n)$, where $q_w \in \mathbb{N}^n$ and*
  $$x_i \in \begin{cases} \{0,1\}^{q_w(i)}, & q_w(i) > 0, \\ \{*\}, & otherwise. \end{cases}$$
  This mapping defines the coding rule from a file of size k bits and a list of memory allocations into processors' memories. A '$*$' represents no data is stored in a processor.

---

[1] A full version of this paper that includes all proofs is available at authors' homepages.

- *Decoding (reconstruction) mapping: $\mathcal{D}(x_1, \ldots, x_n) \mapsto \{0,1\}^k$. where x_i is either a bit string or one of the symbols $\{\phi, *\}$. A '*' in the ith parameter represents that no data was written to the ith processor. A 'ϕ' in the ith parameter represents that the ith processor was not queried.*

Let π denote the following projection function from a list of n parameters $(x_1, \ldots, x_n)$ and a characteristic vector $q \in \{0,1\}^n$ into a list of n items such that the *ith* item is $(\pi((x_1, \ldots, x_n), q))_i = \begin{cases} x_i, & q(i) = 1, \\ \phi, & \text{otherwise.} \end{cases}$. The projection of $(x_1, \ldots x_n)$ by q models that only processors which belong to the support set of q were queried.

The result of the process of encoding a file f using a list of memory allocations q_w and then reading the memories of processors using q_r and decoding, is described as $\mathcal{D}(\pi(\mathcal{E}(f, q_w), q_r))$. The process ends in a recovery of f if $\mathcal{D}(\pi(\mathcal{E}(f, q_w), q_r)) \equiv f$.

Definition 3 (Nonadaptive (ϵ, k)-Storage System). *An (ϵ, k) storage system is a storage system $\mathcal{S} = (\mu_w, \mu_r, \mathcal{E}, \mathcal{D})$ such that:*

$$\forall f \in \{0,1\}^k , Pr[\mathcal{D}(\pi(\mathcal{E}(f, q_w), q_r)) \equiv f] > 1 - \epsilon ,$$

where $q_w \sim \mu_w, q_r \sim \mu_r$ are independent random variables.

Information can be encoded implicitly in the way bits are allocated among processors and not only in the stored bits themselves. The number of saved bits encoded this way can have only relatively small contribution, when the number of processors used for writing/reading is small enough compared to the number of stored bits. We therefore choose to ignore storage systems that make use of such implicit encodings. We regard only storage systems in which the decoding procedure of the retrieval process uses only bits which were explicitly stored. These are systems in which the memory allocation vector (q_w) is distributed independently of the content of the stored file f. In this case Theorem 1 states a necessary information theoretic condition on the read and write strategies of an (ϵ, k) storage system. Such a system must w.h.p. read at least k bits of information during retrieval. Definition 4 captures this property of a pair of read and write strategies.

Definition 4 ((ϵ, k)-Intersection Property). *Let (μ_w, μ_r) be a pair of a write strategy and a read strategy on a set of processors. We say that μ_r, μ_w satisfy the (ϵ, k)-intersection property, if $Pr[\langle q_w, q_r \rangle > k] > 1 - \epsilon$, where $q_w \sim \mu_w$ and $q_r \sim \mu_r$ are independent random variables.*

Theorem 1. *Let $\mathcal{S} = (\mu_w, \mu_r, \mathcal{E}, \mathcal{D})$ be an (ϵ, k) storage system, where the vector of memory allocations, distributed as μ_w, is independent of the content of a file f. Then the write and read strategies (μ_w, μ_r) must satisfy the $(2\epsilon, k)$ intersection property.*

This condition, however, is insufficient. In order to ensure recovery, the retrieval process must yield the correct k bits, i.e. the encoding and decoding schemes must be considered. It turns out that the necessary condition is 'almost' sufficient. Suppose each stored symbol represents the solution to a linear equation over the k bits of a file. To reconstruct the file, it is sufficient to collect the solutions to a set of equations of rank k. It is known that w.h.p, $(1+\gamma)k$ random linear equations over k variables, have a rank k, where γ is a small constant. Hence, by simply storing a random linear combination of the file's bits at each stored symbol, it is sufficient to collect $(1 + \gamma)k$ symbols. Naor and Roth [10] investigate the problem of file distribution in a network. The problem there is different, but the coding methods they suggest can also be used in this context.

For this reason we do not consider any specific coding scheme and simply investigate the pair (μ_w, μ_r) of write and read strategies for which the (ϵ, k)-intersection property holds.

The following definition addresses fault-tolerant storage systems in the non-adaptive adversary model.

Definition 5 (Nonadaptive Fault-Tolerant Storage System). *A k-storage system with write and read strategies μ_w, μ_r is said to be (ϵ, t)-fault-tolerant, if for any set of deleted processors T of size less than t, the induced system (the write and read strategies restricted to $U \setminus T$), satisfies the (ϵ, k)-intersection property. We denote such a system as a (t, ϵ, k)-storage system.*

2.2   Read Write Tradeoff of a Storage System

Given a write strategy μ_w, we are interested in the best read strategy μ_r, in terms of read complexity, such that (μ_w, μ_r) satisfy the (ϵ, k) intersection property.

Lemma 1. *Let μ_w be a write strategy on a universe U of size n. For every read strategy μ_r such that (μ_w, μ_r) satisfy the (ϵ, k)-Intersection Property and $q_r \sim \mu_r$ we have*

$$E[|q_r|] > \frac{1 - \epsilon}{\mathcal{L}(\mu_w)}.$$

Next we turn to analyze fault-tolerant storage systems. We show that in such systems, where the retrieval scheme is nonadaptive, there exists a tradeoff between the read complexity and the write complexity. This is shown by using the power of the adversary to delete any set of size t, and specifically the set composed of the t most write loaded processors.

Theorem 2. *Let (μ_r, μ_w) be the write strategy and read strategy of a (t, ϵ, k) fault-tolerant storage system. Then*

$$E[|q_r|] \cdot E[|q_w|] \geq (1 - \epsilon)t ,$$

where $q_r \sim \mu_r$ and $q_w \sim \mu_w$ are independent of each other.

Sometimes it is desirable to require that the number of processors from which data is retrieved exceeds some threshold (τ). For example when the problem of Byzantine faults is considered and addressed using a majority vote [7, 9]. In that case, the intersection property is defined as $Pr\big[|Q_r \cap Q_w| > \tau\big] > 1 - \epsilon$, where Q_r, Q_w are distributed as μ_r, μ_w respectively. A similar result to Theorem 2 holds in that case.

Theorem 3. *Let (μ_r, μ_w) be the write and read strategies of a (t, ϵ, k) fault-tolerant storage system with threshold τ. Then $E[\|q_r\|] \cdot E[\|q_w\|] \geq (1 - \epsilon)\tau t$, where $q_r \sim \mu_r$ and $q_w \sim \mu_w$ are independent of each other.*

2.3 Bounding the Blowup-Ratio

We bound the minimum number of bits used for the storage of a single file in the nonadaptive model. The following memory model for a processor is considered. It is assumed that each file is encoded and stored separately. In this model a file can be inserted or modified without reading any other file. This assumption (which is implicit in the nonadaptive model) simplifies the storage system and keeps it oblivious to past operations. In that sense, this model suits storage systems for dynamic and scalable networks.

The total storage used for a file is the number of bits assigned over all processors. The blowup-ratio of a storage system is the ratio between the average total storage, and the size of a file which is denoted by k.

Definition 6 (blowup-ratio). *The blowup-ratio $\rho(S)$ of an (ϵ, k) storage system S with a write strategy μ_w, is defined as $\rho(S) \triangleq E_{\mu_w}[\|\|q_w\|\|]/k$, where $\|\cdot\|$ denotes the L_1-norm.*

Obviously it is desirable to have as small as possible blowup-ratio. However, the next theorem shows there is a tradeoff between the read complexity and the blowup-ratio when the reader is nonadaptive.

Theorem 4. *Let S be a (t, ϵ, k) storage system with a read strategy μ_r, then:*

$$\rho(S) > (1 - \epsilon)\frac{t}{E[\|q_r\|]} \ , \ \text{ where } q_r \sim \mu_r.$$

In particular, when $t = \theta(n)$ and the blowup-ratio is a constant, then the read complexity must be $\theta(n)$. In the next section it is shown that this lower bound is outperformed when considering an *adaptive* reader.

3 Fault-Tolerant Adaptive Storage System

In this section we consider a different model in which the adversary is (almost) nonadaptive and the retrieval scheme makes its queries in a logarithmic number of adaptive rounds. For starters, consider a model in which the adversary can make no queries at all (fully nonadaptive) and the reader can query a single processor, before selecting a set to read from. In this model, same results as in the random-fault model can be achieved. The intuition is as follows: A secret permutation π on the processors is stored at each processor. Every read/write operation intended on i is applied to $\pi(i)$ (the reader knows π after he queries a single processor). Since the adversary, being nonadaptive, is unaware of π, the faults look random from the storage system point of view. This solution is simple but not very interesting as it immediately fails when the adversary is given the option to query a small number of processors before selecting the faulty set. Also, selecting and maintaining π requires a centralized solution we wish to avoid. However, this example shows that an advantage in the use of adaptive queries can help a lot.

In contrast, we present in this section a storage system which is fault-tolerant in a slightly enhanced adversarial model, where the adversary is allowed to have a small number of adaptive queries. The 'secret' which is kept from the adversary is only the location of files, no secret key is assumed in our solution. This keeps the system easy to implement in a dynamic and scalable environment.

The storage system we come up with has $O(\sqrt{n})$ write-complexity, $O(\sqrt{n}\log n)$ read-complexity and a constant blowup-ratio. It is resilient against $\theta(n)$ faults in the above model. Adaptive queries to a small set of processors allow to find a large fraction of the ones used for storage. It follows from Theorem 3 that this is not possible in the nonadaptive retrieval model.

3.1   Small Load Implies Some Resiliency Against a Nonadaptive Adversary

We wish to upper bound the probability that a nonadaptive adversary succeeds in failing a set chosen by a write strategy. We show that as long as the load of a write strategy is small enough, a large fraction of a write set survives a nonadaptive attack, with some constant probability.

Suppose that a reader wishes to find a single live element of a write set, sampled from a write strategy μ_w with an almost optimal load of $O(\frac{1}{\sqrt{n}})$ [14]. It follows from the birthday paradox that a randomly chosen set of processors, of size $O(\frac{1}{\mathcal{L}(\mu_w)})$ intersects a previously sampled write set with some constant probability. The intersection is almost uniformly distributed over the elements of the write set. Theorem 5 shows that even after a nonadaptive adversary crashes some constant fraction of the network, with a constant probability at least half the elements of a write set survive. It follows from Lemma 1 that such a reader has an optimal read complexity, up to a constant.

Theorem 5. *Let U be a universe of processors of size n. Let μ be a write strategy on U with load $\mathcal{L}$ and let $Q \sim \mu$. For every set $T \subseteq U$ of faulty processors,*

$$E\big[|T \cap Q|\big] \leq |T| \cdot \mathcal{L} \ .$$

In the above setting, the probability that a constant fraction of a write set survives is

Corollary 1. $Pr_\mu\big[|T \cap Q| > \lambda E[|Q|]\big] \ < \ \frac{|T|\mathcal{L}}{\lambda E[|Q|]} \ .$

In particular, for a system with a fixed write set size $\sqrt{n}$, and write load $\frac{1}{\sqrt{n}}$ that faces up to δn faults, the probability that the majority of processors in a write set are crashed is upper bounded by 2δ.

3.2   A Generic Scheme for a Fault-Tolerant Storage System with a Constant Blowup Ratio

We propose a generic scheme with an adaptive retrieval algorithm which is fault-tolerant in the nonadaptive adversarial model. We saw that when the write load is close to optimal, then with a constant probability a constant fraction of a set chosen by the write strategy survives a nonadaptive attack. Suppose that an adaptive reader can find those surviving elements with a relatively small number of read operations. A pair of such a writer and reader is used to create a fault-tolerant storage system with a constant blowup ratio in the following way: A file f is encoded into ℓ pieces of data, such that any $\frac{\ell}{2}$ of them suffice for reconstructing f. An erasure coding scheme with a constant blowup ratio (e.g. Reed-Solomon) or an IDA scheme [16] is used for this purpose. These pieces of data are then distributed to the ℓ members of a selected write set.

Now, let a nonadaptive adversary crash a δ fraction of the processors in the network, where $0 \leq \delta < \frac{1}{2}$. Corollary 1 implies that a write set chosen by an optimal load strategy, has a probability of at least $1 - 2\delta$ that half of the write set survived. An adaptive reader can then identify the surviving members and reconstruct the file. To ensure reconstruction with an arbitrarily high probability it suffices to write to a constant number of write sets, chosen independently.

The pair of write and read strategies of the ϵ-intersecting QS [8] does not suit this scheme. While having a small write load, a reader must read a constant fraction of the network in order to find a large intersection with a write set (this fact is what makes it resilient against an adaptive adversary). The paths QS presented in [14] was shown to have an optimal load. The elements of a single path can be found with $O(\sqrt{n})$ queries in $O(\sqrt{n})$ rounds, in the presence of faults. Thus, it can be used to create a fault-tolerant storage system with $O(\sqrt{n})$ read and write complexity and a constant blowup ratio. Next we show a write strategy with complexity $O(\sqrt{n})$ and an adaptive reader with complexity $O(\sqrt{n} \log n)$ that requires only $O(\log n)$ rounds.

In this model, when a storage system is $\theta(n)$-fault-tolerant, we cannot expect the product of the read complexity and the write complexity to be $o(n)$. This is due to the fact that adaptiveness does not help before the first element is found. Thus, Theorem 2 can be used to show this lower bound.

3.3   Adaptive Storage System Based on the 'AndOr' System

We present a pair of write strategy and adaptive read algorithm, based on the 'AndOr' quorum system shown in [14] which has an an optimal load of $O(\frac{1}{\sqrt{n}})$. The quorum size is $\sqrt{n}$, and the read algorithm finds a write set in $O(\log n)$ rounds, using $O(\sqrt{n} \log n)$ queries.

We recall the construction of the 'AndOr' system. Consider a complete binary tree of height h, rooted at *root*, and identify the 2^h leaves of the tree with systems processors. We define two collections of subsets of the set of processors, using the following recursive definitions:

(i) For a leaf v, $ANDset(v) = ORset(v) = \{\{v\}\}$.
(ii) $ANDset(v) = \{S \cup R | S \in ORset(v.left) \wedge R \in ORset(v.right)\}$.
(iii) $ORset(v) = ANDset(v.left) \cup ANDset(v.right)$

The AndOr quorum system is then composed of the collections ANDset(*root*) and ORset(*root*). A natural recursive procedure can be used to generate a set $S \in$ ANDset(*root*). The procedure visits nodes of the tree, beginning at the root and propagating downwards. It considers the nodes of the tree as AND/OR gates (on even/odd levels). When visiting an AND gate it continues to both its children, and when visiting an OR gate one of its children is chosen. The leaves visited by the procedure form S. A similar procedure generates a set $R \in$ ORset(*root*). The AndOr structure induces the following properties:

Lemma 2. *(from [14]) Consider a complete binary tree of height h rooted at root. Let $S \in ANDset(root)$ and $R \in ORset(root)$ then $|S \cap R| = 1$, $|R| = 2^{\lfloor \frac{h}{2} \rfloor}$ and $|S| = 2^{\lfloor \frac{h+1}{2} \rfloor}$.*

Adaptive Read Strategy for Finding a Complete and Set. We assume a writer uniformly picks a set $S \in$ ANDset(*root*) to serve as a write set. A uniform sample can be obtained by choosing *left* or *right* with equal probability, in every OR gate during the activation of the recursive procedure. A reader wishes to identify all the members of S.

By probing a processor, the reader finds out whether it belongs to S or not. A single element of S can be identified by probing the $O(\sqrt{n})$ members of an arbitrary set $R \in$ ORset(*root*), as follows from Lemma 2 . After finding a single processor $s \in S$, a large fraction of the original tree can be pruned, as s reveals the choices made at the OR gates on the path from *root* to s. After pruning, the remainder of the tree is composed of complete binary trees of heights $0, 2, 4, \ldots, \log n - 2$. The algorithm is then recursively applied.

Proposition 1. *The read complexity of the algorithm for identifying all the members of $S \in ANDset(root)$, where root is the root of a tree of height h, is $O(\sqrt{n} \log n)$, where $n = 2^h$. The number of adaptive rounds is $\log n$.*

Adaptive Read Strategy in the Presence of Faults. We now assume the existence of up to δn crash faults in the network caused by a nonadaptive adversary, where $0 < \delta < \frac{1}{2}$. Let $S \in$ ANDset(*root*) be chosen at random as described earlier. Corollary 1 implies that with a constant probability at least half the elements of S are not deleted. The reader's algorithm is now required to identify those surviving elements. In this case, finding an element of the chosen S, cannot be guaranteed by querying an arbitrary set in ORset(*root*), as the element in the intersection may be crashed. To overcome this, we may randomly probe processors for membership. To guarantee success with an arbitrarily high probability, it suffices to query $O(\sqrt{n})$ elements as discussed in Section 3.1. The read complexity of the new algorithm remains $O(\sqrt{n} \log n)$. Combining the above write strategy and the adaptive read algorithm, with the generic scheme of Section 3.2, yields the following theorem.

Theorem 6. *The system described above is a $\theta(n)$-fault-tolerant, adaptive storage system, with a constant blowup-ratio, $O(\sqrt{n})$ write complexity and $O(\sqrt{n}\log n)$ read complexity. The number of adaptive rounds is $\log(n)$.*

Theorem 6 considers the fault-tolerance of the described storage system in the (fully) nonadaptive adversarial model. The fault-tolerance properties of the system are preserved even in the presence of a much stronger adversary with the power to query a $o(\sqrt{n})$ processors prior to the selection of the set to crash. Theorem 6 remains correct under this 'almost nonadaptive' adversarial model. The proof relies on the fact that by querying $o(\sqrt{n})$ processors, an adversary is unlikely to identify more than a constant number of elements of a write set.

Dynamically Adjusting the Retrieval Scheme to the Number of Faults.

A drawback of the AndOr storage system, is that even in the case when much fewer than $\theta(n)$ faults occur the read complexity can not be reduced. In [2] Alvisi et al show how a Byzantine quorum system dynamically adjusts to the actual number of faulty processors. It allows them to operate with relatively small quorums in the absence of faults, increasing the quorum size as faults appear. Our system can also be improved so that it reads significantly fewer elements, when there are fewer than $\theta(n)$ faults. The cost of this feature is a $O(\log n)$ blowup-ratio and a multiplicative constant to the write complexity. Unlike [2], no explicit knowledge of the number of faults is required.

The following modifications to the AndOr structure are required: First, each node in the tree represents a processor (not only the leaves). Second, the definitions of the ANDset and ORset collections of sets are changed so as to include all nodes visited by the recursive procedure that generates a set in these collections.

(i) For a leaf v, $ANDset'(v) = ORset'(v) = \{\{v\}\}$.
(ii) $ANDset'(v) = \{\{v\} \cup R \cup S \mid R \in ORset'(v.left) \wedge S \in ORset'(v.right)\}$.
(iii) $ORset'(v) = \{\{v\} \cup S \mid S \in ANDset'(v.left) \cup ANDset'(v.right)\}$

Let $S \in \text{ANDset}'(root)$. We note that the size of S does not change by more than a multiplicative constant. Let S_i denote the members of S in the ith level of the tree. For each i, S_i can be thought of as a set belonging to $\text{ANDset}(root)$ defined on a tree with i levels. The write process encodes a file separately into the set S_i for each i as in the original scheme. This way, reading from the members of a single set S_i (for each i) suffices to reconstruct the file. We therefore achieve $O(\log n)$ blowup-ratio and $O(\sqrt{n})$ write complexity. During retrieval we seek the sets $S_0, \ldots, S_h$ in an increasing order. The members of a set S_i can be identified using the algorithm described in Section 3.3 applied on the tree of height i. The retrieval process stops when a set with a sufficient number of surviving elements is found. It follows from Theorem 6 that when there are g faults, such a set will be found at level of height $\lceil \log g \rceil$ i.e, enough members of $S_{\lceil \log g \rceil}$ survive and can be found. Hence the read complexity is $O(\sqrt{g}\log g)$.

Theorem 7. *The system described above is a $\theta(n)$-fault-tolerant, adaptive storage system, with $O(\log n)$ blowup-ratio, $O(\sqrt{n})$ write complexity and a read complexity that does not exceed $O(\sqrt{g}\log g)$ when up to g faults occur.*

4   Dynamic Implementation of the AndOr Storage System

In this section we adapt the storage system of Section 3 to a dynamic environment using the distance halving (DH) dynamic hash table (DHT) of [11]. We remark that the AndOr system can be implemented on other dynamic hash tables such as Koorde [4] but the analysis is kept much simpler using the continuous approach of the DH graph.

4.1   Some Properties of the Distance Halving Dynamic Network

We recall the construction of the DH-network from [11]. We first define the DH-graph G_c. The vertex set of G_c is the unit interval $I \triangleq [0, 1)$. The edge set of G_c is defined by the following functions: $\ell(y) \triangleq \frac{y}{2}$, $r(y) \triangleq \frac{y+1}{2}$ where $y \in I$, ℓ abbreviates 'left' and r abbreviates 'right'. The edge set of G_c is then $\{(y, \ell(y)), (y, r(y)) \mid y \in I\}$.

Denote by $\boldsymbol{x}$ a set of n points in I. The point x_i is the id. of the ith processor, in a network of n processors. The points of $\boldsymbol{x}$ divide I into n segments. Define the segment of x_i to be $s(x_i) = [x_i, x_{i+1})$ $(i = 1, \ldots, n-1)$ and $s(x_n) = [x_n, 1) \cup [0, x_1)$. In the DH-network, each processor u_i is associated with the segment $s(x_i)$. If a point y is in $s(x_i)$ we say that u_i covers y. Notice that each point $y \in I$ is covered by exactly one processor. When data is written to y it is being stored in the processor that covers y, and remains stored in a single processor throughout the lifetime of the DH-network (when no faults occur). A pair of processors (u_i, u_j) are connected if there exists an edge (y, z) in the DH-graph, such that $y \in s(x_i)$ and $z \in s(x_j)$.

To implement the AndOr system on a DH-network we define the notion of a tree on the DH-graph. The $\ell(\cdot)$ and $r(\cdot)$ functions induce an embedding of a complete binary tree on every point x in I, in a natural way. The left child of a point x is $\ell(x)$ and the right child is $r(x)$. We observe that the distance between every two adjacent points, that represent leaves on the same level ℓ is exactly $\frac{1}{2^\ell}$. Note however, that the distance between two points that represent the two direct children of the same node, is $\frac{1}{2}$. We note that the same tree structure was used in [11] to relieve 'hot spots' (points with high load).

As is common in DHT literature, we make the simplifying assumption that an underlying layer takes care of concurrent operations of Join/Leave/Read/Write, so that the DH-network implementation gets these operations sequentially.

4.2   Dynamic Fault-Tolerant Scheme

We show an implementation of a dynamic storage system, based on the AndOr system over the DH-network. In [11] a file f was stored at a processor that covered $h(f.name)$, where h is a hash function mapping from the domain of file names into I. We use $h(f.name)$ as the root of the AndOr tree. Let $\tau(f)$ denote the tree of height $\log n$ rooted at $root \triangleq h(f.name)$. When f is distributed to a randomly chosen $S \in$ ANDset($root$), it is actually stored in the processors that cover the members of S.

When no δ fraction of the processors cover too large a fraction of I for small enough δ, the system is $\theta(n)$-fault tolerant, because then enough leaves survive an attack. This condition is satisfied when the DH-network is balanced, i.e. no processor cover a segment of size more than $\frac{c}{n}$, for some constant c. Various balancing techniques are described in [11].

Theorem 8. *Assume the DH-network is balanced, then the above storage system is $\theta(n)$-fault tolerant.*

We note that when the id. is uniformly chosen in the join process, the system remains $\theta(n)$-fault tolerant. Uniform choice does not achieve 'balancing', however it remains guaranteed that for small enough δ, no set of δn processors covers too large a fraction of I. Thus, adversary cannot control too many leaves.

Storage Process. Storage can be done in a direct way by using the original routing of the DH-network (see [11]). Another implementation uses a '*gossip protocol*'. The encoded pieces of data start percolating from the root of $\tau(f)$ until they reach S. On even layers (AND gates) the data is equally divided into two parts, each are then 'gossiped' to a different child. On odd layers (OR gates), the data is sent to one of the children chosen at random. After $\log n$ steps the data reaches the members of S randomly chosen from the collection ANDset($root$).

From the writer's point of view the process concludes after writing to the root. At this point the file can already be retrieved. Fault-tolerance is acquired during the percolation. After the gossip has reached at least the nodes of level i, the file becomes $\Omega(2^i)$-fault-tolerant. By letting each processor keep a copy of the data it got during the percolation phase, the system becomes dynamically adjusted to number of faults, as discussed in Section 3.3 .

Retrieval Process. Retrieval is done as in the AndOr system using the routing protocol of the DH-network. Routing dilation is $O(\log n)$, hence retrieval takes $O(\log^2 n)$ steps.

Both storage and retrieval protocols use the the value of $\log n$. Usually, the size of the network n is not available to processors in a dynamic network, so some approximation is required. Such an approximation is suggested in [6] as part of the Viceroy network. The same technique can also be used in the DH-network.

4.3   Dynamic Quorum System

The AndOr system implementation over the DH-network, can serve as a quorum system in a dynamic environment. We need to show how quorums adapt to changes in the size of the network. When a processor that covers a node (point in I) of a quorum senses that $\log n$ has grown it gossips the node to its children on the next layer as described in Section 4.2. When $\log n$ decreases the processor simply deletes the node. Similar techniques to adapt quorums were used in [1]. The optimal load and high availability properties of the AndOr system [14] are maintained.

In comparison with other dynamic constructions of QS, the dynamic AndOr system holds some advantages: The quorum size is $O(\sqrt{n})$ in contrast with [1], where a quorum size of $O(\sqrt{n \log n})$ is required to guarantee an intersection with probability $1 - o(1)$. The join and leave algorithms of the dynamic *'Paths'* system [13] involves a local computation of the Voronoi diagram, whereas in the dynamic AndOr system, a simple step of replication/deletion is required for these operations. Last, the ability to gossip the quorum in logarithmic number of steps is another advantage of our dynamic construction over the dynamic paths.

Acknowledgements

We would like to thank Ilan Gronau for thoroughly reading this paper and the anonymous referees for useful comments.

References

1. I.Abraham and D.Malkhi, Probabilistic quorums for dynamic systems. DISC 2003.
2. L. Alvisi, D. Malkhi, E. Pierce, M. Reiter and R. Wright. Dynamic Byzantine Quorum Systems. Dependable Systems and Networks,(DSN) 2000.
3. A.Fiat and J.Saia. Censorship resistant peer-to-peer content addressable networks. SODA 02.
4. F.Kaashoek, D.R.Karger. Koorde, a simple degree optimal hash table. IPTPS 03.
5. J. Katz and L. Trevisan, On the efficiency of local decoding procedures for error-correcting codes, Proc. STOC 2000.
6. D.Malkhi, M.Naor and D.Ratajczak, Viceroy, a Scalable and dynamic emulation of the buterfly. Proc. PODC 2002.
7. D. Malkhi and M. Reiter. Byzantine Quorum Systems. The Journal of Distributed Computing, 11(4) 1998.
8. D. Malkhi, M. Reiter and R. Wright, Probabilistic quorum systems. PODC 97.
9. D. Malkhi, M. Reiter, A. Wool, and R. Wright. Probabilistic Byzantine Quorum Systems. Proc. PODC 98.
10. M.Naor and R.Roth, Optimal File Sharing in Distributed Networks, SIAM J. Comput. 1995.
11. M.Naor and U.Wieder, Novel architectures for p2p applications: the continuous-discrete approach Proc. SPAA 2003
12. M.Naor and U.Wieder, A Simple fault-tolerant Distributed Hash Table, IPTPS 03.
13. M.Naor and U.Wieder, Scalable and dynamic quorum systems, Proc. PODC 03.
14. M.Naor and A.Wool, The load capacity and availability of quorum systems, SIAM J. on Computing, April 1998.
15. S.Ratnasamy, P.Francis, M.Handley, R.Karp and S.Shenker. A scalable content addressable network. In Proc ACM SIGCOMM 2001.
16. M.O. Rabin. Efficient dispersal of information for security, load balancing, and fault tolerance, J. ACM, 36 (1989).
17. I. Stoica, R. Morris, D. Karger, M. F. Kaashoek, H. Balakrishnan, Chord: a scalable peer-to-peer lookup service for internet applications, ACM SIGCOMM 2001.
18. B.Y. Zhao and Z. Kubiatowicz. Tapestry: An infrastructure for fault-tolerant wide-area location and routing. Technical Report UCB CSD 01-1141. 2001.

Non-skipping Timestamps
for Byzantine Data Storage Systems*

Rida A. Bazzi and Yin Ding

Computer Science Department
Arizona State University
Tempe, Arizona, 85287
{bazzi,yding}@asu.edu

Abstract. We study the problem of implementing a replicated data store with atomic semantics for non self-verifying data in a system of n servers that are subject to Byzantine failures. We present a solution that significantly improves over previously proposed solutions. Timestamps used by our solution cannot be forced to grow arbitrarily large by faulty servers as is the case for other solutions. Instead, timestamps grow no faster than logarithmically in the number of operations. We achieve this saving by defining and providing an implementation for non-skipping timestamps, which are guaranteed not to skip any value. Non-skipping timestamps allow us to reduce the space requirements for readers to $O(max|Q|)$, Where $|Q| \leq n$. This is a significant improvement over the best previously known solution which requires $O(fn)$ space, where f is the maximum number of faulty servers in the system. The solution we present has a low write-load if f is small compared to n, whereas the previously proposed solution always has a high constant write-load.

1 Introduction

We study the problem of implementing a replicated data store in an asynchronous system in which servers can be faulty. We consider a system with an unbounded number of clients in which servers are subject to Byzantine failures and we seek to provide atomic access semantics for non self-verifying data.

Implementations of shared registers with atomic semantics on servers subject to Byzantine failures have been proposed by a number of researchers [11–13]. These solutions typically use Byzantine quorum systems [9]. To write a value, a writer sends the value to all servers in a quorum set, and, to read a value, a reader collects data from all elements of a quorum set to get the most up-to-date value. The non-empty intersection of quorum sets guarantees that the reader can get the most up-to-date value. This simple implementation provides safe semantics [9]. To provide stronger semantics, classical implementation of atomic registers can be used [11]. In [17], Pierce and Alvisi point out the fact that all the then-existing solutions with atomic semantics using non self-verifying data allow only a bounded number of readers and writers. They showed that

* This work is supported in part by the National Science Foundation CAREER award CCR-9876052 and CCR-9972219.

R. Guerraoui (Ed.): DISC 2004, LNCS 3274, pp. 405–419, 2004.

providing atomic semantics in a system with an unbounded number of clients can be reduced to the problem of providing regular semantics, but they did not solve the problem of providing atomic semantics. They presented a protocol providing pseudo-regular semantics which does not require the use of self-verifying data. Their protocol provided atomic semantics for self-verifying data in the presence of an unbounded number of clients and servers subject to Byzantine failures. Martin et al. [13] presented the first solution that provides atomic semantics for non self-verifying data in an asynchronous system with an unbounded number of readers and writers and in which servers are subject to Byzantine failures. Their solution uses a novel technique in which servers forward to clients all late *writes* until the client decides on a value to read. The solution of Martin et al. as well as other implementations that provide atomic semantics in the presence of Byzantine failures can have timestamps that are forced to take arbitrarily large values by Byzantine servers. This problem has not been adequately addressed by previous work.

In this paper, we present a solution to the problem of providing atomic semantics for non self-verifying data in the presence of Byzantine server failures and an unbounded number of clients. Our solution is a significant improvement over previously proposed solutions.

- In contrast to all previous solutions, the size of the timestamps in our solution is bounded by the logarithm of the number of operations and cannot be made arbitrarily large by Byzantine servers as is the case for all previous solutions.
- It requires $O(max|Q|)$, $|Q| \leq n$, space to be used by readers compared to $O(nf)$ space required in [13].
- In [13], each writer writes to all servers in the system which results in a write load equal to 1. In our solution, both read and write are to general Byzantine quorum sets which enable us to use quorums with low load and achieve a load for write operation that is less than or equal to $\sqrt{\frac{4f+1}{n}}$. If $n > 4f + 1$, the load is smaller than the load obtained in [13].
- Our solution allows readers to short-circuit the forwarding of late *writes* by notifying servers of the exact data values they need to complete their read.

In our solution, we do not require self-verifying data to provide atomic semantics. As in [13], we show that by using public-key cryptography, our solution can tolerate clients that fail arbitrarily or by crashing. Both our solution and that of [13] use message forwarding and could potentially require forwarding an unbounded number of late *writes*.

An important contribution of our work is the introduction of non-skipping timestamps. These are timestamps that are guaranteed not to skip any values. Non-skipping timestamps do not increase arbitrarily in size, so they are considerably more space efficient that timestamps used by other solutions. In addition to reducing the size of timestamps, non-skipping timestamps enable us to reduce the space required by readers. Another new tool that we use is *writeback on behalf of a writer*. Writebacks are not new. The idea of a writeback is for a reader to writeback the value it reads so that a later reader is guaranteed to be aware of the value read by the earlier reader (or of later values). In *writeback on behalf of a writer*, the identity of the original writer is included in the writeback. It turns out that this is especially important in the presence of Byzantine failures. It allows us to use arbitrary quorums to write a value instead of writing all values to all servers as is done in [13]. We expect that these tools will be useful in other settings.

2   Related Works

Safe, regular, and Atomic semantics for distributed shared memory were defined by Lamport [7]. Traditional implementations of shared registers with strong semantics using registers with weak semantics assume a bounded number of reader and writers [16]. In this paper, we only consider atomic semantics.

Byzantine quorum systems were introduced by Malkhi and Reiter [9] and further investigated in various works [1, 10, 12, 13]. Our results use non-blocking Byzantine quorum systems [1]. Malkhi and Reiter [9] use Byzantine quorum systems to provide replicated registers with *regular* semantics and provide stronger semantics using traditional implementation of registers with strong semantics from registers with weak semantics. Martin et al. [13] presented the first implementation of a shared store with atomic semantics for non self-verifying data in an asynchronous system in which servers are subject to Byzantine failures and in which the number of readers and writers is unbounded. Their solution uses message forwarding and, as in our solution, could potentially require forwarding an unbounded number of late *writes*. The solution of [13] requires minimal redundancy, $n > 3f$. To achieve the minimal redundancy, it requires every *write* to be executed by all servers in the system, which means that the load for *writes* is equal to 1.

Castro and Liskov [2] described a practical state-machine replication protocol using public-key cryptography techniques that tolerates Byzantine faults in asynchronous networks, requiring $n > 3f$.

One interesting approach for reducing the size of data stored at replicas is voting with witnesses [15]. The idea is to have some data object copies called witnesses that store the latest timestamp of the data. Witnesses can attest to the state of a data object, obsolete or up-to-date, without storing the object. Witnesses were used by Rui and Lynch [3] to provide an implementation of a replicated store with atomic semantics in the presence of an unbounded number of readers and writers subject to crash failures. Their algorithm tolerates crash failures by the servers but does not tolerate Byzantine failures.

Lazy replication has also been proposed to increase the efficiency of reads and writes ([18] for example). The idea is to write to only a few servers, then have the servers diffuse the updates. In this paper, we use information diffusion to tolerate client failures; this is the same approach used by Martin et al. [13].

3   System Model

The system consists of two sets of processes: a set of n server processes (servers) and an unbounded set of client processes (clients). Clients have unique identifiers. The identifiers of writers are elements of a completely ordered set.

Clients communicate with servers and servers communicate with clients using reliable FIFO message passing[1]. To send a message, a process uses the *send* function that takes an intended recipient and a message *content* as parameters. We identify a sent message as a triplet (s, r, c), where s is the sender, r is the recipient and c is the content of the message. Every message sent is guaranteed to be delivered to the intended recipient at a later time, but there is no bound on the time elapsed between the time a message is sent and the time it is delivered. A message delivered to p is of the form (s, c), where (s, p, c) is a message sent at an earlier time. To receive messages, a process p uses the receive function which returns the set of messages that have been delivered to p since the last time p called the receive function.

Each process has an internal state. Server processes follow a protocol that specifies their initial states, the state changes, and the messages to send in response to messages received from other server processes and client processes. Up to f of the server processes can be faulty. Faulty server processes exhibit arbitrary failure behavior: the messages sent by faulty processes as well as their state changes can be arbitrary [6].

Client processes can invoke a "read" or a "write" protocol which specify the state changes and the messages to send to servers to initiate a "read" or a "write" as well as the state changes and messages to send in response to server messages. We consider clients fail by crashing or that are subject to arbitrary failure.

4   Quorums

Quorums have been used for data replication to increase availability and reduce system load. A quorum system is a collection of sets such that any two sets in the collection have non-empty intersection. In a typical implementation of shared storage using quorums, a writer writes its value to all elements of a quorum set of servers. A reader collects values from all elements of a quorum set and returns the most up to date value. The non-empty intersection property guarantees that the reader will always get the most up to date value. In a given implementation with multiple readers and writers, additional measures are needed to handle overlapping writes by different writers and to guarantee strong consistency semantics of the reads and writes. In asynchronous systems in which processes are subject to failures it is not possible to guarantee that all processors in a given quorum will respond to a read request or will acknowledge the receipt of the value from the writer. The problem of ensuring that a response is received from some quorum without contacting too many servers has been studied in [1] and the class of *non-blocking quorum systems* was introduced to that end. The Quorum sets in non-blocking Byzantine systems have an intersection that is larger than that of quorums in traditional Byzantine quorum systems [9]. The larger intersection makes it possible for the client processes to make decisions based on only $|Q| - f$ replies from server processes in a quorum set Q instead of $|Q|$

---

[1] Message passing is assumed to be FIFO to simplify the exposition. All our results can be modified to work for systems with non-FIFO message passing.

replies in traditional quorum systems. In this paper, we require that any two quorum sets have at least $4f + 1$ elements in common.

5   Non-skipping Timestamps

In distributed storage systems, timestamps are used to identify the up-to-date values of an object. When a new value of an object is written, a timestamp value needs to be selected to tag the new value of the object. In traditional implementations, a writer first requests from each server the timestamp value that the server has for the object, then it chooses a timestamp value that is larger than all timestamp values that servers provided. In systems in which servers are subject to arbitrary failures, the size of timestamps can grow arbitrarily large because faulty processors can return arbitrary timestamp values. Techniques to bound the values of timestamps in a shared memory system have been proposed [8], but such techniques assume that the number of clients is bounded and it is not clear that they can be applied to a distributed setting in which servers are subject to Byzantine failures and the number of clients is unbounded. Also, it is important to note that bounding the size of timestamps by recycling old timestamp values is not always appropriate. For instance, in systems that keep a log of all accesses, old object values along with their timestamps need to be recorded and old timestamp values should not be reused.

We propose, and provide an implementation of, *non-skipping* timestamps whose size grow at most logarithmically in the number of write operations in the system. Non-skipping timestamps prevent faulty servers from forcing timestamp values to grow arbitrarily large. In addition, they are guaranteed to be non-skipping in the sense that a new timestamp value is not selected unless *all* smaller timestamp values have been selected. This feature makes it easier to implement a distributed shared register with atomic semantics and can help in reducing the message complexity of such an implementation.

We define non-skipping timestamps as an abstract data type with two operations: *Get* and *Get&Inc*. *Get* returns the value of the timestamp and *Get&Inc* increments the timestamp and returns its value before the increment. The increment *writes* the incremented value to the timestamp and in what follows we say that a *Get&Inc* operation writes a value t when it increments the timestamp value to t. A linearizable implementation of non-skipping timestamps is identical to *fetch&add* [4]. It follows that providing a linearizable wait-free implementation of a non-skipping timestamp is not possible because *fetch&add* has consensus number 2 [4]. Therefore, we have to specify the accepted behavior of implementations of non-skipping timestamps. Valid implementations of non-skipping timestamps should have the following properties:

- *Non-Skipping.* If an operation on a non-skipping timestamp object returns value t_0, then for every timestamp t, $0 < t < t_0$, there exists a *Get&Inc* operation that wrote t at an earlier time.
- *Progress.* Non-overlapping *Get&Inc* operations return different timestamp values, and the value returned by the later operation is greater than that of the earlier one.

- *Partial Linearizability.* There exists a total order of the operations that is consistent with process order and real-time order [5] such that:
  - A *Get* that appears after a *Get&Inc* operation in the global order will not return a value smaller than that written by the *Get&Inc* operation.
  - A value returned by a *Get* operation is not smaller than the value returned by an earlier *Get* operation.

In stating the properties, we assume the existence of a real-time clock to order the events in the system (this clock is not available to clients or servers). Note that the properties allows two *Get&Inc* operations to return the same value; a linearizable implementation of *fetch&add* would not allow that.

5.1 Implementations of Non-skipping Timestamp

The implementation assumes that any two quorums intersect in $4f + 1$ servers, so the total number of servers is $\geq 4f + 1$. In the implementation, each server stores the most up-to-date value of the timestamp that it is aware of. A key observation in the algorithm is that a client need not choose the largest returned timestamp, instead a client can choose the $f + 1$'st largest timestamp. As we will see, this will guarantee that the timestamp selected was actually written by a correct client.

Get. The *Get* operation is simple (See Figure 1). The client maintains a set *received* to store the messages received. It sends GET requests to a quorum Q of servers (lines 1). The client receives from servers replies of the form (s, t), where t is the current timestamp value at server s and stores the reply in the set *received.*. The client waits until it receives $|Q| - f$ replies from different servers (lines 3-6). After enough timestamps are collected, the client sorts the received timestamps in descending order and chooses the $f + 1$'st largest timestamp value as the return value.

Get&Inc. The *Get&Inc* (Figure 2) operation has no input parameter. It returns the current value of the timestamp and increments the timestamp by 1. The client calls the *Get* function, gets the returned timestamp value ts, and then it sends all servers in Q the value of ts incremented by 1 (line 2). After it receives $|Q| - f$ acknowledgments (line 3), it returns ts (line 4).

The server side is simple. Once a server receives a *GET* request, it sends back its timestamp ts. Once a server receives a *INC MESSAGE(ts)*, it updates its timestamp to ts if ts is greater than the current timestamp.

5.2 Proof of Correctness

We only prove the *Non-Skipping* Property. The proofs for the *Progress* and *Partial Linearizability* properties are omitted for lack of space. We assume that the timestamp value is initialized to 0 at all servers.

Get(Q)
1: **send** GET request to servers in Q
2: $received[i] = $ **null**, $1 \le i \le |Q|$
3: **repeat**
4:      **receive** (s, t)
5:      **if** $(received[s] = $ **null**$)$
          $received[s] = t$
6: **until** $|\{i : received[i] \ne $ **null**$\}| \ge |Q| - f$
7: **sort** *received* in descending order of timestamps
8: $ts = received[f + 1]$
9: **return** ts

Fig. 1. *Get*: Client Side.

Get&Inc(Q)
1: $ts = Get(Q)$
2: **send** INC MESSAGE $(ts + 1)$ to servers in Q
3: **wait** for acknowledgments from $|Q| - f$ different servers
4: **return** ts

Fig. 2. *Get&Inc*: Client Side.

Lemma 1 (No Skip). *If an operation on a non-skipping timestamp object returns value t_0, then for every timestamp t, $0 \le t < t_0$, there exists a Get&Inc operation that wrote t at an earlier time.*

Proof. We first note that timestamp values are always non negative as they are never decremented (negative values returned by faulty servers can be ignored). The proof is by induction on t_0. For $t_0 = 0$, the statement of the lemma is vacuously true. Assume the lemma is true for t_0. We show that if an operation returns a timestamp value $t_0 + 1$, then there exists *Get&Inc* that wrote t_0 at an earlier time. By the induction hypothesis, it follows that for every t, $0 \le t < t_0 + 1$, there exists a *Get&Inc* that wrote t at an earlier time.

Assume that an operation returns $t_0 + 1$. Consider the first operation that returns a value t_1 greater than t_0. The operation is either a *Get* operation that computes $ts = t_1$ in line 7 or a *Get&Inc* operation that calls a *Get* operation that returns $ts = t_1$ in line 1. So, without loss of generality, assume that the first operation that returns a value $t_1 \ge t_0 + 1$ is a *Get* operation O_G. O_G must have received $f + 1$ replies all of which are greater than or equal to t_1. Since at most f of the replies can be from faulty servers, it follows that some correct server p_c replied with a timestamp value $\ge t_1$. Consider the *Get&Inc* operation $O_{G\&I}$ that wrote the value t_1 to p_c. $O_{G\&I}$ must have computed a return value equal to $t_1 - 1 \ge t_0$ (line 1) because the value written is always 1 plus the value returned. So, the *Get* operation O_{G_1} that was called by $O_{G\&I}$ in line 1 must have returned $t_1 - 1 \ge t_0$. Since O_G is the first operation to return a value greater than t_0, it follows that O_{G_1} must have returned t_0. So, $O_{G\&I}$ must have written $t_0 + 1$.

6   Distributed Register with Atomic Semantics

In this section, we present a solution to implement a multi-reader/multi-writer atomic distributed register that does not tolerate client failures. In Section 7, we will show how to handle client failures. The solution allows an unbounded number of clients in an asynchronous system in which servers are subject to arbitrary failures. In the solution, writers tag data they write with a timestamp. A timestamp is the form of (ts, w_{id}), where ts is the timestamp value and w_{id} is the unique identifier of the writer. We first give an overview of the main features of the solutions before giving a full description.

6.1   Reducing Reader Memory Requirements

In the solution of [13], readers require $f * (n - f)$ memory locations where each location holds a value and a timestamp. In our solution, we reduce the memory requirement to q_{max} locations, where q_{max} is the size of the largest quorum set in the system. Our solution's memory requirement is considerably smaller than $f * (n - f)$ for large f and is always less than n. The improvement is due to the fact that the reader is able to determine in the first phase of communication with the servers the timestamp value t_r of a *recent* data value that was written immediately before or concurrently with the read; that requires q_{max} memory locations. In a second step, the reader determines a data value that was written with timestamp value t_r. That requires the same locations q_{max} used in the first phase.

The ability of readers to determine the timestamp of a recently written data value is achieved by using the non-skipping timestamps which we already described. In our solution, we do not explicitly use non-skipping timestamp objects; instead we integrate the timestamps into the *read* and *write* protocol.

6.2   Protocol Description

We present the implementation of a read operation and a write operation which specify how clients read and write values and how servers behave in response to read and write requests. The write() operation has as input the value to be written. The read() operation has no input and returns the value read.

Client Side

Write. The writer client maintains a set *received* to store the messages received. The client chooses a quorum Q and sends write requests to all servers in Q (lines 1,2). The client receives from servers in Q replies of the form (s, t), where t is the current timestamp value at server s. The client stores all replies in the set *received* (lines 5,6). The client waits until it receives $|Q| - f$ replies from different servers (lines 4-7). The client computes the $f + 1$'st largest timestamp ts_{max} (line 8-9) and then sends a write message with timestamp value equal $ts_{max} + 1$ (line 10). We should note that lines8-9 find the largest timestamp value that at least $f + 1$ servers are each either faulty or *aware* of the value. So, at least one correct server must be aware of that value. If a correct server sends timestamp value t, then, by the non-skipping property of timestamps, the server can be used as a *witness* for every timestamp less than t. This will be elaborated on in the proofs.

Read. The reader client also maintain an array of *received* messages from the servers. The s entry in the *received* array is of the form (w, t, v), where w is a writer identifier, t is a timestamp value and v is a data value and (w, t, v) was received from server s. The read operation is executed in two phases. In the first phase, the read determines a timestamp value t_{target} of a write that overlaps or immediately precedes the read. In the second phase, the client determines a data value that was written by a correct server with timestamp value t_{target}. This is the data value returned by the read operation (line 21).

The first part of the read is similar to the first part of the write (lines 1-7). In this part the client collects timestamps from the servers in Q and stores each value in a separate entry (one entry per server). After enough timestamps are collected, the client sorts the received timestamps in descending order and chooses the $f + 1$'st largest timestamp value as its target timestamp (lines 8,9)'. In the second phase, the clients starts by erasing all entries in *received* whose timestamp is different from t_{target} (line 10), then the client sends a request to all servers in Q to send a value whose timestamp is equal to t_{target} (this allows short circuiting the forwarding done by servers) (line 11)[2]. Then the client receives from the servers messages of the form (w, t, v), where w is the identifier of a writer that wrote value v with timestamp t (line 13). The clients always maintains the value for the writer with the highest identifier (all these values are written with ts_{target} (lines 14,15). The client keeps on receiving messages until it receives the same (writer,value) pair from $f + 1$ servers (12,16). There might be more than one such pair and the client chooses only one of them (line 17). This is the return value of the read operation (line 21). Before terminating, the client writes back the value it just read (lines 18,19) on behalf of the writer that wrote the value that the client read and then sends END OF READ message to all servers in Q (line 20). It is important to note that the writeback initiated by the client are not simple writebacks of a value; they are writebacks *on behalf of a writer* that contain the identifier of the writer. The reason they are made is to ensure that other readers can have a chance to get the same value that the client just read. The writeback is not needed if we modify the write protocol so that writes are made to all servers in the systems as is done in [13]. The disadvantage of that approach is that the system would have a high load.

Server Side. The code for the server is shown in Figure 5. The server maintains two main values: the current timestamp value ts_{cur} and the current writer w_{cur}.

---

[2] An optimization would have the client send that request only to those servers from which it received initial timestamp value less than or equal to t_{target} from, but that would make the code more cumbersome.

write(in: value)
1: **choose** a quorum Q
2: **send** WRITE request to all elements in Q
3: $received[i] = $ **null**, $1 \leq i \leq |Q|$
4: **repeat**
5:      **receive** (s, t)
6:      **if** $(received[s] = $ **null**$)$
                $received[s] = t$
7: **until** $|\{i : received[i] \neq $ **null**$\}| \geq |Q| - f$
8: **sort** $received$ in descending order of timestamps
9: $t_{max} = received[f + 1]$
10: **send** WRITE MESSAGE $(w_{id}, ts_{max} + 1, value)$ to all elements in Q
11: **wait** for acknowledgments from $|Q| - f$ different servers

Fig. 3. Write: Code execute by client w_{id}.

read(out: value)
//**Phase 1:**
1: **choose** a quorum Q
2: **send** READ REQUEST to all elements in Q
3: $received[i] = $ **null**, $1 \leq i \leq |Q|$
4: **repeat**
5:      **receive** (s, w, t, v)
6:      **if** $(received[s] = $ **null**$)$ **or** $(received[s] < t)$
                or $(received[s] = t$ **and** $received[s] < w)$
                $received[s] = (w, t, v)$
7: **until** $|\{i : received[i] \neq $ **null**$\}| \geq |Q| - f$
8: **sort** $received$ in descending order of timestamps
9: $t_{target} = $ timestamp of $received[f + 1]$
//**Phase 2:**
10: **for** $i = 1$ **to** $|Q|$ **do**
            if $(received[i] = (w, t, v))$ **and** $(t \neq t_{target})$
                $received[i] = $ **null**
11: **send** READ t_{target} to all servers in Q
12: **repeat**
13:     **receive** $(s, w, t_{target}, v))$ // ignore messages with timestamps other than t_{target}
14:     **if** $received[s] \leq w$
15:         $received[s] = (w, v)$
16: **until** $\exists(v, w) : |\{i : received[i] = (v, w)\}| \geq f + 1.$
17: **choose** (v_0, w_0) such that $|\{i : received[i] = (v_0, w_0)\}| \geq f + 1$
18: **send** WRITE MESSAGE (w_0, t_{target}, v_0) to all elements in Q
19: **wait** for acknowledgments from $|Q| - f$ different servers
20: **send** END OF READ message to all servers in Q
21: $value = v_0$

Fig. 4. Read: Client Side.

In addition, the server maintains a set of clients that have initiated a read request (phase 1) and a set of those that have initiated a 'READ ts_{target}' (phase 2). These sets are G_{req} and G_{target} respectively.

Write:
1: upon receipt of a WRITE REQUEST from a client p_w
2:      send ts_{cur} to p_w
3: upon receipt of a WRITE MESSAGE (w, ts, v) from a client p_w
4:      **forall** $(c, ts_c) \in G_{target} \wedge ts_c = ts$
5:          send (w, ts, v) to c
6:      **if** $(ts_{cur} < ts)$ **or** ($ts_{cur} = ts$ **and** $p_w > w_{cur}$) **then**
7:          **forall** $(c, ts_c) \in G_{req}$ **and** $(ts_c < ts_{cur})$
8:              send (w, ts_{cur}, v_{cur}) to c
9:          $w_{cur} = p_w$; $ts_{cur} = ts$; $v_{cur} = v$
10:     send ACK to p_w

Read:
1: upon receipt of a READ REQUEST from a client p_r
2:      send $(w_{cur}, ts_{cur}, v_{cur})$ to p_r
3:      $G_{req} = G_{req} \cup \{(p_r, ts_{cur})\}$
4: upon receipt of a READ ts_{target} message from a client p_r
5:      $G_{req} = G_{req} - \{(p_r, ts_{p_r})\}$
6:      $G_{target} = G_{target} \cup \{(p_r, ts_{target})\}$
7:      **if** $ts_{target} = ts_{cur}$ **then**
8:          send $(w_{cur}, ts_{cur}, v_{cur})$ to p_r
9: upon receipt of a END OF READ message for client p_r
10:     **remove** the entry for p_r from G_{target}

Fig. 5. Write & Read: Server Side.

Handling write operations is done as follows. Upon receipt of a WRITE REQUEST, the server sends the current timestamp value to the writer (lines 1,2). Upon receipt of a WRITE MESSAGE with timestamp value ts (line 3)[3], the server forwards the message to all readers whose target timestamp value is equal to ts (lines 4,5). If the received message is a more up-to-date message (larger timestamp value or same timestamp value but a larger writer identifier), the server replaces the stored value with the new value (along with the writer id and timestamp value) (lines 6,7,9). Also, the server forwards the replaced value to all clients that have pending read requests (line 8). Finally, the server sends an acknowledgment of the WRITE MESSAGE (line 10).

Handling read operations is done as follows. Upon receipt of a READ RE-QUEST from a client p_r, the server sends the reader the stored copy of the latest write and adds the client to the set of clients with pending requests (lines 1,2,3). Upon receipt of READ message from a client p_r, the server removes the client from the request set (lines 4,5) and adds the client to the set of clients with pending READ (line 6). If the target timestamp matches the timestamp of the most up-to-date write, the server forwards the most up to date write to the client (lines 7,8). Upon receipt of a END OF READ message from a client, the server removes the client from the set of servers with pending reads (line 9,10).

---

[3] Note that this client can be either a writer or a reader writing back on behalf of a writer.

Note. In the protocol description, we implicitly assumed that the client is check-ing for the appropriateness of messages received from the servers. For example, in the second phase of a read, the client expects values of a particular form and will ignore all values that are not of that form. Also, we implicitly assume that each operation has a unique identifier and that a client will only process messages with the correct identifier.

6.3   Correctness

Non-skipping Timestamps. It should be clear that the way timestamps are modified by a writer is identical to a $Get\&Inc$ and the timestamps as accessed by a reader is identical to a Get. The writeback simply rewrites a value already written by a writer and it doe not increment the timestamp value. We omit the proofs that the timestamps in the reader and writer protocols are non-skipping as they are identical to those already presented.

Atomic Semantics. We need to prove that the protocol satisfies atomicity and liveness. We only present the proof of liveness and omit the proof of atomicity for lack of space.

Lemma 2 (Liveness). *Both read and write operations eventually terminate.*

Proof (Proof Sketch). **Write Operation:** In the protocol, the writer will wait until it receives $|Q| - f$ replies from the quorum Q it accesses. This is guaranteed to happen because there are at most f failures. We also note that the calcula-tion of ts_{max} always returns a valid value (it returns the $f + 1$'st value among the timestamp values received). **Read Operation:** The reader executes in two phases. In the first phase, the reader has to wait for replies from $|Q| - f$ replies from servers in the quorum Q it accesses. This is guaranteed to happen because there are at most f faulty servers. In the second phase, the reader waits until it receives $f + 1$ replies all with the same value written by one unique writer. It is not obvious why this is guaranteed to happen. We start by examining the properties of ts_{target} that is calculated in the first phase. In the first phase, there are $f + 1$ replies equal to or greater than ts_{target}. There must be at least one correct server among them. Since timestamps are non-skipping, it follows that there must be a correct writer w_{target} that wrote a value with timestamp equal ts_{target} to some quorum Q_{target}. In the first phase, the reader receives at most $f + 1$ values with timestamp greater than or equal to t_{target}. The remaining value have timestamp either equal to t_{target} or less than t_{target}. Those values with timestamps equal to t_{target} are not erased in the loop at line 10. The writer w_{target} that wrote a data value with timestamp value t_{target} must have used a quorum Q_{target} that has $4f + 1$ servers in common with quorum Q used by the reader. Out of these $4f + 1$ servers, f servers might have values with timestamp larger than t_{target} and another f might be faulty. Also f servers from the inter-section might not have sent replies to the reader. All the remaining $f + 1$ servers in the intersection either already sent a value with timestamp equal t_{target} or sent values with timestamps less than t_{target}. Those servers that sent values less than t_{target} will eventually receive the write by w_{target} and forward a value with timestamp t_{target} to the reader (the forwarding will happen because the reader is in their request set after phase 1). Still, this does not guarantee that the client will get $f + 1$ identical values all of them written by the same writer and with timestamp equal t_{target}. In fact, a write by w_{target} might be replaced by another write of a value with timestamp equal t_{target}, but by a writer having a larger identifier. It is enough to consider the last writer who writes a value with timestamp t_{target} to conclude the proof of termination. The number of such writers is finite for we cannot have an infinite number of concurrent writes. Also, any later non-overlapping write will have a larger timestamp value (by the progress property of non-skipping timestamps).

7 Tolerating Faulty Clients

We assume that each writer client has a private key. For every writer, a server keeps the public key, but does not know the private key. In [13], it is assumed that all writers share the same private key. That is adequate for crash failures, but not for Byzantine failures. We can use one private key shared by all writers if writers are not subject to Byzantine failures. In any case, the writers need to be authenticated in order to write and assuming a private/public key pair for each writer is not unreasonable. Our solutions for tolerating faulty clients relies on message diffusion or echo-broadcast. Echo-broadcast is also used in [13] to tolerate crash and Byzantine failures. We only describe the solution for crash failures and we omit the description of the solution for Byzantine failures for lack of space.

A faulty client can crash before it gets a chance to write its value to a sufficient number of servers. So, we need a way to propagate the value written by a client. We use message diffusion at the servers.

To write a value, the writer proceeds as in the fault-free case, with the only difference being that it signs its message with its private key.

After it gets a WRITE MESSAGE, the server first verifies the signature so that a Byzantine faulty server can not forge a message from the client. If the message is correctly verified and a reader is waiting for a value written with that timestamp, the server forwards the written value to the waiting reader. Then if this timestamp value is larger than the current one, it will forward the message to other servers, and forward it to all pending readers, update the data, acknowledge the writer. Hence, even if writer fails at some point, if its correct value is received by a correct server, its value will be updated on all the correct servers in the quorum. If its correct value is not received by a correct server, then at most f faulty servers receive its value. The way these servers act on receiving a write does not affect the correctness of the protocol and they are already handled by the protocol for the fault-free case. If a correct server receives the write, then the server will act as a proxy for the writer and the writer will look like it is correct and the fault-free algorithm on the client side can be used to read its value.

8   Performance

Load. Informally, the load of a processor measures the share it has in handling requests to the quorum system. For a given probabilistic access rule of a quorum system, the load of a quorum system is the probability of accessing the busiest processor. The load of a quorum system is the minimum load over all access probability distributions. A formal definition of load is given in [14], but we omit a formal treatment for lack of space. In the solution of Martin et al., every write accesses all servers in the system. This results in a load equal to 1 for write accesses. In our solution, both reads and writes access servers in a quorum set. It follows that the load our solution depends on the load of the Byzantine quorum system in use. For example, if we use the Byzantine quorum system that is based on projective planes [1], we can get a load that is less than or equal to $\sqrt{\frac{4f+1}{n}}$. This load can be significantly smaller than 1 if f is small compared to n.

Execution Time. In the proof of termination, we did not evaluate the time it takes for read and write operations to terminate. In order to get an idea of the execution time of these operations, we would have to assume an upper bound on the message transmission delay; let d be that bound. Note that this assumption does not contradict the asynchrony assumption we made about the system. It simply gives us an idea about the execution time under bounded delay assumption. We will ignore processing time in the discussion. A write operation requires $4d$ time in order to complete two sets of message exchanges: one exchange to obtain the timestamp and one exchange to write the value and get acknowledgments from enough servers. In [13], $4d$ is also required for writes. A read operation execution time depends on the number of concurrent writes at the time of the execution of the read operation. Consider a read with no concurrent writes. The initial part of a read (lines 1-17) completes in one round of message exchange which requires $2d$. In the final part of a read, the a reader will have to writeback a value, which requires another $2d$ (the reader does not have to choose a timestamp value for writeback). So, the total time required by a reader is at most $4d$ compared to $2d$ for a read that is not concurrent with writes in [13].

Space. The non-skipping timestamps we use do not increase arbitrarily in size and are more efficient than the timestamps of the solution of Martin et al. [13] and other previously proposed solutions. Non-skipping timestamps result in smaller messages. We already noted that readers require $|Q|$ space, where Q is the size of a read quorum. This space is less than or equal to n and can be significantly less than the space required by the solution of Martin et al. [13]. Writers also use $O(n)$ space which is the same as that of the solution of Martin et al. [13]. Servers need to maintain sets of readers in progress in order to forward late messages to them. Maintaining a list of readers in progress is also needed by the solution of Martin et al. This space is proportional to the number of concurrent reads, but is only incurred when there are reads in progress.

References

1. R. A. Bazzi. Access cost for asynchronous byzantine quorum systems. *Distributed Computing Journal*, 14:41–48, January 1992.
2. Castro and Liskov. Practical byzantine fault tolerance. In *OSDI: Symposium on Operating Systems Design and Implementation*. USENIX Association, Co-sponsored by IEEE TCOS and ACM SIGOPS, 1999.
3. R. Fan. Efficient replication of large data objects. In *Thesis, Computer Science and Engineering, MIT*, 2003.
4. M. Herlihy. Wait-free synchronization. *ACM Transactions on Programming Languages and Systems*, 13(1):124–149, January 1991.
5. M. P. Herlihy and J. M. Wing. Linearizability: a correctness condition for concurrent objects. *ACM Transactions on Programming Languages and Systems (TOPLAS)*, 12(3):463–492, 1990.
6. Lamport, Shostak, and Pease. The byzantine generals problem. In *Advances in Ultra-Dependable Distributed Systems, N. Suri, C. J. Walter, and M. M. Hugue (Eds.), IEEE Computer Society Press*. 1995.
7. L. Lamport. On interprocess communication. In *Distributed Computing*, pages 1:76–101, 1986.
8. M. Li, J. Tromp, and P. M. B. Vitányi. How to share concurrent wait-free variables. *Journal of the ACM*, 43(4):723–746, 1996.
9. D. Malkhi and M. Reiter. Byzantine quorum systems. In *Proceedings of the 29th ACM Symposium on Theory of Computing (STOC)*, pages 569–578, 1997.
10. D. Malkhi, M. Reiter, and A. Wool. The load and availability of Byzantine quorum systems. *SIAM J. Computing*, 29(6):1889–1906, 2000.
11. D. Malkhi and M. K. Reiter. Secure and scalable replication in phalanx. In *Symposium on Reliable Distributed Systems*, pages 51–58, 1998.
12. D. Malkhi, M. K. Reiter, and R. N. Wright. Probabilistic quorum systems. In *Symposium on Principles of Distributed Computing*, pages 267–273, 1997.
13. J.-P. Martin, L. Alvisi, and M. Dahlin. Minimal Byzantine storage. In *Distributed Computing, 16th international Conference, DISC 2002*, pages 311–325, October 2002.
14. M. Naor and A. Wool. The load, capacity and availability of quorum systems. *SIAM J. Computing*, 27(2):423–447, April 1998.
15. J.-F. Paris. Voting with witnesses: A consistency scheme for replicated files. In *In Proc. of the 6th International Conference on Distributed Computer Systems*, pages 606–612, 1986.
16. G. Peterson and J. Burns. Concurrent reading while writing ii: The multiwriter case. In *In Proc. 28th IEEE Symp. Found. Comput. Sci.*, pages 383–392, 1987.
17. E. Pierce and L. Alvisi. A framework for semantic reasoning about byzantine quorum systems, 2001.
18. L. S. Rivka Ladin, Barbara Liskov and S. Ghemawat. Providing high availability using lazy replication. *ACM Transaction on Computer Systems*, 10(4):360–391, 1992.

Efficient Verification
for Provably Secure Storage and Secret Sharing in Systems Where Half the Servers Are Faulty

Rida A. Bazzi* and Goran Konjevod**

Computer Science and Engineering Department
Arizona State University
Tempe, AZ 85287-8809
{bazzi,goran}@asu.edu

Abstract. We present new decentralized storage systems that are resilient to arbitrary failures of up to a half of all servers and can tolerate a computationally unbounded adversary. These are the first such results with space requirements smaller than those of full replication without relying on cryptographic assumptions. We also significantly reduce share sizes for robust secret-sharing schemes with or without an honest dealer, again without cryptographic assumptions. A major ingredient in our systems is an information verification scheme that replaces hashing (for storage systems) or information checking protocols (for secret sharing). Together with a new way of organizing verification information, this allows us to use a simple majority algorithm to identify with high probability all servers whose information hasn't been corrupted.

Keywords: Secure storage, secret sharing, Byzantine failures

1 Introduction

In a distributed storage system subject to failures, redundancy needs to be introduced so that data can be correctly retrieved. A simple form of redundancy is full replication. For example, t crash failures can be tolerated by replicating the data on $t + 1$ servers, while t Byzantine failures can be tolerated by replicating the data on $2t + 1$ servers. To retrieve the data, a client reads from all the servers and accepts the value returned by a majority. One can think of replication as a form on *information verification:* the value stored at one server is used to verify the information stored at another. If one server is correct and the value it stores is identical to the value at another server, then the value at the other server is also correct. This is the basis for using majority to retrieve the correct value. In general, the verification information should make it impossible or hard (in

* Research supported in part by the National Science Foundation grants CCR-9972219 and CCR-9876952.
** Research supported in part by the National Science Foundation grant CCR-0209138.

R. Guerraoui (Ed.): DISC 2004, LNCS 3274, pp. 420–434, 2004.

an information-theoretic or a computational sense) for a server to provide corrupt information without being detected. This is the *no cheating* requirement for verification information.

In a secret sharing scheme [1], a dealer has a secret and distributes its *shares* to n participants in such a way that any $t + 1$ shares can be used to recover the secret, but any t shares provide no information about it. A secret sharing scheme consists of two protocols executed by the dealer and the participants. In the *sharing* phase the dealer distributes the shares, and in the *reconstruction* phase the participants *open* their shares (make them available to each other) in order to reconstruct the secret. Robust secret sharing schemes [2] are those that can tolerate faulty participants. In these schemes, the dealer provides participants with verification information that allows detection of corrupt shares during the reconstruction. The definition of secret sharing imposes an additional requirement on the verification information held by any participant: it should leak no information about the *share* (data) that it verifies. This is the *no leakage* requirement for verification information.

The size of the verification information is an important performance measure. In a distributed storage system, the ratio of the total space used to store the data to the size of actual data is called the *space blow-up*. (For full replication, this ratio is equal to n.) By using error-correcting codes [3, 4], the blow-up can be reduced to $n/(n - 2t)$, where $t < n/2$ is the number of faulty servers (it is clear that in general, a correct majority is needed to retrieve the stored data). In a system of n servers, if $2t$ is close to n, this factor becomes $\Omega(n)$ and in fact, Krawczyk [4] proves that $n/(n - 2t)$ is the optimal space blowup unless the solution allows for a positive probability of error. He introduces a *distributed fingerprinting* scheme based on one-way hash functions to circumvent this lower bound. The space blow-up of his method is $n/(n - t)$ in the size of the data file, but it introduces an overhead of $nh/(n - 2t)$ per server, where h is the size of a fingerprint. If $n = 2t + 1$, the space blow-up is 2 and the fingerprinting overhead is nh per server. The additional overhead can be relatively large if the file is not large. Alon et al. [5] further reduce the fingerprinting overhead by using a verification structure where each server stores verification information for data at other servers. They succeed in achieving a blow-up of $2 + \epsilon$ plus an overhead of $\Theta(\log nh)$ per server for $n \geq 2t + 1$, with a hidden constant larger than 1500. Recently, the same authors of [5] developed a scheme that significantly reduces the hidden constant [6]. The schemes of Krawczyk and of Alon et al. use one-way hash functions, so they all rely on unproven assumptions. Hence, the probability of error introduced by their use of hash functions cannot be quantified. By reducing the blow-up factor, the schemes of both Krawczyk and Alon et al. lose an important property of schemes based on error correcting codes: they cannot tolerate computationally unbounded adversaries (for lack of space, we omit the proof of this fact).

The situation is similar for secret sharing. There is a very large body of literature [7], and the vast majority of schemes consider models where information about the secret is not leaked in a computational sense and where faulty participants have bounded computational power. If $n < 3t$, then there is no solution to the problem that does not have a probability of error. Rabin [2] presented a scheme that tolerates $t < (n-1)/2$ faulty participants, but assumes the existence of a broadcast channel to be used by the participants and the dealer. She gave solutions for the case of a correct dealer as well as for the case of a faulty dealer, allowing correct reconstruction of a secret with high probability, without any cryptographic assumptions and in the presence of a computationally unbounded adversary. In her scheme, each server stores n different pieces of verification information, one for each other server, with each piece as large as the share (data) being verified.

Existing work leaves open three important questions for systems in which $n \geq 2t + 1$:

1. Is there a distributed storage scheme that doesn't depend on unproven assumptions, cryptographic or other, and whose space requirements are smaller than those of error correcting codes?

2. Is there a distributed storage scheme that can tolerate a computationally unbounded adversary, and whose space requirements are smaller than those of error correcting codes?

3. Is there a secret sharing scheme that does not depend on unproven assumptions and provides information-theoretic secrecy with high probability, but whose space requirements are smaller than those of Rabin [2]?

We answer all questions in the affirmative by introducing two new techniques for information verification in the presence of a computationally unbounded adversary. The first technique, which we call *private hashing*, allows a server p to verify information of size s of another server q by using $O(hms^{1/m})$ private bits at p and h bits at q. If q changes its information, this will be detected with probability $1 - (1 - 1/2^m)^h$ (for $m = 2$, the detection probability is $1 - (3/4)^h$). Also, p learns nothing about q's information. Our numbers are to be compared to at least $2s$ bits of information at p and at least s bits of information at q that are needed by Rabin's scheme, with detection probability $1 - (1/2)^s$.

Our second technique organizes the verification information in such a way that each server needs to verify only $O(\log n)$ others—in other schemes that tolerate computationally unbounded adversaries, each server verifies the information of all others. This technique relies on the fast majority vote algorithm of Boyer and Moore [8]. (We organize the verification information in such a way that a modified form of the Boyer-Moore algorithm can be used even though every server can only verify $O(\log n)$ others.)

These techniques allow us to achieve the following results.

For distributed storage, we present a scheme with *total* space usage $2S + O(nhm(\log n + k)S^{1/m})$, where S is the total data size, m is a constant and k and h are security parameters. The failure probability is no more than $(9/4)n(1 - 2^{-m})^h + (1/2)^k$. When we take $h \in \Theta(\log n)$ to reduce the error probability to an arbitrary constant $\epsilon < 1$, these numbers guarantee a blow-up less than 2.1 and space overhead in $O((\log n)^2)$, which is independent of the data size. In comparison to the previously proposed schemes, we reduce the storage requirements

significantly without relying on unproven assumptions, and still tolerate computationally unbounded adversaries. Our scheme tolerates an adaptive adversary
that can choose which servers to corrupt next based on publicly available information and the private information of already corrupted servers. Our scheme
does not tolerate a fully adaptive adversary—the difference is that a fully adaptive adversary can look at a server's private data and then decide whether or
not it wants to corrupt it. In practice, the adaptive adversary model is the most
powerful model of interest because we can consider a server compromised as
soon as any of its private data is compromised. As in all previously proposed
schemes, we assume that the clients are correct, but unlike other schemes we
also require that the readers not be subject to Byzantine failures (we discuss
this requirement in Section 2).

For secret sharing, we present a scheme with share size $s + O(\log^2 nms^{1/m})$,
for any constant m, where s is the secret size, for the case of a correct dealer.
This scheme relies on private hashing and our modification of the Boyer-Moore
algorithm. This provides a significant improvement over Rabin's share size of
$(3n + 1)s$. Our secret sharing schemes are formulated in a model identical to
that of Rabin, namely an adaptive computationally unbounded adversary and an
arbitrarily small probability of error. A fully adaptive adversary does not make
sense for secret sharing; if the adversary could access servers' private information,
it could defeat any scheme by reconstructing the secret. Even in the case of
a faulty dealer, we can use our hashing procedure for verification in place of
Rabin's verification procedure and reduce the share size from $s + sf(n)$ to to $s + s^{1/m} f(n)\text{polylog}(n)$ for any constant m (here, f specifies the overhead associated
with the secret-sharing scheme).

2   System Model

Storage System and Secret Sharing. The storage system consists of n servers
$s_1, \ldots, s_n$ and is accessed by external clients. Each server may be *correct* or
faulty, but the number of faulty servers is at most $(n - 1)/2$. The correct servers
work as intended throughout the period in which the system is accessed. The
faulty servers may fail in any arbitrary way at any time. For example, they may
stop responding to requests, modify the data stored on them, or collude with
other faulty servers to modify the data and attempt to mislead the clients that
access them. In secret sharing, the servers are called participants. The dealer can
be thought of as a client and the participant themselves become clients when
the secret is opened.

Communication and Synchrony. We assume reliable and private communication
channels between the clients and the servers. This is the same model assumed
in Rabin's paper [2] and is standard in unconditionally secure secret sharing
schemes. Assuming private communication channels is not standard for the secure storage problem, where existing solutions assume authenticated channels.
In practice, private channels can be implemented using encryption and authentication, but this is not the only way to implement private channels, so assuming

private channels does not imply assuming encrypted channels. We assume a synchronous system, in other words, that it is possible to detect non-responding servers. Even though it has not been explicitly stated in previous work, this assumption is needed to tolerate $(n-1)/2$ arbitrary failures.

Clients. In this work, we assume clients that access the storage system are correct. A writer will correctly follow its protocol and a reader will not divulge private information that it collects during a read operation. The assumption of a correct reader is not significantly stronger than that of a correct writer. In practice, it is not hard to check that a reader will only send read requests and nothing else to servers. This can be enforced locally by restricting read requests to use a well defined interface or by requiring them to go through a trusted proxy. The correct reader assumption only affects the assumptions for the secure storage system, and, as mentioned in the introduction, is not an issue in the model for secret sharing.

Adversary. We consider an adaptive adversary that can choose which servers to corrupt next based on publicly available information and private information of already corrupted servers. The adversary has unbounded computation power. We do not assume a fully adaptive adversary that can decide what to do next based on private information of non-corrupted servers.

3   Efficient Information Checking

In information checking, there are four participants: the dealer, the recipient, the checker, and the verifier (In Rabin's scheme, the recipient is called intermediary, the checker is called the recipient that also functions as a verifier). The dealer sends verification information V to the checker. Also, the dealer sends data S and leakage-prevention information r to the recipient. At a later time, the recipient and the checker pass the information they received to a verifier. Information checking should satisfy the following two properties:

1. No cheating. If the dealer, checker, and verifier are correct, then the recipient cannot provide incorrect data to the verifier without being detected with very high probability.
2. No leakage. If the dealer is correct, then V leaks no information about S.

In our scheme, the verification information V consists of a *private hash* value H and a random selection pattern *Select*. The size of V is considerably smaller than the size of S. Hashing is done recursively by dividing S into pieces, then combining the hash values of the pieces to obtain the hash of S. The space and time complexity of the hashing function depends on a parameter m that determines the depth of the recursion, or number of levels of hashing. We first describe the 1-level base case, then we describe the m-level case.

Figure 1 shows the 1-level and m-level procedures used by the dealer to calculate a single bit of H; to calculate h bits, the same procedure is repeated h times. The h applications of the algorithm are independent and so are the random patterns generated for each of the h bits.

Hash(S: bit string of size $s_m = k^m$, $Select$: matrix of $m \times k$ bits, r: bit)

Hash$_1$($select, S, start, end$)
    Hash$_1 = 0$
    for $i = start$ **to** end **do**
        if $select[i]$ **then**
            Hash$_1 = $ Hash$_1 \oplus S[i]$

Hash$_m$($S, start, end$)
1:   **if** $m = 1$ **then**
2:       Hash$_m = $ Hash$_1(Select[1], S, start, end)$
3:   **else**
4:       Hash$_m = 0$
5:       $s_{m-1} = (end - start + 1)/k$
6:       **for** $i = 0$ **to** k **do**
7:          **if** $Select[m][i]$ **then**
8:          Hash$_m = $ Hash$_m \oplus$ Hash$_{m-1}(S, start + is_{m-1}, start + (i+1)s_{m-1} - 1)$

begin
    Hash $= $ Hash$_m(0, size - 1) \oplus r$
end

Fig. 1. Calculating 1-bit hash value

To produce a single hash bit in 1-level hashing, we calculate the XOR of a randomly selected subset of bits of S. In the function Hash$_1$, a contiguous set of bits of S starting at $start$ and ending at end is hashed. To hash all of S, we use $start = 0$ and $end = \text{size}(S) - 1$ and these are the values used when Hash is called with the number of levels m equal to 1. The function Hash$_1$ has a parameter $Select$, which is a uniformly random string of 0's and 1's, and is used to determine which bits of S are XOR-ed together.

After the appropriate bits are XOR-ed together, a random bit r is XOR-ed with the result in order to prevent leakage; with this addition to the protocol, a checker that stores a hash bit for S cannot learn anything about S.

In m-level hashing, a string of size k^m is divided into k strings of size k^{m-1} each. Then $(m-1)$-level hashing is applied (recursively) to each of the k strings, and finally 1-level hashing (lines 6–8) to the resulting k bits. In the recursion, the selection patterns are not independent: the k hashings at level $(m-1)$ all use the same $(m-1) \times k$ sub-matrix of the $m \times k$ $Select$ matrix. The 1-level hashing done at level m (lines 6–8) uses the remaining $1 \times k$ sub-matrix of the $Select$ matrix.

To summarize: in order to hash an s-bit string into h bits, we use a pattern consisting of $mhs^{1/m}$ bits, and an additional h random bits. The hash can be calculated in no more than mhs steps. Our final algorithm (Section 4.2) requires $2(\log n + k)$ hashes to be stored by each server. The total overhead for calculating all of these is thus $O(hms^{1/m}n \log n)$, where m is an arbitrary constant and s the size of the data. If $h \in \Theta(\log n)$, this reduces to $O(ms^{1/m}n \log^2 n)$.

Lemma 1. *Let Select be an $(m \times k)$-bit matrix where each bit is generated independently uniformly at random. Let r be a bit and S a k^m-bit string, and $H = \text{Hash}(S, Select, r)$ the hash value of S. For k^m-bit string $S' \neq S$ and any bit r', the probability (over the random choice of Select) that*

$$\text{Hash}(S, Select, r) = \text{Hash}(S', Select, r') \tag{1}$$

is at most $p_m = 1 - 2^{-m}$.

Proof. Let $v = r' \oplus r$. Then by the definition of the function Hash, (1) holds if and only if $\text{Hash}_m(S, 0, k^m - 1) \oplus \text{Hash}_m(S', 0, k^m - 1) = v$.

Since the same pattern *Select* is used for S and S', $\text{Hash}_m(S, 0, k^m - 1) \oplus \text{Hash}_m(S', 0, k^m - 1) = \text{Hash}_m(S \oplus S', 0, k^m - 1)$.

To prove the statement of the lemma, we prove by induction on m that for any bit v, the probability that $\text{Hash}_m(S \oplus S', 0, k^m - 1) \neq v$ is at most $1 - 2^{-m}$.

For the base case ($m = 1$), let C_1 be the (non-empty) set of positions on which S and S' differ and let A_1 be the set of positions that are *selected* by Hash_1. Then $\text{Hash}_1(S \oplus S', 0, k^m - 1) = v$ if and only if the parity of $|A_1 \cap C_1|$ is the same as the parity of v. Since A_1 is random, it follows that $A_1 \cap C_1$ is a random subset of C_1. Thus the probability that $|A_1 \cap C_1|$ is even (or odd) is exactly $1/2$. In other words, in the base case the probability that (1) holds is exactly $1/2$.

For the induction step, consider the loop in lines 6–8. The function Hash_{m-1} is applied to k groups $S_1, \ldots, S_k$ of bits of S, resulting in k bits, some of which are then XOR-ed together. The choice of which among the k bits will be XOR-ed together is determined by the k-bit vector $Select[m]$.

Let $C_m = \{i \mid \text{Hash}_{m-1}(S_i) \neq \text{Hash}_{m-1}(S'_i)\}$. (We are abusing the notation slightly here by writing S_i as a parameter of Hash_{m-1} instead of specifying S_i as a subset of S using *start* and *end*.) Since $S \neq S'$, there is an i^* such that $S_{i^*} \neq S'_{i^*}$. The probability that C_m is nonempty is at least the probability that $i^* \in C_m$. By the induction hypothesis, $\text{Hash}_{m-1}(S_{i^*}) \neq \text{Hash}_{m-1}(S'_{i^*})$ with probability at most $1 - 2^{-(m-1)}$ (note that $\text{Hash}_{m-1}(S_{i^*}) \neq \text{Hash}_{m-1}(S'_{i^*})$ if an only if $\text{Hash}_m(S \oplus S', 0, k^m - 1) \neq 0$).

In fact, if C_m contains more than one element, this probability will be even smaller, but in any case it is at most $1 - 2^{-(m-1)}$. Call this probability p_{m-1}. Let $A_m = \{i \mid Select[m][i] = 1\}$, that is, the set of level $m - 1$ hash bits that are selected by Hash_m to calculate the hash bit in line 7. Let $J_m = C_m \cap A_m$. Clearly, $\text{Hash}_m(S \oplus S', 0, k^m - 1) = \bigoplus_{i \in A_m} (\text{Hash}_{m-1}(S_i) \oplus \text{Hash}_{m-1}(S'_i)) = |J_m| \mod 2$.

The above expression is equal to v if and only if the parity of $|J_m|$ is. Since A_m is random, it follows that $J_m = A_m \cap C_m$ is a random subset of C_m. Thus the probability that the parity of $|J_m|$ is equal to v is exactly $1/2$ if C_m is nonempty. If C_m is empty, then the $|J_m| = 0$. Thus for $v = 0$, the probability that $|J_m| \mod 2 = v$ is $(1/2) \cdot p_{m-1} + 1 \cdot (1 - p_{m-1})$. For $v = 1$, on the other hand, this probability is $(1/2) \cdot p_{m-1} + 0 \cdot (1 - p_{m-1})$. In both cases, $|J_m|$ is of equal parity as v with probability $p_m \leq p_{m-1}/2 + (1 - p_{m-1})$. This is maximized for $p_{m-1} = 1 - 2^{-(m-1)}$, which gives $p_m \leq 1 - 2^{-m}$ and proves the induction step.

Lemma 2. *(No cheating.) When using level-m private hashing, if the dealer, checker and verifier are correct, then the recipient cannot provide incorrect data to the verifier without being detected with probability $1 - (1 - 2^{-m})^h$, where h is the length of the verification information.*

Proof. Follows from the description of information checking and Lemma 1 by noting that the h hash bits are independent.

Lemma 3. *(No leakage.) In private hashing, assuming the dealer is correct, the verification information leaks no information about S.*

Proof. The matrix *Select* is generated randomly, independently of S, and $H = $ Hash$(S, Select, r)$ is an XOR with the (uniform and unknown to the checker) random string r, and thus random and independent of S as well.

4   Storage and Recovery

Distributed Storage. When storing the data, a server stores the data pieces computed using IDA [9] with blow-up factor equal to 2. The IDA scheme assumes that data cannot be tampered with, so we need to add extra verification information to detect pieces that have been tampered with and recover the original data. The verification information kept at each server verifies the data as well as the verification information kept at other servers. To retrieve the data, the reader collects all the information (data and verification information) from all the servers. Then, the reader executes an algorithm that enables it to identify (with high probability) a majority of servers whose information has not been tampered with. A basic operation is for the reader to check whether the verification information obtained from one server correctly verifies the information it's supposed to verify. If the verification information has not been tampered with, then with high probability the verified information is correct. The details of the particular algorithm and verification checks are given in subsequent sections.

Secret Sharing. We only present the case in which the dealer is correct. In the sharing phase, the dealer computes the shares using [1] and sends them to the participants; In addition the dealer send the participants verification information for the shares of other participants. In the reconstruction phase, every participant sends all the information it has to all other participants. Then, each participant executes an algorithm that enables it to identify (with high probability) a majority of servers whose information has not been tampered with. This will enable all correct participants to reconstruct the secret.

We start by presenting a scheme in which every server verifies every other server. Then we present a scheme in which every server verifies only $2(\log n + k)$ other servers, where k is a security parameter. This will allow us to achieve the results listed in the introduction.

4.1   Full Verification

In this section we describe a verification scheme in which each server contains information to verify each other server. In this scheme, the servers are arranged on a line from left to right.

```
0: for i = 1 to n do
1:    V[i, 0] = IDA data piece
2: for i = 2 to n do
3:    for j = i − 1 downto 1 do
4:       V[i, j] = H(V[j], R[j])
5:       R[j, i] = the random bits computed in line 4 to prevent leakage
6: for i = n − 1 downto 2 do
7:    for j = i + 1 to n do
8:       V[i, j] = H(V[j])
```

Fig. 2. Full Verification

We can divide the verification information at a given server into two types. The *left-verification* information of a server p is the verification information that p keeps for servers to its left. The *right-verification* information of a server p is the verification information that p keeps for servers to its right. The left-verification information of a server p_r verifies *all* the left-verification information of a server p_l to its left. The right-verification information of a server p_l verifies *all* the verification information (both left- and right-) of a server p_r to its right. We say that the information on two servers is *consistent* if each of the two servers verifies the information of the other server. We will abuse notation and say that the *servers are consistent* and they are related by the *consistency* relation. The algorithm for calculating the verification information is shown in Figure 2. In the algorithm, $V[i, j]$ is i's verification information for j and $R[i, j]$ are the random bits kept at j to prevent leakage to i. In the algorithm, $V[j]$ refers to all of j's verification information at the point it is used in the computation. Similarly we define $R[j]$. In line 4, $V[j]$ is j's left verification information because at that point only j's left verification information has been computed. In line 8, $V[j]$ is j's total verification information.

Majority Elements. A simple approach to recovery would have a reader check that the server's information is consistent with the information of a majority of servers. This will guarantee that all correct servers will pass the check and their information can be used in recovery and also that no information that has been tampered with will be used. Unfortunately, this simple approach will lead to a quadratic number of verifications at recovery time (for now, we will ignore the actual cost of checking whether two servers are consistent). Our goal is to reduce the number of consistency checks to $2n$. We will first find a server p_c whose information is guaranteed to be correct and then find all the correct servers among the subset of servers whose information is verified by p_c. To achieve a linear number of checks, we modify the well-known Boyer-Moore linear-time algorithm [8] for finding a majority element in an array. The linear-time majority element algorithm uses only equality tests. In our setting, we do not have an equality test, but we can check if the information on two servers mutually verifies each other. The consistency relation does not have the same transitivity properties as equality and so we modify the majority algorithm so that the transitivity properties of consistency are sufficient.

Transitivity of Verification. Here we prove the necessary transitivity properties of the verification information.

Lemma 4 (Correctness). *Let p, q be two consistent servers such that p appears before q on the verification line and the information of p is correct. All the information at q is then correct with high probability.*

Proof. Since, p appears to the left of q, it follows that p verifies all the information of q. Since, p is correct, by Lemma 2, if q provides incorrect information it will be verified by p with probability at most $(1 - 2^{-m})^h$, where h is the size of the hash.

Lemma 5 (Right Transitivity). *Let $p_1, \ldots, p_u$ be a sequence of servers that appear in that order on the verification line and such that p_i and p_{i+1} are consistent, for all $1 \leq i \leq u - 1$. If p_1 is correct, then all the information on servers p_u, is correct with probability $1 - (u - 1)(1 - 2^{-m})^h$.*

Proof. If all consecutive pairs of servers are consistent and p_u is incorrect, then one of the verifications along the line (say p_i by p_{i-1}) must have failed. For each i, by Lemma 4, the verification of i by $i - 1$ fails with probability $(1 - 2^{-m})^h$. Thus the probability that there is a failure in at least one of the $u-1$ verifications is $(u - 1)(1 - 2^{-m})^h$.

Lemma 6 (Left Transitivity). *Let $p_1, \ldots, p_u$ be a sequence of servers that appear in that order on the verification line and such that p_i and p_{i+1} are consistent, $1 \leq i \leq u - 1$. If p_u is correct then all the left-verification information on servers p_1 is correct with probability $1 - (u - 1)(1 - 2^{-m})^h$.*

Proof. The proof is similar to the proof of Lemma 5 and is omitted.

In what follows, we assume that the security parameter h is chosen so that the probability of failure is small enough. We will later calculate a value of h that works.

Lemmas 5 and 6 imply that if p_j is correct for some $1 \leq j \leq u$, then all the data on servers $p_1, \ldots, p_u$ is correct with high probability.

The lemmas we have proved enable us to find a server whose data and verification information is correct using the algorithm shown in Figure 3.

The algorithm is almost identical to that of Boyer and Moore [8], but with one important difference. In Boyer and Moore's algorithm, there is no need for the assignment on line 8, whereas in our algorithm, the assignment is crucial to guarantee that the transitivity lemmas can be used. The following theorem

1: $count := 0$
2: **for** $i = 1$ **to** n **do**
3:     **if** $count = 0$ **then**
4:         $correct := i$
5:         $count := 1$
6:     **else**
7:         **if** p_i and $p_{correct}$ are consistent **then**
8:             $correct := i$
9:             $count := count + 1$
10:         **else**
11:             $count := count - 1$

Fig. 3. Finding a correct server

0: **for** $i = 1$ **to** n **do**
1:     $V[i, 0] = $ IDA data piece
2: **for** $i = 2$ **to** n **do**
3:     **for** $j = i - 1$ **downto** $\max(1, i - \ell)$ **do**
4:         $V[i, j] = H(V[j], R[j])$
5:         $R[j, i] = $ the random bits computed in line 4
                to prevent leakage
6: **for** $i = n - 1$ **downto** 2 **do**
7:     **for** $j = i + 1$ **to** $\min(i + \ell, n)$ **do**
8:         $V[i, j] = H(V[j])$

Fig. 4. Verification on an ℓ-Path

(whose proof is omitted for lack of space) shows that the algorithm in Figure 3 will find a correct server (a server whose information has not been tampered with) if a majority of the servers is correct.

Theorem 1. *If a majority of the servers is correct, then with high probability the information of server $p_{correct}$ at the end of the main loop of algorithm of Figure 3 is not tampered with.*

The algorithm allows us to find a server $p_{rightmost}$ with correct data. To find all such servers (this includes all correct ones), we find all servers consistent with $p_{rightmost}$ (note that no server to the right of $p_{rightmost}$ is correct). Finding all correct servers in a set of n thus takes no more than $2n$ consistency checks, therefore the probability that the servers identified as correct really are so is at least $1 - 2n(1 - 2^{-m})^h$.

4.2 Efficient Verification

We present a scheme that relies on the Boyer-Moore majority algorithm, with each server verifying only a small subset of other servers, and achieves very good performance. The scheme guarantees with high probability that the set of correct servers and other servers whose data is not corrupted is identified. It requires $2(\log(n) + k)$ hash values of size h per server to provide a probability of failure at most $(9/4)n(1 - 2^{-m})^h + 2^{-k}$.

The Verification Graph. The verification graph we use is not complete. In the verification algorithm, the servers are arranged in a line $s_1, s_2, \ldots, s_n$ and s_i and s_j verify each other by if and only if $|i - j| \leq \ell$. The resulting graph is called the ℓ-th *power of a path* on n vertices and is denoted by P_n^ℓ. We calculate the verification information as shown in Figure 4, where ℓ is a parameter that determines how many servers each server verifies.

Since each server is verified by only $\ell \ll t$ other servers, an adversary could corrupt all of them and make the now isolated server useless even if it is correct. To prevent this, the writer hides the ordering of the servers in the line by giving each of them a random, unique and private ID. The IDs are used by the reader during reconstruction. However, they are not public information prior to the reconstruction phase and so are unknown to the adversary, who can only learn a server's ID after corrupting the server. Thus the adversary cannot choose a particular ID and then corrupt the server with that ID. So the corrupted server's IDs are selected independently at random. The algorithm must take into account the situations in which corrupted servers report incorrect IDs.

Since at most $t < n/2$ servers are ever corrupted, the probability that a given server is faulty is less than $1/2$, regardless of whether its neighbors in the line are corrupted or not. Thus, given $i \in \{1, 2, \ldots, n - \ell\}$, the probability that ℓ servers immediately following the i-th one are faulty is less than $2^{-\ell}$. If we choose $\ell = 2(\log n + k)$, then the probability that no server is followed by ℓ faulty servers is bounded above by $1/2^k$. It follows that with probability at least $1 - 1/2^k$, in P^ℓ, the set of all correct servers forms a connected component. In what follows we assume without referring to probability (except, of course, when computing the probability of success of the algorithm) that there is no contiguous subsequence of faulty servers of length more than ℓ.

Boyer-Moore Majority for Path Powers. The algorithm is based on the Boyer-Moore majority procedure, but some modifications are necessary to make it run with high probability. First, in Figure 5 we show the initialization.

Since the corrupted servers can advertise themselves under fake names, it may happen that several servers give the same value as their ID. Clearly, at most one of these is correct. During initialization, the servers are sorted into buckets, according to the IDs they report. Each bucket is maintained in the form of a linked list. The (arbitrary) order of servers in each bucket induces, together with the order on the buckets (according to the IDs reported by the servers), an order on the set of servers. It is this order that the algorithm uses to examine the servers one by one.

We assume throughout that there is no contiguous subsequence of more than ℓ buckets containing only faulty servers. This means that even though perhaps we have examined more than ℓ servers between one that reports i as ID and one that reports $i + j$ as ID, as long as $j < \ell$, we expect the two servers to have verification information for each other. However, it may still happen that the basic algorithm (Figure 3) tries to cross-verify a pair of servers not adjacent in the verification graph. We argue that in such a case, we can drop some of the servers, backtrack slightly and continue the algorithm, and still with high probability find a correct server. The algorithm is presented in Figure 6.

```
1:    for i := 1 to n:                    // (1–2): Initialize buckets
2:        list[i] := null
3:    for i := 1 to n:                    // (3–7): Sort servers into buckets,
4:        if list[server[i].ID] = null    // thus creating linked lists.
5:            last[server[i].ID] := server[i]
6:        server[i].next := list[server[i].ID]
7:        list[server[i].ID] := server[i]
8:    i := 1                              // (8–11): Find the first nonempty bucket.
9:    while (list[i] = null) do
10:       i := i + 1
11    start.next := list[i]; startindex := i
12:   i := n                              // (12–15): Find the last nonempty bucket.
13:   while (list[i] = null) do
14:       i := i − 1
15:   endindex := i
16:   for i := startindex to endindex − 1// (16–22) Initialize the remaining
17        if (list[i] ≠ null)             // next pointers.
18:           j := i + 1
19:           while (j ≤ n and list[j] = null) do
20:               j := j + 1
21:           if (j > n) break
22:           last[i].next := list[j]
```

Fig. 5. Finding a correct server: initialization

Underlying the implementation is the notion of a *consistent component*. During the execution of the algorithm, whenever the variable *count* is positive, the algorithm knows a set of at least *count* consistent servers that induce a connected subgraph of the verification graph. The algorithm maintains several pieces of information about the current consistent component: the variable *count* stores the number of consistent servers in the component; *correct* stores the head of the consistent component (the latest server added); *firstnon* and *lastnon*, respectively, point at the first and last element (as ordered by the position in the path) known not to belong to the component; the *next* pointers link the servers known to be inconsistent with the component into a list.

The main actions the algorithm performs are the following: **(1)** Whenever *count* reaches 0, a new consistent component is started. **(2)** Whenever a server p is found to be inconsistent with the head of a component, the last *non-belonging* server (*lastnon*) is linked to p and *lastnon* updated to point to p. **(3)** If the head of the component cannot be checked for consistency against the current server under consideration, the algorithm concludes that the whole component must be faulty (as justified below) and restart the algorithm from *firstnon*.

Note that in the case where more than one server uses the same ID, if one of them is found consistent with the current component, the others servers will be found inconsistent and will consequently be ignored (unless the component is subsequently discarded).

```
23:   i := start; correct := start.next; count := 0; firstnon := null
24:   while (i ≠ null) do
25:        i := i.next
26:        if (|i.ID−correct.ID| > ℓ)
27:             count := 0
28:             i := firstnon
29:             firstnon := null
30:             correct := i
31:        if count = 0 then
32:             correct := i
33:             count := 1
34:        else
35:             if i and correct are consistent
36:                  count := count + 1
37:                  correct := i
38:             else
39:                  count := count − 1
40:                  if (firstnon = null)
41:                       firstnon := i
42:                       lastnon := i
43:                  else
44:                       lastnon.next := i
45:                       lastnon := i
```

Fig. 6. Finding a correct server

We show (using an amortization argument) that the total number of consistency checks is linear (with a small hidden constant) in the number of servers.

Theorem 2. *If a majority of the servers is correct, then, with high probability, the information of server $p_{correct}$ at the end of the main loop of algorithm of Figure 6 is not tampered with.*

Storage Overhead. Since we use patterns to hash strings consisting of, among other things, other patterns, the size of the pattern required is not immediately obvious. According to the rules for storing verification information, each server will store its share of data (size s), the pattern (size p), the $2(\log n + k)$ hashes (each of size h), and the $2(\log n + k)$ random strings (each of size h) used for the data hashed by verifying servers. Thus the total size of data that needs to be hashed by verifying servers is $s + 4h(\log n + k) + p$. Given a string of size s to be hashed into a string of size h, the pattern is of size $hs^{1/m}$. Hence the size of the pattern p must satisfy the inequality $p \geq h(s + p + 4h(\log n + k))^{1/m}$. Under the very reasonable assumption that $\sqrt{s} \geq 4h + 6$, it is enough that $p = hs^{1/m}(\log n + k)^{1/m}$ (we omit the derivation for lack of space).

Running Time. It may not be obvious that the removal of a component and another invocation of the algorithm (and, recursively, possibly more than one) can be performed in a total linear number of consistency verifications.

Theorem 3. *The total number of consistency checks made in the algorithm of Figure 6 before a correct server is found is at most $5n/4$.*

In addition to these $5n/4$ checks, another n may be necessary to find all correct servers. Each consistency check takes time proportional to h times the size of the data stored at a server.

Failure Probability. The algorithm could fail in one of two ways: either one of the consistency checks fails with a false positive, or there is a contiguous sequence of corrupted servers. The first happens with probability $(1 - 2^{-m})^h$ for each check, and the second with probability $(1/2)^k$. Since there are at most $(9/4)n$ consistency checks, the total probability of failure is no more than $(9/4)n(1 - 2^{-m})^h + (1/2)^k$. With $h \in \Theta(\log n)$, this probability can be made an arbitrarily small constant.

References

1. Shamir, A.: How to share a secret. Communications of the ACM **22** (1979) 612–613
2. Rabin, T.: Robust sharing of secrets when the dealer is honest or cheating. Journal of the ACM **41** (1994) 1089–1109
3. MacWilliams, F.J., Sloane, N.J.A.: The Theory of error-correcting codes. North-Holland (1977)
4. Krawczyk, H.: Distributed fingerprints and secure information dispersal. In: Proceedings of the 12th annual ACM symposium on principles of distributed computing. (1993) 207–218
5. Alon, N., Kaplan, H., Krivelevich, M., Malkhi, D., Stern, J.: Scalable secure storage when half the system is faulty. Information and Computation **174** (2002) 203–213
6. Alon, N., Kaplan, H., Krivelevich, M., Malkhi, D., Stern, J.: Addendum to "Scalable secure storage when half the system is faulty". Unpublished Manuscript (2003)
7. Stinson, D., Wei, R.: Bibliography on secret sharing schemes (1998) Available on the Internet at http://www.cacr.math.uwaterloo.ca/~dstinson/ssbib.html.
8. Boyer, R.S., Moore, J.S.: MJRTY—a fast majority vote algorithm. In Boyer, R.S., ed.: Automated reasoning: Essays in honor of Willy Bledsoe. Kluwer (1991) 105–117
9. Rabin, M.O.: Efficient dispersal of information for security, load balancing and fault tolerance. Journal of the ACM **36** (1989) 335–348

Optimal Dispersal of Certificate Chains

Eunjin Jung[1], Ehab S. Elmallah[2], and Mohamed G. Gouda[1]

[1] Department of Computer Sciences
The University of Texas at Austin
Austin, TX USA
[2] Department of Computing Science
University of Alberta
Edmonton, Alberta Canada

Abstract. We consider a network where users can issue certificates that identify the public keys of other users in the network. The issued certificates in a network constitute a set of certificate chains between users. A user u can obtain the public key of other user v from a certificate chain from u to v in the network. For the certificate chain from u to v, u is called the source of the chain and v is called the destination of the chain. Certificates in each chain are dispersed between the source and destination of the chain such that the following condition holds. If any user u needs to securely send messages to any other user v in the network, then u can use the certificates stored in u and v to obtain the public key of v (then u can use the public key of v to set up a shared key with v to securely send messages to v). The cost of dispersing certificates in a set of chains among the source and destination users in a network is measured by the total number of certificates that need to be stored in all users. A dispersal of a set of certificate chains in network is optimal if no other dispersal of the same chain set has a strictly lower cost. In this paper, we show that the problem of computing optimal dispersal of a given chain set is NP-Complete. We also present three polynomial-time algorithms that compute optimal dispersals for three special classes of chain sets.

1 Introduction

We consider a network where users would like to send messages securely to other users. A user who would like to send a secure message is called a *source* and a user who is intended to receive such a message is called a *destination*.

In the Internet, it is common that one source may wish to send messages to many destinations. For example, a source Alice may wish to send her credit card number securely to several destination shopping sites, say Amazon.com, eBay.com, and price-line.com. The secure communication between a source and a destination is protected by encrypting each exchanged message with a shared key only known to the source and destination.

In this network, each user u, whether source or destination, has a private key rk_u and a public key bk_u. In order for a source u to share a key sk with a destination v, u encrypts key sk using the public key bk_v of v and send the result, denoted $bk_v < u, v, sk >$, to v. Only v can decrypt this message and obtain key sk shared with u. This

R. Guerraoui (Ed.): DISC 2004, LNCS 3274, pp. 435–449, 2004.

scenario necessitates that u knows the public key bk_v of v. In the above example, Alice needs to know the public keys of Amazon, eBay, and priceline.

If a user u knows the public key bk_v of another user v in the network, then u can issue a certificate, called a certificate from u to v, that identifies the public key bk_v of v. This certificate can be used by any user that knows the public key of u to further acquire the public key of v.

A certificate from u to v is of the following form:

$$rk_u < u, v, bk_v >$$

This certificate is signed using the private key rk_u of u, and it includes three items: the identity of the certificate issuer u, the identity of the certificate subject v, and the public key of the certificate subject bk_v. Any user that knows the public key bk_u of u can use bk_u to obtain the public key bk_v of v from the certificate from u to v. Note that when a user obtains the public key bk_v of user v from the certificate, the user not only finds out what bk_v is, but also acquires the proof of the association that bk_v is indeed the public key of user v.

The certificates issued by different users in a network can be represented by a directed graph, called the *certificate graph* of the network. Each node in the certificate graph represents a user in the network. Each directed edge from node u to node v in the certificate graph represents a certificate from u to v in the network.

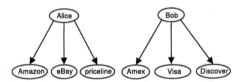

Fig. 1. A certificate graph of Alice and Bob

Fig. 1 shows a certificate graph for a network with two sources, Alice and Bob, and six destinations, Amazon, eBay, priceline, Amex, Visa, and Discover. According to this graph,

Alice issues three certificates
$(Alice, Amazon)$, $(Alice, eBay)$, and $(Alice, priceline)$, and
Bob issues three certificates
$(Bob, Amex)$, $(Bob, Visa)$, and $(Bob, Discover)$

A more efficient way to support secure communication between the sources and the destinations is to introduce some intermediaries between the sources and the destinations. The number of introduced intermediaries is much smaller than the number of sources and the number of destinations. Each intermediary has its own public and private key pair. The sources know the public keys of intermediaries and the intermediaries issue certificates of the public keys of the destinations. For example, two intermediaries, namely VeriSign and CertPlus, can be introduced between the two sources and the six destinations in Fig. 1. The result is the certificate graph in Fig. 2.

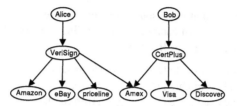

Fig. 2. A certificate graph with intermediaries

According to the certificate graph in Fig. 2, Alice needs to issue only one certificate to VeriSign and Bob needs to issue only one certificate to CertPlus. Alice can then use the two certificates $(Alice, VeriSign)$ and $(VeriSign, Amazon)$ to obtain the public key bk_{Amazon}, and so can securely send messages to Amazon. Also, Bob can use the two certificates $(Bob, CertPlus)$ and $(CertPlus, Visa)$ to obtain the public key bk_{Visa}, and then can securely send messages to Visa.

Note that there is a certificate $(VeriSign, Amex)$ in the certificate graph in Fig. 2 that is not needed to support secure communication between any source and any destination in Fig. 1. This redundancy is removed by specifying which "certificate chains" are being used by the sources and destinations. Certificate chains are defined as follows:

A simple path from a source u to a destination v in a certificate graph G is called a *chain* from u to v in G. u is the *source* of the chain and v is the *destination* of the chain. For users u and v in a certificate graph G, if u wishes to securely send messages to v, then there must be a chain from u to v in G. On the other hand, if there is a chain from u to v, then u does not necessarily wish to securely send messages to v. Fig. 3 shows six chains that are needed to support the secure communications between the two sources and the six destinations in Fig. 1. Since Alice does not need to securely communicate with Amex, the certificate chain $(Alice, VeriSign),(VeriSign, Amex)$ in the certificate graph in Fig. 2 is not included in Fig. 3.

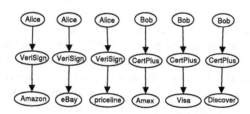

Fig. 3. Certificate chains from Fig. 2

The certificates in each chain need to be dispersed between the source and destination of the chain such that if a source u wishes to securely send a message to a destination v then u can obtain the public key of v from the set of certificates stored in u and v. (Note that to "store a certificate in a user" does not necessarily mean that the user has a local copy of the certificate. Rather, it means that the user only needs to know where to find the certificate, if a need for that certificate arises, either in its local storage or in a remote location.)

For example, assume that each source in Fig. 3 stores its certificate to the corresponding intermediary, and that each destination in Fig. 3 stores the certificate from its corresponding intermediary to itself. Thus,

Alice	stores the certificate $(Alice, VeriSign)$,
Bob	stores the certificate $(Bob, CertPlus)$,
Amazon	stores the certificate $(VeriSign, Amazon)$,
eBay	stores the certificate $(VeriSign, eBay)$,
priceline	stores the certificate $(VeriSign, priceline)$,
Amex	stores the certificate $(CertPlus, Amex)$,
Visa	stores the certificate $(CertPlus, Visa)$, and
Discover	stores the certificate $(CertPlus, Discover)$

In this case, if Alice wishes to securely send messages to priceline, then Alice can use the two certificates stored in Alice's computer and priceline website to obtain the public key of priceline and securely send the messages to priceline. Certificates that are not part of any chain are not stored because they are not needed. This is illustrated by the certificate $(VeriSign, Amex)$, which appears in Fig. 2 but is not stored in Amex.

Dispersal of certificate chains and its cost are defined in Section 2. In Section 3, we show that finding an optimal dispersal of any set of chains is NP-Complete. Then we present three polynomial-time algorithms which compute optimal dispersal of three rich classes of chain sets.

2   Certificate Dispersal

A *certificate graph* G is a directed graph in which each directed edge, called a *certificate*, is a pair (u, v), where u and v are distinct nodes in G. For each certificate (u, v) in G, u is called the *issuer* of the certificate and v is called the *subject* of the certificate. Note that according to this definition no certificate has the same node as both its issuer and subject.

A sequence of certificates $(v_0, v_1), (v_1, v_2), \cdots, (v_{k-1}, v_k)$ in a certificate graph G, where the nodes $v_0, v_1, \cdots, v_k$ are all distinct, is called a *chain* from v_0 to v_k in G. Node v_0 is called the *source* of the chain and node v_k is called the *destination* of the chain. A set of chains in a certificate graph G is called a *chain set* of G.

A *dispersal* D of a chain set CS assigns a set of certificates in CS to each source node and each destination node in CS such that the following condition holds. The certificates in each chain from a source node u to a destination node v in CS are in the set $D.u \cup D.v$, where $D.u$ and $D.v$ are the two sets of certificates assigned by dispersal D to nodes u and v, respectively.

Let D be a dispersal of a chain set CS. The *cost* of dispersal D, denoted $cost.D$, is the sum of cardinalities of the sets assigned by dispersal D to every source or destination node in CS.

$$cost.D = \sum_{v \text{ is a source or destination node in } CS} |D.v|$$

A dispersal D of a chain set CS is *optimal* if and only if for any other dispersal D' of the same chain set CS,

$$cost.D \leq cost.D'$$

Let c be a certificate that appears in one or more chains in a chain set CS, and let D be a dispersal of CS. The *location* of certificate c assigned by D, denoted $D.c$, is defined as a set of all nodes v such that c is in the set of certificates $D.v$.

The location $D.c$ of a certificate c assigned by a dispersal D of a chain set CS is *optimal* if and only if for any other dispersal D' of CS, $|D.c| \le |D'.c|$.

Theorem 1. *Let D be a dispersal of a chain set CS. If D is optimal, then for every certificate c in CS the location $D.c$ is optimal.*

Proof. The proof is by contradiction. Assume that D is optimal, and there exists another dispersal D' of CS and at least one certificate c in CS such that $|D.c| > |D'.c|$.

Let c be a certificate in CS such that $|D.c| > |D'.c|$. Now define a set of certificates $D''.v$ for every node v in CS as follows.

$$D''.x := \begin{cases} D'.x & \text{if } x = c, \\ D.x & \text{if } x \ne c \end{cases}$$

The sets $D''.v$ for every node v in CS constitute a dispersal, D'', because each certificate c' other than c is assigned to the same nodes to which c' is also assigned by D and c is assigned to the same nodes to which c is assigned by D'. The cost of dispersal D'' is computed as follows.

$$cost.D'' = \sum_{v \in CS} |D''.v| = \sum_{c' \in CS, c' \ne c} |D.c'| + |D'.c|$$

By the assumption $|D.c| > |D'.c|$,

$$cost.D'' = \sum_{c' \in CS, c' \ne c} |D.c'| + |D'.c| < \sum_{c' \in CS, c' \ne c} |D.c'| + |D.c| = cost.D$$

Thus, the cost of dispersal D'' is less than the cost of dispersal D contradicting the assumption that D is an optimal dispersal.

Therefore, the location $D.c$ of c is optimal for every certificate c in CS.   □

Theorem 2. *Let D be a dispersal of a chain set CS. If for every certificate c in CS the location $D.c$ is optimal, then D is an optimal dispersal of CS.*

Proof. The proof is by contradiction. Let D be a dispersal for a chain set CS and for every certificate c in CS the location $D.c$ is optimal. Also, let D' be another dispersal of CS where $cost.D' < cost.D$. By the definition of the cost of dispersal,

$$cost.D' = \sum_{c \in CS} |D'.c| < \sum_{c \in CS} |D.c| = cost.D$$

Thus, there must be at least one certificate c in CS such that $|D'.c| < |D.c|$. This contradicts the definition of an optimal location of c.

Therefore, D is an optimal dispersal of the chain set CS.   □

3   NP-Completeness of Optimal Dispersal of Chain Sets

The problem of optimal dispersal of chain sets is to compute an optimal dispersal of any given chain set.

Theorem 3. *The problem of optimal dispersal of chain sets is NP-Complete.*

Proof. The proof of NP-Completeness of an optimal dispersal of a given chain set consists of two parts. First, we prove that there is a polynomial time algorithm which verifies that an assignment of certificates to nodes is a dispersal. Second, we prove that a well-known NP-Complete problem, the vertex cover problem, can be reduced in polynomial time to an optimal dispersal of a chain set.

Proof of First Part:
Given a chain set CS and a set $D.u$ for each node u in CS, we can verify whether D is a dispersal in polynomial time. For each chain from a node u to a node v in CS, reconstruct the chain from the certificates in $D.u$ and $D.v$. If all the chains in the chain set can be reconstructed, then the given set of $D.u$'s is a dispersal. The time complexity of this verification algorithm is $O(p \times n)$, where p is the number of chains in the chain set and n is the length of the longest chain in CS.

Proof of Second Part:
Consider a vertex cover of a directed graph $G=(V, E)$. A vertex cover of G is a subset $VC \subset V$ such that if $(u, v) \in E$, then $u \in VC$ or $v \in VC$ (or both). We show that an algorithm for optimal dispersal can be used to compute a vertex cover of minimum size of any given graph $G=(V, E)$. We consider the set of nodes $V' = V \cup \{x, y\}$, and build, for every edge (u, v) in E, a chain $(u, x); (x, y); (y, v)$. This constitutes our chain set CS.

Let D be an optimal dispersal of CS. By theorem 1, for every certificate c in CS, $D.c$ is optimal, including $c = (x, y)$. For every chain from u to v in CS, $D.u$ or $D.v$ contains (x, y) from the definition of dispersal. Therefore, u or v is in $D.(x, y)$. For every edge (u, v) in G, $D.(x, y)$ contains u or v. Therefore, $D.(x, y)$ is a vertex cover of G.

We show that $D.(x, y)$ is a vertex cover of minimum size by contradiction. Let S be a vertex cover of G where $|S| < |D.(x, y)|$. Since S is a vertex cover of G, for every edge (u, v) in G, node u or node v is in S. Let D' be a dispersal where all certificates other than (x, y) in CS remain in the same node as in D, and (x, y) stored in all the nodes in S. (D' is a dispersal since for every chain from a node u to a node v in CS, all the certificates in the chain are in $D.u \cup D.v$.) Since we constructed D' so that all other certificates than (x, y) in the same nodes as D and (x, y) is stored in fewer nodes by D' than by D,

$$cost.D' = \sum_{c' \in CS, c' \neq c} |D.c'| + |S| < \sum_{c' \in CS, c' \neq c} |D.c'| + |D.c| = \sum_{c \in CS} |D.c| = cost.D$$

This contradicts that D is an optimal dispersal of CS. Hence, $D.(x, y)$ is a vertex cover of G of minimum size.

Therefore, any vertex cover problem can be reduced to an optimal dispersal of an edge in polynomial time and the optimal dispersal of the resulting chain set is equivalent to a vertex cover of minimum size in the original vertex cover problem.

An optimal dispersal problem is verifiable in polynomial time and any vertex cover problem can be reduced to an optimal dispersal problem in polynomial time. If we can find an optimal dispersal of an edge then we can find a vertex cover for any undirected graph. Therefore, an optimal dispersal problem is NP-hard. Furthermore, The vertex cover problem is a well known NP-Complete problem, so the optimal dispersal problem is NP-Complete.   □

4   Optimal Dispersal of Short Chain Sets

In the previous section, we proved that computing an optimal dispersal of any chain set, which includes chains whose length is 3 or more, is NP-Complete. In this section, we show that there is a polynomial-time algorithm that computes an optimal dispersal of any chain set whose chains are all of length 2 or less.

A chain set CS is *short* if and only if the length of the longest chain in CS is at most 2. For example, consider the star certificate graph in Fig. 4(a). In this certificate graph, assume that each satellite node, b, c, or d, wishes to securely communicate with every other satellite node. Fig. 4(b) shows the resulting short chain set.

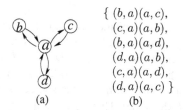

$$\{ \ (b,a)(a,c),$$
$$(c,a)(a,b),$$
$$(b,a)(a,d),$$
$$(d,a)(a,b),$$
$$(c,a)(a,d),$$
$$(d,a)(a,c) \ \}$$

(a)   (b)

Fig. 4. An Example of Short Chain Set

ALGORITHM 1: optimal dispersal of short chain sets
_____
INPUT: a short chain set CS
OUTPUT: a dispersal D of CS

STEPS:
1: **for** each node u in CS, $D.u := \{\}$
2: **for** each certificate (u, v) in CS **do**
3:    **if** there is a node x such that
      the source or destination of every chain that has (u, v) is x
4:        **then** $D.x := D.x \cup \{(u, v)\}$
5:        **else** $D.u := D.u \cup \{(u, v)\}, D.v := D.v \cup \{(u, v)\}$

Consider a certificate (b, a) in the example short chain set. Chains that have (b, a) are $(b, a)(a, c)$ and $(b, a)(a, d)$. So b is the source of every chain that has (b, a). Therefore, (b, a) is stored in $D.b$. After considering all the certificates in the short chain set, the certificates are dispersed by Algorithm 1 as follows:

$$\{D.a = \{\}, D.b = \{(a, b), (b, a)\},$$
$$D.c = \{(a, c), (c, a)\}, D.d = \{(a, d), (d, a)\}\}$$

Theorem 4. *Given a short chain set CS, the dispersal D of CS computed by Algorithm 1 is optimal.*

Proof. The proof consists of two parts. First, we show that Algorithm 1 computes a dispersal D. Second, we show that D is optimal.

Proof of First Part:

By the definition of dispersal in Section 2, if all the certificates in each chain from a source node u to a destination node v in CS are in set $D.u \cup D.v$, then D is a dispersal of CS. In other words, if a certificate (u, v) is stored in the source or destination nodes of every chain that contains (u, v), then D is a dispersal.

By Algorithm 1, every certificate (u, v) is stored either in $D.x$ of some node x, or both $D.u$ and $D.v$. Since the maximum length of a chain in CS is 2, every chain that contains (u, v) starts at u or ends at v. Hence if (u, v) is stored in both $D.u$ and $D.v$ then certificate (u, v) is stored in the source or destination node of every chain that contains (u, v). If (u, v) is stored in node x, by Algorithm 1 x is either the source node or the destination node of every chain that contains (u, v). Therefore, (u, v) is stored in the source or the destination node of every chain that contains (u, v).

Proof of Second Part:

The proof is by contradiction. Let D be the dispersal of a short chain set CS computed by Algorithm 1 and D' be another dispersal of CS. Assume that $cost.D' < cost.D$. There must be at least one certificate c such that $|D'.c| < |D.c|$.

Let (u, v) be such a certificate, $|D'.(u, v)| < |D.(u, v)|$. By Algorithm 1, $|D.(u, v)|$ is either 1 (if there exists some node x that is the source or destination node of every chain that has (u, v)) or 2 (otherwise). Therefore, $|D'.(u, v)| = 1$ and $|D.(u, v)| = 2$, and there exists no node x in CS that is the source or destination node of every chain that has (u, v). By the definition of dispersal, the node w in $D'.(u, v)$ should be the source or a destination of every chain that contains (u, v) in CS. This contradicts that there exists no node x in CS such that x is the source or destination node of every chain that has (u, v).

Therefore, $cost.D \le cost.D'$ for any dispersal D' of CS. Algorithm 1 computes an optimal dispersal of a short chain set CS.   □

The time complexity of Algorithm 1 is $O(ep)$, where e is the number of certificates in the input short chain set and p is the number of chains in the chain set.

5   Optimal Dispersal of Disconnected Chain Sets

In this section, we present an algorithm which computes optimal dispersal for a class of chain sets called disconnected chain sets. A chain set CS is disconnected if and only if for every certificate c in CS, the set of source nodes of the chains that contain c and the set of destination nodes of the chains that contain c are disjoint. Fig. 5 shows an example of a disconnected chain set.

(d, a) has the set of source nodes $\{d\}$ and the set of destination nodes $\{e\}$, which are disjoint. (a, b) has the set of source nodes $\{a\}$ and the set of destination nodes

$$\{ (d,a),$$
$$(a,b)(b,c),$$
$$(a,c)(c,d),$$
$$(a,b)(b,c)(c,d)(d,e)\}$$

Fig. 5. An Example of Disconnected Chain Set

$\{c,e\}$, which are disjoint. Every certificate in this chain set has disjoint sets of source and destination nodes.

Disconnected chain sets represent many useful certificate systems. No strongly-connected certificate graph can produce a disconnected chain set if all possible chains are used. For example, PGP's web of trust[1] commonly results in a certificate graph with a large strongly-connected component. If all the chains are used, it is NP-Complete to compute an optimal dispersal for this strongly-connected component. In fact, not all chains have to be used. As long as the subset of chains in use forms a disconnected chain set, we can find an optimal dispersal in polynomial time.

ALGORITHM 2: optimal dispersal of disconnected chain sets

INPUT: a disconnected chain set CS
OUTPUT: a dispersal D of CS

STEPS:
1: **for** each node u in G, $D.u := \{\}$
2: **for** each certificate (u,v) in G **do**
3:     $G'=(V',E')$ where $V' = \{\}$ and $E' = \{\}$
4:     **for** each chain from node x to node y that contains (u,v) **do**
5:         $V':=V' \cup \{x,y\}$
6:         $E':=E' \cup \{(x,y)\}$
7:     **compute** a minimal vertex cover of the bipartite graph G'
8:     **add** (u,v) to each node in the vertex cover

Consider certificate (a,b) in the example disconnected chain set. G' for (a,b) is $V'=\{a,c,e\}$ and $E'=\{(a,c),(a,e)\}$. Therefore, the vertex cover of minimum size of G' is $\{a\}$. So (a,b) is stored in $D.a$. After considering all certificates in the chain set, the example disconnected chain set is dispersed by Algorithm 2 as follows:

$$\{D.a = \{(a,b),(b,c),(c,d)\}, D.b = \{\}, D.c = \{\},$$
$$D.d = \{(a,c),(d,a)\}, D.e = \{(d,e)\}\}$$

Theorem 5. *Given a disconnected chain set CS, the dispersal D of CS computed by Algorithm 2 is optimal.*

Proof. The proof consists of two parts. First, we show that Algorithm 2 produces a dispersal. Second, we show that the resulting dispersal is optimal.

Proof of First Part:

Let $D.u$ be the set of certificates assigned to a node u in CS by Algorithm 2. Consider any certificate (u, v) in a chain from a source node x to a destination node y in CS. By Algorithm 2, since there is a chain from x to y that goes through (u, v), there is an edge (x, y) in G' for (u, v). By the definition of vertex cover, for edge (x, y) in G', node x or node y is in the vertex cover. Therefore, for the chain from x to y, (u, v) is stored in $D.x$ or $D.y$. This is true for all the certificates in the chain from x to y, for any chain in CS. Hence, D satisfies the dispersal condition in Section 2, so D is a dispersal of CS.

Proof of Second Part:

By Theorem 2, if we can find a dispersal D where $D.c$ of every certificate c in CS is optimal, then D is an optimal dispersal of CS. So we only need to prove that a dispersal computed by Algorithm 2 produces an optimal location of each certificate in CS. The proof is by contradiction. Assume there is another dispersal D' of CS, where $cost.D' < cost.D$. There must be at least one certificate c where $|D'.c| < |D.c|$. For every chain from a node x to a node y that contains c, $D'.c$ should contain x or y. Therefore, $D'.c$ is a vertex cover of the bipartite graph G' constructed for c, where $|D'.c| < |D.c|$. This contradicts that $D.c$ is the vertex cover of minimum size of G' by line 7 in Algorithm 2. Therefore, $D.c$ is an optimal location of c for every certificate c in CS. By Theorem 2, D is optimal.   □

For each certificate (u, v), the graph G' constructed for (u, v) is a bipartite graph. It is because the set of source nodes of the chains that contain (u, v) and the set of the destination nodes of the chains that contain (u, v) are disjoint by the definition of disconnected chain set. Finding a vertex cover in a bipartite graph is a well known problem in graph theory, which takes $O(n'e')$ steps where n' is the number on nodes in G' and e' is the number of edges in G'. In the worst case $n' = n$ and $e' = p$, where n is the number of nodes in CS, and p is the number of chains in CS. Therefore, the time complexity of Algorithm 2 is $O(e \times np) = O(enp)$, where e is the number of certificates in CS.

6   Optimal Dispersal of Concise Graphs

In this section, we present an algorithm which computes optimal dispersal for full chain sets in concise certificate graphs. A chain set is *full* if and only if it contains all chains in a certificate graph. A certificate graph G is called *concise* if and only if it satisfies the following two conditions.

  i. *Short Cycles* : Every simple directed cycle in G is of length 2.
 ii. *Nonredundancy* : G has at most one chain from any node to any other node.

Fig. 6 shows an example of a concise certificate graph. Note that in a concise graph there can be two opposite direction certificates between two adjacent nodes. We refer to any such pair of certificates as *twins*, and we refer to each one of those certificates as the *twin certificate* of the other. Referring to the concise graph in Fig. 6 the two certificates (a, c) and (c, a) are twins. This concept of twin certificates is utilized in

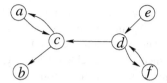

Fig. 6. A concise certificate graph

the following algorithm which computes optimal dispersal of full chain set of concise certificate graphs.

Concise certificate graphs represent many useful certificate systems. For example, a hierarchical certificate system would typically generate a tree-shaped certificate graph. Any tree-shaped certificate graph is a concise certificate graph.

ALGORITHM 3: optimal dispersal of concise certificate graphs

INPUT: a concise certificate graph G
OUTPUT: a dispersal D of the full chain set CS of G

STEPS:
1: **for** each node u in G, $D.u := \{\}$
2: **for** each certificate (u, v) in G **do**
3:     **compute** the set $R.u$ that contains u and every node x from which there is a chain to u in G and this chain does not contain the twin certificate (v, u)
4:     **compute** the set $R.v$ that contains v and every node x to which there is a chain from v in G and this chain does not contain the twin certificate (v, u)
5:     **if** $|R.u| \leq |R.v|$
6:         **then** for every node x in $R.u$, $D.x := D.x \cup \{(u, v)\}$
7:         **else** for every node x in $R.v$, $D.x := D.x \cup \{(u, v)\}$

Consider certificate (a, c) in the example concise certificate graph in Fig. 6. $R.a = \{a\}$ and $R.c = \{b.c\}$ so (a, c) is stored in a. After considering all the certificates in the graph, the example concise certificate graph is dispersed by Algorithm 3 as follows:

$$\{ D.a = \{(a, c), (c, a)\}, D.b = \{(c, b)\}, D.c = \{(d, c)\},$$
$$D.d = \{\}, D.e = \{(e, d)\}, D.f = \{(d, f), (f, d)\} \}$$

Theorem 6. *Given a concise certificate graph G, the dispersal D of the full chain set CS of G computed by Algorithm 3 is optimal.*

Proof. We divide the proof into two parts. First, we show that Algorithm 3 computes a dispersal D. Second, we show that D is optimal.
Proof of First Part:
We show that the certificate subsets $D.x$, computed by Algorithm 3 for every node x in G, satisfy the condition of dispersal in Section 2.

Consider a pair of nodes v_0 and v_k, where there is a chain $(v_0, v_1), (v_1, v_2), \cdots,$ (v_{k-1}, v_k) from v_0 to v_k in G. By the definition of full chain set, chain from v_0 to v_k is in CS. For each certificate (v_i, v_{i+1}) in this chain, the two sets $R.v_i$ and $R.v_{i+1}$ are computed by Algorithm 3. Since there is a chain from v_0 to v_i in G, $R.v_i$ contains v_0. Similarly, since there is a simple directed chain from v_{i+1} to v_k in G, $R.v_{i+1}$ contains v_k. By line 5-7 in Algorithm 3, (v_i, v_{i+1}) is stored either in all nodes in $R.v_i$ or in all nodes in $R.v_{i+1}$. Because $R.v_i$ contains v_0 and $R.v_{i+1}$ contains v_k, certificate (v_i, v_{i+1}) is stored either in $D.v_0$ or in $D.v_k$. Thus, every certificate (v_i, v_{i+1}) in the chain from v_0 to v_k is stored in $D.v_0 \cup D.v_k$. Hence, D is a dispersal of the full chain set CS of G.

Proof of Second Part:

Let D' be another dispersal of CS and (u, v) be any certificate in CS. By the definition of full chain set, if Algorithm 3 is applied to G, then certificate (u, v) is on every directed chain from a node in $R.u$ to a node in $R.v$ in CS, where $R.u$ and $R.v$ are the two sets computed by Algorithm 3 for certificate (u, v). Therefore, $D'.(u, v)$ is a superset of $R.u$ and $R.v$, so $|D'.(u, v)| \geq |R.u \cup R.v| \geq \min(|R.u|, |R.v|) = |D.(u, v)|$. This is true for any certificate (u, v) in CS, thus $cost.D'$ is no less than $cost.D$. Therefore, D computed by Algorithm 3 is optimal. □

The complexity of Algorithm 3 is $O(en)$, where e is the number of certificates in the input concise certificate graph and n is the number of nodes in the concise certificate graph.

7   Related Work

Several papers have investigated the use of certificates for confidentiality, authentication, and authorization. We summarize the results of these papers in the following paragraphs.

Architectures for issuing, storing, discovery, and validating certificates in networks are presented in [2], [3], [4], [5], [6], [7], [8], [9], and [10]. In a large scale network such as today's Internet, one cannot expect to have a central authority to issue, store, and validate all the certificates. A distributed system, where each user participates in issuing, storing, and validating certificates is desirable in such a network.

In [11] and [12], distributed architectures for issuing certificates, particularly in mobile networks, are presented.

In [11], Zhou and Haas present an architecture for issuing certificates in an ad-hoc network. According to this architecture, the network has k servers. Each server has a different share of some private key rk. To generate a certificate, each server uses its own share of rk to encrypt the certificate. If no more than t servers have suffered from Byzantine failures, where $k \geq 3t + 1$, then the resulting certificate is correctly signed using the private key rk, thanks to threshold cryptography. The resulting certificate can be decrypted using the corresponding public key which is known to every node in the ad-hoc network.

In [12], Kong, Perfos, Luo, Lu and Zhang presented another distributed architecture for issuing certificates. Instead of employing k servers in the ad-hoc network, each node in the network is provided with a different share of the private key rk. For a node u to issue a certificate, the node u forwards the certificate to its neighbors and each of them encrypt the certificate using its share of rk. If node u has at least $t + 1$ correct neighbors (i.e. they have not suffered from any failures), the resulting certificate is correctly signed using the private key rk.

Both work assume that a certificate will be signed by a special private key of an authority, and distribute the private key among many servers or users. By contrast, in [13] and this paper, we propose a distributed architecture where every node has both a public key and a private key so it can issue certificates for any other node in the network. This architecture is very efficient in issuing and validating certificates but cannot tolerate Byzantine failures. In particular, if one node suffers from Byzantine failure, then this node can successfully impersonate any other node that is reachable from this node in the certificate graph of the network. This vulnerability to Byzantine failures is not unique to our certificate work. In fact, many proposed certificate architectures, e.g. [2], [3], while [12] , [4], [10], and [9] yield similar vulnerabilities. Recently, we have identified a metric to evaluate the damage from this type of attacks. We call it "vulnerability" of the certificate system and discuss it in more details in [14].

In [10], Li, Winsborough, and Mitchell presented a role-based trust management language RT_0 and suggested the use of strongly typed distributed certificate storage to solve the problem of certificate chain discovery in distributed storage. However, they do not discuss how to efficiently assign certificates among the distributed storages. By contrast, our work focuses on minimizing storage overhead in certificate dispersal among the users while they have enough certificates so that there is no need for certificate chain discovery.

In [15], Ajmani, Clarke, Moh, and Richman presented a distributed certificate storage using peer-to-peer distributed hash table. This work assumes dedicated servers host a SDSI certificate directory and focuses on fast look-up service and load balancing among the servers. By contrast, our work assigns certificates to users such that there is no need for look-up and there are no dedicated certificate storage servers. Our work also focuses on efficient use of storages in all users in network.

In [16], Reiter and Stubblebine investigate how to increase assurance on authentication with multiple independent certificate chains. They introduce two types of independent chains, disjoint paths (no edge is shared by any two chains) and k-connective paths (k certificates need to be compromised to disconnect all these paths). This paper shows that there are no polynomial-time algorithms for locating maximum sets of paths with these properties and presents approximation algorithms.

Perhaps the closest work to ours is [17] where the authors, Hubaux, Buttyán, and Capkun, investigated how to disperse certificates in a certificate graph among the network nodes under two conditions. First, each node stores the same number of certificates. Second, with high probability, if two nodes meet then they have enough certificates for each of them to obtain the public key of the other. By contrast, our work in [13] and here are based on two different conditions. First, different nodes may store different number of certificates, but the number of certificates stored in nodes is minimized. Second, it is guaranteed (i.e. with probability 1) that if two nodes meet then they have enough certificates for each of them to obtain the public key of the other (if there exists a chain between them in the chain set).

Later, the same authors have showed in [18] that a lower bound on the number of certificates to be stored in a node is $\sqrt{n}-1$ where n is the number of nodes in the system. By contrast, we showed in [13] that the tight lower bound on the average number of certificates to be stored in a node is e/n, where e is the number of certificates in the system. Our work here shows that finding an optimal dispersal of a given chain set is NP-Complete, and presents three polynomial-time algorithms which compute optimal dispersal of three classes of chain sets.

8   Conclusion

We have shown that, in general, finding an optimal dispersal of a given chain set is NP-Complete. We have also discussed three polynomial-time algorithms, each of which computes an optimal dispersal for a rich class of chain sets. In [19], we have presented more polynomial-time algorithms which compute an optimal dispersal for more classes of chain sets. This result can be used in any network setting. However, these algorithms are particularly useful when the network is large. In a large scale network such as to-day's Internet, one cannot expect to have a central authority for storing and distributing certificates among all users in the network. Instead, users can store a subset of certificates in the network so that any user can obtain the public key of the other whom the user wants to securely communicate with (if there was a chain in the chain set). More-over, in a large scale network, not all certificate chains in a certificate graph are in use. Computing an optimal dispersal of a chain set instead of the full chain set of a certificate graph reduces the cost of dispersal.

This result can be also used as a metric to evaluate certificate graphs. The optimal dispersal cost is an important property of a certificate graph, since it affects the storage requirement of each node in the network. This is especially important in ad-hoc networks, where mobile nodes may be more restricted in terms of storage than stable nodes can be.

Acknowledgement

The authors would like to thank Jean-Philippe Martin for interesting discussions on the NP-Completeness proof.

References

1. McBurnett, N.: PGP web of trust statistics. http://bcn.boulder.co.us/ neal/pgpstat/ (1996)
2. Rivest, R.L., Lampson, B.: SDSI – A simple distributed security infrastructure. Presented at CRYPTO'96 Rumpsession (1996)
3. Boeyen, S., Howes, T., Richard, P.: Internet X.509 public key infrastructure operational protocols - LDAPv2. RFC 2559 (1999)
4. Myers, M., Ankney, R., Malpani, A., Galperin, S., Adams, C.: X.509 Internet public key infrastructure online certificate status protocol - OCSP. RFC 2560 (1999)
5. Ellison, C., Frantz, B., Lampson, B., Rivest, R., Thomas, B., Ylonen, T.: SPKI certificate theory. RFC 2693 (1999)

6. Blaze, M., Feigenbaum, J., Ioannidis, J., Keromytis, A.: The keynote trust-management system version 2. RFC 2704 (1999)
7. Clarke, D., Elien, J.E., Ellison, C., Fredette, M., Morcos, A., Rivest, R.: Certificate chain discovery in SPKI/SDSI. Journal of Computer Security 9 (2001) 285–322
8. Elley, Y., Anderson, A., Hanna, S., Mullan, S., perlman, R., Proctor, S.: Building certificate paths: Forward vs. reverse. In: Proceedings of the 2001 Network and Distributed System Security Symposium (NDSS '01). (2001) 153–160
9. Freudenthal, E., Pesin, T., Port, L., Keenan, E., Karamcheti, V.: dRBAC: distributed role-based access control for dynamic coalition environments. In: Proceedings of 22nd International Conference on Distributed Computing Systems (ICDCS 02). (2002) 411–420
10. Li, N., Winsborough, W.H., Mitchell, J.C.: Distributed credential chain discovery in trust managemen. Jounal of Computer Security 11 (2003) 35–86
11. Zhou, L., Haas, Z.J.: Securing ad hoc networks. IEEE Network 13 (1999) 24–30
12. Kong, J., Zerfos, P., Luo, H., Lu, S., Zhang, L.: Providing robust and ubiquitous security support for wireless mobile networks. In: Proceedings of Ninth Internation Conference on Network Protocols (ICNP'01). (2001) 251–260
13. Gouda, M.G., Jung, E.: Certificate dispersal in ad-hoc networks. In: Proceedings of the 24th International Conference on Distributed Computing Systems (ICDCS 04), IEEE (2004)
14. Gouda, M.G., Jung, E.: Vulnerability analysis of certificate chains. *in preparation* (2004)
15. Ajmani, S., Clarke, D.E., Moh, C.H., Richman, S.: Conchord: Cooperative sdsi certificate storage and name resolution. In: LNCS 2429 Peer-to-Peer Systems: First International Workshop, IPTPS 2002. (2002) 141–154
16. Reiter, M.K., Stubblebine, S.G.: Resilient authentication using path independence. IEEE Transactions on Computers 47 (1998) 1351–1362
17. Hubaux, J.P., Buttyán, L., Capkun, S.: The quest for security in mobile ad hoc networks. In: Proceedings of the 2001 ACM International Symposium on Mobile ad hoc networking & computing, ACM Press (2001) 146–155
18. Capkun, S., Buttyán, L., Hubaux, J.P.: Self-organized public-key management for mobile ad hoc networks. IEEE Transactions on Mobile Computing 2 (2003) 52–64
19. Jung, E., Elmallah, E.S., Gouda, M.G.: Optimal dispersal of certificate chains. In: to appear in Proceedings of IEEE Global Telecommunications Conference (Globecom 04), IEEE (2004)

On Byzantine Agreement
over $(2,3)$-Uniform Hypergraphs

D.V.S. Ravikant, V. Muthuramakrishnan, V. Srikanth,
K. Srinathan*, and C. Pandu Rangan

Department of Computer Science and Engineering,
Indian Institute of Technology, Madras, Chennai 600036, India
{muthu,ravidvs,srikanth,ksrinath}@meenakshi.cs.iitm.ernet.in,
rangan@iitm.ernet.in

Abstract. In a *Byzantine agreement* protocol, a synchronous network of n interconnected processes of which t may be faulty, starts with an initial binary value associated with each process; after exchanging messages, all correct processes must agree on one of the initial values of the non-faulty processes.

If the network consists of only unicast channels (i.e. a 2-uniform hypergraph), then Byzantine agreement is possible if and only if $n \geq 3t + 1$ (Pease *et. al.* [11]). However, Fitzi and Maurer ([7]) show that if, in addition to all unicast channels, there exists local broadcast among every three processes in the network (i.e. a complete $(2,3)$-uniform hypergraph), $n \geq 2t + 1$ is necessary and sufficient for Byzantine agreement.

In this paper, we show that optimum tolerance of $n \geq 2t + 1$ can be achieved even if a substantial fraction of the local broadcast channels are *not* available. Specifically, we model the network as a $(2,3)$-uniform hypergraph $H = (P, E)$, where P denotes the set of n processes and E is a set of 2-tuples and/or 3-tuples of processes (edges or 3-hyperedges), wherein each 3-hyperedge represents a local broadcast among the three processes; we obtain a characterization of the hypergraphs on which Byzantine agreement is possible. Using this characterization, we show that for $n = 2t + 1$, $\left(\frac{2}{3}t^3 + \Theta(t^2)\right)$ 3-hyperedges are necessary and sufficient to enable Byzantine agreement. This settles an open problem raised by Fitzi and Maurer in [7]. An efficient protocol is also given whenever Byzantine agreement is possible.

1 Introduction

The problem of Byzantine agreement is a classic problem in distributed computing introduced by Lamport et al. in [12]. In many practical situations, it is necessary for a group of processes in a distributed system to agree on some issue, despite the presence of some faulty processes. More precisely, a protocol among a group of n processes (t of which may be faulty), each having a value, is said to achieve Byzantine agreement, if, at the end of the protocol, all honest processes

---

* Financial support from Infosys Technologies Limited, India, is acknowledged.

R. Guerraoui (Ed.): DISC 2004, LNCS 3274, pp. 450–464, 2004.

agree on a value and the following conditions hold: (1) *Agreement:* All honest processes agree on the same value; (2) *Validity:* If all honest processes start with the value $v \in \{0, 1\}$, then all honest processes agree on v; (3) *Termination:* All honest processes eventually agree.

In this paper, we shall use the simple and standard model of a synchronous network wherein any communication protocol evolves as a series of *rounds*, during which the players send messages, receive them and perform (polynomial time) local computations according to the protocol.

The processes' mutual distrust in the network is typically modeled via a (fictitious) centralized adversary that is assumed to control/corrupt the faulty processes. In the threshold adversary model, a fixed upper bound t is set for the number of faulty processes.

Over a complete graph (of point-to-point authenticated channels), it was proved [11] that, Byzantine agreement is achievable on a set of n processes with t (Byzantine) faults if and only if $t < \frac{n}{3}$. Subsequently, there have been (successful) attempts on "improving" the above bound.

One approach has been to study the problem in a non-threshold adversary model like in [8, 6, 1]. In this model the adversary is characterized by an *adversary structure* which is a monotone set of subsets of processes from which processes in any one of the subsets may be corrupted; it was proved [6] that Byzantine agreement is possible if and only if the adversary structure $\mathcal{A}_{adv}$ satisfies $\mathcal{Q}^{(3)}$, i.e., no three sets in $\mathcal{A}_{adv}$ cover the full set of processes.

A second approach is to assume (stronger) communication primitives in addition to the point-to-point authenticated links. For example in [7], a broadcast among three processes was assumed to be available among every set of three processes and the bound was improved to $t < \frac{n}{2}$.

In another line of research, Dolev *et. al.* in [5] study the possibility of Byzantine agreement over incomplete graphs. If $n > 3t$, they prove that Byzantine agreement is achievable if and only if the underlying graph is at least $(2t+1)$-connected. Generalizing this result using the first approach, Kumar *et. al.* [9] show that if the adversary structure $\mathcal{A}$ satisfies $\mathcal{Q}^{(3)}$, Byzantine agreement is achievable if and only if the underlying graph is $\mathcal{A}^{(2)}$-connected, that is, the union of no two sets in the adversary structure is a vertex cut-set of the graph.

With this as the state-of-the-art, the following question (mentioned as an open problem in [7]) arises: *what is a necessary and sufficient condition for achieving Byzantine agreement over incomplete $(2,3)$-uniform hypergraphs?* In this paper, we provide a concise characterization that generalizes the results of [5] (which uses the 1-cast model) to the $(2,3)$-uniform hypergraph model.

2   Motivation and Contributions

In practice one finds local broadcast channels in various networks in the form of LAN (Local Area Network) like an Ethernet or Token ring system. Another example is wireless communication, which is inherently broadcast in nature. A particular case when there is a local broadcast among every three players, that is, a complete $(2,3)$-uniform hypergraph, has been studied in [7]. We investigate the strength of arbitrary $(2,3)$-uniform hypergraphs in the context of achieving Byzantine agreement. Recall that even over *complete* $(2,3)$-uniform hypergraphs on n processes of which up to t may be Byzantine faulty, Byzantine agreement is achievable if and only if $n > 2t$ [7]. We characterize the (im)possibility of Byzantine agreement on an arbitrary network.

Definition 1. *A hypergraph H is said to be (α, β)-hyper-γ-connected if on removal of any $(\gamma - 1)$ vertices, for any partition of the remaining vertices into α sets of maximum size β, there exists a hyperedge which has non-empty intersection with every set of the partition.*

In Section 4 we prove that Byzantine agreement among $n > 2t$ processes connected via a $(2,3)$-uniform hypergraph H is possible if and only if H satisfies the following three conditions: (i) if $n = 2t + 1$, then H is 2-hyperedge complete; (ii) if $n > 2t + 1$, then H is $(2, n)$-hyper-$(2t + 1)$-connected, and (iii) if $2t < n \leq 3t$, then H is $(3, t)$-hyper-$(3t - n + 1)$-connected.

Implicit in the characterization are the principles for fault-tolerant network design using $(2,3)$-hyperedges. Nevertheless, we provide explicit constructions of minimally connected optimally tolerant 3-uniform hypergraphs (in Section 5).

The impact of our results can be seen from the following implications:

Implication 1 *For any $n > 3t$, addition of (any number of) 3-hyperedges does not reduce the $(2t + 1)$-connectivity requirement.*

Remark: Note that any hypergraph H is $(2, n)$-hyper-$(2t + 1)$-connected if and only if its underlying graph is $(2t + 1)$-connected. By underlying graph, we mean the graph obtained by replacing each 3-hyperedge by its corresponding three edges.

Implication 2 *The optimum of $n = (2t + 1)$ can be achieved even if a considerable fraction of the 3-hyperedges are absent. Furthermore, the minimum number of 3-hyperedges necessary to facilitate agreement reduces as (n/t) increases.*

Remark: We will present in Section 5, the design of networks that allow Byzantine agreement with at most $\frac{1}{2}(3t - k - 1)(t + k + 1)(k + 1)$ 3-hyperedges, where $n = 3t - k$, for $0 \leq k < t$.

Implication 3 *There are several scenarios (networks) for which no known protocol can achieve Byzantine agreement while our protocol succeeds.*

Remark: For example, consider the network $H(P, E)$ on five nodes two of which may be faulty and contains eight 3-hyperedges, $P = \{p_1, p_2, p_3, p_4, p_5\}$ and $E_{basis} = \{\{p_1, p_2, p_3\}, \{p_1, p_2, p_4\}, \{p_2, p_3, p_4\}, \{p_3, p_4, p_5\}, \{p_4, p_5, p_1\}, \{p_1, p_2, p_5\}, \{p_2, p_3, p_5\}, \{p_1, p_3, p_5\}\}$. Note that H satisfies the conditions[1] of Theorem 1; hence our protocol of Section 4 achieves agreement while all the extant protocols fail.

---

[1] For any hypergraph on five nodes tolerating two faults, it can in fact be shown that it is impossible to satisfy the conditions of Theorem 1 using any set of seven (or less) 3-hyperedges. Thus, our example is tight.

3   Definitions and the Model

Definition 2. *A hypergraph H is defined as the ordered pair (P, E) where P is a set of vertices and $E \subseteq 2^P$ is a monotone[2] set of hyperedges. A set $e \in E$ is called a $|e|$-hyperedge. The maximal basis of E is $\{e \in E|$ no proper superset of e is in $E\}$.*

We model the network as a hypergraph $H(P, E)$ where $P = \{p_1, p_2, \ldots, p_n\}$ is the set of processes and $\{p_1, p_2, ..., p_k\} \in E$ if and only if $p_1, p_2, ..., p_k$ are connected by a local broadcast.

Definition 3. *A 3-uniform hypergraph is a hypergraph $H(P, E)$ in which all hyperedges in the maximal basis of E are 3-hyperedges. A $(2, 3)$-uniform hypergraph is a hypergraph $H(P, E)$ in which every hyperedge in the maximal basis of E is either a 2-hyperedge or a 3-hyperedge.*

In this paper, we work with networks that are modeled by a $(2, 3)$-uniform hypergraph.

Definition 4. *If $P_1, P_2, \ldots, P_m$ are mutually disjoint non empty sets of size $\leq t$ such that $P_1 \cup P_2 \cup \ldots \cup P_m = P$, then we say $(P_1, P_2, \ldots, P_m)$ forms a (m, t)-partition of P. Formally, $(P_1, P_2, \ldots, P_m)$ forms a (m, t)-partition of P if $1 \leq |P_i| \leq t$ for all i, $1 \leq i \leq m$, $(P_i \cap P_j) = \emptyset$ for all i, j, $1 \leq i < j \leq m$ and $P_1 \cup P_2 \cup \ldots \cup P_m = P$. A hypergraph $H(P, E)$ is said to be (m, t)-hyperconnected if for every (m, t)-partition $(P_1, P_2, \ldots P_m)$ of P, $\exists e \in E$ such that $(e \cap P_i) \neq \emptyset$ for $1 \leq i \leq m$. A hypergraph H is (m, t)-hyper-k-connected if on removal of any $(k - 1)$ vertices, the hypergraph remains (m, t)-hyperconnected.*

Remark: A k-(vertex)connected graph on n nodes is a $(2, n)$-hyper-k-connected hypergraph.

A hypergraph is said to be 2-hyperedge complete if it contains all 2-hyperedges (2-hyperedges among every 2 vertices).

Definition 5. *An adversary structure, $\mathcal{A}_{adv}$, is a monotone[3] set of subsets of the process set P. We abuse the notation $\mathcal{A}_{adv}$ to also denote the maximal basis. Any adversary characterized by $\mathcal{A}_{adv}$ can corrupt the processes in any one set of his choice from $\mathcal{A}_{adv}$. The adversary structure $\mathcal{A}_{adv}$ is said to satisfy $Q^{(k)}$ if the union of no k sets in $\mathcal{A}_{adv}$ equals P.*

4   Characterization of Byzantine Agreement

Theorem 1. *Let $H(P, E), |P| = n$ be a $(2, 3)$-uniform hypergraph. There exists a deterministic protocol for Byzantine agreement on H tolerating t faults if and only if all the following hold:*

1. *If $n = 2t + 1$, then H should have all 2-hyperedges.*
2. *If $n > 2t + 1$, then H is $(2, n)$-hyper-$(2t + 1)$-connected.[4]*
3. *If $2t < n \leq 3t$, then H is $(3, t)$-hyper-$(3t - n + 1)$-connected.*

---

[2] If $S \in E$ and $S' \subseteq S$ then $S' \in E$.
[3] If $S \in \mathcal{A}_{adv}$ then $S' \in \mathcal{A}_{adv}$ for every $S' \subset S$
[4] This condition implies that we still need $(2t + 1)$-edge connectivity with respect to 2-hyperedges.

Proof (Necessity of conditions 1 and 2): The proof is similar to the proof for $(2t + 1)$-connectivity on normal graphs in [10]. The main idea of the proof is illustrated in the Lemma 1.

The key idea behind Lemma 1 is to design a distributed system with contradicting behavior assuming the existence of a protocol satisfying the conditions stated in the lemma. Note that the newly constructed system need not solve the Byzantine agreement problem. The processors in the new system behave exactly as specified in the (assumed) protocol.

Lemma 1. *Byzantine agreement is not achievable on a four node hypergraph H tolerating one fault if the hypergraph is not $(2,4)$-hyper-3-connected.*

Proof: Suppose, for the sake of contradiction, that there is a protocol A that achieves agreement among the four players p_1, p_2, p_3 and p_4 connected by a hypergraph H which is not $(2,4)$-hyper-3-connected.

Assume without loss of generality that $\{p_2, p_4\}$ disconnects H. The maximal hypergraph H_1 that is not $(2,4)$-hyper-3-connected which has $\{p_2, p_4\}$ as a cut-set is as shown in Figure 1. The only two 3-hyperedges possible in H_1 are $\{p_1, p_2, p_4\}$ and $\{p_2, p_3, p_4\}$. Since H is a subgraph of H_1, the protocol also works on H_1. Without loss of generality assume that all communication is through the two 3-hyperedges $\{p_1, p_2, p_4\}$ and $\{p_2, p_3, p_4\}$[5].

Let $\pi_1, \pi_2, \pi_3, \pi_4$ denote the local programs of p_1, p_2, p_3, p_4 respectively.[6] For each $i \in \{0, \ldots, 3\}$ let p'_i be an identical copy of player p_i.

We construct a new system S of eight players (the original ones along with their copies) connected by the hypergraph H'_1 as shown in the Figure 1. The 3-hyperedges in H'_1 are $\{\{p_1, p_2, p'_4\}, \{p_2, p_3, p_4\}, \{p'_1, p'_2, p_4\}, \{p'_2, p'_3, p'_4\}\}$. In S, both p_i and its copy p'_i run the same local program π_i. Notice that some hyperedges to which p_i was connected in the original network H_1 are substituted by other hyperdeges in the new network H'_1. For each player p_i, we specify a mapping $M_{p_i} : E(H_1) - > E(H'_1)$ such that if p_i communicates along $e \in H_1$ in A then it communicates along $M_{p_i}(e)$ in the new system.
$M_{p_1}(\{p_1, p_2, p_4\}) = \{p_1, p_2, p'_4\}, M_{p_3}(\{p_2, p_3, p_4\}) = \{p_2, p_3, p_4\}$,
$M_{p_2}(\{p_1, p_2, p_4\}) = \{p_1, p_2, p'_4\}, M_{p_2}(\{p_2, p_3, p_4\}) = \{p_2, p_3, p_4\}$,
$M_{p_4}(\{p_1, p_2, p_4\}) = \{p'_1, p'_2, p_4\}, M_{p_4}(\{p_2, p_3, p_4\}) = \{p_2, p_3, p_4\}$
The mapping for p'_i is obtained by substituting p'_j for p_j and vice versa in the mapping for p_i. The mapping becomes clear from Figure 1.

The rest of the proof follows as in the proof of Theorem [6.39] of [10]. □

Observe that in the proof, we only used the corruptibility of the processes p_2 and p_4. Thus we have the following

---

[5] If p_1 wants to send some message to p_2 along $\{p_1, p_2\}$, he sends it along $\{p_1, p_2, p_4\}$ and addresses it to p_2. If p_2 wants to send a message to p_4 he sends it along $\{p_1, p_2, p_4\}$ and $\{p_2, p_3, p_4\}$ and addresses them to p_4.

[6] By 'local program' we mean the version of the protocol as run at a particular player. An execution of a local program is dependent only on his input value and on the messages he receives during the course of the protocol.

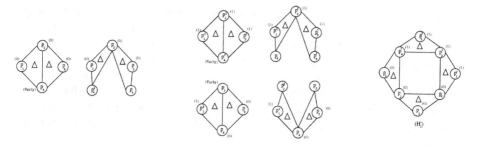

Fig. 1. Views: $\{p_1, p_2, p_3\}, \{p'_1, p'_2, p'_3\}$ & $\{p'_1, p_4, p_3\}$.

Observation 1 *Byzantine agreement is not achievable on four node hypergraph H tolerating the adversary $\mathcal{A}$ characterized by the adversary structure $\mathcal{A}_{adv} = \{\{p_2\}, \{p_4\}\}$ if $\{p_2, p_4\}$ disconnects the hypergraph.*

We shall now continue with the proof of the necessity of conditions 1 and 2 of Theorem 1. Specifically we prove that Byzantine agreement is not achievable among n processes tolerating t faults if the hypergraph is not $(2, n)$-hyper-$(2t + 1)$-connected.

On the contrary, assume a protocol Π exists for Byzantine agreement on some hypergraph $H(P, E)$ that is not $(2, n)$-hyper-$(2t+1)$-connected. The main idea of the proof is to construct a protocol Π' that achieves Byzantine agreement on a four node hypergraph H' tolerating the adversary $\mathcal{A}$ characterized by the adversary structure $\mathcal{A}_{adv} = \{\{p_2\}, \{p_4\}\}$ where $\{p_2, p_4\}$ disconnects the hypergraph H'. This leads to a contradiction since existence of such Π' violates Observation 1.

Let $n > (2t+1)$, assume that $H(P, E)$ is not $(2, n)$-hyper-$(2t + 1)$-connected. That is there exist a set of $2t$ processes that disconnect H. Partition this set into two sets of t processes each, say P_2 and P_4. On removal of the $2t$ processes, the hypergraph disconnects into at least two components, let the processes in one component be P_1 and the processes in the remaining components be P_3. Processes in P_1 and P_3 are disconnected from each other. Thus there does not exist a hyperedge in E which has non empty intersection with both P_1 and P_3.

Construct a hypergraph $H'(P', E')$ on four processes where $P' = \{p_1, p_2, p_3, p_4\}$, $\{p_i, p_j\} \in E'$ if P_i and P_j are connected in H (there is a hyperedge $e \in E$ that has non empty intersection with each of P_i, P_j) and $\{p_i, p_j, p_k\} \in E'$ if P_i, P_j and P_k are connected in H (there is a hyperedge $e \in E$ that has non empty intersection with each of P_i, P_j, P_k). It follows from the earlier argument that $\{p_1, p_3\} \notin E'$ and hence $\{p_2, p_4\}$ disconnects H'.

Using the protocol Π, construct a protocol Π' for Byzantine agreement among the processes in P' connected by the hypergraph H' by allowing p_i simulate the behavior of processes in P_i for $i = 1, 2, 3, 4$. Processes p_i simulate the behavior of processes in P_i as follows: (a) Set the inputs of all players in P_i as the input of p_i, (b) In each round, messages sent among $p \in P_i$ and $q \in P_j$ using the hyperedge $\{p, q\} \in E$ are sent using the hyperedge $\{i, j\} \in E'$ ($\{i, j\} \in E'$

by the definition of E') and messages sent among $p \in P_i$, $q \in P_j$ and $r \in P_k$ using the hyperedge $\{p, q, r\} \in E$ are sent using the hyperedge $\{i, j, k\} \in E'$ ($\{i, j, k\} \in E'$ by the definition of E') and (c) At the end of simulation of Π, p_i accepts the value of a process in P_i.

Observe that if Π tolerates t faults, specifically if Π tolerates the adversary characterized by the adversary structure $\{P_2, P_4\}$ where $P_2 \cup P_4$ disconnects H then Π' tolerates the adversary characterized by the adversary structure $\{\{p_2\}, \{p_4\}\}$ where $\{p_2, p_4\}$ disconnects H'. This leads to a contradiction to Corollary 1.

To prove the case for $n = (2t+1)$, assume the contrary i.e., there is a protocol that achieves Byzantine agreement on a $(2t + 1)$-node hypergraph that is not 2-hyperedge complete. Consider the set of P' of $(2t - 1)$ processes that disconnect H. Partition P' into two sets P_2 and P_4 of sizes t and $(t - 1)$ respectively and continue as in the above case. This completes the proof of the necessity of conditions 1 and 2 of Theorem 1 □

We shall now turn to the proof of the necessity of condition 3 of Theorem 1. It is crucial to understand connectivity of hypergraphs from a set theoretic view at this point.

Lemma 2. *Let* $|\mathcal{P}| = n$, $2t < n \leq 3t$, $P_1, P_2, P_3 \subset \mathcal{P}$ *and* $|P_1| = |P_2| = |P_3| = t$. *If* $(P_1 \cup P_2 \cup P_3) = \mathcal{P}$ *then* $|P_1 - (P_2 \cup P_3)| + |P_2 - (P_1 \cup P_3)| + |P_3 - (P_2 \cup P_1)| \geq (2n - 3t)$.

Proof:
$|P_1 - (P_2 \cup P_3)| + |P_2 - (P_1 \cup P_3)| + |P_3 - (P_2 \cup P_1)|$
$= n - |(P_1 \cap P_2) - P_3| - |(P_2 \cap P_3) - P_1| - |(P_1 \cap P_3) - P_2| - |P_1 \cap P_2 \cap P_3|$
$= n - |P_1 \cap P_2| - |P_2 \cap P_3| - |P_3 \cap P_1| + 2|P_1 \cap P_2 \cap P_3|$
$= n - (3t - n + |P_1 \cap P_2 \cap P_3|) + 2|P_1 \cap P_2 \cap P_3|$
$= 2n - 3t + |P_1 \cap P_2 \cap P_3| \geq 2n - 3t.$ □

Lemma 3. *Let* $|P| = n$, $2t < n \leq 3t$. *Hypergraph* $H(P, E)$ *is* $(3, t)$-*hyper*-$(3t - n+1)$-*connected if and only if for every* $P_1 \cup P_2 \cup P_3 = P$ *and* $|P_1| = |P_2| = |P_3| = t$, *there exists a 3-hyperedge across* $P_1 - (P_2 \cup P_3)$, $P_2 - (P_1 \cup P_3)$, $P_3 - (P_2 \cup P_1)$ *i.e.,* $\exists i \in P_1 - (P_2 \cup P_3)$, $j \in P_2 - (P_1 \cup P_3)$, $k \in P_3 - (P_2 \cup P_1)$ *such that* $\{i, j, k\} \in E$.

Proof: ($\Longrightarrow$) Let $H(P, E)$ be $(3, t)$-hyper-$(3t - n + 1)$-connected. $|(P_1 \cap P_2) - P_3| + |(P_2 \cap P_3) - P_1| + |(P_1 \cap P_3) - P_2| + |P_1 \cap P_2 \cap P_3| \leq 3t - n$ from proof of Lemma 2. Further each of the sets $P_1 - (P_2 \cup P_3)$, $P_2 - (P_1 \cup P_3)$ and $P_3 - (P_2 \cup P_1)$ are non empty since $|P_i \cup P_j| \leq 2t < n$. Since H is $(3, t)$-hyper-$(3t - n + 1)$-connected, there is a 3-hyperedge across the sets $P_1 - (P_2 \cup P_3)$, $P_2 - (P_1 \cup P_3)$ and $P_3 - (P_2 \cup P_1)$.

($\Longleftarrow$) Assume the contrary, i.e. there exists a hypergraph $H(P, E)$ such that for some t ($2t < n \leq 3t$) H is not $(3, t)$-hyper-$(3t-n+1)$-connected but there exists a 3-hyperedge across $P_1 - (P_2 \cup P_3)$, $P_2 - (P_1 \cup P_3)$, $P_3 - (P_2 \cup P_1)$ whenever $P_1 \cup P_2 \cup P_3 = P$ and $|P_1| = |P_2| = |P_3| = t$. Since H is not $(3, t)$-hyper-$(3t - n + 1)$, there exists a set C of $(3t - n)$ nodes and a partition of $P - C$ into 3 sets S_1, S_2, S_3 with $1 \leq |S_i| \leq t$, such that there is no 3-hyperedge across S_1, S_2, S_3.

Partition C into 3 sets C_1, C_2, C_3 such that $|C_i| = 2t + |S_i| - n$. Construct P_1, P_2, P_3 such that $P_1 = S_1 \cup C_2 \cup C_3$, $P_2 = S_2 \cup C_1 \cup C_3$ and $P_3 = S_3 \cup C_1 \cup C_2$. Observe that $P_1 \cup P_2 \cup P_3 = S_1 \cup S_2 \cup S_3 \cup C = P$. Further $|P_1| = |S_1| + |C_2| + |C_3| = |S_1| + |C| - |C_1| = |S_1| + 3t - n - 2t - |S_i| + n = t$. Similarly, $|P_2| = |P_3| = t$. So there exists a 3-hyperedge across S_1, S_2, S_3. This is a contradiction. Hence H is $(3, t)$-hyper-$(3t - n + 1)$-connected. $\qquad\square$

Proof (Necessity of the condition 3): Assume the contrary, i.e., $H(P, E)$ is not $(3, t)$-hyper-$(3t - n + 1)$-connected. Then, from Lemma 3 it follows that there exist $P_1, P_2, P_3 \in \mathcal{A}_{adv}$ such that $|P_1| = |P_2| = |P_3| = t$, $P_1 \cup P_2 \cup P_3 = P$ with no 3-hyperedge across $P_1 - (P_2 \cup P_3), P_2 - (P_1 \cup P_3), P_3 - (P_2 \cup P_1)$. Let Π be the protocol for Byzantine agreement tolerating the adversary $\mathcal{B}$ characterized by the adversary structure $\mathcal{A}_{adv}$, the protocol also tolerates the adversary $\mathcal{B}'$ characterized by the adversary structure $\mathcal{A}'_{adv} = \{P_1, P_2, P_3\}$. We show that there cannot exist a protocol for Byzantine agreement among the processes of $P_1 \cup P_2 \cup P_3$ tolerating the adversary $\mathcal{B}'$ when $P_1 - (P_2 \cup P_3), P_2 - (P_1 \cup P_3), P_3 - (P_2 \cup P_1)$ are not connected by a 3-hyperedge.

Assume that the protocol runs for r rounds. Informally, the proof aims to construct three *scenarios* of protocol execution by defining the process inputs and behavior in each case such that the requirements of Byzantine agreement in these three scenarios imply a contradiction. The proof is similar to the proof of Theorem 3.1 in [1].

Before proceeding to the proof, we first introduce some notation. We denote the messages sent from process x to process y in round r as $M^r_{xy}(\delta)$ where δ is the scenario under consideration. We also let $\mathcal{M}^r_x(\delta)$ denote the ordered list of all the messages sent to the process x through rounds $1, 2, ..., r$. We define two scenarios X and Y to be *indistinguishable* with respect to process x after r rounds if $\mathcal{M}^r_x(X) = \mathcal{M}^r_x(Y)$ and the process x's input in X and Y is the same. We now describe three scenarios, α, β and γ of protocol execution and show

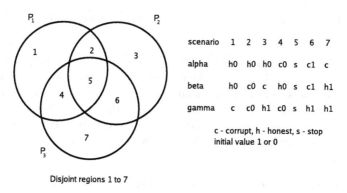

scenario	1	2	3	4	5	6	7
alpha	h0	h0	h0	c0	s	c1	c
beta	h0	c0	c	h0	s	c1	h1
gamma	c	c0	h1	c0	s	h1	h1

c - corrupt, h - honest, s - stop
initial value 1 or 0

Disjoint regions 1 to 7

Fig. 2. Scenarios α, β and γ.

that the requirements of Byzantine agreement in these three scenarios imply a contradiction to the existence of a protocol. For each scenario we specify the behavior of players belonging to each adversary set.

- **Scenario** α: In this scenario, the adversary corrupts processes belonging to the set P_3. Processes in $(P_1 \cup P_2) - P_3$ are all honest and start with input 0.
- **Scenario** β: The adversary corrupts processes belonging to the set P_2. Processes in $P_3 - (P_1 \cup P_2)$ have input 1 while processes in $P_1 - P_2$ have input 0.
- **Scenario** γ: The adversary corrupts processes belonging to the set P_1. Processes in $(P_3 \cup P_2) - P_1$ are honest and start with input 1.

We now describe the adversary strategy for each of the scenarios.

- In scenario α, the faulty processes imitate their behavior in scenario β. Formally, $M^r_{zx}(\alpha) = M^r_{zx}(\beta) \ \forall r, z \in P_3$,(i.e. In the first round every one acts honestly in all three scenarios. From the next round every player in P_3 in scenario α would behave as how they would behave in scenario β in that round.)
- In scenario γ, the faulty processes imitate their behavior in scenario β. Formally, $M^r_{zx}(\gamma) = M^r_{zx}(\beta) \ \forall r, z \in P_1$.
- In scenario β, the adversary corrupts processes belonging to the adversary set P_2. In their communication with processes in $P_1 - (P_2 \cup P_3)$ the faulty processes send the same messages that were sent by them in scenario α. And in their communication with players in $P_3 - (P_2 \cup P_1)$ the faulty processes send the same messages that were sent by them in scenario γ[7].
- Processes belonging to more than one adversary set send the same messages as in the scenario in which they are honest. Therefore, they send the same messages in all the three scenarios.

We complete the proof by separately proving the following statement: No protocol can achieve agreement in all three scenarios (see Lemma 6). Evidently the above statement completes the contradiction to the assumption that Byzantine agreement is possible if the hypergraph is not $(3, t)$-hyper-$(3t - n + 1)$-connected.

Lemma 4. *The two scenarios, α and β are indistinguishable to any process belonging to $P_1 - (P_2 \cup P_3)$.*

Proof: Processes belonging to $P_1 - (P_2 \cup P_3)$ start with the same inputs in both the scenarios α and β. Hence they behave similarly in the first round of both the scenarios. By the specified adversarial strategy, processes belonging to P_2 and P_3 send the same message to processes in $P_1 - (P_2 \cup P_3)$ in both the scenarios. By induction on the number of rounds, it follows that processes in $P_1 - (P_2 \cup P_3)$ receive the same messages in both the scenarios, i.e., $\forall r \ \mathcal{M}^r_x(\alpha) = \mathcal{M}^r_x(\beta)$, $x \in P_1 - (P_2 \cup P_3)$. $\qquad \square$

Lemma 5. *The two scenarios, β and γ are indistinguishable to any process belonging to $P_3 - (P_1 \cup P_2)$.*

---

[7] Had there been a 3-hyperedge across $P_2 - (P_1 \cup P_3)$, $P_1 - (P_2 \cup P_3)$ and $P_3 - (P_2 \cup P_1)$, the protocol would have forced the players in $P_2 - (P_1 \cup P_3)$ to use the 3-hyperedges whenever they have to send messages to $P_1 - (P_2 \cup P_3)$ or $P_3 - (P_2 \cup P_1)$. This would have prevented the double dealing of the processes that is being described here.

Proof: Similar to the proof of Lemma 4.   □

Lemma 6. *No protocol can achieve agreement in all three scenarios.*

Proof: Suppose there exists a protocol which achieves agreement in all the three scenarios. From the validity condition for agreement, it follows that the honest processes must agree on the value 0 in scenario α, and the value 1 in the scenario γ. Processes in $P_1 - (P_2 \cup P_3)$, who behave honestly in both the scenarios, α and β perceive both these scenarios to be indistinguishable (Lemma 4), hence decide on the same value in both the scenarios, viz, 0. Similarly, the processes in $P_3 - (P_1 \cup P_2)$ decide on the same value in scenarios β and γ, namely 1. This contradicts the agreement condition for Byzantine agreement in scenario β.   □
This completes the proof of necessity of all the conditions for Theorem 1. We shall now prove the sufficiency of the three conditions stated in Theorem 1.

Proof Sufficiency: [4] gives a protocol for achieving consensus tolerating Byzantine faults whenever $n > 3t$ and the conditions of Theorem 1 are satisfied. When $n \leq 3t$, we give a protocol (Figure 3) that achieves consensus tolerating Byzantine faults whenever a hypergraph $H(P, E)$ satisfies the conditions of Theorem 1. We only use the 3-hyperedges of H.

In a hypergraph $H(P, E)$, every 3-hyperedge $e \in E$ can locally agree on a single value by a triple majority voting protocol (MVP)[8] [7]. Thus the set e can act as a virtual process P_e, as exploited by [1]. We denote the set of virtual processes $\{P_e | e \in E \text{ and } |e| = 3\}$ as $\mathcal{VP}$.

Observe that the value of a virtual process $P_{\{p,q,r\}}$ can be successfully reconstructed by a honest process whenever two or more processes of $\{p, q, r\}$ are honest. We say that a set A_i in the adversary structure $\mathcal{A}_{adv}$ *dominates* a virtual process $e = \{p, q, r\} \in E$ if $|e \cap A_i| \geq 2$. The value of a virtual process p_e that is dominated by A_i might not be uniquely re-constructable by all honest processes when A_i dominates p_e, so p_e can behave "dishonestly" when A_i is corrupted. The combined adversary set over real and virtual processes $\mathcal{A}^{\mathcal{P} \cup \mathcal{VP}}_{adv}$ is given by $\{B(A_i) | A_i \in \mathcal{A}\}$ where $B(A_i) = \bigcup_j \{e_j \text{ where } e_j \in E, \text{ and } A_i \text{ dominates } e_j\} \cup A_i$.

From Lemma 3 it follows that for every three (adversary) sets from $\mathcal{A}^{(\mathcal{P} \cup \mathcal{VP})}_{adv}$ we have a virtual player $\{i, j, k\}$ such that no two of $\{i, j, k\}$ belongs to a single adversary set (among the three). This means that none of the three adversary sets can corrupt this virtual player. Thus the adversary structure satisfies $\mathcal{Q}^{(3)}$. Hence a simple extension of the Phase King protocol as described in [2,3] achieves Byzantine agreement.   □

Complexity of the protocol: Real players can exchange values reliably since the hypergraph is $(2,n)$-hyper-$(2t + 1)$-connected. A universal exchange among the virtual players can be simulated by a universal exchange among the real players, followed by a local computation of all the virtual players values. The reconstruction is successful if the virtual player is honest. This reduces the complexity of universal exchange in each phase from $O(|\mathcal{VP}|^2)$ to $O(|\mathcal{P}| \cdot |\mathcal{VP}|)$. As in

---

[8] In a MVP every process broadcasts its value and agrees via a local majority

```
for k = 1 to |P| do         (* Set of kings *)
begin                       (* Start of a phase *)
       send(value)ᵃ         (*Universal Exchange 1*)
       receive(V)
       Vⁱ = {r ∈ P ∪ VP, r sent i}, i = 0, 1
       if V⁰ ⊂ of some adversary set in 𝒜⁽ᴾ∪ⱽᴾ⁾ₐdᵥ
           send(1)
       else
           send(0)          (*Universal Exchange 2*)
       receive(R)
       Rⁱ = {r ∈ P ∪ VP, r sent i }, i = 0, 1
       if R¹ ⊄ of any adversary set in 𝒜⁽ᴾ∪ⱽᴾ⁾ₐdᵥ
           value = 1
       else
           value = 0
       (for the king pₖ only)
           send(value)      (* King's Broadcast *)
       receive(king's value)
       if R⁰ ⊂ of some adversary set in 𝒜⁽ᴾ∪ⱽᴾ⁾ₐdᵥ
           value =1
       if R¹ ⊂ of some adversary set in 𝒜⁽ᴾ∪ⱽᴾ⁾ₐdᵥ
           value =0
       else  value = king's value
end                         (* End of the phase *)

――――――――
ᵃ By send(x) we mean sending x reliably to all processes
  (if required) using a sub-protocol like that of [5].
```

Fig. 3. Description of the Phase King protocol for a process in $P \cup VP$.

[5, 10], $O(t)$ communication is required for reliably communicating 1 bit between v_i, v_j if $\{v_i, v_j\} \notin E$. Further since $|VP| = O(t^3)$, the complexity of each phase is $O(nt^4)$ and hence the above protocol has an overall bit complexity of $O(nt^5)$.

5   Network Design

For $n > 3t$, Byzantine agreement is possible if and only if the graph is $(2t + 1)$-connected [4, 10]. Therefore the graph with the minimal number of edges on which Byzantine agreement is possible is a graph on n nodes that is $(2t + 1)$-connected and has the minimal number of edges. The problem of finding the minimal edge graph on n nodes that is k-connected is a well studied problem in graph theory.

In this section we ask a similar question, for $2t < n \leq 3t$, what is the "minimal" $(2, 3)$-hypergraph on which Byzantine agreement is possible. We assume that the hypergraph is 2-hyperedge complete and give a placement of (nearly) as few 3-hyperedges as possible satisfying the conditions of Theorem 1. In other words, for $n = (3t-k)$, $0 \leq k < t$, we give a $(3, t)$-hyper-$(3t-n+1)$-connected hypergraph that has $O(kt^2)$ 3-hyperedges. For $n = 3t$ this implies that an addition of $O(t^2)$ 3-hyperedges makes Byzantine agreement possible among $3t$ players. Furthermore, for $n = (2t + 1)$ we give a construction that provably uses an asymptotically optimum (ratio bound $1 + o(1)$) number of 3-hyperedges.

5.1   Design for $n = (3t - k)$

Definition 6 (Edge Graph). *Given a 3-uniform hypergraph $H(P, E)$, the edge graph of a node $v \in P$ is defined as $G_v(P_v, E_v)$ where $P_v = P - \{v\}$ and $E_v = \{\{i, j\} | \{i, j, v\} \in E\}$.*

For constructing a $(3,t)$-hyper-$(3t - n + 1)$-connected hypergraph $H(P, E)$ on $n = (3t - k)$ nodes, we consider $P' = \{v_0, v_1, v_2, \ldots, v_k\} \subset P$ and place 3-hyperedges such that for each i, $0 \le i \le k$, v_i's edge graph is $(t + k)$-connected. The edge graph is isomorphic to $G(V, E)$ where $V = \{1, 2, \ldots, n-1\}$ and $\{i, j\} \in E$ whenever $(i - j) \bmod (n - 1) \le \lceil \frac{t+k}{2} \rceil$. Clearly $G(V, E)$ is $(t + k)$-connected.

Claim. $H(P, E)$ is $(3,t)$-hyper-$(3t - n + 1)$-connected.

Proof: Consider a partition of P into P_1, P_2, P_3 each of size t. It is enough to show that there exists a hyperedge across $P_1 - (P_2 \cup P_3), P_2 - (P_1 \cup P_3), P_3 - (P_2 \cup P_1)$ (Lemma 3). Let us call these sets P_1', P_2' and P_3' respectively. These sets are disjoint and of size $\le t$ by definition and from Lemma 2, $|P_1' \cup P_2' \cup P_3'| = |P_1'| + |P_2'| + |P_3'| \ge (2n - 3t) = (3t - 2k)$. Hence $|P - (P_1' \cup P_2' \cup P_3')| \le k$.

Since $|P'| = (k + 1)$, there exists a $v \in P'$ such that $v \in P_1' \cup P_2' \cup P_3'$. Without loss of generality let $v \in P_1'$. Let G be the subgraph induced by $P_2' \cup P_3'$ on G_v. Note that G is obtained from G_v by removing $\le t + k - 1$ nodes from P_v ($|P_v| = 3t - k - 1$ and $|P_2' \cup P_3'| \ge 2t - 2k$). Since G_v is $(t + k)$ connected, G is 1-connected. This means there exists a pair (i, j) with $i \in P_2'$ and $j \in P_3'$ such that the edge $\{i, j\} \in E_v$, i.e. $\{i, j, v\} \in E$. Therefore the required 3-hyperedge across P_1', P_2' and P_3' is $\{i, j, v\}$.   □

In H each of the $(k+1)$ nodes of P' are part of $O(k+t)n = O(t^2)$ hyperedges. Therefore the total number of 3-hyperedges in our construction $= O(kt^2)$.

5.2   Lower Bound for $n = (2t + 1)$

Claim. Consider any hypergraph $H(P, E)$ on $|P| = (2t + 1)$ nodes such that Byzantine Agreement is possible between the nodes (processes) in P tolerating t faults. Every pair of nodes in $H(P, E)$ is part of at least t 3-hyperedges.

Proof: On the contrary, suppose there exist nodes p_1 and p_2 such that they form less than t 3-hyperedges i.e. $|P'| = \{p|\{p, p_1, p_2\} \in E\}| < t$. Consider the partition of a $(t + 2)$ subset of $P - P'$ into 3 sets P_1, P_2, P_3, such that $P_1 = \{p_1\}, P_2 = \{p_2\}$. Since Byzantine Agreement is possible among the nodes in P tolerating t faults, from Theorem 1, H must be $(3, t)$-hyper-t-connected, i.e. there exists a 3-hyperedge $\{p_1, p_2, p_3\} \in E$ such that $p_1 \in P_1, p_2 \in P_2, p_3 \in P_3$. But $P_3 \cap P' = \emptyset$; this is a contradiction.   □

Observation 2 *From the above claim we find that the total number of 3-hyper-edges is at least* $\frac{\binom{2t+1}{2} \times t}{3} = \frac{(2t+1)t^2}{3}$

5.3   Design for $n = (2t + 1)$

We give an inductive construction which yields an asymptotically optimum number of 3-hyperedges.

Basis: The base case starts with $t = 1$ ($n = 3$). Since there are only 3 nodes, one 3-hyperedge is necessary and sufficient.

Induction: Given a hypergraph $H(P, E)$ on $n = (2t + 1)$ nodes ($t \geq 1$) which is $(3, t)$-hyper-t-connected, we give a construction of a hypergraph $H'(P', E')$ on $n = (2t + 3)$ nodes that is $(3, t + 1)$-hyper-$(t + 1)$-connected. We construct $H'(P', E')$ by extending $H(P, E)$ i.e., $P \subset P', E \subset E'$. Let the two additional nodes be x and y i.e. $P' = P \cup \{x, y\}$.

Consider the complete 2-uniform hypergraph on the vertex set P; it can be decomposed into t vertex disjoint Hamilton cycles $C_1, C_2, C_3, \ldots, C_t$. Define

$$\left.\begin{array}{l} C_x = C_1 \cup C_2 \cup \ldots \cup C_{\frac{t}{2}} \\ C_y = C_{\frac{t}{2}+1} \cup C_{\frac{t}{2}+2} \cup \ldots \cup C_t \end{array}\right\} t \text{ even} \qquad \left.\begin{array}{l} C_x = C_1 \cup C_2 \cup \ldots \cup C_{\frac{t+1}{2}} \\ C_y = C_{\frac{t+1}{2}} \cup C_{\frac{t+1}{2}+1} \cup \ldots \cup C_t \end{array}\right\} t \text{ odd}$$

Let the subgraphs induced by C_x and C_y be $G_x(P, C_x)$ and $G_y(P, C_y)$ respectively. Note that G_x and G_y are $(2,n)$-hyper-t-connected and their union is the complete 2-uniform hypergraph. The additional 3-hyperedges added are: $E_x = \{\{x\} \cup e | e \in C_x\}, E_y = \{\{y\} \cup e | e \in C_y\}, E_{xy} = \{\{x, y, v\} | v \in P\}, E' = E \cup E_x \cup E_y \cup E_{xy}$

Lemma 7. *The hypergraph $H'(P', E')$ is $(3, t + 1)$-hyper-$(t + 1)$-connected.*

Proof: We need to show that for every partition of any $(t + 3)$ subset S of P' into 3 sets S_1, S_2, and S_3, there is a 3-hyperedge that has non empty intersection with each of S_1, S_2, S_3. We consider the different cases of partitions that arise for the $(t + 3)$ set.

Case $S \subset P$: By induction hypothesis we know that for every 3 partition of any $(t + 2)$ subset of P the condition is satisfied and hence will be satisfied for any 3 partition of a $(t + 3)$ subset also.

Case $S - \{x\} \subset P$ and $x \in P_1$: Two cases arise depending on the size of the partition P_1.

If $|P_1| > 1$, consider the $(t + 2)$ set $S' = S - \{x\}$ (subset of P). By induction hypothesis, the result is true on S' with the partition $P_1 - \{x\}, P_2$, and P_3.

In the case $|P_1| = 1$ i.e., $P_1 = \{x\}$. The pair of nodes in P which forms 3-hyperedges with x are precisely the edges in C_x. We need one of those edges to be across P_2 and P_3 for the condition to be valid. This means that the subgraph induced by $P_2 \cup P_3$ on G_x must be $(2,n)$-hyperconnected. Now $|P_2 \cup P_3| = (t+2)$ implying that G_x must be $(2,n)$-hyper-t-connected.

Case $\{x, y\} \subset S$: Two cases arise depending on whether x and y occur in the same partition or in different partitions.

If they occur in the same partition say P_1, then by virtue of the fact that every pair of nodes in P forms a 3-hyperedge with either x or y since $G_x \cup G_y$ is the complete 2-uniform hypergraph on $2t + 1$ nodes we get that for any $u \in P_2$ and $v \in P_3$ the 2-hyperedge $\{u, v\}$ must form a triangle with either x or y.

If they occur in different partitions, $x \in P_1$ and $y \in P_2$, then for any $v \in P_3$ we have the hyperedge $\{x, y, v\} \in E_{xy} \subset E'$.   □

Let $N(k)$ denote the number of 3-hyperedges in the above construction for $n = (2k + 1)$ then $N(k)$ is given by:

$$N(k+1) = N(k) + |E_x(k)| + |E_y(k)| + |E_{xy}(k)| = \begin{cases} N(k) + 2k^2 + 3k + 1 \ (t \text{ even}) \\ N(k) + 2k^2 + 5k + 2 \ (t \text{ odd}) \end{cases}$$

Solving the recursion we find $N(k) = \frac{2}{3}t^3 + \Theta(t^2)$. Since the lower bound on the minimum number of 3-hyperedges required is $\frac{(2t+1)t^2}{3}$, the above construction is asymptotically optimum with ratio bound $1 + o(1)$.

6   Conclusion

In this paper, we generalized the following well-known theorem in the literature:
Theorem([5, 10]): Byzantine agreement in a graph (or 2-uniform hypergraph) of n processes of which up to t may be faulty is possible if and only if $n > 3t$ and the graph is $(2t + 1)$-connected.
Our Generalization: See Theorem 1.

Using this generalization, we solve an open problem of [7], viz., *for $n = (2t + 1)$, what is the minimum number of 3-hyperedges required to enable Byzantine agreement?* We show that $\left(\frac{2}{3}t^3 + \Theta(t^2)\right)$ 3-hyperedges are necessary and sufficient.

Whenever $n > 2t$ and the minimal connectivity requirements (or more) are satisfied, we presented efficient protocols for Byzantine agreement over $(2,3)$-hypergraphs.

There are many interesting open questions in a wide variety of directions. We list four natural directions that could be explored.

First, one could consider the complexity issues regarding Byzantine agreement protocols over hypergraphs. For instance, on a complete 2-uniform hypergraph, $t + 1$ rounds are necessary and sufficient for agreement; what is the round complexity for the case of hypergraphs?(See [13] for some results).

Next, the lower bounds on the minimum number of hyperedges to achieve agreement seem to be interestingly connected to extremal hypergraph theory. For instance, when $n = 3t$ computing the lower bound in the case of 3-hyperedges becomes the problem of computing a specific *Hypergraph Turan number.*[9]

A third interesting line of research is about the complexity of the following decision problem: *given the required fault-tolerance, is Byzantine agreement possible on the given hypergraph?* For instance, in the case of 2-uniform hypergraphs, verifying $2t + 1$-connectivity is easy (polynomial time algorithms exist); however, for 3-uniform hypergraphs, the status is unknown; nevertheless, there exist very interesting connections to algorithmic hypergraph theory.

Finally, one could extend our results to the non-threshold adversarial model. A straightforward application of the ideas of this paper would result in the following characterization.

---

[9] The *Turan number* for a hypergraph H denoted as $ex(n, H)$ is the maximum number of hyperedges on a n vertex hypergraph which (up to an isomorphism) does not contain H as its subgraph.

Theorem 2. *Byzantine agreement on a $(2,3)$-uniform hypergraph $H(P,E)$ tolerating any adversary characterized by the adversary structure $\mathcal{A}_{adv}$ that satisfies $\mathcal{Q}^{(2)}$ is possible if and only if*

1. *For every node v such that there exist two sets A and B in $\mathcal{A}_{adv}$ with $P - (A \cup B) = \{v\}$, the edge $\{v,w\}$ belongs to E for every $w \in P$ where $w \neq v$.*
2. *If for all A and B in $\mathcal{A}_{adv}$, $|A \cup B| < (n-1)$, then the underlying graph of $H(P,E)$ is $\mathcal{A}^{(2)}$-connected.*
3. *If $\mathcal{A}_{adv}$ does not satisfy $\mathcal{Q}^{(3)}$, then for every three sets S_1, S_2 and S_3 in $\mathcal{A}_{adv}$ such that $(S_1 \cup S_2 \cup S_3) = P$, there exists $e \in E$ such that e has non empty intersection with the sets $S_1 - (S_2 \cup S_3), S_2 - (S_1 \cup S_3)$ and $S_3 - (S_1 \cup S_2)$.*

However, complexity and placement issues for the non-threshold model are still to be looked into.

References

1. S. Amitanand, I. Sanketh, K. Srinathan, V. Vinod, and C. Pandu Rangan. Distributed consensus in the presence of sectional faults. In *22nd ACM PODC*, pages 202–210, July 2003.
2. P. Berman and J. A. Garay. Asymptotically optimal distributed consensus. In *ICALP*, volume 372 of *LNCS*, pages 80–94, 1989.
3. P. Berman, J.A. Garay, and K.J. Perry. Towards optimal distributed consensus. In *21st IEEE FOCS*, pages 410–415, 1989.
4. D. Dolev. The byzantine generals strike again. *Jl. of Algorithms*, 3(1):14–30, 1982.
5. D. Dolev, C. Dwork, O. Waarts, and M. Yung. Perfectly secure message transmission. *JACM*, 40(1):17–47, 1993.
6. M. Fitzi and U. Maurer. Efficient byzantine agreement secure against general adversaries. In *DISC*, volume 1499 of *LNCS*, pages 134–148, Springer-Verlag, 1998.
7. M. Fitzi and U. Maurer. From partial consistency to global broadcast. In *32nd ACM STOC*, pages 494–503, 2000.
8. M. Hirt and U. Maurer. Complete characterization of adversaries tolerable in secure multiparty computation. In *16th ACM PODC*, pages 25–34, 1997.
9. M.V.N. Ashwin Kumar, P.R. Goundan, K. Srinathan, and C. Pandu Rangan. On perfectly secure communication over arbitrary networks. In *21st ACM PODC*, pages 193-202, 2002.
10. N. Lynch. *Distributed Algorithms*. Morgan Kaufmann, 1997.
11. M. Pease, R. Shostak, and L. Lamport. Reaching agreement in the presence of faults. *Journal of ACM*, 27:228–234, April 1980.
12. M. Pease, R. Shostak, and L. Lamport. The byzantine generals problem. *ACM Transactions on Programming Languages and Systems*, 4(3):382–401, July 1982.
13. D.V.S. Ravikant, V. Muthuramakrishnan, V. Srikanth, K. Srinathan, and C. Pandu Rangan. Brief Announcement: On the round complexity of distributed consensus over synchronous networks. In *23rd ACM PODC*, 2004. To appear.

Author Index

Lecture Notes in Computer Science

For information about Vols. 1–3148

please contact your bookseller or Springer

Vol. 3205: N. Davies, E. Mynatt, I. Siio (Eds.), UbiComp 2004: Ubiquitous Computing. XVI, 452 pages. 2004.

Vol. 3203: J. Becker, M. Platzner, S. Vernalde (Eds.), Field Programmable Logic and Application. XXX, 1198 pages. 2004.

Vol. 3202: J.-F. Boulicaut, F. Esposito, F. Giannotti, D. Pedreschi (Eds.), Knowledge Discovery in Databases: PKDD 2004. XIX, 560 pages. 2004. (Subseries LNAI).

Vol. 3201: J.-F. Boulicaut, F. Esposito, F. Giannotti, D. Pedreschi (Eds.), Machine Learning: ECML 2004. XVIII, 580 pages. 2004. (Subseries LNAI).

Vol. 3199: H. Schepers (Ed.), Software and Compilers for Embedded Systems. X, 259 pages. 2004.

Vol. 3198: G.-J. de Vreede, L.A. Guerrero, G. Marín Raventós (Eds.), Groupware: Design, Implementation and Use. XI, 378 pages. 2004.

Vol. 3195: C.G. Puntonet, A. Prieto (Eds.), Independent Component Analysis and Blind Signal Separation. XXIII, 1266 pages. 2004.

Vol. 3194: R. Camacho, R. King, A. Srinivasan (Eds.), Inductive Logic Programming. XI, 361 pages. 2004. (Subseries LNAI).

Vol. 3193: P. Samarati, P. Ryan, D. Gollmann, R. Molva (Eds.), Computer Security – ESORICS 2004. X, 457 pages. 2004.

Vol. 3192: C. Bussler, D. Fensel (Eds.), Artificial Intelligence: Methodology, Systems, and Applications. XIII, 522 pages. 2004. (Subseries LNAI).

Vol. 3191: M. Klusch, S. Ossowski, V. Kashyap, R. Unland (Eds.), Cooperative Information Agents VIII. XI, 303 pages. 2004. (Subseries LNAI).

Vol. 3190: Y. Luo (Ed.), Cooperative Design, Visualization, and Engineering. IX, 248 pages. 2004.

Vol. 3189: P.-C. Yew, J. Xue (Eds.), Advances in Computer Systems Architecture. XVII, 598 pages. 2004.

Vol. 3187: G. Lindemann, J. Denzinger, I.J. Timm, R. Unland (Eds.), Multiagent System Technologies. XIII, 341 pages. 2004. (Subseries LNAI).

Vol. 3186: Z. Bellahsène, T. Milo, M. Rys, D. Suciu, R. Unland (Eds.), Database and XML Technologies. X, 235 pages. 2004.

Vol. 3185: M. Bernardo, F. Corradini (Eds.), Formal Methods for the Design of Real-Time Systems. VII, 295 pages. 2004.

Vol. 3184: S. Katsikas, J. Lopez, G. Pernul (Eds.), Trust and Privacy in Digital Business. XI, 299 pages. 2004.

Vol. 3183: R. Traunmüller (Ed.), Electronic Government. XIX, 583 pages. 2004.

Vol. 3182: K. Bauknecht, M. Bichler, B. Pröll (Eds.), E-Commerce and Web Technologies. XI, 370 pages. 2004.

Vol. 3181: Y. Kambayashi, M. Mohania, W. Wöß (Eds.), Data Warehousing and Knowledge Discovery. XIV, 412 pages. 2004.

Vol. 3180: F. Galindo, M. Takizawa, R. Traunmüller (Eds.), Database and Expert Systems Applications. XXI, 972 pages. 2004.

Vol. 3179: F.J. Perales, B.A. Draper (Eds.), Articulated Motion and Deformable Objects. XI, 270 pages. 2004.

Vol. 3178: W. Jonker, M. Petkovic (Eds.), Secure Data Management. VIII, 219 pages. 2004.

Vol. 3177: Z.R. Yang, H. Yin, R. Everson (Eds.), Intelligent Data Engineering and Automated Learning – IDEAL 2004. XVIII, 852 pages. 2004.

Vol. 3176: O. Bousquet, U. von Luxburg, G. Rätsch (Eds.), Advanced Lectures on Machine Learning. IX, 241 pages. 2004. (Subseries LNAI).

Vol. 3175: C.E. Rasmussen, H.H. Bülthoff, B. Schölkopf, M.A. Giese (Eds.), Pattern Recognition. XVIII, 581 pages. 2004.

Vol. 3174: F. Yin, J. Wang, C. Guo (Eds.), Advances in Neural Networks - ISNN 2004. XXXV, 1021 pages. 2004.

Vol. 3173: F. Yin, J. Wang, C. Guo (Eds.), Advances in Neural Networks – ISNN 2004. XXXV, 1041 pages. 2004.

Vol. 3172: M. Dorigo, M. Birattari, C. Blum, L. M. Gambardella, F. Mondada, T. Stützle (Eds.), Ant Colony, Optimization and Swarm Intelligence. XII, 434 pages. 2004.

Vol. 3171: A.L.C. Bazzan, S. Labidi (Eds.), Advances in Artificial Intelligence – SBIA 2004. XVII, 548 pages. 2004. (Subseries LNAI).

Vol. 3170: P. Gardner, N. Yoshida (Eds.), CONCUR 2004 - Concurrency Theory. XIII, 529 pages. 2004.

Vol. 3166: M. Rauterberg (Ed.), Entertainment Computing – ICEC 2004. XXIII, 617 pages. 2004.

Vol. 3163: S. Marinai, A. Dengel (Eds.), Document Analysis Systems VI. XI, 564 pages. 2004.

Vol. 3162: R. Downey, M. Fellows, F. Dehne (Eds.), Parameterized and Exact Computation. X, 293 pages. 2004.

Vol. 3160: S. Brewster, M. Dunlop (Eds.), Mobile Human-Computer Interaction – MobileHCI 2004. XVII, 541 pages. 2004.

Vol. 3159: U. Visser, Intelligent Information Integration for the Semantic Web. XIV, 150 pages. 2004. (Subseries LNAI).

Vol. 3158: I. Nikolaidis, M. Barbeau, E. Kranakis (Eds.), Ad-Hoc, Mobile, and Wireless Networks. IX, 344 pages. 2004.

Vol. 3157: C. Zhang, H. W. Guesgen, W.K. Yeap (Eds.), PRICAI 2004: Trends in Artificial Intelligence. XX, 1023 pages. 2004. (Subseries LNAI).

Vol. 3156: M. Joye, J.-J. Quisquater (Eds.), Cryptographic Hardware and Embedded Systems - CHES 2004. XIII, 455 pages. 2004.

Vol. 3155: P. Funk, P.A. González Calero (Eds.), Advances in Case-Based Reasoning. XIII, 822 pages. 2004. (Subseries LNAI).

Vol. 3154: R.L. Nord (Ed.), Software Product Lines. XIV, 334 pages. 2004.

Vol. 3153: J. Fiala, V. Koubek, J. Kratochvíl (Eds.), Mathematical Foundations of Computer Science 2004. XIV, 902 pages. 2004.

Vol. 3152: M. Franklin (Ed.), Advances in Cryptology – CRYPTO 2004. XI, 579 pages. 2004.

Vol. 3150: G.-Z. Yang, T. Jiang (Eds.), Medical Imaging and Augmented Reality. XII, 378 pages. 2004.

Vol. 3149: M. Danelutto, M. Vanneschi, D. Laforenza (Eds.), Euro-Par 2004 Parallel Processing. XXXIV, 1081 pages. 2004.